ActionScript Cookbook

Other resources from O'Reilly

ActionScript Cookbook

Joey Lott

O'REILLY®

Beijing · Cambridge · Farnham · Köln · Paris · Sebastopol · Taipei · Tokyo

ActionScript Cookbook
by Joey Lott

Published by O'Reilly & Associates, Inc., 1005 Gravenstein Highway North, Sebastopol, CA 95472.

O'Reilly & Associates books may be purchased for educational, business, or sales promotional use. Online editions are also available for most titles (*safari.oreilly.com*). For more information, contact our corporate/institutional sales department: (800) 998-9938 or *corporate@oreilly.com*.

Editor:	Bruce Epstein
Production Editor:	Matt Hutchinson
Cover Designer:	Emma Colby
Interior Designer:	David Futato

Printing History:

July 2003:	First Edition.

ISBN: 0-596-00490-7

[M]

Table of Contents

Part I.   Local Recipes

Part III. Applications

Preface

The *ActionScript Cookbook* is written with all levels of ActionScript developers in mind—people like you, who want practical solutions to common problems. Keep this book next to your computer to tackle programming challenges such as how to use ActionScript to draw a circle or load images at runtime, or work with Flash Communication Server (FlashCom) and Flash Remoting. This book is filled with exciting yet accessible and practical examples, solutions, and insights into the situations that Flash and ActionScript developers are sure to encounter.

The book is divided into three parts. The first two parts follow the classic O'Reilly Cookbook series format, in which each recipe presents the problem, the solution, and a discussion of the solution. You can quickly locate the recipe that most closely matches your situation and get the solution without having to read the whole book to understand the underlying code. The Discussion sections of each recipe offer a deeper analysis of how the solution works and possible design choices and ramifications. So you get the best of both worlds—quick and easy access to the answers you want and deeper insights into the nature of both the problem and the solution. The *ActionScript Cookbook* helps you develop your understanding of concepts by applying them in real situations.

Part I contains "local recipes," which address problems that involve client-side ActionScript only (scripting within the Flash movie). These recipes cover working with color, movie clips, text, forms, and so on.

Part II contains "remote recipes," which involve some kind of server interaction. For example, Part II includes recipes on working with FlashCom applications; loading external assets such as MP3s, SWFs, and JPEGs; using XML with your Flash movies; and using Flash Remoting.

Part III diverges somewhat from the classic O'Reilly Cookbook recipe approach, but I'm particularly excited about this part of the book. Each of the chapters in Part III show you, step by step, how to create complete applications that incorporate many of the recipes from Parts I and II. These chapters help you understand how to use many of the techniques in the context of a complete application.

What's Not in This Book

This book contains a lot of information on a wide range of topics. It covers the gamut of client-side ActionScript, plus recipes involving FlashCom, Flash Remoting, ColdFusion, PHP, ASP.NET, and more. Every recipe is presented in the context of an applied solution or example. While the book discusses some minimal theory, it is not intended as an introduction to any of these subjects. If you need more theory and introductory information on ActionScript, you should check out *ActionScript for Flash MX: The Definitive Guide*, Second Edition by Colin Moock (O'Reilly).

Although this book is aimed at a broad spectrum of developers, it doesn't cover the absolute basic ActionScript familiar to most casual scripters, such as the *gotoAndStop()* command. For such basic ActionScript, consult the recipes in the *Flash Cookbook*, the companion volume to this book due out in late 2003. Prior to publication, sample ActionScript-related chapters from the *Flash Cookbook* are available at *http://www.person13.com/fcb*. For additional Flash and ActionScript resources, see *http://moock.org/moockmarks* and *http://www.person13.com/ascb*.

Flash Naming Conventions

With the introduction of the MX family of products, including Flash MX, Macromedia abandoned a standard numeric versioning system for its Flash authoring tool. The Flash Player, however, is still versioned numerically. Table P-1 describes the naming conventions for Flash used in this book.

Table P-1. Flash naming conventions used in this book

Name	Meaning
Flash MX	The Flash MX authoring tool (as opposed to the Flash Player).
Flash Player 6	The Flash Player, version 6. The Flash Player is a browser plugin for major web browsers on Windows, Macintosh, and Linux. The platform-specific versions of the plugin are referred to collectively as "Flash Player 6," except where noted.
Flash Player x.0.y.0	The Flash Player, specifically the release specified by x and y, as in Flash Player 6.0.47.0.
Flash 6	Short name for "Flash Player 6," used where the distinction between Flash MX (the authoring tool) and Flash Player 6 (the browser plugin) is irrelevant.
Flash 5 authoring tool	The Flash 5 authoring tool, which came before Flash MX (as opposed to the Flash Player).
Flash Player 5	The Flash Player, version 5.
Flash 5	Short name for "Flash Player 5," used where the distinction between Flash 5 (the authoring tool) and Flash Player 5 (the browser plugin) is irrelevant.
Flash 2, Flash 3, and Flash 4	Versions of the Flash Player prior to version 5.
Standalone Player	A version of the Flash Player that runs directly off the local system rather than as a web browser plugin or ActiveX control.
Projector	A self-sufficient executable that includes both a *.swf* file and a Standalone Player. Projectors can be built for either the Macintosh or Windows operating system using Flash's File → Publish feature.

The Code

This book contains a lot of ActionScript (or more colloquially, *code*). Many recipes offer suggested custom classes and custom methods for built-in ActionScript classes that I have found to be invaluable. I trust you will find them useful as well. I also recommend that you organize these classes and methods into ActionScript library files that you can save to your Flash *Include* directory so you can include them in your Flash movies with relative ease. (The *Include* folder is a special subdirectory under the Flash installation directory in which Flash automatically looks for included files. You may need to create this subdirectory manually.) You can skip or ignore these custom classes and methods if you don't think they are relevant to the kind of applications you build. Alternatively, you can enter the code from this book into your own ActionScript libraries; going through the code line by line will deepen your understanding of how it works.

 To save time or avoid errors when hand-entering the code, you can download the complete ActionScript libraries from *http://www. person13.com/ascb*.

In addition to the ActionScript libraries, there are also some other important code examples within the recipes, such as custom components and server-side scripts (ASP.NET, CFML, etc.). The corresponding Flash documents and scripts are also available for download at the same web site. The complete applications from Part III are available for download as well. To successfully use the Flash applications from Part III, you must also have downloaded the necessary ActionScript libraries from Parts I and II.

Typographical Conventions

To indicate the various syntactic components of ActionScript, this book uses the following conventions:

Menu options
> Menu options are shown using the → character, such as File → Open.

`Constant width`
> Indicates code samples, clip instance names, frame labels, property names, and variable names. Variable names often end with the standard suffixes that activate code-hinting (such as _mc for variables that refer to movie clip instances). Although using these suffixes is considered the best practice, for brevity or clarity, the preferred suffixes have sometimes been omitted.

Italic

> Indicates function names, method names, class names, layer names, symbol link-age identifiers, URLs, filenames, and file suffixes such as *.swf*. In addition to being italicized, method and function names are also followed by parentheses, such as *duplicateMovieClip()*.

`Constant width bold`

> Indicates text that you must enter verbatim when following a step-by-step procedure, although it is sometimes used within code examples for emphasis, such as to highlight an important line of code in a larger example.

`Constant width italic`

> Indicates code that you must replace with an appropriate value (e.g., *your name here*). `Constant width italic` is also used to emphasize variable, property, method, and function names referenced in comments within code examples.

When referring to properties and methods of objects and classes, I use these conventions:

- Class-level (static) properties are shown with the both the class name and property in `constant width` because they should both be entered verbatim. For example, `Stage.width` or `Math.NaN`.

- Instance-level properties are shown with the class or object instance in `constant width italic` because it should be replaced by a specific instance. The property itself is shown in `constant width` and should be entered as shown. For example, `Button.tabEnabled`.

- Method and function names, and the class or object to which they pertain, are always shown in italics and followed by parentheses, as in *MovieClip. duplicateMovieClip()*. Refer to the online help or *ActionScript for Flash MX: The Definitive Guide* to know whether to include the class name literally (i.e., if it is a so-called *static method*), as in *TextField.getFontList()*, or replace it with an instance name, such as *ball_mc.duplicateMovieClip()*.

- For brevity, I often omit the class name when discussing a property or method of a class. For example, if discussing the `htmlText` property of the *TextField* class, when I say "set the `htmlText` property," you should infer from context that I mean, "set the `someField_txt`.`htmlText` property, where `someField_txt` is the identifier for your particular text field."

- In some cases, an object property will contain a reference to a method or call-back handler. It wasn't always clear whether I should have used `constant width` to indicate that it is a property (albeit one storing a method name) or *italics* and parentheses to indicate it is a method (albeit one stored in a property). If the line between a property referring to a method versus the method itself is sometimes blurred, forgive me. To constantly harp on the technical difference would have made the text considerably less accessible and readable.

Pay special attention to notes and warnings set apart from the text with the following icons:

This is a tip. It contains useful information about the topic at hand, often highlighting important concepts or best practices.

This is a warning. It helps you solve and avoid annoying problems or warns you of impending doom. Ignore at your own peril.

We'd Like to Hear from You

We at O'Reilly have tested and verified the information in this book to the best of our ability, but you may find that features have changed (or even that we have made mistakes!). Please let us know about any errors you find, as well as your suggestions for future editions, by writing to:

O'Reilly & Associates, Inc.
1005 Gravenstein Highway North
Sebastopol, CA 95472
(800) 998-9938 (in the United States or Canada)
(707) 829-0515 (international/local)
(707) 829-0104 (fax)

We have a web page for the book, where we list errata, examples, or any additional information. You can access this page at:

http://www.oreilly.com/catalog/actscptckbk

To comment or ask technical questions about this book, send email to:

bookquestions@oreilly.com

For more information about our books, conferences, software, Resource Centers, and the O'Reilly Network, see our web site at:

http://www.oreilly.com

Acknowledgments

While there is only one name that goes on the cover, this book was not produced by one person alone. There are many, many acknowledgments I would like to make to all the people who have made this possibility a reality.

First of all, thanks go to Bruce Epstein—editor extraordinaire and (I suspect) super-hero as well. Bruce's patience with my seemingly endless emails, his faith, and his support have proved invaluable. And he has helped to transform my words into something akin to prose.

I would also like to thank all the people at O'Reilly who have helped out with all their talents. There is so much more that goes into a book than simply writing some words, and I am grateful for all the people who have contributed in their many ways. My thanks to Matt Hutchinson, Claire Cloutier, Glenn Bisignani, Rob Romano, Johnna Dinse, Reg Aubry, Sarah Sherman, Emma Colby, David Futato, Andrew Savikas, and everyone in the marketing, sales, tools, design, and production departments.

I am grateful to Tim O'Reilly for maintaining a vision for a publishing company that is dedicated to such high quality. It shows at every step along the way, and it is reflected in the end product. It is truly a pleasure and honor to work with O'Reilly.

I would like to acknowledge my agent, David Fugate, of Waterside Productions. David always makes sure that things are working well for everyone involved. He is absolutely great to work with, and his enthusiasm and dedication make a difference.

I would like to thank Robert Reinhardt, my friend and sometimes co-author, for all that he has done for me and all that he continues to do. Robert is always there to help me test out new ideas and to offer his encouragement.

Also, I would like to thank Colin Moock for indirectly providing the opportunity to write this book by paving the way with *ActionScript for Flash MX: The Definitive Guide*. I would also like to thank him for graciously allowing me to adapt or reproduce several tables from his well-respected book, which was a frequent companion during the writing and reviewing process.

I would like to thank the Macromedians who develop and improve Flash, without whom there would be nothing to write about. And on a related note, thanks go to the entire Flash community for embracing Flash and ActionScript and for creating the demand for a book like this one.

This book has been transformed from its earlier stages into what you are about to read with the much appreciated assistance of technical reviewers who were kind enough to lend their time and expertise. Specifically, I would like to thank Sham Bhangal, Gareth Downes-Powell, and Devon O'Dell for their feedback for the entire manuscript. Thanks also to Brian Lesser for his comments on the recipes relating to FlashCom and Pavils Jurjans for his careful review of the recipes on regular expressions. Thanks are also due to John Viega and Andy Oram for reviewing the encryption/security recipe. Last, but not least, I would like to thank Gareth and Devon for providing assistance with PHP scripts, Arun Bhalla for his assistance with Perl scripts, and Peter deHaan for his assistance with ColdFusion scripts. I would also like to thank other technical reviewers who offered feedback on one or more chapters, including Kathryn Aaker, Beau Ambur, Jeffrey Bardzell, Eric Bell, David Humphreys, Chafic Kazoun, Danny Kodicek, Tom Muck, Samuel Neff, Jesse Warden, and Edoardo Zubler. I apologize if I accidentally omitted anyone from the list.

Thanks are definitely due to the many readers, to the developers on numerous mailing lists, and to all the people who post to various newsgroups and user forums. All the questions and answers and feedback are more beneficial than you can know.

Certainly not least of all, I would sincerely like to thank all the wonderful people in my life who love, support, and encourage me.

And without a doubt I acknowledge the oneness, the great mystery that makes all things possible.

Joey Lott
Los Angeles, California
May 2003

## PART I

Local Recipes

## CHAPTER 1

ActionScript Basics

1.0   Introduction

Using ActionScript, you can create Flash movies that do just about anything you can imagine. But before launching into the vast possibilities, let's start with the basic foundation. The good news is that ActionScript commands follow a well-defined pattern, sharing similar syntax, structure, and concepts. Mastering the fundamental grammar puts you well on the way to mastering ActionScript.

This chapter addresses the frequent tasks and problems that relate to core Action-Script knowledge. Whether you are a beginner or master—or somewhere in between—these recipes help you handle situations that arise in every ActionScript project.

This book assumes you are familiar with the Flash authoring tool and have entered some basic ActionScript in the past, perhaps using the built-in Actions. ActionScript code is entered in the Actions panel (Window → Actions), as shown in Figure 1-1.

We'll be entering our code in Expert Mode, which allows us to type the desired code into the Actions panel's script pane, also shown in Figure 1-1. Activate Expert Mode using the pop-up Options menu in the Actions panel, as shown in Figure 1-2. The menu in Figure 1-2 also displays useful configuration options, such as whether to display line numbers or auto-format your ActionScript code.

ActionScript's *trace()* command is used to display text in the Output window during authoring, as seen in Figure 1-3. To enter a script, you'll highlight a frame in the timeline and then open the Actions panel (the easiest way to open the Actions panel is using the shortcut key, F9). Code can also be attached directly to a movie clip or button, but attaching code to the timeline is usually preferred. Many developers add a *scripts* layer to their timeline, and that is where they attach their code.

The Output window is useful for debugging and is displayed automatically whenever *trace()* actions are executed (but only in the Test Player.) Recipes 8.9 and 11.15 display text at runtime to provide user feedback or assist in debugging.

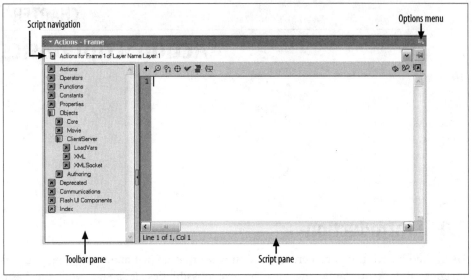

Figure 1-1. The Actions panel in Expert Mode

Now that you know where to enter code, for beginners, here is quick primer on terminology. These definitions are very approximate and are intended to orient people who have never programmed before. They are not technically exact or complete in every regard. If you already know what these terms mean, then please excuse what may be perceived as imprecise definitions, which are presented here for clarity and brevity.

Variables

> *Variables* are convenient placeholders for data in our code, and we can name them anything we like, provided the name isn't already reserved by ActionScript and the name starts with a letter, underscore, or dollar sign (but not a number). Variables are convenient for holding interim information, such as a sum of numbers, or to refer to something, such as a text field or movie clip. Local variables are preferably *declared* with the var keyword the first time they are used in a script. Global variables and timeline variables are discussed in Recipe 1.12. You can assign a value to a variable using the equals sign (=), which is also known as the *assignment operator*.

Functions

> For our purposes, *functions* are blocks of code that do something. We can *call* or *invoke* a function (that is, execute it) by using its name. Commands such as *trace()* are functions that come built into the Flash Player.

Scope

> A variable's *scope* describes when and where the variable can be manipulated by the code in a movie. Scope defines a variable's life span and from where in our code we can set or retrieve the variable's value. A function's scope determines

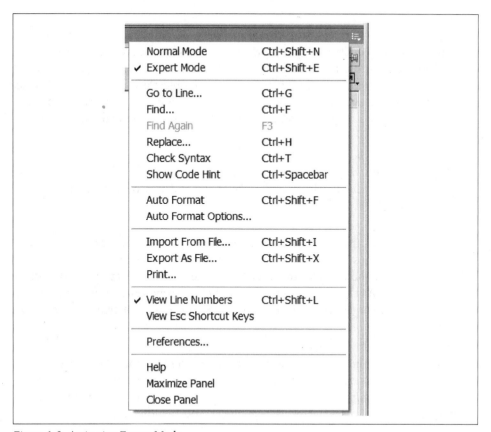

Figure 1-2. Activating Expert Mode

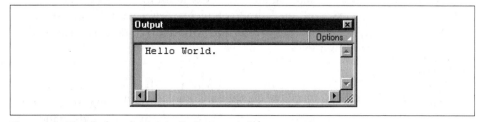

Figure 1-3. The Flash authoring tool's Output window

where and when the function is accessible to other blocks of code. Recipe 1.7 deals with issues of scope.

Handler

A *handler* is a function that is executed in response to an event, such as a mouse-click, a keystroke, or the movement of the playhead in the timeline.

Objects and classes

An *object* is something you can manipulate programmatically in ActionScript, such as a movie clip. There are other types of objects, such as those used to manipulate colors, dates, and text fields. Objects are instances of *classes*. That is, a class is a template for creating objects, and an object is a particular occurrence of that class. If you get confused, think of it in biological terms: you can consider yourself an object (instance) that belongs to the general class known as humans.

Methods

A *method* is a function associated with an object that operates on the object. For example, a text field object's *replaceSel()* method can be used to replace the selected text in the field.

Properties

A *property* is an attribute of an object, which can be read and/or set. For example, a movie clip's horizontal location is specified by its _x property, which can be both tested and set. On the other hand, a text field's length property, which indicates the number of characters in the field, can be tested but cannot be set directly (it can be affected indirectly, however, by adding or removing text from the field).

Statements

ActionScript commands are entered as a series of one or more *statements*. A statement might tell the playhead to jump to a particular frame, or it might change the size of a movie clip. Most ActionScript statements are terminated with a semicolon (;). This book uses the terms "statement" and "action" interchangeably.

Comments

Comments are notes within code that are intended for other humans and ignored by Flash. In ActionScript, single-line comments begin with // and terminate automatically at the end of the current line. Multiline comments begin with /* and are terminated with */.

Interpreter

The *ActionScript interpreter* is that portion of the Flash Player that examines your code and attempts to understand and execute it. Following ActionScript's strict rules of grammar ensures that the interpreter can easily understand your code. If the interpreter encounters an error, it often fails silently, simply refusing to execute the code rather than generating a specific error message.

Directives and pragmas

A line of code that begins with a # is a *directive* or *pragma*, which provides special instructions to Flash at compilation time (when the *.fla* is converted into a *.swf*). The most common directive is #include, which is used to include ActionScript code contained in an external *.as* file. Do not include a terminating semicolon on lines of code containing directives or pragmas.

Don't worry if you don't understand all the specifics. You can use each recipe's solution without understanding the technical details, and this primer should help you understand the terminology.

Many of the recipes in this book require you to access a movie clip's methods or properties. Sometimes these clips are created at runtime via ActionScript, but often you'll want to adapt a recipe to work with your author-time content. ActionScript can refer by name to a movie clip instance created in the authoring tool.

> ActionScript refers to authoring-time movie clips using the name of the movie clip instance on the Stage (not the name of the Library symbol from which the clip is derived). Therefore, you must set a movie clip's instance name using the Property inspector, as shown in Figure 1-4, before you can access it via ActionScript. See Recipe 7.19 for information on creating movie clip instances from a Library symbol at runtime.

Figure 1-4 shows a movie clip on the Stage with its instance name set to "semiCircle_mc" in the Property inspector.

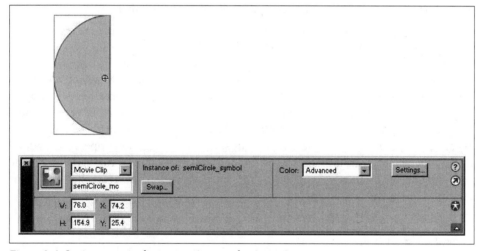

Figure 1-4. Setting a movie clip instance's name for ActionScript access

1.1   Using Mathematical Operators

Problem

You want to modify something over time, such as the rotation or position of a movie clip.

Solution

Use the compound assignment operators to change a variable or property in increments. Or, if incrementing or decrementing by one, use the prefix or postfix increment or decrement operators.

Discussion

Often, you'll want the new value of a variable or property to depend on the previous
value. For example, you might want to move a movie clip to a new position that is 10
pixels to the right of its current position.

In an assignment statement—any statement using the assignment operator (an
equals sign)—the expression to the right of the equals sign is evaluated and the result
is stored in the variable or property on the left side. Therefore, you can modify the
value of a variable in an expression on the right side of the equation and assign that
new value to the very same variable on the left side of the equation.

Although the following may look strange to those who remember basic algebra, it is
very common for a variable to be set equal to itself plus a number:

```
// Add 6 to the current value of myNum and assign that new value back to myNum. For
// example, if myNum was 3, this statement sets it to 9.
myNum = myNum + 6;
```

However, when performing mathematical operations, it is often more convenient to
use one of the *compound assignment operators*, which combine a mathematical operator with the assignment operator. The +=, -=, *=, and /= operators are the most
prevalent compound assignment operators. When you use one of these compound
assignment operators, the value on the right side of the assignment operator is added
to, subtracted from, multiplied by, or divided into the value of the variable on the
left, and the new value is assigned to the same variable. The following are a few
examples of equivalent statements.

These statements both add 6 to the existing value of myNum:

```
myNum = myNum + 6;
myNum += 6;
```

These statements both subtract 6 from the existing value of myNum:

```
myNum = myNum - 6;
myNum -= 6;
```

These statements both multiply myNum by anotherNum:

```
myNum = myNum * anotherNum;
myNum *= anotherNum;
```

These statements both divide myNum by anotherNum:

```
myNum = myNum / anotherNum;
myNum /= anotherNum;
```

There should be no space between the two symbols that make up a compound assignment operator.

Additionally, if you are incrementing or decrementing a variable by 1, you can use the increment or decrement operators (-- and ++).

This statement adds 1 to myNum:

```
myNum++;
```

and has the same effect as either of these statements:

```
myNum = myNum + 1;
myNum += 1;
```

This statement subtracts 1 from myNum:

```
myNum--;
```

and has the same effect as either of these statements:

```
myNum = myNum - 1;
myNum -= 1;
```

You can use the increment and decrement operators before or after the variable or property on which they operate. If used before the operand, they are called *prefix operators*. If used after the operand, they are called *postfix operators*. The prefix and postfix operators modify the operand in the same way but at different times. In some circumstances, there is no net difference in their operation, but the distinction is still important in many cases. When using prefix operators, the value is modified before the remainder of the statement or expression is evaluated. And if using postfix operators, the value is modified after the remainder of the statement has executed. Note how the first example increments myNum after displaying its value, whereas the second example increments myNum before displaying its value:

```
myNum = 5;
trace(myNum++);   // Displays: 5
trace(myNum);     // Displays: 6

myNum = 5;
trace(++myNum);   // Displays: 6
trace(myNum);     // Displays: 6
```

Getting back to our original problem, you can use mathematical operators to modify a property over time. This example causes the specified movie clip to rotate by 5 degrees for each tick of the frame rate:

```
myClip_mc.onEnterFrame = function () {
  this._rotation += 5;
};
```

1.2   Checking Equality or Comparing Values

Problem

You want to check if two values are equal.

Solution

Use the equality (or inequality) or strict equality (or strict inequality) operator to compare two values. To check whether a value is a valid number, use *isNaN()*.

Discussion

Equality expressions always return a Boolean value indicating whether the two values are equal. The equality (and inequality) operators come in both regular and strict flavors. The regular equality and inequality operators check whether the two expressions being compared can be resolved to the same value after converting them to the same datatype. For example, note that the string "6" and the number 6 are considered equal because the string "6" is converted to the number 6 before comparison:

```
trace(5 == 6);    // Displays: false
trace(6 == 6);    // Displays: true
trace(6 == "6");  // Displays: true
trace(5 == "6");  // Displays: false
```

The logical inequality operator (!=) returns false if two values are equal and true if they are not equal. If necessary, the operands are converted to the same datatype before the comparison:

```
trace(5 != 6);    // Displays: true
trace(6 != 6);    // Displays: false
trace(6 != "6");  // Displays: false
trace(5 != "6");  // Displays: true
```

On the other hand, the strict equality and inequality operators first check whether the values being compared are of the same datatype before performing the comparison. Differences in datatype cause the strict equality operator to return false and the strict inequality operator to return true:

```
trace(6 === 6);    // Displays: true
trace(6 === "6");  // Displays: false
trace(6 !== 6);    // Displays: false
trace(6 !== "6");  // Displays: true
```

 There is a big difference between the assignment operator (=) and the equality operator (==). If you use the assignment operator instead of the equality operator, you change the variable's value rather than testing its current value.

Using the wrong operator leads to unexpected results. In the following example, myVar equals 5 at first, so you might expect the subsequent *if* statement to always evaluate to false, preventing the *trace()* from being executed:

```
var myVar = 5;
// The following code is wrong. It should be if (myVar == 6) instead
if (myVar = 6) {
  trace("Rabbits are bunnies.");
}
trace("myVar is " + myVar);  // Displays: myVar is 6
```

However, the example mistakenly uses the assignment operator (=) instead of the equality operator (==). That is, the expression *myVar* = 6 sets myVar to 6 instead of testing whether myVar is 6. When used in an *if* clause, the expression *myVar* = 6 is treated as the number 6. Because any nonzero number used in a test expression converts to the Boolean true, the *trace()* action is called. Replace the test expression with *myVar* == 6 instead.

You can check an item's datatype using the *typeof* operator, as follows:

```
var myVar = 5;
if (typeof myVar == "number") {
  trace("Yippee. It's a number.");
}
```

But some numeric values are invalid. The following example results in myVar being set equal to NaN (a constant representing invalid numbers, short for "Not-a-Number") because the calculation cannot be performed in a meaningful way:

```
var myVar = 15 - "coffee";
```

Despite its name, NaN is a recognized value of the *number* datatype:

```
trace(typeof myVar);   // Displays: "number"
```

Therefore, to test if something is not only a number, but a valid number, you might try this:

```
var myVar = 15 - "coffee";
if (typeof myVar == "number") {
  // Nice try, but this won't work.
  if (myVar != NaN) {
    trace("Yippee. It's a number.");
  }
}
```

 You can't simply compare a value to the constant NaN to check whether it is a valid number. Instead, you must use the special *isNaN()* function to perform the test.

To determine if a number is invalid, use the special *isNaN()* function, as follows:

```
var myVar = 15 - "coffee";
if (isNaN(myVar)) {
```

```
      trace("Sorry, that is not a valid number.");
    }
```

To test the opposite of a condition (i.e., whether the condition is not true) use the logical *NOT* operator (!). For example, to check whether a variable contains a *valid* number, use *!isNAN()*, as follows:

```
var myVar = 15 - "coffee";
if (!isNaN(myVar)) {
  // The number is not invalid, so it must be a valid number.
  trace ("That is a valid number.");
  // This jumps to another frame, assuming you've labeled a frame "SuccessScreen".
  gotoAndStop ("SuccessScreen");
}
```

Of course, you can perform comparisons using the well-known comparison operators. For example, you can use the > and < operators to check if one value is less than or greater than another value:

```
trace(5 < 6);    // Displays: true
trace(5 > 5);    // Displays: false
```

Similarly, you can use the >= and <= operators to check if one value is less than or equal to, or greater than or equal to, another value:

```
trace(5 <= 6);   // Displays: true
trace(5 >= 5);   // Displays: true
```

You should also be aware that ActionScript compares different datatypes differently. ActionScript data can be categorized into *primitive* datatypes (*string*, *number*, and *Boolean*) or *composite* datatypes (*object*, *movieclip*, and *array*). When you compare primitive datatypes, ActionScript compares them "by value." In this example, myVar and myOtherVar are considered equal because they both contain the value 6.

```
var myVar = 6;
var myOtherVar = 6;
trace (myVar == myOtherVar);        // Displays: true
```

However, when you compare composite datatypes, ActionScript compares them "by reference." Comparing items by reference means that the two items are considered equal only if both point to exactly the same object, not merely to objects with matching contents. For example, two arrays containing exactly the same values are not considered equal:

```
// Create two arrays with the same elements.
arrayOne = new Array("a", "b", "c");
arrayTwo = new Array("a", "b", "c");
trace(arrayOne == arrayTwo);        // Displays: false
```

Two composite items are equal only if they both refer to the identical object, array, or movie clip. For example:

```
// Create a single array
arrayOne = new Array("a", "b", "c");
```

```
// Create another variable that references the same array.
arrayOne = arrayTwo;
trace(arrayOne == arrayTwo);          // Displays: true
```

See Also

Recipe 6.8

1.3   Performing Actions Conditionally

Problem

You want to perform an action only when a condition is true.

Solution

Use an *if* statement or a *switch* statement.

Discussion

You often need your ActionScript code to make decisions, such as whether to execute a particular action or group of actions. To execute an action under certain circumstances, use one of ActionScript's *conditional* statements: *if*, *switch*, or the ternary conditional operator (? :).

The conditional statements allow you to make logical decisions, and you'll learn from experience which is more appropriate for a given situation. The *if* statement is most appropriate when you want to tell your Flash movie to do something only when a certain condition is met (i.e., when the condition is true). When you have several possible conditions to test, you can use the *switch* statement instead. And you can use Flash's ternary conditional operator to perform conditional checking and assignment on a single line.

First, we'll look at the *if* statement. Of the conditional statements in ActionScript, the *if* statement is the most important to understand. In its most basic form, an *if* statement includes the keyword if followed by the test expression whose truthfulness you want to evaluate to determine which action or actions to execute. The test expression must be in parentheses, and the statement(s) to be executed should be within curly braces (the latter is mandatory if there is more than one statement in the statement block).

Here, we check whether animalName contains the word "turtle". This might be used to check whether the user answered a quiz question correctly (here, animalName is a variable assumed to contain the user's answer). Note that the double equals sign (==)

is used to test whether two items are equal. It should not be confused with the single equals sign (=), which is used to assign a value to an item.

```
if (animalName == "turtle") {
  // This trace( ) statement executes only when animalName is equal to "turtle".
  trace("Yay! 'Turtle' is the correct answer.");
}
```

Additionally, you can add an *else* clause to an *if* statement to perform alternative actions if the condition is false. Note that the *trace()* command has no effect when the Flash movie is running in a browser, so it is intended for testing purposes only. We use the *gotoAndStop()* command to jump to a different frame (presumably one that displays an appropriate message) depending on whether the user answered the question correctly or incorrectly.

```
if (animalName == "turtle") {
  // These statements execute only when animalName is equal to "turtle".
  trace("Yay! 'Turtle' is the correct answer.");
  gotoAndStop("CongratulationsScreen");
}
else {
  // These statements execute only when animalName is not equal to "turtle".
  trace("Sorry, you got the question wrong.");
  gotoAndStop("TryAgainScreen");
}
```

 The *gotoAndStop()* command jumps to a frame with the specified label or frame number and is used in this example to illustrate typical real-world usage. The example assumes you've created a Flash movie with frames labeled "CongratulationsScreen" and "TryAgainScreen." To label a frame, highlight one of the layers in the timeline and add a label using the Frame field in the Property inspector.

You can add an *else if* clause to an *if* statement. If the *if* condition is true, the *else if* clause is skipped. If the *if* condition is false, the ActionScript interpreter checks to see if the *else if* condition is true.

```
if (animalName == "turtle") {
  // This trace( ) statement executes only when animalName is equal to "turtle".
  trace("Yay! 'Turtle' is the correct answer.");
}
else if (animalName == "dove") {
  // This trace( ) statement executes only when animalName is not "turtle" but is
  // "dove".
  trace("Sorry, a dove is a bird, not a reptile.");
}
```

What if the preceding example was written as two separate *if* statements (one to check if animalName is "turtle" and another to check if it is "dove")? The example would work as intended, but it would be less efficient. Using the *else if* statement guarantees that if animalName is "turtle", we don't bother checking if it is also equal to "dove".

If your two conditions are mutually exclusive, use an *else if* clause to check the second condition. If your two conditions are not mutually exclusive, and you want to perform both statement blocks when both conditions are met, use two separate *if* statements.

When you use an *if* statement with both *else if* and *else* clauses, the *else* clause must be the last clause in the statement. The final *else* clause is convenient as a catchall; it's where you can put statements that take the appropriate action if none of the other conditions are met.

```
if (animalName == "turtle") {
  // This trace( ) statement executes only when animalName is equal to "turtle".
  trace("Yay! 'Turtle' is the correct answer.");
}
else if (animalName == "dove") {
  // This statement executes only when animalName is not "turtle" but is "dove".
  trace("Sorry, a dove is a bird, not a reptile.");
}
else {
  // This statement executes only when animalName is neither "turtle" nor "dove".
  trace("Sorry, try again.");
}
```

You can also include more than one *else if* clause in an *if* statement. However, in that case, you should most likely use a *switch* statement instead; generally, *switch* statements are more legible and succinct than the comparable *if* statement. Where performance is critical, some ActionScripters prefer to use *if* statements, which allow somewhat greater control for optimization purposes.

A *switch* statement is composed of three parts:

The switch *keyword*
Every *switch* statement must begin with the switch keyword.

Test expression
This is an expression, enclosed in parentheses, whose value you want to test in order to determine which actions to execute.

The switch statement body
The statement body, enclosed in curly braces, is composed of *cases*. Each case is composed of the following parts:

The case *or* default *keyword*
Each case must begin with a case keyword. The exception is the default case (analogous to an *else* clause in an *if* statement), which uses the default keyword.

Case expression
This is an expression whose value is compared to the *switch* statement's test expression. If the two values are equal, the code in the case body is executed.

The default case (the case that uses the default keyword) does not need a case expression.

Case body

This is one or more statements, usually ending in a *break* statement, to be performed if the *case* is true.

The switch keyword is always followed by the test expression in parentheses. Then, the *switch* statement body is enclosed in curly braces. There can be one or more *case* statements within the *switch* statement body. Each case (other than the default case) starts with the case keyword followed by the case expression and a colon. The default case (if one is included) starts with the default keyword followed by a colon. Therefore, the general form of a *switch* statement is:

```
switch (testExpression) {
  case caseExpression:
    // case body
  case caseExpression:
    // case body
  default:
    // case body
}
```

Here is an example. Note that once a case tests true, all the remaining actions in all subsequent cases within the *switch* statement body also execute. This example is most likely not what the programmer intended:

```
var animalName = "dove";

/* In the following switch statement, the first trace() statement does not execute
   because animalName is not equal to "turtle". But both the second and third trace()
   statements execute, because once the "dove" case tests true, all subsequent code
   is executed.
*/
switch (animalName) {
  case "turtle":
    trace("Yay! 'Turtle' is the correct answer.");
  case "dove":
    trace("Sorry, a dove is a bird, not a reptile.");
  default:
    trace("Sorry, try again.");
}
```

Normally, you should use *break* statements at the end of each case body to exit the *switch* statement after executing the actions under the matching case.

> The *break* statement terminates the current *switch* statement, preventing statements in subsequent case bodies from being executed erroneously.

You don't need to add a *break* statement to the end of the last *case* or *default* clause, since it is the end of the *switch* statement anyway:

```
var animalName = "dove";

// Now, only the second trace( ) statement executes.
switch (animalName) {
  case "turtle":
    trace("Yay! 'Turtle' is the correct answer.");
    break;
  case "dove":
    trace("Sorry, a dove is a bird, not a reptile.");
    break;
  default:
    trace("Sorry, try again.");
}
```

The *switch* statement is especially useful when you want to perform the same action for one of several matching possibilities. Simply list multiple case expressions one after the other. For example:

```
switch (animalName) {
  case "turtle":
  case "alligator":
  case "iguana":
    trace("Yay! You named a reptile.");
    break;
  case "dove":
  case "pigeon":
  case "cardinal":
    trace("Sorry, you specified a bird, not a reptile.");
    break;
  default:
    trace("Sorry, try again.");
}
```

ActionScript also supports the ternary conditional operator (? :), which allows you to perform a conditional test and an assignment statement on a single line. A "ternary" operator requires three operands, as opposed to the one or two operands required by unary and binary operators. The first operand of the conditional operator is a conditional expression that evaluates to true or false. The second operand is the value to assign to the variable if the condition is true, and the third operand is the value to assign if the condition is false.

```
varName = (conditional expression) ? valueIfTrue : valueIfFalse;
```

One common use of the ternary operator is in assigning default values to variables in functions if a parameter value was omitted when calling the function. For example:

```
function myFunction (param) {
  var val = (param != undefined) ? param : "default value";
}
```

The preceding example can be written using an *if* statement:

```
function myFunction (param) {
  var val;
  if (param != undefined) {
    val = param;
  } else {
    val = "default value";
  }
}
```

Either way is correct; however, the ternary operator requires fewer lines of code and executes faster.

Here is an example in which salutation defaults to "Hello" if no greeting was specified; otherwise, salutation is set to greeting's value.

```
function welcome (greeting) {
  var salutation = (greeting != undefined) ? greeting: "Hello";
  trace (salutation + " Sailor!")
}
```

Here are some examples of the results:

```
welcome();         // Displays: Hello Sailor!
welcome("Ahoy");   // Displays: Ahoy Sailor!
```

1.4   Performing Complex Conditional Testing

Problem

You want to make a decision based on multiple conditions.

Solution

Use the logical *AND* (&&), *OR* (||), and *NOT* (!) operators to create compound conditional statements.

Discussion

Many statements in ActionScript can involve conditional expressions, including *if*, *while*, and *for* statements, and statements using the ternary conditional operator. To test whether two conditions are both true, use the logical *AND* operator (&&), as follows (see Chapter 10 for details on working with dates):

```
// Check if today is April 17th.
now = new Date();
if (now.getDate() == 17 && now.getMonth() == 3) {
  trace ("Happy Birthday, Bruce!");
}
```

You can add extra parentheses to make the logic more apparent:

```
// Check if today is April 17th.
if ((now.getDate() == 17) && (now.getMonth() == 3)) {
  trace ("Happy Birthday, Bruce!");
}
```

Here we use the logical *OR* operator (||) to test whether either condition is true:

```
// Check if it is a weekend.
if ((now.getDay() == 0) || (now.getDay() == 6) ) {
  trace ("Why are you working on a weekend?");
}
```

You can also use a logical *NOT* operator (!) to check if a condition is not true:

```
// Check to see if the name is not Bruce.
if (!(name == "Bruce")) {
  trace ("This application knows only Bruce's birthday.");
}
```

The preceding example could be rewritten using the inequality operator (!=):

```
if (name != "Bruce") {
  trace ("This application knows only Bruce's birthday.");
}
```

Any Boolean value, or an expression that converts to a Boolean, can be used as the test condition:

```
// Check to see if a movie clip is visible. If so, display a message. This condition
// is shorthand for myMovieClip._visible == true.
if (myMovieClip._visible) {
  trace("The movie clip is visible.");
}
```

The logical *NOT* operator is often used to check if something is false, rather than true:

```
// Check to see if a movie clip is invisible (not visible). If so, display a message.
// This condition is shorthand for myMovieClip._visible != true or
// myMovieClip._visible == false.
if (!myMovieClip._visible) {
  trace("The movie clip is invisible. Set it to visible before trying this action.");
}
```

The logical *NOT* operator is often used in compound conditions along with the logical *OR* operator:

```
// Check to see if the name is neither Bruce nor Joey. (This could also be rewritten
// using two inequality operators and a logical AND.)
if (!((name == "Bruce") || (name == "Joey"))) {
  trace ("Sorry, but only Bruce and Joey have access to this application.");
}
```

Note that ActionScript does not bother to evaluate the second half of a logical *AND* statement unless the first half of the expression is true. If the first half is false, the overall expression is always false, so it would be inefficient to bother evaluating the second half. Likewise, ActionScript does not bother to evaluate the second half of a logical *OR* statement unless the first half of the expression is false. If the first half is true, the overall expression is always true.

1.5 Repeating an Operation Many Times

Problem

You want to perform a task multiple times within a single frame.

Solution

Use a loop to perform the same task multiple times within a single frame. For example, you can use a *for* statement:

```
for (var i = 0; i < 10; i++) {
  // Display the value of i.
  trace(i);
}
```

Discussion

When you want to execute the same action (or slight variations thereof) multiple times within a single frame, use a looping statement to make your code more succinct, easier to read, and easier to update. You can use a *while* statement or a *for* statement for this purpose, but generally a *for* statement is the better choice. Both statements achieve the same result, but the *for* statement is more compact and more familiar to most programmers.

The syntax of a *for* statement consists of five basic parts:

The for *keyword*
> Every *for* statement must begin with a for keyword.

Initialization expression
> The loop typically employs an *index variable* (a.k.a. a *loop counter*) that is initialized when the statement is first encountered. The initialization is performed only once regardless of how many times the loop is repeated.

Test expression
> A loop should include a test expression that returns true or false. The test expression is evaluated once each time through the loop. Generally, the test expression compares the index variable to another value, such as a maximum number of loop iterations. The overall expression must evaluate to true for the *for* statement's body to execute (contrast this with a *do…while* loop, which executes at least once, even if the test expression is false). On the other hand, if the

test expression never becomes false, you'll create an infinite loop, resulting in a warning that the Flash Player is running slowly (which appears after 15 seconds).

Update expression

The update expression usually updates the value of the variable used in the test expression so that, at some point, the test expression becomes false and the loop ends. The update expression is executed once each time through the loop. An infinite loop is often caused by failing to update the appropriate variable in the update expression (usually the same variable used in the test expression).

Statement body

The statement body is a block of substatements enclosed in curly braces that is executed each time through the loop. If the test expression is never true, the *for* statement's body won't be executed.

The for keyword should come first, and it should be followed by the initialization, test, and update expressions enclosed in parentheses. Semicolons must separate the three expressions from one another (although the initialization, test, and update statements are optional, the semicolons are mandatory). The remainder of the *for* loop is composed of the statement body enclosed in curly braces. The general form is:

```
for (initialization; test; update) {
  statement body
}
```

Here is an example of a *for* statement that outputs the numbers 0 to 999. Because the index variable i is a local variable, we preface it with the var keyword in the initialization expression.

```
for (var i = 0; i < 1000; i++) {
  trace(i);
}
trace ("That's the end.");
```

To understand the *for* statement, you can follow along with the ActionScript interpreter as it processes the command. In the preceding example, the for keyword tells the interpreter to perform the statements within the *for* loop as long as the conditional expression is true. The initialization expression is executed only once, and it sets the variable i to 0. Next, the interpreter checks the test expression (*i < 1000*). Because i is 0, which is less than 1000, the expression evaluates to true and the *trace()* action within the *for* statement body is executed. The ActionScript interpreter then executes the update statement, in this case i++, which increments i by 1. The interpreter then repeats the process from the top of the loop (but skips the initialization step). So the interpreter again checks whether the test expression is true and, if so, executes the statement body again. It then executes the update statement again. This process repeats until the test expression is no longer true. The last value displayed in the Output window is 999, because once i is incremented to 1000, the test expression no longer evaluates to true and the loop comes to an end. Once the loop terminates, execution continues with whatever commands follow the loop.

Both the initialization and update expressions can include multiple actions separated by commas. The following example simultaneously increments i and decrements j, and displays their values in the Output window:

```
for (var i = 0, j = 10; i < 10; i++, j--) {
  trace("i is " + i);
  trace("j is " + j);
}
```

The preceding example is not the same as using two nested *for* statements (which is shown in the next code block).

It is also common to use nested *for* statements. When you use a nested *for* statement, use a different index variable than that used in the outermost *for* loop. By convention, the outermost *for* loop uses the variable i, and the nested *for* loop uses the variable j. For example:

```
for (var i = 1; i <= 3; i++) {
  for (var j = 1; j <= 2; j++) {
    trace(i + " X " + j + " = " + (i * j));
  }
}
```

The preceding example displays the following multiplication table in the Output window:

```
1 X 1 = 1
1 X 2 = 2
2 X 1 = 2
2 X 2 = 4
3 X 1 = 3
3 X 2 = 6
```

It is possible to nest multiple levels of *for* statements. By convention, each additional level of nesting uses the next alphabetical character as the index variable. Therefore, the third level of nested *for* statements typically uses k as the index variable:

```
for (var i = 1; i <= 3; i++) {
  for (var j = 1; j <= 3; j++) {
    for (var k = 1; k <= 3; k++) {
      trace(i + " X " + j + " X " + k + " = " + (i * j * k));
    }
  }
}
```

Additionally, you can use *for* statements to loop backward:

```
// Count backward from 10 to 1.
for (var i = 10; i > 0; i--) {
  trace(i);
}
```

You should not use a *for* statement to perform tasks over time.

Many programmers make the mistake of trying to use *for* statements to animate movie clips. For example:

```
for (var i = 0; i < 20; i++) {
  myMovieClip._x += 10;
}
```

Although the preceding code moves the movie clip 200 pixels to the right of its starting point, all the updates take place within the same frame. There are two problems with this. First of all, the Stage updates only once per frame, so only the last update is shown on the Stage (causing the movie clip to jump 200 pixels suddenly rather than moving smoothly in 20 steps). And second, even if the Stage updates more often, each iteration through the *for* loop takes only a few milliseconds, so the animation would happen too quickly. For actions that you want to take place over time, use an *onEnterFrame()* handler (see Recipe 1.6) or set an interval using the *setInterval()* function (see Recipe 1.7).

Moreover, tight repeating loops should not be used to perform lengthy processes (anything that takes more than a fraction of a second). The Flash Player displays a warning whenever a single loop executes for more than 15 seconds. Using an *onEnterFrame()* handler or the *setInterval()* function avoids the warning message and allows Flash to perform other actions in addition to the repeated actions that are part of the loop.

See Also

The *for* statement is used in many practical situations, and you can see examples in a great many of the recipes throughout this book. See Recipes 6.2 and 9.10 for some practical examples, and Recipe 2.3, in which the *break* command is used to exit the loop prematurely. Recipe 6.13 discusses *for...in* loops, which are used to enumerate the properties of an object or array.

1.6   Performing an Action
   Once per Frame Update

Problem

You want to perform an action or actions at the frame rate of the movie.

Solution

Use an *onEnterFrame()* handler.

Discussion

The *onEnterFrame()* event handler method for movie clips is the appropriate choice when you want to perform actions continuously at the same speed as the frame rate of the movie. See Recipes 1.1 and 7.8.

1.7   Repeating a Task at Timed Intervals

Problem

You want to perform an action or actions at a specific timed interval.

Solution

Use the *setInterval()* function.

Discussion

The *setInterval()* function allows you to specify an interval (in milliseconds) at which your Flash movie will invoke a function. Use *setInterval()* to perform a particular action over time but not necessarily at the frequency of the frame rate of the movie.

```
// Define a function.
function myIntervalFunction ( ) {

    // Output the difference between the current timer value and its value from the
    // last time the function was called.
    trace(getTimer( ) - lastTime);
    lastTime = getTimer( );
}

// Set up an interval that attempts to invoke myIntervalFunction( ) once every
// millisecond.
setInterval(myIntervalFunction, 1);
```

In the preceding example, even though the interval is theoretically one millisecond, in practice, its accuracy and granularity depend on computer playback performance in relation to other tasks being demanded of the processor. There are two implications to this:

- Don't rely on intervals to be extremely precise.
- Don't rely on intervals to be smaller than a few milliseconds.

The *setInterval()* function returns an identifier for the newly created interval. If you want to be able to stop the interval at a later time, you must store the return value, as follows:

```
// Set an interval such that someFunction() is called approximately once per second.
// Assign setInterval()'s return value to the variable myIntervalID for later use.
myIntervalID = setInterval(someFunction, 1000);
```

You can use the *clearInterval()* function to stop an interval if you know the interval's identifier:

```
clearInterval(myIntervalID);
```

If you want the interval to invoke the method of an object instead of a standalone function, you can use the variation of the *setInterval()* function in which you pass it three parameters—a reference to the object, the name of the function (as a string), and the interval in milliseconds— instead of just two:

```
// Create a simple object using the Object constructor.
obj = new Object();

// Assign a method named myMethod to an object, obj.
obj.myMethod = function () {
  trace("obj.myMethod() has been called");
};

// Use setInterval() to tell the movie to invoke the myMethod() method of the obj
// object approximately every six seconds.
setInterval(obj, "myMethod", 6000);
```

Whichever variation of the *setInterval()* function you use, any additional parameters that you pass to the *setInterval()* function are passed along to the function or method:

```
// Define a function that accepts a parameter and displays it in the Output window.
function displayValue (val) {
  trace(val);
}

// Use setInterval() to call displayValue() once per minute. The third parameter is
// passed to the function when it is called so that each time "Bunny rabbits go
// hippity-hop" is displayed in the Output window.
setInterval(displayValue, 60000, "Bunny rabbits go hippity-hop");
```

Be aware that any values that you pass to a function or method by way of the *setInterval()* function are evaluated only at the time the interval is initialized. So the same parameter values are always passed to a function or method that is called via *setInterval()*:

```
obj = new Object();

obj.traceAnimalName = function (name) {
  trace(name);
};
```

```
myAnimalName = "cub";

setInterval(obj, "traceAnimalName", 30, myAnimalName);

// Even if myAnimalName is assigned a new value, the value "cub" is always passed to
// traceAnimalName( ), because myAnimalName was "cub" when setInterval( ) was first
// called.
myAnimalName = "puppy";
```

One of the neat things you can do with *setInterval()* is create animations that are independent of the movie's frame rate. Remember that the *onEnterFrame()* method executes at the same interval as the frame rate, so using that technique ties you to the movie's properties. But with *setInterval()* you can call a function or method at any interval you want. Here is an example in which two intervals are set—one for a square movie clip (every 50 milliseconds) and one for a circle movie clip (every 100 milliseconds):

```
// Define the function first. This function takes three parameters: a reference to
// the movie clip object, the change in x, and the change in y.
function moveObj (obj, dx, dy) {

  // Increment the movie clip's x and y coordinates.
  obj._x += dx;
  obj._y += dy;

  // In case the interval is less than the movie's frame rate, you need to use the
  // built-in updateAfterEvent( ) method to refresh the Stage.
  updateAfterEvent( );
}

// Create two intervals. Each invokes the moveObj( ) function, but at different
// intervals and with different movie clip references as parameters.
squareInterval = setInterval(moveObj, 50,  square, 1, 1);
circleInterval = setInterval(moveObj, 100, circle, 1, 1);
```

1.8 Creating Reusable Code

Problem

You want to perform a series of actions at various times without duplicating code unnecessarily throughout your movie.

Solution

Create a function and then call (i.e., invoke) it by name whenever you need to execute those actions.

There is more than one way to create (i.e., define or declare) a function. Here is how to create a *named function*:

```
function functionName () {
  // Statements go here.
}
```

To call (i.e., execute) the named function, refer to it by name, such as:

```
functionName();
```

Here is how to create a *function literal*:

```
functionName = function () {
  // Statements go here.
};
```

Although not strictly required, it is considered a best practice to include a semicolon following the closing curly brace when defining a function literal.

Discussion

Grouping statements into a function allows you to define the function once but execute it as many times as you'd like. This is useful when you need to perform similar actions at various times without duplicating the same code in multiple places. Keeping your code centralized in functions makes it easier to understand (because you can write the function once and then ignore the details when using it) and easier to maintain (because you can make changes in one place rather than in multiple places).

There are two common ways of defining ActionScript functions: as named functions or function literals (a.k.a. *anonymous functions*). Each of these ways of declaring a function has its own use.

The named function declaration is the most common choice (when not defining a function to be used as a method) and has at least one advantage over function literals: named functions are accessible within the entire keyframe (or *on()* or *onClipEvent()* handler) even if they come after the call to the function.

For example, even though the *writeMessage()* function is not declared until after it is invoked, the function is still available:

```
// Invoke the writeMessage() function, which is declared later in the script.
writeMessage();

// Declare (define) the writeMessage() function as a named function.
function writeMessage () {
  trace("Hello, friend.");
}

// The function is available before or after it has been declared.
writeMessage();
```

In contrast, a function literal is accessible only from lines of code that come after the declaration:

```
// The ActionScript interpreter will not be able to find a function with this name,
// and so nothing happens (it fails silently).
writeMessage2();

// Declare (define) the writeMessage2() function as an anonymous function literal
writeMessage2 = function () {
  trace("Hello, friend.");
};

// However, the function is available from lines of code after it has been declared.
writeMessage2();
```

However, there are several reasons to use function literals:

- You can assign a function literal to a global variable so that the function can be accessed from any timeline.
- Function literals offer a convenient, compact, and intuitive way to define methods for objects.
- Function literals can be treated like other variables, in that they can be passed to other functions or have their values reassigned.

Here, we assign a function literal as a property of the _global object:

```
_global.launchBookExamples = function () {
  getURL("http://www.person13.com/ascb", "_blank");
};
```

Therefore, from anywhere on any timeline, you can execute the function by simply using its name. For example, you might attach this script to a button:

```
myButton.onRelease = function () {
  launchBookExamples();
};
```

Here, we define the function as a method of a movie clip (where *onEnterFrame()* is a special, built-in method for movie clips that you need to define before it can be used):

```
myClip_mc.onEnterFrame = function () {
  trace("Hooray for methods!");
};
```

Of course, you can define custom methods as well by simply assigning the function literal to a new property of the object:

```
myClip_mc.myCustomMethod = function () {
  trace("Hooray for methods!");
};
```

It is also worth noting that you can set one method equal to another method. This technique is often used to assign the same actions to a movie clip or button for two different events. You can define an anonymous function and assign it to one of the event handler methods, and then simply assign one event handler method to the other. A common example of this is when you want to define the same actions for when a user releases a button or movie clip and when they release outside:

```
// Define an onRelease() method for a movie clip.
myMovieClip.onRelease = function () {
  trace("Hooray for methods!");
};

// Assign the same method definition to the onReleaseOutside() method as well.
myMovieClip.onReleaseOutside = myMovieClip.onRelease;
```

Functions can also be passed as data. You can conveniently pass a function literal to another function that requires a function as one of its arguments, such as *setInterval()* or the *Array.sort()* method:

```
// Set an interval that calls a function that increments a variable, i, and displays
// the value.
setInterval(function () {trace(++i);}, 1000);
```

Functions are subject to the same scope limitations as variables. Timeline functions are accessible only while the timeline on which they are defined exists. A timeline function can be a named function or an anonymous function assigned to a timeline variable. Additionally, timeline functions can be called only by using the proper target path. When you access the function from the same timeline, you do not need to include the target path, but when you want to access the function from another timeline, you need to make sure you provide the correct path.

```
// Explicitly invoke a function that is defined on the main timeline.
_root.myFunction();
```

If your function is used within the same timeline only, you don't need to worry about scope issues. However, if you intend to use the function throughout many timelines, two solutions are generally employed:

- Define the function as a global function. If you make a function a global function, you can call it by name from any timeline in the movie without having to worry about scope:

```
_global.myFunction = function () {
  trace("Global functions are fun!");
};
```

- Define the function as a (static) method of a global class. All of the built-in classes are global by default, and if you define a class with a global constructor (see Recipe 12.5), then even your custom classes can be global. This technique is really a variation on the first, but with the advantage that classes offer you a way of organizing your functions in a potentially meaningful way (for example, the built-in *Math* class organizes many mathematical functions).

1.9 Generalizing a Function to Enhance Reusability

Problem

You want to perform slight variations of an action without having to duplicate multiple lines of code to accommodate the minor differences.

Solution

Add parameters to your function to make it flexible enough to perform slightly different actions when it is invoked rather than performing exactly the same action or producing the same result each time.

Define the parameters that account for the variability in what you want the function to do:

```
function myParamsFunction (param1, param2, param3) {
  trace("The average is " + (param1 + param2 + param3)/3);
}
```

If you don't know the exact number of parameters the function will receive, use the built-in arguments array to handle a variable number of parameters.

Discussion

A function that doesn't accept parameters generally produces the same result each time it is invoked. But you often need to perform almost exactly the same actions as an existing function, but with minor variations. Duplicating the entire function and then making minor changes to the second version is a bad idea in most cases. Usually, it makes your code harder to maintain and understand. More importantly, you'll usually find that you need not only two variations but many variations of the function. It can be a nightmare to maintain five or six variations of what should ideally be wrapped into a single function. The trick is to create a single function that can accept different values to operate on.

For example, if you have an *average()* function, you want to specify arbitrary values to be averaged each time it is invoked, instead of having it always average the same two numbers. You can accomplish this goal using *parameters*.

The most common way to work with parameters is to list them within the parentheses in the function declaration. The parameter names should be separated by commas, and when you invoke the function you should pass it a comma-delimited list of *arguments* that correspond to the parameters it expects.

The terms "parameters" and "arguments" are often used interchangeably to refer to the variables defined in the function declaration or the values that are passed to a function when it is invoked.

Here is a simple example of a function declaration using parameters and a function invocation in which arguments are passed during the function call:

```
// Define the function such that it expects two parameters: a and b.
function average (a, b) {
  trace("The average is " + (a + b)/2);
}
```

```
// When you invoke the function, pass it two arguments, such as 6 and 12, that
// correspond to the a and b parameters.
// This call to average( ) displays: "The average is 9"
average(6, 12);
```

Parameters work in exactly the same way with function literals as they do with named functions:

```
average = function (a, b) {
  trace("The average is: " + (a + b)/2);
};
```

In most situations it is best to declare the parameters that the function should expect. However, there are some scenarios in which the number of parameters is unknown. For example, if you want the *average()* function to average any number of values, you can use the built-in arguments array, which is available within any function's body. All the parameters that are passed to a function are automatically placed into that function's arguments array.

```
// There is no need to specify the parameters
// to accept when using the arguments array.
function average () {
  var result = 0;

  // Loop through each of the elements of the arguments array
  // and add that value to result.
  for (var i = 0; i < arguments.length; i++) {
    result += arguments[i];
  }
  // Then divide by the total number of arguments.
  trace("The average is " + result/arguments.length);
}
```

```
// You can invoke average( ) with any number of parameters.
// In this case, the function will display: "The average is 7.5".
average (3, 6, 9, 12);
```

Technically, arguments is an object with additional properties beyond that of a basic array. However, while arguments is a special kind of array, you can still work with it in the same ways that you would a regular array.

1.10 Exiting a Function

Problem

You want to exit a function.

Solution

Functions terminate automatically after the last statement within the function executes. Use a *return* statement to exit a function before reaching its end.

Discussion

The *return* statement exits the current function, and the ActionScript interpreter continues the execution of the script that initially invoked the function. Any statements within the function body that follow a *return* statement are ignored.

```
function myFunction ( ) {
  return;
  trace("Never called");
}

myFunction( );
// Execution continues here after returning from the myFuction( ) invocation.
```

In the preceding example, the *return* statement causes the function to terminate before performing any actions, so it is not a very useful function. More commonly, you will use a *return* statement to exit a function under certain conditions. This example exits the function if the password is wrong:

```
function checkPassword (password) {

  // If password is not "SimonSays", exit the function.
  if (password != "SimonSays") {
    return;
  }

  // Otherwise, perform the rest of the actions.
  gotoAndStop ("TreasureMap");
}
```

```
// This function call uses the wrong password, and so the function exits.
checkPassword("MotherMayI");

// This function uses the correct password, and so the function jumps to the
// TreasureMap frame.
checkPassword("SimonSays");
```

1.11   Obtaining the Result of a Function

Problem

You want to perform a function and return the results to the script that invoked the function.

Solution

Use a *return* statement that specifies the value to return.

Discussion

The *return* statement, when used without any parameters, simply terminates a function. Technically, *return* returns the value undefined to the caller if no value is specified. Likewise, if there is no *return* statement, the function returns undefined when it terminates. But any value specified after the return keyword is returned to script that invoked the function. Usually, the returned value is stored in a variable for later use:

```
function average (a, b) {
  // Return the average of a and b.
  return (a + b)/2;
}

var playerScore ;
// Call the average() function and store the result in a variable.
playerScore = average(6, 12);
// Use the result in some way.
trace("The player's average score is " + playerScore);
```

You can use the return value of a function, without storing it in a variable, by passing it as a parameter to another function:

```
trace("The player's average score is " + average(6, 12));
```

Note, however, that if you do nothing with the return value of the function, the result is effectively lost. For example, this statement has no detectable benefit because the result is never displayed or used in any way:

```
average(6, 12);
```

1.12   Avoiding Conflicting Variables

Problem

You want to make sure that variables within a function do not interfere with variables in other functions or within the timeline in which the function is defined.

Solution

Use the var keyword to declare local variables.

Discussion

Generally, you should declare variables used within functions as *local variables*. Local variables are known only within the function. Therefore, they do not conflict with variables of the same name in other functions or within the timelines in which the functions are defined. To make a variable local, declare it with the var keyword. Parameters are automatically treated as local variables, so you do not need to include the var keyword when declaring parameters for a function.

```
function localVarsFunction (param1, param2) {
  var myVar;
  myVar = "Local variables are fun.";
}
```

Or, more succinctly, you can write:

```
function localVarsFunction (param1, param2) {
  var myVar = "Local variables are fun.";
}
```

Variables declared without the var keyword are implicitly scoped to the timeline on which they reside (note that unlike some languages, ActionScript doesn't require you to declare a variable before assigning it a value for the first time). In this case, myVar is a *timeline variable*, not a local variable, even though it is declared within a function:

```
function timelineVarsFunction () {
  myVar = "Timeline variables are fun but not usually a good choice in functions.";
}
```

To declare a *global variable*, attach it as a property to the _global object, as follows:

```
_global.companyName = "Person13";
```

Once declared, a global variable can be accessed from anywhere in the movie by simply using its name, as follows:

```
trace ("Welcome to the " + companyName + "web site.");
```

However, a local variable of the same name will override the global variable:

```
function localVarsFunction () {
  var companyName = "Macromedia";
```

```
// This displays "Welcome to the Macromedia web site."
trace ("Welcome to the " + companyName + "web site.");

// To access the global variable of the same name, precede it with _global.
// This displays "Welcome to the Person 13 web site."
trace ("Welcome to the " + _global.companyName + "web site.");
}
```

For this reason, make sure that you always prefix a global variable reference with _global when you want to set its value. Otherwise, Flash will create a new local variable with the same name, which can potentially cause problems.

1.13   Reusing and Organizing Code in Multiple Movies

Problem

You want to reuse code that you've created for one project in another Flash movie. Or you want to write your ActionScript code in an external text editor.

Solution

Place your ActionScript code in external *.as* files and use the #include directive to add them to your Flash movies:

```
// Adds all the code within MyActionScriptFile.as to your Flash movie.
#include "MyActionScriptFile.as"
```

Discussion

Use the #include directive to incorporate code from external text files into your Flash movie during compilation from a *.fla* file to a *.swf* file. When you export a *.swf* file, Flash replaces the #include directive with the contents of the specified file. The external file must be a text file with valid ActionScript code in it. By convention the file should be named with the *.as* extension, though it is not absolutely necessary:

```
#include "ASutils.as"
```

Notice that the #include directive is not followed by a semicolon. Adding a semicolon causes an error.

Additionally, Flash must be able to locate the file when you export the movie. Therefore, you should place the file in a location relative to where the Flash document is saved. For example, the previous example looks for a file named *ASutils.as* in the same directory as the *.fla* document. You can also place the file in a subdirectory of the directory in which the Flash document is saved:

```
// Look for a file named ASutils.as in a subdirectory named myASFiles.
#include "myASFiles/ASutils.as"
```

You can also place the ActionScript files in the Flash installation's *Include* directory. And, in fact, this is recommended for all ActionScript files that you anticipate you might use in multiple movies. If Flash cannot find a file with the specified name relative to the *.fla* file, it looks in the *Configuration\Include* subdirectory of the directory in which Flash is installed. For example, on Windows-based computers, the default *Include* folder is located in *C:\Program Files\Macromedia\Flash MX\Configuration\ Include*.

If Flash is unable to find the external file in the folder specified by the #include directive (by default, the same directory as the *.fla* file) and is unable to find the file within the Flash *Include* directory, it displays an error message.

You should not upload your *.as* files along with your *.swf* file. The contents of the external text file are added to the *.swf* file when it is exported. Because the contents are not loaded into the *.swf* file dynamically at runtime, you must reexport the *.swf* file if the external *.as* file changes. Remember that future changes to the *.as* file will affect any movie that includes it the next time the movie is reexported. To prevent future changes in an external file from affecting a given movie, you can copy and paste the external code into the particular *.fla* and remove the original #include statement.

There is one additional consideration when working with external ActionScript files: it is good practice to add at least one blank line to the end of each *.as* file. This is because when Flash includes the code from the external file, it can sometimes combine the last line of the external file with the next line of code within the Flash document. This can sometimes cause errors if the last line in the external file contains code. But if the last line is blank, you can avoid these sorts of problems.

Note also that an included file can include another file (a nested #include). But paths inside an included file are relative to the original *.fla* file, not relative to the parent file location. Developers typically use a package-style reference incorporating their domain name or a project name as a directory for included files to avoid name collisions with other libraries. For example:

```
#include "com/person13/utilities/ASutils.as"
```

## CHAPTER 2

Runtime Environment

2.0   Introduction

Flash Player 6 offers a relatively large amount of information about and control over the runtime environment. ActionScript's System.capabilities object returns information about the Player and the computer on which it is running, such as the operating system, language, and audio capabilities. The *System* object also allows you to control some elements of the Player such as the right-click menu under Windows (Ctrl-click on the Macintosh) and the Settings dialog box. The *Stage* object controls the scaling and alignment of the movie within the Player.

2.1   Detecting the Player Version

Problem

You want to know the user's Flash Player version.

Solution

Use a plugin-detection script that runs in the browser before loading the Flash Player, or use ActionScript (System.capabilities.version, *getVersion()*, or $version) within the Flash Player, as supported by the minimum Player version you expect to encounter.

Discussion

There are two broad categories of Flash Player version detection: you can attempt to detect the Player version with a browser-based script before the Player loads, or you can use ActionScript within the Flash Player to check the version that is currently running.

The problem with the first method is that it doesn't work on all platforms and with all browsers, as explained in part at *http://www.macromedia.com/support/flash/ts/documents/browser_support_matrix.htm.*

Therefore, you should guard against a "false negative" in your detection approach; even if you fail to detect the Flash Player plugin, you should give the user the option of telling you that he has the plugin installed and would like to view your Flash content (i.e., don't force visitors to the Macromedia Flash installation page just because you can't detect their Player version).

There is a wealth of existing documentation on detecting the presence and version of the Flash Player plugin with a browser script, so refer to the following URLs for explanations and examples.

Macromedia Technote 14526, "How to detect the presence of the Flash Player," is a good starting point:

> *http://www.macromedia.com/support/flash/ts/documents/uber_detection.htm*

See also the Player-detection discussion in the Flash Deployment Kit:

> *http://www.macromedia.com/support/flash/player/flash_deployment_readme/*

The standard third-party browser-based Flash plugin-detection tool is the Moock Flash Player Inspector:

> *http://www.moock.org/webdesign/flash/detection/moockfpi/*

Testing the Flash Player version from ActionScript can be problematic because the user might not have the Player installed at all (in which case your movie and its ActionScript code are never executed), or the installed version may not support the latest ActionScript techniques. Therefore, it is typical to use the lowest common denominator for checking Flash Player versions (you can use the more modern techniques if you are sure the user will have at least a known minimum version). Naturally, if your movie is running in the Standalone Player, you can't use the browser-based plugin-detection scripts, but you can build the executable with whatever version of Flash you choose.

For maximum compatibility, use the _level0.$version property, which returns a string of the form:

```
OS MajorVersion,MinorVersion,Build,Patch
```

The $version property is supported in Flash Player 4.0.11.0 and later. For example, the following returned string indicates the Windows Player version 6.0, build number 40.0:

```
WIN 6,0,40,0
```

You can extract the operating system, major version, and minor version using the *String.split()* method, making it easier to work with the results:

```
// Split $version into an array with two elements using a space as the delimiter.
// This creates an array with two elements, such as "WIN" and "6,0,40,0".
playerParts = _root.$version.split(" ");

// Store the OS name in playerOS.
playerOS = playerParts[0];

// Split the remaining version string using a comma as the delimiter. This creates an
// array with four elements, such as "6", "0", "40", and "0".
playerVersion = playerParts[1].split(",");

// Convert the major and minor version, the build, and the patch into numbers and
// store them for later use.
playerMajorMinor = Number(playerVersion[0] + "." + playerVersion[1]);
playerBuild = Number(playerVersion[2]);
playerPatch = Number(playerVersion[3]);
```

You can use the version number to make a decision, such as sending the user to an error page that says, "This site requires Flash 5 or later":

```
if (playerMajorMinor < 5.0) {
  getURL ("http://www.person13.com/flashplugin/versionerrorpage.html");
} else {
  getURL ("http://www.person13.com/ascb/modernmovie.swf");
}
```

Why check the Player version from within Flash at all? Why not just publish a Flash 5 *.swf* file if your site requires the Flash 5 Player? In some browsers, such as Internet Explorer for Windows, the browser will automatically attempt to load the later plugin if the currently installed plugin is too old. But by using a Flash-based detection script, you can detect the plugin more accurately than you can in some browsers. Furthermore, you can customize the user experience to make it more user-friendly. Therefore, if you expect visitors to have older versions of the plugin, you should publish a Flash 4 *.swf* file that acts as a gatekeeper to Flash content requiring newer versions of the plugin. That is, the Flash 4 *.swf* should detect the version and then branch to another *.swf* file containing code implemented in the more modern version you are supporting.

Flash 5 added support for the *getVersion()* global function, which returns the same version information string as $version. Use $version to detect the Player version unless you are sure that the user has at least Flash 5 installed. Likewise, Flash 6 supports the more modern System.capabilities.version property, which again returns the same string as $version. The advantage of $version is, of course, that it is supported in older versions of the Player. And since the purpose in most cases is to detect the correct Player version, it doesn't generally make sense to use a technique that is not available in older versions of the Player. The exception is if you want to detect only versions and revisions since the Flash 5 and Flash 6 Players, respectively.

Put the following code in a *System.as* file and include it (using the #include directive) to more readily perform version checking in your movies. This code will work with Flash 5 or later.

```
// Create a System object if it doesn't exist already.
if (System == undefined) {
  System = new Object( );
}

// Create a System.capabilities object if it doesn't exist already.
if (System.capabilities == undefined) {
  System.capabilities = new Object( );
}

// The extractPlayer( ) method extracts the OS and major and minor versions of the
// Player and saves them as properties of the System.capabilities object.
System.capabilities.extractPlayer = function ( ) {
  var playerParts = _level0.$version.split(" ");
  this.playerOS = playerParts[0];
  var playerVersion = playerParts[1].split(",");
  this.playerMajorMinor = Number(playerVersion[0] + "." + playerVersion[1]);
  this.playerBuild = Number(playerVersion[2]);
  this.playerPatch = Number(playerVersion[3]);
}

// The following methods return the playerOS, playerMajorMinor, playerBuild, and
// playerPatch. If necessary, extractPlayer( ) is called first.
System.capabilities.getPlayerOS = function ( ) {
  if (this.playerOS == undefined) {
    this.extractPlayer( );
  }
  return this.playerOS;
}

System.capabilities.getPlayerMajorMinor = function ( ) {
  if (this.playerMajorMinor == undefined) {
    this.extractPlayer( );
  }
  return this.playerMajorMinor;
}

System.capabilities.getPlayerBuild = function ( ) {
  if (this.playerBuild == undefined) {
    this.extractPlayer( );
  }
  return this.playerBuild;
}

System.capabilities.getPlayerPatch = function ( ) {
  if (this.playerPatch == undefined) {
    this.extractPlayer( );
  }
  return this.playerPatch;
}
```

```
// Test each get method to see that it works.
trace(System.capabilities.getPlayerOS( ));
trace(System.capabilities.getPlayerMajorMinor( ));
trace(System.capabilities.getPlayerBuild( ));
trace(System.capabilities.getPlayerPatch( ));
```

You can use the preceding code to easily check the various portions of the version string. For example, if your movie uses scroll pane components, you should require Player 6.0.40.0 or later because previous revisions had bugs related to scroll panes. For example:

```
// Display an error message if not using at least version 6.0.40.0.
if ( !(System.capabilities.getPlayerMajorMinor( ) >= 6 &&
        System.capabilities.getPlayerBuild( ) >= 40) ) {
  outputTextField.text = "You need version 6.0.40.0 or later of the " +
                         "Flash Player in order to view this movie correctly."
}
```

For testing purposes, older versions of the Flash Player can be obtained from:

http://www.macromedia.com/support/flash/ts/documents/oldplayers.htm

2.2   Detecting the Operating System

Problem

You want to know the operating system under which the Flash movie is being played, perhaps to indicate which operating systems are not supported or to implement a platform-specific feature.

Solution

Use the $version or System.capabilities.os property.

Discussion

In Recipe 2.1, we saw that the $version property string includes the operating system on which the Player is running. The operating system can be either "MAC", "WIN", or "UNIX".

```
playerParts = _level0.$version.split(" ");
switch (playerParts[0]) {
  case "MAC":
    gotoAndStop ("WelcomeMac");
    break;
  case "WIN":
    gotoAndStop ("WelcomeWindows");
    break;
  case "UNIX":
    gotoAndStop ("WelcomeUnix");
}
```

As of Flash 6, you can use the System.capabilities.os property, which returns a string indicating the operating system and version name. Possible values include "Windows XP", "Windows 2000", "Windows NT", "Windows 98/Me", "Windows 95", and "Windows CE". On the Macintosh, the string includes the version number, such as "MacOS 9.2.1" or "MacOS 10.1.4".

You can make design choices based on the operating system. For example, your movie might load different assets depending on the user's operating system, or you may simply want to record the operating systems of the users who view your movies for statistical analysis.

If all you care about is the general platform type instead of the specific version, you can check just the first three letters of the string, as follows:

```
os = System.capabilities.os.substr(0, 3);
if (os == "Win") {
    // Windows-specific code goes here.
} else if (os == "Mac") {
    // Mac-specific code goes here.
} else {
    // Must be Unix or Linux
}
```

2.3   Checking the System Language

Problem

You want to know what language is used on the computer playing the movie.

Solution

Use the System.capabilities.language property.

Discussion

You can use the System.capabilities.language property to determine the language of the computer that is playing the movie. The property returns a two-letter ISO-639-1 language code (i.e., "fr" for French). Where applicable, a two-letter country code is appended, separated from the language code with a hyphen (i.e., "en-US" for U.S. English and "en-UK" for U.K. English).

For a summary of language codes, see the following resources:

http://lcweb.loc.gov/standards/iso639-2/englangn.html
http://www.iso.org/iso/en/prods-services/iso3166ma/02iso-3166-code-lists/list-en1.html

Here is an example of how to use the `language` property:

```
// Example output: en-US
trace(System.capabilities.language);
```

You can use this property to dynamically load content in the appropriate language:

```
// Create an associative array with language codes
// for the keys and greetings for the values.
greetings = new Array();
greetings["en"] = "Hello";
greetings["es"] = "Hola";
greetings["fr"] = "Bonjour";

// Extract the first two characters from the language code.
lang = System.capabilities.language.substr(0, 2);

// Use a default language if the language is not in the list.
if (greetings[lang] == undefined) {
  lang = "en";
}

// Display the greeting in the appropriate language.
trace(greetings[lang]);
```

When you want to offer multiple language capabilities in your movies, you can choose from several different approaches. One approach, as shown in the preceding code, is to create associative arrays for all the text that appears in the movie. Another is to create static content in multiple movies (one for each language) and load those movies based on the language code. With this technique, each *.swf* filename should include the language code, such as *myMovie_en.swf*, *myMovie_es.swf*, *myMovie_fr.swf*, etc.

```
// Get the language from the capabilities object.
lang = System.capabilities.language.substr(0, 2);

// Create an array of the languages you are supporting (i.e., the languages for which
// you have created movies).
supportedLanguages = ["en", "es", "fr"];

// Set a default language in case you don't support the user's language.
useLang = "en";

// Loop through the supported languages to find a match to the user's language. If
// you find one, set useLang to that value and then exit the for statement.
for (var i = 0; i < supportedLanguages.length; i++) {
  if (supportedLanguages[i] == lang) {
    useLang = lang;
    break;
  }
}

// Load the corresponding movie.
_root.loadMovie("myMovie_" + useLang + ".swf");
```

2.4   Detecting Display Settings

Problem

You want to know the display settings for the device on which the movie is being played.

Solution

Use the `screenResolutionX` and `screenResolutionY` properties of the `System.capabilities` object.

Discussion

You should use the `System.capabilities` object to determine the display settings of the device that is playing the movie. The `screenResolutionX` and `screenResolutionY` properties return the display resolution in pixels.

```
// Example output:
// 1024
// 768
trace(System.capabilities.screenResolutionX);
trace(System.capabilities.screenResolutionY);
```

You can use these values to determine how to display a movie or even which movie to load. These decisions are increasingly important as more handheld devices support the Flash Player. For example, the dimensions of a cell phone screen and a typical desktop computer display are different, so you should load different content based on the playback device:

```
resX = System.capabilities.screenResolutionX;
resY = System.capabilities.screenResolutionY;

// If the resolution is 240 × 320 or less, then load the PocketPC movie version.
// Otherwise, assume the device is a desktop computer and load the regular content.
if ( (resX <= 240) && (resY <= 320) ) {
  _root.loadMovie("main_pocketPC.swf");
}
else {
  _root.loadMovie("main_desktop.swf");
}
```

You can also use the screen-resolution values to center a pop-up browser window:

```
resX = System.capabilities.screenResolutionX;
resY = System.capabilities.screenResolutionY;

// Set variables for the width and height of the new browser window.
winW = 200;
winH = 200;
```

```
// Determine the x and y values in order to center the window.
winX = (resX / 2) - (winW / 2);
winY = (resY / 2) - (winH / 2);

// Create the code that, when passed to getURL( ), opens the new browser window.
jsCode = "javascript:void(newWin=window.open('http://www.person13.com/'," +
         "'newWindow', 'width=" + winW +
         ", height=" +  winH + "," +
         "left=" + winX + ",top=" + winY + "'));";

// Call the JavaScript function using getURL( ).
_root.getURL(jsCode);
```

Additionally, it is worth considering using the screen-resolution values to determine whether to scale a movie. For example, when users have their resolution set to a high value such as 1600×1200, some fonts may appear too small to read.

2.5   Scaling the Movie

Problem

You want to control how a movie fits in the Player, including the scaling.

Solution

Use the Stage.scaleMode property.

Discussion

The Flash Player defaults to a scale mode of "showAll" (except the test Player, which defaults to "noScale"). In "showAll" mode, the Flash movie scales to fit the Player while maintaining the movie's original aspect ratio. The result is that the movie can have borders on the sides if the Player aspect ratio does not match the movie aspect ratio. You can set a movie to "showAll" mode, as follows:

```
Stage.scaleMode = "showAll";
```

The "noBorder" mode scales a movie to fit the Player while maintaining the original aspect ratio, but it forces the Player to display no borders around the Stage. If the aspect ratio of the Player does not match that of the movie, some of the movie will be cut off around the edges. You can set a movie to "noBorder" mode, as follows:

```
Stage.scaleMode = "noBorder";
```

The "exactFit" mode scales a movie to fit the Player and alters the movie's aspect ratio, if necessary, to match that of the Player. The result is that the movie always exactly fills the Player, but the elements of the movie may be distorted. For example:

```
Stage.scaleMode = "exactFit";
```

In "noScale" mode, the movie is not scaled, and it maintains its original size and aspect ratio regardless of the Stage's size. When you use the "noScale" mode, also set the movie's alignment (see Recipe 2.6). For example:

```
Stage.scaleMode = "noScale";
```

The scaleMode property's value does not prevent the user from being able to scale the movie using the right-click/Ctrl-click menu. However, you can disable those options in the menu, as shown in Recipe 2.9.

See Also

Additionally, you can affect scaling (among other things) in Standalone Projectors using a third-party utility such as SWF Studio (see Recipe 2.10).

2.6   Changing the Alignment

Problem

You want to change the alignment of the movie within the Player.

Solution

Use the Stage.align property.

Discussion

Flash movies appear in the center of the Player by default. You can control the alignment of a movie within the Player by setting the Stage.align property, as shown in Table 2-1.

Table 2-1. Alignment as controlled by Stage.align

Value	Horizontal alignment	Vertical alignment
"T"	Center	Top
"B"	Center	Bottom
"L"	Left	Center
"R"	Right	Center
"C" or " "	Center	Center
"LT" or "TL"	Left	Top
"RT" or "TR"	Right	Top
"LB" or "BL"	Left	Bottom
"RB" or "BR"	Right	Bottom

There is no "official" value to center the Stage both vertically and horizontally in the Player. Technically, any string that doesn't match one of the other modes will center the Stage. The value "C" is listed in Table 2-1 because it is convenient to remember and it will work.

The following code demonstrates the effects of both the scale mode and alignment of a movie within the Player. This code relies on the *DrawingMethods.as* file from Chapter 4 (specifically, the *drawRectangle()* method). Additionally, make sure to include the PushButton component in the movie's Library (see Recipe 11.1). Once you have added this code to a new movie's main timeline, test the movie in the Standalone Player. Experiment by scaling the Player and clicking on the different buttons to see the effects.

```
// Include DrawingMethods.as from Chapter 4 for the drawRectangle( ) method.
#include "DrawingMethods.as"

// Create a movie clip and draw a rectangle in it. The rectangle is 550 × 400 (the
// dimensions of the default movie), and it is positioned so that the upper-left
// corner of the rectangle is at (0,0) within the Stage. This movie clip allows you
// to see the boundaries of the Stage when the movie is scaled.
_root.createEmptyMovieClip("background", 1);
background.lineStyle(0, 0, 0);
background.beginFill(0xFF00FF);
background.drawRectangle(550, 400, 0, 0, 275, 200);
background.endFill( );

// Array of possible values for scaleMode
scaleLabels = ["noScale", "exactFit", "showAll", "noBorder"];

// Create push buttons for each scale mode.
for (var i = 0; i < scaleLabels.length; i++) {
  btn = _root.attachMovie("FPushButtonSymbol", "scaleBtn" + i, (i + 2),
       {_y: (i * 25)});
  btn.setLabel(scaleLabels[i]);
  btn.onRelease = function ( ) {
    Stage.scaleMode = this.getLabel( );
  };
}

// Array of possible alignment values
alignLabels = ["T", "B", "L", "R", "C", "LT", "RT", "LB", "RB"];

// Create push buttons for each alignment option.
for (var i = 0; i < alignLabels.length; i++) {
  btn = _root.attachMovie("FPushButtonSymbol", "scaleBtn" + (i + 4), (i + 6),
       {_x: 200, _y: (i * 25)});
  btn.setLabel(alignLabels[i]);
  btn.onRelease = function ( ) {
    Stage.align = this.getLabel( );
  };
}
```

2.7 Detecting the Device's Audio Capabilities

Problem

You want to determine the audio capabilities of the device on which the Player is running.

Solution

Use the hasAudio and hasMP3 properties of the System.capabilities object.

Discussion

Desktop versions of Flash Player 6 and later support MP3 playback and the ability to encode audio from a microphone or similar device. However, Flash Players for other devices do not necessarily support all, or possibly any, audio capabilities. The System.capabilities.hasAudio property returns true if the Player has any audio capabilities and false otherwise. This is extremely important for playing movies on multiple devices. If a device has no audio support, you should avoid forcing users to download something they cannot hear (especially because audio can be quite large):

```
// Load a .swf containing sound only if the Player can play audio.
if (System.capabilities.hasAudio) {
  mySoundHolder.loadMovie("sound.swf");
} else {
  mySoundHolder.loadMovie("silent.swf");
}
```

Just because a Player has audio capabilities, however, does not necessarily mean that it can play back MP3 sounds. Therefore, if publishing MP3 content, you should test for MP3 capabilities using the System.capabilities.hasMP3 property. MP3 sounds are preferable, if supported, because they offer better sound-quality-to-file-size ratios than ADCP sounds.

```
// If the Player can play MP3s, load an MP3 using a Sound object. Otherwise, load a
// .swf containing ADCP sound into a nested movie clip.
if (System.capabilities.hasMP3) {
  mySound = new Sound(mySoundHolder);
  mySound.load("sound.mp3", false);
} else {
  mySoundHolder("adcpSound.swf");
}
```

It is important to understand that the hasAudio and hasMP3 property settings are based on the capabilities of the Player and not of the system on which the Player is running. The desktop system players (for Windows, Mac OS, and Linux) always return true for both properties regardless of whether the system actually has the hardware (i.e., soundcard and speakers) to play back sounds. However, players for other devices may return false if the device does not support the audio or MP3 features.

2.8 Prompting the User to Change Player Settings

Problem

You want to open the user's Flash Player Settings dialog box to prompt her to allow greater access to her local system.

Solution

Use the *System.showSettings()* method.

Discussion

The *System.showSettings()* method opens the Flash Player Settings dialog box, which includes four tabs. The number in parentheses is the value you pass to *showSettings()* to open that particular tab.

Privacy (0)
> Allows the user to specify whether to allow Flash access to her camera and microphone.

Local Storage (1)
> Allows the user to specify how local shared objects are stored, including the maximum allowable disk usage.

Microphone (2)
> Allows the user to select a microphone and adjust the volume.

Camera (3)
> Allows the user to select a camera.

If you don't pass any parameters to the *showSettings()* method, it opens the Settings dialog box to the tab that was opened the last time the Settings dialog box was used. Here, we open the Settings dialog box to the Local Storage tab by explicitly specifying a value of 1:

```
// Open the Settings dialog box to the Local Storage tab.
System.showSettings(1);
```

 Out of courtesy, you should prompt the user to open the Settings dialog box with a button rather than simply opening it without warning. Also, you should alert the user beforehand as to which settings to change.

See Also

Recipe 16.4

2.9   Hiding the Flash Player's Menu Items

Problem

You want to hide the right-click menu under Windows (Ctrl-click on the Macintosh).

Solution

You can't disable the Flash Player's pop-up menu entirely, but you can minimize the options shown in the menu by setting the `Stage.showMenu` property to `false`.

Discussion

By default, the following options appear in the Flash Player's pop-up menu when the user right-clicks in Windows (or Ctrl-clicks on the Macintosh):

Zoom In
Zoom Out
100%
Show All
Quality (Low, Medium, or High)
Settings
Print
About Flash Player 6

You can remove most of the menu options with the following line of ActionScript code, although the Settings and About options remain in place:

```
Stage.showMenu = false;
```

Unfortunately, Flash does not provide a way to disable the menu entirely. Furthermore, Windows users are accustomed to using right-click to display a pop-up browser menu that allows them to open a link in a new window, for example. Such options are not available due to the Flash pop-up menu's presence. It is possible to use a third-party utility such as SWFKit or SWF Studio to completely disable the menu for enhanced Standalone Projectors (Windows versions only), as shown in Recipe 2.10.

See Also

See Recipe 2.8 for a way to display Flash's Settings dialog box without requiring the user to right-click (in Windows) or Ctrl-click (on Macintosh).

2.10 Enhancing Standalone Projectors

Problem

You want to create an enhanced Standalone Projector with features such as border-less playback, custom titles, no Flash menus, and so on.

Solution

Use a third-party tool such as SWF Studio or SWFKit to create the Projector from your completed Flash movie.

Discussion

SWF Studio is a third-party utility that helps you overcome some of the limitations of regular standalone Flash Projectors. However, SWF Studio produces Windows projectors only. Also note that the resultant projector files are rather hefty (minimum file size is around 1.5 MB). Therefore, projectors created with SWF Studio are more suited for distribution via CD-ROM or a kiosk than via download.

SWF Studio has many features, as described on the official product site (*http://www. northcode.com*). SWFKit (*http://www.swfkit.com*) offers similar feature enhancements, but we cover only SWF Studio in detail here.

However, regardless of the Projector enhancements you want to achieve, there are several steps necessary in any project that uses SWF Studio:

1. Create your Flash movie by exporting the *.swf* file from Flash.

2. Open SWF Studio. The program automatically starts with a new project opened, so you don't need to create a new project.

3. On the left side of the application window is the Project Tree (see Figure 2-1). Locate the Layout option at the end of the list and click on it.

4. In the right pane, click on the Layout Options button. A menu appears from which you should select Add Movie (see Figure 2-1).

5. A new Movie is added to the project and appears as an item under the Layout option in the Project Tree. The Movie option should be selected automatically, and the right pane should now contain a File form field. Click on the Browse button to the right of the form field, select the *.swf* file you want to add to the project, and click OK.

6. Select the enhancements you want to add to your projector (the default settings disable the right-click menu entirely).

7. After you have chosen the settings for the Projector, click Build to export the EXE. If you saved the project previously, SWF Studio exports the EXE with that name; otherwise, it exports the EXE as *Untitled.exe*. If you do not specify an output directory, the EXE appears on the desktop.

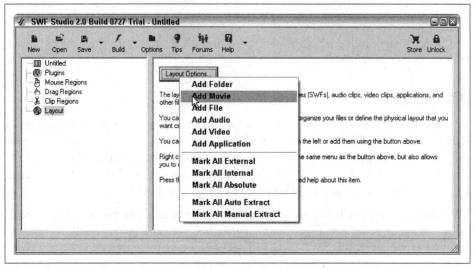

Figure 2-1. SWF Studio Project Tree window

See Also

Third-party tools: SWF Studio (*http://www.northcode.com*) and SWFKit (*http://www.swfkit.com*). See Recipes 2.9, 2.11, and 2.12 for details on several of their benefits.

2.11 Setting the Dimensions of a Projector

Problem

You want to specify the dimensions of a Projector.

Solution

Use SWF Studio to create the Projector (Windows only). Set the size settings prior to building the project.

Discussion

If you are creating a Windows Projector, you can use SWF Studio to set the dimensions of the movie. Follow the steps in Recipe 2.10, substituting the following tasks for step 6:

1. Choose the first item from the Project Tree. If you have saved your project, the item has the same name as your project; otherwise, the item is labeled Untitled.

2. On the right, the Project Options pane appears, and the Output tab is selected by default. You can leave the output settings at their default values.

3. Select the Window tab.

4. In the Window tab, choose one of the following options:

   Full Screen
   > This option forces the Projector to full screen, matching the monitor resolution at runtime.

   Fixed Size
   > If you select this option, you must specify the dimensions (in pixels) to use for the Projector. The default is 500 × 400.

   % of Desktop
   > This option scales the Projector to fit a percentage of the user's desktop. Because users can have different resolution settings on their computers, choosing a percentage can have different results than using Fixed Size.

   Match the Size of your Main Movie
   > This option leaves the movie's dimensions as they are.

See Also

See Recipe 2.10 for more information on how to use SWF Studio.

2.12 Specifying Where on Screen a Projector Opens

Problem

You want to specify a location on the screen where a Projector should open.

Solution

Use SWF Studio to create the Projector (Windows only) and specify the position settings.

Discussion

One of the many useful features of SWF Studio is the ability to specify where on screen the Projector should open. Standard Flash Projectors don't offer this option, but SWF Studio can set the percentage values in the x and y directions at which the Projector should open. To accomplish this, complete the steps in Recipe 2.10, substituting the following for step 6:

1. Choose the first item from the Project Tree. If you have saved your project, the item has the same name as your project; otherwise, the item is labeled Untitled.

2. On the right, the Project Options pane appears and the Output tab is selected by default. You can leave all the output settings at their default values.

3. Select the Window tab.

4. In the Window tab locate the Size and Position portion of the settings. To the right is a controller that allows you to adjust the position at which the movie opens on screen. The black rectangle represents the user's screen, and the white rectangle represents the Projector. By moving the horizontal and vertical sliders you can adjust the relative position of the Projector.

## CHAPTER 3

Color

3.0   Introduction

Color objects can control colors programmatically, which means you can create dynamically colored elements in your movies. You can change background colors, animate colors over gradations, and allow user control over colors (with sliders, buttons, and so on).

To work effectively with colors, you must understand how to specify color values. ActionScript colors have four parts: red, green, blue, and alpha (or transparency). For the color components—each ranging in value from 0 to 255 (in standard, decimal format)—higher numbers mean brighter colors. When red, green, and blue are all 0, the resulting color is black. When red, green, and blue are all 255, the resulting color is white. When red, green, and blue are all equal, the resulting color is a shade of gray.

The alpha value determines the transparency: a value of 0 is completely transparent, and the maximum value, which depends on the method or property used to set the alpha value, is fully opaque. The maximum value for alpha is 100 when specified using the _alpha property; the maximum alpha value is 255 when specified as part of a color transformation along with RGB components.

For example, a pure blue, fully opaque color would have the following components:

```
Red: 0, Green: 0, Blue: 255, Alpha: 255
```

For colors in which you don't want to change the alpha (which defaults to the value set for the object during authoring) you can represent the RGB parts as a single value ranging from 0 to 16777215, but using the hexadecimal equivalent is much more practical.

The hexadecimal representation of an ActionScript color begins with 0x and is followed by six bytes (two bytes each for red, green, and blue), so it takes the form 0x*RRGGBB*. For example, pure red is 0xFF0000, pure green is 0x00FF00, and pure blue is 0x0000FF. All other colors are some combination of red, green, and blue. For example, a nice lime green is 0xA9FC9C. The Flash Color Mixer panel (Shift + F9) shows the hexadecimal value for the selected color under the swatch in the lower-left portion of the panel, as shown in Figure 3-1.

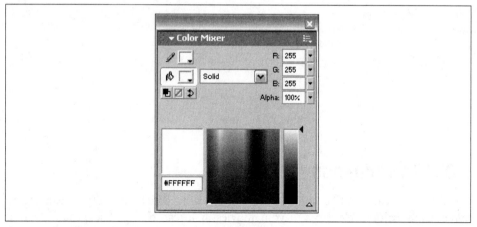

Figure 3-1. The Color Mixer panel

Hexadecimal format makes it easy to identify the red, green, and blue components of a color. However, you are free to use the decimal equivalent. For example, 11140252 is the decimal equivalent of the hexadecimal number 0xA9FC9C.

3.1   Setting the Color of a Movie Clip

Problem

You want to control the color of a movie clip dynamically (at runtime, rather than during authoring).

Solution

Create a *Color* object that targets the desired movie clip, and then use the *Color.setRGB()* method.

Discussion

You can't change the color of a movie clip directly. Instead, you must first create a *Color* object that targets the movie clip of interest, as follows:

```
my_color = new Color(myMovieClip);
```

You can alternatively specify the movie clip name as a string:

```
my_color = new Color("myMovieClip");
```

The target movie clip, as specified when creating a *Color* object, must correspond to the name of a movie clip instance on the Stage, not the name of the Library symbol from which the clip is derived. Therefore, you must set the target clip's instance name using the Property inspector before you can target it using a *Color* object.

A *Color* object can target a movie clip on any timeline using an absolute or relative reference, such as:

```
my_color = new Color(_root.myMovieClip);
my_color = new Color(_parent.myMovieClip);
```

Once you have created a *Color* object, you can use it to control the color of the targeted movie clip instance.

The *Color.setRGB()* method applies a single color value to the movie clip targeted by the *Color* object (as specified when the *Color* object was created), filling the entire movie clip shape with a single color. The color value can be of any valid Action-Script numeric format.

The following examples both apply a solid blue color to the targeted movie clip:

```
my_color.setRGB(0x0000FF);    // Hexadecimal
my_color.setRGB(255);         // Decimal
```

The following examples both apply a solid lime green color to the targeted movie clip:

```
my_color.setRGB(0xA9FC9C);    // Hexadecimal
my_color.setRGB(11140252 );   // Decimal
```

See Also

Recipe 5.2

3.2   Specifying RGB Values

Problem

You want to create an RGB value to use with *setRGB()* based on the red, green, and blue part values.

Solution

Use the bitshift left and bitwise *OR* operators.

Discussion

The easiest way to combine individual red, green, and blue components into a single RGB value is to use bitwise operations. Simply shift the red value left by 16 bits and the green value left by 8 bits, then combine them with the blue value using the bitwise *OR* operator, as follows:

```
red   = 100;
green = 100;
blue  = 100;
rgb = (red << 16) | (green << 8) | (blue);

// Create the Color object.
my_color = new Color(myMovieClip);

// Set the RGB color.
my_color.setRGB(rgb);
```

The bitshift left operator (<<) effectively multiplies a number by two for each bit position that the number is shifted (this is similar to how shifting a decimal number one decimal place to the left effectively multiplies it by 10). In this context, the bitwise *OR* operator (|) essentially concatenates the shifted numbers together. Therefore, assuming that red, green, and blue are each in the range of 0 to 255, the following:

```
rgb = (red << 16) | (green << 8) | (blue);
```

is equivalent to:

```
rgb = (red * Math.pow(2,16)) + (green * Math.pow(2,8)) + blue;
```

or:

```
rgb = (red * 65536) + (green * 256) + blue;
```

In practice, it is often easier to use *Color.setTransform()*—in which the red, green, and blue components are specified as separate properties of a transform object—to alter the targeted clip's color. Furthermore, *setTransform()* allows you to set the alpha value for a color, which *setRGB()* does not.

See Also

Recipe 3.7

3.3   Decoding an RGB Value

Problem

You want to extract the red, green, and blue components from an RGB value returned by *Color.getRGB()*.

Solution

Use the bitshift right and bitwise *AND* operators.

Discussion

You can extract the red, green, and blue components from the single RGB value returned by *Color.getRGB()* using the bitshift right (>>) and bitwise *AND* (&) operators. You can extract one or more of the colors individually as follows:

```
// Create the Color object.
my_color = new Color(myMovieClip);

// Get the current RGB color.
rgb = my_color.getRGB( );

// rgb contains an RGB color value in decimal form, such as 14501017 (rosy pink),
// which is stored internally as its hex equivalent, such as 0xDD4499.
red   = (rgb >> 16);
green = (rgb >> 8) & 0xFF;
blue  =  rgb & 0xFF;
```

Although displayed as a decimal number, remember that each color is stored internally in its hexadecimal form: 0xRRGGBB. For example, the color value 14501017 (which is rosy pink) is stored internally as 0xDD4499. In this format, it is easy to see that the red component is DD in hex (221 in decimal), the green component is 44 in hex (68 in decimal), and the blue component is 99 in hex (153 in decimal).

The preceding transformation effectively separates a 24-bit value into its three 8-bit components (the leftmost eight bits represent red, the middle eight bits represent green, and the rightmost eight bits represent blue). The bitshift right operator is used to shift the eight bits of interest to the rightmost position. Using the bitwise *AND* operator with 0xFF retains the rightmost eight bits only, effectively masking off any unwanted bits on the left.

In practice, it is often easier to use *Color.getTransform()*—in which the red, green, and blue components are returned as separate properties of a transform object—to determine a clip's color. Furthermore, *getTransform()* also returns the alpha value for a color, which *getRGB()* does not.

See Also

Recipe 3.7

3.4 Setting the RGB Relative to Its Current Value

Problem

You want to modify the RGB value of a movie clip relative to its current value.

Solution

Use *Color.getRGB()* to retrieve the current value, then perform bitwise operations to modify the value, and set the new value using *Color.setRGB()*.

Discussion

We saw in Recipe 3.3 how to retrieve the current RGB value of a movie clip using *Color.getRGB()* and then use bitwise operations to extract the red, blue, and green components. To perform a relative color adjustment, simply modify the individual color components and reapply the new color using *Color.setRGB()*. For example, you could brighten a movie clip's color by increasing the red, green, and blue components by a certain amount:

```
// Create the Color object.
my_color = new Color(myMovieClip);

// Retrieve the current RGB setting.
rgb = my_color.getRGB( );
red   = (rgb >> 16);
green = (rgb >> 8) & 0xFF;
blue  =  rgb & 0xFF;

// Brighten the colors by increasing their magnitude. This assumes that the red,
// green, and blue values are no more than 245 prior to the operation.
red   += 10;
green += 10;
blue  += 10;

// Combine the components into a single RGB value and apply it with Color.setRGB( ).
rgb = (red << 16) | (green  << 8) | blue;
my_color.setRGB(rgb);
```

3.5 Tinting a Movie Clip's Color

Problem

You want to modify the color tint of a movie clip (as opposed to applying a single color to the whole shape).

Solution

Use the *setTransform()* method of the *Color* object that targets the movie clip.

Discussion

Using *Color.setRGB()* to fill a movie clip with a solid color overrides any color contrast within the movie clip. To apply a tint to a movie clip, use *Color.setTransform()* instead.

Flash records the color values set for a movie clip during authoring. A single clip might contain hundreds of colors. However, *setRGB()* applies the same RGB value to every color region within a movie clip. On the other hand, *setTransform()* can modify colors relative to their original values. For example, consider a movie clip that contains a JPEG with hundreds of colors. Using *setRGB()* applies one color to the whole movie clip, resulting in a solid-colored rectangle. But with *setTransform()*, you can adjust the red, green, and blue levels of each original color, effectively tinting the image without losing the initial contrast.

The *setTransform()* method accepts a single parameter: a *transform object* that includes the eight properties shown in Table 3-1.

Table 3-1. Properties of a color transform object

Property	Range	Description
ra	−100 to 100	Red percentage transformation
rb	−255 to 255	Red offset
ga	−100 to 100	Green percentage transformation
gb	−255 to 255	Green offset
ba	−100 to 100	Blue percentage transformation
bb	−255 to 255	Blue offset
aa	−100 to 100	Alpha percentage transformation
ab	−255 to 255	Alpha offset

The values in Table 3-1 are used to transform the existing color values within the movie clip using the following formulas:

```
red   = originalRed   * (ra/100) + rb
green = originalGreen * (ga/100) + gb
blue  = originalBlue  * (ba/100) + bb
alpha = originalAlpha * (aa/100) + ab
```

If any of the resulting values (red, green, blue, or alpha) are outside of the 0 to 255 range, it becomes more difficult to predict the resulting effect on the color. Therefore, it is generally wise to specify property values such that the resulting color remains in the valid range.

You can create the transform object by creating a generic instance of the base *Object* class and adding properties to it, as follows:

```
myColorTransform = new Object( );
myColorTransform.ra = 100;
myColorTransform.rb = 50;
myColorTransform.ga = 100;
myColorTransform.gb = 50;
myColorTransform.ba = 100;
myColorTransform.bb = 50;
myColorTransform.aa = 100;
myColorTransform.ab = 0;
```

Or you can create an equivalent transform object using object literal notation:

```
myColorTransform = {ra: 100, rb: 50, ga: 100, gb: 50,
                    ba: 100, bb: 50, aa: 100, ab: 0};
```

Any properties that are omitted from the preceding transform object are given a value of 0.

After defining a transform object, apply it to the targeted movie clip via *Color. setTranform()*, as follows:

```
my_color = new Color(myMovieClip);
my_color.setTranform(myColorTransform);
```

The values involved in transforming a movie clip's colors can sometimes appear a bit daunting and confusing at first. Familiarize yourself with how these values work together to produce a single color transformation by experimenting with the advanced color settings in the Flash MX authoring tool. The advanced settings correspond to the properties that make up a transform object, and they have the same effect—albeit at authoring time instead of runtime. You can access the advanced color settings at authoring time by following these steps:

1. Select a movie clip instance on the Stage.
2. Open the Property inspector (Window → Properties).
3. Select Advanced from the Color dropdown list in the Property inspector.
4. The Settings button appears to the right of the Color dropdown list. Click the Settings button to open the Advanced Effects dialog box.

3.6   Setting a Movie Clip's Transparency

Problem

You want to adjust a movie clip's transparency.

Solution

Set the _alpha property for the movie clip instance, or set the aa and ab properties of the clip's transform object when using *Color.setTransform()*.

Discussion

You can set a movie clip's alpha value (transparency) anywhere from completely transparent (0) to fully opaque (100). The most direct, and generally the most common, way to adjust a movie clip's transparency is by setting the movie clip's _alpha property. You can assign the _alpha property any numeric value, but only values in the range of 0 to 100 will effect a predictable visible change. This sets the clip to be partially transparent:

```
myMovieClip._alpha = 63;
```

For more information on how you can animate the _alpha property over time to create fade effects, see Recipe 7.9.

In addition, you can use a *Color* object to modify a movie clip's transparency. Use a *Color* object's *setTransform()* method (see Recipe 3.5) to assign color transformations to a movie clip. Among the properties of a color transform object are the aa (alpha offset) and ab (alpha percentage) properties. Therefore, you can use these properties to assign new transparency settings to a movie clip:

```
// Get the current transform object and modify the aa and ab properties.
// See Recipe 3.7 for details on modifying a transform object's properties.
my_color = new Color(circle_mc);
transformObj = my_color.getTransform( );
transformObj.aa = 63;
transformObj.ab = 0;
my_color.setTransform(transformObj);
```

Modifying a movie clip's alpha using *Color.setTransform()* requires much more code than simply setting the movie clip's _alpha property. However, if you are already setting a movie clip's color values using *Color.setTransform()*, it is convenient to set the alpha at the same time using this technique.

Note that all changes made to the *MovieClip.*_alpha property are reflected in the transform object returned by *Color.getTransform()*. Similarly, changes made via *Color.setTransform()* are reflected in the *MovieClip.*_alpha property.

See Also

Recipe 7.9 for important information on modifying the _alpha property over time

3.7   Transforming a Movie Clip's Current Color

Problem

You want to modify a movie clip's color relative to the current color transformation, instead of relative to the author-time color values.

Solution

Use the *getTransform()* and *setTransform()* methods of the *Color* object that targets the movie clip.

Discussion

The *Color.getTransform()* method returns the transform object last applied to the targeted movie clip. For example, if you had previously applied a transform object that set the movie clip's alpha percentage to 42, *getTransform()* would return an object with the following values:

```
{ra: 100, rb: 0, ga: 100, gb: 0, ba: 100, bb: 0, aa: 42, ab: 0}
```

The transform object reflects changes made to a movie clip's color either at authoring time or at runtime. If you modify the color values using the Property inspector at authoring time, those values are indicated in the movie clip's transform object. You can make changes to a movie clip's color at runtime by using the *setTransform()* or *setRGB()* methods of its *Color* object, and you can adjust the movie clip's _alpha property separately. All runtime changes—not just the changes made using *setTransform()*—are reflected in the transform object. If you have not applied any color changes at runtime or authoring time then *getTransform()* returns the following value (a neutral transform object):

```
{ra: 100, rb: 0, ga: 100, gb: 0, ba: 100, bb: 0, aa: 100, ab: 0}
```

You can modify the properties of the transform object returned by *getTransform()* and then apply the modifications using *setTransform()*:

```
// Create the Color object.
my_color = new Color(myMovieClip);

// Get the transform object.
myTransformObject = my_color.getTransform( );

// Set the green percentage of all colors within the movie clip to 50% of the current
// value.
myTransformObject.ga = 50;

// Apply the transform object.
my_color.setTransform(myTransformObject);
```

The preceding example retains the previously applied transform values, with the exception of ga, which is set to 50. You can instead increment or decrement the properties relative to their current values:

```
// Get the transform object.
myTransformObject = my_color.getTransform( );

// Increment the red, green, and blue offsets by 10 to brighten the object's colors.
myTransformObject.rb += 10;
myTransformObject.gb += 10;
myTransformObject.bb += 10;

// Set the transform object.
my_color.setTransform(myTransformObject);
```

 Transformations applied with *setTransform( )* occur relative to the colors in the original movie clip symbol, independent of any previous transformations. In other words, the transformations are not cumulative. We simulated a cumulative transformation by basing the new transformation on the previous values, as returned by *getTransform( )*.

3.8   Restoring a Movie Clip's Original Color

Problem

You want to restore the original symbol's color values to a movie clip.

Solution

Reset the transformation object using the *setTransform( )* method of the *Color* object that targets the movie clip.

Discussion

No matter what changes you made to a movie clip's color using *setTransform( )* and *setRGB( )* (or made at authoring time), you can restore the original color values using a *reset transform object* (one with 100 for the percentages and 0 for the offsets):

```
resetTransform = {ra: 100, rb: 0, ga: 100, gb: 0, ba: 100, bb: 0, aa: 100, ab: 0};
```

When this reset transform object is passed to the *setTransform( )* method, the colors in the targeted movie clip are set to those of the Library symbol on which the clip is based:

```
// Create the Color object.
my_color = new Color(myMovieClip);

// Apply a unity transformation.
resetTransform = {ra: 100, rb: 0, ga: 100, gb: 0, ba: 100, bb: 0, aa: 100, ab: 0};
my_color.setTransform(resetTransform);
```

3.9   Controlling a Movie Clip's Color with Sliders

This recipe presents a full application that creates sliders for the red, green, blue, and alpha values that control a movie clip's color:

1. Create a new Flash document and save it.

2. On the main timeline, rename the default layer as *movieClips* and create a new layer named *actions*.

3. Create a movie clip symbol and draw a circle in it. The circle should be approximately 120 × 120 pixels.

4. Return to the main timeline and create an instance of the circle movie clip on the Stage on the *movieClips* layer. Place the instance on the left side of the Stage. Name the instance circle_mc using the Property inspector.

5. Open the Components panel (Window → Components) and drag four instances of the ScrollBar component onto the Stage on the *movieClips* layer. Name these instances red_sb, green_sb, blue_sb, and alpha_sb. Line them up horizontally on the right side of the Stage.

6. Select the keyframe of the *actions* layer and open the Actions panel.

7. Add the following code to the Actions panel and test the movie (Control → Test Movie). The scrollbars are automatically colorized to indicate the color components they control. Moving the thumb sliders on the scrollbars adjusts the circle's color.

```
// Define a function that will initialize the scrollbar instances as sliders to
// control the color values.
function initSliders () {

    // First, set the scroll properties of each of the scrollbars. For the red,
    // green, and blue scrollbars, the values should range from 0 to 255. Use a
    // pageSize of 120 for the color sliders to create a proportional thumb bar.
    // The alpha range is from 0 to 100, and so the pageSize should be 47 to create
    // a thumb bar that is proportional with the other sliders.
    red_sb.setScrollProperties  (120, 0, 255);
    green_sb.setScrollProperties(120, 0, 255);
    blue_sb.setScrollProperties (120, 0, 255);
    alpha_sb.setScrollProperties(47,  0, 100);

    // Colorize the sliders themselves. Make the red_sb slider red and, similarly,
    // make green_sb green and blue_sb blue. Make the alpha_sb slider white.
    red_sb.setStyleProperty  ("face", 0xFF0000);
    green_sb.setStyleProperty("face", 0x00FF00);
    blue_sb.setStyleProperty ("face", 0x0000FF);
    alpha_sb.setStyleProperty("face", 0xFFFFFF);

    // Set the initial position for the color sliders. alpha_sb remains at 100%.
    red_sb.setScrollPosition  (127);
    green_sb.setScrollPosition(127);
    blue_sb.setScrollPosition (127);
}
```

```
function initColor () {
  // Store a new Color object in a property of circle_mc.
  my_color = new Color(circle_mc);
  circle_mc.col = my_color;

  // Store references to the four scrollbars as properties of circle_mc.
  circle_mc.red   = red_sb;
  circle_mc.green = green_sb;
  circle_mc.blue  = blue_sb;
  circle_mc.alpha = alpha_sb;
}

// Initialize the sliders and the Color object.
initSliders();
initColor();

// Update the color of the circle_mc movie clip based on the slider positions.
circle_mc.onEnterFrame = function () {
  // Retrieve the current position of the color and alpha sliders.
  var r = 255 - this.red.getScrollPosition();
  var g = 255 - this.green.getScrollPosition();
  var b = 255 - this.blue.getScrollPosition();
  var a = 100 - this.alpha.getScrollPosition();

  // Set up the transformation object properties to set circle_mc's color.
  transformObj = new Object();
  transformObj.ra = 0;
  transformObj.rb = r;
  transformObj.ga = 0;
  transformObj.gb = g;
  transformObj.ba = 0;
  transformObj.bb = b;
  transformObj.aa = a;
  transformObj.ab = 0;
  this.col.setTransform(transformObj);
}
```

CHAPTER 4
Drawing and Masking

4.0 Introduction

The ActionScript Drawing API, introduced in Flash MX, allows you to draw inside movie clips at runtime. The handful of primitive Drawing API methods let you draw almost any imaginable shape, as demonstrated in this chapter's recipes. The Drawing API uses a *pen* metaphor, akin to a CAD line plotter, in which an imaginary pen is moved around the drawing canvas. The pen's stroke attributes can be customized, and the pen can draw lines or curves. Shapes can be empty or filled. Note that the coordinates are relative to the movie clip's registration point. Use the *MovieClip._x* and *MovieClip._y* properties to reposition the entire clip on the Stage.

The Drawing API is a subset of the methods of the *MovieClip* class, and therefore most of the recipes in this chapter are implemented as custom methods of the *MovieClip* class. You should add these custom methods to an ActionScript file named *DrawingMethods.as* (or download the final version from the URL cited in the Preface) and include it in your own projects.

All paths and shapes drawn with the Drawing API are drawn inside the movie clip from which the methods are invoked. For this reason the *createEmptyMovieClip()* method is often used in conjunction with any runtime drawing. The *createEmptyMovieClip()* method does just what its name implies—it creates a new, empty movie clip nested within the movie clip on which it is invoked:

```
// Create a new movie clip named myMovieClip_mc with a depth of 1 inside of _root.
_root.createEmptyMovieClip("myMovieClip_mc", 1);
```

You can specify the pen style with the *MovieClip* class's *lineStyle()* method and draw lines and curves with the *lineTo()* and *curveTo()* methods. The pen can be repositioned without drawing anything by calling the *moveTo()* method.

Many of these recipes use the custom *Math.degToRad()* method from Recipe 5.12 to convert angles from degrees to radians. Your *DrawingMethods.as* file should include *Math.as* from Chapter 5 by using this statement on the first line:

```
#include "Math.as"
```

Also see Recipes 5.13 and 5.14 for an explanation of how to calculate X and Y coordinates using trigonometry, which is called for in some of this chapter's recipes.

4.1   Drawing a Line

Problem

You want to draw a line using ActionScript.

Solution

Use the *lineStyle()* method to specify the thickness, color, and transparency of the line. Then use the *lineTo()* method to draw a line from the current pen position to a destination point.

Discussion

Before you can draw anything using ActionScript, you need to tell Flash what kind of line style to use. The line style consists of the line's thickness, color, and alpha value (opacity), and you can set these values using the *lineStyle()* method on the movie clip in which you wish to draw. The line's thickness should be specified in pixels, but any value less than 1 draws lines with hairline thickness. Color values should be specified as numbers, as explained in the Introduction to Chapter 3. The alpha value should be anywhere from 0 (completely transparent) to 100 (completely opaque).

```
// Set a 1-pixel, blue, completely opaque line style.
myMovieClip_mc.lineStyle(1, 0x0000FF, 100);
```

The most basic type of drawing that you can do with ActionScript is drawing a straight line. Flash uses the current pen position as the starting point, so you need to provide only the coordinates of the destination point. Use the *MovieClip.lineTo()* method to create a line from the current pen position to the specified destination point:

```
// Draws a line from the current pen position to (100,100) within the coordinate
// system of myMovieClip_mc.
myMovieClip_mc.lineTo(100, 100);
```

When you use ActionScript methods to draw, all the lines and fills are drawn within the movie clip from which the methods are invoked. For example, in the preceding code, the line is drawn within myMovieClip_mc. Additionally, the line style must be defined for each movie clip. If you define a line style for myMovieClip_mc, but then you try to use the *lineTo()* method with another movie clip instance, Flash does not draw anything.

As mentioned previously, when you use the Drawing API methods such as *lineTo()*, Flash draws the line beginning at the current pen position. If you have not otherwise moved the pen (by calling a *lineTo()*, *curveTo()*, or *moveTo()* method), the pen is positioned at the origin of the movie clip's coordinate system, point (0,0). The origin is the clip's registration point, which resides at the clip's center by default. You can move the pen without drawing a line by using the *moveTo()* method. The *moveTo()* method simply relocates the pen to the coordinate you specify.

```
// Move the pen in myMovieClip_mc to (300,30).
myMovieClip_mc.moveTo(300, 30);
```

The *moveTo()* method is important in situations in which you want to begin drawing from a point other than the movie clip's center or draw lines or shapes without necessarily connecting all the lines:

```
// Create an empty movie clip to act as the drawing canvas.
_root.createEmptyMovieClip("myMovieClip_mc", 1);

// Set a 1-pixel, black, completely opaque line style.
myMovieClip_mc.lineStyle(1, 0x000000, 100);

// Draw a dashed line using a series of lines and spaces.
myMovieClip_mc.moveTo( 0, 0);
myMovieClip_mc.lineTo(10, 0);
myMovieClip_mc.moveTo(15, 0);
myMovieClip_mc.lineTo(25, 0);
myMovieClip_mc.moveTo(30, 0);
myMovieClip_mc.lineTo(40, 0);
myMovieClip_mc.moveTo(45, 0);
myMovieClip_mc.lineTo(55, 0);
```

See Also

Recipe 7.17

4.2   Drawing a Curve

Problem

You want to draw a curve using ActionScript.

Solution

Set a line style with *lineStyle()* and then use the *curveTo()* method.

Discussion

When drawing lines or curves with ActionScript, the first thing you must do is define the line style, as shown in Recipe 4.1.

Once you have set a line style, you can draw a curve using the *curveTo()* method. The *curveTo()* method draws an approximation of a Bézier curve (though optimized for performance), which requires three points: a starting point, a control point, and a destination point. The starting point is always determined by the current pen position. The destination point is simply the point on the canvas to which you wish to draw. The control point is the point that determines the shape of the curve; it is calculated by determining where the tangents to the curve at the starting and destination points intersect. The control point is not actually on the curve, as shown in Figure 4-1.

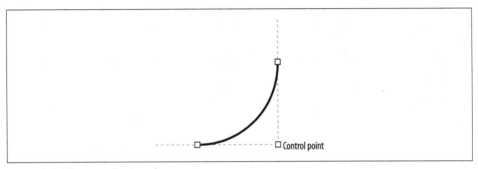

Figure 4-1. The control point of a curve

This simple example draws a curve:

```
// Draw a curved line in myMovieClip_mc with a control point at (0,100) and a
// destination point of (100,100).
this.createEmptyMovieClip("myMovieClip_mc", 1);
myMovieClip_mc.lineStyle(1, 0x000000, 100);
myMovieClip_mc.curveTo(0, 100, 100, 100);
```

4.3   Drawing a Rectangle

Problem

You want to draw a rectangle at runtime.

Solution

Create a custom *MovieClip.drawSimpleRectangle()* method using the Drawing API and invoke it on a movie clip.

Discussion

To draw a simple rectangle, specify the stroke's attributes using the *lineStyle()* method and then draw four lines using the *lineTo()* method:

```
// Create rectangle_mc with a depth of 1 on the main timeline.
_root.createEmptyMovieClip("rectangle_mc", 1);

// Specify a one-pixel, solid, black line.
rectangle_mc.lineStyle(1, 0x000000, 100);

// Draw four lines to form the perimeter of the rectangle.
rectangle_mc.lineTo(100,  0);
rectangle_mc.lineTo(100, 50);
rectangle_mc.lineTo(  0, 50);
rectangle_mc.lineTo(  0,  0);
```

Thus, drawing a simple rectangle is no huge feat. To draw multiple rectangles with various dimensions, you should create a custom *drawSimpleRectangle()* method for the *MovieClip* class, as follows:

```
// Define the custom method on MovieClip.prototype so that it's available to all
// movie clip instances.
MovieClip.prototype.drawSimpleRectangle = function (width, height) {
  this.lineTo(width, 0);
  this.lineTo(width, height);
  this.lineTo(0, height);
  this.lineTo(0, 0);
}

// Invoke the custom method like this.
_root.createEmptyMovieClip("rectangle_mc", 1);
rectangle_mc.lineStyle(1, 0x000000, 100);
rectangle_mc.drawSimpleRectangle(100, 50);
```

The dimensions of the rectangle are 102 × 52 pixels due to the line thickness. Reduce the dimensions by two pixels in each direction to create a rectangle whose outside dimensions match the intended size.

See Also

See Recipe 4.4 for an enhanced rectangle-drawing routine that adds several features, such as optional rounded corners, offset, and rotation.

4.4 Drawing a Rounded Rectangle

Problem

You want to draw a rectangle with rounded corners, an offset, or rotation.

Solution

Create a custom *MovieClip.drawRectangle()* method using the Drawing API and invoke it on a movie clip.

Discussion

The *drawSimpleRectangle()* method from Recipe 4.3 is, as the name suggests, quite simple.

Let's create a more complex version that also:

- Draws a rectangle with a specified angle of rotation
- Let's you specify the rectangle center's coordinates
- Can draw a rectangle with rounded corners

The *drawRectangle()* method accepts six parameters:

width
: The width of the rectangle in pixels

height
: The height of the rectangle in pixels

round
: The radius (in pixels) of the arc that is used to round the corners. If the value is undefined or 0, the corners remain square.

rotation
: The clockwise rotation to apply to the rectangle in degrees. If undefined, the rectangle is not rotated.

x
: The x coordinate of the center point for the rectangle. If undefined, the rectangle is centered at x = 0.

y
: The y coordinate of the center point for the rectangle. If undefined, the rectangle is centered at y = 0.

Here is our enhanced *drawRectangle()* method, defined on MovieClip.prototype, so it's available to all movie clip instances:

```
// Include the custom Math library from Chapter 5 to access Math.degToRad().
#include "Math.as"

MovieClip.prototype.drawRectangle = function (width, height, round, rotation, x, y) {
  // Make sure the rectangle is at least as wide and tall as the rounded corners.
  if (width < (round * 2)) {
    width = round * 2;
  }
  if (height < (round * 2)) {
    height = round * 2;
  }
```

```
// Convert the rotation from degrees to radians.
rotation = Math.degToRad(rotation);

// Calculate the distance from the rectangle's center to one of the corners (or
// where the corner would be in rounded-cornered rectangles). See the line labeled
// r in Figure 4-2.
var r = Math.sqrt(Math.pow(width/2, 2) + Math.pow(height/2, 2));

// Calculate the distance from the rectangle's center to the upper edge of the
// bottom-right rounded corner. See the line labeled rx in Figure 4-2. When round
// is 0, rx is equal to r.
var rx = Math.sqrt(Math.pow(width/2, 2) + Math.pow((height/2) - round, 2));

// Calculate the distance from the rectangle's center to the lower edge of the
// bottom-right rounded corner. See the line labeled ry in Figure 4-2. When round
// is 0, ry is equal to r.
var ry = Math.sqrt(Math.pow((width/2) - round, 2) + Math.pow(height/2, 2));

// Calculate angles. r1Angle is the angle between the X axis that runs through the
// center of the rectangle and the line rx. r2Angle is the angle between rx and r.
// r3Angle is the angle between r and ry. And r4Angle is the angle between ry and
// the Y axis that runs through the center of the rectangle.
var r1Angle = Math.atan( ((height/2) - round) /( width/2) );
var r2Angle = Math.atan( (height/2) / (width/2) ) - r1Angle;
var r4Angle = Math.atan( ((width/2) - round) / (height/2) );
var r3Angle = (Math.PI/2) - r1Angle - r2Angle - r4Angle;

// Calculate the distance of the control point from the
// arc center for the rounded corners.
var ctrlDist = Math.sqrt(2 * Math.pow(round, 2));

// Declare the local variables used to calculate the control point.
var ctrlX, ctrlY;

// Calculate where to begin drawing the first side segment and then draw it.
rotation += r1Angle + r2Angle + r3Angle;
var x1 = x + ry * Math.cos(rotation);
var y1 = y + ry * Math.sin(rotation);
this.moveTo(x1, y1);
rotation += 2 * r4Angle;
x1 = x + ry * Math.cos(rotation);
y1 = y + ry * Math.sin(rotation);
this.lineTo(x1, y1);

// Set rotation to the starting point for the next side segment and calculate the x
// and y coordinates.
rotation += r3Angle + r2Angle;
x1 = x + rx * Math.cos(rotation);
y1 = y + rx * Math.sin(rotation);

// If the corners are rounded, calculate the control point for the corner's curve
// and draw it.
if (round > 0) {
  ctrlX = x + r * Math.cos(rotation - r2Angle);
```

```
    ctrlY = y + r * Math.sin(rotation - r2Angle);
    this.curveTo(ctrlX, ctrlY, x1, y1);
}

// Calculate the end point of the second side segment and draw the line.
rotation += 2 * r1Angle;
x1 = x + rx * Math.cos(rotation);
y1 = y + rx * Math.sin(rotation);
this.lineTo(x1, y1);

// Calculate the next line segment's starting point.
rotation += r2Angle + r3Angle;
x1 = x + ry * Math.cos(rotation);
y1 = y + ry * Math.sin(rotation);

// Draw the rounded corner, if applicable.
if (round > 0) {
    ctrlX = x + r * Math.cos(rotation - r3Angle);
    ctrlY = y + r * Math.sin(rotation - r3Angle);
    this.curveTo(ctrlX, ctrlY, x1, y1);
}

// Calculate the end point of the third segment and draw the line.
rotation += 2 * r4Angle;
x1 = x + ry * Math.cos(rotation);
y1 = y + ry * Math.sin(rotation);
this.lineTo(x1, y1);

// Calculate the starting point of the next segment.
rotation += r3Angle + r2Angle;
x1 = x + rx * Math.cos(rotation);
y1 = y + rx * Math.sin(rotation);

// If applicable, draw the rounded corner.
if (round > 0) {
    ctrlX = x + r * Math.cos(rotation - r2Angle);
    ctrlY = y + r * Math.sin(rotation - r2Angle);
    this.curveTo(ctrlX, ctrlY, x1, y1);
}

// Calculate the end point for the fourth segment and draw it.
rotation += 2 * r1Angle;
x1 = x + rx * Math.cos(rotation);
y1 = y + rx * Math.sin(rotation);
this.lineTo(x1, y1);

// Calculate the end point for the next corner arc and, if applicable, draw it.
rotation += r3Angle + r2Angle;
x1 = x + ry * Math.cos(rotation);
y1 = y + ry * Math.sin(rotation);
if (round > 0) {
    ctrlX = x + r * Math.cos(rotation - r3Angle);
```

```
        ctrlY = y + r * Math.sin(rotation - r3Angle);
        this.curveTo(ctrlX, ctrlY, x1, y1);
    }
}
```

Figure 4-2 shows the geometry when drawing the rounded corners for the rectangle.

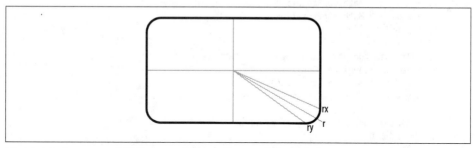

Figure 4-2. A conceptual illustration of drawing a rounded rectangle

The preceding example will be clearer with a closer examination.

The ActionScript trigonometric methods require angles measured in radians. Therefore, whenever you specify an angle in degrees (which is generally easier for humans), you must convert the units to radians before passing them to ActionScript's trigonometric methods. In this case, we convert the rotation parameter from degrees to radians using the *Math.degToRad()* method from Recipe 5.12:

```
rotation = Math.degToRad(rotation);
```

The length of the three imaginary lines used for drawing the rounded corners, as shown in Figure 4-2, are calculated using the Pythagorean theorem, as discussed in Recipe 5.13. In our example, these distances are:

```
var r  = Math.sqrt(Math.pow(width/2, 2) + Math.pow(height/2, 2));
var rx = Math.sqrt(Math.pow(width/2, 2) + Math.pow((height/2) - round, 2));
var ry = Math.sqrt(Math.pow((width/2) - round, 2) + Math.pow(height/2, 2));
```

Next, we must calculate the angles formed between the axes and the lines r, rx, and ry. These angles are used to determine the x and y coordinates of the starting and ending side segments. If you know the lengths of the sides of a right triangle, you can determine the angles that they form. Because the axes and the lines r, rx, and ry can be formed into right triangles you can determine the angles these lines form using the tangent and arctangent. The tangent in a right triangle is defined as the ratio of the side opposite the angle to the side adjacent to the angle. The arctangent is the inverse of the tangent function, so we use the following to determine the angles:

```
var r1Angle = Math.atan(((height/2) - round)/(width/2));
var r2Angle = Math.atan((height/2)/(width/2)) - r1Angle;
var r4Angle = Math.atan(((width/2) - round)/(height/2));
var r3Angle = (Math.PI/2) - r1Angle - r2Angle - r4Angle;
```

The corners are each composed of a single curve that is a semicircle. To determine the distance between the semicircle's center point and the control point used to draw that curve, again use the Pythagorean theorem:

```
var ctrlDist = Math.sqrt(2 * Math.pow(round, 2));
```

The first thing you want to do when you draw the rectangle is to move the imaginary pen to a starting point on the rectangle without actually drawing a line. In this example, the calculated starting point is at the right end of the bottom segment (of an unrotated rectangle). If you know the distance between two points and the angle (the opposite angle formed by an imaginary right triangle with the known line being the hypotenuse), you can calculate the x and y coordinates of the destination point using trigonometric functions. The x coordinate is determined by the distance times the cosine of the angle. The y coordinate is determined by the distance times the sine of the angle. In this example the x and y coordinates (x1 and y1) are also offset by the x and y parameters to draw a rectangle whose center is not at (0, 0):

```
rotation += r1Angle + r2Angle + r3Angle;
var x1 = x + ry * Math.cos(rotation);
var y1 = y + ry * Math.sin(rotation);
this.moveTo(x1, y1);
```

The remainder of the example follows the same pattern: draw a line, draw a rounded corner (if applicable), and then move to the next side segment. The new coordinates for each segment are calculated using the same process as described previously. Once you have defined and included the *drawRectangle()* method in your Flash document, you can quickly draw a rectangle within any movie clip instance. Don't forget that you still need to define the line style (see Recipe 4.1) before Flash will actually draw anything.

```
// Create a new movie clip into which to draw the rectangle.
this.createEmptyMovieClip("rectangle_mc", 1);

// Define a 1-pixel, black, solid line style.
rectangle_mc.lineStyle(1, 0x000000, 100);

// Draw a rectangle with dimensions of 100 × 200. The rectangle has rounded corners
// with radii of 10, and it is rotated 45 degrees clockwise.
rectangle_mc.drawRectangle(100, 200, 10, 45);
```

You can draw a square by using the *drawRectangle()* method with equal height and width values:

```
this.createEmptyMovieClip("square_mc", 1);
square_mc.lineStyle(1, 0x000000, 100);
square_mc.drawRectangle(100, 100);
```

You can draw filled rectangles by invoking *beginFill()* or *beginGradientFill()* before *drawRectangle()* and invoking *endFill()* after *drawRectangle()*:

```
this.createEmptyMovieClip("filledRectangle_mc", 1);
filledRectangle_mc.lineStyle(1, 0x000000, 100);    // Define a black, 1-pixel border.
```

```
filledRectangle_mc.beginFill(0x0000FF);          // Define a solid blue fill.
filledRectangle_mc.drawRectangle(100, 200);
filledRectangle_mc.endFill( );
```

See Also

Recipes 4.3, 4.8, 4.9, 5.12, 5.13, and 5.14

4.5   Drawing a Circle

Problem

You want to draw a circle at runtime.

Solution

Create a custom *MovieClip.drawCircle()* method using the Drawing API and invoke it on a movie clip.

Discussion

You can create a circle in ActionScript with eight curves. Fewer curves results in a distorted circle and too many curves hinders performance. Let's create a custom method of the *MovieClip* class for drawing circles. This method, *drawCircle()*, allows for three parameters:

radius
> The radius of the circle

x   The x coordinate of the circle's center point. If undefined, the circle is centered at x = 0.

y   The y coordinate of the circle's center point. If undefined, the circle is centered at y = 0.

Define the custom *drawCircle()* method on MovieClip.prototype to make it available to all movie clip instances:

```
MovieClip.prototype.drawCircle = function (radius, x, y) {
    // The angle of each of the eight segments is 45 degrees (360 divided by 8), which
    // equals π/4 radians.
    var angleDelta = Math.PI / 4;

    // Find the distance from the circle's center to the control points for the curves.
    var ctrlDist = radius/Math.cos(angleDelta/2);
```

```
// Initialize the angle to 0 and define local variables that are used for the
// control and ending points.
var angle = 0;
var rx, ry, ax, ay;

// Move to the starting point, one radius to the right of the circle's center.
this.moveTo(x + radius, y);

// Repeat eight times to create eight segments.
for (var i = 0; i < 8; i++) {

    // Increment the angle by angleDelta (π/4) to create the whole circle (2π).
    angle += angleDelta;

    // The control points are derived using sine and cosine.
    rx = x + Math.cos(angle-(angleDelta/2))*(ctrlDist);
    ry = y + Math.sin(angle-(angleDelta/2))*(ctrlDist);

    // The anchor points (end points of the curve) can be found similarly to the
    // control points.
    ax = x + Math.cos(angle)*radius;
    ay = y + Math.sin(angle)*radius;

    // Draw the segment.
    this.curveTo(rx, ry, ax, ay);
}
}
```

How the *drawCircle()* method functions is better understood with a little explanation.

The distance of the control point for each segment from the circle's center is found using a trigonometric formula that states that the cosine of an angle is equal to the adjacent side over the hypotenuse. In the case of the circle, the angle that bisects a segment (thus also intersecting its control point) is $\pi/8$ (angleDelta/2). The distance to the control point from the center of the circle forms the hypotenuse of the right triangle, as you can see in Figure 4-3.

```
var ctrlDist = radius/Math.cos(angleDelta/2);
```

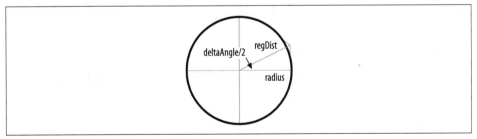

Figure 4-3. Calculating a point approximating a circular path

Basic trigonometric formulas can be used to find the x and y coordinates along the circle's circumference given the angle and the hypotenuse. For the control point, the hypotenuse value is ctrlDist, and the angle is angle − angleDelta/2, since this angle bisects the segment. The anchor point is found using the value of angle, which is calculated to be the angle that intersects the anchor point, and the circle's radius (since the anchor point should always be on the circle's circumference). Thus, it follows:

```
rx = x + Math.cos(angle-(angleDelta/2))*(ctrlDist);
ry = y + Math.sin(angle-(angleDelta/2))*(ctrlDist);
ax = x + Math.cos(angle)*radius;
ay = y + Math.sin(angle)*radius;
```

Once you have defined the *drawCircle()* method and included it in your Flash document, you can quickly draw a circle with just a few lines of code. Remember that you still need to define a line style before Flash will draw anything.

```
// Create a movie clip instance in which you will draw the circle.
this.createEmptyMovieClip("circle_mc", 1);

// Define a 1-pixel, black, solid line style.
circle_mc.lineStyle(1, 0x000000, 100);

// Draw a circle of radius 100, centered at (50,75).
circle_mc.drawCircle(100, 50, 75);
// Draw a circle of radius 65, centered at (0,0).
circle_mc.drawCircle(65);
```

You can fill a circle by invoking *beginFill()* or *beginGradientFill()* before *drawCircle()* and invoking *endFill()* after *drawCircle()*:

```
this.createEmptyMovieClip("circle_mc", 1);
circle_mc.lineStyle(1, 0x000000, 100);   // Use a 1-pixel, black, solid border.
circle_mc.beginFill(0x0000FF);            // Use a solid blue fill.
circle_mc.drawCircle(100);
circle_mc.endFill();
```

4.6   Drawing an Ellipse

Problem

You want to draw an ellipse (oval) at runtime.

Solution

Create a custom *MovieClip.drawEllipse()* method using the Drawing API and invoke it on a movie clip.

Discussion

You can create a method of the *MovieClip* class to draw an ellipse that is very similar to the *drawCircle()* method in Recipe 4.5. In fact, the *drawCircle()* method is merely a degenerate version of *drawEllipse()*, in which the radii in the x and y directions are the same.

The custom *drawEllipse()* method accepts four parameters:

xRadius
> The radius of the ellipse in the x direction (major axis).

yRadius
> The radius of the ellipse in the y direction (minor axis).

x   The x coordinate of the center of the ellipse.

y   The y coordinate of the center of the ellipse.

Refer to Recipe 4.5 for those aspects of the *drawEllipse()* method that are not commented on here.

```
MovieClip.prototype.drawEllipse = function (xRadius, yRadius, x, y) {
  var angleDelta = Math.PI / 4;

  // While the circle has only one distance to the control point for each segment,
  // the ellipse has two distances: one that corresponds to xRadius and another that
  // corresponds to yRadius.
  var xCtrlDist = xRadius/Math.cos(angleDelta/2);
  var yCtrlDist = yRadius/Math.cos(angleDelta/2);
  var rx, ry, ax, ay;
  this.moveTo(x + xRadius, y);
  for (var i = 0; i < 8; i++) {
    angle += angleDelta;
    rx = x + Math.cos(angle-(angleDelta/2))*(xCtrlDist);
    ry = y + Math.sin(angle-(angleDelta/2))*(yCtrlDist);
    ax = x + Math.cos(angle)*xRadius;
    ay = y + Math.sin(angle)*yRadius;
    this.curveTo(rx, ry, ax, ay);
  }
}
```

Once you have defined and included the *drawEllipse()* method in your Flash document, you can draw an ellipse rather easily. Use the *drawEllipse()* method the same way you used the *drawCircle()* method in Recipe 4.5 but provide both x and y radii instead of just a single radius. Remember that you still need to define the line style before you call the *drawEllipse()* method.

```
// Create an ellipse with minor and major axes of 100 and 200, respectively.
this.createEmptyMovieClip("ellipse", 1);
ellipse.lineStyle(1, 0x000000, 100);    // Use a one-pixel, black, solid border
ellipse.drawEllipse(100, 200);
```

Having defined *drawEllipse()*, we can rewrite the *drawCircle()* method, as follows:

```
MovieClip.prototype.drawCircle = function (radius, x, y) {
  // Call drawEllipse() with the same radius for both x and y.
  this.drawEllipse (radius, radius, x, y);
}
```

See Also

Recipe 4.5

4.7   Drawing a Triangle

Problem

You want to draw a triangle at runtime.

Solution

Create a custom *MovieClip.drawTriangle()* method using the Drawing API and invoke it on a movie clip.

Discussion

You can determine and plot the vertices of a triangle given the lengths of two sides and the angle between them. This is a better approach than specifying the lengths of the three sides because knowing the lengths of two sides and the angle between them always determines a triangle, whereas three arbitrary sides may not fit together to make a triangle.

The custom *drawTriangle()* method accepts six parameters:

ab   The length of the side formed between points *a* and *b*, as shown in Figure 4-4.

ac   The length of the side formed between points *a* and *c*, as shown in Figure 4-4.

angle
    The angle (in degrees) between sides *ab* and *ac*.

rotation
    The rotation of the triangle in degrees. If 0 or undefined, side *ac* parallels the x axis.

x   The x coordinate of the centroid (the center point) of the triangle.

y   The y coordinate of the centroid of the triangle.

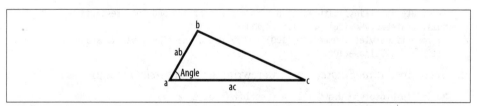

Figure 4-4. The parameters used in the drawTriangle() method

Define the custom *drawTriangle()* method on `MovieClip.prototype` to make it available to all movie clip instances:

```
// Include the custom Math library from Chapter 5 to access Math.degToRad().
#include "Math.as"

MovieClip.prototype.drawTriangle = function (ab, ac, angle, rotation, x, y) {

    // Convert the angle between the sides from degrees to radians.
    angle = Math.degToRad(angle);

    // Convert the rotation of the triangle from degrees to radians.
    rotation = Math.degToRad(rotation);

    // Calculate the coordinates of points b and c.
    var bx = Math.cos(angle - rotation) * ab;
    var by = Math.sin(angle - rotation) * ab;
    var cx = Math.cos(-rotation) * ac;
    var cy = Math.sin(-rotation) * ac;

    // Calculate the centroid's coordinates.
    var centroidX = (cx + bx)/3 - x;
    var centroidY = (cy + by)/3 - y;

    // Move to point a, then draw line ac, then line cb, and finally ba (ab).
    this.moveTo(-centroidX, -centroidY);
    this.lineTo(cx - centroidX, cy - centroidY);
    this.lineTo(bx - centroidX, by - centroidY);
    this.lineTo(-centroidX, -centroidY);
}
```

There are a few points about this method that bear further discussion.

Point *a* will always be the point of rotation, so you don't need to calculate it's coordinates. However, points *b* and *c* need to be calculated (using basic trigonometric ratios). We define point *b* at the end of line *ab* at an angle of `angle` in an unrotated triangle. To factor in rotation we subtract `rotation` from `angle`. We define point c to be at the end of line *ac*. In an unrotated triangle, point *c* is on the same x axis as point *a*, but to factor in rotation you should subtract `rotation` from the angle between line *ac* (and itself, which is, of course, 0). This leads us to:

```
var bx = Math.cos(angle - rotation) * ab;
var by = Math.sin(angle - rotation) * ab;
var cx = Math.cos(-rotation) * ac;
var cy = Math.sin(-rotation) * ac;
```

The x coordinate of the centroid of a triangle is calculated by adding together the x coordinates of the vertices and dividing by three. The y coordinate is found in an analogous manner. In our *drawTriangle()* method, the coordinates of point *a* are always (0, 0), so it doesn't factor into the equation. We subtract the x and y inputs from the centroid coordinates to account for any user-defined offset:

```
var centroidX = (cx + bx)/3 - x;
var centroidY = (cy + by)/3 - y;
```

Here is an example of how to use the *drawTriangle()* method. Notice that you still have to define the line style before invoking the *drawTriangle()* method.

```
// Draw a triangle with sides of 100 and 200 pixels and an angle of 30 degrees.
this.createEmptyMovieClip("triangle_mc", 1);
triangle_mc.lineStyle(1, 0x000000, 100);        // Use a one-pixel, black, solid border
triangle_mc.drawTriangle(100, 200, 30);
```

See Also

You can draw an isosceles triangle using the *drawRegularPolygon()* method of Recipe 4.8 (and specifying a shape with three sides).

4.8   Drawing Regular Polygons

Problem

You want to draw a regular polygon (a polygon in which all sides are equal length) at runtime.

Solution

Create a custom *MovieClip.drawRegularPolygon()* method using the Drawing API and invoke it on a movie clip.

Discussion

You can create a method to draw a regular polygon using basic trigonometric ratios to determine the necessary angles and coordinates of the segments.

The *drawRegularPolygon()* accepts five parameters:

sides
> The number of sides in the polygon

length
> The length of each side in pixels

rotation
> The number of degrees by which the polygon should be rotated

x   The x coordinate of the center of the polygon

y   The y coordinate of the center of the polygon

Define the custom *drawRegularPolygon()* method on MovieClip.prototype to make it available to all movie clip instances:

```
// Include the custom Math library from Chapter 5 to access Math.degToRad().
#include "Math.as"
```

```
MovieClip.prototype.drawRegularPolygon = function (sides, length, rotation, x, y) {

    // Convert rotation from degrees to radians.
    rotation = Math.degToRad(rotation);

    // The angle formed between the segments from the polygon's center as shown in
    // Figure 4-5. Since the total angle in the center is 360 degrees (2π radians),
    // each segment's angle is 2π divided by the number of sides.
    var angle = (2 * Math.PI) / sides;

    // Calculate the length of the radius that circumscribes the polygon (which is also
    // the distance from the center to any of the vertices).
    var radius = (length/2)/Math.sin(angle/2);

    // The starting point of the polygon is calculated using trigonometry, where radius
    // is the hypotenuse and rotation is the angle.
    var px = (Math.cos(rotation) * radius) + x;
    var py = (Math.sin(rotation) * radius) + y;

    // Move to the starting point without yet drawing a line.
    this.moveTo(px, py);

    // Draw each side. Calculate the vertex coordinates using the same trigonometric
    // ratios used to calculate px and py earlier.
    for (var i = 1; i <= sides; i++) {
      px = (Math.cos((angle * i) + rotation) * radius) + x;
      py = (Math.sin((angle * i) + rotation) * radius) + y;
      this.lineTo(px, py);
    }
}
```

Figure 4-5 shows the angle used when calculating how to draw a regular polygon.

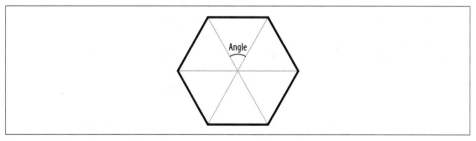

Figure 4-5. Drawing a regular polygon

Once you have defined the *drawRegularPolygon()* method and included it in your Flash document, you can quickly draw regular polygons with any number of sides (with a minimum of three sides, of course, for it to be a valid polygon.) Remember, as with all the other drawing methods in this chapter, you must define a line style prior to invoking the *drawRegularPolygon()* method.

```
// Create the movie clip into which to draw the polygon.
this.createEmptyMovieClip("polygon_mc", 1);

// Use a 1-pixel, black, solid line style for the border.
polygon_mc.lineStyle(1, 0x000000, 100);

// Draw a regular nonagon (a nine-sided polygon) with sides of length 30.
polygon_mc.drawRegularPolygon(9, 30);
```

As with all the custom methods in this chapter that define shapes, you can create a filled polygon by invoking *beginFill()* or *beginGradientFill()* before *drawRegularPolygon()* and invoking *endFill()* after *drawRegularPolygon()*.

```
this.createEmptyMovieClip("polygon_mc", 1);
polygon_mc.lineStyle(1, 0x000000, 100);    // Define a black, 1-pixel border.
polygon_mc.beginFill(0x00FF00);            // Define a solid green fill.
polygon_mc.drawRegularPolygon(9, 30)
polygon_mc.endFill();
```

4.9   Filling a Shape with a Solid or Translucent Color

Problem

You want to draw a shape and fill it with a solid or translucent color at runtime.

Solution

Use the *beginFill()* and *endFill()* methods to initiate and close a shape drawn at runtime.

Discussion

To draw a filled shape, call *beginFill()* prior to any other drawing methods, including the custom methods you have defined such as *drawCircle()* and *drawPolygon()*. Invoke *endFill()* after calling other drawing methods to create the shape.

 You cannot apply a fill to an existing shape drawn at authoring time or runtime. You must invoke *beginFill()* before drawing the shape to be filled.

This example creates a solid blue circle with a radius of 100 pixels:

```
_root.createEmptyMovieClip("shape_mc", 1);

// Tell ActionScript to begin a solid, blue fill.
shape_mc.beginFill(0x0000FF, 100);
```

```
// Invoke a custom drawing method, such as drawCircle( ), or invoke lineTo( ) or
// curveTo( ) multiple times to create a closed shape.
shape_mc.drawCircle(100);

// Call endFill( ) to close the shape after other drawing methods have been called.
shape_mc.endFill( );
```

The *beginFill()* method requires two parameters:

fillColor
> The RGB value to use for the fill

alpha
> The value between 0 (transparent) and 100 (opaque) that controls the opacity

To create a translucent, filled shape, specify an *alpha* less than 100. If *alpha* is 0, the shape will appear unfilled. Don't forget to define a line style if you want the outline to be visible.

The *endFill()* method does not require any parameters. It simply ends the fill initiated with *beginFill()* or *beginGradientFill()*. To avoid unexpected results, ensure that the pen returns to the starting point to complete the shape before invoking *endFill()*.

See Also

Recipes 3.2 and 4.10

4.10 Filling a Shape with a Gradient

Problem

You want to draw a shape and fill it with a gradient at runtime.

Solution

Use the *beginGradientFill()* and *endFill()* methods to initiate and close a shape drawn at runtime.

Discussion

In a *gradient fill*, there is a graded change in colors. Flash supports linear gradients, in which one color fades into the next from left to right. Flash also supports radial gradients, in which the colors radiate out from a center point. You can initiate a gradient-filled shape using *beginGradientFill()* in the same way you initiate a solid-filled shape with *beginFill( )*. The difference is that the call to *beginGradientFill( )* requires a more complex set of parameters:

gradientType
> Either "linear" for a linear gradient, or "radial" for a radial gradient.

colors
> An array of RGB values for the colors to use in the gradient. They are displayed in the gradient from left to right in a linear gradient, or from the center outward in a radial gradient.

alphas
> An array of alpha values that correspond to the colors in the *colors* parameter array.

ratios
> An array whose elements are numbers corresponding to the *colors* and *alphas* elements. The values in the *ratios* array indicate the point within the gradient at which each color is pure. The range of values for the *ratios* should be from 0 (leftmost point in a linear fill, or innermost point in a radial fill) to 255 (rightmost or outermost).

matrix
> An object with the following properties:
>
> *matrixType*
>> This value should always be "box".
>
> *x*   The x coordinate of the bottom-left corner of the gradient.
>
> *y*   The y coordinate of the bottom-left corner of the gradient.
>
> *width*
>> The width of the gradient in pixels.
>
> *height*
>> The height of the gradient in pixels.
>
> *r*   The rotation of the gradient in radians (not degrees).

Here is an example that uses a linear gradient to fill a rectangle:

```
// Include the drawing methods, which are needed for the drawRectangle( ) method.
#include "DrawingMethods.as"

// Define the width and height of the rectangle to be drawn and filled.
rectWidth  = 100;
rectHeight = 200;

// Create an empty clip into which we will draw the shape.
_root.createEmptyMovieClip("shape_mc", 1);
shape_mc.lineStyle(3, 0, 100);
```

```
// Create a colors array with RGB values for blue, green, and red.
colors = [0x0000FF, 0x00FF00, 0xFF0000];

// Create an alphas array in which the colors are 100% opaque.
alphas = [100, 100, 100];

// Create a ratios array where pure blue is at the left edge of the gradient, pure
// green is in the center, and pure red at the right edge.
ratios = [0, 127.5, 255];

// Create the matrix object. Set the x and y coordinates so that the bottom-left
// corner of the gradient lines up with the bottom-left corner of the rectangle. Set
// the width and height of the gradient to match the rectangle.
matrix = {matrixType: "box", x: -rectWidth/2, y: -rectHeight/2, w: rectWidth,
          h: rectHeight, r:0};

// Call beginGradientFill() so that the rectangle will be
// filled with a linear gradient.
shape_mc.beginGradientFill("linear", colors, alphas, ratios, matrix);

// Draw the rectangle with rounded corners (requires DrawingMethods.as).
shape_mc.drawRectangle(rectHeight, rectWidth, 10);

// End the fill.
shape_mc.endFill();
```

Note that the *endFill()* method is used to end a drawing operation begun with either *beginFill()* or *beginGradientFill()*.

Here is an example of a radial, gradient fill used to fill an ellipse:

```
// Include the drawing methods, which are needed for the drawEllipse() method.
#include "DrawingMethods.as"

// Define the width and height of the ellipse to be drawn and filled.
ellipseWidth  = 100;
ellipseHeight = 200;

_root.createEmptyMovieClip("shape_mc", 1);
shape_mc.lineStyle(3, 0x000000, 100);

// Create colors, alphas, and ratios arrays for white and black, both 100% opaque.
// Pure white starts in the center and grades into pure black at the outside edge.
colors = [0xFFFFFF, 0x000000];
alphas = [100, 100];
ratios = [0, 255];

// Define the matrix object.
matrix = {matrixType: "box", x: -ellipseWidth/2, y: -ellipseHeight/2,
          w: ellipseWidth, h: ellipseHeight, r:0};

// Begin the radial fill.
shape_mc.beginGradientFill("radial", colors, alphas, ratios, matrix);
```

```
// Draw the ellipse (requires DrawingMethods.as).
shape_mc.drawEllipse(ellipseWidth/2, ellipseHeight/2);

// End the fill.
shape_mc.endFill( );
```

See Also

See Recipes 4.4 and 4.6 for implementations of the custom *drawRectangle()* and *drawEllipse()* methods. See Recipe 4.11 for details on creating a custom gradient fill.

4.11   Filling a Shape with a Complex Gradient

Problem

You want to draw a gradient-filled shape at runtime, but the box-style gradient matrix doesn't offer sufficient control.

Solution

Use the *beginGradientFill()* and *endFill()* methods in conjunction with a *TransformMatrix* object.

Discussion

In Recipe 4.10, we used a box-style gradient to apply a simple fill pattern. However, you can attain precise control over the gradient by passing a transformation matrix as the *matrix* parameter sent to the *beginGradientFill()* method.

ActionScript uses a 3 × 3 transformation matrix to apply a custom gradient. Working directly with the transformation matrix can be a bit more complicated than it is worth, so you should take advantage of the *TransformMatrix* class, which makes this process much easier. You need to include *TransformMatrix.as* in any Flash document in which you wish to work with a transform matrix:

```
#include "TransformMatrix.as"
```

The *TransformMatrix.as* file is not part of the standard Flash installation, but it is included on the Flash CD-ROM under *Goodies\Macromedia\Other Samples\ transformmatrix.as*. You should copy the file from the CD-ROM to Flash's *Include* directory (*Flash Intallation\Configuration\Include*).

First, create a *TransformMatrix* object using the standard constructor method:

```
matrix = new TransformMatrix( );
```

Thereafter, you can call any of the five available methods:

translate(x, y)
> The *translate()* method offsets the bottom-left corner (for linear gradients) or the center (for radial gradients) of the gradient. By default, the gradient is positioned at (0,0). The two parameters specify the number of pixels by which to translate the gradient in the x and y directions.

scale(width, height)
> The *scale()* method scales the gradient to the specified width and height.

rotate(degrees)
> The *rotate()* method rotates the gradient clockwise by the specified number of degrees (not radians).

skew(degrees)
> The *skew()* method skews the gradient by the number of degrees specified, creating a stretching effect.

shear(x, y)
> The *shear()* method shears the gradient. The two parameters specify the number of pixels by which to shear the gradient in the x and y directions.

Unlike the standard 3 × 3 transformation matrix, the *TransformMatrix* class uses a gradient that is 1 × 1 pixels until you scale it. Therefore, when working with a transformation matrix, you should use the *scale()* method, either by itself or in conjunction with the other methods, to ensure that the gradient is appropriately sized.

This example applies the *translate()* method with the *scale()* method:

```
// Include the drawing methods, which are needed for the drawRectangle() method.
#include "DrawingMethods.as"

// Include the file that implements the TransformMatrix class.
#include "TransformMatrix.as"

// Create an empty movie clip for drawing.
_root.createEmptyMovieClip("shape_mc", 1);

// Create the colors, alphas, and ratios arrays just as you would when working with a
// box-style gradient.
colors = [0x0000FF, 0x00FF00, 0xFF0000];
alphas = [100, 100, 100];
ratios = [0, 127.5, 255];

// Create a new TransformMatrix object.
matrix = new TransformMatrix();

// Scale the gradient to 100 × 200 pixels and offset it 20 pixels to the right.
matrix.scale(100, 200);
matrix.translate(20, 0);

// Use a 1-pixel, black, solid border.
shape_mc.lineStyle(1, 0x000000, 100);
```

```
// Call beginGradientFill() just as you would when working with a box-style gradient,
// except the matrix parameter is a TransformMatrix object.
shape_mc.beginGradientFill("linear", colors, alphas, ratios, matrix);

// Draw a rectangle (requires DrawingMethods.as).
shape_mc.drawRectangle(100, 200);
shape_mc.endFill();
```

You can achieve animation effects by repeatedly redrawing the same shape and applying different transformations to the gradient fill:

```
// Include the drawing methods, which are needed for the drawCircle() method.
#include "DrawingMethods.as"
// Include the file that implements the TransformMatrix class.
#include "TransformMatrix.as"

_root.createEmptyMovieClip("shape_mc", 1);

// Call the following actions repeatedly by placing them within the shape_mc clip's
// onEnterFrame() method.
shape_mc.onEnterFrame = function () {

    // Create the colors, alphas, and ratios arrays as usual.
    var colors = [0x0000FF, 0x00FF00, 0xFF0000];
    var alphas = [100, 100, 100];
    var ratios = [0, 127.5, 255];

    // Create the TransformMatrix object.
    var matrix = new TransformMatrix();

    // Increment a custom scaleFactor property and pass that value to the transform
    // matrix's scale() method. This will scale the gradient in the x and y directions
    // uniformly, increasing over time.
    var sf = this.scaleFactor++;
    matrix.scale(sf, sf);

    // Clear the previously drawn shape. Otherwise, Flash will get bogged down trying
    // to keep track of all the old shapes.
    this.clear();

    // Draw a circle with a gradient fill. Each time this circle is redrawn the
    // gradient will be larger.
    this.lineStyle(1, 0x000000, 100);   // Use a one-pixel, black, solid border
    this.beginGradientFill("radial", colors, alphas, ratios, matrix);
    this.drawCircle(100);        // Requires DrawingMethods.as
    this.endFill();
}
```

See Also

Recipes 4.4, 4.5, and 4.10

4.12   Scripting Masks

Problem

You want to create a mask at runtime.

Solution

Use the Drawing API to create a shape and then use *MovicClip.setMask()* to apply the mask.

Discussion

Masks can be used to create unique shapes or visual effects. For example, you can use masks to create wipes and transitions or interesting animations in which only the masked portion of the artwork is visible at a given time. You can even create masks that change shape over time, and use them to mask bitmapped graphics (in movie clips).

You can use any movie clip as a mask of another movie clip using the *setMask()* method. The *setMask()* method is called from the movie clip to be masked, and you should pass it a reference to the movie clip that acts as the mask:

```
maskedMovieClip.setMask(maskMovieClip);
```

In most cases, masks are simple shapes, such as rectangles or circles. You do not need to use the Drawing API to draw the mask movie clip, but it is recommended that you do so unless the mask is of an unusual shape.

First, here is an example in which a mask follows the mouse. The mask is assigned to a movie clip containing a loaded image, so the effect is that the user can see only the portion of the image over which he has positioned the mouse.

```
// Include the drawing methods, which are needed for the drawCircle() method.
#include "DrawingMethods.as"

// Create a movie clip and a nested movie clip for loading an image. See Recipe 15.3
// for more information on the need for creating nested movie clips when loading
// external JPEGs.
_root.createEmptyMovieClip("image_mc", 1);
_root.image_mc.createEmptyMovieClip("imageHolder_mc", 1);

// Load the image into the movie clip. You can use this URL if you want, but it will
// work only while you are using the test or standalone players. See Recipe 15.3 for
// more information on loading JPEGs.
image_mc.imageHolder_mc.loadMovie("http://www.person13.com/ascb/images/image1.jpg");

// Draw the masking movie clip.
_root.createEmptyMovieClip("mask_mc", 2);
mask_mc.lineStyle(3, 0x000000, 0);
```

```
mask_mc.beginFill(0, 100);
mask_mc.drawCircle(60);
mask_mc.endFill( );

// Call the setMask( ) method on the masked movie clip and pass it the masking movie
// clip as a parameter.
image_mc.setMask(mask_mc);

// Call the startDrag( ) method of the masking movie clip so that the mask can be
// moved with the cursor.
mask_mc.startDrag(true);
```

Next, here is an example in which a mask is used to create a wipe transition between two loaded images.

```
#include "DrawingMethods.as"

// Create a movie clip and a nested movie clip and load the first image into it.
_root.createEmptyMovieClip("image0_mc", 1);
_root.image0_mc.createEmptyMovieClip("imageHolder_mc", 1);
image0_mc.imageHolder_mc.loadMovie("http://www.person13.com/ascb/images/image1.jpg");

// Create another movie clip and nested movie clip and load the second image into it.
// Both image0_mc and image1_mc are created at (0,0). This means that they will
// overlap. This is what we want.
_root.createEmptyMovieClip("image1_mc", 2);
_root.image1_mc.createEmptyMovieClip("imageHolder_mc", 1);
image1_mc.imageHolder_mc.loadMovie("http://www.person13.com/ascb/images/image2.jpg");


// Draw the masking movie clip. The dimensions of the images are 640 × 480 (if you
// load the images using the URLs provided) and so the mask should be a rectangle
// with the same dimensions.
_root.createEmptyMovieClip("mask_mc", 3);
mask_mc.lineStyle(3, 0x000000, 0);
mask_mc.beginFill(0, 100);
mask_mc.drawRectangle(640, 480);
mask_mc.endFill( );

// Position the mask so that it is off to the left side of the Stage.
mask_mc._x = -320;
mask_mc._y = 240;

// Call the setMask( ) method to set mask_mc as the mask for image1_mc. This causes
// image0_mc to display initially, even though it is below image1_mc.
image1_mc.setMask(mask_mc);

// Define an event handler method for image0_mc so that the mask movie clip moves
// when the user clicks on image0_mc.
image0_mc.onRelease = function ( ) {

    // Use an onEnterFrame( ) event handler method to move the mask. This assumes you
    // have the default frames per second setting of 12.
    _root.mask_mc.onEnterFrame = function ( ) {
```

```
    // Move the mask to the right by 12 pixels.
    this._x += 12;

    // If the mask is fully masking the image, then delete the onEnterFrame( ) method.
    if (this._x >= 320) {
      this._x = 320;
      delete this.onEnterFrame;
    }
  }
}
}
```

If you use the URLs provided in this example, then the images that are
loaded have dimensions of 640 × 480. Therefore, you might need to
increase the dimensions of your movie to see the full images. If you use
your own images, they must be of the same resolution for the effect to
work as described.

## CHAPTER 5

Numbers and Math

5.0 Introduction

Although numbers aren't always in the spotlight, don't overlook their power and importance in your code. Numbers come in all shapes and sizes—from binary to decimal to hexadecimal. Each type of representation has its own particular niche in which it is most valuable. For example, hexadecimal numbers are often used to represent RGB color values because they make it easy to discern each of the three color components. See Recipe 5.2 to learn how to convert between different number bases.

Closely related to numbers is the subject of mathematics. Without mathematical operations, your Flash movies would be rather dull. Simple operations such as addition and subtraction are essential to even the most basic ActionScript applications, and more advanced math, such as random-number generation and trigonometric calculations, is equally essential to advanced applications.

The *Math* object supports methods and properties useful in a range of mathematical operations. In the recipes throughout this chapter, you can discover how to extend the functionality of the *Math* object to perform more advanced operations, such as financial calculations. See *http://www.person13.com/ascb* for the final version of the *Math.as* file used throughout this chapter.

5.1 Representing Numbers in Different Bases

Problem

You want to specify a value as a binary, octal, or hexadecimal number.

Solution

Hexadecimal literals start with 0X or 0x (where the first character is a zero, not an "oh"), and octal literals start with 0 (again, zero, not "oh"). Binary numbers can't be represented directly, but you can specify their octal or hexadecimal equivalent.

Discussion

You can represent numbers in ActionScript using whichever format is most convenient, such as decimal or hexadecimal notation. For example, if you set the value of the *MovieClip._rotation* property, it is most convenient to use a decimal number:

```
myMovieClip._rotation = 180;
```

On the other hand, hexadecimal numbers are useful for specifying RGB colors. For example, you can set the RGB value for a *Color* object in hexadecimal notation (in this example, 0xF612AB is a hex number representing a shade of pink):

```
myColor = new Color(myMovieClip);
myColor.setRGB(0xF612AB);
```

Any numeric literal starting with 0X or 0x is presumed to be a *hexadecimal number* (a.k.a. *hex* or base-16). Allowable digits in a hexadecimal number are 0–9 and A–F (both uppercase and lowercase letters are allowed).

Any numeric literal starting with 0, but not 0x or 0X, is presumed to be an *octal number* (a.k.a. base-8). Allowable digits in an octal number are 0–7. For example, 0777 is an octal number. Most developers don't ever use octal numbers in Action-Script.

The only digits allowed in *binary numbers* (a.k.a. base-2) are 0 and 1. Although you can't specify a binary number directly, you can specify its hexadecimal equivalent. Four binary digits (*bits*) are equivalent to a single hex digit. For example, 1111 in binary is equal to F in hex (15 in decimal). The number 11111111 in binary is equal to FF in hex (255 in decimal). Binary numbers (or rather their hexadecimal equivalents) are most commonly used with ActionScript's bitwise operators (&, |, ^, >>, <<, and >>>).

See Also

Recipes 3.2, 3.3, 3.4, and 5.2

5.2   Converting Between Different Number Systems

Problem

You want to convert a number between different bases (decimal, binary, hexadecimal, etc.).

Solution

Use the *parseInt()* function with the *radix* parameter (the *radix* is the number's base) to convert a string to a decimal representation. Use the *Number.toString()* method with the *radix* parameter to convert a decimal number to a string representation of the value in another base.

Discussion

No matter how you set a number value in ActionScript, the result is always retrieved as a decimal (base-10) number.

```
// Create a Color object.
myColor = new Color(this);

// Set the RGB value as a hexadecimal.
myColor.setRGB(0xF612AB);

// This displays the value as decimal: 16126635
trace(myColor.getRGB());
```

However, if you want to output a value in a different base, you can use *Number.toString(radix)* to convert any number value to a string representing that number in the specified base.

These two examples convert numeric literals to *Number* objects and output the string representations in base-2 (binary) and base-16 (hexadecimal) format:

```
// The radix is 2, so output as binary.
trace(new Number(51).toString(2));  // Displays: "110011"
// The radix is 16, so output as hex.
trace(new Number(25).toString(16)); // Displays: "19"
```

This example assigns a primitive number to a variable and calls the *toString()* method to output the value in hexadecimal:

```
myNum = 164;
trace(myNum.toString(16)); // Displays: "A4"
```

Note that the results from these examples are not numeric literals, but rather strings, such as "110011", "19", and "A4".

This example sets the RGB value of a *Color* object, then calls *toString()* on the result to display the value as a hexadecimal (as it had been input, although the alpha digits are converted to lowercase, and the result is a string, not a number):

```
myColor = new Color(this);
myColor.setRGB(0xF612AB);
trace(myColor.getRGB().toString(16));  // Displays: "f612ab"
```

The valid range for the *radix* parameter of the *toString()* method is from 2 to 36. If you call *toString()* with no *radix* parameter or an invalid value, decimal format (base-10) is assumed.

You can achieve the inverse of the *toString()* process using the *parseInt()* function with the *radix* parameter. The *parseInt()* function takes a string value and returns a number. This is useful if you want to work with inputs of bases other than 10.

These examples parse the numbers from the string in base-2 (binary), base-16 (hexadecimal), and base-10, respectively. Note that the result is always a decimal.

```
trace(parseInt("110011", 2));  // Displays: 51
trace(parseInt("19", 16));     // Displays: 25
trace(parseInt("17", 10));     // Displays: 17
```

If omitted, the *radix* is assumed to be 10, unless the string starts with 0X or 0, in which case hexadecimal or octal is assumed:

```
trace(parseInt("0x12"));    // The radix is implicitly 16. Displays: 18
trace(parseInt("017"));     // The radix is implicitly 8. Displays: 15
```

An explicit *radix* overrides an implicit one. In the next example, the result is 0, not 12. When the number is treated as base-10, conversion stops when a nonnumeric character—the *x*—is encountered.

```
// The number is treated as a decimal, not a hexadecimal number.
trace(parseInt("0x12", 10));   // Displays: 0 (not 12 or 18)
```

Here, although the leading zero doesn't prevent the remaining digits from being interpreted, it is treated as a decimal number, not an octal number:

```
// The number is treated as a decimal, not an octal number.
trace(parseInt("017", 10));   // Displays: 17 (not 15)
```

Due to a deviation from the ECMA-262 standard, ActionScript gets confused by the "0x" that prefixes a hexadecimal number if you specify an explicit *radix* of 16. Therefore, if you specify an explicit radix, don't prefix the number with "0x". For example, although the following should, according to the ECMA-262 standard, return the decimal equivalent of 0xA9FC9C, it returns 0 instead:

```
trace (parseInt("0xA9FC9C", 16));   // Displays: 0
```

Either of these will work as expected:

```
trace (parseInt("0xA9FC9C"));       // Displays: 11140252 (implicit radix)
trace (parseInt("A9FC9C", 16));     // Displays: 11140252 (explicit radix)
```

Conversely, don't forget to include either "0x" or an explicit radix. The following interprets the string as a decimal and returns NaN (Not-a-Number) because "A" can't be converted to an integer:

```
trace(parseInt("A9FC9C"));     // NaN
```

5.3   Rounding Numbers

Problem

You want to round a number to the nearest integer, decimal place, or interval (such as to the nearest multiple of 5).

Solution

Use *Math.round()* to round a number to the nearest integer. Use *Math.floor()* and *Math.ceil()* to round a number down or up, respectively. Create a custom *roundTo()* method to round a number to a specified number of decimal places or to a specified multiple.

Discussion

There are numerous reasons to round numbers. For example, when displaying the results of a calculation, you might display only the intended precision. Because all arithmetic in ActionScript is performed with floating-point numbers, some calculations result in unexpected floating-point numbers that must be rounded. For example, the result of a calculation may be 3.9999999 in practice even though it should be 4.0 in theory.

The *Math.round()* method returns the nearest integer value of any parameter passed to it:

```
trace(Math.round(204.499));  // Displays: 204
trace(Math.round(401.5));    // Displays: 402
```

The *Math.floor()* method rounds down, and the *Math.ceil()* method rounds up:

```
trace(Math.floor(204.99));   // Displays: 204
trace(Math.ceil(401.01));    // Displays: 402
```

To round a number to the nearest decimal place:

1. Decide the number of decimal places to which you want to round. For example, if you want to round 90.337 to 90.34, then you will round to two decimal places, which means that you will round to the nearest .01.

2. Divide the input value by the number chosen in Step 1 (in this case, .01).

3. Use *Math.round()* to round the calculated value from Step 2 to the nearest integer.

4. Multiply the result of Step 3 by the same value that you used to divide in Step 2.

For example, to round 90.337 to two decimal places, you could use:

```
trace (Math.round(90.337 / .01) * .01);   // Displays: 90.34
```

You can use the identical math to round a number to the nearest multiple of an integer. For example, this rounds 92.5 to the nearest multiple of 5:

```
trace (Math.round(92.5 / 5)  * 5);   // Displays: 95
```

As another example, this rounds 92.5 to the nearest multiple of 10:

```
trace (Math.round(92.5 / 10) * 10);   // Displays: 90
```

You can create a custom *Math.roundTo()* method that encapsulates this functionality. The custom method takes two parameters:

num
>   The number to round.

roundToInterval
>   The interval to which to round *num*. For example, if you want to round to the nearest tenth, use 0.1 as the interval. Or, to round to the nearest multiple of six, use 6.

Here is our custom *roundTo()* method, which is attached directly to the *Math* object, so it is available throughout the entire movie. You can add this custom method to a *Math.as* file for easy inclusion in other projects.

```
Math.roundTo = function (num, roundToInterval) {
  // roundToInterval defaults to 1 (round to the nearest integer).
  if (roundToInterval == undefined) {
    roundToInterval = 1;
  }
  // Return the result.
  return Math.round(num / roundToInterval) * roundToInterval;
};
```

Here is an example of how to use the *Math.roundTo()* method, assuming it is stored in an external file named *Math.as*:

```
#include "Math.as"
trace(Math.roundTo(Math.PI));         // Displays: 3
trace(Math.roundTo(Math.PI, .01));    // Displays: 3.14
trace(Math.roundTo(Math.PI, .0001));  // Displays: 3.1416
trace(Math.roundTo(123.456, 1));      // Displays: 123
trace(Math.roundTo(123.456, 6));      // Displays: 126
trace(Math.roundTo(123.456, .01));    // Displays: 123.46
```

You might prefer a custom *Math.roundDecPl()* method that rounds a number to a specified number of decimal places. Our custom method takes two parameters:

num
>   The number to round

decPl
>   The number of decimal places to which to round *num*

Here is our custom *roundDecPl()* method, which is attached directly to the *Math* object, so it is available throughout the entire movie:

```
Math.roundDecPl = function (num, decPl) {

  // decPl defaults to 0 (round to the nearest integer).
  if (decPl == undefined) {
    decPl = 0;
  }
  // Calculate the value used to multiply the original number,
  // which is 10 raised to the power of decPl.
  var multiplier = Math.pow(10, decPl);
  // Return the result.
  return Math.round(num * multiplier ) / multiplier;
};
```

Here is an example of how to use *Math.roundDecPl()*, assuming it is stored in an external file named *Math.as*:

```
#include "Math.as"
trace(Math.roundDecPl(Math.PI));      // Displays: 3
trace(Math.roundDecPl(Math.PI, 2));   // Displays: 3.14
trace(Math.roundDecPl(Math.PI, 4));   // Displays: 3.1416
```

5.4   Inserting Leading or Trailing Zeros

Problem

You want to add leading or trailing zeros to a number to display it as a string.

Solution

Create a custom *Math.zeroFill()* method.

Discussion

You might need to format numbers with leading or trailing zeros for display purposes, such as when displaying times or dates. For example, you would want to format 6 hours and 3 minutes as 6:03 or 06:03, not 6:3. And when you display monetary values, you often want to ensure that two digits appear after the decimal place so that 23 dollars and 40 cents is formatted as $24.40, not $23.4.

To add leading zeros, follow these steps:

1. Convert the number into a string using the *String()* function.

2. Determine the number of zeros to add by subtracting the string length from the number of places you want in the resulting value.

3. Use a *for* loop to prepend the necessary number of zeros (as strings) to the number.

To add trailing zeros, follow the same steps, but append the zeros instead of prepending them.

You can define a custom method, *Math.zeroFill()*, to format a number with leading or trailing zeros and invoke it whenever it is needed.

The *Math.zeroFill()* method accepts up to three parameters (it returns a string):

num
> The number you want to format.

places
> The number of total digits that should be filled in the resulting, formatted numeric string.

trailing
> If true, then the zeros are appended to the string. Otherwise, the zeros are prepended.

Here's the custom *zeroFill()* method that you can add to your *Math.as* file for easy inclusion in any Flash movie:

```
Math.zeroFill = function (num, places, trailing) {

  // Convert the number to a string.
  var filledVal = String(num);

  // Get the length of the string.
  var len = filledVal.length;

  // Use a for statement to add the necessary number of characters.
  for (var i = 0; i < (places - len); i++) {
    // If trailing is true, append the zeros; otherwise, prepend them.
    if (trailing) {
      filledVal += "0";
    } else {
      filledVal = "0" + filledVal;
    }
  }
  // Return the string.
  return filledVal;
};
```

Here is an example that uses *zeroFill()* to display the binary representation of a number. The first *trace()* statement simply displays the value returned by *Number.toString()*. The second *trace()* statement displays the zero-filled version showing all eight bits of the number instead of just six.

```
#include "Math.as"
val = 42;
trace(val.toString(2));                  // Displays: "101010"
trace(Math.zeroFill(val.toString(2), 8)); // Displays: "00101010"
```

See Also

Recipes 5.2 and 5.6

5.5   Formatting Numbers for Display

Problem

You want to format a number with a custom decimal delimiter, thousands delimiters, and/or leading spaces.

Solution

Create a custom *Math.formatNumber()* method.

Discussion

ActionScript does not include a built-in way to format numbers as strings, so you need to create a custom method to handle this for you. Furthermore, the delimiter used to indicate decimals and thousands varies by country. For example, the number represented as 1,234.56 in the United States is written as 1.234,56 in many countries. Using some basic string, array, and mathematical methods, we can create a custom method to format numbers with a configurable decimal delimiter (i.e., 123.4 or 123,4), configurable thousands delimiters (i.e., 1,234 or 1.234), and optional leading spaces (to align values when using a monospace font).

Our custom *Math.formatNumber()* method accepts four parameters:

num
> The number you want to format

thousandsDelim
> The value to use for delimiting the thousands, millions, billions, etc. places

decimalDelim
> The value to use for delimiting the decimal places

spaceFill
> Specifies the number of total spaces the formatted string should occupy (optional)

Here is our method definition, which can be added to *Math.as* for easy inclusion in your projects:

```
Math.numberFormat = function (num, thousandsDelim, decimalDelim, spaceFill) {
    // Default to a comma for thousands and a period for decimals.
    if (thousandsDelim == undefined) {thousandsDelim = ",";}
    if (decimalDelim   == undefined) {decimalDelim= ".";}
```

```
// Convert the number to a string and split it at the decimal point.
parts = String(num).split(".");

// Take the whole number portion and store it as an array of single characters.
// This makes it easier to insert the thousands delimiters, as needed.
partOneAr = parts[0].split("");

// Reverse the array so we can process the characters right to left.
partOneAr.reverse();

// Insert the thousands delimiter after every third character.
for (var i = 0, counter = 0; i < partOneAr.length; i++) {
  counter++;
  if (counter > 3) {
    counter = 0;
    partOneAr.splice(i, 0, thousandsDelim);
  }
}

// Reverse the array again so that it is back in the original order.
partOneAr.reverse();

// Create the formatted string using decimalDelim, if necessary.
var val = partOneAr.join("");
if (parts[1] != undefined) {
  val += decimalDelim + parts[1];
}

// If spaceFill is defined, add the necessary number of leading spaces.
if (spaceFill != undefined) {
  // Store the original length before adding spaces.
  var origLength = val.length;
  for (var i = 0; i < spaceFill - origLength; i++) {
    val = " " + val;
  }
}

// Return the value.
return val;
};
```

Note that in the preceding example, we store the length of the string prior to prepending it with spaces. If we checked the length within the loop, as follows, the length itself would change for each iteration (because it would count the spaces already added):

```
// This leads to the wrong result!
for (var i = 0; i < spaceFill - val.length; i++) {
  val = " " + val;
}
```

Here is another way the loop could be implemented. This time, we intentionally retest the length of the string with each loop iteration. Note that the loop's initialization and update expressions are empty; only the loop's conditional test is used.

```
for (; val.length < spaceFill; ) {
  val = " " + val;
}
```

Here are a few examples of how to use *numberFormat( )*:

```
trace(Math.numberFormat(1234.2));              // Displays: "1,234.2"
trace(Math.numberFormat(1234.2, ".", ","));    // Displays: "1.234,2"
// Note the extra leading spaces in the result of the following example.
trace(Math.numberFormat(1234.2, ",", ".", 10)); // Displays: "   1,234.2"
```

See Also

Recipes 5.3 and 5.4 can be used to ensure that a certain number of digits are displayed past the decimal point. Then, if you are using a monospaced font, aligning numbers is simply a matter of setting the text field's format to right justification using the *TextFormat*.align property. Also refer to Recipe 5.6.

5.6   Formatting Currency Amounts

Problem

You want to format a number as currency, such as dollars.

Solution

Create a custom *Math.currencyFormat( )* method.

Discussion

Unlike some other languages, such as ColdFusion, ActionScript does not have a built-in function for formatting numbers as currency amounts. That's the bad news. The good news is that it is not too difficult to create a custom method to format numbers as currency amounts.

Our custom *Math.currencyFormat( )* method accepts up to seven parameters:

num
> The number to format.

decimalPl
> The number of decimal places in the formatted number.

currencySymbol
> The symbol, such as a dollar sign ($), to use.

thousandsDelim

The characters used to delimit thousands, millions, etc.

decimalDelim

The characters used to delimit the fractional portion from the whole number.

truncate

If true, truncate the number to the specified number of decimal places; otherwise, round the number.

spaceFill

The number of spaces the entire formatted string should occupy.

Here is our custom *Math.currencyFormat()* method. The method converts a numeric parameter into a currency-formatted string. Include this method within *Math.as* along with the custom *roundDecPl()*, *numberFormat()*, and *zeroFill()* methods in this chapter, on which this example relies.

```
Math.currencyFormat = function (num, decimalPl, currencySymbol, thousandsDelim,
                        decimalDelim, truncate, spaceFill) {

  // Default to two decimal places, a dollar sign ($), a comma for thousands, and a
  // period for the decimal point. We implemented the defaults using the conditional
  // operator. Compare with Recipe 5.5.
  decimalPl      = (decimalPl == undefined)      ? 2   : decimalPl;
  currencySymbol = (currencySymbol == undefined) ? "$" : currencySymbol;
  thousandsDelim = (thousandsDelim == undefined) ? "," : thousandsDelim;
  decimalDelim   = (decimalDelim == undefined)   ? "." : decimalDelim;

  // Split the number into the whole and decimal (fractional) portions.
  var parts = String(num).split(".");

  // Truncate or round the decimal portion, as directed.
  if (truncate) {
    parts[1] = Number(parts[1]) * Math.pow(10, -(decimalPl - 1));
    parts[1] = String(Math.floor(parts[1]));
  } else {
    // Requires the roundDecPl() method defined in Recipe 5.3
    parts[1] = Math.roundDecPl(Number("." + parts[1]), decimalPl);
    parts[1] = String(parts[1]).split(".")[1];
  }

  // Ensure that the decimal portion has the number of digits indicated.
  // Requires the zeroFill() method defined in Recipe 5.4.
  parts[1] = Math.zeroFill(parts[1], decimalPl, true);

  // If necessary, use the numberFormat() method from Recipe 5.5 to format the number
  // with the proper thousands delimiter and leading spaces.
  if (thousandsDelim != "" || spaceFill != undefined) {
    parts[0] = Math.numberFormat(parts[0], thousandsDelim, "",
            spaceFill - decimalPl - currencySymbol.length);
  }
```

```
    // Add a currency symbol and use String.join() to merge the whole (dollar) and
    // decimal (cents) portions using the designated decimal delimiter.
    return currencySymbol + parts.join(decimalDelim);
};
```

Here are a few examples of *Math. currencyFormat ()* in action:

```
trace(Math.currencyFormat(1.2));             // Displays: $1.20
trace(Math.currencyFormat(.3));              // Displays: $0.30
trace(Math.currencyFormat(1234567));         // Displays: $1,234,567.00
trace(Math.currencyFormat(12.34, 2, "\u20AC"));  // Displays: €12.34 (euros)
trace(Math.currencyFormat(12.34, 2, "\u00a3"));  // Displays: £12.34 (pounds)
trace(Math.currencyFormat(12.34, 2, "\u00a5"));  // Displays: ¥12.34 (yen)
trace(Math.currencyFormat(1.2, 2, "", ".", ","));  // Displays: 1,20
trace(Math.currencyFormat(1234, 2, "", ".", ","));  // Displays: 1.234,00
```

See Also

Recipes 5.3 and 5.5. See Appendix A for creating special characters, including the
euro, yen, and British pound symbols. To align currency amounts in text fields, use a
monospaced font and set the field's format to right justification using the
TextFormat.align property.

5.7   Generating a Random Number

Problem

You want to generate a random number within a certain range.

Solution

Use *Math.random()* as the basis for a custom *randRange()* method.

Discussion

You can use the *Math.random()* method to generate a random floating-point number from 0 to 0.999999999. In most cases, however, programs call for a random integer, not a random floating-point number. Furthermore, you may want a random
value within a specific range. If you do want a random floating-point number, you
will ordinarily want to specify its precision (the number of decimal places).

Here is the basic process for generating random numbers of this type:

1. Calculate the range difference and then add 1. For example, if you want to generate random numbers between 4 and 10, the range is 10–4 (which equals 6). To
   ensure an equal distribution, add 1 to this range.

2. If you want the random number to include decimal places, multiply the range
   by the correct multiple of 10 prior to adding 1. For example, to create random

numbers with one decimal place, multiply the range by 10. To create random numbers with two decimal places, multiply the range by 100, etc.

3. Multiply the value from step 2 by the value returned by *Math.random()*. This will give you a value between 0 and the value from step 2 (with decimal places).

4. Use the *Math.floor()* method to get the integer part of the value from step 3.

5. Divide the result from step 4 by the same multiple of 10 that you used in step 2. For example, if you originally multiplied by 10, divide by 10. This step converts the result to the correct number of decimal places.

6. Add the value from step 5 to the smallest value in the range. This offsets the value to be within the specified range.

A custom *Math.randRange()* method encapsulates the process so that you can generate random numbers while blissfully ignoring the details.

The custom *randRange()* method should take up to three parameters:

minNum
> The smallest value in the range.

maxNum
> The largest value in the range.

decPl
> The number of decimal places to which to round the random number. If 0 or omitted, the number is returned as an integer.

Here is our custom *randRange()* method, which is attached directly to the *Math* object, so it is available throughout the entire movie. It assumes that *minNum* is always less than *maxNum*. You can add this custom method to the *Math.as* file for easy inclusion in other projects.

```
Math.randRange = function(minNum, maxNum, decPl) {

    // Default to zero decimal places (generate a random integer).
    decPl = (decPl == undefined) ? 0 : decPl;

    // Calculate the range, multiply by 10 to the power of the number of decimal
    // places, and add 1. We'll call this "delta".
    var rangeDiff = (maxNum - minNum) * Math.pow(10, decPl) + 1;

    // Multiplying delta by Math.random() generates a value from 0 to 0.999 * delta.
    var randVal = Math.random() * rangeDiff;

    // Truncate the value to the integer part.
    randVal = Math.floor(randVal);

    // Restore the proper number of decimal places.
    randVal /= Math.pow(10, decPl);
```

```
// Add minNum as an offset to generate a random number in the correct range.
randVal += minNum;

// Return the random value. Use the custom roundTo( ) method from Recipe 5.3 to
// ensure that the result is rounded to the proper number of decimal places.
return Math.roundTo(randVal, Math.pow(10, -decPl));
};
```

Here is an example of how to use the *randRange()* method, assuming it has been stored in an external ActionScript text file named *Math.as*:

```
#include "Math.as"

// Generate a random integer from 5 to 10, inclusive.
trace(Math.randRange(5, 10));

// Generate a random number, rounded to two decimal places from -5 to 5.
trace(Math.randRange(-5, 5, 2));
```

You can use *randRange()* when you don't want an even distribution from 0 to the maximum value in the range. Here is an example of how to use *randRange()* to generate a random alpha value for a movie clip in the range of 75 to 100. It allows a clip to have a random alpha while avoiding clips that are too transparent.

```
myMovieClip._alpha = Math.randRange(75, 100);
```

Random numbers generated by traditional programming languages are not truly random. Rather, they are derived from a pseudorandom algorithm fed by an initial *random seed*. ActionScript does not allow you to specify the random seed (Flash presumably uses an essentially random starting point, such as the time in milliseconds). Don't confuse a random number with a unique number because random numbers are not guaranteed to be unique.

See Also

Recipes 5.3 and 5.11

5.8   Simulating a Coin Flip

Problem

You want to simulate a coin flipping or other Boolean (true/false) event in which there is a 50% chance of either outcome.

Solution

Use the *randRange()* method to generate an integer that is either 0 or 1 and then correlate each possible answer with one of the desired results.

Discussion

You can use the *randRange()* method from Recipe 5.7 to generate a random integer in the specified range. To relate this result to an event that has two possible states, such as a coin flip (heads or tails) or a Boolean condition (true or false), treat each random integer as representing one of the possible states. By convention, programmers use 0 to represent one state (such as "off") and 1 to represent the opposite state (such as "on"), although you can use 1 and 2 if you prefer.

For example, here is how you could simulate a coin flip:

```
#include "Math.as"

function coinFlip () {
  flip = Math.randRange(0, 1);
  if (flip == 0) {
    return "heads";
  } else {
    return "tails";
  }
}

// Example usage:
trace ("The result of the coin flip was " + coinFlip());
```

Here, we write a function that tests our *coinFlip()* routine to see if it is reasonably even-handed. Do you expect a perfect 50/50 distribution regardless of the number of coin flips? Test it and see.

```
#include "Math.as"

function testCoinFlip (numFlips) {
  // We'll count how many of each result occurs. Initialize them to 0.
  var heads = 0;
  var tails = 0;

  // Repeat the process numFlips times and keep tabs on the results.
  for (var i = 0; i < numFlips; i++) {
    flip = Math.randRange(0, 1);
    if (flip == 0) {
      heads++;
    } else {
      tails++;
    }
  }
  // Display the results. Will it be 50/50?
  trace ("The result of " + numFlips + " coin flips was:");
  trace ("Heads: " + heads);
  trace ("Tails: " + tails);
}
```

```
// Example usage:
testCoinFlip(10);
testCoinFlip(100);
testCoinFlip(1000);
```

Applying a similar principle, here is a function that returns a random "yes" or "no" reply:

```
function randomReply () {
  reply = Math.randRange(0, 1);
  if (reply == 0) {
    return "yes";
  } else {
    return "no";
  }
}
```

We can use a shortcut when creating a function that generates a Boolean (true or false) value. Here, we take advantage of the fact that the *Boolean()* method will convert the number 0 to false and the number 1 to true. In this case, using a range from 1 to 2 won't work because both 1 and 2 convert to the Boolean value true.

```
function trueOrFalse () {
  return Boolean(Math.randRange(0, 1));
}
```

 If you are testing the value of your random number, be sure to save the result in a variable (and test the saved result) rather than generating a new random number each time you perform the test.

The following is wrong because it generates independent random numbers in the dependent *else if* clauses. In some cases, none of the conditions will be true and the function will return undefined.

```
function guessABC () {
  if (Math.randRange(1, 3) == 1) {
    return "A";
  } else if (Math.randRange(1, 3) == 2) {
    return "B";
  } else if (Math.randRange(1, 3) == 3) {
    return "C";
  }
  // We may arrive here unintentionally, due to our buggy implementation...in which
  // case undefined is returned.
}
```

This is the correct way to accomplish our goal:

```
function guessABC () {
  // Store the random number.
  guess = Math.randRange(1, 3);
  // Now test it as many times as necessary.
  if (guess == 1) {
```

```
      return "A";
   } else if (guess == 2) {
      return "B";
   } else if (guess == 3) {
      return "C";
   }
}
```

5.9   Simulating Dice

Problem

You want to mimic rolling dice.

Solution

Use the *randRange()* method to generate random numbers in the desired range.

Discussion

You can use the *randRange()* method from Recipe 5.7 to generate random integer
values to simulate rolling a die or dice in your Flash movies. Mimicking the rolling of
dice is an important feature in many games you might create using ActionScript, and
the *randRange()* method makes your job easy.

```
// Include Math.as to have access to Math.randRange().
#include "Math.as"

// Calling Math.randRange() with min = 1 and max = 6 generates
// a random number as though you are rolling a six-sided die.
die1 = Math.randRange(1, 6);

// Add the results of two "rolls" together to simulate a pair of six-sided dice.
dice = Math.randRange(1, 6) + Math.randRange(1, 6);
```

Math.randRange(1, 12) does not correctly simulate a pair of six-sided
dice because the results must be between 2 and 12, not 1 and 12.
Does *Math.randRange(2, 12)* give the correct result? No, it does not!
Math.randRange(2, 12) results in a smooth distribution of numbers
from 2 to 12, whereas in games played with two dice, 7 is much more
common than 2 or 12. Therefore, you must simulate each die separately and then add the results together. Furthermore, in many
games, such as backgammon, game play depends on the individual
value of each die, not simply the total of both dice, so you'll want to
keep these results separate.

It is not uncommon to want to generate a random number and then store it for later
use. If you want to reuse an existing random number, be sure to save the result rather

than generating a new random number, as per the warning in Recipe 5.8. Note the difference in the following two scenarios. In the first scenario, dice will always be the sum of die1 plus die2:

```
die1 = Math.randRange(1, 6);
die2 = Math.randRange(1, 6);
dice = die1 + die2;
```

In the second scenario, there is no relation between the value of dice and the earlier random values stored in die1 and die2. In other words, even if die1 and die2 add up to 7, dice stores a completely different value between 2 and 12:

```
die1 = Math.randRange(1, 6);
die2 = Math.randRange(1, 6);
dice = Math.randRange(1, 6) + Math.randRange(1, 6);
```

You can call *Math.randRange()* with any range to simulate a multisided die. Here, we call it with a range from 1 to 15 to generate a random number as though the user is rolling a 15-sided die, as might be found in a role-playing game such as *Dungeons and Dragons*:

```
myRoll = Math.randRange(1, 15);
```

Here is an example that uses the drawing methods to simulate a single 15-sided die. It uses the *randRange()* method to generate random values when the user clicks on the die_mc movie clip.

```
// Include both Math.as and DrawingMethods.as (from Chapter 4) to access the methods
// used in this example.
#include "Math.as"
#include "DrawingMethods.as"

// Create a die_mc clip on _root. Within that clip, create a shape_mc clip and draw a
// filled (white fill, black outline) square using drawRectangle().
_root.createEmptyMovieClip("die_mc", 1);
die_mc.createEmptyMovieClip("shape_mc", 1);
die_mc.shape_mc.lineStyle(1, 0x000000, 100);
die_mc.shape_mc.beginFill(0xFFFFFF, 100);
die_mc.shape_mc.drawRectangle(50, 50);

// Create a text field within die_mc and set the font size to 24.
die_mc.createTextField("num", 2, 0, 0, 0, 0);
die_mc.num.autoSize = true;
tf = new TextFormat();
tf.size = 24;
die_mc.num.setNewTextFormat(tf);

// Move die_mc so that it is visible on stage.
die_mc._x = 200;
die_mc._y = 200;

// Create a method that generates random numbers and sets
// the text field of the die to display those values.
die_mc.onToss = function () {
```

```
// Generate a random number from 1 to 15 to mimic a 15-sided die.
var randNum = Math.randRange(1, 15);

// Display the value in the text field and center the text field on the die.
this.num.text = randNum;
this.num._x = -(this.num._width/2);
this.num._y = -(this.num._height/2);

// Count to 20 and set the onEnterFrame() method to null. This animates the die for
// 21 frames and then stops until it is clicked again.
this.count++;
if (this.count > 20) {
  this.count = 0;
  this.onEnterFrame = null;
}
};

// When the user clicks on the die_mc movie clip, set onEnterFrame to the onToss()
// method so it is called at the frame rate until 20 frames have animated. After
// which, onEnterFrame() becomes null and nothing more happens until the user clicks
// on it again.
die_mc.onRelease = function () {
  this.onEnterFrame = this.onToss;
};
```

5.10   Simulating Playing Cards

Problem

You want to use ActionScript to deal cards for a card game using a standard 52-card deck (without jokers).

Solution

Create a custom *Cards* class that uses the *randRange()* method to deal the cards.

Discussion

To work with playing cards within your Flash movies, you should create a custom *Cards* class. The *Cards* class should have an array property that contains all the cards in the deck and a *deal()* method that deals the cards to a specified number of players. Additionally, you should define a supporting class named *CardPlayer*. The *CardPlayer* class represents each player in a card game, including their hands of cards. Let's take a look at the example code first:

```
// Include the Math.as file on whose methods this recipe relies.
#include "Math.as"
```

```javascript
// When a new card player is created by way of its constructor, pass it a reference
// to the card deck and give it a unique player ID.
function CardPlayer (deck, id) {
  this.hand = null;
  this.deck = deck;
  this.id = id;
}

// The setHand( ) method sets the cards in a player's hand.
CardPlayer.prototype.setHand = function (hand) {
  this.hand = hand;
};

// The getHand( ) method returns the cards in a player's hand.
CardPlayer.prototype.getHand = function ( ) {
  return this.hand;
};

// The draw( ) method deals the specified number of cards to the player.
CardPlayer.prototype.draw = function (num) {
  this.deck.draw(this.id, num);
};

// The discard( ) method discards the cards specified
// by their indexes in the player's hand.
CardPlayer.prototype.discard = function (cardsArIds) {
  cardsArIds.sort( );
  for (var i = 0; i < cardsArIds.length; i++) {
    this.hand.splice(cardsArIds[i] - i, 1);
  }
};

// The Cards constructor creates a deck of cards.
function Cards ( ) {

  // Create a local array that contains the names of the four suits.
  var suits = ["Hearts", "Diamonds", "Spades", "Clubs"];

  // The cards property is an array that is populated with all the cards.
  this.cards = new Array( );

  // Specify the names of the cards for stuffing into the cards array later.
  var cardNames = ["2", "3", "4", "5", "6", "7", "8", "9", "10",
                   "J", "Q", "K", "A"];

  // Create a 52-card array. Each element is an object that contains properties for
  // the card's integer value (for sorting purposes), card name, suit name, and
  // display name. The display name combines the card's name and suit in a single
  // string for display to the user.
  for (var i = 0; i < suits.length; i++) {
    // For each suit, add 13 cards.
    for (var j = 0; j < 13; j++) {
      this.cards.push(
```

```
                    {val: j,
                     name: cardNames[j],
                     suit: suits[i],
                     display: cardNames[j] + " " + suits[i]});
    }
  }
}

// The deal() method needs to know the number of players in the game and the number
// of cards to deal each player. If the cardsPerPlayer parameter is undefined, then
// it deals all the cards.
Cards.prototype.deal = function (numOfPlayers, cardsPerPlayer) {

  // Create an array, players, that holds the cards dealt to each player.
  var players = new Array();

  // The players array contains CardPlayer objects. Each card player is given a
  // reference to this deck of cards, as well as a unique player ID.
  for (var i = 0; i < numOfPlayers; i++) {
    players.push(new CardPlayer(this, i));
  }

  // Make a copy of the deck of cards from which we'll deal. This way, we can always
  // recreate a fresh deck from the original cards property.
  this.cardsToDeal = this.cards.concat();

  // If a cardsPerPlayer value was passed in, deal that number of cards. Otherwise,
  // divide the number of cards (52) by the number of players.
  var cardsEach = cardsPerPlayer;
  if (cardsPerPlayer == undefined) {
    cardsEach = Math.floor(this.cards.length / numOfPlayers);
  }

  // Deal the specified number of cards to each player.
  var rand, hand;
  for (var i = 0; i < numOfPlayers; i++) {

    hand = new Array();

    // Deal a random card to each player. Remove that card from the
    // CardsToDeal array so that it cannot be dealt again.
    for (var j = 0; j < cardsEach; j++) {
      rand = Math.randRange(0, this.cardsToDeal.length - 1);
      hand.push(this.cardsToDeal[rand]);
      this.cardsToDeal.splice(rand, 1);
    }

    // Use Cards.orderHand() to sort a player's hand and use setHand() to assign it
    // to the card player object.
    players[i].setHand(Cards.orderHand(hand.concat()));
  }

  // Return the players array.
  return players;
};
```

```
// The Cards.draw( ) method is called from CardPlayer.draw( ) to draw the specified
// number of cards from the deck and add them to the player's hand.
Cards.prototype.draw = function (player, numToDraw) {

    // Get the player's current hand.
    var hand = players[player].getHand( );

    // Add the specified number of cards to the hand.
    for (var i = 0; i < numToDraw; i++) {
        rand = Math.randRange(0, this.cardsToDeal.length - 1);
        hand.push(this.cardsToDeal[rand]);
        this.cardsToDeal.splice(rand, 1);
    }

    // Sort the hand and reassign it to the player object.
    var orderedHand = Cards.orderHand(hand);
    players[player].setHand(orderedHand);
};

// Used by sort( ) in the orderHand( ) method to sort the cards by suit and rank
Cards.sorter = function(a, b) {
    if (a.suit > b.suit) {
        return 1;
    } else if (a.suit < b.suit) {
        return -1;
    } else {
        return (Number(a.val) > Number(b.val))
    }
};

// This method sorts an array of cards by calling the sort( ) method on that array
// with a sorter method of Cards.sorter( ).
Cards.orderHand = function(hand) {
    hand.sort(Cards.sorter);
    return hand;
};
```

Now let's look more carefully at some of the pieces of the *CardPlayer* and *Cards* classes and what they do.

First, we define the *CardPlayer* class constructor. Each *CardPlayer* object contains three properties: the hand (which is an array of cards), a reference to the deck from which the game is being played (an instance of the *Card* class), and a player ID that is unique within the game (i.e., each player is identified by a number, such as 0, 1, 2, or 3). The *CardPlayer* class defines getter and setter methods for the hand property and *draw()* and *discard()* methods to obtain new cards and remove old ones.

The first part of the *Card* class is the constructor method, which creates an array of all possible cards. There are many ways to approach this. The example uses nested *for* statements to create a 52-card array (the loop executes 13 times for each of the 4 suits). First, it creates an array specifying the names of the four suits and another array specifying the names of each card. Then, it populates the cards array by creating 13 cards for each suit. The *push()* method appends a new object for each card, which becomes an element of the cards array.

The *deal()* method creates an array of card players. It returns an array of *CardPlayer* objects (one for each player in the game). The number of players is determined by the *numOfPlayers* parameter, allowing for flexibility in how the cards are dealt. The code "deals" the cards by randomly selecting an element (card) from the cardsToDeal array and adding it to a player's hand. It is important that the selected element is removed from cardsToDeal, as shown using *splice()* in this example, so that it is not dealt twice. Next, each player's hand is sorted using the *orderHand()* method, and then each player's hand's contents are set for each player's *CardPlayer* object.

The *orderHand()* and *sorter()* methods work together to sort a user's hand by suit and then by rank. The *orderHand()* method calls the *sort()* method on the array, with *sorter()* as the custom sorter function.

Additionally, the *Card* class defines a *draw()* method, which is useful for games such as poker in which players can draw additional cards. The *draw()* method draws a specified number of cards from the deck and adds them to a player's hand.

This example code tests the *Cards* class:

```
// First, create a new Cards object.
c = new Cards();

// Call the deal() method, specifying four players and six cards per player.
players = c.deal(4, 6);

// For each player...
for (var i = 0; i < players.length; i++) {

  // Display the player number.
  trace("player " + i);

  // Display the player's cards.
  for (var j = 0; j < players[i].getHand().length; j++) {
    trace("  " + players[i].getHand()[j].display);
  }
}

// Now, for the first player, discard the first and third cards from the hand and
// draw two new cards.
players[0].discard([0, 2]);
players[0].draw(2);

// Now display the players' hands again. Notice that the first player has two
// different cards while the rest of the players have the same hands as before.
for (var i = 0; i < players.length; i++) {

  // Display the player number.
  trace("player " + i);
```

```
// Display the player's cards.
for (var j = 0; j < players[i].getHand( ).length; j++) {
  trace("  " + players[i].getHand( )[j].display);
}
}
```

Note that our code draws cards from the deck randomly rather than from the "top." This is necessary because we added the cards in rank and suit order, so drawing from the top would not give a randomized deal. An alternative solution is to randomize (shuffle) the cards when creating the array and then deal the cards in order from the deck. In that case, the programmer should be careful to shuffle the cards again each time a new deck of cards is created from the master copy (rather than shuffling the master copy, which would result in all games being played with the same deck of cards).

Also note that our example doesn't deal gracefully with games in which you might run out of cards. It assumes that 52 cards is sufficient for the current hand and that a new deck will be created for each subsequent hand. Enhancing the example is left to you as an exercise.

5.11   Generating a Unique Number

Problem

You want to generate a unique number to append to a URL to prevent the browser from retrieving the asset from the local cache.

Solution

Use the number of milliseconds elapsed since January 1, 1970, as returned by *Date().getTime()*.

Discussion

Unique numbers are most commonly used to generate a unique URL (to prevent an asset from being retrieved from the local cache). That is, by appending a unique number to the end of a URL, it is unlike any previous URL; therefore, the browser obtains the data from the remote server instead of the local cache.

Assuming you need a unique number less frequently than once per millisecond, the number of milliseconds returned by *Date().getTime()* is essentially unique (at least during the execution of your movie).

Note that you do not want to use the milliseconds of an existing *Date* object because its time value doesn't automatically increase as your movie runs. Instead, generate a new *Date* object representing "now" each time you need to extract a unique number.

Here, we define our custom *Math.getUniqueID()* method to encapsulate the code to generate the unique number. By default, the method automatically generates a new value each time it is called. However, if you pass it a useCached parameter of true, the method returns the same ID that it generated the last time it was called. This can be useful if you want to create a single ID for a movie and access it multiple times.

```
Math.getUniqueID = function (useCached) {

  // If the unique ID has already been created and if useCached is true, return the
  // previously generated value.
  if (this.uniqueID != undefined && useCached) {
    return this.uniqueID;
  }

  var now = new Date();          // Generate a Date object that represents "now."
  this.uniqueID = now.getTime(); // Get the elapsed milliseconds since Jan 1, 1970.
  return this.uniqueID;
};
```

Note that you shouldn't use the *Date.getMilliseconds()* method to generate unique numbers because it returns the milliseconds of a *Date* object (i.e., the fractional remainder of the number of seconds), which is always in the range of 0 to 999.

As already noted, the *getUniqueID()* method generates a unique value only if at least one millisecond elapses between invocations. If you call it more frequently, it returns the same value twice.

```
// Each of these calls returns the same value because they are all called within one
// millisecond of each other.
timeOne   = Math.getUniqueID();
timeTwo   = Math.getUniqueID();
timeThree = Math.getUniqueID();
trace(timeOne);
trace(timeTwo);
trace(timeThree);
```

5.12   Converting Angle Measurements

Problem

You want to work with angle values in ActionScript, but you must convert to the proper units.

Solution

Create custom *degToRad()* and *radToDeg()* methods.

Discussion

The _rotation property of a movie clip object is measured in degrees. Every other angle measurement in ActionScript, however, uses radians, not degrees. This can be a problem in two ways. First of all, if you want to set the _rotation property based on the output of one of ActionScript's trigonometric methods, you must convert the value from radians to degrees. Second, humans generally prefer to work in degrees, which we must convert to radians before feeding to any of the trigonometric methods. Fortunately, the conversion between radians and degrees is simple. You should add the following *degToRad()* and *radToDeg()* methods to your *Math.as* file for converting from degrees to radians and vice versa. Note that they are attached directly to the top-level *Math* object, making them available throughout your movie.

```
// Convert degrees to radians by multiplying by π and dividing by 180.
Math.degToRad = function(deg){
  return (Math.PI * deg) / 180;
};

// Convert radians to degrees by multiplying by 180 and dividing by π.
Math.radToDeg = function(rad){
  return (rad * 180) / Math.PI;
};
```

This following code demonstrates how the methods work:

```
trace(Math.degToRad(90));        // Displays: 1.5707963267949 (which is π/2)
trace(Math.radToDeg(Math.PI));   // Displays: 180
```

These two methods are invaluable when you want to use the trigonometric methods:

```
// Use degToRad() to convert degrees to radians before passing the value to
// Math.cos() (which expects radians).
trace(Math.cos(Math.degToRad(36)));

// Get the angle (in radians) for a cosine of .75 using the inverse cosine.
angle = Math.acos(.75);
// Set MovieClip._rotation to the degree equivalent of the angle in radians.
myMovieClip._rotation = Math.radToDeg(angle);
```

See Also

Recipe 5.15

5.13 Calculating the Distance Between Two Points

Problem

You want to calculate the distance between two points.

Solution

Create custom *Math.getDistance()* method.

Discussion

You can calculate the distance (in a straight line) from any two points by using the *Pythagorean theorem*. The Pythagorean theorem states that in any right triangle (a triangle in which one of the angles is 90 degrees), the length of the *hypotenuse* (the long side) is equal to the square root of the sum of the squares of the two other sides (referred to as the *legs* of the triangle). The Pythagorean theorem is usually written as:

$$a^2 + b^2 = c^2$$

You can use this formula to calculate the distance between any two points, where *a* is the difference between the points' x coordinates, *b* is the difference between their y coordinates, and *c* (the distance to be determined) equals the square root of ($a^2 + b^2$). In ActionScript, this is written as:

```
var c = Math.sqrt(Math.pow(a, 2) + Math.pow(b, 2));
```

How do you calculate the distance between two points using a right triangle? While it might not seem immediately obvious, you can form an imaginary right triangle using any two points in the Flash coordinate system, as shown in Figure 5-1.

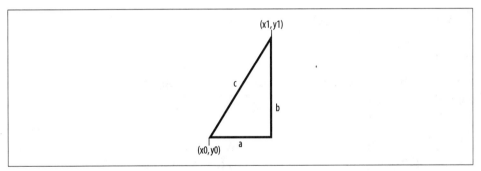

Figure 5-1. The hypotenuse of a right triangle is drawn between two points to calculate the distance between the points

The hypotenuse of the imaginary triangle is formed by the line connecting the two points. The legs of the triangle are formed by lines extending horizontally and vertically from the two points. You can find the lengths of the legs by finding the differences between the x and y coordinates. The length of leg *a* is determined by the difference in the points' x coordinates, and the length of leg *b* is determined by the difference in the points' y coordinates. Once you know the lengths of legs *a* and *b*, you can use the Pythagorean theorem to calculate the length of the hypotenuse, *c*, which represents the distance between the points (our original quarry).

It is convenient to encapsulate this calculation in a method that you can reuse. The custom *Math.getDistance()* method we define here accepts the x and y coordinates of the two points as its four parameters:

```
Math.getDistance = function (x0, y0, x1, y1) {

    // Calculate the lengths of the legs of the right triangle.
    var dx = x1 - x0;
    var dy = y1 - y0;

    // Find the sum of the squares of the legs of the triangle.
    var sqr = Math.pow(dx, 2) + Math.pow(dy, 2);

    // Return the square root of the sqr value.
    return (Math.sqrt(sqr));
};
```

Here is an example of the *Math.getDistance()* method being used to calculate the distance between two points at (300,400) and (0,0):

```
trace(Math.getDistance(300, 400, 0, 0));  // Displays: 500
```

See Also

Recipe 4.7

5.14 Determining Points Along a Circle

Problem

You want to calculate the coordinates of a point along a circle given the circle's radius and the sweep angle.

Solution

Use the *Math.sin()* and *Math.cos()* methods to calculate the coordinates using basic trigonometric ratios.

Discussion

Finding the coordinates of a point along a circle is easy with some trigonometry. So let's look at the formulas you can use within your ActionScript code and the theory behind them.

Given any point on the Stage—a point we'll call p0, with coordinates (x0, y0)—plus a distance and the angle from the horizontal, you can find the coordinates of another point—which we'll call p1, with coordinates (x1, y1)—using some basic trigonometric ratios. The angle is formed between a conceptual line from p0 to p1 and a line parallel to the X axis, as shown in Figure 5-2. The *opposite side* (O) is the side furthest away from the angle. The *adjacent side* (A) is the side that forms the angle with the help of the hypotenuse (H).

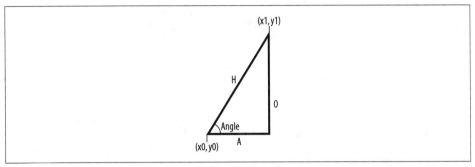

Figure 5-2. The angle, adjacent side, opposite side, and hypotenuse of a right triangle

If you know the distance between two points and the angle to the horizontal, as shown in Figure 5-2, you can calculate the x and y coordinates of the destination point using trigonometric functions. The trigonometric sine of the angle is equal to the ratio of the opposite side over the hypotenuse:

```
sine(angle) = opposite/hypotenuse
```

Solving for the opposite side's length, this can be written as:

```
opposite = sine(angle) * hypotenuse
```

You can see from Figure 5-2 that the opposite side represents the change in the y direction.

The trigonometric cosine of the angle is equal to the ratio of the adjacent side over the hypotenuse:

```
cosine(angle) = adjacent/hypotenuse
```

Solving for the adjacent side's length, this can be written as:

```
adjacent = cosine(angle) * hypotenuse
```

You can see from Figure 5-2 that the adjacent side represents the change in the x direction.

Because the lengths of the opposite and adjacent sides yield the changes in the x and y directions, by adding the original x and y coordinates to these values you can calculate the coordinates of the new point.

So how does this help in determining a point along a circle's perimeter? Figure 5-3, which shows our familiar triangle inscribed within a circle, emphasizes the equivalency: the triangle's hypotenuse (H) equates to the circle's radius, and the triangle's angle equates to the sweep angle to the point of interest along the circle's perimeter.

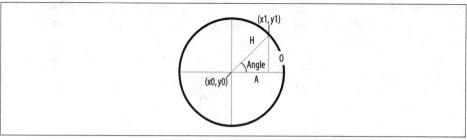

Figure 5-3. Using trigonometry to determine a point along a circle's perimeter

Therefore, the x coordinate of a point along the circle's perimeter is determined by the radius times the cosine of the angle. The y coordinate is determined by the radius times the sine of the angle. Here is the ActionScript code for finding the coordinates of p1 when the circle's radius and center point (p0) are known:

```
x1 = x0 + (Math.cos(angle) * radius);
y1 = y0 + (Math.sin(angle) * radius);
```

Therefore, these formulas can be used to determine any point along a circle's perimeter, given the circle's center point and radius. By changing the angle over time, you can trace the path of a circle. Here are a few examples:

```
// Include DrawingMethods.as from Chapter 4.
#include "DrawingMethods.as"
#include "Math.as"

// Create a square_mc movie clip.
_root.createEmptyMovieClip("square_mc", 1);
square_mc.lineStyle(1, 0x000000, 100);
square_mc.drawRectangle(10, 10);

// Move the square in a circular path with a radius of 50. The larger the value by
// which angle is incremented, the faster the movement.
square_mc.onEnterFrame = function () {
  this._x = Math.cos(Math.degToRad(this.angle)) * 50;
  this._y = Math.sin(Math.degToRad(this.angle)) * 50;
  this.angle += 5;
};

// Create another square movie clip.
_root.createEmptyMovieClip("square2_mc", 2);
square2_mc.lineStyle(1, 0x000000, 100);
square2_mc.drawRectangle(10, 10);

// Make the square spiral outward in 30-degree increments, increasing the radius by
// two pixels per frame.
square2.onEnterFrame = function () {
  this._x += Math.cos(Math.degToRad(30)) * 2;
  this._y += Math.sin(Math.degToRad(30)) * 2;
};
```

See Also

Recipes 4.5 and 4.6

5.15 Converting Between Units of Measurement

Problem

You want to convert between Fahrenheit and Centigrade, pounds and kilograms, or other units of measurement.

Solution

Write a custom method to perform the conversion and add it to the *Math* class.

Discussion

There are various systems of measurement used throughout the world. For example, temperature is commonly measured with both the Fahrenheit and Centigrade scales, and weight is commonly measured using both pounds and kilograms. For these reasons, you may need to convert from one unit of measurement to another.

Each of these conversions has its own algorithm. For example, to convert from Centigrade to Fahrenheit, you should multiply by 9/5 and then add 32 (to convert from Fahrenheit to Centigrade, subtract 32 and multiply by 5/9). Likewise, you can multiply by 2.2 to convert pounds to kilograms, and you can divide by 2.2 to convert kilograms to pounds. We also saw in Recipe 5.12 how to convert angles from degrees to radians and vice versa.

Here is a temperature converter. The method takes three parameters: the name of the units from which you are converting, the name of the units to which you are converting, and the value to convert. In this example code, we define conversions between Fahrenheit and Centigrade ("F" is interpreted to mean "Fahrenheit"; "C" and "Celsius" are recognized alternatives to "Centigrade"):

```
Math.convertTemperature = function (fMeasure, tMeasure, val) {
    // Convert all names to lowercase to match any capitalization.
    fMeasure = fMeasure.toLowerCase( );
    tMeasure = tMeasure.toLowerCase( );

    if ( (fMeasure == "centigrade" || fMeasure == "celsius" || fMeasure == "c")
        && (tMeasure == "fahrenheit" || tMeasure == "f") ) {
      // Convert Centigrade to Fahrenheit.
      return (val * 9/5) + 32;
    } else if ( (fMeasure == "fahrenheit" || fMeasure == "f") &&
        (tMeasure == "centigrade" || tMeasure == "celsius" || tMeasure == "c") ) {
      // Convert Fahrenheit to Centigrade.
      return (val - 32) * 5/9;
```

```
        } else {
            trace ("Invalid conversion type from " + fMeasure + " to " + tMeasure);
            return NaN;
        }
};
```

Here are examples of how to use this function:

```
trace(Math.convertTemperature ("Centigrade", "Fahrenheit", 0));    // Displays: 32
trace(Math.convertTemperature ("c", "f", 0));                      // Displays: 32
trace(Math.convertTemperature ("fahrenheit", "centigrade", 212)); // Displays: 100
trace(Math.convertTemperature ("fahrenheit", "celsius", 212));     // Displays: 100
```

You could modify the preceding function to also support degrees Kelvin. However, if you support more than two units of measure, the number of possible permutations (and the number of required *else if* clauses) multiplies rapidly. In such a case, you can convert all values to an interim unit of measurement to reduce the number of transformations required. For example, you can convert all temperatures to and from Centigrade, as follows:

```
Math.convertToCentigrade = function (fMeasure, val) {
    fMeasure = fMeasure.toLowerCase();
    if (fMeasure == "kelvin" || fMeasure == "k") {
        return (val - 273.15);
    } else if ( fMeasure == "fahrenheit" || fMeasure == "f" ) {
        return (val - 32) * 5/9;
    } else if (fMeasure == "centigrade" || fMeasure == "celsius" || fMeasure == "c") {
        return val;
    } else {
        return NaN;
    }
};

Math.convertFromCentigrade = function (tMeasure, val) {
    tMeasure = tMeasure.toLowerCase();
    if (tMeasure == "kelvin" || tMeasure == "k") {
        return (val + 273.15);
    } else if ( tMeasure == "fahrenheit" || tMeasure == "f" ) {
        return (val * 9/5) + 32;
    } else if (tMeasure == "centigrade" || tMeasure == "celsius" || tMeasure == "c") {
        return val;
    } else {
        return NaN;
    }
};
```

This allows our *Math.convertTemperature()* method to be simplified, as follows:

```
Math.convertTemperature = function (fMeasure, tMeasure, val) {
    var centigradeVal = Math.convertToCentigrade (fMeasure, val);
    return Math.convertFromCentigrade (tMeasure, centigradeVal );
};
```

Here are examples of how to use this function:

```
trace(Math.convertTemperature ("centigrade", "Kelvin", 0));   // Displays: 273.15
trace(Math.convertTemperature ("k", "f", 0));                 // Displays: -459.67
trace(Math.convertTemperature ("fahrenheit", "kelvin", 212)); // Displays: 373.15
trace(Math.convertTemperature ("K", "celsius", 0));           // Displays: -273.15
```

Or, if you prefer, you could write single-purpose functions, such as *Math.fahrToCent()*, *Math.centToFahr()*, and *Math.fahrToKelvin()*, that simply accept the value to convert.

Here is another function that converts between pounds and kilograms using the same structure shown earlier:

```
Math.convertWeights = function (fMeasure, tMeasure, val) {
  if (fMeasure == "pounds" && tMeasure == "kilograms") {
    return val / 2.2;
  } else if (fMeasure == "kilograms" && tMeasure == "pounds") {
    return val * 2.2;
  } else {
    return "invalid conversion type";
  }
};
```

Here are some examples of its use:

```
trace(Math.convertWeights ("pounds", "kilograms", 0));    // Displays: 0
trace(Math.convertWeights ("kilograms", "pounds", 100));  // Displays: 220
```

You can add support for conversion to other units of weight by inserting additional *else if* statements following the same pattern. Or you can use the technique demonstrated for temperature, in which all values are first converted to a common unit.

See Also

For an example of using a hardcoded function to perform a single type of unit conversion, refer to Recipe 5.12, which includes a function to convert angles from degrees to radians and another function that does the opposite.

5.16 Calculating Asset Appreciation (Future Value)

Problem

You want to know how much something will be worth in the future, given its value today and an expected interest rate, i (for example, calculating the amount of money you can accumulate in a savings account given an initial deposit).

Solution

You must calculate the appreciation of an asset over time at the assumed interest rate. This is often referred to as the *future value* of an asset. For a given interest rate, i, an asset appreciates by a factor of $(1 + i)$ for each period (such as a year).

Discussion

For the purposes of illustration, let's calculate the future value of an asset using the brute-force method.

If you deposit $1 in a bank account that earns 5% interest per year, one year from now, you will have earned 5 cents in interest. The total account, including principal and interest, will be worth $1.05. The math for this is:

```
FV = PV * (1 + i);
```

where *FV* is the future value (the amount of money you'll have next year, sometimes called *FV1*), *PV* is the *present value* (the amount of money you deposited initially, sometimes called *FV0*), and i is the interest rate (expressed as a decimal, such as 0.05).

So if you deposit $100 at a 5% interest rate, the future value at the end of one year is $105, which is determined as follows:

```
FV1 = 100 * (1 + .05);
```

Typically, interest is compounded over time, so at the end of the second year, the value is:

```
FV2 = FV1 * (1 + i);
```

Here is a function that calculates the future value by brute force for an arbitrary number of periods. We name the parameter that represents the interest rate `interest` (instead of i) so as not to mistake it for an index variable (and we'll use `periods` as our loop variable to avoid the reverse confusion):

```
Math.bruteFutureValue = function (interest, n, PV) {
   // PV       = initial deposit (present value)
   // interest = periodic interest rate
   // n        = number of periods

   // Start with the future value equal to the present value.
   FV = PV;

   // Now compound it over n periods at an interest rate of interest.
   for (var periods = 1; periods <= n; periods++) {
     FV = FV * (1 + interest);
   }
   return FV;
};
```

```
// Example usage:
// How much will $500 appreciate in 10 years at a 5% rate?
trace ("It will be worth: " + Math.bruteFutureValue(.05, 10, 500));
```

You can use the custom *CurrencyFormat()* method from Recipe 5.6 to format the result for display.

It doesn't matter whether the interest is compounded daily, weekly, monthly, or annually, provided that the specified interest rate is correct for the number of periods. For example, if compounding monthly, be sure to multiply the number of years by 12 and divide the annual interest rate by 12.

```
// How much will $500 appreciate in 10 years at a 5% rate with monthly compounding?
trace ("It will be worth: " + Math.bruteFutureValue(.05/12, 10*12, 500));
```

So the brute-force method appears to work, but it has two drawbacks. One drawback is that it can be slow if you are doing a lot of calculations. The other problem is that it can't be used to calculate so-called *continuous compounding*.

Let's revisit this formula for the value of the account at the end of the second year:

```
FV2 = FV1 * (1 + i);
```

Substituting *PV * (1 + i)* for *FV1*, we get:

```
FV2 = (PV * (1 + i)) * (1 + i);
```

This can also be written as:

```
FV2 = PV * ((1 + i) * (1 + i));
```

The last portion is *(1 + i)* squared, so the formula can be written as:

```
FV2 = PV * Math.pow((1 + i), 2);
```

where 2 is the number of periods.

Extrapolating, you can guess that the future value after *n* periods would be:

```
FVN = PV * Math.pow((1 + i), n);
```

So we can speed up our calculation by using the following implementation:

```
Math.futureValue = function (interest, n, PV) {
    // PV       = initial deposit (present value)
    // interest = periodic interest rate
    // n        = number of payment periods
    multiplier = Math.pow ((1 + interest), n);
    return (PV * multiplier);
};
```

You'll see that you get the same result as with our earlier brute-force approach:

```
// How much will $500 appreciate in 10 years at a 5% rate with monthly compounding?
trace ("It will be worth: " + Math.futureValue(.05/12, 10*12, 500));
```

but our new code will be much faster for a large number of periods (when *n* is large).

However, to perform continuous compounding, the number of periods, *n*, becomes infinite. Although the derivation for the formula is beyond the scope of this book, continuous compounding can be implemented as follows:

```
Math.continuousCompounding = function (interest, n, PV) {
    // PV       = initial deposit (present value)
    // interest = periodic interest rate
    // n        = number of payment periods
    multiplier = Math.pow (Math.E, n*interest);
    return (PV * multiplier);
};
// How much will $500 appreciate in 10 years at a 5% rate with continuous
// compounding?
trace ("It will be worth: " + Math.continuousCompounding (.05, 10, 500));
```

The above calculations assume an interest rate, *i*, which may not be known or even predictable in many scenarios. For example, you can't predict the exact return of the stock market over any given period (although you can make educated guesses based on historic data if the time period is long enough). So, typically, you should allow the user to specify an interest rate and perform the calculations under various scenarios.

 Remember to represent the interest rate as a decimal, such as 0.01. If you specify an interest rate of 1.0, it is equivalent to 100% interest! And be sure to specify the correct interest rate for the chosen number of periods (such as the monthly interest rate rather than the annual interest rate).

If you are calculating the future value of a fixed investment (such as a bond or certificate of deposit), you would know the fixed rate it returns. However, you might not be able to predict the rate of inflation. Everyone knows that inflation reduces the effective value of money in the future. To calculate the so-called *real rate of interest*, subtract the rate of inflation from the stated interest rate. For example, if your bond earns 5%, but you expect inflation to be 4%, you can use the above examples with an interest rate of 1% to calculate how much your money will be worth in the future relative to today's dollars.

See Also

Recipes 5.6, 5.17, 5.18, and 5.19. For the exact derivation of continuous compounding and other financial formulas, see any competent college-level financial accounting or applied mathematics book. You can find much of the interesting math online by Googling for "continuous compounding derivation." For example, see *http://ljsavage.wharton.upenn.edu/~waterman/Teaching/IntroMath99/Class04/Notes/node13.htm*.

5.17 Calculating Retirement Savings

Problem

You want to calculate how much money you'll have at retirement, assuming you'll receive a series of equal periodic payments.

Solution

Calculate the future value of a series of periodic payments using the custom *Math.FV()* function.

Discussion

Suppose you are implementing a retirement calculator. People commonly deposit a certain amount of money each month into their retirement account. Typically, they want to know how much money they'll accumulate in the account at some time in the future. There are two components to the accumulation of funds: the interest earned each period, plus the periodic payment that is added. The total value also includes a third component: the principal in the account at the beginning of the calculation.

Here is an enhanced version of the *futureValue()* function presented in Recipe 5.16. It calculates the future value based on an initial payment plus periodic payments. We calculate the final amount by adding together the appreciation of the principal and the appreciation of the periodic payments. If the periodic payment is 0, the calculation reduces to the equation from Recipe 5.16 (in which there is principal and interest only). If there is no initial deposit, you can use 0 for the *PV* parameter. You can add this to your *Math.as* file to use it in other projects.

```
Math.FV = function (interest, n, PMT, PV) {
    // PV       = initial deposit (present value)
    // interest = periodic interest rate
    // n        = number of payment periods
    // PMT      = periodic payment
    // FV       = future value

    // Financial equations for a series of payments compounded over n periods:
    // multiplier     = Math.pow ((1 + interest ), n)
    // FV of principle = PV * Math.pow ((1 + interest ), n)
    //                = PV * multiplier
    // FV of payments  = PMT * ((Math.pow ((1 + interest ), n) - 1) / interest)
    //                = PMT * ((multiplier-1)/interest)

    multiplier = Math.pow ((1 + interest), n);
    // Add FV of principal and FV of payments together to get total value.
    FV = PV * multiplier + PMT * ( (multiplier-1) / interest);
```

```
  return FV;
};
```

You can use the custom *Math.FV()* method as follows:

```
// How much money will I have in 30 years if it appreciates at 6%, starting with
// $50,000 and paying $400/month?
trace (Math.FV(.06/12, 30*12, 400, 50000));
```

Again, you can consult a financial textbook for the derivation of the preceding formulas. You can confirm their accuracy by testing them against the value derived from the brute-force method:

```
Math.bruteFV = function (interest, n, PMT, PV) {
  FV = PV;
  for (var periods = interest; periods <= n; periods++) {
    FV = FV * (1 + interest) + PMT;
  }
  return FV;
};
```

 You can and should confirm your calculations against the values returned by a commercial spreadsheet or actuarial table. For example, our custom *Math.FV()* function returns the same value, as the one obtained in Microsoft Excel using the Insert → Function → Financial → FV formula.

See Also

Recipes 5.6, 5.16, 5.18, and 5.19

5.18   Calculating the Loan (Mortgage) You Can Afford

Problem

You want to calculate how large a loan you can get assuming you make a given monthly payment.

Solution

Calculate the present value of a series of equal future periodic payments using the custom *Math.PV()* function.

Discussion

Suppose you are a bank with a big pile of money and you want to lend it to someone to earn some interest. The borrower might come to you and say, "I can pay you back

$1,000 per month for 30 years. How much money will you loan me?" The answer requires you to calculate how much the money that you will receive at various times in the future (as a series of periodic payments) is worth today.

The following custom *Math.PV()* function returns the same value as the one obtained in Microsoft Excel using the Insert → Function → Financial → PV formula. You can add this to your *Math.as* file for easy inclusion in other projects.

```
Math.PV = function (i, n, PMT) {
   // i   = periodic interest rate
   // n   = number of payment periods
   // PMT = periodic payment

   // Present value compounded over n periods:
   // PV = PMT * ( (multiplier-1)/(i*multiplier))
   // where multiplier = Math.pow ((1 + i), n)

   multiplier = Math.pow ((1 + i), n);
   PV = PMT * (multiplier-1) / (i*multiplier);
   return PV;
};
```

You can use the custom *Math.PV()* method as follows:

```
// How much will the bank loan me if I can pay $1000/month for 30 years (6% rate)?
trace (Math.PV(.06/12, 30*12, 1000));
```

See Also

Recipes 5.6, 5.16, 5.17, and 5.19. You can consult a financial textbook for the derivation of the preceding formula. It is essentially based on the reverse of the process used in Recipe 5.16 to calculate the future value..

5.19 Calculating Loan Amortization or Annuities

Problem

You want to determine the monthly payment it takes to pay off a loan (i.e., *amortize* the loan). Alternatively, you want to know how much money you can withdraw from a retirement account on a periodic basis.

Solution

Calculate the payments using the custom *Math.PMT()* function.

Discussion

Suppose you want to borrow $100,000 from a bank, and you need to know the required monthly payment to pay back the loan. The answer requires the bank to calculate how much money is needed to pay off the principal and the interest that accrues before the loan is finally paid off in full. The calculation is equivalent to the one needed to calculate how much money you can take out monthly from a retirement account. However, in the case of a so-called *annuity*, you start with the lump sum and extract a series of periodic payments. The math still answers the question, "Given an initial pile of money and the prevailing interest rate, how much money can I take out (or must I pay back) each month before the balance is zero?"

The following custom *Math.PMT()* function returns the same value as the one obtained in Microsoft Excel using the Insert → Function → Financial → PMT formula. You can add this to your *Math.as* file for easy inclusion in other projects.

```
Math.PMT = function (i, n, PV) {
    // PV  = initial savings deposit or loan amount (present value)
    // i   = periodic interest rate
    // n   = number of payment periods
    // PMT = periodic payment

    // Calculate the periodic payment needed to amortize (pay back) a loan.
    multiplier = Math.pow((1 + i), n);

    return (PV * i * multiplier / (multiplier - 1));
};

// Example usage:
// What monthly payment pays back a $100,000 mortgage (30-year fixed at 6%)?
trace("Your monthly payment is " + Math.PMT (0.06/12, 30*12, 100000));
```

See Also

Recipes 5.6, 5.16, 5.17, and 5.18. You can consult a financial textbook for a discussion of annuities and loan amortization or see online resources such as *http://www.mortgage-calc.com*.

## CHAPTER 6

Arrays

6.0 Introduction

Arrays are essential to successful ActionScript programming. At its most basic, an array can be thought of as a series of variables that can be referred to using a single, common name, which is often easier than having separate variable names for each datum. And what's more, the data in an array is ordered and enumeratable, providing a convenient way to organize, sort, and access the values.

Arrays provide a way of grouping together, organizing, and processing related data elements. The concept of an array should not be foreign to you. If fact, we use the concept of arrays in everyday life all the time. A simple grocery list or to-do list can be thought of as an array. Your address book is an array containing people's names and addresses. Libraries keep track of books using an indexing system whereby each book becomes, conceptually, an element in a library's array. You'll ordinarily use arrays to hold a series of related items, such as playing cards in a deck, as seen in Recipe 5.10.

In ActionScript, there are two kinds of arrays: *integer-indexed* and *associative*. Unless otherwise specified, the term "array" usually refers to an integer-indexed array. Both types of arrays group together related data, but they use different means of accessing the data. An integer-indexed array uses integers (numbers) as unique identifiers for each element in the array. Such arrays are ordered by *index* (i.e., element number), starting from 0. Each element occupies a numbered slot in the array. Integer-indexed arrays are ideal for sets of data that you want to work with in sequential order. Associative arrays use string *keys* to access each value. You can read more about associative arrays in Recipe 6.12.

Integer-indexed arrays are the focus of the majority of the recipes in this chapter, and so you should know how to create an array first. There are two ways to construct a new array in ActionScript: with the constructor function or as an array literal. All arrays are members of the *Array* class. You can use the *Array()* constructor function to instantiate new array objects in one of three ways:

```
myArray = new Array();          // Create an empty array.
myArray = new Array(numElems);  // Create an array with numElems undefined elements.
myArray = new Array(elem0,...elemn); // Create an array with specified elements.
```

The array literal notation also creates a new array but without having to use the constructor function. Literal notation is convenient for specifying elements at the time of creation, such as:

```
myArray = ["a", "b", "c"];
```

Some methods of the *Array* class modify the existing array on which the method is called, and others return a new array (offering an indirect way to create arrays).

You can retrieve and set array elements using the array-access operator (square brackets) and the index of the element you wish to get or set. For example:

```
// Set the fifth element of the array to "apples" (array indexes start at 0).
myArray[4] = "apples";

// Display the fifth element in the Output window.
trace(myArray[4]);   // Displays: apples
```

ActionScript doesn't care what kind of values you store in arrays. You can store strings, numbers, Booleans, or any kind of objects. And, unlike stricter programming languages, you can even store different datatypes in a single array. For example, this array stores a string, an integer, a Boolean, and an object:

```
myArray = ["a", 2, true, new Object()];
```

Unlike many languages, ActionScript doesn't require you to specify the number of elements in an array when it is declared (a.k.a. *dimensioned* or *allocated*).

6.1   Adding Elements to the Start or End of an Array

Problem

You want to add elements to an existing array.

Solution

Use the *push()* method to append elements to an array; use the *unshift()* method to insert elements at the beginning of an array.

Discussion

You can append elements to an existing array using the *Array.push()* method, passing it one or more values to be appended:

```
myArray = new Array( );
myArray.push("val 1", "val 2");
```

You can also append a single element using the array's length property as the index. Because ActionScript array indexes are zero-relative (meaning that the first index is 0, not 1), the last element is at an index of Array.length − 1.

```
myArray[myArray.length] = "val 3";
```

If you try to set an element with an index that does not yet exist, the array is extended to include the necessary number of elements automatically (in which case intervening elements are initialized to undefined). For example, after executing the following statements, myArray contains the elements ["a", "b", "c", undefined, undefined, "f"]:

```
myArray = ["a", "b", "c"];
myArray[5] = "f";
```

Appending elements onto an array is common when you want to build an array incrementally or when you want to store the history of a user's actions for the purpose of implementing a Back button or history feature.

To add elements to the beginning of an array, use the *unshift()* method, which shifts the existing elements by one index position, and inserts the new element at index 0:

```
// Create an array with four elements: "a", "b", "c", and "d".
myArray = new Array( );
myArray.push("a", "b", "c", "d");

// Add "z" to the beginning of the array. This shifts all the other elements so that
// the value "a" moves from index 0 to index 1, etc.
myArray.unshift("z");

// Display the results by looping through the elements. See Recipe 6.2.
for (var i = 0; i < myArray.length; i++) {
  trace(myArray[i]);
}
```

Should you add elements to the beginning or the end of an array? That depends on your goal. It also depends on how you intend to access or remove the elements at a later time. For example, if you want to access items in last-in-first-out (LIFO) order, you might use *Array.push()* to add elements to an array and *Array.pop()* to remove the elements in reverse order.

6.2 Looping Through an Array

Problem

You want to access or process all of the elements of an array in sequential order.

Solution

Use a *for* loop that increments an index variable from 0 to *Array*.length − 1. Use the index to access each element in turn.

Discussion

To access the values stored in the elements of an array, loop through the array's elements using a *for* loop. Because the first index of an array is 0, the index variable in the *for* statement should start at 0. The last index of an array is always 1 less than the length property of that array. Within the *for* statement, you can use the loop index variable within square brackets to access array elements. For example:

```
myArray = ["a", "b", "c"];
for (var i = 0; i < myArray.length; i++) {
  // Display the elements in the Output window.
  trace("Element " + i + ": " + myArray[i]);
}
```

The looping index variable (*i* in the example code) should range from 0 to one less than the value of the length property. Remember that the last index of an array is always one less than its length.

Alternatively, you can also use a *for* statement that loops backward from *Array*.length − 1 to 0, decrementing by one each time. Looping backward is useful when you want to find the last matching element rather than the first (see Recipe 6.3). For example:

```
myArray = ["a", "b", "c"];
for (var i = myArray.length - 1; i >= 0; i--){
  // Display the elements in the Output window in reverse order.
  trace("Element " + i + ": " + myArray[i]);
}
```

There are many examples in which you might want to loop through all the elements of an array. For example, by looping through an array containing references to movie clips, you can perform a particular action on each of the movie clips:

```
for (var i = 0; i < myArray.length; i++){
  // Move each movie clip one pixel to the right.
  myArray[i]._x++;
}
```

You can improve the performance of a loop by storing the array's length in a variable rather than computing it during each loop iteration. For example:

```
var len = myArray.length;
for (var i = 0; i < len; i++){
  // Move each movie clip one pixel to the right.
  myArray[i]._x++;
}
```

This works as expected only if the length of the array does not change during the loop, which assumes that elements are not being added or removed.

See Also

See Recipe 5.5 for some correct and incorrect ways to loop through characters in a string. See Recipe 6.13 for details on enumerating elements of an associative array.

6.3 Searching for Matching Elements in an Array

Problem

You want to find the first element in an array that matches a specified value.

Solution

Use a *for* statement to loop through an array, and use a *break* statement once a match has been found.

Discussion

When you are searching for the first element in an array that matches a specified value, you should use a *for* statement, as shown in Recipe 6.2, but with the addition of a *break* statement to exit the loop once the match has been found.

A *break* statement used within a *for* statement causes the loop to exit once it is encountered. Note that the *break* statement is generally placed within an *if* statement, so it is reached only when a certain condition is met. The importance of the *break* statement when searching for the first matching element is two-fold. First of all, you should not needlessly loop through the remaining elements of an array once the match has been found, since it would waste processing time. In the following example, the *break* statement exits the loop after the second iteration, saving six more needless iterations. Imagine the savings if there were a thousand more elements. Furthermore, the *break* statement is vital when searching for the first match because it ensures that only the first element is matched and that subsequent matches are ignored. If the *break* statement is omitted in the following example, all matching elements are displayed, as opposed to the first one only.

```
// Create an array with eight elements.
myArray = ["a", "b", "c", "d", "a", "b", "c", "d"];

// Specify what we want to search for.
searchString = "b";

// Use a for statement to loop through, potentially, all the elements of the array.
for (var i = 0; i < myArray.length; i++) {

  // Check whether the current element matches the search value.
  if (myArray[i] == searchString) {

    // Do something with the matching element, if necessary. In this example, display
    // a message in the Output window for testing purposes.
    trace("Element with index " + i + " found to match " + searchString);

    // Include a break statement to exit the for loop once a match has been found.
    break;
  }
}
```

You can also search for the *last* matching element of an array by reversing the order in which the *for* statement loops through the array. Initialize the index variable to *Array*.length − 1 and loop until it reaches 0 by decrementing the index variable, as follows:

```
myArray = ["a", "b", "c", "d", "a", "b", "c", "d"];

searchString = "b";

// Loop backward through the array. In this example, we'll find the "b" at index 5.
for (var i = myArray.length - 1; i >= 0; i--) {
  if (myArray[i] == searchString) {
    trace("Element with index " + i + " found to match " + searchString);
    break;
  }
}
```

See Also

Recipe 6.10

6.4   Removing Elements

Problem

You want to remove an element or elements from an array and shift any remaining elements to fill the vacant indexes.

Solution

Use the *splice()* method to remove elements in the middle of the array. You can use *pop()* to remove the last element or *shift()* to remove the first element.

Discussion

You can remove elements from an array starting at a specified index using the *splice()* method. When using *splice()* to delete elements, you should pass it two parameters:

start
> The index of the array from which to start deleting elements.

deleteCount
> The number of elements to delete. If this value is undefined, all the elements from *start* to the end of the array are deleted:

```
myArray = ["a", "b", "c", "d"];

// Remove one element from myArray starting at index 1.
myArray.splice(1, 1);

// Display the results. The array now contains three elements: "a", "c", and "d".
for (var i = 0; i < myArray.length; i++) {
  trace(myArray[i]);
}
```

The *splice()* method also returns a new array containing the deleted elements. For example:

```
myArray = ["a", "b", "c", "d"];

// Remove two elements from myArray starting at index 0.
deletedElems = myArray.splice(0, 2);

// Display the deleted elements: "a" and "b".
for (var i = 0; i < deletedElems.length; i++) {
  trace(deletedElems [i]);
}
```

If deleting a single element from the beginning or end of the array, you can use the *shift()* and *pop()* methods. The *shift()* method removes the first element of the array and returns its value. The *pop()* method removes the last element of the array and returns its value.

```
myArray = ["a", "b", "c", "d"];

// Remove the first element and display its value.
trace(myArray.shift());

// Remove the last element and display its value.
trace(myArray.pop());
```

```
// Display the remaining elements. The array has two elements left: "b" and "c".
for (var i = 0; i < myArray.length; i++) {
  trace(myArray[i]);
}
```

6.5   Inserting Elements in the Middle of an Array

Problem

You want to insert elements in the middle of an array.

Solution

Use the *splice()* method.

Discussion

You can use the *splice()* method to insert elements as well as delete them. Any values passed as parameters to the *splice()* method following the first and second parameters are inserted into the array starting at the index specified by the *start* parameter. All existing elements following that index are shifted to accommodate for the inserted values. If 0 is passed to the *splice()* method for the *deleteCount* parameter, no elements are deleted, but the new values are inserted:

```
myArray = ["a" ,"b", "c", "d"];

// Insert three string values—"one", "two", and "three"—starting at index 1.
myArray.splice(1, 0, "one", "two", "three");

// myArray now contains seven elements: "a", "one", "two", "three", "b", "c", and
// "d".
for (var i = 0; i < myArray.length; i++) {
  trace(myArray[i]);
}
```

You can also delete elements and insert new elements at the same time:

```
myArray = ["a" ,"b", "c", "d"];

// Remove two elements and insert three more into myArray starting at index 1.
myArray.splice(1, 2, "one", "two", "three");

// myArray now contains five elements: "a", "one", "two", "three", and "d".
for (var i = 0; i < myArray.length; i++) {
  trace(myArray[i]);
}
```

6.6   Converting a String to an Array

Problem

You have a list of values as a string and you want to parse it into an array of separate elements.

Solution

Use the *String.split()* method.

Discussion

You can split any list of values (a string) into an array using the *split()* method of the *String* class. The list must be delimited by a uniform substring. For example, the list "Susan,Robert,Paula" is one in which the elements of the list are delimited by commas.

The *split()* method takes up to two parameters:

delimiter

> The substring that is used to delimit the elements of the list. If undefined, the entire list is placed into the first element of the new array.

limit

> The maximum number of elements to place into the new array. If undefined, all the elements of the list are placed into the new array.

You can use a space as the delimiter to split a string into an array of words:

```
myList = "Peter Piper picked a peck of pickled peppers";

// Split the string using the space as the delimiter. This puts
// each word into an element of the new array, myArray.
myArray = myList.split(" ");
```

The *split()* method can be extremely useful when values are loaded into Flash using *loadVariables()* or a *LoadVars* object. For example, a list of names might be retrieved from the server as a string:

```
names=Michael,Peter,Linda,Gerome,Catherine
```

You can make it easier to use the names by parsing them into an array using the *split()* method:

```
namesArray = names.split(",");
```

See Also

Recipe 6.7

6.7 Converting an Array to a String

Problem

You want to convert an array to a string.

Solution

Use the *join()* method.

Discussion

ActionScript provides you with a built-in way to quickly convert arrays to strings (assuming, of course, that the array elements themselves are either strings or another datatype that ActionScript can automatically cast to a string) using the *join()* method. You should provide the *join()* method with a parameter that tells Flash which delimiter to use to join the elements:

```
myArray = ["a", "b", "c"];
trace(myArray.join("|"));    // Displays: a|b|c
```

If you don't provide a delimiter, Flash uses a comma by default:

```
myArray = ["a", "b", "c"];
trace(myArray.join());       // Displays: a,b,c
```

 The *toString()* method does the same thing as calling the *join()* method either with no parameters or with the comma as the parameter. And, in fact, if you try to use an array in a situation in which a string is required, Flash will automatically call the *toString()* method:

```
myArray = ["a", "b", "c"];
trace(myArray);  // Displays: a,b,c
```

See Also

Recipe 6.6

6.8 Creating a Separate Copy of an Array

Problem

You want to copy an array, but you want the duplicate to be dissociated from the original array.

Solution

Use the *concat()* method or the *slice()* method.

Discussion

Because arrays are a composite datatype, they are copied and compared differently from primitive data. A variable that holds an array doesn't truly contain all of the array's data. Instead, the variable simply points to the place in the computer's memory where the array's data resides. This makes sense from an optimization standpoint. Primitive data tends to be small, such as a single number or a short string. But composite data, such as an array, can be very large. It would be very inefficient to copy an entire array every time you wanted to perform an operation on it or pass it to a function. Therefore, when you try to copy an array, ActionScript doesn't necessarily make a separate copy of the array's data. A simple example illustrates this.

First, let's look at how primitive data is copied from the variable myNumber to another variable, myOtherNumber:

```
// Assign the number 5 to a variable.
var myNumber = 5;
// Copy myNumber's value to another variable, myOtherNumber.
var myOtherNumber = myNumber;
// Change myNumber's value.
myNumber = 29;

trace(myNumber);        // Displays: 29
trace(myOtherNumber);   // Displays: 5
```

When the copy is made, the contents of myNumber are copied to myOtherNumber. After the copy is made, subsequent changes to myNumber have no effect on myOtherNumber because primitive data is said to be *copied by value*.

Now, let's look at an analogous operation with arrays, but note the substantial difference from the preceding example. Data is copied from the variable myArray to the variable myOtherArray, but the two variables remain joined! When the value of myArray changes, the changes are reflected in myOtherArray!

```
// Assign elements of an array.
var myArray = ["a", "b", "c"];
// Copy myArray to another variable, myOtherArray.
var myOtherArray = myArray;

// Both arrays contain the same values, as expected.
trace(myArray);         // Displays: "a,b,c"
trace(myOtherArray);    // Displays: "a,b,c"

// Change myArray's value.
myArray = ["d", "e", "f"];
```

```
// Surprise! Both arrays contain the new values. The old values are lost!
trace(myArray);        // Displays: "d,e,f"
trace(myOtherArray);   // Displays: "d,e,f" (not "a,b,c")
```

Is the relationship between two copies of an array a good thing or a bad thing? The answer depends on what you expect and what you need to accomplish. Let's first understand what is happening, then learn how to address it.

In the preceding example, the following line does not make a copy of myArray's contents, as it would if myArray held a primitive datum:

```
var myOtherArray = myArray;
```

Instead, it says to Flash, "Make myOtherArray point to whatever myArray points to, even if the contents change in the future." So the two variables myArray and myOtherArray always point to the same data in memory. If it helps, you can think of this arrangement as being similar to a file shortcut on Windows (which is called an alias on the Macintosh). A shortcut simply points to another file located elsewhere. Whether you open the original file directly or access it via the shortcut, there is only one physical file that contains the content of interest. If the file's contents change, the shortcut still offers access to the current contents of the file. If you wanted two independent files, you'd have to duplicate the original file rather than simply create a shortcut to it.

So, is it a good thing if two arrays refer to the same data? As explained earlier, in the natural course of things, it increases efficiency to avoid copying the contents of an array unnecessarily. But you might wish to operate on a copy of an array so as not to alter the original. For example, in Recipe 5.10, we set up a deck of cards as an array and make a copy of it before dealing. That way, when we want a new deck, we can easily make a new copy from the pristine original without having to recreate it from scratch.

You can create a copy of an array that is separate from the original using *concat()*:

```
// Assign elements of an array.
var myArray = ["a", "b", "c"];
// Create an independent copy of myArray using concat(), which returns a new array.
var myOtherArray = myArray.concat();

// Both arrays contain the same values, as expected.
trace(myArray);        // Displays: "a,b,c"
trace(myOtherArray);   // Displays: "a,b,c"

// Change myArray's value.
myArray = ["d", "e", "f"];

// Unlike preceding examples, the arrays are independent.
trace(myArray);        // Displays: "d,e,f"
trace(myOtherArray);   // Displays: "a,b,c"
```

In line 4 of the preceding example, you could also use *slice()* instead of *concat()*, as follows:

```
var myOtherArray = myArray.slice(0);
```

6.9   Storing Complex or Multidimensional Data

Problem

You have two or more sets of related data and you want to be able to keep track of the relationships between the elements.

Solution

Use parallel arrays, an array of arrays (a multidimensional array), or an array of objects.

Discussion

You can create two or more *parallel arrays* in which the elements with the same index in each array are related. For example, the *beginGradientFill()* method, discussed in Recipe 4.10, uses three parallel arrays for the colors, alphas, and ratios of the values used in the gradient. In each array, the elements with the same index correspond to one another.

To create parallel arrays, populate multiple arrays such that the elements with the same index correspond to one another. When you use parallel arrays, you can easily retrieve related data since the indexes are the same across the arrays. For example:

```
colors = ["maroon", "beige",    "blue",    "gray"];
years  = [1997,     2000,       1985,      1983];
makes  = ["Honda",  "Chrysler", "Mercedes", "Fiat"];

// Loop through the arrays. Since each array is the same length, you can use the
// length property of any of them in the for statement. Here, we use makes.length.
for (var i = 0; i < makes.length; i++) {
  // Outputs:
  // A maroon 1997 Honda
  // A beige 2000 Chrysler
  // A blue 1985 Mercedes
  // A gray 1983 Fiat

  // Display the elements with corresponding indexes from the arrays.
  trace("A " + colors[i] + " " + years[i] + " " + makes[i]);
}
```

Another option for working with multiple sets of data is to create a *multidimensional array*, which is an array of arrays (i.e., an array in which each element is another array):

```
// Create an array, cars, and populate it with elements that are arrays. Each element
// array represents a car and contains three elements (make, year, and color).
cars = new Array();
cars.push(["maroon", 1997, "Honda"]);
cars.push(["beige", 2000, "Chrysler"]);
cars.push(["blue", 1985, "Mercedes"]);
cars.push(["gray", 1983, "Fiat"]);

// Loop through the elements of the cars array.
for (var i = 0; i < cars.length; i++) {
    // The output is the same as in the earlier parallel arrays example:
    // A maroon 1997 Honda
    // A beige 2000 Chrysler
    // A blue 1985 Mercedes
    // A gray 1983 Fiat

    // Output each element of each subarray, cars[i]. Note the use of two successive
    // indexes in brackets, such as cars[i][0].
    trace("A " + cars[i][0] + " " + cars[i][1] + " " + cars[i][2]);
}
```

Here is another way to view the two-dimensional cars array's contents. This displays the elements in a long list (the formatting isn't as nice as in the previous example, but it shows the array structure more clearly).

```
// Loop through the elements of the cars array.
for (var i = 0; i < cars.length; i++) {
    // Loop through the elements of each subarray, cars[i].
    for (var j = 0; j < cars[i].length; j++) {
        // Note the use of two successive indexes in brackets, cars[i][j].
        trace("Element [" + i + "][" + j + "] contains: " + cars[i][j]);
    }
}
```

In the preceding example (the array of arrays), it is hard to discern the meaning of something like cars[i][0] or cars[i][j]. Furthermore, if the order of elements in a subarray changes, we would have to modify our code (or it might erroneously display "A Honda maroon 1997" instead of "A maroon 1997 Honda").

One alternative is to work with related data using an array of objects. This technique is similar to working with an array of arrays, but it offers the advantage of named properties. When you use an array of arrays, you must reference each value by its numbered index. However, when you use an array of objects, you can reference the data by property name instead of index number. We can specify the properties of the object in any order we like, because we'll refer to them later by name, not by number.

```
// Create an array, cars, and populate it with objects. Each object has a make
// property, a year property, and a color property.
cars = new Array();
```

```
// Here, we use object literals to define three properties for each car and then add
// the object literals to the main array.
cars.push({make: "Honda",    year: 1997, color: "maroon"});
cars.push({make: "Chrysler", year: 2000, color: "beige"});
cars.push({make: "Mercedes", year: 1985, color: "blue"});
cars.push({make: "Fiat",     year: 1983, color: "gray"});

// Loop through the cars array.
for (var i = 0; i < cars.length; i++) {
  // The output is the same as in the earlier examples, but each value is referenced
  // by its property name, which is more programmer-friendly.
  trace("A " + cars[i].color + " " + cars[i].year + " " + cars[i].make);
}
```

See Also

Recipe 6.12 covers associative arrays, in which elements are accessed by name instead of number.

6.10   Sorting or Reversing an Array

Problem

You want to sort the elements of an array.

Solution

Use the *sort()* method. For arrays of objects, you can also use the *sortOn()* method.

Discussion

You can perform a simple sort on an array using the *sort()* method. The *sort()* method, without any parameters, sorts the elements of an array in ascending order. Elements are sorted according to the Unicode code points of the characters in the string (roughly alphabetical for Western European languages). However, the sort is also case-sensitive, and it sorts numbers "alphabetically" instead of numerically. See Recipe 6.11 for details on creating custom sorting algorithms that are case-insensitive.

```
words = ["tricycle", "relative", "aardvark", "jargon"];
words.sort();
trace(words);    // Displays: aardvark,jargon,relative,tricycle
```

The *reverse()* method reverses the order of the elements in an array:

```
words = ["tricycle", "relative", "aardvark", "jargon"];
words.reverse();
trace(words);    // Displays: jargon,aardvark,relative,tricycle
```

If you want to sort the elements of an array in descending order, use the *sort()* method followed by the *reverse()* method:

```
words = ["tricycle", "relative", "aardvark", "jargon"];
words.sort();
words.reverse();
trace(words); // Displays: tricycle,relative,jargon,aardvark
```

You can sort arrays of objects using the *sortOn()* method. The *sortOn()* method requires a string parameter specifying the name of the property on which to sort the elements:

```
cars = new Array();
cars.push({make: "Honda",    year: 1997, color: "maroon"});
cars.push({make: "Chrysler", year: 2000, color: "beige"});
cars.push({make: "Mercedes", year: 1985, color: "blue"});
cars.push({make: "Fiat",     year: 1983, color: "gray"});

// Sort the cars array according to the year property of each element.
cars.sortOn("year");

for (var i = 0; i < cars.length; i++) {
  // Outputs:
  // A gray 1983 Fiat
  // A blue 1985 Mercedes
  // A maroon 1997 Honda
  // A beige 2000 Chrysler
  trace("A " + cars[i].color + " " + cars[i].year + " " + cars[i].make);
}
```

To sort the elements of an array of objects in descending order, call the *reverse()* method after calling *sortOn()*.

Sorted arrays can be useful in many scenarios. For example, if you want to display the elements of an array in a UI component or a text field, you often want to list the elements in alphabetical order.

See Also

The *sort()* and *sortOn()* methods make changes to the order of the original array; they do not return a new array. See Recipe 6.8 to make a separate copy of an array on which you can perform destructive operations. See Recipe 6.11 for details on case-insensitive sorting and numeric sorting, as well as custom sorting in general.

6.11   Implementing a Custom Sort

Problem

You want to sort an array in a way such that the basic *sort()* and *sortOn()* methods do not suffice. You want to sort an array in a case-insensitive manner, perform a numeric sort, or use another custom or multikey criterion.

Solution

Use the *sort()* method and pass it a reference to a *compare function*.

Discussion

If you want complete control over sorting criteria, use the *sort()* method with a custom *compare function* (also called a *sorter function*). The compare function is called repeatedly by the *sort()* method to reorder two elements of the array at a time. The compare function receives two parameters (let's call them *a* and *b*), which it should compare to determine which one should be ordered first. Your custom compare function should return a positive number, a negative number, or 0, depending on how the elements are to be sorted. If the function returns a negative number, *a* is ordered before *b*. If the function returns 0, then the current order is preserved. If the function returns a positive number, *a* is ordered after *b*. Your compare function is called with every relevant combination of elements until the entire array has been properly ordered. Using a custom compare function is easier than it sounds. You do not need to concern yourself with the details of the sorting algorithm; you simply specify the criteria for comparing any two elements.

Here is a simple compare function that performs a case-insensitive sort:

```
function insensitiveSorter(a, b) {
  itemOne = a.toUpperCase( );
  itemTwo = b.toUpperCase( );
  if (itemOne > itemTwo) {
    return 1;
  } else if (itemOne < itemTwo) {
    return -1;
  } else {
    return 0
  }
}
```

Case-insensitive sorting is useful when you have an array of values with mixed cases, because Flash automatically sorts all uppercase letters before lowercase letters by default:

```
myArray = ["cardinal", "California", "camel", "Chicago"];
myArray.sort( );
trace(myArray);  // Displays: California,Chicago,camel,cardinal
```

However, when you use the case-insensitive sort utilizing the custom sorter function as defined previously, Flash sorts the values in alphabetical order regardless of case:

```
myArray = ["cardinal", "California", "camel", "Chicago"];
myArray.sort(insensitiveSorter);
trace(myArray);  // Displays: California,camel,cardinal,Chicago
```

When sorting numbers, the standard *sort()* method produces unexpected results. Numbers are sorted "alphabetically" instead of numerically. After the following example, myArray is [1,12,2,3,4,43], not [1,2,3,4,12,43]:

```
myArray = [1, 12, 2, 3, 43, 4];
myArray.sort( )
trace (myArray);  // Displays: 1,12,2,3,4,43 not 1,2,3,4,12,43
```

Here is a simple compare function that performs a numeric sort, instead of a string-based sort, even if the elements are strings, such as "1", "2", "3":

```
function numberSorter(a, b) {
  itemOne = parseInt(a);
  itemTwo = parseInt(b);
  if (itemOne > itemTwo) {
    return 1;
  } else if (itemOne < itemTwo) {
    return -1;
  } else {
    return 0
  }
}
```

You can use it as follows:

```
myArray = [1, 12, 2, 3, 43, 4];
myArray.sort(numberSorter);
trace (myArray);  // Displays: 1,2,3,4,12,43
```

In the *numberSorter()* function, the difference between the two numbers yields a positive result if *a* is greater than *b*, and a negative result if the opposite is true. It yields 0 if they are equal. Therefore, numeric comparisons of the previous type can be simplified as follows.

```
function numberSorter(a, b) {
  itemOne = parseInt(a);
  itemTwo = parseInt(b);
  return (itemOne - itemTwo);
}
```

You can easily modify the sort function to sort the numbers in reverse order, as follows:

```
function reverseSorter(a, b) {
  itemOne = parseInt(a);
  itemTwo = parseInt(b);
  return (itemTwo - itemOne);
}
```

Here is a full-fledged example that sorts the cars array by make and year:

```
// Create an array with elements that have some matching make properties but
// different year and color properties.
cars = new Array( );
cars.push({make: "Honda",   year: 1997, color: "maroon"});
cars.push({make: "Chrysler", year: 2000, color: "beige"});
cars.push({make: "Mercedes", year: 1985, color: "blue"});
```

```
cars.push({make: "Fiat",     year: 1983, color: "gray"});
cars.push({make: "Honda",    year: 1982, color: "white"});
cars.push({make: "Chrysler", year: 1999, color: "green"});
cars.push({make: "Mercedes", year: 2002, color: "tan"});
cars.push({make: "Fiat",     year: 1981, color: "brown"});

// Create the custom compare function. The function is always passed two elements as
// parameters. It is convenient to call them a and b.
function sorter(a, b) {

  // If the make property of a is larger than (meaning it comes alphabetically after)
  // the make property of b, return 1 to sort a after b. If the make property of a is
  // less than the make property of b, then return -1 to sort a before b. Otherwise
  // (if a.make and b.make are the same), perform the comparison on the year
  // property. We use String.toUpperCase( ) to ensure a case-insensitive comparison.
  // We also convert the year to an integer and use the aforementioned shortcut for
  // numeric comparison.
  makeOne = a.make.toUpperCase( );
  makeTwo = b.make.toUpperCase( );
  if (makeOne > makeTwo ) {
    return 1;
  } else if (makeOne < makeTwo) {
    return -1;
  } else {
    return (parseInt(a.year) - parseInt(b.year))
  }
}

// Call the sort( ) method and pass it a reference to the sorter( ) compare function.
cars.sort(sorter);

// Loop through the array and output the results.
for (var i = 0; i < cars.length; i++) {
  // Displays the results alphabetically by make, then by year:
  // A green 1999 Chrysler
  // A beige 2000 Chrysler
  // A brown 1981 Fiat
  // A gray 1983 Fiat
  // A white 1982 Honda
  // A maroon 1997 Honda
  // A blue 1985 Mercedes
  // A tan 2002 Mercedes

  trace("A " + cars[i].color + " " + cars[i].year + " " + cars[i].make);
}
```

6.12   Creating an Associative Array

Problem

You want to create an array that uses named elements instead of numbered indexes.

Solution

Create an associative array.

Discussion

When you are working with sets of data in which each element has a specific meaning or importance, a typical, number-indexed array does not always suffice.

For example, if you are working with a set of data such as the names of members of a committee, a number-indexed array is sufficient:

```
members = new Array("Franklin", "Gina", "Sindhu");
```

However, if each member of the committee plays a special role, a standard array offers no way to indicate that. To address the issue, you can use an *associative array* (sometimes called a *hash table* or simply an *object*). An associative array uses named elements rather than numeric indexes. The names used to refer to elements are often called *keys* or *properties*. The keys can give a meaningful context to the associated element value.

You can create an associative array in ActionScript using *object literal notation* (which will be shown shortly) or by adding elements to an object. Despite their name, you don't use the *Array* class to create associative arrays. The *Array* class provides methods and properties that work with number-indexed arrays only and not with associative arrays. Associative arrays must be instances of the *Object* class. Technically, since the *Object* class is the base class for all ActionScript classes, all ActionScript objects are associative arrays. You can use this fact to your advantage when working with movie clips (see Recipe 7.10). But when you are creating an object explicitly for the purpose of forming an associative array, you should use an instance of the generic *Object* class.

One way you can create an associative array is by using object literal notation. With this technique you use curly braces ({ }) to enclose a comma-delimited list of keys and values, which are separated by a colon (:). Here is an example:

```
members = {scribe: "Franklin", chairperson: "Gina", treasurer: "Sindhu"};
```

For readability, this can be written as:

```
members = {scribe: "Franklin",
           chairperson: "Gina",
           treasurer: "Sindhu"};
```

You can also create an associative array using the following multiline technique with the *Object* constructor. Although the object literal notation is fine for creating small associative arrays in a single step, you should use the *Object* constructor technique for creating larger associative arrays. It improves readability and lets you add properties to an associative array by assigning the properties (keys) on subsequent lines. For example:

```
members = new Object( );
members.scribe = "Franklin";
members.chairperson = "Gina";
members.treasurer = "Sindhu";
```

Although using an *Object* constructor is more common, you can initialize the associative array object using an empty object literal in place of the *Object* constructor:

```
members = {};
```

You can retrieve the values from an associative array in two ways. The first way is to access the elements using property notation (with the dot operator):

```
trace(members.scribe); // Displays: Franklin
```

The other option for retrieving values from an associative array is using array-access notation. To use array-access notation, reference the associative array followed by the array-access operator ([]). Within the array-access operator, you must use the *string* value of the name of the key you wish to access:

```
trace(members["scribe"]); // Displays: Franklin
```

Array-access notation is extremely useful in situations in which there are multiple keys with names in a sequence. This is because you can dynamically generate the key string value, whereas you cannot do this with property notation. For example:

```
members = new Object( );
members.councilperson1 = "Beatrice";
members.councilperson2 = "Danny";
members.councilperson3 = "Vladamir";

for (var i = 1; i <= 3; i++) {
  trace(members["councilperson" + i];
}
```

You can use either the property notation or array-access notation to read or write the values of an associative array:

```
members = new Object( );
members["councilperson"] = "Ruthie";
trace(members.councilperson);          // Displays: Ruthie
members.councilperson = "Rebecca";
trace(members["councilperson"]);       // Displays: Rebecca
```

See Also

Recipe 6.13 contains more details on accessing named elements of an associative array.

6.13   Reading Elements of an Associative Array

Problem

You want to enumerate the elements of an associative array.

Solution

Use a *for...in* statement.

Discussion

You can iterate through the elements of integer-indexed arrays using a *for* statement. However, named elements in associative arrays cannot be accessed by a numeric index, and the order of associative array elements is not guaranteed, regardless of the order in which the elements are added to the array.

Fortunately, you can loop through the enumerable elements of an associative array using a *for...in* statement. That is, a *for...in* statement iterates through all the readable properties of the specified object. The syntax for a *for...in* statement is as follows:

```
for (key in object) {
  // Actions
}
```

The *for...in* statement doesn't require an explicit update statement because the number of loop iterations is determined by the number of properties in the object being examined. Note that *key* is a variable name that will be used to store the property name during each iteration, not the name of a specific property or key. On the other hand, *object* is the specific object whose properties you want to read. For example:

```
members = new Object();
members.scribe = "Franklin";
members.chairperson = "Gina";
members.treasurer = "Sindhu";

// Use a for...in statement to loop through all the elements.
for (var role in members) {
  // Outputs:
  // treasurer: Sindhu
  // chairperson: Gina
  // scribe: Franklin
  trace(role + ": " + members[role]);
}
```

When you use a *for...in* statement, you must use array-access notation (square brackets) with the associative array. If you try to use property notation (with the dot operator) it will not work properly. This is because the value that is assigned to the key iterator variable is the *string* name of the key, not the key's identifier.

A *for…in* loop does not display all built-in properties of an object. For example, it displays custom properties added at runtime, but it does not enumerate methods of built-in objects, even though they are stored in object properties.

See Also

Recipes 6.2 and 7.10

CHAPTER 7
Movie Clips

7.0   Introduction

Movie clips are at the very core of ActionScript. Without movie clips there would be no visual element to a Flash movie, so you can see why they are incredibly important.

Unlike many other object types, movie clips are never instantiated using a constructor function (the *MovieClip* class constructor is used only when creating subclasses, as in Recipe 12.12). Instead, movie clips are created in one of four ways:

- Manually (at authoring time)
- Attached from the Library at runtime, using *attachMovie()*
- Duplicated from another movie clip at runtime, using *duplicateMovieClip()*
- Created as a new, empty movie clip at runtime, using *createEmptyMovieClip()*

Once a movie clip has been instantiated, it can be controlled in a variety of ways. The timelines of movie clips can be controlled using playback methods such as *play()*, *stop()*, and *gotoAndPlay()*. Movie clips can be assigned actions that occur when certain events are triggered, and movie clip attributes can be controlled such that you can affect position, rotation, transparency, and so on.

To control a movie clip using ActionScript, you must know the target path to that instance. Each movie clip in a movie can be targeted in one of two ways: using a relative path or an absolute path. In relative paths there is a known relationship between the timeline from which the instructions are being issued and the movie clip to which they are being addressed. For example, a movie clip can address itself in a relative fashion using the keyword this:

```
// Instruct a movie clip to play from within its own timeline.
this.play( );
```

Generally, if the this keyword is omitted, it is assumed:

```
// Instruct a nested movie clip to set its x position to 50.
this.myNestedMovieClip._x = 50;
```

```
// Perform same task. In this example, this is assumed.
myNestedMovieClip._x = 50;
```

However, in some cases, omitting this can be problematic because there are global functions with the same names as movie clip methods. For example, if you use the command *stop()*, Flash might think you are using the global *stop()* function rather than the *MovieClip.stop()* method. Therefore, as a best practice, you should always explicitly use this when referring to the current timeline rather than relying on Flash to assume it.

You can also target a nested movie clip's parent using the _parent keyword.

 When you use _parent, you should always use an explicit reference to the starting point. In some cases Flash assumes this, but in other cases it does not, leading to unexpected results. To solve the problem, specify the movie clip you are starting from, as seen in the following examples:

```
// Set the rotation of a parent movie clip to 36.
this._parent._rotation = 36;
```

```
// Set the alpha of a parent clip's parent to 50.
this._parent._parent._alpha = 50;
```

Absolute paths do not require you to know the relationship of the timeline from which the instructions are being issued to the targeted movie clip. Rather, you need to know only the full path to the movie clip from the main, or root, movie clip. The main movie clip in a Flash movie is given a special name, _root. Therefore, absolute target paths begin with _root (or _level*n* in some cases, though this is not recommended):

```
// Instruct myNestedMovieClip to play. This instruction can be issued from any
// timeline with success.
_root.myMovieClip.myNestedMovieClip.play();
```

 Using the global function *loadMovieNum()*, it is possible to load *.swf* files into different levels within the same movie. In these cases, each movie can be referenced using absolute paths that begin with _level0, _level1, _level2, etc. However, the *loadMovie()* method is the preferred technique for loading content into your movie, and it does not use levels (see Recipe 15.1).

7.1 Referring to Movie Clips via ActionScript

Problem

You need to refer to a movie clip programmatically.

Solution

If you are creating the movie clip at authoring time, select the movie clip on stage and specify an instance name for it using the Property inspector. Then you can refer to it by that name via ActionScript.

Discussion

We saw in the Introduction how to refer to movie clips throughout your Action-Script code. But what names should you substitute for *myMovieClip* or *myNestedMovieClip* in the earlier examples to refer to your own movie clips?

The instance name you use in your code must match the name of the movie clip instance on stage, not the name of the Library symbol from which the clip is derived. Therefore, you must set the clip's instance name using the Property inspector before you can refer to it from ActionScript (see Figure 1-4). For example, if you've set the instance name of a movie clip to "circle_mc" using the Property inspector, you can control it via ActionScript:

```
circle_mc._xscale = 200;
```

See Also

For information on working with runtime-generated movie clips, see Recipes 7.2, 7.18, and 7.19. Also refer to Recipe 3.1.

7.2   Targeting Movie Clips with Dynamic Names

Problem

You want to target a movie clip in which the clip's name is generated dynamically.

Solution

Use array-access notation (square brackets) and string concatenation (the + operator).

Discussion

If you know a movie clip's name, you can target it using standard dot notation:

```
// Target a movie clip named myMovieClipA that is within a clip named holderClip that
// is, in turn, within _root.
_root.holderClip.myMovieClipA._x = 25;
```

However, the situation is a little different when the movie clip's name (or any part of the path) is not explicitly known. For example, if you have the movie clip's name

---

stored in a variable, you may make the common mistake of trying to use the variable name within the target path:

```
// This will not work! It will look for a movie clip named "myVar" instead of a movie
// clip with the same name as the value of myVar.
_root.holderClip.myVar._x = 25;    // Wrong!
```

Instead, you should use array-access notation. All objects, including movie clips, can be treated as associative arrays. This means that you can access any element of a movie clip—even a nested movie clip—using the array-access operator ([ ]). Note that while standard dot notation expects a movie clip reference, array-access notation expects a string or a variable that contains a string value:

```
// This works! It evaluates myVar through the use of array-access notation. It
// targets the clip within holderClip that has the same name as the value of myVar.
_root.holderClip[myVar]._x = 25;
```

Another common mistake when using array-access notation is to accidentally use a dot before the array-access operator:

```
// This will not work! There should not be a dot between holderClip and the
// array-access operator.
_root.holderClip.[myVar]._x = 25;    // Wrong!
```

Using array-access notation is extremely beneficial when you have sequentially named movie clips that you want to target:

```
// These few lines of code can set the _visible property to false for 50 movie clips
// named myMovieClip0 thru myMovieClip49.
for (var i = 0; i < 50; i++) {
  _root["myMovieClip" + i]._visible = false;
}
```

See Also

Recipe 7.1

7.3   Affecting Playback

Problem

You want to control the playhead of a movie clip's timeline.

Solution

Use the global functions and movie clip methods that control the playhead.

Discussion

You can use the timeline-affecting methods, shown in Table 7-1, to control the playback of a movie clip. These methods are most meaningful for movie clips that have more than one frame in their timelines. Therefore, movie clips created using the *createEmptyMovieClip()* method cannot be usefully affected by the timeline-affecting methods because they have only one frame, and there is no way to programmatically add more frames.

Table 7-1. The timeline-affecting methods

Method	Description
play()	Plays the movie clip's timeline from the current frame. If the timeline is already playing, this has no effect.
stop()	Stops the movie clip's timeline at the current frame. If the timeline is already stopped, this has no effect. Flash continues to render the Stage and process events even when a clip is stopped.
gotoAndPlay()	Plays the timeline from a particular frame regardless of the current frame. The frame can be specified as a frame number or a frame label.
gotoAndStop()	Moves the playhead to a particular frame and stops the play head. The frame can be specified as a frame number or a frame label.
nextFrame()	Moves the playhead to the frame after the current frame and stops the play head.
prevFrame()	Moves the playhead to the frame just before the current frame and stops the play head.

There are many potential uses for each of these methods. You should use them to meet the needs of your movie. Here are some tips for how you might use each method.

You can use the *play()* method to play the timeline of an animation when the user rolls over the movie clip:

```
myMovieClip.onRollOver = function () {
  this.play();
};
```

You can also use *play()* to play the timeline of a movie clip once a callback method, such as the *onLoad()* method of a *LoadVars* object, has been invoked. This can be useful for situations in which you want to ensure that data has been loaded into the movie before allowing the user to see a particular part of it. It is also useful when the movie clip depends on loaded data to work properly.

```
// lv is a LoadVars object.
lv.onLoad = function () {
  // Process the loaded data.

  // Call the play() method of a movie clip on _root.
  _root.myMovieClip.play();
};
```

You can use the *stop()* method to stop the playback of a movie clip at the outset. This is useful if you want to prevent playback until certain conditions are met, such as when the user rolls over the movie clip or when data loads into the movie, etc. Movie clips always play by default, so you have to explicitly tell them to stop:

```
myMovieClip.stop();
```

By default, movie clip timelines continue to loop (playback begins again at the first frame after the playhead reaches the last frame). If you want a timeline to play only once, you should use the *stop()* method on the last frame of the movie clip's timeline:

```
this.stop();
```

You can use the *gotoAndPlay()* method to play a particular section of a timeline when a user performs an action, such as clicking on a navigational button. Generally, it is not the best practice to create multiple sections of a timeline. Rather, each timeline should be a distinct unit. However, you may have good reason in some cases to have a single timeline in which many parts of an animation take place, and in these cases *gotoAndPlay()* is a useful method. (That said, ActionScript doesn't mesh well with scenes, so Flash scenes should generally be avoided in ActionScript-heavy movies.) Here are two examples:

```
// When the user clicks and releases myButtonMovieClip
// (presumed to be a navigational button in your movie),
// tell the main timeline (_root) to begin playback from frame 33.
myButtonMovieClip.onRelease = function () {
  _root.gotoAndPlay(33);
};

// This example is the same as the previous one, except it uses the frame label
// "section b" instead of a frame number. You can apply frame labels by selecting the
// frame and entering a value into the Frame field of the Property inspector.
myButtonMovieClip.onRelease = function () {
  _root.gotoAndPlay("section b");
};
```

You can use the *gotoAndStop()* method to go to a single frame of a timeline when a user performs an action, such as rolling out of a movie clip. Recipe 7.5 discusses how movie clips used as buttons automatically have a *gotoAndStop()* method applied for the _up, _over, and _down labels within the movie clip, if they exist. You could make a more interesting movie clip button by also adding _rollout and other such labels to the timeline and using *gotoAndStop()* within the appropriate event handler methods:

```
myButtonMovieClip.onRollOut = function () {
  this.gotoAndStop("_rollout");
};
```

You can use the *nextFrame()* and *prevFrame()* methods to navigate back and forth along a movie clip's timeline, such as in a slide presentation:

```
// This code allows a user to move back and forth along the frames of the main
// timeline. prevBtn and nextBtn are buttons or movie clips that act as buttons.
prevBtn.onRelease = function () {
```

```
    _root.prevFrame();
};

nextBtn.onRelease = function () {
    _root.nextFrame();
};
```

You can also use the _currentframe property in conjunction with *gotoAndStop()* or *gotoAndPlay()* to instruct the playhead to move to a frame on the timeline relative to the current frame:

```
forwardFiveBtn.onRelease = function () {
    _root.gotoAndStop(_currentframe + 5);
};
```

7.4   Reversing Playback

Problem

You want to play a movie clip's timeline in reverse.

Solution

Use an *onEnterFrame()* event handler with the *prevFrame()* method.

Discussion

You can programmatically reverse the playback of a movie clip's timeline with ActionScript. The *onEnterFrame()* event handler of a movie clip is called repeatedly at the same frequency as the movie's frame rate. Therefore, if you create an *onEnterFrame()* method definition for a movie clip that includes a call to the *prevFrame()* method, the movie clip's timeline will continually move to the previous frame at the movie's frame rate:

```
myMovieClip.onEnterFrame = function () {
    this.prevFrame();
};
```

If the movie clip's playhead is already on the first frame, *prevFrame()* has no effect. Therefore, to loop the movie clip's timeline while playing in reverse, add a conditional statement that goes to the last frame of the movie clip if it is already on the first frame. The current frame number is determined using the _currentframe property, and the last frame is determined using the _totalframes property:

```
myMovieClip.onEnterFrame = function () {
    if (this._currentframe > 1) {
      // Play the clip backwards.
      this.prevFrame();
    } else {
```

```
        // Loop back to the end if we're already at the beginning.
        this.gotoAndStop(this._totalframes);
    }
};
```

See Also

Recipe 7.8

7.5 Using Movie Clips as Buttons

Problem

You want to use a movie clip as a button.

Solution

Use the button event handler methods with the movie clip.

Discussion

Button symbols are still appropriate choices when you want to create simple, authoring-time buttons with basic button states. However, in most cases, you should use movie clips as buttons instead because movie clips can handle all the button events, and ActionScript gives you much more programmatic control over movie clips than buttons. For example, you can attach movie clips to a timeline from the Library, programmatically control the contents of a movie clip such as text labels, and use drawing methods to draw inside movie clips.

While it is not technically improper to apply event handlers to the physical instances of movie clips on the Stage, using the event handler methods (introduced in Flash MX) offers several advantages. First of all, they enable you to keep your code centralized rather than applying the code to each instance. Furthermore, you can assign event handler methods to dynamically created movie clips as well as manually created instances.

The button event handler methods include those shown in Table 7-2.

Table 7-2. The button event handler methods

Event handler method	Description
onPress( )	Triggered when the user clicks on the instance.
onRelease( )	Triggered when the user releases the mouse following a click on the instance.
onReleaseOutside( )	Triggered when the user releases a mouseclick outside the instance. In other words, the user clicked on the instance, moved the cursor off the instance while still pressing on the mouse button, and then released the button.

Table 7-2. The button event handler methods (continued)

Event handler method	Description
onRollOver( )	Triggered when the user moves the pointer over the instance.
onRollOut( )	Triggered when the user moves the pointer off the instance.
onDragOver( )	Triggered when the user drags the pointer onto the instance while the mouse button is pressed. However, the mouse must have been pressed while initially over another button or movie clip with button handlers.
onDragOut( )	Triggered when the user drags the pointer off the instance while the mouse button is pressed.
onSetFocus( )	Triggered when the focus is set to the instance.
onKillFocus( )	Triggered when the focus leaves the instance.

Here is an example you can use to understand how the button events work with a movie clip. You use the *drawCircle( )* method from Recipe 4.5 to draw a circle movie clip and then apply the button event handler methods to it.

```
// Include the DrawingMethods.as file from Chapter 4 for its drawCircle( ) method.
#include "DrawingMethods.as"

// Create a circle_mc clip and draw a blue circle at the center of the Stage.
_root.createEmptyMovieClip("circle_mc", 1);
circle_mc.lineStyle(1, 0x000000, 100);
circle_mc.beginFill(0x0000FF, 100);
circle_mc.drawCircle(100, Stage.width/2, Stage.height/2);
circle_mc.endFill( );

// Next, apply the button event handler methods so that when each event is triggered,
// a message is written to the Output window.
circle_mc.onPress = function ( ) {
  trace("pressed");
};

circle_mc.onRelease = function ( ) {
  trace("released");
};

circle_mc.onReleaseOutside = function ( ) {
  trace("released outside");
};

circle_mc.onRollOver = function ( ) {
  trace("rolled over");
};

circle_mc.onRollOut = function ( ) {
  trace("rolled out");
};

circle_mc.onDragOver = function ( ) {
  trace("dragged over");
};
```

```
circle_mc.onDragOut = function () {
  trace("dragged out");
};

circle_mc.onSetFocus = function () {
  trace("focus set");
};

circle_mc.onKillFocus = function () {
  trace("focus removed");
};

// Use the Selection.setFocus( ) method to set the focus to the circle_mc movie clip,
// and then use it to remove the focus. This will trigger the onSetFocus( ) and
// onKillFocus( ) methods of circle_mc.
Selection.setFocus(circle_mc);
Selection.setFocus(null);
```

When you create a movie clip to use as a button, you can also apply frame labels of _ up, _over, and _down to the frame of the movie clip that represents each button state. When a button event handler is applied to such a movie clip, Flash automatically goes to and stops at the frame label that matches the current button state. You must also place a *stop()* action on the first frame; otherwise, Flash automatically plays the timeline until one of the button states is activated. If you create an animation sequence for each button state, add a *this.play()* method call to the _up, _over, and _down frames within the movie clip; otherwise, the subsequent frames will not play back.

7.6 Defining Hit Areas for Movie Clips

Problem

You want to define a hit area for a movie clip used as a button.

Solution

Create a second movie clip to serve as the hit area. Then assign a reference to the hit area movie clip to the hitArea property of the button movie clip.

Discussion

When you create button symbols at authoring time, you can create alternate hit areas using the Hit frame of the button's timeline. This can be very useful if the artwork in the button is not solid or if you want to define a hit area that is otherwise different from the shape defined by the button's artwork.

You can also define hit areas for movie clips used as buttons. All movie clips have a built-in property named hitArea. If hitArea is left undefined, Flash automatically uses the movie clip's artwork as the hit area. However, you can assign the hitArea property a reference to another movie clip to serve as the hit area.

The following example shows how a custom hit area can be useful when dealing with odd shapes or outlines. Using code, we generate a movie clip that contains 100 small, unfilled circles that are aligned to form a square grid. We then assign an *onRelease()* event handler method to the movie clip instance. Testing the code reveals that the movie clip's rollover state is activated only when the mouse pointer is directly over one of the circle outlines.

```
// Include the DrawingMethods.as file from Chapter 4 for its drawCircle() method.
#include "DrawingMethods.as"

// Create the button movie clip. Name it myButton_mc.
this.createEmptyMovieClip("myButton_mc", 1);

// Use a for statement to create 100 small circles and align them in 10 rows of 10 to
// form a square grid.
for (var i = 0, x = 0, y = 0; i < 100; i++) {
  myButton_mc.createEmptyMovieClip("circle_mc" + i, i);
  circle_mc = myButton_mc["circle_mc" + i];
  circle_mc.lineStyle(0, 0, 100);
  circle_mc.drawCircle(1);
  circle_mc._x = x;
  circle_mc._y = y;
  // Space the circles in a row by five pixels.
  x += 5;

  // Start the next row of circles.
  if (x > 45) {
    x = 0;
    y += 5;
  }
}
myButton_mc.onRelease = function () {
  trace("you clicked the button");
};
```

We can create a solid, filled, transparent square movie clip and overlay it on top of the square grid composed of circles. Then, by assigning the new movie clip to the button movie clip's hitArea property, Flash uses its shape to define the hit area for the button movie clip.

```
// Create the new movie clip.
this.createEmptyMovieClip("hitArea_mc", 2);

// Draw a square in the movie clip with the dimensions of myButton_mc.
hitArea_mc.lineStyle(1, 0, 0);
hitArea_mc.beginFill(0, 0);
hitArea_mc.drawRectangle(myButton_mc._width, myButton_mc._height);

// Position hitArea_mc so that it overlays myButton_mc.
hitArea_mc._x = myButton_mc._x + hitArea_mc._width/2;
hitArea_mc._y = myButton_mc._y + hitArea_mc._height/2;
```

```
// Assign hitArea_mc as the hit area for myButton_mc.
myButton_mc.hitArea = hitArea_mc;
```

See Also

Recipe 7.15

7.7   Checking for Mouseover

Problem

You want to check whether the mouse pointer is over a movie clip.

Solution

Use the *onRollover()* event handler, or use the *hitTest()* method within an *onEnterFrame()* method.

Discussion

In many cases, the *onRollOver()* and *onRollOut()* event handler methods, as shown in Recipe 7.5, are the easiest way to respond to the mouse pointer rolling over a movie clip. However, this technique fails when you drag one clip over another, such as when using a clip as a custom mouse pointer. Here is an example to illustrate the point:

```
// Include the DrawingMethods.as file from Chapter 4 for its drawRectangle() and
// drawCircle() methods.
#include "DrawingMethods.as"

// Create a rectangle_mc movie clip on the Stage.
_root.createEmptyMovieClip("rectangle_mc", 1);
rectangle_mc.lineStyle(1, 0x000000, 100);
rectangle_mc.beginFill(0, 100);
rectangle_mc.drawRectangle(100, 200, 10);
rectangle_mc.endFill();
rectangle_mc._x = 100;
rectangle_mc._y = 100;

// Create onRollOver() and onRollOut() methods such that when the mouse rolls on and
// off the movie clip, it goes to 50% transparency and back.
rectangle_mc.onRollOver = function () {
  this._alpha = 50;
};

rectangle_mc.onRollOut = function () {
  this._alpha = 100;
};
```

```
// Create a circle_mc movie clip.
_root.createEmptyMovieClip("circle_mc", 2);
circle_mc.lineStyle(1, 0x000000, 100);
circle_mc.beginFill(0xFFFFFF, 100);
circle_mc.drawCircle(50);
circle_mc.endFill();

// Create onPress() and onRelease() methods such
// that circle_mc is draggable when clicked.
circle_mc.onPress = function () {
  this.startDrag();
};

circle_mc.onRelease = function () {
  this.stopDrag();
};
```

Testing this example reveals that mousing over the rectangle normally works just fine. But when you drag the circle over the rectangle, the *rectangle_mc.onRollOver()* event handler is not triggered.

The workaround is to use an *onEnterFrame()* method instead of *onRollOver()* and *onRollOut()* and check whether the mouse pointer's coordinates overlap the movie clip using *hitTest()*. You should use _root._xmouse and _root._ymouse as the x and y parameters for *hitTest()*.

```
// Include the DrawingMethods.as file from Chapter 4 for its drawRectangle() and
// drawCircle() methods.
#include "DrawingMethods.as"

_root.createEmptyMovieClip("rectangle_mc", 1);
rectangle_mc.lineStyle(1, 0x000000, 100);
rectangle_mc.beginFill(0, 100);
rectangle_mc.drawRectangle(100, 200, 10);
rectangle_mc.endFill();
rectangle_mc._x = 100;
rectangle_mc._y = 100;

// Use an onEnterFrame() method instead of onRollOver() and onRollOut().
rectangle_mc.onEnterFrame = function () {

  // Check whether the mouse pointer, at coords (_root._xmouse, _root._ymouse),
  // overlaps the movie clip using the hitTest() method. If it overlaps, set _alpha
  // to 50; otherwise, set _alpha to 100.
  if (this.hitTest(_root._xmouse, _root._ymouse)) {
    this._alpha = 50;
  } else {
    this._alpha = 100;
  }
};

_root.createEmptyMovieClip("circle_mc", 2);
circle_mc.lineStyle(1, 0x000000, 100);
```

```
circle_mc.beginFill(0xFFFFFF, 100);
circle_mc.drawCircle(50);
circle_mc.endFill( );

circle_mc.onPress = function ( ) {
  this.startDrag( );
};

circle_mc.onRelease = function ( ) {
  this.stopDrag( );
};
```

There is an additional issue that arises with this technique. In the preceding example code, the _alpha property is set to 50 continuously as long as the mouse pointer is over the movie clip, and it is set to 100 continuously as long as the mouse pointer is not over the movie clip. In this example this is not particularly a problem, but in some applications it is important that the code be executed only once on mouseover and once on mouseout. You can accomplish this task by the addition of a custom property and a little bit of extra logic, as shown by the bold text in the following example:

```
rectangle_mc.onEnterFrame = function ( ) {
  // Check whether the mouse pointer is over the movie clip and whether the custom
  // property, mouseover, is false. If both conditions are true, perform the
  // mouseover actions. Otherwise, if the mouse pointer is not over the movie clip
  // and the mouseover property is true, perform the mouseout actions.
  if (this.hitTest(_root._xmouse, _root._ymouse) && !this.mouseover) {
    trace("setting _alpha = 50");
    this._alpha = 50;

    // Set mouseover to true to prevent mouseover actions from executing again.
    this.mouseover = true;
  }
  else if (!this.hitTest(_root._xmouse, _root._ymouse) && this.mouseover) {
    trace("setting _alpha = 100");
    this._alpha = 100;

    // Set mouseover to false to prevent mouseout actions from executing again.
    this.mouseover = false;
  }
};
```

7.8   Performing Repeated Actions on Movie Clips

Problem

You want to perform a particular action on a movie clip repeatedly.

Solution

Use an *onEnterFrame()* event handler method or use *setInterval()*.

Discussion

Every movie clip's *onEnterFrame()* method is called repeatedly during a Flash movie's playback. If a movie clip's *onEnterFrame()* method is defined, any actions it contains are automatically invoked at the frequency of the movie's frame rate. For example, if a movie's frame rate is set to 12 frames per second, actions defined within a movie clip's *onEnterFrame()* method are invoked 12 times per second. Here is an example using *onEnterFrame()*, which shows that it is called at approximately the frame rate. You will notice that it is not exact. The precision to which the movie plays back at the correct frame rate depends on the computer's processor and what else is being processed at the same time as the Flash movie.

```
// Define an onEnterFrame() method for an existing movie clip named myMovieClip.
myMovieClip.onEnterFrame = function () {

  // Store the number of milliseconds since the movie started to play.
  var currentTime = getTimer();

  // Calculate the difference between the current time and the time of the previous
  // call to onEnterFrame(), which gives you the elapsed time between calls. The
  // first time through, prevTime is undefined.
  var timeElapse = currentTime - this.prevTime;

  // Display the timeElapse times 12 (or the movie's frame rate if it is not 12).
  // This will tell you how many milliseconds it takes for 12 calls to the
  // onEnterFrame() method. The output should generally be around 1000 milliseconds,
  // which means that the method is called 12 times per second.
  trace(timeElapse * 12);

  // Set prevTime to the current time. prevTime needs to be a property so that it is
  // accessible the next time onEnterFrame() is called. Local variables disappear
  // between calls to the method.
  this.prevTime = currentTime;
};
```

There are many useful things you can do using an *onEnterFrame()* method. For example, you can continuously animate a movie clip's position by adjusting its _x and/or _y properties:

```
// At the current frame rate, increment myMovieClip's _x and _y properties. This
// animates the movie clip slowly in a diagonal to the lower-right corner and
// eventually off the Stage.
myMovieClip.onEnterFrame = function () {
  this._x++;
  this._y++;
};
```

onEnterFrame()'s only limitation is that it is always called at the frame rate of the movie. If you want to create intervals that differ from the movie's frame rate, use the *setInterval()* function. If the screen updates should be more frequent than the frame rate, make sure to include a call to *updateAfterEvent()* at the end of your interval function.

```
function myIntervalFunction ( ) {
  myMovieClip._x++;
  updateAfterEvent( );
}

myMovieClipInterval = setInterval(myIntervalFunction, 10);
```

See Also

For more details on how to use *setInterval()*, see Recipe 1.7. To test a movie's frame rate, see the time-tracker tool at *http://www.moock.org/webdesign/flash/actionscript/ fps-speedometer*.

7.9   Fading a Movie Clip

Problem

You want to programmatically fade a movie clip.

Solution

Create a *fade()* method that uses the *onEnterFrame()* event handler method and the movie clip's _alpha property.

Discussion

You can set the value of a movie clip's _alpha property to adjust its transparency. Thus, if you want to set a movie clip's transparency to a single value, you can do so with a single statement such as:

```
// Set the movie clip's transparency to 50%.
myMovieClip._alpha = 50;
```

You can repeat this process to achieve a fading effect on the same movie clip. You should do this by placing the property assignment statement within the *onEnterFrame()* method of the movie clip:

```
// Repeatedly decrement the _alpha of the movie clip.
myMovieClip.onEnterFrame = function ( ) {
  this._alpha--;
};
```

The valid range for the _alpha property of a movie clip is from 0 (completely transparent) to 100 (fully opaque). However, because ActionScript allows you to set the value outside that range, use an *if* statement to safeguard against inappropriate values:

```
// Continuously decrement _alpha, provided it is greater than 0.
myMovieClip.onEnterFrame = function () {
  this._alpha--;
  if (this._alpha <= 0) {
    delete this.onEnterFrame;
  }
};
```

The preceding code works, but it is not completely efficient and has the potential for some minor errors. The reason is that the working range for _alpha is from 0 to 100, but internally Flash converts all the numbers to a range of 0 to 255. As a result, you can end up with incorrect values using the preceding technique. You can test this for yourself by adding a *trace()* statement to the code:

```
myMovieClip.onEnterFrame = function () {
  this._alpha--;
  trace(this._alpha);
  if (this._alpha <= 0) {
    delete this.onEnterFrame;
  }
};
```

Testing the example reveals that the _alpha value is not decremented by 1 each time, as you might expect, and the final result can be negative. To solve this problem, you can use another variable as an intermediary:

```
myMovieClip.onEnterFrame = function () {

  // Use alphaCount as an intermediate variable. If the value is undefined,
  // initialize it to 99; otherwise, decrement it by 1.
  this.alphaCount = (this.alphaCount == undefined) ? 99 : --this.alphaCount;

  // Assign the value of alphaCount to _alpha. The alphaCount value is always an
  // integer, which is what we want.
  this._alpha = this.alphaCount;
  if (this._alpha <= 0) {
    delete this.onEnterFrame;
  }
};
```

And, of course, you can do the reverse to fade up a movie clip:

```
myMovieClip.onEnterFrame = function () {

  // Use alphaCount as an intermediate variable. If the value is undefined,
  // initialize it to 0; otherwise, increment it by 1.
  this.alphaCount = (this.alphaCount == undefined) ? 0 : ++this.alphaCount;

  // Assign the value of alphaCount to _alpha. The alphaCount value is always an
  // integer, which is what we want.
```

```
    this._alpha = this.alphaCount;

    // Make sure the value does not exceed 100.
    if (this._alpha >= 100) {
      delete this.onEnterFrame;
    }
};
```

If you work with programmatically generated fades often, you should create a *fade()* method for all *MovieClip* objects and add it to a *MovieClip.as* file for easy inclusion in future projects. The method should accept two parameters:

rate

> The rate at which to increment or decrement the movie clip's _alpha property. In most cases, it should be from 1 to 20. If the value 0 is used, then no changes occur to the _alpha property.

up   A Boolean that indicates whether to fade up (if true) or fade down (if false).

Here is our custom *fade()* method:

```
MovieClip.prototype.fade = function (rate, up) {

    // Create a new, nested movie clip to monitor the fade progress. This avoids
    // interfering with any existing onEnterFrame() method applied to the movie clip.
    this.createEmptyMovieClip("fadeMonitor_mc", this.getNewDepth());

    // Define a new onEnterFrame() method for the monitor movie clip.
    this.fadeMonitor_mc.onEnterFrame = function () {

      // Set a Boolean property, isFading, so that other methods know if the movie clip
      // is being faded.
      this._parent.isFading = true;

      // Check whether the movie clip is being faded up or down.
      if (up) {
        // Use an intermediate property to determine the new alpha value.
        this.alphaCount = (this.alphaCount == undefined) ? 0 :
                           this.alphaCount + rate;

        // If the current _alpha of the clip is under 100, assign the new value;
        // otherwise, set the value to 100 and delete the onEnterFrame() method.
        if (this._parent._alpha < 100) {
          this._parent._alpha = this.alphaCount;
        } else {
          this._parent._alpha = 100;
          delete this.onEnterFrame;

          // Set isFading to false since the fade is completed.
          this._parent.isFading = false;
        }
      } else {
        // Use alphaCount as an intermediate property to determine the alpha value.
        this.alphaCount = (this.alphaCount == undefined) ? 100 :
                          this.alphaCount - rate;
```

```
      // If the current _alpha is greater than 0, assign the new value; otherwise,
      // set the value to 0 and delete the onEnterFrame() method.
      if (this._parent._alpha > 0) {
        this._parent._alpha = this.alphaCount;
      } else {
        this._parent._alpha = 0;
        delete this.onEnterFrame;

        // Set isFading to false since the fade is completed.
        this._parent.isFading = false;
      }
    }
  }
};
```

Here is an example that uses the custom *fade()* method to fade a movie clip from
total opacity to total transparency. This example does not demonstrate the ability of
the *fade()* method to incorporate an existing *onEnterFrame()* method.

```
// Include DrawingMethods.as from Chapter 4 for its drawCircle() method.
#include "DrawingMethods.as"
// Include MovieClip.as from this chapter for its custom fade() method.
#include "MovieClip.as"

// Draw a circle.
_root.createEmptyMovieClip("myMovieClip", 1);
myMovieClip.lineStyle(1, 0x000000, 100);
myMovieClip.drawCircle(100);

// Call fade() with a rate of 5. This fades the movie clip down in 20 frames.
myMovieClip.fade(5);
```

When you use the *fade()* method on a movie clip where you are also defining an
onEnterFrame() method, you must define the *onEnterFrame()* method before you
call *fade()*. Here is an example of how to use the *fade()* method in such a scenario:

```
_root.createEmptyMovieClip("myMovieClip", 1);
myMovieClip.lineStyle(1, 0x000000, 100);
myMovieClip.drawCircle(100);

// Set the _alpha property to 0 initially so that it can fade up from nothing.
myMovieClip._alpha = 0;

// Create an onEnterFrame() method that moves the movie clip.
myMovieClip.onEnterFrame = function () {
  this._x++;
  this._y++;
};

// Call fade() to fade up. Notice that the fade and the movement defined in the
// onEnterFrame() method work simultaneously. If the onEnterFrame() method is
// defined after the call to fade(), the fade() method does not work.
myMovieClip.fade(5, true);
```

7.10   Discovering Nested Movie Clips

Problem

You want to use ActionScript to retrieve an array of movie clip instances nested within a specific movie clip.

Solution

Use a *for...in* statement to loop through all the contents of the movie clip, and if the content is an instance of the *MovieClip* class (as indicated by the *instanceof* operator), add it to an array of the nested movie clips.

Discussion

Movie clips can be nested within other movie clips. A nested clip instance is stored as a property of its parent clip. Since movie clip instances are objects, you can access all the nested movie clips using a *for...in* statement. However, a basic *for...in* statement lists other properties in addition to nested movie clips. This example displays not only movie clips nested in _root, but also any timeline variables, functions, and the built-in $version variable:

```
for (var item in _root) {
  trace(item + ": " + _root[item]);
}
```

To separate nested movie clips from the rest of a clip's contents, you can use the *instanceof* operator to check if an item is an instance of the *MovieClip* class, as follows:

```
// The if statement disregards everything but movie clips.
for (var item in _root) {
  if (_root[item] instanceof MovieClip) {
    trace(item + ": " + _root[item]);
  }
}
```

You can also write a simple custom method for the *MovieClip* class that returns an array of nested movie clips:

```
MovieClip.prototype.getMovieClips = function () {

  // Define the array to contain the movie clip references.
  var mcs = new Array( );

  // Loop through all the contents of the movie clip.
  for (var i in this) {
    // Add any nested movie clips to the array.
    if (this[i] instanceof MovieClip) {
      mcs.push(this[i]);
    }
  }
```

```
      return mcs;
  };
```

Here is an example that uses the *getMovieClips()* method to display all the movie clips within _root:

```
trace(_root.getMovieClips());
```

Here is a version that recursively displays all movie clips in a tree:

```
MovieClip.prototype.showMovieClips = function () {
  // Loop through all the contents of the movie clip.
  for (var i in this) {
    // Add any nested movie clips to the array.
    if (this[i] instanceof MovieClip) {
      trace (this[i]);
      // Recursively call this function to show any nested clips
      this[i].showMovieClips();
    }
  }
};
// Example usage:
_root.showMovieClips();
```

See Also

Recipe 6.13

7.11 Getting Unique Depths

Problem

You want to easily ensure that you always get a unique depth when creating a new movie clip using *createEmptyMovieClip()*, *attachMovie()*, or *duplicateMovieClip()*.

Solution

Create and use a custom *MovieClip.getNewDepth()* method.

Discussion

Only one movie clip can exist at each depth within a parent clip, so if you specify an existing depth when using *createEmptyMovieClip()*, *attachMovie()*, or *duplicateMovieClip()*, the movie clip already on that depth is overwritten. Unless you want to overwrite an existing movie clip, you must always use a unique depth when using these methods.

ActionScript does not provide native support for generating a unique movie clip depth. You must keep track of all the used depths yourself. When you add only a few movie clips programmatically, this does not pose a problem; however, if you programmatically generate many movie clips, it becomes difficult to track which depths are already used. Fortunately, you can solve this problem easily with a few lines of code.

You can add a *getNewDepth()* method to the *MovieClip* class so that every movie clip inherits it, as shown in the following code block. The process is not complex. If the movie clip does not yet have a custom currentDepth property defined, we define it and initialize it to the value of 1. The value 1 is used because that is the first depth you want to assign to any programmatically generated nested movie clip in most cases. Once the method ensures that the currentDepth property exists, it returns that property's value and increments it by 1 so that the next time the method is called, a new depth value is returned.

```
MovieClip.prototype.getNewDepth = function () {
  // If no currentDepth is defined, initialize it to 1.
  if (this.currentDepth == undefined) {
    this.currentDepth = 1;
  }
  // Return the new depth and increment it by 1 for next time.
  return this.currentDepth++;
};
```

Here is an example of the *getNewDepth()* method being used:

```
// This assumes our custom getNewDepth() method is defined in MovieClip.as.
#include "MovieClip.as"

// Create two new movie clips in _root and assign them unique depths using the
// getNewDepth() method.
_root.createEmptyMovieClip("circle_mc", _root.getNewDepth());
_root.createEmptyMovieClip("square_mc", _root.getNewDepth());
```

The *getNewDepth()* method defaults the currentDepth property to a value of 1 when it is initialized. There are some cases in which you want to use depths starting below 1. For example, movie clips placed on the Stage at authoring time begin with a depth of −16383. You can programmatically create movie clips that appear below manually created movie clips if you assign them a depth less than −16383. You can still use the *getNewDepth()* method in these cases by assigning a value to the movie clip's currentDepth property before invoking *getNewDepth()*.

```
// Include MovieClip.as from this chapter and DrawingMethods.as from Chapter 4.
#include "MovieClip.as"
#include "DrawingMethods.as"

// Set the currentDepth property so that the next programmatically created movie clip
// can be made to appear below any manually created instance.
_root.currentDepth = -16384;

// Create a movie clip using getNewDepth() to retrieve a depth value. The value
// -16384 is used. Be aware that the value is then incremented to -16383, which is
// the depth of the first manually created instance.
_root.createEmptyMovieClip("circle_mc", _root.getNewDepth());
```

```
circle_mc.lineStyle(1, 0x000000, 0);
circle_mc.beginFill(0, 100);
circle_mc.drawCircle(100, 100, 100);
circle_mc.endFill( );
```

When you use this technique of setting the currentDepth property, be aware that it can overwrite manually created movie clips if you are not careful. For example, in the preceding code block, the depth of the circle_mc movie clip is −16384. The first manually created movie clip always has a depth of −16383; therefore, if you use *getNewDepth()* again and it assigns a depth of −16383, the new programmatic clip overwrites the first manually created clip in your movie. You can solve this dilemma by again setting the value of currentDepth. For example, the following code block programmatically creates a movie clip below any manually created instances. It then sets the currentDepth to 1 so that future programmatically created instances are placed above all manually created instances.

```
#include "MovieClip.as"

_root.currentDepth = -16384;
_root.createEmptyMovieClip("circle_mc", _root.getNewDepth( ));
_root.currentDepth = 1;
```

See Also

Recipe 7.16

7.12   Getting a Movie Clip's Boundaries

Problem

You want to know the minimum and maximum x and y coordinates that determine the edges of a movie clip (its bounding box).

Solution

Use the *getBounds()* method.

Discussion

You can determine the left, right, top, and bottom coordinates of a movie clip within its parent movie clip using a combination of the _x, _y, _width, and _height properties:

```
left   = myMovieClip._x;
right  = left + myMovieClip._width;
top    = myMovieClip._y;
bottom = top + myMovieClip._height;
```

While this technique works, it is rather intensive and inefficient when compared to the *getBounds()* method. The *getBounds()* method returns an object with four properties:

xMin

> The leftmost x coordinate of the movie clip

xMax

> The rightmost x coordinate of the movie clip

yMin

> The topmost y coordinate of the movie clip

yMax

> The bottommost y coordinate of the movie clip

The four properties define the bounding box of the visible content within the movie clip. (Note that y coordinates increase as you move down the screen, which is the opposite of the Cartesian coordinate system.) When you call *getBounds()* without parameters, it returns an object with values relative to the movie clip's coordinate system. You can also pass the method a reference to a target coordinate system (another movie clip) for which you want the returned object's values to be given:

```
// Include DrawingMethods.as from Chapter 4 for its drawCircle() method.
#include "DrawingMethods.as"

// Create a new movie clip and draw a circle in it.
_root.createEmptyMovieClip("circle_mc", 1);
circle_mc.lineStyle(1, 0x000000, 100);
circle_mc.drawCircle(100);

// Move the circle to (200,200) within _root.
circle_mc._x = 200;
circle_mc._y = 200;

// Get the bounds of the circle within circle_mc as well as relative to the _root
// coordinate space.
insideBounds = circle_mc.getBounds();
parentBounds = circle_mc.getBounds(_root);

// Loop through the bounds objects and list the values.
trace("inside bounds:");
for (var val in insideBounds) {
  trace(val + ": " + insideBounds[val]);
}

trace("parent bounds:");
for (var val in parentBounds) {
  trace(val + ": " + parentBounds[val]);
}

/* Output window shows:
inside bounds:
yMax: 101
```

```
yMin: -101
xMax: 101
xMin: -101
parent bounds:
yMax: 301
yMin: 99
xMax: 301
xMin: 99
*/
```

See Also

Recipe 7.17

7.13   Creating a Draggable Movie Clip

Problem

You want a user to be able to drag a movie clip with the mouse.

Solution

Use the *startDrag()* method.

Discussion

You can allow the user to drag any movie clip with the mouse by invoking the *startDrag()* method on the clip. When invoked without parameters, *startDrag()* moves the movie clip relative to the pointer at the moment the method was invoked (the clip moves with the pointer but maintains the same distance from the pointer). You can see this for yourself.

1. Place the following code on the first frame of the main timeline of a new Flash document:

   ```
   // Include DrawingMethods.as from Chapter 4 for its drawCircle() method.
   #include "DrawingMethods.as"

   // Create a movie clip and draw a circle in it.
   _root.createEmptyMovieClip("circle_mc", 1);
   circle_mc.lineStyle(1, 0x000000, 100);
   circle_mc.drawCircle(100);

   // Call the startDrag() method from circle_mc.
   circle_mc.startDrag();
   ```

2. Move the pointer so that it appears on the right side of the Player when you test it.

3. Test the movie. Notice that the movie clip moves with the pointer but always maintains the same distance.

The *startDrag()* method can be called with no parameters, as shown in the previous example. Optionally, you can also specify one Boolean parameter that explicitly tells the movie clip whether or not to snap to the mouse pointer:

```
_root.createEmptyMovieClip("circle_mc", 1);
circle_mc.lineStyle(1, 0x000000, 100);
circle_mc.drawCircle(100);

// Call the startDrag( ) method from circle_mc, passing it the value true. This will
// cause the movie clip to automatically snap to the pointer. This use of the
// startDrag( ) method can be useful for situations such as creating custom pointers
// (see Recipe 7.14).
circle_mc.startDrag(true);
```

Additionally, you can define a rectangular area within which the movie clip can be dragged by specifying values for the optional second through fifth parameters of the *startDrag()* method. The following is a complete list of possible parameters for *startDrag()*:

lockCenter
> If true, the movie clip snaps to the pointer; otherwise, the movie clip moves relative to its position to the pointer when the method was called.

left
> A number indicating the leftmost pixel value to which the movie clip can be dragged.

top
> A number indicating the topmost pixel value to which the movie clip can be dragged.

right
> A number indicating the rightmost pixel value to which the movie clip can be dragged.

bottom
> A number indicating the bottommost pixel value to which the movie clip can be dragged.

Here is an example that demonstrates the optional constraining feature of *startDrag()*:

```
// Create a new movie clip and draw a circle within it.
_root.createEmptyMovieClip("circle_mc", 1);
circle_mc.lineStyle(1, 0x000000, 100);
circle_mc.drawCircle(100);

// Create a new movie clip and draw a rectangle within it at (200,200).
_root.createEmptyMovieClip("rectangle_mc", 2);
rectangle_mc.lineStyle(1, 0x000000, 100);
rectangle_mc.drawRectangle(300, 300);
rectangle_mc._x = 200;
rectangle_mc._y = 200;
```

```
// Determine the bounding area within which the circle can be dragged. Figure it such
// that the circle never leaves the boundaries of the rectangle.
rb = rectangle_mc.getBounds(_root);
l = rb.xMin + circle_mc._width/2;
r = rb.xMax - circle_mc._width/2;
t = rb.yMin + circle_mc._width/2;
b = rb.yMax - circle_mc._width/2;

// Invoke startDrag() on circle_mc, telling it to snap circle_mc to the pointer and
// passing the bounding box limits within which circle_mc can be dragged.
circle_mc.startDrag(true, l, t, r, b);
```

The preceding code snippets show how to make a movie clip draggable from the beginning of playback. Another popular place for *startDrag()* is within an *onPress()* event handler method, where it makes a movie clip draggable as soon as it is clicked. To stop the clip from dragging when the user releases the mouse button, call *stopDrag()* from within the movie clip's *onRelease()* event handler method:

```
// Draw a filled circle movie clip.
_root.createEmptyMovieClip("circle_mc", 1);
circle_mc.lineStyle(1, 0x000000, 100);
circle_mc.beginFill(0, 100);
circle_mc.drawCircle(100);
circle_mc.endFill();

// When the user clicks anywhere on the circle, allow it to be dragged.
circle_mc.onPress = function () {
  this.startDrag();
};

// When the user releases the mouse button, stop the drag action. This drops the
// movie clip on the Stage wherever the user released the mouse button.
circle_mc.onRelease = function () {
  this.stopDrag();
};
```

7.14 Creating a Custom Mouse Pointer

Problem

You want to create a custom mouse pointer in place of the usual arrow or hand cursor.

Solution

Simulate a mouse pointer using a movie clip. Use a movie clip with an *onEnterFrame()* method to continually update its position to match the mouse pointer, and use *Mouse.hide()* to hide the standard pointer.

Discussion

You can effectively replace the mouse pointer with a custom movie clip using a simple, two-step technique. First, you should hide the default arrow pointer from view with the static method, *Mouse.hide()*. You saw in Recipe 7.13 how you can cause a movie clip to move with the pointer using the *startDrag()* method. It seems logical to use this approach to make a custom pointer movie clip follow the mouse movement on stage; however, only one movie clip can follow the mouse movement at one time using the *startDrag()* method. This limitation can cause problems if you want to use *startDrag()* for both a custom pointer and to implement drag-and-drop functionality. To avoid this conflict, use an *onEnterFrame()* method to continually update the custom pointer movie clip's position on stage so that it matches the built-in _xmouse and _ymouse properties of the clip's parent, as follows:

```
myCustomPointer.onEnterFrame = function ( ) {
  this._x = this._parent._xmouse;
  this._y = this._parent._ymouse;
};
```

Or, if you prefer, you can use the *setInterval()* technique in place of *onEnterFrame()* (see Recipe 7.8). Using *setInterval()* is advisable in situations in which the frame rate is too low to update the custom pointer position quickly enough.

```
function updatePointer (pointerClip) {
  pointerClip._x = pointerClip._parent._xmouse;
  pointerClip._y = pointerClip._parent._ymouse;
  updateAfterEvent( );
}

pointerInterval = setInterval(updatePointer, 10, mousePointer);
```

Follow these steps to replace the mouse pointer:

1. Create a movie clip instance to be used as the new mouse pointer. You should make sure the depth of the movie clip is higher than any other clip so that it does not disappear behind other movie clips on the Stage.

2. Define an *onEnterFrame()* method or an interval function that continually sets the _x and _y properties of the mouse pointer movie clip to the _xmouse and _ymouse values of its parent movie clip.

3. Call the *Mouse.hide()* method to hide the default pointer.

Let's create a simple working example. The following code creates a circle movie clip that uses the custom *fade()* method (see Recipe 7.9) to continually fade the circle in and out. Then, using an interval, Flash continually updates the position of the movie clip to follow the mouse movement. And to show that there is no conflict between the custom mouse pointer and draggable movie clips, we add a draggable square movie clip as well.

```
// Include DrawingMethods.as from Chapter 4 for its custom drawing methods. Include
// MovieClip.as from this chapter for its custom fade() method.
#include "DrawingMethods.as"
#include "MovieClip.as"

// Create a custom pointer movie clip with a depth of 10000 to ensure that it appears
// in front of all other movie clips on the Stage. In this example, draw a small
// filled circle in the movie clip.
_root.createEmptyMovieClip("mousePointer", 10000);
mousePointer.lineStyle(1, 0x000000, 100);
mousePointer.beginFill(0, 100);
mousePointer.drawCircle(9);
mousePointer.endFill();
// Add an onEnterFrame() method to mousePointer that causes the movie clip to
// continually fade up and down.
mousePointer.onEnterFrame = function () {

  // If the movie clip is not currently being faded, call fade().
  if (!this.isFading) {

    // Call fade() with a rate of 5 and with the value of property this.up. The
    // this.up property is a custom property created for this situation. At first,
    // this.up has the value undefined, which is like passing false to fade(). After
    // each call to fade(), toggle this.up so that it alternates between true and
    // false, causing the clip to fade up and down repeatedly.
    this.fade(5, this.up);
    this.up = !this.up;
  }
};

// Create an interval to update the position of the custom pointer movie clip.
function updatePointer (pointerClip) {
  pointerClip._x = pointerClip._parent._xmouse;
  pointerClip._y = pointerClip._parent._ymouse;

  // Use updateAfterEvent() to make sure that the screen updates often enough.
  updateAfterEvent();
}

// Set the interval on which updatePointer() is called.
pointerInterval = setInterval(updatePointer, 100, mousePointer);

// Hide the default pointer.
Mouse.hide();

// Create a square movie clip.
_root.createEmptyMovieClip("square_mc", 1);
square_mc.lineStyle(1, 0x000000, 100);
square_mc.beginFill(0, 0);
square_mc.drawRectangle(100, 100);
square_mc.endFill;

// Make the square draggable when clicked.
square_mc.onPress = function () {
```

```
    this.startDrag();
};
square_mc.onRelease = function () {
    this.stopDrag();
};
```

To show the default pointer again in place of the custom pointer, follow these steps:

1. Remove the custom pointer movie clip using *removeMovieClip()* or hide it by setting its _visible property to false:

    ```
    mousePointer._visible = false;
    ```

2. Call the *Mouse.show()* method:

    ```
    Mouse.show();
    ```

7.15 Checking for Overlapping Movie Clips (Performing Hit Tests)

Problem

You want to find out if two movie clips are overlapping.

Solution

Use the *hitTest()* method. Or, for testing collisions between two complex shapes, create and utilize a custom *hitTestOutline()* method.

Discussion

The *hitTest()* method enables you to determine one of three things:

- Whether any point within the bounding box of one movie clip overlaps any point in the bounding box of another movie clip
- Whether a specific coordinate is within the bounding box of a movie clip
- Whether a specific coordinate is within the outline of a movie clip's shape

The easiest way to test whether a movie clip overlaps another clip is to call *hitTest()* from one movie clip instance and pass it a reference to the other movie clip instance:

```
// Returns true if myMovieClipA overlaps myMovieClipB, and false otherwise. This
// tests whether the bounding boxes overlap. If the shapes are nonrectangular, this
// technique may not be appropriate.
myMovieClipA.hitTest(myMovieClipB);
```

Here is a working example that draws a circle and a rectangle. Then, using the *startDrag()* method, the code causes the circle movie clip to follow the pointer. Using an *onEnterFrame()* method in conjunction with *hitTest()*, the code continually checks whether the circle overlaps the rectangle. If you test the example, you can see that there are times when the hit test returns true even though the circle shape does not overlap the rectangle. This is because the circle's bounding box might overlap with the rectangle even though its outline does not.

```
// Include DrawingMethods.as from Chapter 4 for its custom drawing methods.
#include "DrawingMethods.as"

// Draw a circle.
_root.createEmptyMovieClip("circle_mc", 1);
circle_mc.lineStyle(1, 0x000000, 100);
circle_mc.drawCircle(20);

// Draw a rectangle and position it at (200,200).
_root.createEmptyMovieClip("rectangle_mc", 2);
rectangle_mc.lineStyle(1, 0x000000, 100);
rectangle_mc.drawRectangle(100, 100);
rectangle_mc._x = 200;
rectangle_mc._y = 200;

// Tell the circle to snap to the pointer and follow it around.
circle_mc.startDrag(true);

// Use an onEnterFrame() method to continually check hitTest()'s value.
circle_mc.onEnterFrame = function () {
  // Use trace() to output the value of the hit test.
  trace(this.hitTest(_root.rectangle_mc));
};
```

Another way to use *hitTest()* is to check whether a coordinate is within the bounding box of the movie clip. When you use *hitTest()* in this way, you do not need to specify another movie clip instance, just the x and y coordinates against which you wish to test. Additionally, you should set the third, *shapeFlag* parameter to false to let *hitTest()* know you want to perform a test on the bounding box of the movie clip and not its outline. Here is an example that checks to see if the coordinates of the mouse pointer are within a rectangle:

```
// Include DrawingMethods.as from Chapter 4 for its drawRectangle() method.
#include "DrawingMethods.as"

_root.createEmptyMovieClip("rectangle_mc", 1);
rectangle_mc.lineStyle(1, 0x000000, 100);
rectangle_mc.drawRectangle(100, 100);
rectangle_mc._x = 200;
rectangle_mc._y = 200;

rectangle_mc.onEnterFrame = function () {
  // Perform a hit test using the _xmouse and _ymouse properties of _root. This will
  // test true if the mouse pointer is over the rectangle and false otherwise.
  trace(this.hitTest(_root._xmouse, _root._ymouse, false));
};
```

If you want to test whether coordinates are within a movie clip's shape instead of simply testing for hits within the bounding box, use the same basic technique as shown in the preceding example but set the *shapeFlag* parameter to true. This is great for testing to see if a coordinate is within a complex (nonrectangular) shape. Here is an example that does just that:

```
// Include DrawingMethods.as from Chapter 4 for its drawCircle() method.
#include "DrawingMethods.as"

_root.createEmptyMovieClip("circle_mc", 1);
circle_mc.lineStyle(1, 0x000000, 100);
circle_mc.drawCircle(60);
circle_mc._x = 200;
circle_mc._y = 200;

circle_mc.onEnterFrame = function () {
  trace(this.hitTest(_root._xmouse, _root._ymouse, true));
};
```

 All hit tests are performed using global coordinates—i.e., coordinates within the _root object's coordinate system.

Notice that in the preceding example, the mouse pointer coordinates were obtained using the _xmouse and _ymouse properties of _root. You would not get the same results if you used the mouse pointer coordinates relative to the rectangle or circle clips. This is important to understand in situations in which you want to test to see if a coordinate within one movie clip is overlapping another movie clip. In these cases you need to convert the local coordinates to global coordinates using the *localToGlobal()* method and test using the resulting values. The following example demonstrates this:

```
// Include DrawingMethods.as from Chapter 4 for its drawCircle() method.
#include "DrawingMethods.as"

// Draw a filled circle and position it at (200,200).
_root.createEmptyMovieClip("staticCircle_mc", 2);
staticCircle_mc.lineStyle(1, 0x000000, 100);
staticCircle_mc.beginFill(0xFF, 33);
staticCircle_mc.drawCircle(100);
staticCircle_mc.endFill();
staticCircle_mc._x = 200;
staticCircle_mc._y = 200;

// Create a movie clip that will follow the mouse pointer. Inside that movie clip,
// create a nested movie clip and draw a small circle in it.
_root.createEmptyMovieClip("bouncingCircleHolder", 1);
bouncingCircleHolder.createEmptyMovieClip("bouncingCircle_mc", 1);
bouncingCircleHolder.bouncingCircle_mc.lineStyle(1, 0, 100);
bouncingCircleHolder.bouncingCircle_mc.drawCircle(3);
```

```
// Tell the bouncingCircle_mc movie clip to move back and forth within the
// bouncingCircleHolder movie clip.
bouncingCircleHolder.bouncingCircle_mc.velocity = 3;
bouncingCircleHolder.bouncingCircle_mc.onEnterFrame = function () {

  // Change the x position of bouncingCircle_mc by the velocity.
  this._x += this.velocity;

  // If the x position is outside of the range of -30 to 30, then reverse the
  // velocity so that it begins moving back in the opposite direction.
  if (this._x < -30 || this._x > 30) {
    this.velocity *= -1;
  }

  // Create a point object for use with the localToGlobal() method. Assign it the x
  // and y values from bouncingCircle_mc.
  var pnts = {x: this._x, y: this._y};

  // Use localToGlobal() to convert the points' object values
  // to their global equivalents.
  this._parent.localToGlobal(pnts);

  // Output the hit test results for staticCircle_mc within the coordinates of
  // bouncingCircle_mc (as they have been converted to their global equivalents).
  trace(_root.staticCircle_mc.hitTest(pnts.x, pnts.y, true));
};

// Instruct the boundingCircleHolder movie clip to follow the mouse pointer.
bouncingCircleHolder.startDrag(true);
```

In the preceding example, you cannot get accurate results by simply performing a hit test between staticCircle_mc and bouncingCircle_mc. This is because such a hit test would be performed between the bounding boxes of the two movie clips, and they are each circles. Notice, however, that while this example works more or less when bouncingCircle_mc is relatively small, a larger version would not produce very accurate results. The reason for this is that the hit test is being performed between staticCircle_mc and the center point of bouncingCircle_mc, not the entire bouncingCircle_mc shape.

ActionScript does not provide a simple way to perform a hit test between two circles. However, you can perform such a test by checking whether the centers of the circles are within a distance that is less than the sum of their radii, as shown in the following example (see Recipe 5.13 for more information):

```
// Include DrawingMethods.as from Chapter 4 for its drawCircle() method.
#include "DrawingMethods.as"

// Create two circle movie clips: circle0 and circle1.
_root.createEmptyMovieClip("circle0", 1);
circle0.lineStyle(1, 0x000000, 100);
circle0.drawCircle(60);
circle0._x = 200;
circle0._y = 200;
```

```
_root.createEmptyMovieClip("circle1", 2);
circle1.lineStyle(1, 0x000000, 100);
circle1.drawCircle(60);
circle1.startDrag(true);

// Continually check to see if the circles overlap.
circle1.onEnterFrame = function () {

  // Find the difference in x and y coordinates between
  // the centers of the two circles.
  var dx = circle0._x - this._x;
  var dy = circle0._y - this._y;

  // Calculate the distance between the centers of the two circles.
  var dist = Math.sqrt(Math.pow(dx, 2) + Math.pow(dy, 2));

  // If the distance between the centers is less than the sum of
  // the two radii, the circles overlap.
  if (dist < (circle0._width + this._width)/2) {
    trace("circles touching");
  }
};
```

There is no trivial way to perform hit tests between two complex shapes in Action-Script. However, it can be done with a little bit of work. The premise is that while you cannot use *hitTest()* to test only the shapes of two movie clips (and not their bounding boxes), you can mimic this by performing a shape-sensitive hit test between one of the objects and a series of movie clips that outline the shape of the other. Traditionally, people have accomplished this by creating a series of small, circle movie clips around the outline of one of the shapes at authoring time. However, you can do even better than that. The following code illustrates how to create a series of small circles to outline a shape at runtime and how to use them to perform a hit test between two complex movie clips:

```
// Include DrawingMethods.as from Chapter 4 for its drawCircle() method.
#include "DrawingMethods.as"

// The outline() method creates a series of small circles within the movie clip that
// outline the shape. The optional circleRadius parameter defines the radii of the
// circles. The smaller the circles, the more accurate the hit test, but it is also
// more processor-intensive. The optional show parameter allows you to show the
// circles for testing purposes.
MovieClip.prototype.outline = function (circleRadius, show) {
  // Use a default radius of 3 pixels.
  if (circleRadius == undefined) {
    circleRadius = 3;
  }

  // Create an array for holding the references to the outline circles.
  this.outlines = new Array();
```

```
// Get the coordinates of the bounding box and set the x and y variables
// accordingly. The x variable must be more than the minimum x boundary because
// otherwise the method will not be able to locate the shape.
var bounds = this.getBounds(this);
var x = bounds.xMin + circleRadius;
var y = bounds.yMin;

// Begin by outlining the shape from the top-left corner
// and moving to the right as x increases.
var dir = "incX";
goodToGo = true;
var pnts;
var i = 0;

// The goodToGo variable is true until the last circle is drawn.
while (goodToGo) {
  i++;

  // Create the new circle outline movie clip and draw a circle in it.
  this.createEmptyMovieClip("outline" + i, i);
  var mc = this["outline" + i];
  mc.lineStyle(0, 0x0000FF, 100);
  mc.drawCircle(circleRadius);

  // Set the circle visibility to false unless show is true.
  mc._visible = show ? true : false;

  // Add the circle movie clip to the outlines array for use during the hit test.
  this.outlines.push(mc);

  // Check to see in which direction the outline is being drawn.
  switch (dir) {
    case "incX":

      // Increment the x value by the width of one of the circles to move the next
      // circle just to the right of the previous one.
      x += mc._width;

      // Create a point object and call localToGlobal( ) to convert the values to
      // the global equivalents.
      pnts = {x: x, y: y};
      this.localToGlobal(pnts);

      // If the center of the circle does not touch the shape within the movie
      // clip, increment y and calculate the new global equivalents for another hit
      // test. This moves the circle down until it touches the shape.
      while (!this.hitTest(pnts.x, pnts.y, true)) {
        y += mc._width;
        pnts = {x: x, y: y};
        this.localToGlobal(pnts);
      }
```

```
// If the maximum x boundary has been reached, set the new direction to begin
// moving in the increasing y direction.
if (x >= bounds.xMax - (mc._width)) {
  dir = "incY";
}

// Set the coordinates of the circle movie clip.
mc._x = x;
mc._y = y;

// Reset y to the minimum y boundary so that you can move the next circle
// down from the top until it touches the shape.
y = bounds.yMin;
break;

case "incY":
  // The remaining cases are much like the first, but they move in different
  // directions.
  y += mc._width;
  pnts = {x: x, y: y};
  this.localToGlobal(pnts);
  while (!this.hitTest(pnts.x, pnts.y, true)) {
    x -= mc._width;
    pnts = {x: x, y: y};
    this.localToGlobal(pnts);
  }
  if (y >= bounds.yMax - (mc._width)) {
    dir = "decX";
  }
  mc._x = x;
  mc._y = y;
  x = bounds.xMax;
  break;

case "decX":
  x -= mc._width;
  pnts = {x: x, y: y};
  this.localToGlobal(pnts);
  while (!this.hitTest(pnts.x, pnts.y, true)) {
    y -= mc._width;
    pnts = {x: x, y: y};
    this.localToGlobal(pnts);
  }
  if (x <= bounds.xMin + (mc._width)) {
    dir = "decY";
  }
  mc._x = x;
  mc._y = y;
  y = bounds.yMax;
  break;

case "decY":
  y -= mc._width;
  pnts = {x: x, y: y};
```

```
            this.localToGlobal(pnts);
            while (!this.hitTest(pnts.x, pnts.y, true)) {
              x += mc._width;
              pnts = {x: x, y: y};
              this.localToGlobal(pnts);
            }
            if (y <= bounds.yMin + (mc._width)) {
              goodToGo = false;
            }
            mc._x = x;
            mc._y = y;
            x = bounds.xMin;
            break;
        }
    }
};

// Perform a hit test between a movie clip with outline circles and another movie
// clip you specify in the parameter.
MovieClip.prototype.hitTestOutline = function (mc) {

  // Loop through all the elements of the outlines array.
  for (var i = 0; i < this.outlines.length; i++) {

    // Create a point object and get the global equivalents.
    var pnts = {x:this.outlines[i]._x, y:this.outlines[i]._y};
    this.localToGlobal(pnts);

    // If the mc movie clip tests true for overlapping with any of the outline
    // circles, then return true. Otherwise, the method returns false.
    if (mc.hitTest(pnts.x, pnts.y, true)) {
      return true;
    }
  }
  return false;
};

// In this example, create two movie clips with complex shapes. Create instances
// named mc1 and mc2. This code creates an outline on mc1 (and for testing purposes
// it shows you the circles).
mc1.outline(3, true);

// Continually perform a hit test between the two shapes. The hitTestOutline() method
// must be invoked from the movie clip with the outlines.
mc1.onEnterFrame = function () {
  trace(this.hitTestOutline(mc2));
};

// Tell mc2 to follow the mouse pointer.
mc2.startDrag(true);
```

See Also

Recipes 7.6 and 7.17

7.16 Changing Stacking Order

Problem

You want to swap the depths of two movie clips.

Solution

Use the *swapDepths()* method.

Discussion

The *swapDepths()* method swaps the depths of any two movie clips. You should call it from one of the two movie clips and pass it a reference to the other:

```
myMovieClip1.swapDepths(myMovieClip2);
```

One way in which this method is particularly useful is in swapping the depths of two movie clips when *hitTest()* detects that one overlaps the other. The following example uses this concept but also illustrates the problem that can occur when trying to use this technique.

 The following example shows a white circle and a black circle that overlap and rapidly change depths. The result is a very fast blinking effect, which may be induce seizures in readers prone to epilepsy or may induce nausea in sensitive viewers. Please exercise caution.

The following code swaps two clips' depths when they overlap:

```
// Include DrawingMethods.as from Chapter 4 for its drawCircle() method.
#include "DrawingMethods.as"

// Draw two circle movie clips: one black and one white.
_root.createEmptyMovieClip("circle1", 1);
circle1.lineStyle(1, 0x000000, 100);
circle1.beginFill(0xFFFFFF, 100);
circle1.drawCircle(100);
circle1.endFill();

_root.createEmptyMovieClip("circle2", 2);
circle2.lineStyle(1, 0x000000, 100);
circle2.beginFill(0, 100);
circle2.drawCircle(100);
circle2.endFill();
```

```
// Set each movie clip to be on the visible part of the Stage.
circle1._x = circle2._x = 200;
circle1._y = circle2._y = 200;

// Make each movie clip draggable when clicked.
circle1.onPress = function () {
  this.startDrag();
};

circle1.onRelease = function () {
  this.stopDrag();
};

circle2.onPress = function () {
  this.startDrag();
};

circle2.onRelease = function () {
  this.stopDrag();
};

// Continually check to see if circle1 and circle2 overlap. If so, call the
// swapDepths() method to switch their depths.
_root.onEnterFrame = function () {
  if (circle1.hitTest(circle2)) {
    circle1.swapDepths(circle2);
  }
};
```

As you can see, the depths swap back and forth over and over. You need to add more logic to the code to instruct the movie how to perform a more intelligent swap. The basic process is that the *onEnterFrame()* method needs to know which movie clip should remain on top, and it should perform that swap only if the movie clip is not already on top. Here is how you can rewrite the previous code to fix the problem (changes are shown in bold).

```
...
circle1.onPress = function () {
  this.startDrag();

  // Set a dragged property in _root, so _root knows that
  //   circle1 is being dragged. And set a nondragged property in _root,
  // so _root knows that circle2 is not being dragged.
  _root.dragged = this;
  _root.nondragged = _root.circle2;
};

circle1.onRelease = function () {
  this.stopDrag();
};

circle2.onPress = function () {
  this.startDrag();
```

```
// Set the dragged and nondragged properties as before, but with the values
// reversed from when circle1 was being dragged.
_root.dragged = this;
_root.nondragged = _root.circle1;
};

circle2.onRelease = function ( ) {
  this.stopDrag( );
};

_root.onEnterFrame = function ( ) {

  // Now check to see if the two movie clips are overlapping and see if the dragged
  // movie clip is below the nondragged movie clip. If so, swap them.
  if (this.dragged.hitTest(this.nondragged) &&
      this.dragged.getDepth( ) < this.nondragged.getDepth( )) {
    this.dragged.swapDepths(this.nondragged);
  }
};
```

See Also

Recipe 7.11

7.17 Converting Between Coordinate Spaces

Problem

You want to convert between the movie clip's coordinate space and the Stage's coordinate space, or vice versa.

Solution

Create a point object and use *localToGlobal( )* or *globalToLocal( )*.

Discussion

The most common reason for needing to convert coordinates from one coordinate space to another is to perform hit tests (see Recipe 7.15). But regardless of why you want to perform the coordinate conversions, you can quickly accomplish your task using the *localToGlobal( )* and *globalToLocal( )* methods. Each method requires you to first create a *point object*. A point object is an instance of the *Object* class with x and y properties set to the x and y coordinates of the point of interest.

You can define a point object using an object literal. For example:

```
pnts = {x: 24, y:42};
```

If the point object represents a point in the global coordinate system that you want to convert to the local equivalent, you should use the *globalToLocal()* method and invoke it from the target movie clip:

```
localMovieClip.globalToLocal(pnts);
```

If you want to convert a local point to a point in the global coordinate system, you should use the *localToGlobal()* method instead:

```
localMovieClip.localToGlobal(pnts);
```

See Also

Recipe 7.15

7.18   Duplicating Movie Clips

Problem

You have an existing movie clip on the Stage and you want to create duplicates of it.

Solution

Use the *duplicateMovieClip()* method.

Discussion

You can create a duplicate of any existing movie clip (except _root) by calling the *duplicateMovieClip()* method from it. The duplicate movie clip is created within the same timeline as the original, and it inherits all the settings of standard movie clip properties (such as _x, _y, _rotation, etc.) as well as *onClipEvent()* handlers from the original clip. While the duplicated movie clip does not inherit any custom properties or any event handler methods from the original, you can use an initialization object to copy properties to the new object (see Recipe 7.19). The *duplicateMovieClip()* method requires at least two parameters: the name and depth of the new movie clip.

```
// This example creates a new movie clip named myDupMovieClip1 at depth 1. The new
// movie clip is a copy of myMovieClip and resides on the same timeline.
myMovieClip.duplicateMovieClip("myDupMovieClip1", 1);

// This example creates a movie clip named myDupMovieClip2 with a depth of 2. It is
// initialized such that the _x property is set to 20.
myMovieClip.duplicateMovieClip("myDupMovieClip2", 2, {_x: 20});
```

When you use *duplicateMovieClip()*, you often want to create slightly customized duplicates. In other words, all the duplicates share the same basic core but might be customized with various color settings, etc. For example, you might want to create 30 duplicates of a balloon movie clip, positioning each at random points on the

Stage. A basic *for* statement can be useful when creating the duplicates. Also, though this aspect is undocumented, the method returns a reference to the duplicate movie clip, which can be useful in many situations.

```
// Use a for statement to loop 30 times.
for (var i = 0; i < 30; i++) {

    // Generate random x and y coordinates.
    x = Math.random( ) * 550;
    y = Math.random( ) * 400;

    // Create the duplicate movie clip with names balloon0, balloon1, etc. from the
    // original movie clip named balloonBase_mc. Each duplicate is positioned randomly
    // using the init object. The returned reference to the new movie clip is assigned
    // to the variable balloonDuplicate.
    balloonDuplicate = balloonBase_mc.duplicateMovieClip("balloon" + i, i,
                            {_x: x, _y: y});

    // Create a Color object to control the new movie clip. Assign it to a custom
    // property of the new movie clip so that you can differentiate easily between
    // Color objects.
    balloonDuplicate.col = new Color(balloonDuplicate);

    // Set the RGB for the new movie clip to a random number.
    balloonDuplicate.col.setRGB(Math.random( ) * 255 * 255 * 255);
}
```

Even though the *duplicateMovieClip()* method does not apply custom properties and methods (including event handler methods) to the new movie clip, there is a technique that you can use as a short workaround. When you use a *for...in* statement to loop through all the properties of a movie clip, only custom properties and methods show up. Therefore, you can use a *for...in* loop to create an initialization object to pass to the *duplicateMovieClip()* method:

```
// Create an initialization object with the Object constructor, then use a for...in
// loop to create elements within the initialization object that correspond to the
// elements within the original movie clip.
init = new Object( );
for (var item in myMovieClip) {
    init[item] = myMovieClip[item];
}

// Call duplicateMovieClip( ) to create a new movie clip that inherits the standard
// properties (as do all duplicated movie clips) and the custom properties and
// methods by way of the initialization object.
myMovieClip.duplicateMovieClip("myDupMovieClip2", 2, init);
```

See Also

Recipe 7.19

7.19   Adding Movie Clips from the Library with ActionScript

Problem

You want to add a movie clip to your movie from the library without having to create an instance manually at authoring time.

Solution

Use the *attachMovie()* method.

Discussion

You should make a practice of using the *attachMovie()* method to add movie clips to your movies for any instances that are controlled entirely by ActionScript. The *attachMovie()* method allows you to add a movie clip using ActionScript at runtime instead of having to add the movie clip manually at authoring time. This is advantageous for several reasons, including:

- With *attachMovie()*, you can add movie clips dynamically. This is extremely important for any movies in which you need to load movie clips based on user information or data drawn from an XML file or a database.

- It is bad practice to add movie clips to the Stage at authoring time that will be controlled exclusively by ActionScript. Don't add movie clips to your Stage at authoring time unless they are being manually animated or you need to visually lay them out.

To use *attachMovie()*, you must export the movie clip Library symbols. Library symbols are automatically exported with the movie when you create instances of them at authoring time. However, if a symbol is not explicitly used within the movie as a manually created instance, it is not automatically included in the *.swf* file (this saves space by not including unused symbols). In these cases, you need to tell Flash to export the symbol so that you can use it from ActionScript at runtime. To do this, follow these steps:

1. Select a Library symbol and open the Linkage properties from the Library panel's pop-up Options menu.

2. In the Linkage Properties dialog box, select the Export for ActionScript and Export in First Frame checkboxes (see Figure 7-1).

3. You should also give the symbol a *linkage identifier*. The linkage identifier is the name that you use with the *attachMovie()* method. Give the symbol a linkage identifier that is descriptive, so it is easier to remember. As a best practice, you

should give your symbols linkage identifiers that end with `Symbol`. For example, `largeCircleSymbol` is a much better identifier than `Symbol 1`.

4. Click on OK to close the Linkage Properties dialog box.

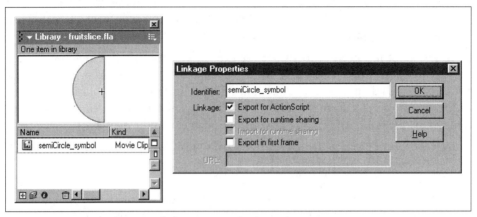

Figure 7-1. Setting a Library symbol's properties for ActionScript access

Figure 7-1 shows a Library symbol with its symbol linkage identifier set to "semiCircle_symbol" in the Linkage Properties dialog box (accessible from the Library panel's Options pop-up menu).

The preceding steps explain what is perhaps the most common way of exporting movie clip symbols for use at runtime. If you are creating a movie that will be distributed on a CD-ROM or other non-Internet-based medium, or if you will require that the user download the entire movie prior to beginning playback (i.e., a nonstreaming movie) then the preceding technique will work perfectly for you. However, because the technique exports all the movie clips on the first frame of the movie, it can cause a long initial wait for movies that are intended to stream. In these cases, you can modify the technique slightly so that the movie clips are not exported on the first frame, but instead on the frames where they are used. To do this, follow these steps:

1. Select a Library symbol and open the Linkage properties from the Library panel's pop-up Options menu.

2. In the Linkage Properties dialog box, select the Export for ActionScript checkbox.

3. Uncheck the Export in First Frame checkbox. You deselect this option because you will manually export the movie clip at the appropriate frame.

4. Give the symbol a linkage identifier.

5. Click on OK to close the Linkage Properties dialog box.

6. On the timeline on which you wish to attach the movie clip, create a new layer named *Exported Clips* and create a new keyframe on the frame where you want to attach the movie clip.

7. Create an instance of the movie clip symbol on the keyframe from Step 6. You don't need to name the instance. And, typically, you will want to create the instance off stage and/or set the _alpha property to 0.

Once a symbol has been properly set for export, you can use ActionScript to add instances to the movie. You can call the *attachMovie()* method from any existing movie clip, including _root. The method adds an instance of the Library symbol within the movie clip from which it is called. The method requires at least three parameters: the linkage name, the new instance name, and the depth.

```
// Create an instance of the largeCircleSymbol symbol. The new movie clip is named
// myCircle1, and it has a depth of 1.
_root.attachMovie("largeCircleSymbol", "myCircle1", 1);

// Once the instance has been created, you can do anything with it that you can do
// with any other movie clip. For example, here myCircle1 is moved to x = 120.
myCircle1._x = 120;
```

The *attachMovie()* method also allows for a fourth, optional parameter: an initialization object. The initialization object should be an instance of the *Object* class (whether created with the constructor or as an object literal), and the properties of that object are then applied to the new movie clip. This is a convenient way to initialize a movie clip. It is possible to accomplish the same task without the initialization object, but in most cases it is easier to use the initialization object.

```
// This one line of code accomplishes the same task as the two lines of code in the
// previous code block.
_root.attachMovie("largeCircleSymbol", "myCircle1", 1, {_x: 120});
```

The initialization object is most useful when you want to initialize multiple properties within the new movie clip:

```
// In this example four properties are initialized after creating the new movie clip.
// This requires five lines total.
_root.attachMovie("largeCircleSymbol", "myCircle1", 1);
myCircle1._x = 120;
myCircle1._y = 90;
myCircle1._xscale = 50;
myCircle1._yscale = 50;

// You can accomplish the same task with fewer lines using the initialization object.
_root.attachMovie("largeCircleSymbol", "myCircle1", 1,
                  {_x: 120, _y: 90, _xscale: 50, _yscale: 50});
```

You can use *attachMovie()* to create dynamically named movie clips. This is particularly useful when you want to create movie clips with sequential names, such as mc0, mc1, mc2, and so on.

```
// This for statement creates 10 instances of largeCircleSymbol
// and names them mc0 through mc9.
for (var i = 0; i < 10; i++) {
  _root.attachMovie("largeCircleSymbol", "mc" + i,  i, {_x: i*20, _y: i*20});
}
```

The *attachMovie()* method also returns a reference to the movie clip it creates. This can be useful in cases where you use *attachMovie()* to create movie clips with dynamic names. For example, you might use the contents of an XML document to dynamically create button movie clips in your movie, in which the buttons are named in sequence, such as myButton0, myButton1, myButton2, etc:

```
/* This example shows the onLoad() method of an XML object that loads the following
   document:
   <navigation>
     <button label="Housewares" categoryId="12" />
     <button label="Books" categoryId="99" />
     <button label="Electronics" categoryId="63" />
     <button label="Software" categoryId="24" />
     <button label="Furniture" categoryId="42" />
   </navigation>

   The attachMovie() method returns a reference to the movie clip that it creates. In
   this example, it is assigned to the variable btn. Without the use of the btn
   reference, the subsequent lines of code would have to substitute
   _root["myButton" + i] in place of btn.
*/
myXML.onLoad = function () {
  var categories = this.firstChild.childNodes;
  var btn;
  for (var i = 0; i < categories.length; i++) {
    btn = _root.attachMovie("FPushButtonSymbol", "myButton" + i,  i);
    btn.label  = categories[i].attributes.label;
    btn._y = i * 25;
    btn.onRelease = function () {
      trace(this.label);
    };
  }
};
```

The preceding example is more useful with Flash 5 movies than with later versions of Flash because you can use the initialization object to accomplish the same task since its availability in Flash MX. You can even use the initialization object to assign methods to a movie clip created with *attachMovie()*!

```
// Here is the previous example rewritten to use an initialization object.
myXML.onLoad = function () {
  var categories = this.firstChild.childNodes;

  // Create a variable, init, to be the initialization object.
  var init;
  for (var i = 0; i < categories.length; i++) {
```

```
// For each element from the XML document, create a new initialization object
// using the Object class constructor. Then, assign to init all the properties
// (and methods) you want assigned to the new movie clip.
init = new Object();
init.label  = categories[i].attributes.label;
init._y = i * 25;
init.onRelease = function () {
  trace(this.label);
};

// Call attachMovie( ) and pass it init.
_root.attachMovie("FPushButtonSymbol", "myButton" + i,  i, init);
  }
};
```

## CHAPTER 8

Text

8.0 Introduction

Flash MX introduces a rich ActionScript API for working with text in movies. Prior versions didn't allow much more than being able to control the value displayed in manually created text fields.

The *TextField* class is used to create and manipulate text at runtime (though the text itself can be created either at runtime or authoring time). Through methods and properties of a text field you can alter text visibility, change the position of the text within the movie, enable user input, and much more. In addition, there are two "helper" classes—*TextFormat* and *Selection*—that play a supporting role. *TextFormat* objects are used to apply formatting options such as font, font size, indentation, and margins to text fields. The *Selection* object allows programmatic control over keyboard focus and is helpful for selecting and deselecting text fields and the text within them.

Text fields share similar properties with *MovieClip* and *Button* objects to control an object's position, rotation, and visibility, plus others shown in Table 8-1 (for a complete list of *TextField* properties, refer to the online help under Help → ActionScript Dictionary).

Table 8-1. TextField graphical display properties

Property	Description
_x	x coordinate of the text field relative to its parent
_y	y coordinate of the text field relative to its parent
_width	Width of the text field in pixels
_height	Height of the text field in pixels
_xscale	Horizontal scale of the text field as a percentage
_yscale	Vertical scale of the text field as a percentage
_alpha	Transparency of the text field (range of 0 to 100)

Table 8-1. TextField graphical display properties (continued)

Property	Description
_visible	Visibility of the text field object (`true` or `false`)
_rotation	Clockwise rotation of the text field in degrees
_xmouse	The cursor's x coordinate relative to the text field's coordinate system
_ymouse	The cursor's y coordinate relative to the text field's coordinate system

8.1   Referring to a Text Field via ActionScript

Problem

You want to refer to a text field via ActionScript.

Solution

Refer to author-time text fields by their instance names.

Discussion

Many of the recipes in this chapter require you to access a text field's methods or properties. Sometimes text fields are created at runtime via ActionScript, but often you'll want to adapt a recipe to work with your author-time content.

ActionScript refers to author-time text fields using the text field instance name, which must be set, as follows:

1. Select the text field instance on the Stage.

2. Open the Property inspector.

3. Change the text field's type from "Static Text" to "Dynamic Text" (change it to "Input Text" if you want to allow user input at runtime).

4. Specify an instance name in the Property inspector (the instance name field appears once you complete Step 3).

See Also

To refer to a text field created at runtime, use the *TextField* instance returned by *MovieClip.createTextField()*, as demonstrated in Recipe 8.2. For details on creating editable text fields, see Recipe 8.5.

8.2 Creating a Text Field

Problem

You want to create a text field at runtime that you can use in your Flash movie.

Solution

You can create a text field using the *MovieClip.createTextField()* method.

Discussion

You can create a text field at authoring time using Flash's Text tool. Manual creation lets you see the layout of the objects on the Stage. However, many projects benefit from creating text fields dynamically. For example:

- An animation with randomized text elements
- A user interface in which items (and their labels) are created dynamically based on data loaded into the movie from a text file, XML document, or other source
- A form that automatically adapts to a user's input
- Word games

The *MovieClip.createTextField()* method creates a text field at runtime. Note that the *createTextField()* method is invoked on a *MovieClip* object, not a text field. (If we had a text field already, we wouldn't need the recipe, now would we?)

The *createTextField()* method takes six required parameters:

```
parentMovieClip.createTextField(name, depth, x, y, width, height);
```

where the parameters are as follows:

name
: The instance name of the new text field

depth
: The depth (within the *MovieClip* object) of the new text field

x   The x position relative to *parentMovieClip*'s registration point

y   The y position relative to *parentMovieClip*'s registration point

width
: The width of the field in pixels

height
: The height of the field in pixels

The new text field is created within the movie clip from which the method is invoked, which is called the *parent clip* or *container clip*.

This example creates a new text field named myText—with a depth of 1, positioned at (0, 0), and with a width of 100 and a height of 20—within _root:

```
_root.createTextField("myText", 1, 0, 0, 100, 20);
```

Once the text field is created, it can be targeted using *parentMovieClip. newTextFieldName*, as follows:

```
_root.myText._x = 100;
```

The parent clip can be _root (the main timeline) or a movie clip created either at runtime or authoring time. You can use the *duplicateMovieClip()*, *attachMovie()*, and *createEmptyMovieClip()* methods of the *MovieClip* class to dynamically create a parent movie clip to hold the text field:

```
_root.createEmptyMovieClip("myTextHolder", 1);
_root.myTextHolder.createTextField("myText", 1, 0, 0, 100, 20);
_root.myTextHolder.myText.text = "This is a new text object";
```

You can remove a *TextField* created with *createTextField()* simply by invoking the *removeTextField()* method on that object, as follows:

```
myText.removeTextField( );
```

See Also

Recipe 7.11

8.3   Creating an Outline Around a Text Field

Problem

You want to make a border around a text field.

Solution

Set the text field's border property to true. Additionally, you can change the color of the border by setting the object's borderColor property.

Discussion

By default, a text field lacks a visible border, which may be desirable. For example, you may not want a border around an item label. However, user input fields have borders by convention. The border shows the user where to click to input a value. Simply setting a text field's border property to true turns on the border around the object.

```
myTextField.border = true;
```

To turn off the border, simply set the border property to false.

The default border color is black but can be changed by setting the `borderColor` property, which accepts a hex RGB value corresponding to the desired color:

```
myTextField.borderColor = 0xFF00FF;   // Make the border violet.
```

See Also

Recipes 3.2 and 8.4

8.4   Creating a Background for a Text Field

Problem

You want to make a visible background behind the text in a text field.

Solution

Set the text field's background property to true. Additionally, you can change the color of the background by setting the object's `backgroundColor` property.

Discussion

Text fields lack a visible background by default (in other words, the background is transparent). However, you can create a background for a text field by setting the background property to true for that object:

```
myTextField.background = true;
```

By default, the background for a text field is white (if made visible). You can, however, assign the background color by setting the value of the object's `backgroundColor` property, which accepts a hex RGB value corresponding to the desired color:

```
myTextField.backgroundColor = 0x00FFFF; // Set the background to light blue.
```

8.5   Making a User Input Field

Problem

You want to create a user input field to allow the user to enter text.

Solution

Set the text field's type property to "input". Alternatively, you can create and use a custom *createInputTextField()* method.

Discussion

When a text field is created using *createTextField()*, it defaults to being a dynamic field. This means that it can be controlled with ActionScript but the user cannot input text into it. To enable the field for user input, set the type property to "input", like so:

```
myTextField.type = "input";
```

Though it isn't a requirement, input fields generally also have a border and a background; otherwise, the user may have difficulty finding and selecting the field so as to enter a value into it:

```
myTextField.border = true;
myTextField.background = true;
```

For a user to be able to input text, the field's selectable property must be true, which is the default. You do not need to explicitly set the selectable property to true unless you previously set it to false.

As you can see, several steps are required to successfully make an input text field using ActionScript. While none of them are particularly difficult, they can be a bit tedious when you are creating multiple input text fields. Therefore, it is convenient to create a custom *createInputTextField()* method for the *MovieClip* class that takes care of these steps with a single method call. You should add the following code to a *TextField.as* file in your Flash *Include* directory for easy inclusion in other projects. You may prefer to add it to the *MovieClip.as* file used throughout Chapter 7, since it adds a method to the *MovieClip* class.

```
MovieClip.prototype.createInputTextField = function (name, depth, x, y, w, h) {

    // Define a default width and height for text fields created with this method
    // (width defaults to 100 and height defaults to 20).
    if (w == undefined) {
      w = 100;
    }
    if (h == undefined) {
      h = 20;
    }

    // Create the text field using the built-in MovieClip.createTextField() method.
    this.createTextField(name, depth, x, y, w, h);

    // Then assign the necessary values to the object to make it an input field.
    this[name].border = true;
    this[name].background = true;
    this[name].type = "input";
};
```

You can use the custom *createInputTextField()* method in your Flash movies to create an input text field with a single line of code. The method takes the same parameters in the same order as the *createTextField()* method, but it automatically makes the text field an input field with the border and background turned on. Additionally, with the *createInputTextField()* method, you can omit the *w* and *h* parameters and allow the text field to use default settings (as opposed to the *createTextField()* method, which requires that you provide all parameters):

```
// Make sure to include the necessary ActionScript file. This assumes you added the
// custom createInputTextField() method to TextField.as and not MovieClip.as.
#include "TextField.as"

// Create an input text field allowing the x and y coordinates to default to (0,0)
// and the width and height to default to 100 × 20.
_root.createInputTextField("myInputText", 1);
```

8.6 Making a Password Input Field

Problem

You want to create an input text field so that characters entered into it are displayed as asterisks—a feature commonly used on password input fields.

Solution

Set the text field's `password` property to `true`.

Discussion

When a user enters a password into a field, you generally do not want observers to be able to read the password. This is a basic security precaution. The common convention is to display only asterisks in the field as the user types. This way, the user can see that he is successfully entering a value without observers being able to easily read the password.

To create an input field that is automatically masked with asterisks, you only need to set the *TextField*.`password` property to `true`:

```
myTextField.password = true;
```

When you set the password property to `true`, all text entered into the text field, either programmatically or by user input, displays as asterisks:

```
myTextField.password = true;
myTextField.text = "some text";  // Text field displays: *********
```

See Also

Recipe 8.5. Password text fields only obscure the display of the text; the value contained by the text property is unaltered. Therefore, when you send the password value across an Internet connection, it is not encrypted. If you need additional security when sending the password, you should use HTTPS or use an encryption technique such as a crypto-graphic hash algorithm, as Branden Hall discusses at *http://www.macromedia.com/ desdev/mx/flash/extreme/extreme003.html*. Also, read Macromedia Flash Security white-paper *http://www.macromedia.com/devnet/mx/flash/whitepapers/security.pdf*. See Recipe 11.19 for information on transmitting data securely.

8.7   Filtering Text Input

Problem

You want to restrict the characters that a user can type into an input field.

Solution

Set the `restrict` property of the text field.

Discussion

By default, a user can type any character into an input field. However, in many sce-narios you might want to restrict the allowable characters. For example, you might restrict characters to numbers and dashes in the case of an input field for telephone numbers.

The *TextField*.`restrict` property lets you specify the allowed characters for user input in a field. Specify a string containing the allowable characters, such as:

```
myTextField.restrict = "abcdefg";
```

This example lets the user enter any of the following allowable characters: a, b, c, d, e, f, or g. Other characters are disallowed. If the user tries to enter "freedom", only "feed" will appear, since the letters r, o, and m are not in the allowable character set.

 If the `restrict` string is set to the empty string, then *all* characters are allowed. To prevent input entirely, set the text field's type to "dynamic".

Also note that ActionScript distinguishes between upper- and lowercase characters. In other words, there is a difference between *a* and *A*. If the `restrict` property is set to "abcdefg", the uppercase variants of the allowable characters (such as *A*, *B*, *C*) will be entered as the lowercase (allowable) equivalents *a*, *b*, and *c*. The same is true in reverse: if a lowercase character is entered when only the uppercase counterpart is allowed, the character will be converted to uppercase.

The restrict property supports certain regular expressions, as described in Recipe 9.6. Therefore, you can also enter ranges by indicating the first character in the range and the last character in the range separated by a dash (-):

```
myTextField.restrict = "a-zA-Z";    // Allows only upper- and lowercase letters
myTextField.restrict = "a-zA-Z ";   // Allows only letters and spaces
myTextField.restrict = "0-9";       // Allows only numbers
```

In addition to specifying allowable characters, you can also disallow characters with a restrict string by using the caret character (^). All characters and ranges in a restrict string following the caret will be disallowed. For example:

```
myTextField.restrict = "^abcdefg"; // Allows all except lowercase a–g
myTextField.restrict = "^a-z";     // Disallows all lowercase letters (but allows all
                                   // other characters, including uppercase)
myTextField.restrict = "0-9^5";    // Allows numbers only, with the exception of 5
```

You can also specify allowable characters using Unicode escape sequences. For example, if you want to disallow users from entering the → character (Ctrl-Z) into a field, you can specify its Unicode code point in the restrict property, as follows:

```
myTextField.restrict = "^\u001A";
```

To allow a literal character that has a special meaning when used in a restrict string (such as a dash or caret), you must *escape* the character in the restrict string by preceding it with two backslashes (not just one):

```
myTextField.restrict = "0-9\\-";    // Allows numbers and dashes
myTextField.restrict = "0-9\\^";    // Allows numbers and caret marks
```

If you want to escape the backslash character, you must precede it with three backslashes for a total of four backslashes:

```
myTextField.restrict = "0-9\\\\";   // Allows numbers and backslashes
```

See Also

Recipe 9.6. Also refer to Table A-1, which lists the Unicode code points for Latin 1 characters.

8.8   Restricting the Maximum Field Length

Problem

You want to limit the length of the string input in a text field.

Solution

Set the text field's maxChars property.

Discussion

By default, an input text field allows a user to type in as many characters as she desires. However, you may have good reason to want to set a maximum. For example, if an input field prompts a user for her two-character country code, you might want to prevent the user from entering more than two characters. Setting the maxChars property to a number limits the user input to that many characters.

```
myTextField.maxChars = 6;  // Maximum of six characters can be input
```

Set maxChars to null to allow an entry of unlimited length.

See Also

Recipe 8.7

8.9   Displaying Dynamic Text at Runtime

Problem

You want to display text within a movie.

Solution

Set the text property of a text field.

Discussion

Aside from being used as input fields, text fields are often used to display text to the user. Setting a text field's text property causes the corresponding text to display in the field.

```
myTextField.text = "this will display in the field";
```

> The Flash 5 technique of assigning a variable to a text field is still available, though not preferred. However, if exporting to Flash 5 format, you can assign a variable name to the text field using the variable property.

Special characters, such as \t for tab and \n for newline, can be used within a text string.

Displaying text programmatically in a movie is useful for many reasons. If a movie contains dynamic or frequently updated text, the values can be loaded from an external source, such as a database or XML document, and then programmatically displayed in text fields.

The *trace()* command displays text in Flash's Output window, but the window is available during authoring only. You can use a text field to display output at runtime using a custom function:

```
function traceText (msg) {
  myTextField.text += msg + newline;
}
traceText ("Here's my message");
```

See Also

Recipes 8.1 and 8.2. See Recipe 8.10 for information on support for HTML-formatted text.

8.10   Displaying HTML-Formatted Text

Problem

You want to display HTML content in a text field.

Solution

Set the text field's html property to true, and set the htmlText property to the value of the HTML content to display.

Discussion

Text fields can interpret and display basic HTML tags, if properly configured. Using HTML in a text field is a convenient way to add links and simple formatting, such as font color and bold text.

Text fields display plain text by default. To enable HTML formatting, set the field's html property to true:

```
myTextField.html = true;
```

Once the html property is set to true, the value of the object's htmlText property will be interpreted as HTML:

```
myTextField.htmlText = "<u>this will display as underlined text</u>";
```

Set the html property to true before setting the htmlText property; otherwise, the value of htmlText will not be interpreted as HTML.

When the html property is false (which is the default), the htmlText property value is rendered as regular text. But when html is set to true, the htmlText property is rendered as HTML complete with <p> and <font> markup tags:

```
myTextField.html = false;
myTextField.htmlText = "test";
```

```
trace(myTextField.htmlText);
/* Output window displays:
test
*/
myTextField.html = true;
myTextField.htmlText = "test";
trace(myTextField.htmlText);
/* Output window displays:
<P ALIGN="LEFT"><FONT FACE="Times New Roman"
    SIZE="12" COLOR="#000000">test</FONT></P>
*/
```

No matter what, the text property of a text field is rendered as plain text. This means that even if the html property is true, if the text property is set to <u>test</u>, the object will display <u>test</u> instead of <u>test</u>.

Despite the fact that they appear to be two properties, text and htmlText are linked such that when one is altered, the other is as well. This means that you should not try to assign different values to each. Whatever value is assigned to text is also assigned to htmlText (with additional HTML flourish if the html property is set to true), and vice versa. You can test this for yourself, as follows:

```
myTextField.html = true;
myTextField.htmlText = "htmlText value";
trace(myTextField.text);
trace(myTextField.htmlText);
myTextField.text = "text value";
trace(myTextField.text);
trace(myTextField.htmlText);
/* Output window displays:
htmlText value
<P ALIGN="LEFT"><FONT FACE="Times New Roman"
    SIZE="12" COLOR="#000000">htmlText value</FONT></P>
text value
<P ALIGN="LEFT"><FONT FACE="Times New Roman"
    SIZE="12" COLOR="#000000">text value</FONT></P>
*/
```

The htmlText property is a little quirky. Each time you append a new value to the htmlText property, the appended value is wrapped in a <p> element. Therefore, if you assign a value to an object's htmlText property and then append another value to htmlText, the two values will be displayed on two different lines even if no line-breaking tags were specified:

```
myTextField.html = true;
myTextField.htmlText = "a";
myTextField.htmlText += "b";
trace(myTextField.htmlText);
/* Output window displays:
<P ALIGN="LEFT"><FONT FACE="_sans" SIZE="12"
    COLOR="#000000">a</FONT></P>
<P ALIGN="LEFT"><FONT FACE="_sans" SIZE="12"
    COLOR="#000000">b</FONT></P>
*/
```

A simple solution to this problem is to append the values to a string variable and then assign that variable's value to the htmlText property in a single assignment statement:

```
myTextField.html = true;
var htmlTextVal = "a";
htmlTextVal += "b";
myTextField.htmlText = htmlTextVal;
trace(myTextField.htmlText);
/* Output window displays:
<P ALIGN="LEFT"><FONT FACE="_sans" SIZE="12" COLOR="#000000">ab</FONT></P>
*/
```

If you want to display HTML code in its unrendered format, set the html property to false and assign the HTML value to the text property of the text field, as follows:

```
myTextField.html = false;
myTextField.text = "<u>underlined text</u>";
/* Text field displays:
<u>underlined text</u>
*/
```

This can be a useful technique if, for example, you want to show both the rendered HTML and the HTML source code in side-by-side text fields:

```
htmlCode = "<i>italicized text</i>";
sourceHTML.html = false;
sourceHTML.text = htmlCode;
renderedHTML.html = true;
renderedHTML.htmlText = htmlCode;
```

You cannot display both rendered and unrendered HTML in the same text field. If you try to do so, you will end up with unreliable results.

Additionally, you cannot toggle between the viewing of rendered and unrendered HTML in a text field. For example, if you set a text field's html property to true, add HTML content, and set the html property to false, the displayed text appears as rendered HTML, not as HTML source code.

The set of HTML tags supported by Flash 5 text fields includes: <B>, <I>, <U>, <FONT> (with FACE, SIZE, and COLOR attributes), <P>, <BR>, and <A>. Flash 6 adds support for <LI> and <TEXTFORMAT> (with LEFTMARGIN, RIGHTMARGIN, BLOCKINDENT, INDENT, LEADING, and TABSTOPS attributes corresponding to the *TextFormat* class's properties of the same names).

See Also

Appendix E of *ActionScript for Flash MX: The Definitive Guide* gives full details on Flash's support for HTML tags.

8.11 Condensing Whitespace

Problem

You want to condense whitespace in an HTML text field display.

Solution

Set the object's condenseWhite property to true.

Discussion

When you use HTML in a text field, the optional condenseWhite setting condenses whitespace, as is done in most HTML browsers. For example, the following text would be rendered in a web browser with only a single space between "hello" and "friend" in spite of the fact that the original source has multiple spaces between the two words:

```
hello          friend
```

In ActionScript text fields, however, all of the spaces are displayed unless you set the condenseWhite property to true.

```
myTextField.html = true;
myTextField.condenseWhite = true;
myTextField.htmlText = "hello          friend";   // Displays: "hello friend"
```

The condenseWhite property works only when the html property is true.

See Also

Recipe 8.10 and the *XML*.ignoreWhite property

8.12 Sizing Text Fields to Fit Contents

Problem

You want to size a text field's viewable area to fit the text it contains.

Solution

Use the autoSize property, or create and use a custom *createAutoTextField()* method.

Alternatively, you can also set the _width and _height properties based on the values of the textWidth and textHeight properties.

Discussion

You can set the autoSize property of a text field so that it automatically resizes itself in order to fit its contents. By default, autoSize is set to "none", meaning that the text field does not automatically resize. There are six possible values for the autoSize property, but two possible values are redundant, leaving four effective settings:

"left" or true

Set the property to "left" or true if you want the text field to resize while fixing the upper-left corner's position. In other words, the text field's lower-right corner will be the point that moves when it expands and contracts.

```
// These two lines do the same thing.
myTextField.autoSize = "left";
myTextField.autoSize = true;
```

"center"

Set the property to "center" if you want the text field to be anchored at its center point. While the top of the object remains fixed, it will expand and contract downward and equally to the right and left.

```
myTextField.autoSize = "center";
```

"right"

Set the property to "right" if you want the upper-right corner of the text field to remain steady while the object expands and contracts in the direction of the lower-left corner:

```
myTextField.autoSize = "right";
```

"none" or false

Set the property to "none" or false if you want to turn off the autosize functionality, in which case the text field dimensions do not adjust automatically:

```
// These two lines do the same thing.
myTextField.autoSize = "none";
myTextField.autoSize = false;
```

It is convenient to create auto-sizing text fields using a custom *createAutoTextField()* method. You should add the following code to your *TextField.as* file (or the *MovieClip.as* file from Chapter 7) for easy inclusion in other projects:

```
MovieClip.prototype.createAutoTextField = function (name,
                                    depth,
                                    x, y,
                                    w, h,
                                    val,
                                    align) {

// The align parameter is assigned to the text field's autoSize property.
// Defaults to true (same as "left"). Ignored if width, w, is specified.
if (align == undefined) {
  align = true;
}
```

```
        // Create the text field using the built-in MovieClip.createTextField() method.
        this.createTextField(name, depth, x, y, w, h);

        // If the width, w, was 0 or unspecified, set the autoSize property so that the
        // text field resizes to fit its contents.
        if (w == undefined || w == 0) {
          this[name].autoSize = align;
        }

        // If a value was provided, assign it to the text field's text property.
        if (val != undefined) {
          this[name].text = val;
        }
    };
```

You can use the custom *createAutoTextField()* method as you would use the built-in *createTextField()* method. The primary difference is that *createAutoTextField()* creates an auto-sizing text field with a single method invocation. Additionally, the val parameter allows you to assign text to the text field when creating it.

```
    // Make sure to include the necessary ActionScript file. This assumes you added the
    // custom createAutoTextField() method to TextField.as and not MovieClip.as
    #include "TextField.as"

    // Create a text field that autosizes and give it a text value of "init value".
    _root.createAutoTextField("myAutoText", 1, 0, 0, 0, 0, "init value");
```

If you do not want to use the auto-size feature, you can manually adjust the _width and _height properties. This might be useful if, for example, you want to fix the text field width but adjust the height manually to fit the content. You can retrieve the contents' width and height using the textWidth and textHeight properties. Then you can set the _width or _height properties accordingly.

Because a text field's total width and height are slightly larger than the width and height of the text it contains, you will likely find that if you set the _width and _ height properties to the textWidth and textHeight properties, the text may be cut off. You can account for this discrepancy by adding a margin as necessary. This example resizes the text field a little larger than the reported property values to accommodate the contents:

```
    myTextField._width  = myTextField.textWidth + 5;
    myTextField._height = myTextField.textHeight + 5;
```

See Also

Recipe 8.8

8.13 Scrolling Text with the ScrollBar Component

Problem

You want to create a scrolling text field with a scrollbar.

Solution

Use the Flash UI Components ScrollBar component.

Discussion

Using the ScrollBar component, you can easily add both vertical and horizontal scrolling capabilities to a text field. If the text field is created during authoring, you can simply drag a scrollbar instance from the Components panel onto the text field itself. The ScrollBar component will automatically snap (if View → Snap to Objects is enabled) to the side on which it is dropped (top, bottom, left, or right) and will automatically size itself to match the text field object. Additionally, the scrollbar instance will automatically set its scroll target to be the text field onto which it was dropped.

You can also add a scrollbar to a dynamically created text field, or add the scrollbar dynamically for other reasons (such as when a text field is resized or its contents change). To make the process fully dynamic, add the scrollbar using *MovieClip.attachMovie( )* (see Recipe 7.19). To accomplish this, you must first make sure that the ScrollBar component is included in the movie's Library by dragging an instance of it from the Components panel to the Stage. This action will automatically link the ScrollBar component for export with the identifier *FScrollBarSymbol*. With the symbol in the Library, you can attach the component using ActionScript, as follows:

```
_root.attachMovie("FScrollBarSymbol", "myScrollBar_sb", 2);
```

To specify the text field to control, specify it as the *target* parameter for the Scroll-Bar component's *setScrollTarget( )* method:

```
myScrollBar_sb.setScrollTarget(myTextField);
```

While this is all that is technically required for a scrollbar to control the scrolling of a text field, there are generally additional considerations. For example, you usually will want to position the scrollbar adjacent to the text field. Likewise, you typically will want the scrollbar's dimensions to match the width or height of the text field it controls (depending on whether it is a horizontal or vertical scrollbar).

To align a vertical scrollbar instance so that it is flush with the top of the text field it controls, set its _y property to match the text field's _y property. To align the same scrollbar instance so that it touches the right side of the text field, offset its _x property by the text field's width value. For example:

```
myScrollBar_sb._x = myTextField._x + myTextField._width;
myScrollBar_sb._y = myTextField._y;
```

To set the size of a scrollbar instance, use the *setSize()* method, which accepts the size (the height) of the instance in pixels. To match the scrollbar length to the text field, pass the text field's _height property to the *setSize()* method:

```
myScrollBar_sb.setSize(myTextField._height);
```

If you want the scrollbar to control the horizontal scrolling of a text field, use the *setHorizontal()* method, passing it the value true. (This also orients the scrollbar horizontally.)

```
myScrollBar_sb.setHorizontal(true);
```

When a scrollbar instance is horizontal, *setSize()* sets its width instead of its height.

See Also

Recipe 8.14

8.14   Scrolling Text Programmatically

Problem

You want to scroll text in a text field via ActionScript without requiring user input.

Solution

Use the `scroll`, `maxscroll`, `bottomScroll`, `hscroll`, and `maxhscroll` properties of the text field.

Discussion

You can control the scrolling of a text field with ActionScript and without the aid of a scrollbar. For example, you may want to scroll the contents of a text field automatically to display a word or selection within the text. Or perhaps you don't want to use the ScrollBar component for file size–optimization reasons. Regardless, you can programmatically control a text field's scrolling in both the vertical and horizontal directions using some built-in properties. You should use the `scroll`, `maxscroll`, and `bottomScroll` properties to control vertical scrolling, and use the `hscroll` and `maxhscroll` properties to control horizontal scrolling.

Every text field has a number of lines, whether it is 1 or 100. Each of these lines is identified by a number starting at one. Some of these lines may be visible, and some may be beyond the border of the text field. Therefore, to view the lines that extend beyond the visible portion of the text field you must scroll to them. Figure 8-1 illustrates this point. It depicts a text field's display, in which the solid line indicates the object's border—the visible area—and the dotted line surrounds the rest of the text contained within the object but lying outside the its visible area. To the left of the text field are line numbers for each line of text. The three labels—scroll, bottomScroll, and maxscroll—indicate the meaning of the text field properties of the same name.

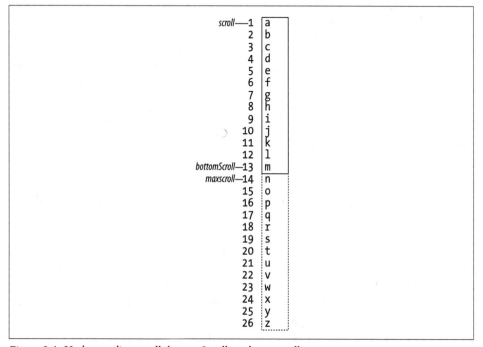

Figure 8-1. Understanding scroll, bottomScroll, and maxscroll

The scroll property is a read/write property that indicates the top line of the text field's visible area. In Figure 8-1, the scroll property's value is 1. To scroll the contents of a text field, assign a new line number to the scroll property. Setting scroll to 6, for example, scrolls the contents of the text field up until line 6 is the topmost line displayed. The value of scroll should always be an integer. Flash cannot scroll to noninteger values.

```
myTextField.scroll = 1;    // Scroll to the top.
myTextField.scroll += 1;   // Scroll to the next line.
myTextField.scroll = 6;    // Scroll to line 6.
```

You can scroll to the next page of a text field's contents using the bottomScroll property, which indicates the bottommost visible line in the text field. While you cannot set bottomScroll, you can use it to determine the new value to assign to scroll. In

Figure 8-1, `bottomScroll` is 13. If `scroll` is set to 6, then `bottomScroll` is automatically updated to 18.

```
// Scroll to the next page with the previous page's bottom line at the top.
myTextField.scroll = myTextField.bottomScroll;
// Scroll to the next complete page without the bottom line from the previous page.
myTextField.scroll = myTextField.bottomScroll + 1;
```

You should use the `maxscroll` property to scroll to the last page of contents within a text field. The `maxscroll` property is also a read-only property. This property contains the value of the maximum line number that can be assigned to `scroll`. Therefore, the `maxscroll` property changes only when the number of lines in the text field changes (either through user input or through ActionScript assignment). In Figure 8-1, `maxscroll` is 14. This is because with 26 total lines in the text field, and with 13 visible lines, when `scroll` is set to 14, the last visible line is 26 (the last line in the text field).

Don't try to set `scroll` to a value less than 1 or greater than the value of `maxscroll`. Although this won't cause an error, it won't scroll the text beyond the contents. Add blank lines to the beginning or end of the text field's contents to artificially extend its scrolling range:

```
myTextField.scroll = myTextField.maxscroll;    // Scroll to the bottom.
```

The vertical scrolling properties are in units of lines, but the horizontal scrolling properties (`hscroll` and `maxhscroll`) are in units of pixels. Other than that, `hscroll` and `maxhscroll` work more or less in the same fashion as `scroll` and `maxscroll` (although there is no property for horizontal scrolling that corresponds to `bottomScroll`). The `hscroll` property is a read/write property that allows you to control the value of the leftmost visible pixel starting with 0. The `maxhscroll` property is a read-only property that indicates the pixel value of the maximum value that can be assigned to `hscroll`.

```
myTextField.hscroll = 0;                  // Scroll to the far left.
myTextField.hscroll += 1;                 // Scroll to the right one pixel.
myTextField.hscroll = myTextField.maxhscroll; // Scroll to the far right.
```

Figure 8-2 depicts `maxhscroll` for a dynamic text field (a field whose type is set to "dynamic"). Text shown in gray is outside the visible area of the text field.

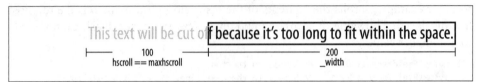

Figure 8-2. The maxhscroll property for a dynamic text field

Figure 8-3 depicts maxhscroll for an input text field (a field whose type is set to "input"). Note that Flash automatically adds buffer space to allow room for user input. Again, text shown in gray is outside the visible area of the text field.

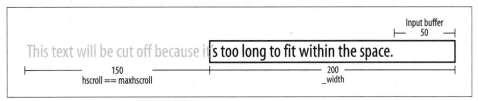

Figure 8-3. The maxhscroll property for an input text field

8.15   Responding to Scroll Events

Problem

You want to have some actions performed when a text field's contents are scrolled.

Solution

Define the text field's *onScroller()* event handler method. Alternatively, you can use a listener object.

Discussion

When a text field is scrolled vertically or horizontally (meaning that the scroll or hscroll property has been changed either by your custom ActionScript code or by a scrollbar), the *onScroller()* method is automatically invoked. By default, a text field's *onScroller()* method is undefined, but you can assign it a reference to a function:

```
myTextField.onScroller = function () {
  trace("text is scrolled");
};
```

You can also create *listener objects* for a text field that are notified when the text is scrolled. Listener objects can be any kind of object, such as another text field, a movie clip, or a custom object type. You should define an *onScroller()* method for the listener object, then register the object to the text field using the *addListener()* method. Call the *addListener()* method from the text field and pass it a parameter that references the listener object (the object with *onScroller()* defined). For example:

```
myListener = new Object();
myListener.onScroller = function () {
  // Actions go here.
};
myTextField.addListener(myListener);
```

You can add multiple listeners to one text field. Working with listeners is a powerful technique because it allows you to define actions that should occur on multiple objects when a text field is changed in some way. This is much more powerful than placing all the actions within a single method assigned to the text field for several reasons. For one thing, it is a good practice to keep actions specific to an object assigned to that object and not to other objects. (For example, a ScrollBar component configures itself as a listener for the targeted text field. If the text field changes programmatically, the ScrollBar component independently updates its own scroller position to match the text field.) Additionally, the listener objects can reference themselves with the this keyword, which keeps your code as abstract as possible. Here, two objects are added as listeners:

```
myListener = new Object( );
myListener.onScroller = function ( ) {
  // Actions go here.
};

myMovieClip.onScroller = function ( ) {
  this._x++;
};

myTextField.addListener(myMovieClip);
myTextField.addListener(myListener);
```

You can remove a listener by invoking the text field's *removeListener()* method, passing it a reference to the listener object to remove:

```
myTextField.removeListener(myListener);
```

See Also

For more information on listeners, see Recipe 12.11, along with Recipes 8.26 and 8.27.

8.16   Formatting Existing Text

Problem

You want to format the existing text in a text field.

Solution

Pass a *TextFormat* object to the *TextField.setTextFormat()* method.

Discussion

A text field allows minimal control over the formatting of the text it displays, such as by setting the htmlText property. Although you can set the color of the entire contents of the text field using the textColor property, for example, the *TextField* class doesn't offer precise control over character formatting. However, the *TextFormat* class is a "helper" class; *TextFormat* objects can format the text displayed in text fields.

The first step in formatting text is to create a *TextFormat* object using the constructor method:

```
myTextFormat = new TextFormat( );
```

Next, assign values to the *TextFormat* object's properties as you desire:

```
myTextFormat.align = "center";   // Center-align the text.
myTextFormat.bold = true;        // Bold the text.
myTextFormat.color = 0xFFFF00;   // Make the text yellow.
myTextFormat.blockIndent = 5;    // Adjust the margin by five pixels.
```

You can apply text formatting to the existing text for an entire text field by passing a *TextFormat* object to the text field's *setTextFormat()* method:

```
myTextField.setTextFormat(myTextFormat);
```

When you invoke the *setTextFormat()* method in this way, the formatting from the *TextFormat* object is applied to the text already assigned to the text field. The formatting does not apply to any text assigned to the text field after the *setTextFormat()* method is invoked. If additional text is entered by the user, the original text retains its applied formatting, but the inserted text does not have any special formatting applied to it. All formatting is removed if the text value is modified by appending a value by way of ActionScript.

```
myTextField.text = "this is some text";
myTextField.setTextFormat(myTextFormat); // Formatting applied
myTextField.text = "this is other text"; // No formatting applied
myTextField.setTextFormat(myTextFormat); // Formatting reapplied
myTextField.text += "appended text";     // Formatting removed
```

If you make changes to the *TextFormat* object, you should reapply the formatting to the text field by passing the modified object to the *setTextFormat()* method. Otherwise, the changes are not automatically displayed.

See Also

Recipe 8.10 explains how to use HTML-formatted text, Recipe 8.17 explains how to apply formatting to new text rather than existing text, and Recipe 8.18 applies formatting to individual characters rather than an entire field.

8.17   Formatting User-Input Text

Problem

You want to apply formatting to text as it is entered into a text field by the user.

Solution

Apply a *TextFormat* object using the *setNewTextFormat()* method of the text field.

Discussion

You should use the *setNewTextFormat()* method of a text field object to apply text formatting to text as it is entered by the user. You should create a *TextFormat* object as in Recipe 8.16 and then pass that object to the text field's *setNewTextFormat()* method:

```
myTextFormat = new TextFormat( );
myTextFormat.color = 0x0000FF;      // Make the text blue.
myTextField.setNewTextFormat(myTextFormat);
```

When you use *setNewTextFormat()*, the formatting is applied to text that the user types into the field.

See Also

Recipe 8.18

8.18   Formatting a Portion of a Text Field

Problem

You want to add formatting to some, but not all, text in a text field, or you want to apply different formatting to various parts of a text field.

Solution

Create a *TextFormat* object and use it to format a substring of the text field using one of the *setTextFormat()* method variations.

Discussion

You can format an entire text field as shown in Recipe 8.16, or you can use one of the versions of the *setTextFormat()* method to format just a portion of a text field. These variations allow you to apply formatting to the specified character range only.

You can set the formatting for a single character within a text field by invoking the *setTextFormat()* method and passing it two parameters:

`index`
> The zero-relative index of the character to which the formatting should be applied

`textFormatObj`
> A reference to a *TextFormat* object

This example applies the formatting to the first character only:

```
myTextField.setTextFormat(0, myTextFormat);
```

Alternatively, if you want to apply the formatting to a range of characters, you can invoke *setTextFormat()* with three parameters:

`startIndex`
> The beginning, zero-relative character index

`endIndex`
> The index of the character after the last character in the desired range

`textFormatObj`
> A reference to a *TextFormat* object

This example applies the formatting to the 1st through 10th characters:

```
myTextField.setTextFormat(0, 10, myTextFormat);
```

You may notice that certain formatting options are not applied under certain circumstances when you try to format portions of a text field. For example, the text alignment will be applied only if the formatting is applied to the first character in a line.

See Also

Recipe 8.16

8.19 Setting a Text Field's Font

Problem

You want to use ActionScript to change the font used for some displayed text.

Solution

Set the font property of a *TextFormat* object and apply the formatting to the text field.

Discussion

You can programmatically specify the font that is used to display text using the font property of a *TextFormat* object. You can assign to this property the string name of the font (or fonts) that should be used:

```
myTextFormat.font = "Arial";
```

The font specified must be available on the computer on which the movie is running. Because some computers may not have the preferred font installed, you can specify multiple font names separated by commas, as follows:

```
myTextFormat.font = "Arial, Verdana, Helvetica";
```

The first font is used unless it cannot be found, in which case the Player attempts to use the next font in the list.

Apply the font change to a text field, as follows:

```
myTextField.setTextFormat(myTextFormat);
```

If none of the specified fonts are found, the default system font is used.

See Also

Recipes 8.16, 8.18, and 8.20

8.20   Embedding Fonts

Problem

You want to ensure that text will display properly even if the intended font is not installed on the user's computer.

Solution

Export the font in the movie's Library, set the text field's embedFonts property to true, and use a *TextFormat* object, setting its font property to the linkage identifier for the embedded font.

Discussion

You should embed fonts if you want to ensure that text will display using the intended font even if the font is not installed on the user's computer. To embed a font, follow these steps:

1. Open the Flash document's Library and select New Font from the pop-up Options menu (see Figure 8-4). A Font Symbol Properties dialog box appears.

2. In the Name field, specify the name given to the symbol in the Library. Any name will suffice, so specify a name that makes sense to you.

3. From the Font drop-down list, select the font that you wish to embed.

4. If you wish to include the bold and/or italic versions of the font as well, select the appropriate checkboxes. Be aware that including bold and italic font outlines will increase the file size significantly, so do so only if you really need them.

5. Click OK in the Font Symbol Properties dialog box.

6. Select the new Font symbol in the Library and choose Linkage from the pop-up Options menu.

7. In the Linkage Properties dialog box, select the Export for ActionScript and Export in First Frame checkboxes.

8. Give the symbol a linkage identifier. This is the name that will be used in the ActionScript code. The linkage identifier should be something that corresponds to the font. For example, if the font you are embedding is Garamond, you might give it a linkage identifier of *garamondEmbedded.*

9. Click OK in the Linkage Properties dialog box.

10. Set the `embedFonts` property of the text field to `true`. By default, the property is `false`, which means that Flash uses device fonts. By setting the `embedFonts` property to `true`, the text field can use embedded fonts only. If you attempt to assign a device font to a text field with `embedFonts` set to `true`, nothing will be displayed.

    ```
    myTextField.embedFonts = true;
    ```

11. Set the `TextFormat.font` property to the linkage identifier of the embedded font. If this value is not found, no text is displayed.

    ```
    myTextFormat.font = "garamondEmbedded";
    ```

12. Apply the *TextFormat* object to the text field using *setTextFormat()*:

    ```
    myTextField.setTextFormat(myTextFormat);
    ```

See Also

Recipes 8.16 and 8.19

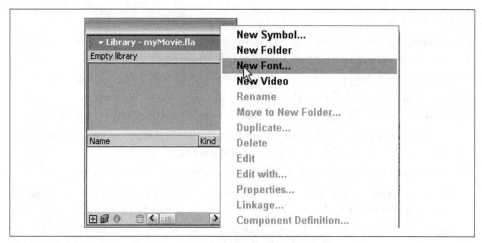

Figure 8-4. Selecting New Font from the Library's pop-up Options menu

8.21 Creating Text That Can Be Rotated

Problem

You want to make sure that text will continue to display even when it is rotated.

Solution

Use embedded fonts.

Discussion

Unless you specifically use an embedded font, text fields use device fonts. For most situations, this is perfectly workable. However, in situations in which you want to animate a text field (or its parent movie clip) by changing its _rotation property, you must use embedded fonts. Device fonts will disappear in a rotated text field.

See Also

Recipe 8.20 explains how to embed fonts.

8.22 Displaying Unicode Text

Problem

You want to display Unicode text in your movie, possibly including non-English characters.

Solution

Use the Unicode escape sequences for the characters within the assignment to the text field's text property. You can also include the Unicode text directly in an external ActionScript file and use an #include directive.

Discussion

All text in Flash MX is treated as Unicode text. Therefore, you can display any Unicode character within a text field. If you know the escape sequence for the character, you can assign it to a text field's text property. All Unicode escape sequences in ActionScript begin with \u and are followed by four-digit hexadecimal numbers. The escape sequences must be enclosed in quotes.

```
// Display a famous equation with a superscripted 2.
myTextField.text = "E = MC\u00B2";
```

You can also display Unicode text without using escape sequences by inserting the desired characters directly into an external ActionScript file and using the #include directive to load the text into the Flash movie. This is necessary because Flash does not allow you to enter Unicode characters directly into the Actions panel. You must make sure that the text editor you use allows you to enter Unicode text and save it as UTF-8–encoded format (Notepad and TextEdit both allow for this). You must also include the special //!-- UTF8 comment at the beginning of the file to indicate that it contains UTF-8–encoded text. For example, you can save this text in a file named *UTFcontent.as*:

```
//!-- UTF8
// This is the ActionScript file saved as something like UTFcontent.as.
mySpanish = "Español";
myJapanese = "尤 民";
myHebrew = "א ב";
```

 Notice that non-English characters can be directly inserted into the external file. Some of these characters might require the user to have the proper language pack installed on his computer.

In the Flash document, include the external file and assign the loaded variables containing Unicode characters to the text properties of existing text fields as desired. For example:

```
#include "UTFcontent.as"
mySpanishTextField.text = mySpanish;
myJapaneseTextField.text = myJapanese;
myHebrewTextField.text = myHebrew;
```

See Also

Table A-1 lists the Unicode escape sequences. If you want a Unicode character reference online, you can open up the Character Map utility under Windows using Start → Programs → Accessories → System Tools → Character Map.

8.23 Assigning Focus to a Text Field

Problem

You want to use ActionScript to bring focus to a text field.

Solution

Use the *Selection.setFocus()* method.

Discussion

You should use the *Selection* class's static *getFocus()* method to assign focus to a specific text field programmatically. The method assigns focus to the object whose name is passed in as a parameter. You should pass *getFocus()* a string value that evaluates to the path to the object. You can specify the parameter as an absolute or relative path, such as:

```
// The following are equivalent, assuming that myTextField exists within _root.
Selection.setFocus("myTextField");
Selection.setFocus("_root.myTextField");
```

Additionally, to support Flash 4 and Flash 5 movies, the parameter passed to *setFocus()* can be a string that evaluates to the path of the variable associated with the text field, and the path can be given in slash notation if desired. For example:

```
Selection.setFocus("/myTextFieldVar");
```

To remove focus from a text field, you should call the *setFocus()* method and pass it the null value:

```
Selection.setFocus(null);
```

See Also

Recipe 11.21

8.24 Selecting Text with ActionScript

Problem

You want to highlight a portion of the text within a text field.

Solution

Use the *Selection.setSelection()* method.

Discussion

The *Selection* class has a static method, *setSelection()*, which highlights a portion of the text in the text field. The selection is applied to the text field that has focus (see Recipe 8.23). The *setSelection()* method takes two parameters:

startIndex
    The beginning, zero-relative index of the text to highlight

endIndex
    The index of the character after the text to highlight

For example:

```
myTextField.text = "this is some text";  // Set the text value.
Selection.setFocus("myTextField");       // Bring focus to the text field.
Selection.setSelection(0, 4);            // Highlight the word "this".
```

See Also

Recipes 8.25 and 8.26

8.25   Setting the Insertion Point in a Text Field

Problem

You want to use ActionScript to set the insertion point in a text field.

Solution

Use the *Selection.setSelection()* method, specifying the same value for the starting and ending indexes.

Discussion

You can use *Selection.setSelection()* to set the cursor position in a text field by setting the beginning and ending index parameters to the same value. This example sets the cursor position in the text field that has focus:

```
// Positions the insertion point before the first character
Selection.setSelection(0, 0);
```

See Also

Recipe 8.24

8.26 Responding When Text Is Selected or Deselected

Problem

You want to perform a task when a text field is selected or deselected.

Solution

Assign a function definition to the text field's *onSetFocus()* and/or *onKillFocus()* methods.

Discussion

You should define the *onSetFocus()* method for any text field for which you want certain actions to be performed when focus is brought to the field. Likewise, you should define the *onKillFocus()* method for any text field for which you want certain actions to be performed when focus leaves the field. These methods are invoked automatically when focus changes on a text field, though by default the methods are undefined.

```
myTextField.onSetFocus = function (prevFocus) {
  trace(this._name + " selected, previously selected was " + prevFocus._name);
};
myTextField.onKillFocus = function (newFocus) {
  trace(this._name + " deselected, new selection is " + newFocus._name);
};
```

In each case, the method is automatically passed a parameter. In the case of *onSetFocus()*, the parameter is a reference to the object that previously had focus and for *onKillFocus()*, the parameter is a reference to the object that is gaining focus. In either case, you are not required to handle this parameter or do anything with it, but it is there if you want or need it.

A handy use of the *onSetFocus()* event handler method might be to set the value of an instructional output field's text when a particular input field is selected in a form:

```
myInputField.onSetFocus = function () {
  _root.myOutputField.text = "instructions for this form field";
};
```

A useful implementation of the *onKillFocus()* event handler method might be to check the value of a form field once it loses focus:

```
myInputField.onKillFocus = function () {
  if (this.text != "valid answer") {
    _root.myOutputField.text = "invalid answer supplied";
  }
};
```

8.27   Responding to User Text Entry

Problem

You want to perform a task when the content of a text field is modified by user input.

Solution

Assign a function definition to the text field's *onChanged()* event handler method. Alternatively, you can use a listener object with a defined *onChanged()* method and register it with the text field using *addListener()*.

Discussion

You can specify actions to be performed each time the content of a text field is changed by user input, whether that change be deleting or cutting characters, typing in characters, or pasting characters. You can define the text field's *onChanged()* event handler method:

```
myTextField.onChanged = function () {
  trace("the value has been modified");
};
```

When a user makes any change to the value of an input text field with an *onChanged()* handler defined, the actions defined in the *onChanged()* handler are executed.

You can also define an *onChanged()* method for a listener object (or listener objects). If multiple objects need to be updated when a change occurs in the input text field's value, you should register those objects as listeners. You should define an *onChanged()* method for the listener object and then register the listener with the text field's *addListener()* method. The *addListener()* method takes a reference to the listener object. For example:

```
myListener = new Object();
myListener.onChanged = function () {
  // Actions go here.
};
myTextField.addListener(myListener);
```

You can use *addListener()* to register as many listener objects as you need. In this way, each listener object handles only the functionality that is applicable to it.

If you want to unregister a listener object, call the *removeListener()* method of the text field at any time, passing it a reference to the listener object to be removed:

```
myTextField.removeListener(myListener);
```

Whether using the event handler method or using a listener object, attempt to keep your *onChanged( )* definition as streamlined as possible. Remember that the method is invoked every time the user types a character into the text field, so if you try to do too much at once, you can put unnecessary strain on your Flash movie.

See Also

Recipe 8.15

8.28 Adding a Hyperlink to Text

Problem

You want to hyperlink some of the text displayed in a text field.

Solution

Use HTML <a href> tags within the object's htmlText property. Alternatively, use a *TextFormat* object with a value assigned to the url property.

Discussion

Both solutions to this problem require you to set the text field's html property to true:

```
myTextField.html = true;
```

If you want to use HTML to add a hyperlink, add an <a href> tag to the text field's htmlText property, as follows:

```
myTextField.htmlText = "<a href=\"http://www.person13.com/\">click here</a>";
```

You can specify a target window in which to open the link by adding a target attribute to the <a href> HTML tag. For example:

```
myTextField.htmlText = "<a href=\"http://www.person13.com/\" target=\"_blank\">click
here</a>";
```

When text is hyperlinked in Flash, the mouse cursor changes to a hand when it is over the linked text. Flash does not inherently provide any indication that the text is linked, as do most HTML browsers (with an underline and color change). For this reason, it is helpful to add HTML markup that underlines and colors the linked text:

```
htmlLink = "<font color=\"#0000FF\"><u>";    // Add the color and underline.
htmlLink += "<a href=\"http://www.person13.com/\">click here</a>";
htmlLink += "</u></font>";
myTextField.htmlText = htmlLink;             // Close the color and underline.
```

You can accomplish the same tasks without HTML by using a *TextFormat* object. The *TextFormat* class includes a `url` property for just this purpose. Assigning the URL to the `url` property will link the formatted text. For example:

```
myTextField.text = "click here";
myTextFormat = new TextFormat( );
myTextFormat.url = "http://www.person13.com/";
myTextField.setTextFormat(myTextFormat);
```

To specify a target window in which to open the link, set the value of the *TextFormat* object's target property, as follows:

```
myTextField.text = "click here";
myTextFormat = new TextFormat( );
myTextFormat.url = "http://www.person13.com/";
myTextFormat.target = "_blank";
myTextField.setTextFormat(myTextFormat);
```

As with the HTML technique, when using a *TextFormat* object to create a hyperlink, Flash does not offer any indication as to the link's presence other than the hand cursor when it is moused over. You can add color and/or an underline to the linked text to let the user know that it is a link. You should use the *TextFormat* object's color and underline properties for this purpose:

```
myTextField.text = "click here";
myTextFormat = new TextFormat( );
myTextFormat.color = 0x0000FF;
myTextFormat.underline = true;
myTextFormat.url = "http://www.person13.com/";
myTextField.setTextFormat(myTextFormat);
```

You can use either of the techniques in this recipe to add links that point not only to *http* and *https* protocols, as shown in the examples, but also links to other protocols. For example, you can use the same techniques to open a new email message:

```
myTextField.text = "email me";
myTextFormat = new TextFormat( );
myTextFormat.color = 0x0000FF;
myTextFormat.underline = true;
myTextFormat.url = "mailto:joey@person13.com";
myTextField.setTextFormat(myTextFormat);
```

Be aware, however, that many other types of links (such as *mailto* links) will work only when the movie is being played in a web browser in which a default client for the protocol has been defined.

See Also

Recipes 8.10 and 8.18. Recipe 9.6 shows how to test whether a string has the form of a valid email address. Recipe 18.4 explains how to send data to a server-side script, which could then send the email for you. Recipe 20.10 explains how to call ColdFusion functions from Flash. You can use Cold Fusion's `<cfmail>` tag to send email from a ColdFusion server.

CHAPTER 9

Strings

9.0 Introduction

Strings are the fundamental textual element of the ActionScript language. You should use strings for any data in your application that uses characters for any reason. For example:

```
myString = "this is a string";
myString = 'this is also a string';
myString = "strings can contain characters such as -(*+5~";
```

String values must always be enclosed within quotes. You can use either single or double quotes, but the starting and ending quotes enclosing a string must be of the same type.

```
// Both of these strings cause errors because of mismatched quotes.
myString = "an incorrect string';      // Ending quote should be double
myString = 'another incorrect string";  // Ending quote should be single
```

ActionScript provides functionality that allows you to work with strings in many ways. Although ActionScript does not provide native support for regular expressions (pattern matching), the third-party *RegExp* class described in Recipe 9.6 does.

9.1 Joining Strings

Problem

You want to concatenate (join) together two or more strings into a single value.

Solution

Use the string concatenation operator (+) or the combination concatenation-assignment operator (+=). Alternatively, use the *concat()* method.

Discussion

You can join together multiple strings in a single expression using the concatenation operator (+) between the two string operands:

```
// Results in a single value of "Thisworks" (no space)
myString = "This" + "works";
```

If you want to join together more than two strings, use additional concatenation operators and string value operands in the appropriate order:

```
// Results in a single value of "This works" (with a space)
myString = "This" + " " + "works";
```

In the preceding examples, there is little reason why you would need to join together the string literals instead of assigning a single string value ("This works" instead of "This" + " " + "works"). However, this demonstrates the technique you'll use when working with dynamic values. You can use the concatenation operator to join together not only string literals, but also variables containing string values (or values that can be converted to strings). For example:

```
num = 24.
// Results in a single value of "There are 24 people"
myString = "There are " + num  + " people";
```

The concatenation operator automatically converts any non-string values to strings, as long as at least one of the operands in the statement is a string. In the preceding example, the number value, 24, is converted to the string value "24" automatically before being joined with the other strings. However, if all the operands are numbers, the ActionScript interpreter treats the + operator as the addition operator instead of the concatenation operator:

```
num1 = 24;
num2 = 42;
// Results in a number value of 66
myString = num1 + num2;
```

You can concatenate, rather than add, two or more numbers in several ways. One way is to concatenate an empty string to the beginning of the statement:

```
num1 = 24;
num2 = 42;
// Results in a string value of "2442"
myString = "" + num1 + num2;
```

The empty string must be placed first in the expression because if the two numbers appear first, they are added rather than concatenated, even though the final value is still converted to a string:

```
num1 = 24;
num2 = 42;
// Results in a string value of "66"
myString = num1 + num2 + "";
```

Another option is to use the *String()* function to ensure that at least one of the numbers is converted to a string before performing the concatenation:

```
num1 = 24;
num2 = 42;
// Results in a string value of "2442"
myString = String(num1) + num2;
```

When you use this technique for only two numbers, it does not matter which one you convert to a string (or you can convert both). But if you are joining more than two numbers, you should convert the first or second number to a string. Otherwise, the numbers preceding the value that is converted to a string will be added rather than concatenated.

```
num1 = 24;
num2 = 42;
num3 = 21;
// Results in a string value of "6621"
myString = num1 + num2 + String(num3);
```

If you want to add, rather than concatenate, two number values in the middle of a string concatenation statement, you should enclose that expression in parentheses. This evaluates the expression first, treating it as an addition operation rather than a concatenation operation.

```
num1 = 24;
num2 = 42;
// Results in "There are 66 people"
myString = "There are " + (num1 + num2) + " people";
```

You can also append text to strings using multiple lines of code rather than trying to cram it all into one statement. You should use the combination concatenation-assignment operator in these cases.

```
myString = "a ";
myString += "quick ";
myString += "brown ";
myString += "fox";
```

This technique can be useful for several reasons. First of all, sometimes you want to join together long string values, and your code remains more readable when you break it up into multiple lines:

```
myString = "This is the first line of a long paragraph of text.\n";
myString += "By adding line by line to the string variable you make ";
myString += "your code more readable.";
```

You may have a good reason to append more text to a string over time rather than all at once. For example, your movie may periodically poll a server-side script that returns updated data. You can append this new data to an existing string using the combination concatenation-assignment operator. For example:

```
// lv is a LoadVars object.
lv.onLoad = function () {
```

```
// Assume the server script returns a variable named newData. You can append its
// value (and a newline) to an existing string named myString.
_root.myString += this.newData + newline;
};
```

You can also use the *String.concat()* method to append new values to the end of an existing string. The *concat()* method does not affect the original string. Instead, it returns a new string containing the concatenated value.

```
myString = "first string value.";
```

```
// Set myNewString to "first string value.second string value."
// The value of myString remains unchanged.
myNewString = myString.concat("second string value.");
```

Flash 4 used the & operator for string concatenation. Flash converts the & operator to the *add* operator when updating Flash 4 files to Flash 5 or Flash 6 format. The + operator is the preferred string concatenation operator in Flash 5 and later.

9.2   Using Quotes and Apostrophes in Strings

Problem

You want to use quotes or apostrophes within a string value.

Solution

Use a backslash to escape the quotes or apostrophes contained within the string. Alternatively, use single quotes within double quotes, or vice versa.

Discussion

The ActionScript interpreter always matches up quotes of the same kind (single quotes with single quotes and double quotes with double quotes) when used in strings. Therefore, if you enclose a string literal within quotes of one type and try to include the same kinds of quotes in the string value, ActionScript fails to interpret it as you intended.

This string assignment causes an error because of mismatched quotes. Flash interprets the " character before the Y as the end of the string; it does not understand what to do with the remaining characters.

```
myString = "He said, "Yes.""; // Wrong!
```

One possible solution is to use single quotes to enclose a string literal that contains double quotes, or double quotes to enclose a string literal that contains single quotes:

```
// This assignment works. The result is a string: He said, "Yes."
myString = 'He said, "Yes."';
```

```
// This assignment also works. The result is a string: He said, 'Yes.'
myString = "He said, 'Yes.'";
```

However, if the string value contains both single and double quotes, this technique does not work. Furthermore, you have to pay close attention to what type of quotes are used where. An alternative solution, which will work all the time, is to use the backslash to escape any quote used within the string value (i.e., escape the quote by preceding it by the backslash character):

```
// This assignment works. The result is a string: He said, "Yes."
myString = "He said, \"Yes.\"";
```

The backslash character tells the ActionScript interpreter to interpret the next character literally, and not with any special meaning it might normally have. Therefore, when you precede a quotation mark within a string value with the backslash character, you tell the ActionScript interpreter that the quote does not signal the boundary of the string value, as it normally would.

9.3   Inserting Special Whitespace Characters

Problem

You want to add whitespace characters such as tabs or newline characters to your string.

Solution

Use the escape sequences for the special characters.

Discussion

There are five special whitespace characters with escape sequences, as shown in Table 9-1.

Table 9-1. Whitespace escape sequences

Whitespace character	Escape sequence
Newline	\n
Tab	\t
Backspace	\b
Form feed	\f
Carriage return	\r

You can use these escape sequences within a string. They are most useful when displaying a string value in a text field:

```
// Results in a string value: these    words    are    separated    by    tabs
myString = "these\twords\tare\tseparated\tby\ttabs";
```

```
/* Results in a string value:
these
words
are
separated
by
newlines
*/
myString = "these\nwords\nare\nseparated\nby\nnewlines";
```

ActionScript also provides a constant, newline, which can be used in place of the \n escape sequence. The result is the same:

```
/* Results in a string value:
two
lines
*/
myString = "two" + newline + "lines";
```

Within Flash, the newline, form feed, and carriage return characters all result in the same display. However, when you load content into Flash from external sources, some values will have newline characters, some will have form feeds, and some will have carriage returns.

9.4   Searching for a Substring

Problem

You want to find a value within a string.

Solution

Use the *indexOf()* or *lastIndexOf()* methods.

Discussion

You can use the *indexOf()* and *lastIndexOf()* methods to determine whether a string contains a specified substring value. Each method returns the starting index of the substring if it is found. If the substring is not found, the value −1 is returned.

The *indexOf()* method takes up to two parameters:

substring
   The substring value for which you want to search.

startIndex
   The zero-relative starting position from which to search within the string. If undefined, the method begins the search from the beginning of the string.

If you want to test whether a string contains another string, you can use the *indexOf()* method with only one parameter. For example:

```
myString = "This string contains the word cool twice. Very cool!";

// Get the index of the first occurrence of the substring "cool" within myString.
indexOfCool = myString.indexOf("cool");

// If the indexOf() method returns -1, no occurrences of "cool" were found.
if (indexOfCool != -1) {
  // Displays: "String contains word cool at index 30", because the first occurrence
  // of the substring appears starting at index 30 within myString.
  trace("String contains word cool at index " + indexOfCool);
}
```

You can get the indexes of subsequent occurrences of a substring by specifying the second, optional parameter of the *indexOf()* method, *StartIndex*. A simple and effective way to search for the next occurrence of a substring is to pass the method a starting index parameter value of one more than what was returned by the previous search:

```
myString = "This string contains the word cool twice. Very cool!";

// Get the index of the first occurrence of the substring "cool" within myString.
indexOfCool = myString.indexOf("cool");

if (indexOfCool != -1) {
  // Displays: "String contains word cool at index 30"
  trace("String contains word cool at index " + indexOfCool);
}

// Get the index of the second occurrence of the substring "cool" within myString.
// Pass the method the previous value of indexOfCool + 1. This starts the search past
// the starting index of the previous occurrence, thus finding the next occurrence.
// If you do not add 1 to indexOfCool when passing it to indexOf(), the method
// returns the location of the first occurrence again.
indexOfCool = myString.indexOf("cool", indexOfCool + 1);

if (indexOfCool != -1) {
  // Displays: "String contains word cool at index 47", because the next occurrence
  // of the substring appears starting at index 47 within myString.
  trace("String contains word cool at index " + indexOfCool);
}
```

You can use *indexOf()* in a *while* statement to get the indexes of every occurrence of a substring. For example:

```
myString = "This string contains the word cool thrice. Very cool! Yes, cool!";

// Initialize indexOfCool to -1 so that the while statement searches the string from
// the 0 index (starting at indexOfCool + 1).
indexOfCool = -1;

// Loop until indexOf() returns -1.
while ( (indexOfCool = myString.indexOf("cool", indexOfCool + 1)) != -1 ) {
```

```
/* Displays:
    String contains word cool at index 30
    String contains word cool at index 48
    String contains word cool at index 59
*/
    trace("String contains word cool at index " + indexOfCool);
}
```

The *while* conditional in the preceding code looks more complicated than it really is. If you take it apart, you can see that it is composed of manageable and understandable parts. The first part assigns to indexOfCool the value returned by the *indexOf()* method:

```
indexOfCool = myString.indexOf("cool", indexOfCool + 1);
```

The first time that this statement is encountered, the initial value of indexOfCool is −1 because it was set to −1 prior to the *while* statement. This is necessary to start the search at index 0 because 1 is added to that value each time. If indexOfCool is undefined, the ActionScript interpreter resolves it to 0; adding 1 to 0 causes Flash to search the string starting at index 1 instead of 0, potentially missing a match if the search string occurs at the beginning of the searched string. Each subsequent time the *while* condition is evaluated, the value of indexOfCool has the value of the starting index of the previously found match.

The second part of the *while* conditional tests to make sure that the result of the *indexOf()* method is not −1. This is important because without it, the *while* loop would continue indefinitely. When *indexOf()* returns −1, it means that no more matches exist, so the *while* loop terminates.

You can also search backward in a string. The *lastIndexOf()* method always returns the starting index of the last occurrence of the substring (it returns the position of the beginning of the found string, not its end, even though the search is performed backward). Therefore, it takes only one parameter: the substring for which to search. If no match is found, *lastIndexOf()* returns −1.

```
myString = "This string contains the word cool twice. Very cool!";

// Get the index of the last occurrence of the substring "cool" within myString.
indexOfCool = myString.lastIndexOf("cool");

if (indexOfCool != -1) {
    // Displays: "String contains word cool at index 47", because the last occurrence
    // of the substring appears starting at index 47 within myString.
    trace("String contains word cool at index " + indexOfCool);
}
```

Both the *indexOf()* and *lastIndexOf()* methods are case-sensitive in their searches. For example, the substring "cool" would not be found in the string "Cool" because the cases are not the same. To perform a case-insensitive search, use the *toLowerCase()* method in conjunction with the *indexOf()* or *lastIndexOf()* method:

```
// Create a string that spells "cool" as both "cool" and "Cool".
myString = "Cool! This is a string with the word cool. It spells cool as both ";
myString += "cool (lowercase) and Cool (capitalized).";

search = "cool";

// Output the index of the first occurrence of "cool". The result is 37 because it
// does not find "Cool" due to the case-sensitive search.
trace(myString.indexOf(search));

// Output the index of the first occurrence of "cool" after lowercasing the string
// with toLowerCase(). The result is 0 because it now finds "Cool" (which has been
// converted to "cool") at the beginning of the string.
trace(myString.toLowerCase().indexOf(search));

// Output the index of the last occurrence of "cool". The result is 66 because it
// does not find the last "Cool" due to the case-sensitivity.
trace(myString.lastIndexOf("cool"));

// Output the index of the last occurrence of cool after lowercasing the string. The
// result is 87 because it finds the last "Cool".
trace(myString.toLowerCase().lastIndexOf(search));

// Now change the search string to "Cool" (capitalized).
search = "Cool";

// Output the index of the first occurrence of "Cool" after lowercasing the string.
// The result is -1 because "Cool" doesn't exist in the lowercase string.
trace(myString.toLowerCase().indexOf(search));

// This is similar to the preceding line of code, but the search string is also
// converted to lowercase. Therefore, the result is 0 because the starting index of
// the first occurrence of "cool" (regardless of case) is 0. Lowercasing both the
// string being searched and the substring for which you are searching ensures that a
// completely case-insensitive search is performed.
trace(myString.toLowerCase().indexOf(search.toLowerCase()));
```

You can use the *indexOf()* method to create a find feature for text fields:

```
// Include DrawingMethods.as from Chapter 4 for its drawRectangle() method.
#include "DrawingMethods.as"

// Add the custom find() method to TextField.prototype so that it is available to
// all text fields. The method takes three parameters: search is the search string,
// startIndex is the index from which to perform the search, and matchCase is a
// Boolean that specifies if the search should be case-sensitive. If matchCase is
// undefined, the search is case-insensitive.
TextField.prototype.find = function (search, startIndex, matchCase) {
```

```
// Initialize the local variable, index.
var index;

// If matchCase is false or undefined, perform a case-insensitive search.
// Otherwise, do a case-sensitive match.
if (!matchCase) {
  index = this.text.toLowerCase().indexOf(search.toLowerCase( ), startIndex);
} else {
  index = this.text.indexOf(search, startIndex);
}

// Set the focus to the text field in case it is not already set.
Selection.setFocus(this);

// If the search string was found, set the selection to highlight the match within
// the text field. Otherwise, position the cursor at the beginning of the text
// field.
if (index != -1) {
  Selection.setSelection(index, index + search.length);
} else {
  Selection.setSelection(0, 0);
}

// Return the index of the match so that it can be used to pass the next startIndex
// value to this method when called again.
return index;
};

// Example usage:

// Create a text field.
_root.createTextField("myText", 1, 100, 100, 0, 0);
myText.autoSize = true;
myText.border = true;
myText.text = "This is a text field with text. And more text.";

// Create a button movie clip.
_root.createEmptyMovieClip("myButton_mc", 2);
myButton_mc.lineStyle(0, 0x000000, 100);
myButton_mc.beginFill(0, 100);
myButton_mc.drawRectangle(100, 20);
myButton_mc.endFill( );
myButton_mc._x = 400;
myButton_mc._y = 300;

// When the button is clicked, call the find( ) method of the myText text field. Pass
// it the search string text. The myButton_mc.currentIndex is set with each call to
// find( ) to the value of the starting index of the found match. Therefore, passing
// currentIndex + 1 to find( ) makes it look for the next match.
myButton_mc.onRelease = function ( ) {
  this.currentIndex = _root.myText.find("text", this.currentIndex + 1, false);
};
```

9.5   Extracting a Substring

Problem

You want to extract a substring from a string.

Solution

Use the *substring()*, *substr()*, or *slice()* methods.

Discussion

The *substring()*, *substr()*, and *slice()* methods all return the value of a substring without affecting the original string. The only difference between the three methods is in the parameters they accept.

The *substr()* method takes up to two parameters:

startIndex

> The position of the first character of the substring. The value can be negative, in which case the index is calculated from the end of the string, where −1 is the last character, −2 is the second-to-last character, and so on.

length

> The number of characters in the substring to extract. If this parameter is omitted, all the characters from *startIndex* to the end are used:

```
myString = "Bunnies";
trace(myString.substr(0));       // Displays: Bunnies
trace(myString.substr(0, 3));    // Displays: Bun
trace(myString.substr(3, 3));    // Displays: nie
trace(myString.substr(-1));      // Displays: s
trace(myString.substr(-2, 5));   // Displays: es
```

The *substring()* and *slice()* methods each take the same parameters:

startIndex

> The position of the first character of the substring to extract.

endIndex

> The position of one character after the last character in the substring to extract. If this parameter is omitted, all the characters from the *startIndex* to the end are used.

The *substring()* and *slice()* methods differ in that *substring()* accepts positive index values only; it interprets negative values as 0. Also, if *endIndex* is less than *startIndex*, the *substring()* method automatically reverses them before executing. The *slice()* method, on the other hand, accepts negative values for both *startIndex* and *endIndex*; it interprets negative values as counting back from the end of the string. The *slice()* method fails if you specify an *endIndex* that is less than *startIndex*.

```
myString = "Rabbits";

// Both of these output the entire string, beginning at index 0 and going to the last
// index (the value of which is myString.length - 1).
trace(myString.substring(0));        // Displays: Rabbits
trace(myString.slice(0));            // Displays: Rabbits

// The substring() method outputs nothing because it converts the negative indexes to
// 0. The slice() method outputs "it", which is the substring from the third-to-last
// character (index -3) to the next-to-last character (index -1).
trace(myString.substring(-3, -1));  // Displays nothing
trace(myString.slice(-3, -1));      // Displays: it

// Both of these output the substring "ab".
trace(myString.substring(1, 3));    // Displays: ab
trace(myString.slice(1, 3));        // Displays: ab

// The substring() method outputs the substring "ab" because it reverses the order of
// the parameters automatically. The slice() method outputs nothing because the
// slice() method does not reverse the order of the parameters.
trace(myString.substring(3, 1));    // Displays: ab
trace(myString.slice(3, 1));        // Displays nothing
```

You will commonly use the substring-extraction methods in conjunction with the *indexOf()* and *lastIndexOf()* methods. You can use the *indexOf()* and *lastIndexOf()* methods to search for the substring within a string, and then you can use the substring-extraction methods to get the substrings.

This example extracts a file's extension and its filename (without the extension), which are presumed to be separated from each other by a period:

```
filename = "mydocument.jpg";
// Find the location of the period.
extIndex = filename.lastIndexOf(".");

// The extensionless filename ("mydocument") is everything before the period.
strippedFileName = filename.substr(0, extIndex);
trace ("The filename is " + strippedFileName);

// The extension ("jpg") is everything after the period.
extension = filename.substr(extIndex + 1, filename.length);
trace ("The file extension is " + extension);
```

You can also use the *split()* method, assuming there is only one period in the filename:

```
filename = "mydocument.jpg";
// Split the string wherever the period occurs.
nameArray = filename.split(".");

// The first element is "mydocument" (everything before the first period).
strippedFileName = nameArray[0];
trace ("The filename is " + strippedFileName);
```

```
// The next element is "jpg" (anything after the first
// period and before the next one).
extension = nameArray[1];
trace ("The file extension is " + extension);
```

Compare the two preceding examples. What happens if the filename contains no periods, such as "mydocument"? (Hint: The first example fails in that case.) What if the filename contains more than one period, such as "ascb_fig8.1.bmp"? (Hint: The second example fails in that case.)

Here is a general solution:

```
// This function returns everything before the last period, if any.
function stripExtension (filename) {
  // Find the location of the period.
  extIndex = filename.lastIndexOf(".");
  if (extIndex == -1) {
    // Oops, there is no period. Just return the filename.
    return filename;
  } else {
    return filename.substr(0, extIndex);
  }
}

// This function returns everything after the last period, if any.
function extractExtension (filename) {
  // Find the location of the period.
  extIndex = filename.lastIndexOf(".");
  if (extIndex == -1) {
    // Oops, there is no period, so return the empty string
    return "";
  } else {
    return filename.substr(extIndex + 1, filename.length);
  }
}
// Example usage:
trace(stripExtension("mydocument.jpg"));       // Displays: mydocument
trace(stripExtension("mydocument"));           // Displays: mydocument
trace(stripExtension("mydocument.1.jpg"));     // Displays: mydocument.1
trace(extractExtension("mydocument.jpg"));     // Displays: jpg
trace(extractExtension("mydocument"));         // Displays nothing
trace(extractExtension("mydocument.1.jpg"));   // Displays: jpg
```

See Also

Recipe 9.8

9.6 Matching Patterns with Regular Expressions

Problem

You want to match a pattern within a string instead of finding a specific substring.

Solution

Use a regular expression and the *RegExp.exec()* method.

Discussion

Many programming languages support *regular expressions* to match patterns in strings. (You may be familiar with other types of pattern matching. For example, Windows' file search feature lets you use pattern matching with wildcards, such as * and ?. But regular expressions support much more sophisticated pattern matching.) ActionScript does not provide native support for regular expressions. However, there are several third-party classes that are publicly available. One such class is the *RegExp* class by Pavils Jurjans, which is very similar to the JavaScript 1.3 *RegExp* class (JavaScript 1.5 implements new *RegExp* features not supported by the Action-Script *RegExp* class).

Table 9-2 summarizes regular expression pattern-matching operations.

Table 9-2. Regular expressions

Expression	Matches	Example
?	The preceding character zero or one time (i.e., preceding character is optional).	ta?k matches "tak" or "tk" but not "tik" or "taak"
*	The preceding character zero or more times.	wo*k matches "wok", "wk", or "woook", but not "wak"
+	The preceding character one or more times.	craw+l matches "crawl" or "crawwl" but not "cral"
. (period)	Any one character except newline.	c.ow matches "crow" or "clow" but not "cow"
^	Specified string at beginning of a line.	^wap matches "wap" but not "swap"
$	Specified string at the end of a line. (The "$" metacharacter should be at the end of the pattern, such as w$. Though *RegExp* accepts it at the beginning of the pattern, such as $w, this feature is not supported by the ECMA standard.)	ow$ matches "ow" but not "owl"
x|y	Either statement.	one|two matches "one" or "two" but not "ten"

Table 9-2. Regular expressions (continued)

Expression	Matches	Example
[abc]	Any of the characters within the brackets.	l[aeo]g matches "lag", "leg", or "log" but not "lig"
[a–z]	Any characters within the range.	[0-3]* matches "1320" but not "4523"
[^abc]	Any character other than those listed.	l[^aeo]g matches "lig" but not "lag", "leg", or "log"
[^a–z]	Any characters not in the range.	[^0-3]* matches "4758" but not "4931"
{n}	Exactly *n* occurrences of the preceding character.	cre{2}l matches "creel" but not "crel" or "creeel"
{n,m}	At least *n* but no more than *m* instances of the preceding letter.	cre{2,3}l matches "creel" or "creeel" but not "crel"
\b	Word boundary.	up\brow matches "up row" but not "uprow"
\B	Letter not at the beginning of a word.	up\Brow matches "uprow" but not "up row"
\d	Any numeric digit; same as [0–9].	\d* matches "13243" but not "13A46"
\D	Any non-digit character; same as [^0–9].	\D* matches "1ABC3" but not "13946"
\s	Single whitespace character (space, tab, line feed, or form feed).	\s matches the space in "King Tut"
\S	Single non-whitespace character.	\STut matches "gTut" but not "Tut"
\w	Any alphanumeric character; same as [A–Za–z0–9]	a\wm matches "arm" but not "a8m"
\W	Any nonalphanumeric character.	a\Wm matches "a7m" but not "aim"
\x	Escaped character (non-metacharacters) specified by *x*.	\/ finds slashes; \(finds parentheses, etc.

The *RegExp* class does not try to interpret escape sequences that are natively interpreted by Flash. The ActionScript *RegExp* class interprets the escape sequences \d, \D, \s, \S, \w, \W, \b, and \B, but other escape sequences, such as \n and \t, are interpreted by Flash itself. Therefore, if you want to match a newline character, you should use the pattern "\n", but if you want to match a digit, you use the pattern "\\d" (note the double backslash before "d").

You must first download and install the *RegExp* class if you wish to use it in your Flash documents. You can download it from Pavils's web site:

http://www.jurjans.lv/flash/RegExp.html

You can download the ActionScript file itself (*RegExp.as*) or a zip file (*RegExp.zip*) that contains additional support files. Whichever download you choose, copy the *RegExp.as* file into your Flash installation's *Include* directory (*Flash Installation/Configuration/Include*). From there, you can easily include it in any Flash document.

The main difference between Pavils's ActionScript *RegExp* class and its JavaScript kin is that there is no way to define a regular expression using an object initializer. Instead, you must always use the constructor method:

```
// This will work in JavaScript but not in ActionScript.
re = /[a-z]*/;

// This is the proper way to create a regular expression in ActionScript.
re = new RegExp("[a-z]*");

// Create a regular expression that matches a backslash.
re = new RegExp("\\\\");
```

 Because the *RegExp* object is created by passing a string to the constructor, all references to \ within the string must be escaped as \\. Since \ is also a special character in *RegExp* patterns, to search for a backslash in a regular expression, you must escape it like this: "\\\\".

When constructing a regular expression, you can specify a second parameter containing flags that modify its behavior. The most common flags are "i" for case-insensitive matches and "g" for global matching (finds all matches at once and returns them in an array). For example:

```
// This matches all letters a, b, c, A, B, and C.
re = new RegExp("[a-c]", "ig");
```

Once you have created a regular expression that describes the pattern for which you want to search within the string, use the *regExp.exec()* method to perform the search. The *exec()* method takes the string as a parameter, and it returns the match. Each call to *exec()* searches for the next match. If no match is found, it returns null.

```
// You must include the third-party RegExp.as file from
// http://www.jurjans.lv/flash/RegExp.html.
#include "RegExp.as"

// Create a regular expression that matches three-letter words.
re = new RegExp("\\b[a-z]{3}\\b", "g");

myString = "This string has two three-letter words";

// Search the string for the pattern and display the first result: has.
match = re.exec(myString);
trace(match);

// Search the string again for the pattern and display the next result: two.
match = re.exec(myString);
trace(match);

// Search the string again. No more matches, so the result is null.
match = re.exec(myString);
trace(match);
```

The *exec()* method continues to cycle through the string with each call. After the method returns null, it will return to the beginning of the string for the next search.

You can use a *while* statement with the *exec()* method to find all the matches, like so:

```
#include "RegExp.as"

// Create a regular expression that matches three-letter words.
re = new RegExp("\\b[a-z]{3}\\b", "g");
myString = "This string has two three-letter words";

/* Loop until the exec( ) method returns null. This while loop outputs:
    has
    two
*/
while ((match = re.exec(myString)) != null) {
  trace(match);
}
```

The *RegExp.test()* method tests whether a string contains a match to a regular expression. The method returns true if the pattern is matched, and false otherwise. You can use *test()* to test whether a string is valid for a particular use, such as whether it takes the form of a valid email address. For example:

```
#include "RegExp.as"

// Create a regular expression that matches an email pattern.
re = new RegExp("^([\\w\-\\.]+)@(([\\w\\-]+\\.)+[\\w\\-]+)$");

// Create an array of strings that may or may not be valid emails.
emails = new Array( );
emails.push("someone@someserver.com");
emails.push("your.name@someplace.org");
emails.push("email goes here");

/* Test each array element to see whether it is a valid email. The results are:
    true
    true
    false
*/
for (var i = 0; i < emails.length; i++) {
  trace(re.test(emails[i]));
}
```

See Also

A detailed discussion of regular expressions is beyond the scope of this book. A good primer on the JavaScript *RegExp* class can be found at *http://devedge.netscape.com/library/manuals/2000/javascript/1.3/guide/regexp.html*. *JavaScript: The Definitive Guide* by David Flanagan (O'Reilly) includes detailed coverage of using regular expressions in JavaScript. See *Mastering Regular Expressions* by Jeffrey E. F. Friedl (O'Reilly) for extensive practice with regular expressions. Also refer to Recipes 9.4 and 9.7. Recipe 9.9 demonstrates using regular expressions to remove nonalphanumeric characters in a string. Also see Recipe 8.7, which covers filtering text input. Table A-1 lists the Unicode code points for the Latin 1 character set. Recipe 11.4 discusses validating data input.

9.7   Looking for a Pattern Match

Problem

You want to search a string for every match to a pattern.

Solution

Use the custom *String.match()* method.

Discussion

The native ActionScript *String* class does not provide a *match()* method that allows you to find matches to a pattern within a string. However, the custom *RegExp.as* file (see Recipe 9.6) adds a *match()* method to the *String* class.

You should call the *match()* method from a string and pass it a regular expression as a parameter. The method searches the string for all matching substrings and places them in a new array:

```
// You must include the third-party RegExp.as file from Recipe 9.6.
#include "RegExp.as"

myString = "Twenty twins went toward them";

// Create a new regular expression to perform a case-insensitive match on an entire
// string for any words that begin with "tow" or "tw".
re = new RegExp("\\bt(o)?w[\\w]+\\b", "ig");

// Find all the matches and put them in an array.
matches = myString.match(re);

/* Loop through the array and display the results. The output is:
   Twenty
   twins
   toward
*/
for (var i = 0; i < matches.length; i++) {
  trace(matches[i]);
}
```

See Also

Recipe 9.6

9.8 Parsing a String into Words

Problem

You want to process a string one word at a time.

Solution

Use the *split()* method.

Discussion

The *split()* method (see Recipe 6.6) splits a string into an array using the specified delimiter. To split a string into separate words, use the *split()* method with a space as the delimiter:

```
// Create a string with multiple words.
myString = "this is a string of words";

// Split the string into an array of words using a space as the delimiter.
words = myString.split(" ");

// Loop through the array and do something with each word. In this example, we just
// output the values.
for (var i = 0; i < words.length; i++) {
  /* Displays:
    this
    is
    a
    string
    of
    words
  */
  trace(words[i]);
}
```

You can process the individual words in many ways. Here is an example that uses this technique to split a string into words and then creates movie clips containing those words. The user can then drag the words around on stage to form various sentences or statements, as in the popular magnetic poetry kits.

```
// Create a string and split the string into an array of words.
myString = "This is a string of ActionScript poetry words";
words = myString.split(" ");

// Loop through all the words in the array.
for (var i = 0; i < words.length; i++) {
```

```
// Create a new movie clip for each word.
word_mc = _root.createEmptyMovieClip("word" + i, i);

// Create a text field within each movie clip.
word_mc.createTextField("word_txt", 1, 0, 0, 0, 0);

// The text field should autosize to fit its contents. It should also have a border
// and background so that it mimics the look of poetry magnets.
word_mc.word_txt.autoSize   = true;
word_mc.word_txt.border     = true;
word_mc.word_txt.background = true;

// Set each movie clip's text field value to one of the words from the array.
word_mc.word_txt.text = words[i]

// The movie clip is draggable when clicked and stops
// being draggable when released.
word_mc.onPress = function () {
  this.startDrag();
};
word_mc.onRelease = function () {
  this.stopDrag();
};

// Randomize the position of the movie clips containing words.
rx = Math.random() * Stage.width  - word_mc._width;
ry = Math.random() * Stage.height - word_mc._height;
word_mc._x = rx;
word_mc._y = ry;
}
```

The preceding use of *split()* by itself is all that you need when the original string value contains words and spaces but no punctuation. If the string has punctuation or other miscellaneous characters, you should remove them first by using a regular expression and the custom *String.replace()* method included in *RegExp.as*. The regular expression to remove everything except letters, numbers, and spaces is [^a-zA-Z0-9]:

```
// You must include the third-party RegExp.as file from Recipe 9.6.
#include "RegExp.as"

// Create a string that uses punctuation.
myString = "Here are some words. Also, here is some punctuation!";

// Create an array of words from the string without first removing punctuation.
words = myString.split(" ");

// Display the elements of the array. Some of the elements also contain
// punctuation. This is most likely undesirable.
for (var i = 0; i < words.length; i++) {

  /* Outputs:
     Here
     are
```

```
        some
        words.
        Also,
        here
        is
        some
        punctuation!
    */
    trace(words[i]);
}
// Create a regular expression that can be used to remove all nonalphanumeric
// characters and spaces.
re = new RegExp("[^a-zA-Z0-9 ]", "g");

// Call the replace() method of myString. Pass it the regular expression, re, and
// tell it to replace all nonmatching characters with the empty string.
nString = myString.replace(re, "");

// Split nString, the result of the replace() method call, into an array of words.
words = nString.split(" ");

// Output all the elements of the words array. This time each element is a word, and
// none of the elements include punctuation.
for (var i = 0; i < words.length; i++) {

    /* Outputs:
       Here
       are
       some
       words
       Also
       here
       is
       some
       punctuation
    */
    trace(words[i]);
}
```

Including the *RegExp.as* file also enhances the *String.split()* method to support regular expressions as a parameter directly. Therefore, instead of calling *String.replace()* separately, as shown in the preceding example:

```
re = new RegExp("[^a-zA-Z0-9 ]", "g");
nString = myString.replace(re, "");
words = nString.split(" ");
```

you can pass the *RegExp* object directly to *split()*, as follows:

```
re = new RegExp("[^a-zA-Z0-9]", "g");
words = myString.split(re);
```

See Also

Recipes 6.6, 9.6, 9.5, and 9.9

9.9 Removing and Replacing Characters

Problem

You want to remove characters from a string and optionally replace them.

Solution

Create a custom *String.simpleReplace()* method. Alternatively, for replacing patterns, use the *String.replace()* method included in *RegExp.as*.

Discussion

ActionScript does not provide a native method that replaces substrings within a string. Therefore, you must use a custom method to do so. If you want to replace instances of a specific substring, you can create a custom *simpleReplace()* method for the *String* class. This method should accept up to three parameters:

search
> The substring you want to find and replace.

replace
> The value with which to replace the occurrences of the *search* substring.

matchCase
> If true, the method performs a case-sensitive search. Otherwise, it performs a case-insensitive search.

Here is our custom *String.simpleReplace()* method:

```
String.prototype.simpleReplace = function (search, replace, working) {

  // temp stores the string value with the replaced substrings.
  var temp;

  // working holds the value of the string.
  var working = this;

  // Perform a case-insensitive search if so directed.
  if (!matchCase) {
    working = this.toLowerCase();
    search = search.toLowerCase();
  }
```

```
// searchIndex holds the starting index of a matches. startIndex stores the value
// of the index after the replaced substring.
var searchIndex = -1;
var startIndex = 0;

// Find each match to the search substring.
while ((searchIndex = working.indexOf(search, startIndex)) != -1) {

    // Append to temp the string value from the end of the last match to just before
    // the current match. Then, append the replace string in place of the search
    // substring.
    temp += this.substring(startIndex, searchIndex);
    temp += replace;

    // startIndex holds the index one after the final character of the matched
    // substring. This starts the next search-and-replace operation after the
    // substring that is being replaced.
    startIndex = searchIndex + search.length;
}

// Return the temp value plus the remainder of the original
//string value (after the last match).
return temp + this.substring(startIndex);
};

// Create a string to test.
myString = "It's a bird, it's a plane, it's ActionScript Man!";

// Replace all instances of "it's" with "it is". Perform a case-insensitive match.
// Outputs: it is a bird, it is a plane, it is ActionScript Man!
trace(myString.simpleReplace("it's", "it is", false));
```

In cases where you need to perform pattern matching as part of the replacement within a string, you should use the custom *String.replace()* method, which is available only if you include the *RegExp.as* file. This method allows you to match and replace using a regular expression instead of a string literal, which offers a great deal more flexibility.

You should first create a regular expression using the *RegExp* constructor. The regular expression should be the pattern that you want to match and replace in your string. Then pass that regular expression as the first parameter to the *String.replace()* method. The second parameter should be a string literal that you want to use to replace all occurrences of the pattern.

```
// You must include the third-party RegExp.as file from Recipe 9.6.
#include "RegExp.as"

// Create a string that includes people and telephone numbers. The telephone numbers
// follow the same pattern, so you can use a regular expression to replace them.
myString = "Regina [555-1212], Henriette [555-1234]";

// Create a regular expression that matches the telephone number pattern and searches
// globally. This pattern matches U.S. telephone number patterns (without area codes)
```

```
// and is provided for demo purposes only. You must adapt it to match telephone
// number patterns in your country. You could also use "\\d" instead of "[0-9]" in
// the following expression.
re = new RegExp("[0-9]{3}-[0-9]{4}", "g");

// Output the string with the telephone numbers replaced by X's. The result is:
// Regina [XXX-XXXX], Henriette [XXX-XXXX]
trace(myString.replace(re, "XXX-XXXX"));
```

9.10   Processing One Character at a Time

Problem

You want to process a string one character at a time.

Solution

Use a *for* statement and the *String.charAt()* method. Alternatively, use *String.split()*
with the empty string as the delimiter to split the string into an array of all the characters, then use a *for* statement to loop through the array.

Discussion

The simplest way to process each character of a string is to use a *for* statement that
loops from 0 to the length of the string, incrementing by 1. Within the *for* statement
body, you can use the *charAt()* method to extract each character for processing.

```
myString = "a string";

// Loop from 0 to the length of the string.
for (var i = 0; i < myString.length; i++) {
  /* Output each character, one at a time. This displays:
    a

    s
    t
    r
    i
    n
    g
  */
  trace(myString.charAt(i));
}
```

You can achieve the same effect by using the *split()* method to first split the string
into an array of characters and then looping through the array to process each character. You should use the empty string as the delimiter parameter for the *split()*
method to split between each character.

```
myString = "a string";

// Split the string into an array of characters (one-character strings).
chars = myString.split("");

// Loop through all the elements of the chars array.
for (var i = 0; i < chars.length; i++) {
  /* Output each character element. This displays:
     a

     s
     t
     r
     i
     n
     g
  */
  trace(chars[i]);
}
```

Both techniques are generally interchangeable, though the second offers some advantages if you want to process the characters using common array methods. For example, if you first split a string into an array of characters, you can sort that array. This is not as easily done when you use the *charAt()* technique:

```
myString = "a string";

chars = myString.split("");

// Alphabetically sort the array of characters.
chars.sort( );

for (var i = 0; i < chars.length; i++) {
  /* Displays:

     a
     g
     i
     n
     r
     s
     t
  */
  trace(chars[i]);
}
```

Also, if you want to use this process to remove every instance of a particular character, it is easier with an array than with the *charAt()* technique:

```
myString = "a string";

chars = myString.split("");

for (var i = 0; i < chars.length; i++) {
```

```
      // Remove all "r" elements from the array. Be sure to decrement i if an element is
      // removed. Otherwise, the next element is improperly skipped.
      if (chars[i] == "r") {
        chars.splice(i, 1);
        i--;
      }
    }
  }

  // Displays: a sting
  trace(chars.join(""));
```

See Also

Though the preceding technique for replacing characters works for simple cases, you should see Recipe 9.9 for more capable alternatives.

9.11   Converting Case

Problem

You want to change the case of a string or perform a case-insensitive comparison.

Solution

User the *toUpperCase()* and *toLowerCase()* methods.

Discussion

The *toUpperCase()* and *toLowerCase()* methods return new strings in which all the characters are uppercase or lowercase, respectively. This is useful in situations in which you want to ensure uniformity of case. For example, you can use *toLowerCase()* or *toUpperCase()* to perform case-insensitive searches within strings, as shown in Recipe 9.4. Both methods affect alphabetical characters only, leaving nonalphabetic characters unchanged.

```
  myString = "What case?";

  // Displays: what case?
  trace(myString.toLowerCase());

  // Displays: WHAT CASE?
  trace(myString.toUpperCase());

  // The original string value is unchanged: What case?
  trace(myString);
```

Both methods return a new string. To alter the original string, reassign the return value to it, as follows:

```
  myString = myString.toLowerCase();
```

You can use *toLowerCase()* and *toUpperCase()* in concert to capitalize the first letter of a word, as implemented in the following custom *toInitialCap()* method:

```
String.prototype.toInitialCap = function () {
  // Convert the first character to uppercase and the remainder to lowercase.
  return this.charAt(0).toUpperCase() + this.substr(1).toLowerCase();
};
```

```
myString = "bRuCE";
trace(myString.toInitialCap());     // Displays: Bruce
```

Here is another function that converts a string to so-called *title case* (initial letters capitalized). Unlike the preceding example, it doesn't lowercase subsequent characters.

```
String.prototype.toTitleCase = function () {
  working = this;
  var words = working.split(" ");
  for (var i = 0; i < words.length; i++) {
    words[i] = words[i].charAt(0).toUpperCase() + words[i].substr(1)
  }
  return (words.join(" "));
};
```

```
myString = "the actionScript cookbook";
trace(myString.toTitleCase ());     // Displays: The ActionScript Cookbook
```

9.12   Trimming Whitespace

Problem

You want to trim the whitespace from the beginning and end of a string.

Solution

Write a custom *trim()* method that splits the string into an array of characters, removes the whitespace from the beginning and end, and then returns the character array as a string using *join()*.

Discussion

Extra whitespace at the beginning and end of a string is a common enough annoyance that you should have a way of dealing with it. ActionScript does not provide a native *trim()* method, so you have to write your own.

The custom *trim()* method presented here:

1. Splits the string into an array or characters
2. Removes whitespace elements at the beginning of the array until it finds an element that is not a whitespace character (tab, form feed, carriage return, newline, or space)

3. Removes whitespace elements at the end of the array

4. Uses *join()* to form the array characters into a single string and returns that value

Here is our custom *String.trim()* function. You can add it to a *String.as* file for easy inclusion in other projects.

```
String.prototype.trim = function () {

  // Split the string into an array of characters.
  var chars = this.split("");

  // Remove any whitespace elements from the beginning of the array using splice().
  // Use a break statement to exit the loop when you reach a non-whitespace character
  // to prevent it from removing whitespace in the middle of the string.
  for (var i = 0; i < chars.length; i++) {
    if (chars[i] == "\r" ||
        chars[i] == "\n" ||
        chars[i] == "\f" ||
        chars[i] == "\t" ||
        chars[i] == " ") {
      chars.splice(i, 1);
      i--;
    } else {
      break;
    }
  }

  // Loop backward through the array, removing whitespace elements until a
  // non-whitespace character is encountered. Then break out of the loop.
  for (var i = chars.length - 1; i >= 0; i--) {
    if (chars[i] == "\r" ||
        chars[i] == "\n" ||
        chars[i] == "\f" ||
        chars[i] == "\t" ||
        chars[i] == " ") {
      chars.splice(i, 1);
    } else {
      break;
    }
  }

  // Recreate the string with the join() method and return the result.
  return chars.join("");
};

// Create a string with beginning and ending whitespace.
myString = "\n\r\f\ta string\t\t\n\n";

/* Display the value before calling the trim() method. Displays:
this string value is:


  a string
```

```
<end>
*/
trace("this string value is: " + myString + "<end>");

// Set myString to the value returned by the trim( ) method.
myString = myString.trim( );

/* Now, display the value again using the same trace( ) statement. Displays:
this string value is: a string<end>
*/
trace("this string value is: " + myString + "<end>");
```

For good measure, here is a trim function implemented using the *RegExp* class:

```
// You must include the third-party RegExp.as file from Recipe 9.6.
#include "RegExp.as"
var trimRe = new RegExp("^\\s*|\\s*$");
var myString = "\r\n\f\t test string \r\n\f\t";
trace(myString.replace(trimRe, ""));  // Displays: test string
```

9.13   Reversing a String by Word or by Letter

Problem

You want to reverse a string either by word or by letter.

Solution

Use the *split()* method to create an array of the words/characters and use the *reverse()* and *join()* methods on that array.

Discussion

You can reverse a string by word or by character using the same process. The only difference is in the delimiter you use in the *split()* method and the joiner you use in the *join()* method. In either case, you should first split the string into an array—using a space as the delimiter for words or the empty string as the delimiter for characters. Then call the *reverse()* method of the array, which reverses the order of the elements. Finally, use the *join()* method to reconstruct the string. When reversing by word, use a space as the joiner, and when reversing by character, use the empty string as the joiner.

```
myString = "hello dear reader";

// Split the string into an array of words.
words = myString.split(" ");

// Reverse the array.
words.reverse( );
```

```
// Join the elements of the array into a string using spaces.
myStringRevByWord = words.join(" ");

// Outputs: reader dear hello
trace(myStringRevByWord);

// Split the string into an array of characters.
chars = myString.split("");

// Reverse the array elements.
chars.reverse( );

// Join the array elements into a string using the empty string.
myStringRevByChar = chars.join("");

// Outputs: redaer raed olleh
trace(myStringRevByChar);
```

9.14 Converting Between Strings and Unicode or ASCII

Problem

You want to convert between characters and their corresponding Unicode code point (a.k.a. character codes) or ASCII codes.

Solution

Use the *String.charCodeAt( )* and *String.fromCharCode( )* methods.

Discussion

You can use *fromCharCode( )* to display characters that you cannot enter into your Flash document directly. The method is a static method, which means that it is invoked from the top-level *String* object instead of from a string instance. For values less than 128, *fromCharCode( )* essentially converts a numeric ASCII code to its equivalent character.

```
/* Outputs:
   New paragraph: ¶
   Cents: ¢
   Name: Joey
*/
trace("New paragraph: " + String.fromCharCode(182));
trace("Cents: " + String.fromCharCode(162));
trace("Name: " + String.fromCharCode(74, 111, 101, 121));
```

You can use the *charCodeAt()* method to retrieve the code point of the character at a particular index of a string. For characters whose Unicode code point is less than 128, *charCodeAt()* essentially converts a character to its equivalent ASCII code.

```
myString = "abcd";

// Outputs the code point, 97, of the first character, a
trace(myString.charCodeAt(0));
```

The *fromCharCode()* method is an alternative to using Unicode escape sequences to display special characters. However, you can also use *fromCharCode()* in concert with *charCodeAt()* to test for the existence of special characters:

```
myString = String.fromCharCode(191) + "Donde es el ba" +
           String.fromCharCode(241)  + "o?";

// Test whether the first character of the string has the code point of 191. If so,
// displays: The string "¿Donde es el baño?" has a ¿ at the beginning.
if (myString.charCodeAt(0) == 191) {
  message = "The string \"" + myString + "\" has a " + String.fromCharCode(191) +
            " at the beginning.";
  trace(message);
}
```

 The following methods are useful for creating cryptographic word games, but they are not secure and should not be used for sensitive data.

You can use the *charCodeAt()* and *fromCharCode()* methods in concert to encode and decode a string:

```
String.prototype.encode = function () {

  // The codeMap property is assigned to the String class when the encode() method is
  // first run. Therefore, if no codeMap is defined, it needs to be created.
  if (String.codeMap == undefined) {

    // The codeMap property is an associative array that maps each original code
    // point to another code point.
    String.codeMap = new Object();

    // Create an array of all the code points from 0 to 255.
    var origMap = new Array();
    for (var i = 0; i <= 255; i++) {
      origMap.push(i);
    }

    var rand;

    // Create a temporary array that is a copy of the origMap array.
    var charTemp = origMap.concat();
```

```
    // Loop through all the character code points in origMap.
    for (var i = 0; i < origMap.length; i++) {

        // Create a random number that is between 0 and the last index of charTemp.
        rand = Math.round(Math.random( ) * (charTemp.length-1));

        // Assign to codeMap values such that the keys are the original code points and
        // the values are the code points to which they should be mapped.
        String.codeMap[origMap[i]] = charTemp[rand];

        // Remove the elements from charTemp that were just assigned to codeMap. This
        // prevents duplicates.
        charTemp.splice(rand, 1);
    }
  }

  // Split the string into an array of characters.
  var chars = this.split("");

  // Replace each character in the array with the corresponding value from codeMap.
  for (var i = 0; i < chars.length; i++) {
      chars[i] = String.fromCharCode(String.codeMap[chars[i].charCodeAt(0)]);
  }

  // Return the encoded string.
  return chars.join("");
};

String.prototype.decode = function ( ) {

  // Split the encoded string into an array of characters.
  var chars = this.split("");

  // Create an associative array that reverses the keys and values of codeMap. This
  // allows you to do a reverse lookup based on the encoded character rather than the
  // original character.
  var reverseMap = new Object( );
  for (var key in String.codeMap) {
    reverseMap[String.codeMap[key]] = key;
  }

  // Loop through all the characters in the array and replace
  // them with the corresponding value from reverseMap, thus
  // recovering the original character values.
  for (var i = 0; i < chars.length; i++) {
    chars[i] = String.fromCharCode(reverseMap[chars[i].charCodeAt(0)]);
  }

  // Return the decoded string.
  return chars.join("");
};

// Example usage:
myString = "She sells sea shells by the sea shore";
```

```
// Create the encoded version of myString using the encode( ) method.
encoded = myString.encode( );

// Output the value of the encoded string. This will be randomly generated each time
// you run the movie. It might look something like this:
// êEk¶˘k§§˘¶˚k¬¶˚Ek§§˘¶v_¶¥Ek¶˚k¬¶˚E _k
trace(encoded);

// Output the value returned by the decode( ) method.
// Displays: She sells sea shells by the sea shore
trace(encoded.decode( ));
```

See Also

Table A-1 lists the Unicode code points for the Latin 1 character set.

## CHAPTER 10

Dates and Times

10.0 Introduction

Dates and times are important to many ActionScript applications, particularly when you develop more robust applications that offer users services. Date and time values are important for determining the amount of time that has elapsed for timed operations, for determining whether a user's trial membership is active, and for storing transaction dates, to name but a few scenarios.

ActionScript stores dates and times internally as *Epoch milliseconds*, which are the number of milliseconds that have elapsed since the *Epoch*, namely midnight, January 1, 1970 Coordinated Universal Time (UTC). For our purposes, UTC is essentially equivalent to the more familiar Greenwich Mean Time (GMT). (See *http://aa.usno.navy.mil/faq/docs/UT.html* to learn about the subtle distinctions.) Many programming languages store dates in terms of the Epoch (often in seconds instead of milliseconds); therefore, you can readily work with date and time values that have been imported from other sources (and vice versa).

In addition, the *Date* class allows you to set and get date and time values in terms of years, months, days, and so on, using methods such as *getFullYear()*, *setFullYear()*, *getMonth()*, and *setMonth()*. These methods are for your convenience, but the values are stored internally as Epoch milliseconds.

10.1 Finding the Current Date and Time

Problem

You want to know the current date and time.

Solution

Create a new date using the *Date()* constructor with no parameters. Alternatively, use a CGI script or any other server-side language to return the server time, and create a new *Date* object from that value.

Discussion

The date and time that ActionScript can calculate on its own is based on the client computer's date and time settings. Therefore, if the user's computer has the incorrect time, so will the Flash movie. With that caveat in mind, you can retrieve the current client-side date and time by creating a new *Date* object using the *Date()* constructor with no parameters, as follows:

```
// Create a new Date object.
today = new Date( );

// Displays client-side date and time
trace(today);
```

 Avoid the temptation to name your date variable date. Unlike in Java-Script, ActionScript identifiers (including variable and class names) are case-insensitive. Date is the name of the constructor function for the *Date* class; therefore, naming a variable date disables the *Date* constructor.

If an active Internet connection is available, the Flash movie can try to retrieve the date and time from a server. This technique can ensure more accurate dates and times. Although the server's time settings might be inaccurate, at least the time will be consistent for all client movies.

The basic process when reading the time from a server is as follows:

1. Create a CGI script on the web server that outputs a name/value pair, in which the value is the number of seconds since midnight January 1, 1970 (the Epoch).

2. Within the Flash movie, use a *LoadVars* object (or the *loadVariables()* method) to load the Epoch seconds.

3. Convert the loaded seconds from a string to a number, multiply by 1000, and construct a new *Date* object by passing the value to the *Date()* constructor.

PHP is a scripting language that can be found on a large number of web hosts. It is quite simple to create a PHP page to output the current time and date as the number of seconds since the Epoch. All you need to do is create a PHP document with the following content and upload it to the server:

```
now=<?php echo time( );?>
```

If you don't have PHP on your server, or if you are simply more comfortable with Perl (another language that is almost universally available on web servers), then here is a Perl script that outputs the number of seconds since the Epoch:

```perl
#!/usr/local/bin/perl
print "Content-type:text/plain\n\n";
print "now=";
print time;
```

There are a few tips to keep in mind when setting up this script on your server:

- The first line indicates where the Perl interpreter can be found. The value given in the example is fairly universal. However, contact your web server administrator if you encounter problems.

- Many servers disable the remote execution of scripts without particular file extensions. The *.cgi* extension is commonly allowed. Try naming the script *getDate.cgi*.

- Most web servers limit CGI access to specific directories. Normally, these directories are found in the account root directory (or within the web root of the account), and are named either *cgi* or *cgi-bin*. Make sure you save the script in the correct directory.

- On Unix servers, your CGI script must have its permissions set to 755. Most FTP programs allow you to change permissions. If you are working from a shell script, use the following command:

  ```
  chmod 755 filename
  ```

Within the Flash document, you need to load the time value from the server. The best way to accomplish this is to use a *LoadVars* object. The *LoadVars* class was introduced in Flash MX. For compatibility with earlier Flash Player versions, use the *MovieClip.loadVariables()* method instead.

If you pass the *Date()* constructor a single value, ActionScript interprets it as the number of milliseconds since the Epoch and creates a new *Date* object that corresponds to that value. Therefore, you must multiply the value returned by the script (which is in seconds) by 1,000.

```
// Create a LoadVars object.
lv = new LoadVars( );

// Use the load( ) method to call the CGI script on the server. If using PHP, this
// should point to the appropriate PHP page, such as getDate.php, instead.
lv.load("http://www.person13.com/cgi-bin/getDate.cgi");

// onLoad( ) is invoked automatically when the server returns a response.
lv.onLoad = function ( ) {

    // Create a Date object by passing (seconds * 1000) to the Date( ) constructor. The
    // value returned by the server is this.nameOfVariable, in this case, this.now.
    // Convert the string value to a number before multiplying it by 1000.
    var serverDate = new Date(Number(this.now) * 1000);
```

```
    // Display the date and time returned by the server (in this case, with time zone
    // offsets for the user's computer settings).
    trace(serverDate);
};
```

The date is always stored in ActionScript as the milliseconds since the Epoch, but it is always displayed with proper offsets based on the user's local time zone setting (unless you specifically use the UTC methods). So if the user's computer has the incorrect time zone setting, the display might be incorrect. However, the actual date (as stored in Epoch milliseconds) is still correct.

See Also

If your server's time is not reliable or accurate enough for your needs, there are many existing date and time servers on the Internet from which you can retrieve reasonably accurate date and time information. For example, see *http://tycho.usno.navy.mil*. For details on synchronizing time via the Network Time Protocol, see *http://www.ntp.org* and Recipe 10.7.

10.2   Retrieving the Day or Month Name

Problem

You want to retrieve the name of the day or the month.

Solution

Create arrays that contain the string values for the names of the days of the week and the names of the months of the year. Use the numeric day and month to extract the string values from the arrays.

Discussion

The ActionScript *Date* class provides the *getDay()* and *getMonth()* methods, which return integer values representing the day of the week (from 0 to 6) and the month of the year (from 0 to 11). However, you may want the name of the day or month instead of its zero-relative number. To address this, create arrays containing the names of the days and months. The best way to do this is to define these arrays as properties of the *Date* class and store this information in a *Date.as* file that you can include in other projects:

```
    // Create days and months arrays as properties of the Date class.
    Date.days = ["Sunday", "Monday", "Tuesday", "Wednesday", "Thursday",
                 "Friday", "Saturday"];
    Date.months = ["January", "February", "March", "April", "May", "June", "July",
                   "August", "September", "October", "November", "December"];
```

```
// Create a Date object for December 1, 2002, which is a Sunday.
myDate = new Date(2002, 11, 1);

// Displays: Sunday
trace(Date.days[myDate.getDay( )]);

// Displays: December
trace(Date.months[myDate.getMonth( )]);
```

See Also

Recipe 10.3

10.3   Formatting the Date and Time

Problem

You want to display a formatted date and/or time value.

Solution

Use *Date.toString()*, or create a custom *Date.format()* method that returns the date and time as a string in the requested format.

Discussion

The *Date.toString()* method returns a user-friendly string version of the target *Date* object. For example:

```
// Displays: Mon May 26 11:32:46 GMT-0400 2003
trace(new Date().toString( ));
```

Because ActionScript automatically invokes the *toString()* method on any object used in a string context, you can obtain the same result even if you omit *toString()*, as in the following example:

```
// Also displays: Mon May 26 11:32:46 GMT-0400 2003
trace(new Date( ));
```

You can rewrite the *Date.toString()* method to return a different date format:

```
Date.prototype.toString = function ( ) {
  return "Milliseconds since the Epoch: " + this.getTime( );
};
// Both display: Milliseconds since the Epoch: 1053963542360
trace (new Date().toString( ));
trace (new Date( ));
```

However, a better approach is to implement a flexible, custom formatting method that accepts a parameter specifying the desired date format. Fortunately, there is a standard implementation for date formatting in languages such as Java, which you can imitate. Table 10-1 shows the symbols you should use in creating the formatting string that is passed to the custom *format()* method.

Table 10-1. Date and time symbols

Symbol	Meaning	Example
y	Year	2002
M	Month in year	December or 12 (depends on context: MM means 12 ; MMM means December)
d	Day in month	01
h	Hour in A.M./P.M. (1–12)	12
H	Hour in day (0–23)	21
m	Minute in hour	24
s	Second in minute	33
S	Millisecond in second	960
E	Day in week	Sunday or Sun (depends on context: E means Sunday; EEE means Sun)
a	A.M./P.M.	AM or PM

The custom *format()* method should accept a string parameter indicating the date/time format. It should use a *switch* statement to return the value in the designated format. The Date.days and Date.months arrays (see Recipe 10.2) must be accessible for the following example code to work properly. (You should include this code in your *Date.as* file along with the Date.days and Date.months arrays.)

```
Date.days = ["Sunday", "Monday", "Tuesday", "Wednesday", "Thursday",
            "Friday", "Saturday"];
Date.months = ["January", "February", "March", "April", "May", "June", "July",
            "August", "September", "October", "November", "December"];

// This custom helper method converts a number value to a two-digit string so that
// single-digit values are formatted correctly (e.g., 5 becomes 05).
Date.toTens = function (val) {
  if (val < 10) {
    return "0" + val;
  } else {
    return String(val);
  }
};

// Converts the integer time to a string representation. The 24-hour clock (where
// hours is from 0 to 23) in converted to a 12-hour clock with AM/PM indictor.
Date.toTwelveHour = function (hour, min) {
  var amPm = "AM";
  if (hour > 12) {
    hour = hour - 12;
    amPm = "PM";
  } else if (hour == 0) {
```

```
        hour = 12;
    }
    return Date.toTens(hour) + ":" + Date.toTens(min) + " " + amPm;
};

Date.prototype.format = function (format) {

    // Create local variables with the date's values.
    var day       = this.getDay();
    var monthDate = this.getDate();
    var month     = this.getMonth();
    var year      = this.getFullYear();
    var hour      = this.getHours();
    var min       = this.getMinutes();
    var sec       = this.getSeconds();
    var millis    = this.getMilliseconds();

    // Return a string with the date and/or time in the requested format, such as
    // "MM-dd-yyyy". You may want to add more cases to implement the remaining formats
    // within Table 10-1.
    switch (format) {
      case "MM-dd-yyyy":
        return Date.toTens(month + 1) + "-" + Date.toTens(monthDate) + "-" + year;
      case "MM/dd/yyyy":
        return Date.toTens(month + 1) + "/" + Date.toTens(monthDate) + "/" + year;
      case "dd-MM-yyyy":
        return Date.toTens(monthDate) + "-" + Date.toTens(month + 1) + "-" + year;
      case "dd/MM/yyyy":
        return Date.toTens(monthDate) + "/" + Date.toTens(month + 1) + "/" + year;
      case "hh:mm a":
        return Date.toTwelveHour(hour, min);
      case "EEE, MMM dd, yyyy":
        return Date.days[day].substr(0, 3) + ", " + Date.months[month] + " " +
            Date.toTens(monthDate) + ", " + year;
      case "E, MMM dd, yyyy":
        return Date.days[day] + ", " + Date.months[month] + " " +
            Date.toTens(monthDate) + ", " + year;
    }
};
```

Here are a few examples of the *format()* method being used:

```
// Create a date for December 1, 2002, which is a Sunday. The time is 06:09PM.
myDate = new Date(2002, 11, 1, 18, 9);

trace(myDate.format("MM-dd-yyyy"));   // Displays: 12-01-2002
trace(myDate.format("MM/dd/yyyy"));   // Displays: 12/01/2002
trace(myDate.format("dd-MM-yyyy"));   // Displays: 01-12-2002
trace(myDate.format("dd/MM/yyyy"));   // Displays: 01/12/2002
trace(myDate.format("hh:mm a"));      // Displays: 06:09 PM
// Displays: Sun, December 01, 2002
trace(myDate.format("EEE, MMM dd, yyyy"));
// Displays: Sunday, December 01, 2002 06:09 PM
trace(myDate.format("E, MMM dd, yyyy") + " " + myDate.format("hh:mm a"));
```

See Also

It is possible to enhance the *format()* method by adding more cases to the *switch* statement. This is left to you as an exercise. You may find the information at *http://www.php.net/manual/en/function.date.php* useful as a reference. Also refer to Recipe 10.4.

10.4   Formatting Milliseconds as Minutes and Seconds

Problem

You want to display milliseconds in minutes and seconds (*mm:ss*) format.

Solution

Create and use a custom, static method, *Date.formatMilliseconds()*.

Discussion

Many values in ActionScript are given in milliseconds. For example, sound lengths are given in milliseconds. However, in most cases, you want to format the value as minutes and seconds when displaying it to the user. You can accomplish this with a short custom method that we'll add to the *Date* class.

Here's our static method—a static method is called directly from the class, rather than on an object instance—that converts milliseconds to the format *mm:ss*. Add this code to your *Date.as* file for easy inclusion in other projects.

```
Date.formatMilliseconds = function (millis) {

  // Determine the minutes and seconds portions of the time.
  var seconds = millis / 1000;
  var m = Math.floor(seconds/60);
  var s = Math.round(seconds - (m * 60));

  // Add leading zeros to one-digit numbers.
  if (m < 10) {
    m = "0" + m;
  }
  if (s < 10) {
    s = "0" + s;
  }
  return m + ":" + s;
};
```

Here's an example of how you can use this method:

```
#include "Date.as"

// Assuming mySound_sound is a Sound object, get its duration in milliseconds.
dur = mySound_sound.duration;

// Create a text field to display the value.
this.createTextField("displayTime_txt", 1, 0, 0, 100, 20);

// Display the time value formatted as mm:ss.
displayTime_txt.text = Date.formatMilliseconds(dur);
```

See Also

Recipes 10.3 and 10.5

10.5 Converting Between DMYHMSM and Epoch Milliseconds

Problem

You want to convert between DMYHMSM format (days, months, years, hours, minutes, seconds, milliseconds) and Epoch milliseconds.

Solution

Use the *getTime()* and *setTime()* methods.

Discussion

Most of us are more comfortable thinking of dates and times in terms of components such as hours, days, and years than working with Epoch milliseconds or seconds. For example, it is generally more meaningful to humans to discuss the time and date 3:55 A.M., Friday, October 13, 1978 than to discuss the corresponding Epoch milliseconds value of 277124100000. However, languages such as ActionScript store times in Epoch milliseconds (or Epoch seconds) format. Therefore, it is important to be able to convert between different formats when displaying dates and times to users or when sharing dates between applications that use different formats.

When constructing a date in ActionScript, you can use the DMYHMSM approach, as follows:

```
// Construct a date for 3:55 AM, Friday, October 13, 1978.
myDate = new Date(1978, 9, 13, 3, 55, 0, 0);
```

ActionScript automatically performs the conversion and stores the date as the corresponding Epoch milliseconds value. To retrieve that value, call the *getTime()* method from the *Date* object:

```
// For Pacific Standard Time, displays: 277124100000
// The output may vary depending on your time zone.
trace(myDate.getTime( ));
```

You can pass the Epoch seconds value returned by *getTime()* to another application (such as a CGI script) or use it to perform date mathematics (see Recipe 10.6).

On the other hand, you may want to set a date using the Epoch milliseconds. For example, in Recipe 10.1, the CGI script returns the current server time to Flash in Epoch seconds (which needs to be converted to milliseconds by multiplying by 1,000). Also, when performing date mathematics you may want to set a date according to Epoch milliseconds. You have two options for setting a date according to Epoch milliseconds. One choice is to pass the milliseconds value to the *Date* constructor as the only parameter, and the other is to pass the milliseconds value to the *setTime()* value of an existing date. Both techniques are effectively the same. The only reason to use the *setTime()* technique rather than the *Date* constructor is if you have assigned any custom properties to an existing date that would be lost by calling the constructor.

```
// Construct a new Date object for 3:55 AM, Friday, October 13, 1978. Here, we use
// the value displayed in the Output window from the preceding example.
myDate = new Date(277124100000);

// Displays: Fri Oct 13 03:55:00 GMT-0700 1978 (timezone offset may vary)
trace(myDate);

// Create a Date object.
myDate = new Date( );

// Assign a custom property to the Date object.
myDate.label = "This is a special day!";

// Use the setTime( ) method to set the date to 3:55 AM, Friday, October 13, 1978.
// This doesn't overwrite the label property, as calling the Date constructor would.
myDate.setTime(277124100000);

// Displays: Fri Oct 13 03:55:00 GMT-0700 1978 (timezone offset may vary)
trace(myDate);
```

See Also

After assigning a value to a date using the *setTime()* method, you can use *getDate()*, *getMonth()*, *getYear()*, *getHours()*, *getSeconds()*, *getMinutes()*, and *getMilliseconds()* methods to retrieve the individual DMYHMSM values in the local time. To retrieve the UTC date and time, use *getUTCDate()*, *getUTCMonth()*, *getUTCHours()*, *getUTCSeconds()*, *getUTCMinutes()*, and *getUTCMilliseconds()* instead. See Recipe 10.6.

10.6 Calculating Elapsed Time or Intervals Between Dates

Problem

You want to calculate an elapsed time, elapsed date, or relative time.

Solution

For simple elapsed time, add and subtract from the Epoch milliseconds or the value returned by *getTimer()*. For more complex conversions, create custom *Date.doMath()* and *Date.elapsedTime()* methods.

Discussion

For simple conversions such as adding or subtracting an hour, day, or week to or from a date, simply add or subtract from the date's Epoch milliseconds value. For this purpose, note that a second is 1,000 milliseconds, a minute is 60,000 milliseconds, an hour is 3,600,000 milliseconds, a week is 604,800,000 milliseconds, and so on. Unless you have a spectacular gift for remembering these conversion values, storing them as constants of the *Date* class is the easiest option. You can add the following constants to your *Date.as* file for convenience:

```
// There are 1000 milliseconds in a second, 60 seconds in a minute, 60 minutes in an
// hour, 24 hours in a day, and 7 days in a week.
Date.SEC  = 1000;
Date.MIN  = Date.SEC * 60;
Date.HOUR = Date.MIN * 60;
Date.DAY  = Date.HOUR * 24;
Date.WEEK = Date.DAY * 7;
```

You can use the *Date.getTime()* method to retrieve a date's current value in Epoch milliseconds, and you can set the new value using the *Date.setTime()* method. The following example adds one day to a given *Date* object.

```
#include "Date.as"
myDate = new Date(1978, 9, 13, 3, 55, 0, 0);

// Displays: Fri Oct 13 03:55:00 GMT-0700 1978
trace(myDate);

// Add one day to the previous date by setting the new date/time to the original
// date/time plus Date.DAY (the number of milliseconds in a day).
myDate.setTime(myDate.getTime( ) + Date.DAY);
```

```
// Displays: Sat Oct 14 03:55:00 GMT-0700 1978
trace(myDate);
```

Here are some more examples of simple conversions using *Date.getTime()*, *Date. setTime()*, and the aforementioned constants:

```
#include "Date.as"
myDate = new Date(1978, 9, 13, 3, 55, 0, 0);

// Subtract one week from the date.
// Displays : Fri Oct 6 03:55:00 GMT-0700 1978 (timezone offset may vary)
myDate.setTime(myDate.getTime( ) - Date.WEEK);
trace(myDate);

// Add one week and one day to the date.
// Displays: Sat Oct 14 03:55:00 GMT-0700 1978 (timezone offset may vary)
myDate.setTime(myDate.getTime( ) + Date.WEEK + Date.DAY);
trace(myDate);

// Subtract 3 hours and 55 minutes from the date.
// Displays: Sat Oct 14 00:00:00 GMT-0700 1978 (timezone offset may vary)
myDate.setTime(myDate.getTime( ) - (3 * Date.HOUR) - (55 * Date.MIN));
trace(myDate);
```

You'll often want to calculate an elapsed time to create a timer for a game or other activity. Calculating the elapsed time is simply a matter of recording the time during initialization and then later comparing it to the current time at some later point during execution. For example, to calculate how long a movie has been running, you can use the following code (note that the *new Date()* constructor always returns the current time):

```
// Record the starting time.
var startingTime = new Date( );
// Create a text field to display the current time.
this.createTextField("timer_txt", 1, 100, 100, 50, 20);

// Check the elapsed time during each tick of the frame rate.
this.onEnterFrame = function ( ) {
  // Determine the elapsed time.
  var elapsedTime = new Date().getTime() - startingTime.getTime( );
  // Convert from milliseconds to seconds and round to the nearest second.
  this.timer_txt.text = Math.round(elapsedTime / 1000);
};
```

The global *getTimer()* function, not to be confused with the *Date.getTime()* method, returns the number of milliseconds since the Player started running. Therefore, by checking its value at successive times, it can also be used to determine the elapsed time. This alternative to the preceding example uses the global *getTimer()* function in place of *new Date()*:

```
var startingTime = getTimer( );
this.createTextField("timer_txt", 1, 100, 100, 50, 20);
```

```
    this.onEnterFrame = function () {
      // Determine the elapsed time.
      var elapsedTime = getTimer() - startingTime;
      // Convert from milliseconds to seconds and round to the nearest second.
      this.timer_txt.text = Math.round(elapsedTime / 1000);
    };
```

Note that the following code is not necessarily an acceptable alternative to the preceding example. The global *getTimer()* function returns the number of milliseconds since the Player started running, not since the current movie started running. In this example, the timer is not reset when a new movie loads:

```
    this.createTextField("timer_txt", 1, 100, 100, 50, 20);
    this.onEnterFrame = function () {
      // Convert from milliseconds to seconds and round to the nearest second.
      this.timer_txt.text = Math.round(getTimer()/ 1000);
    };
```

We can adapt the earlier example to create a countdown timer. This example jumps to the frame labeled "OutOfTime" after 60 seconds:

```
    // Record the starting time.
    var startingTime = getTimer();
    // Create a text field to display the current time.
    this.createTextField("timer_txt", 1, 100, 100, 50, 20);
    // Count down from 60 seconds
    var maxTime = 60

    // Check the elapsed time during each tick of the frame rate.
    this.onEnterFrame = function () {
      // Determine the elapsed time.
      var elapsedTime = getTimer() - startingTime;
      // Convert from milliseconds to seconds and round to the nearest second.
      elapsedTime = Math.round(elapsedTime / 1000);
      if (elapsedTime >= maxTime) {
        this.timer_txt.text = "0";
        gotoAndPlay("OutOfTime");
      } else {
        this.timer_txt.text = maxTime - elapsedTime;
      }
    };
```

Let's return to our earlier example in which we calculated elapsed times using *Date* objects. When it comes to adding and subtracting years and months from dates, we cannot rely on constants. This is because the number of milliseconds in a month varies with the number of days in the month, and leap years have more milliseconds than other years. However, the *Date* class handles wrap-around calculations transparently when using the getter and setter methods. The most effective way to handle date math is to create a *Date.doMath()* method that performs the calculations for you. Such a method should take up to seven numeric parameters, each of which can be positive or negative:

years
> The number of years to add to the date

months
> The number of months to add to the date

days
> The number of days to add to the date

hours
> The number of hours to add to the date

minutes
> The number of minutes to add to the date

seconds
> The number of seconds to add to the date

milliseconds
> The number of milliseconds to add to the date

Here is the custom *Date.doMath()* method, which you can add to your *Date.as* file for easy inclusion in other projects:

```
Date.prototype.doMath = function (years, months, days, hours, minutes,
                                  seconds, milliseconds) {

    // Perform conversions on a copy so as not to alter the original date.
    var d = new Date(this.getTime( ));

    // Add the specified intervals to the original date.
    d.setYear(d.getFullYear( ) + years);
    d.setMonth(d.getMonth( ) + months);
    d.setDate(d.getDate( ) + days);
    d.setHours(d.getHours( ) + hours);
    d.setMinutes(d.getMinutes( ) + minutes);
    d.setSeconds(d.getSeconds( ) + seconds);
    d.setMilliseconds(d.getMilliseconds( ) + milliseconds);

    // Return the new date value.
    return d;
};

// Example usage:
#include "Date.as"
myDate = new Date(1978, 9, 13, 3, 55, 0, 0);

// Add 1 year and subtract 3 hours and 55 minutes.
// Displays: Sat Oct 13 00:00:00 GMT-0700 1979
trace(myDate.doMath(1, 0, 0, -3, -55));
```

```
// You can also add 365 days and subtract 235 minutes to arrive at the same date as
// the previous statement. Displays: Sat Oct 13 00:00:00 GMT-0700 1979
trace(myDate.doMath(0, 0, 365, 0, -235));

// Add 24 years. Displays: Sun Oct 13 03:55:00 GMT-0700 2002
trace(myDate.doMath(24));
```

The preceding example demonstrates how to create a new *Date* object based on an elapsed time from an existing *Date* object. However, you may want to calculate the elapsed time between two existing *Date* objects, which is not as trivial as you might assume. You might try subtracting the return value of the *getTime()* method of one *Date* object from another, but this doesn't offer a general solution for calculating the elapsed time between two *Date* objects. Although the operation yields the number of milliseconds between the two dates, the result isn't convenient to manipulate when the times are not within the same day. Manually converting the number of milliseconds to a number of years, months, and days is difficult due to the varying number of days per month, leap year, etc. Furthermore, handling negative elapsed times can be cumbersome.

Therefore, it is easiest to create a custom *Date.elapsedTime()* method that returns a *Date* object representing an elapsed time. This allows us to use the *Date* class's built-in methods to calculate the number of years, months, and days between two *Date* objects. There are several caveats, however. Although ActionScript internally stores dates relative to the Epoch time (midnight on January 1, 1970), most *Date* class methods return absolute values, not values relative to the Epoch. For example, the year for a date in 1971 is returned as 1971, not 1. For our elapsed-time object to be optimally useful, we must define custom *elapsedYears()* and *elapsedDays()* methods to return values that are relative to the Epoch time. (The month, hour, minute, second, and millisecond of the Epoch time are all 0, so there is no need for custom methods to return relative offsets for these values.)

Our custom *elapsedTime()* method presented here creates a new *Date* object that represents the elapsed time between the *Date* object on which it is invoked and another *Date* object. If no secondary *Date* object is specified, the elapsed time is calculated relative to the current time ("now"). The elapsed time is always stored as a positive number, regardless of which *Date* object represents a later time. You should add the *elapsedTime()*, *elapsedYears()*, and *elapsedDays()* methods to your *Date.as* file for easy inclusion in other projects.

```
// Calculate the elapsed time (as an absolute value) between a Date object and a
// specified date.
Date.prototype.elapsedTime = function (t1) {
  // Calculate the elapsed time relative to the specified Date object.
  if (t1 == undefined) {
    // Calculate the elapsed time from "now" if no object is specified.
    t1 = new Date( );
  } else {
```

```
    // Make a copy so as not to alter the original.
    t1 = new Date(t1.getTime( ));
  }
  // Use the original Date object's time as one endpoint. Make a copy so as not to
  // alter the original.
  var t2 = new Date(this.getTime( ));

  // Ensure that the elapsed time is always calculated as a positive value.
  if (t1 < t2) {
   temp = t1;
   t1 = t2;
   t2 = temp;
  }
  // Return the elapsed time as a new Date object.
  var t = new Date(t1.getTime() - t2.getTime( ));
  return t;
};
```

The *elapsedYears()* and *elapsedDays()* methods return the year and day relative to the Epoch time.

```
Date.prototype.elapsedYears = function ( ) {
  return this.getUTCFullYear( ) - 1970;
};

Date.prototype.elapsedDays = function ( ) {
  return this.getUTCDate( ) - 1;
};
```

Here are some examples of how to use the custom methods. Note that the built-in *Date* class methods can be used to retrieve the elapsed months, hours, minutes, seconds, and milliseconds, but the custom *elapsedYears()* and *elapsedDays()* methods must be used to retrieve the elapsed years and days.

```
#include "Date.as"
// Calculate someone's age based on his birthday.
birthday = new Date(1966, 3, 17);
age = birthday.elapsedTime( );
trace("Elapsed Years "        + age.elapsedYears( ));
trace("Elapsed Months "       + age.getUTCMonth( ));
trace("Elapsed Days "         + age.elapsedDays( ));
trace("Elapsed Hours "        + age.getUTCHours( ));
trace("Elapsed Minutes "      + age.getUTCMinutes( ));
trace("Elapsed Seconds "      + age.getUTCSeconds( ));
trace("Elapsed Milliseconds " + age.getUTCMilliseconds( ));

// Calculate an interval between two dates.
firstDay = new Date(1901, 0, 1, 0, 0, 0, 0);
lastDay  = new Date(2000, 11, 31, 23, 59, 59, 999);
century = firstDay .elapsedTime(lastDay);
trace("Elapsed Years "        + century.elapsedYears( ));
trace("Elapsed Months "       + century.getUTCMonth( ));
trace("Elapsed Days "         + century.elapsedDays( ));
trace("Elapsed Hours "        + century.getUTCHours( ));
```

```
trace("Elapsed Minutes "      + century.getUTCMinutes());
trace("Elapsed Seconds "      + century.getUTCSeconds());
trace("Elapsed Milliseconds " + century.getUTCMilliseconds());
```

Naturally, there are many other potential ways to implement the elapsed date/time functionality. We have chosen the simplest for illustration purposes. For a more elegant and time-consuming solution, you could implement an *elapsedDate* class as a subclass of the *Date* class. The custom class could override the built-in *getUTCFullYear()*, *getUTCDate()*, *getYear()*, *setUTCDate()*, *setUTCFullYear()*, and *setYear()* to get and set values relative to the Epoch instead of absolute values. Such an implementation is left as an exercise to the reader.

See Also

Recipe 10.8

10.7   Parsing a Date from a String

Problem

You want to create a *Date* object from a string.

Solution

Create a custom *parseDate()* method that parses the individual date components (year, month, etc.) from the string using regular expressions and then assembles a new date.

Discussion

ActionScript does not provide any native methods for parsing a string into a *Date* object. This limitation does not necessarily pose a problem. For example, Flash Remoting allows you to return native *Date* objects from other applications. Even if you are not working with Flash Remoting, you can pass values between Flash and other applications using Epoch seconds/milliseconds. However, if you need to parse a string into a date, you should use a custom *parseDate()* method. This method takes the string value as a parameter, parses out each of the date's parts (the year, hour, etc.), and then returns a new *Date* object. Add the following code to your *Date.as* file for easy inclusion in other projects. The following code uses the custom *RegExp* class. See Recipe 9.6.

```
// You must include the third-party RegExp.as file from Recipe 9.6. One way to ensure
// this is to add #include "RegExp.as" to the Date.as file in which you also add the
// parseDate() method.
#include "RegExp.as"
```

```
// This method also relies on the Date.months array from Recipe 10.2.
Date.parseDate = function (dateStr) {

  // Create local variables to hold the year, month, date of month, hour, minute, and
  // second. Assume that there are no milliseconds in the date string.
  var year, month, monthDate, hour, minute, second;

  // Use a regular expression to test whether the string uses ActionScript's date
  // string format. Other languages and applications may use the same format. For
  // example: Thu Dec 5 06:36:03 GMT-0800 2002
  var re = new RegExp(
    "[a-zA-Z]{3} [a-zA-Z]{3} [0-9]{1,2} [0-9]{2}:[0-9]{2}:[0-9]{2} .* [0-9]{4}",
    "g");
  var match = re.exec(dateStr);

  // If the date string matches the pattern, parse the date from it and return a new
  // Date object with the extracted value.
  if (match != null) {

    // Split the match into an array of strings. Split it on the spaces so the
    // elements will be day, month, date of month, time, timezone, year.
    var dateAr = match[0].split(" ");

    // Set the month to the second element of the array. This is the abbreviated name
    // of the month, but we want the number of the month (from 0 to 11), so loop
    // through the Date.months array until you find the matching element, and set
    // month to that index.
    month = dateAr[1];
    for (var i = 0; i < Date.months.length; i++) {
      if (Date.months[i].indexOf(month) != -1) {
        month = i;
        break;
      }
    }
  }

  // Convert the monthDate and year from the array from strings to numbers.
  monthDate = Number(dateAr[2]);
  year = Number(dateAr[dateAr.length - 1]);

  // Extract the hour, minute, and second from the time element of the array.
  var timeVals = dateAr[3].split(":");
  hour   = Number(timeVals[0]);
  minute = Number(timeVals[1]);
  second = Number(timeVals[2]);

  // If the array has six elements, there is a timezone offset included (some date
  // strings in this format omit the timezone offset).
  if (dateAr.length == 6) {
    var timezone = dateAr[4];

    // Multiply the offset (in hours) by 60 to get minutes.
    var offset = 60 * Number(timezone.substr(3, 5))/100;
```

```
    // Calculate the timezone difference between the client's computer and the
    // offset extracted from the date string.
    var offsetDiff = offset + new Date().getTimezoneOffset( );

    // Add the timezone offset, in minutes. If the date string and the client
    // computer are in the same timezone, the difference is 0.
    minute += offsetDiff;
  }

  // Return the new date.
  return new Date(year, month, monthDate, hour, minute, second);
}

// If the date string didn't match the standard date string format, test whether it
// includes either MM-dd-yy(yy) or MM/dd/yy(yy).
re = new RegExp("[0-9]{2}(/|-)[0-9]{2}(/|-)[0-9]{2,}", "g");
match = re.exec(dateStr);
if (match != null) {
  // Get the month, date, and year from the match. First, use the forward slash as
  // the delimiter. If that returns an array of only one element, use the dash
  // delimiter instead.
  var mdy = match[0].split("/");
  if (mdy.length == 1) {
    mdy = match[0].split("-");
  }

  // Extract the month number and day-of-month values from the date string.
  month = Number(mdy[0]) - 1;
  monthDate = Number(mdy[1]);

  // If the year value is two characters, then we must add the century to it.
  if (mdy[2].length == 2) {
    twoDigitYear = Number(mdy[2]);
    // Assumes that years less than 50 are in the 21st century
    year = (twoDigitYear < 50) ? twoDigitYear + 2000 : twoDigitYear + 1900;
  } else {
    // Extract the four-digit year
    year = mdy[2];
  }
}

// Check whether the string includes a time value of the form of h(h):mm(:ss).
re = new RegExp("[0-9]{1,2}:[0-9]{2}(:[0-9]{2,})?", "g");
match = re.exec(dateStr);
if (match != null) {
  // If the length is 4, the time is given as h:mm. If so, then the length of the
  // first part of the time (hours) is only one character. Otherwise, it is two
  // characters in length.
  var firstLength = 2;
  if (match[0].length == 4) {
    firstLength = 1;
  }
```

```
// Extract the hour and minute parts from the date string. If the length of the
// match is greater than five, assume that it includes seconds.
hour = Number(dateStr.substr(match.index, firstLength));
minute = Number(dateStr.substr(match.index + firstLength + 1, 2));
if (match[0].length > 5) {
  second = Number(dateStr.substr(match.index + firstLength + 4, 2));
}
}

// Return the new date.
return new Date(year, month, monthDate, hour, minute, second);
};
```

Here are a few examples that show how you can use the *parseDate()* method to create a new *Date* object from a string. As with many of the examples in this chapter, the actual output will vary depending on your time zone settings.

```
#include "Date.as"

// Displays: Sat Oct 9 00:00:00 GMT-0700 1982
trace(Date.parseDate("10/09/1982"));

// Displays: Fri Oct 13 03:55:00 GMT-0700 1978
trace(Date.parseDate("It was 3:55 on 10-13-78"));

// Displays: Tue Dec 3 06:36:02 GMT-0800 2002
trace(Date.parseDate("Fri Dec 2 14:36:02 GMT+0800 2002"));
```

10.8   Creating Timers and Clocks

Problem

You want to create a timer or perform actions at set intervals.

Solution

Use the *setInterval()* function.

Discussion

This recipe explains how to perform actions at set intervals and create a clock showing the absolute time. Refer to Recipe 10.6 for details on creating timers that show the elapsed time.

The *setInterval()* function, added in Flash MX, lets you set up a timer that calls a function or a method at a specific time interval. The function returns a reference to the interval so that you can abort the action in the future. You can choose from several variations depending on how you want to use *setInterval()*. If you want to call a function at a specific interval without passing it any parameters, you can call *setInterval()* with a reference to the function and the number of milliseconds between function invocations.

```
// This example uses the custom format( ) method, so it requires the Date.as file.
#include "Date.as"

// This function is called by setInterval( ), and it displays the current time.
function displayTime( ) {
  var d = new Date( );
  trace(d.format("hh:mm a"));
}

// This example invokes displayTime every 60,000 milliseconds (once per minute).
dtInterval = setInterval(displayTime, 60000);
```

 The *setInterval()* function invokes the function or method at approximately the specified interval. The interval between calls is dependent on the processor of the client computer and is not exact or consistent.

You can also use *setInterval()* to pass parameters to the called function. When you pass additional parameters to the *setInterval()* function, those values are passed along to the function that is called at the interval. You should note, however, that the parameters sent to the function cannot be dynamically updated with each call. The *setInterval()* function calls the function multiple times, but *setInterval()* itself is called only once. Therefore, the values of the parameters that are passed to the function are evaluated only once as well:

```
// Create a function that displays the value passed to it.
function displayValue (val) {
  trace(val);
}

// Create an interval such that displayValue( ) is called every five seconds and is
// passed a parameter. Notice that even though the parameter is Math.random( ) (a
// method that generates a random value between 0 and 1), the same value is always
// passed to displayValue( ) because Math.random( ) is evaluated only once.
dvInterval = setInterval(displayValue, 5000, Math.random( ));
```

You can also use *setInterval()* to call methods of an object, in which case you must pass it at least three parameters. The first parameter is a reference to the object, the second parameter is the string name of the method, and the third parameter is the number of milliseconds for the interval.

```
// Include the DrawingMethods.as file from Chapter 4 for its drawTriangle( ) method.
#include "DrawingMethods.as"

// Create a movie clip object and draw a triangle in it.
_root.createEmptyMovieClip("triangle", 1);
triangle.lineStyle(1, 0x000000, 100);
triangle.drawTriangle(300, 500, 60);
```

```
// Add a method to the triangle that moves the
// movie clip 10 pixels in the x and y directions.
triangle.move = function () {
  this._x += 10;
  this._y += 10;
};

// Call the move() method of the triangle movie clip every two seconds.
trInterval = setInterval(triangle, "move", 2000);
```

You can pass parameters to an object's method via *setInterval()* by listing the parameters after the *milliseconds* parameter in the *setInterval()* call:

```
// Include the DrawingMethods.as file from Chapter 4 for its drawTriangle() method.
#include "DrawingMethods.as"

_root.createEmptyMovieClip("triangle", 1);
triangle.lineStyle(1, 0x000000, 100);
triangle.drawTriangle(300, 500, 60);

// Modify the move() method to accept parameters.
triangle.move = function (x, y) {
  this._x += x;
  this._y += y;
};

// Call the move() method every two seconds and pass it the values 10 and 10.
trInterval = setInterval(triangle, "move", 2000, 10, 10);
```

The following example uses *setInterval()* to create a clock movie clip in which the display is updated once per second:

```
// Include the DrawingMethods.as file from Chapter 4 for its drawCircle() method.
#include "DrawingMethods.as"

// Create the clock_mc movie clip on _root and place it so it is visible on stage.
// This movie clip contains the hands and face movie clips.
_root.createEmptyMovieClip("clock_mc", 1);
clock_mc._x = 200;
clock_mc._y = 200;

// Add a face_mc movie clip to clock_mc and draw a circle in it.
clock_mc.createEmptyMovieClip("face_mc", 1);
clock_mc.face_mc.lineStyle(1, 0x000000, 100);
clock_mc.face_mc.drawCircle(100);

// Add the hour, minute, and second hands to clock_mc. Draw a line in each of them.
clock_mc.createEmptyMovieClip("hourHand_mc", 2);
clock_mc.hourHand_mc.lineStyle(3, 0x000000, 100);
clock_mc.hourHand_mc.lineTo(50, 0);
clock_mc.createEmptyMovieClip("minHand_mc", 3);
clock_mc.minHand_mc.lineStyle(3, 0x000000, 100);
clock_mc.minHand_mc.lineTo(90, 0);
clock_mc.createEmptyMovieClip("secHand_mc", 4);
```

```
clock_mc.secHand_mc.lineStyle(1, 0x000000, 100);
clock_mc.secHand_mc.lineTo(90, 0);

// Create a method for the clock_mc movie clip that updates the clock display based
// on the client computer's current time.
clock_mc.updateDisplay = function () {

    // Extract the hour, minute, and second from the current time.
    var d = new Date( );
    var hour = d.getHours( );
    var min = d.getMinutes( );
    var sec = d.getSeconds( );

    // Set the rotation of the hands according to the hour, min, and sec values, The
    // _rotation property is in degrees, so calculate each value by finding the
    // percentage of the hour, min, or sec relative to a full rotation around the clock
    // (and multiply by 360 to get the degrees). Also, subtract 90 degrees from each
    // value to correctly offset the rotation from 12 o'clock rather than from the 3
    // o'clock position.
    this.hourHand_mc._rotation = (((hour + min/60)/12) * 360) - 90;
    this.minHand_mc._rotation = (((min + sec/60)/60) * 360) - 90;
    this.secHand_mc._rotation = ((sec/60) * 360) - 90;
};

// Call the updateDisplay( ) method of the clock_mc movie clip once per second.
clockInterval = setInterval(clock_mc, "updateDisplay", 1000);
```

See Also

It is left as an exercise for you to add a digital display to the preceding clock example using the techniques shown in Recipes 10.6 and 10.3. Also refer to Recipe 1.7.

## CHAPTER 11

Forms

11.0 Introduction

Forms are the primary means through which applications accept user input. They are used for a wide variety of purposes, such as gathering user information, performing searches, and placing orders for products and services. But whatever the purpose of a specific form, they all share several common features:

- A form is composed of input text fields, menus, checkboxes, radio buttons, push buttons, and possibly other custom control types such as sliders, dials, calendars, and even images.

- A form submits data to be processed further, often by a server-side script.

- Many forms validate their data before submitting it for processing to ensure that all necessary information has been entered properly.

- A form may be limited to one page (screen) or be spread across several pages, depending on its length and appropriate user considerations.

ActionScript provides text fields as well as standard UI components for creating the elements of a form, but it does not provide a native *Form* class to manage the user input process or the form as a whole. However, this chapter includes recipes that enable you to create and utilize forms effectively in your Flash movies. These recipes extend the functionality of existing UI components, define a *Form* class, and define a *MultiPageForm* class. You should place all of this code in a *Form.as* file and save it to your Flash *Include* directory so that you can reuse the code easily in your applications.

11.1 Adding UI Components at Runtime

Problem

You want to add UI components such as combo boxes, list boxes, and push buttons to a movie at runtime.

Solution

Add the component to the Library at authoring time and use *attachMovie()* to create a runtime instance.

Discussion

You can use *attachMovie()* to add UI components to your movies at runtime, just as you would any other movie clip. However, you must first add the components to the movie's Library. To do so, you must drag a component from the Components panel to the Stage during authoring, which also places a copy of the component in your Library under the heading "Flash UI Components." Flash automatically copies over any subcomponents that are needed; for example, dragging a list box to the Stage copies both the ListBox component and the ScrollBar component, on which list boxes rely, to the Library.

You can optionally delete the component instances from the Stage, but the components remain accessible in the Library. The component symbols are automatically set for export, and you should leave the linkage identifier names at their defaults, as listed in Table 11-1.

Table 11-1. UI component linkage identifiers

Component	Linkage identifier
List box	*FListBoxSymbol*
Combo box	*FComboBoxSymbol*
Checkbox	*FCheckBoxSymbol*
Radio button	*FRadioButtonSymbol*
Push button	*FPushButtonSymbol*
Scrollbar	*FScrollBarSymbol*
Scroll pane	*FScrollPaneSymbol*
Message box	*FMessageBoxSymbol*

Once a component symbol is within a movie's Library, the procedure for adding instances at runtime with *attachMovie()* is exactly the same as with any other movie clip. For example, this code creates a new movie clip instance of the CheckBox UI component and names it myCheckBox_ch:

```
_root.attachMovie("FCheckBoxSymbol", "myCheckBox_ch", 1);
```

See Also

Recipes 7.1, 7.19, 11.3, 11.7, 11.10, and 11.15

11.2 Positioning Form Elements

Problem

You want to programmatically position form elements.

Solution

Set the _x and _y properties of each element.

Discussion

Components are derived from movie clips, so they support the basic movie clip properties and methods, including the _x and _y properties. You can set the _x and _y properties of any component to position it on stage, just as you would with a movie clip:

```
myComponentInstance._x = 90;
myComponentInstance._y = 180;
```

See Also

For more complex positioning, see Recipes 11.8 and 11.22

11.3 Adding Menus to a Form

Problem

You want to add menus to your form.

Solution

Use combo boxes or list boxes.

Discussion

You can choose from two types of form menus in your Flash movies: combo boxes and list boxes. A combo box is analogous to the standard HTML <SELECT> tag, which is often referred to as a pop-up menu or drop-down list. A combo box allows a user to select one item at a time, and it displays only the selected item when the menu is not in use. Additionally, if you set a combo box's editable property to true (using *setEditable(true)*), the user can enter a value by typing it into the text area associated with the combo box.

You can populate a combo box one item at a time using the *addItem()* and *addItemAt()* methods. However, it is usually easier to use the *setDataProvider()* method to assign all the menu items at once. You can pass the *setDataProvider()* method a reference to an array or any object that inherits from the *DataProvider* class, such as a *RecordSet* object. The combo box is automatically populated with the data provider elements in the order they appear within the data provider object. Here is an example:

```
// Create a new combo box.
_root.attachMovie("FComboBoxSymbol", "myComboBox_cb", 1);

// Place the combo box at (100,100).
myComboBox_cb._x = 100;
myComboBox_cb._y = 100;

// Create an array to use as the data provider.
menuItems = ["item a", "item b", "item c", "item d"];

// Populate the combo box.
myComboBox_cb.setDataProvider(menuItems);
```

A list box allows the user to see more than one item at a time. You can populate a list box the same way you would a combo box, that is, by using *setDataProvider()*. List boxes also have two additional initialization parameters: the number of menu items to display at a time and a Boolean indicating whether to allow multiple selections. List boxes default to six visible menu items, but you can change this value with *setRowCount()*. List boxes do not allow for multiple selections by default, but you can change this using *setSelectMultiple(true)*. Users can then select multiple values by Shift-clicking to select multiple contiguous values or Ctrl-clicking (Windows) or Cmd-clicking (Macintosh) to select multiple, noncontiguous values. Here is an example:

```
// Create a new list box.
_root.attachMovie("FListBoxSymbol", "myListBox_lb", 1);

// Place the list box at (100,100).
myListBox_lb._x = 100;
myListBox_lb._y = 100;

// Create an array to use as the data provider.
menuItems = ["item a", "item b", "item c", "item d"];

// Populate the list box.
myListBox_lb.setDataProvider(menuItems);

// Set the list box to display three menu items at a time.
myListBox_lb.setRowCount(3);

// Allow the user to select multiple items at once.
myListBox_lb.setSelectMultiple(true);
```

Each menu item has two properties: label and data. The label value is displayed in the menu, while the data value is available behind the scenes. This allows you to associate data with each item displayed in the menu. When you populate a menu with an array of strings, as shown earlier, the label properties of the menu items correspond to the array elements, but the data properties are left as undefined. It is a best practice to associate both label and data values with each menu item, which you can accomplish using an array of objects, where each object contains both label and data properties. For example:

```
// Create an array of objects. Each element should have both label and data
// properties. The label is displayed in the menu, while data is available for
// programmatic use.
menuItems = [{label: "item a", data: "test a"}, {label: "item b", data: "test b"}];

// Populate the menu using the setDataProvider() method, as usual.
myListBox_lb.setDataProvider(menuItems);
```

See Also

Recipe 11.6

11.4 Making Dependent Menus

Problem

You want to make the items in one menu (list box or combo box) dependent on the user's selection in another form element.

Solution

Create a custom *makeDependent()* method for all combo boxes and list boxes.

Discussion

Making a menu depend on the value of another form element is a common practice. For example, you might want to present a list of minivans instead of sports cars if the customer indicates that safety and seating capacity are his top priorities when choosing a new car.

You can create a dependent menu by following these steps:

1. Create an array of data providers (i.e., an array of arrays) for the dependent menu. Each data provider element should correspond to an item in the master menu. In other words, the index of each data provider element should match up with the index of an item in the master menu.

2. Define the *setChangeHandler()* method of the master menu so that it automatically calls a function when the user selects an item from the master menu.

3. In the callback function, use the *getSelectedIndex()* method to determine the selected index of the master menu. Then set the data provider of the dependent menu to the element from the data providers array of the same index.

This feature set is much easier to implement if you make a custom *makeDependent()* method for *FSelectableListClass*. This class is the superclass for both list boxes and combo boxes, so our custom method is available to both kinds of menus. The *makeDependent()* method should take two parameters:

multiDataProvider
This should be a reference to an array of data providers. Each element of the array should match up with one of the items in the master menu.

master
This is a reference to the master menu.

Here is our custom *makeDependent()* method:

```
FSelectableListClass.prototype.makeDependent = function (multiDataProvider, master) {
    // Set the master menu's change handler to the updateView() method (see following)
    // for the dependent menu.
    master.setChangeHandler("updateView", this);

    // Set the dependent menu's properties to the values passed in as parameters.
    this.multiDataProvider = multiDataProvider;
    this.master = master;
};

// updateView() is called whenever the user selects an item from the master menu.
FSelectableListClass.prototype.updateView = function () {

    // Get the index of the selected menu item from the master menu.
    var selectedIndex = this.master.getSelectedIndex();

    // Get the data provider that corresponds to the selected index.
    var dp = this.multiDataProvider[selectedIndex];

    // Set the data provider for the dependent menu.
    this.setDataProvider(dp);
};
```

Here is an example of the *makeDependent()* method in use:

```
// In this example, create two combo boxes. Space them 150 pixels apart.
_root.attachMovie("FComboBoxSymbol", "myComboBox1", 1);
_root.attachMovie("FComboBoxSymbol", "myComboBox2", 2, {_x: 150});

// Create the master menu's data provider array and use it to populate the menu.
items1 = ["a", "b", "c"];
myComboBox1.setDataProvider(items1);
```

```
// Create the multiDataProvider array. It has three elements, each corresponding to
// an item in the master menu. Each element is a data provider. In this case, they
// are each simple array data providers.
items2 = new Array();
items2.push(["1 a", "2 a", "3 a"]);
items2.push(["1 b", "2 b", "3 b"]);
items2.push(["1 c", "2 c", "3 c"]);

// Call the makeDependent() method from the dependent menu. Pass it the
// multiDataProvider and a reference to the master menu.
myComboBox2.makeDependent(items2, myComboBox1);
```

It is important to note that the *makeDependent()* method sets the master menu's change handler, which would conflict with another change handler defined for the master menu. In the majority of situations this should not be an issue because it is unlikely that you will need to add any other actions to the master menu's change handler. However, should you decide to do this, make sure to include a call to the master menu's *updateView()* method in the new change handler function. For example:

```
function newOnChange(masterMenu) {

  // You must include a call to the menu's updateView() method.
  masterMenu.updateView();

  // Additional actions go here.
}

myComboBox1.setChangeHandler("newOnChange");
```

11.5   Resizing Menus to Fit Their Contents

Problem

You want to adjust the width of a menu to accommodate the widest menu item.

Solution

Create and invoke a custom *adjustWidth()* method.

Discussion

Both combo boxes and list boxes default to a width of 100 pixels, and they do not automatically resize to fit their contents when you populate them. Therefore, the text of menu items wider than 100 pixels is cut off. Although the menu components offer no documented means of adjusting the width to fit the contents, there are several undocumented properties you can use to create a custom method that sizes the menus appropriately. Menu components (list boxes and combo boxes) are subclasses of

FSelectableListClass. Therefore, if you add a custom *adjustWidth()* method to *FSelectableListClass*, it is accessible to both list boxes and combo boxes.

Furthermore, all objects derived from *FSelectableListClass* have three undocumented properties that are valuable in calculating the necessary width to accommodate all the menu items:

labels

An array of string values displayed in the menu when the menu is populated from the Parameters panel at authoring time.

dataprovider

A reference to a *DataProvider* object that is created when the menu is populated at runtime by the *setDataProvider()* method. It has an items property that is an array of objects with label properties (yielding the needed string values).

textstyle

A reference to the *TextFormat* object used to format the menu items.

You can use these properties to determine the text width of each menu item (using the *TextFormat.getTextExtent()* method).

Here is our custom *FSelectableListClass.adjustWidth()* method:

```
// Add the adjustWidth() method to FSelectableListClass.
FSelectableListClass.prototype.adjustWidth = function () {

  // maxW stores the largest text extent.
  var maxW = 0;

  // w stores the text extent of each label element.
  var w;

  // The local variable labels is an array of the string values for each menu item.
  // Assign it the value of the labels property to begin with.
  var labels = this.labels;

  // If the menu was not populated at authoring time, set labels to an array of the
  // values obtained from the data provider.
  if (labels == undefined) {
    labels = new Array();

    // Append the label property for each data provider to the labels array.
    for (var i = 0; i < this.dataprovider.getLength(); i++) {
      labels.push(this.dataprovider.getItemAt(i).label);
    }
  }

  // Loop through all the elements of the labels array.
  for (i = 0; i < labels.length; i++) {

    // Use textstyle.getTextExtent() to obtain the width of each label (it returns an
    // object with width and height properties, and we extract width here).
    w = this.textstyle.getTextExtent(labels[i]).width;
```

```
    // Store the width of the widest label in maxW.
    maxW = Math.max(w, maxW);
  }

  // Use setSize() to set the menu width to maxW + 25. The 25 is padding so that menu
  // items are not cut off by scrollbars. Pass the current height to setSize() to
  // leave the list box's height unchanged (height does not apply to combo boxes).
  this.setSize(maxW + 25, this._height);
};
```

You can test the custom *adjustWidth()* method as follows:

```
// Create a new list box.
_root.attachMovie("FListBoxSymbol", "myListBox_lb", 1);

// Create an array to use as the data provider.
menuItems = ["item a", "item b", "item c", "item d"];

// Populate the list box.
myListBox_lb.setDataProvider(menuItems);

// Call adjustWidth() to set the menu width to fit the contents.
myListBox_lb.adjustWidth();
```

11.6   Detecting the Selected Menu Items

Problem

You want to get the user-selected value(s) from a menu.

Solution

Use *getSelectedItem()* (for both combo boxes and list boxes) or *getSelectedItems()* (for list boxes only).

Discussion

You can use the *getSelectedItem()* method to get the selected value from a menu. The method returns an object with a label and a data property, representing the user-selected menu item. The *getSelectedItem()* method works for both combo boxes and single-selection list boxes. If you use *getSelectedItem()* with a multiple-selection list box, it returns the last selected item in the list:

```
// Displays the label property of the selected item from a combo box.
trace(myComboBox_cb.getSelectedItem().label);

// Displays the data property of the selected item from a combo box.
trace(myComboBox_cb.getSelectedItem().data);
```

Generally, the label property is used for display purposes, while the data property is used to submit the form data to a server for further processing.

If implementing a list box that allows multiple selections at once (see Recipe 11.3), you should retrieve the selections using *getSelectedItems()*, which returns an array of objects with label and data properties:

```
// Store the array of selected items in selectedItems.
selectedItems = myListBox_lb.getSelectedItems();

// Display the label and data properties of each element in the selectedItems array.
for (var i = 0; i < selectedItems.length; i++) {
  trace(selectedItems[i].label);
  trace(selectedItems[i].data);
}
```

Typically, ActionScript developers use either *getSelectedItem()* or *getSelectedItems()* within the click handler for a form's Submit button:

```
function onClick () {
  var selectedVal = myListBox_lb.getSelectedItem().data;

  // Do something with data here.
}

submitBtn.setClickHandler("onClick");
```

11.7   Adding Radio Buttons to a Group

Problem

You want to add a group of radio buttons to your form.

Solution

Add radio button instances and assign them to a group using *setGroupName()*.

Discussion

Use the radio button UI component to present several mutually exclusive choices. Radio buttons work best with a limited number of items. For a choice among many items, use a combo box or list box. When you create a radio button, you must assign it a label and, in many cases, some data. The label is the text displayed next to the radio button, and the data is stored for programmatic processing when the radio button has been selected and submitted. Even in cases where the label and data are the same, you should still assign a value for the data. This is because it is good practice to retrieve the value for a selected radio button from its data value, not from its label.

You should set these values using the *setLabel()* and *setData()* methods. The label should be a string value, but the data can be of any datatype.

This example shows that the data can be a complex object, which can be stored, used for processing or transmitted to a server when the radio button is selected:

```
// Create a radio button named myRadioButton0_rb.
_root.attachMovie("FRadioButtonSymbol", "myRadioButton0_rb", 1);

// Set the label so that the radio button displays the text "item 1".
myRadioButton0_rb.setLabel("item 1");

// Assign a data object with id and description properties.
myRadioButton0_rb.setData({id: 25, description: "this is an item"});
```

Every radio button must belong to a radio button group so that ActionScript can ensure that radio buttons within the group are mutually exclusive.

 If you want to allow a user to select multiple options from a list, use multiple checkboxes or a multiple-selection list box instead of radio buttons. If there is only one choice, use a checkbox.

You should add each radio button to a group using the *setGroupName()* method, which takes a string parameter specifying the name of the group to which the radio button should be assigned:

```
myRadioButton0_rb.setGroupName("myRadioButtons");
```

Radio button group names are arbitrary, but it is good practice to give each group a name that relates to its purpose and name each radio button in a numbered sequence. Here is an example that illustrates this point with a radio button group for travel preferences:

```
// Create four radio buttons, travelPrefs0_rb through travelPrefs3_rb, and assign
// them to the "travelPrefs" group. Note that the label and data are both set for
// each button, as is good practice, even though both contain the same value.
_root.attachMovie("FRadioButtonSymbol", "travelPrefs0_rb", 1);
_root.attachMovie("FRadioButtonSymbol", "travelPrefs1_rb", 2);
_root.attachMovie("FRadioButtonSymbol", "travelPrefs2_rb", 3);
_root.attachMovie("FRadioButtonSymbol", "travelPrefs3_rb", 4);

travelPrefs0_rb.setGroupName("travelPrefs");
travelPrefs1_rb.setGroupName("travelPrefs");
travelPrefs2_rb.setGroupName("travelPrefs");
travelPrefs3_rb.setGroupName("travelPrefs");

travelPrefs0_rb.setLabel("spring");
travelPrefs0_rb.setData ("spring");
travelPrefs1_rb.setLabel("summer");
travelPrefs1_rb.setData ("summer");
travelPrefs2_rb.setLabel("fall");
travelPrefs2_rb.setData ("fall");
```

```
travelPrefs3_rb.setLabel("winter");
travelPrefs3_rb.setData ("winter");

// Position the radio buttons.
travelPrefs0_rb._y = 100;
travelPrefs1_rb._y = 120;
travelPrefs2_rb._y = 140;
travelPrefs3_rb._y = 160;
```

There are two important potential problems that become apparent when you start programmatically adding radio buttons. First of all, the labels appear on the right side of the buttons by default. Fortunately, you can use *setLabelPlacement("left")* to place the label to the left of the radio button. Furthermore, to set the same placement for all radio buttons in a group, you can invoke *setLabelPlacement()* on the radio group object (the group object is automatically created with the name passed to *setGroupName()*). You must create the radio buttons and assign them to the group before invoking *setLabelPlacement()* on the group object. For example:

```
// Align the labels to the left of the radio buttons in the travelPrefs group.
travelPrefs0_rb.setGroupName("travelPrefs");
travelPrefs1_rb.setGroupName("travelPrefs");
travelPrefs2_rb.setGroupName("travelPrefs");
travelPrefs3_rb.setGroupName("travelPrefs");
travelPrefs.setLabelPlacement("left");
```

Another problem becomes apparent when you add labels that extend beyond the default width of the radio button, in which case the text is cut off in the display. You can create a custom method for *FRadioButtonGroupClass* (the class for radio button groups) to automatically resize the labels of all the radio buttons in the group. To do so, you must be able to reference the text fields containing the radio buttons' label text. The path to the text field of a radio button is undocumented, but it can be referenced as this.fLabel_mc.labelField from each radio button. You also must be able to reference each radio button from the group object. Radio button groups have an undocumented property—an array named radioInstances containing references to the radio button instances—that works perfectly for this purpose.

Here is a custom *adjustWidth()* method for the *FRadioButtonGroupClass* class, which you can add to your *Form.as* file for easy inclusion in future projects:

```
FRadioButtonGroupClass.prototype.adjustWidth = function () {
  var tf;

  // Loop through all the radio buttons in the group.
  for (var i = 0; i < this.radioInstances.length; i++) {

    // Set each label text field to auto size.
    tf = this.radioInstances[i].fLabel_mc.labelField;
    tf.autoSize = true;
```

```
    // Set the width of each radio button to the width of the text field plus 13. The
    // 13 pixels account for the width of the button graphic.
    this.radioInstances[i].setSize(tf._width + 13);
  }
};
```

11.8   Aligning Radio Buttons Automatically

Problem

You want to align all the radio buttons in a group into one or more columns.

Solution

Create and invoke a custom *setPositions()* method for *FRadioButtonGroupClass*.

Discussion

Another problem that very quickly presents itself after you add more than one radio button is that of placement on the Stage. You can position each radio button (each of which is a movie clip) individually using the _x and _y properties. On the other hand, you can also add a custom method to *FRadioButtonGroupClass* that automatically aligns all the radio buttons within the group. You can use the radioInstances property (see Recipe 11.7) to loop through each button in a radio button group and space them evenly.

Our custom *setPositions()* method accepts up to four parameters:

x   The x coordinate within the parent movie clip where the first radio button should be placed. If undefined, then 0 is assumed.

y   The y coordinate within the parent movie clip where the first radio button should be placed. If undefined, then 0 is assumed.

cols
    The number of columns into which the radio buttons should be organized. If undefined, the radio buttons are aligned in one vertical column.

spacing
    The vertical spacing between the radio buttons, in pixels. If undefined, defaults to 15. The horizontal spacing is five pixels more than the widest item in the column

Here, then, is our custom *setPositions()* method, which you should add to your *Form.as* file for easy inclusion in future projects:

```
FRadioButtonGroupClass.prototype.setPositions = function (x, y, cols, spacing) {

  // Set the spacing to 15 pixels, if undefined.
  if (spacing == undefined) {
    spacing = 15;
  }
```

```
// If the value of cols is either undefined or greater than the number of items,
// use one column.
if ( (cols == undefined) || (cols > this.radioInstances.length) ) {
  cols = 1;
}

// The itemsPerColumn array is used to determine how many items are placed into
// each column. Initialize remainingItems to the number of elements in the
// radioInstances array.
var itemsPerColumn = new Array();
var remainingItems = this.radioInstances.length;

// Determine how many items to place in each column.
for (var i = 0; i < cols; i++) {

  // Divide the number of items remaining by the number of columns minus i. This
  // tells you how many items should go into the column.
  itemsPerColumn[i] = Math.round(remainingItems / (cols - i));

  // Update the number of remaining items for the next iteration.
  remainingItems -= itemsPerColumn[i];

  // If this is the last column, add all remaining items to the column.
  if (i == (cols - 1)) {
    itemsPerColumn[i] += remainingItems;
  }
}

// The index variable is incremented with each iteration through the nested for
// loop to successfully loop through each element of the radioInstances array.
var index = 0;

// maxW stores the maximum width of any item in a column.
var maxW = 0;

// colStartX is used to track the x coordinate for each column. The initial x
// coordinate is specified by the x parameter.
var colStartX = x;
var item;

// Loop through each item in each column using nested for statements. i is the
// current column, and j is the current item within the current column.
for (var i = 0; i < itemsPerColumn.length; i++) {
  for (var j = 0; j < itemsPerColumn[i]; j++) {

    // Set item to the current radio button reference.
    item = this.radioInstances[index];

    // Record the width of the widest button in the column so far, in maxW.
    maxW = Math.max(item._width, maxW);

    // The x coordinate is the same for each radio button in a given column. The y
    // coordinate depends on the y and spacing parameters plus the item number
    // within the column.
```

```
    item._x = colStartX;
    item._y = (j * spacing) + y;

    // Increment index to refer to the next radio button the next time around.
    index++;
  }

  // To set the starting position for the next column, add the maximum width of
  // this column plus five pixels to provide some spacing between columns.
  colStartX += maxW + 5;

  // Reset maxW so that it does not carry over to the next column
  maxW = 0;
  }
};
```

You should call the *setPositions()* method only after you have added all the radio buttons to the group using the *setGroupName()* method for each radio button. Here is an example that uses *setPositions()* to place four radio buttons in two columns:

```
#include "Form.as"

// Create four radio buttons, named emailPrefs0_rb through emailPrefs3_rb, and assign
// them to the "emailPrefs" group.
_root.attachMovie("FRadioButtonSymbol", "emailPrefs0_rb", 1);
_root.attachMovie("FRadioButtonSymbol", "emailPrefs1_rb", 2);
_root.attachMovie("FRadioButtonSymbol", "emailPrefs2_rb", 3);
_root.attachMovie("FRadioButtonSymbol", "emailPrefs3_rb", 4);

emailPrefs0_rb.setGroupName("emailPrefs");
emailPrefs1_rb.setGroupName("emailPrefs");
emailPrefs2_rb.setGroupName("emailPrefs");
emailPrefs3_rb.setGroupName("emailPrefs");

// Add labels and data.
emailPrefs0_rb.setLabel("once a day");
emailPrefs0_rb.setData ("day");
emailPrefs1_rb.setLabel("once a week");
emailPrefs1_rb.setData ("week");
emailPrefs2_rb.setLabel("once a year");
emailPrefs2_rb.setData ("year");
emailPrefs3_rb.setLabel("no email");
emailPrefs3_rb.setData ("none");

// Position the radio buttons.
emailPrefs.setPositions(10, 10, 2, 30);
```

11.9   Getting the Selected Radio Button Value

Problem

You want to get the value of the selected radio button from a group.

Solution

Use the *getValue()* method.

Discussion

First, create two radio buttons and assign them to the same group (named "answer-Group"):

```
_root.attachMovie("FRadioButtonSymbol", "answer0_rb", 1);
_root.attachMovie("FRadioButtonSymbol", "answer1_rb", 2);

answer0_rb.setGroupName("answerGroup");
answer1_rb.setGroupName("answerGroup");
answer0_rb.setLabel("Hot");
answer0_rb.setData (212);
answer1_rb.setLabel("Cold");
answer1_rb.setData (32);

answerGroup.setPositions( );
```

Some time later, you can obtain the data value of the selected radio button by invoking the *getValue()* method on the radio button group. The radio button group is created automatically when a radio button is added to a group using *setGroupName()*. In this example, the return value is either 212 or 32, not the string "Hot" or "Cold". That is, *getValue()* returns the selected button's data property, not its label property.

```
selectedVal = answerGroup.getValue( );
```

As with getting the selected values for other UI components, you typically get the values for radio button groups once the user clicks on the Submit button:

```
function onClick ( ) {
  var selectedVal = answerGroup.getValue( );

  // Do something with data here.
}

submitBtn.setClickHandler("onClick");
```

See Also

Recipes 11.6, 11.7, and 11.11

11.10 Adding Checkboxes to a Form

Problem

You want to add checkboxes to your form.

Solution

Use checkbox UI components.

Discussion

You should use checkboxes in situations in which you want a user to be able to select multiple options from a list, but you do not wish to use a list box. Or, alternatively, you should use a checkbox in any situation that calls for a simple yes/no or true/false answer. Checkboxes function similarly to radio buttons, except for a few important distinctions:

- You cannot set a data value for a checkbox. Checkboxes have only two possible values: true (checked) or false (unchecked).
- Checkboxes do not have a natively available group as radio buttons do.
- Multiple checkboxes should not be used for mutually exclusive choices.

You can set the label of a checkbox with the *setLabel()* method, and you can set the placement of the label (right or left) using the *setLabelPlacement()* method, just as with radio buttons.

The fact that checkboxes don't provide native support for grouping, as radio buttons do, is not necessarily a problem. However, by adding grouping functionality to checkboxes (and coding the checkbox group class to inherit from the radio button group class), you can easily leverage the resizing and positioning code from Recipes 11.7 and 11.8 for radio button groups to work with checkboxes.

You can create a custom checkbox group class as follows:

1. Create a *FCheckBoxGroupClass* constructor.
2. Designate *FCheckBoxGroupClass* to inherit from *FRadioButtonGroupClass*.
3. Define *setGroupName()* and *addToRadioGroup()* methods for *FCheckBoxClass* (the class for checkboxes). These methods can be copied from *FRadioButtonClass* and modified slightly.

 The following code uses variables and properties with "radio" in their names instead of "checkbox." Do not be confused by this. This is merely because the checkbox group class inherits from the radio button group class, and therefore the references are to radio buttons even though in truth they are checkboxes.

Here is our custom *setGroupName()* code for the *FCheckBoxGroupClass* class:

```
// FCheckBoxGroupClass should be defined globally just as the other UI component
// classes. Set the class to inherit from FRadioButtonGroupClass. This means that all
// the functionality of FRadioButtonGroupClass is accessible to the new class.
_global.FCheckBoxGroupClass = function () {};
FCheckBoxGroupClass.prototype = new FRadioButtonGroupClass();
```

```
// Define a setGroupName( ) method for checkboxes, which is the
// same as the one for radio buttons.
FCheckBoxClass.prototype.setGroupName = function (groupName) {
  for (var i = 0; i < this._parent[this.groupName].radioInstances.length; i++) {
    if (this._parent[this.groupName].radioInstances[i] == this) {
      delete this._parent[this.groupName].radioInstances[i];
    }
  }
  this.groupName = groupName;
  this.addToRadioGroup( );
};

// Define addToRadioGroup( ) for checkboxes. This method is called from
// setGroupName( ). It is the same method as the addToRadioGroup( ) method for radio
// buttons, except it creates a new instance of FCheckBoxGroupClass instead of
// FRadioButtonGroupClass.
FCheckBoxClass.prototype.addToRadioGroup = function ( ) {
  if (this._parent[this.groupName] == undefined) {
    this._parent[this.groupName] = new FCheckBoxGroupClass( );
  }
  this._parent[this.groupName].addRadioInstance(this);
};
```

Once you have defined the preceding code, and added it to *Forms.as*, you can assign checkboxes to checkbox groups as you would assign radio buttons to radio button groups:

```
#include "Forms.as"
myCheckBox0_ch.setGroupName("myCheckBoxGroup");
```

The methods of radio button groups are then available to checkbox groups. Though most of the methods are not applicable, the custom *setPositions( )* and *adjustWidth( )* methods from Recipes 11.7 and 11.8 are:

```
// You can call the adjustWidth( ) and setPositions( ) methods from checkbox groups.
myCheckBoxGroup.adjustWidth( );
myCheckBoxGroup.setPositions(100, 100, 2);
```

Another useful feature of checkbox groups is that you can also call the *setLabelPlacement( )* method from the group, as you can from a radio button group!

```
// Set the label placement for all the checkboxes in the group to the left.
myCheckBoxGroup.setLabelPlacement("left");
```

11.11 Getting Checkbox Values

Problem

You want to determine the values (true or false) of checkboxes.

Solution

Use the *getValue()* method for each checkbox, or create a custom *getValues()* method for the checkbox group.

Discussion

The *getValue()* method returns true if a checkbox is checked and false if the checkbox is unchecked:

```
trace(myCheckBox0_ch.getValue());
```

If you have created a checkbox group (see Recipe 11.10), you can add a custom method, *getValues()*, that returns an array of the values for each checkbox in the group. The elements of the returned array contain three properties:

name
> The name of the checkbox instance

label
> The label value of the checkbox

value
> The value of the checkbox (true or false)

Here is our custom *getValues()* method, which you should add to your *Form.as* file for easy inclusion in future projects:

```
// Create the new method, getValues(), for the FCheckBoxGroupClass.
FCheckBoxGroupClass.prototype.getValues = function () {

    // The dataAr array is populated with the objects for each checkbox in the group.
    var dataAr = new Array();

    // Create two local variables for use in the for statement.
    var cb, obj;

    // Loop through every checkbox in the group.
    for (var i = 0; i < this.radioInstances.length; i++) {

        // cb refers to the current checkbox.
        cb = this.radioInstances[i];

        // For each checkbox, create an object with name, label, and value properties.
        obj = new Object();
        obj.name = cb._name;
        obj.label = cb.getLabel();
        obj.value = cb.getValue();

        // Add the object to the array.
        dataAr.push(obj);
    }
```

```
    // Return the array of values.
    return dataAr;
};
```

See Also

Recipes 11.9 and 11.10

11.12 Assembling an Advanced Form

Problem

You want to put together a form to which you can add advanced features such as one-step submission, validation, and multipage forms.

Solution

Create a custom *Form* class.

Discussion

In HTML, forms are created within the structure of a FORM element. Because HTML forms provide a container into which all the form elements can be added, it is possible to add more advanced functionality to them. ActionScript does not provide an analogous structure, however. Therefore, Flash offers nothing that inherently holds multiple elements on a page together into a true form. If you want to add advanced features to your forms, you must create a *Form* class to act as the container for all the form elements.

The *Form* class's primary function is to keep track of the otherwise disparate elements (text fields, list boxes, etc.) that you want to be part of a single form. To accomplish this, your *Form* class needs to have an array property to which elements can be added. In the example code, this array property is named formElements. Next, the *Form* class also needs a method, *addElement()*, by which elements can be added to forms.

Here is the basic implementation of our *Form* class:

```
// Define the Form constructor as a global class, as with other UI components.
_global.Form = function () {

  // Initialize the formElements array to store references to all the elements.
  this.formElements = new Array();
};

// The addElement() method adds an element to the formElements array.
Form.prototype.addElement = function (element) {
  this.formElements.push(element);
};
```

The *Form* class serves as the foundation of all the advanced form features in the recipes that follow. Store it in a *Form.as* file and include it in any projects that require advanced form management.

11.13 Submitting a Form

Problem

You want to submit a form to a URL, such as a CGI script.

Solution

Use a *LoadVars* object with properties and values corresponding to each element of the form to be submitted. Or, alternatively, write a *submitToURL()* method for the custom *Form* class to handle this process dynamically for any form.

Discussion

Here are the steps for submitting form data to a URL using *LoadVars*:

1. Create a *LoadVars* object.
2. Add a property to the *LoadVars* object for each form element. The property name should be the name of the form element. For list boxes, combo boxes, text fields, and checkboxes, the property name is the value of the element's instance name (programmatically, this is the _name property value). For radio buttons, the name of the property should be the group name. The value of each property should be the value of the element as retrieved using the recipes in this chapter.
3. Call the *send()* method of the *LoadVars* object to send all the properties and values to a specified URL.

Here is a code snippet that uses this process with just a few form elements:

```
lv = new LoadVars( );
lv.myListBox_lb        = myListBox_lb.getSelectedIndex( ).data;
lv.myCheckBox0_ch      = myCheckBox0_ch.getValue( );
lv.myRadioButtonGroup = myRadioButtonGroup.getValue( );
lv.send("http://www.yourdomain.com/cgi/getFormData.cgi");
```

The preceding process is not too taxing, as long as there are only a few simple elements in the form. However, as you add more elements to the form, the process becomes more burdensome and error-prone. You can simplify the process by creating a *submitToURL()* method for the *Form* class (see Recipe 11.12) and using it for all your form submission needs.

The *submitToURL()* method shown in the following example accepts a single parameter: the URL to which to submit the form data. The *submitToURL()* method (shown later) also relies on another custom method, *getValues()*, which populates an associative array with the form element names and their values, and then returns that array.

```
Form.prototype.getValues = function () {

    // Create the associative array to hold the form element names and values.
    var obj = new Array();
    var values, value, elem;

    // Loop through all the form elements in the form.
    for (var i = 0; i < this.formElements.length; i++) {
        elem = this.formElements[i];

        // Process each form element, as appropriate to its type. The instanceof operator
        // indicates whether the element is of the specified class.
        if (elem instanceof TextField) {
            // Store each text field's value in the array
            // with the text field name as the key.
            value = elem.text;
            obj[elem._name] = value;
        }
        else if (elem instanceof FCheckBoxClass) {
            // Get the value of the checkbox, and assign it to an element of the
            // associative array using the checkbox's name as the key.
            value = elem.getValue();
            obj[elem._name] = value;
        }
        else if (elem instanceof FCheckBoxGroupClass) {
            // Get the values within the checkbox group (requires custom checkbox group
            // class (see Recipe 11.11).
            values = elem.getValues();

            // Store each checkbox value in the array, where the key is the name property
            // of the element returned by the checkbox group.
            for (var j = 0; j < values.length; j++) {
                obj[values[i].name] = values[i].value;
            }
        }
        else if (elem instanceof FRadioButtonGroupClass) {
            // Store the active radio button's value (obtained from getValue()), where the
            // key is the radio button group name.
            value = elem.getValue();
            obj[elem.getGroupName()] = value;
        }
        else if (elem instanceof FComboBoxClass) {
            // For a combo box, retrieve the data property of the object returned by the
            // getSelectedItem() method, unless it is undefined, in which case use the
            // label property.
            value = (elem.getSelectedItem().data == undefined) ?
                    elem.getSelectedItem().label: elem.getSelectedItem().data;

            // If value is an object (and not a primitive string), this means that the data
            // property was assigned a reference to an object. In that case, assign to
```

```
      // value the value property from the data object. (See Recipe 12.3 regarding
      // assigning data objects.)
      if (value instanceof Object) {
        value = value.value;
      }

      // Store the value, using a key that is the name of the combo box.
      obj[elem._name] = value;
    }
    else if (elem instanceof FListBoxClass) {

      // Retrieve the values from the list box.
      values = elem.getSelectedItems();

      // Create an element whose key is the list box name. Assign to this element a
      // new array filled with the values from the list box (potentially multiple).
      obj[elem._name] = new Array();

      // For each selected item in the list box, add its value to the array. The
      // logic for getting each value is the same as used earlier for combo boxes.
      for (var j = 0; j < values.length; j++) {
        value = (values[j].data == undefined) ? values[j].label : values[j].data;
        if (value instanceof Object) {
          value = value.value;
        }
        obj[elem._name].push(value);
      }
    }
  }
}

  // Return the associative array containing all the form values.
  return obj;
};


// The submitToURL() method should be called from your Form object to submit the form
// data to a URL.
Form.prototype.submitToURL = function (url) {

  // Create a new LoadVars object for sending the form data to the URL.
  var lv = new LoadVars();

  // Get the form values by calling the getValues() method (defined earlier).
  var vals = this.getValues();

  // Add each form element to the LoadVars object so they will be submitted.
  for (var item in vals) {
    lv[item] = vals[item];
  }

  // Send the data to the server script at the specified URL.
  lv.send(url);
};
```

See Also

Recipe 11.12

11.14 Validating Form Input

Problem

You want to validate user input before allowing a form to be submitted for processing.

Solution

Write a custom *validate()* method for the *Form* class that checks each form element.

Discussion

ActionScript does not provide a native means by which to validate form input. However, you can add a small amount of code to the custom *Form* class, with which you can then quickly add validation code to any form. You should add two methods to the custom *Form* class and add one line of code to the existing constructor.

One method, *setValidator()*, should be used to set the validators for any elements requiring validation. The method should take two parameters: the name of the form element as a string and the validator.

The validator can have one of three types of values:

true
> If the Boolean true is specified, the element must contain a value. Use this for mandatory form elements.

"email"
> If the string "email" is specified, the element's value must be in the format of a valid email address.

Regular expression
> If a regular expression is specified, it defines the pattern that the element value must match.

The *setValidator()* method adds new elements to an associative array in which the key is the element name and the value is the validator. You should, therefore, initialize the associative array in the constructor method.

The *validate()* method performs the validation based on the validators that have been specified using *setValidator()*. The *validate()* method should loop through the elements of the form and, if a validator has been assigned for the element, verify that the element value meets the criteria. The *validate()* method returns the name of the first element that fails the validation test. Otherwise, the method returns true, indicating that the form validated successfully. The following is a partial listing of our enhanced *Form* class, which should be stored in a *Form.as* file. Everything in this listing should be added to the existing contents of *Form.as*, with one exception. The constructor method shown here should replace the existing constructor code.

```
// Make sure to include RegExp.as (see Recipe 9.6) in the Form.as file. The
// validation methods require it.
#include "RegExp.as"

_global.Form = function () {
  this.formElements = new Array();

  // Our updated constructor creates the validators associative array.
  this.validators = new Object();
};

// The setValidator() method adds elements to the validators associative array.
Form.prototype.setValidator = function (elementName, validator) {
  this.validators[elementName] = validator;
};

// The validate() method attempts to validate the form.
Form.prototype.validate = function () {

  // Retrieve the form's values using getValues().
  var values = this.getValues();
  var valid, re;

  // Loop through all the values.
  for (var item in values) {

    // Get the validator for the current form element.
    valid = this.validators[item];

    // Validate the element based on its validator (true, "email", or a reg exp).
    // Remember that the condition (valid) is the same as (valid == true).
    if (valid) {
      // If the validator is true, check whether the element has some value.
      if ( (values[item] == undefined) || (values[item] == null)
          || (values[item] == "")) {
        // If no valid value exists, return this item as an error.
        return item;
      }
    } else if (valid == "email") {
      // If the validator is "email", make sure it is an email address of the form
      // something@somewhere.topleveldomain.
      re = new RegExp("^([\\w\-\\.]+)@(([\\w\\-]+\\.)+[\\w\\-]+)$");
      if (!re.test(values[item])) {
        // If it doesn't match an email pattern, return the item as an error.
        return item;
      }
    } else if (valid != undefined) {
```

```
    // If the validator is not true or "email", assume it's a regular expression
    // string. Create a regular expression from the string and test for a match.
    re = new RegExp(valid);
    if (!re.test(values[item])) {
      // If it doesn't match the reg exp, return the item as an error.
      return item;
    }
   }
  }
 }
 // Return true to indicate successful validation
 return true;
};
```

You can use the validation methods in a form before submitting it. If the *validate()*
method returns true, then the form is ready to submit; otherwise, you can direct the
user to correct the errors on the form. The following is an example of its use. Note
that this example uses a *trace()* statement to display the error in the Output window. However, the Output window is available only when testing during authoring.
For more details on how to effectively alert the user with messages when the Flash
Player is running in a browser, see Recipe 11.15.

```
#include "Form.as"

// Create two text fields and a push button.
_root.createTextField("name_txt", 1, 100, 100, 100, 20);
_root.createTextField("email_txt", 2, 100, 130, 100, 20);
_root.attachMovie("FPushButtonSymbol", "btn_pb", 3, {_x: 100, _y: 160});

// Set the text fields so that they have a border and allow input.
name_txt.border  = true;
name_txt.type    = "input";
email_txt.border = true;
email_txt.type   = "input";

// Create the form.
myForm = new Form();

// Add the text fields to the form and set validators for them. The name_txt field
// must contain some text, and email_txt must have a valid email format.
myForm.addElement(name_txt);
myForm.setValidator("name_txt", true);
myForm.addElement(email_txt);
myForm.setValidator("email_txt", "email");

btn_pb.onRelease = function () {

  // Call the validate() method of the form.
  var valid = _root.myForm.validate();

  // If the form validates, submit the form. Otherwise, display the name of the form
  // element that needs to be corrected.
  if (valid) {
```

```
      // Submit form.
   } else {
     trace(valid);
   }
};
```

See Also

Recipes 9.6, 11.12, and 11.15

11.15 Alerting Users to Validation Errors

Problem

You want to alert the user when there is a validation error in the form data.

Solution

Use a message box.

Discussion

The MessageBox component is the perfect way to alert users when there is a form validation error. The MessageBox component can be found in Flash UI Components Set 2, which is available for free from the Macromedia Flash Exchange (*http://www.macromedia.com/exchange/flash*). You can add a message box programmatically using *attachMovie( )*, as you can with any other component. You only need to make sure that the component symbol is included in the Flash document's Library, as described in Recipe 11.1. The linkage identifier for the symbol is *FMessageBoxSymbol*.

```
    this.attachMovie("FMessageBoxSymbol", "myMessageBox", 1);
```

Normally, you don't want a message box to be visible when the movie starts. Instead, you want to make the message box visible only if and when there is something about which to alert the user. Therefore, you should initialize a message box by setting its _visible property to false. You can do this either after attaching the movie clip or during the *attachMovie( )* invocation by using an initialization object, as follows:

```
    this.attachMovie("FMessageBoxSymbol", "myMessageBox", 1, {_visible: false});
```

Additionally, when you attach a message box programmatically, you must specify the buttons to include in the message box using the *setButtons( )* method. The method expects an array of labels for the buttons. Typically, a message box has only one button—an OK button.

```
    myMessageBox.setButtons(["OK"]);
```

You can programmatically set the message that the user sees with the *setMessage()* method:

```
myMessageBox.setMessage("Hello, friend.");
```

The following is an example of a message box used in conjunction with form validation. To test this code, you need to add both the PushButton and MessageBox component symbols to the movie's Library. You also need to make sure that your *Form.as* file includes all the necessary functionality. If in doubt, download the completed *Form.as* file from *http://www.person13.com/ascb*.

```
#include "Form.as"

// Create a text field and a push button.
_root.createTextField("email_txt", 1, 100, 130, 100, 20);
_root.attachMovie("FPushButtonSymbol", "btn_pb", 2, {_x: 100, _y: 160});

// Create the message box. Initialize it with _visible set to false.
// Also, create an OK button.
_root.attachMovie("FMessageBoxSymbol", "messageBox", 3,
                   {_x: 200, y: 200, _visible: false});
messageBox.setButtons(["OK"]);

// Set the text field so that it has a border and allows input.
email_txt.border = true;
email_txt.type   = "input";

// Create the form.
myForm = new Form( );

// email_txt must have a valid email format.
myForm.addElement(email_txt);
myForm.setValidator("email_txt", "email");

btn_pb.onRelease = function ( ) {

  // Call the validate( ) method of the form.
  var valid = _root.myForm.validate( );

  // If the form validates, submit it. Otherwise, display the name of the problematic
  // form element in the message box.
  if (valid) {
    // Submit form.
  } else {
    _root.messageBox.setMessage("You must fill out a valid entry for " + valid);
    _root.messageBox._visible = true;
  }
};
```

See Also

Recipe 11.14

11.16 Making a Multipage Form

Problem

You want to create a form that spans multiple "pages" rather than being all on one screen.

Solution

Create a custom *MultiPageForm* class.

Discussion

You can create multipage forms in Flash without having to create a custom class. However, there are several drawbacks to this approach:

- The most convenient way to do it is to create a form that spans multiple frames. Flash does not automatically remember the values the user selected for form elements across frames. Therefore, you have to programmatically store and repopulate the user's selections for the form pages when they click back and forth.

- The process requires a lot of custom coding each time you want to create a new multipage form rather than relying on an existing infrastructure. Basically, it means a lot of duplicated effort and code.

- It is possible, but not very easy, to leverage the functionality of the *Form* class.

For these reasons, it is far superior to create a class that handles all the details of working with a multipage form. By creating a *MultiPageForm* class, you can use and reuse the functionality easily.

The *MultiPageForm* class has the following characteristics:

- The class has an array property that contains *Form* objects. A multipage form is composed, therefore, of multiple forms that are stored in an array property.

- The class has methods that set the current visible page of the form by making the other pages invisible. All forms are created on the same frame.

Here is the next enhancement to the *Form* class, a *setVisible()* method, which should be added to our *Form.as* file:

```
// setVisible() accepts a Boolean value–true or false–and uses it to set the
// _visible property of each element. Thus, it hides or shows an entire form page.
Form.prototype.setVisible = function (visible) {
  for (var i = 0; i < this.formElements.length; i++) {

    // If the element is a radio button group (or a checkbox group, which inherits
    // from the same class), set the visibility of each item in the group.
    if (this.formElements[i] instanceof FRadioButtonGroupClass) {
      for (var j = 0; j < this.formElements[i].radioInstances.length; j++) {
```

```
            this.formElements[i].radioInstances[j]._visible = visible;
          }
      } else {
        // Otherwise, set the _visible property of the individual element.
        this.formElements[i]._visible = visible;
      }
    }
};
```

And here is our *MultiPageForm* class, which should also be added to our *Form.as* file:

```
// Create the MultiPageForm class constructor.
_global.MultiPageForm = function () {
  // Initialize currentPage to display the first page of the form.
  this.currentPage = 1;

  // Create an array to hold all the form "pages".
  this.forms = new Array();

  // If the caller passed in any parameters, assume they are references to existing
  // Form objects to add to this multipage form. Therefore, loop through the
  // arguments array and invoke the addForm() method for each argument.
  for (var i = 0; i < arguments.length; i++) {
    this.addForm(arguments[i]);
  }
};

// Add a Form object to the MultiPageForm object.
MultiPageForm.prototype.addForm = function (frm) {
  this.forms.push(frm);
};

// setPage() sets the current page. The first page of the form is 1.
MultiPageForm.prototype.setPage = function (page) {

  // Show the current page and hide all the other pages.
  for (var i = 0; i < this.forms.length; i++) {
    if (page == (i + 1)) {
      this.forms[i].setVisible(true);
    } else {
      this.forms[i].setVisible(false);
    }
  }

  // Remember the current page.
  this.currentPage = page;
};

// nextPage() goes to the next page (or to the first page if this is the last page).
MultiPageForm.prototype.nextPage = function () {

  // Increment the current page.
  this.currentPage++;
```

```
  // If we're past the last page, go to the first page instead.
  if (this.currentPage > this.forms.length) {
    this.currentPage = 1;
  }

  // Display the new current page and hide the other pages.
  this.setPage(this.currentPage);
};

// prevPage() goes to the previous page (or the last page if this is the first one).
MultiPageForm.prototype.prevPage = function () {

  // Decrement the current page.
  this.currentPage--;

  // If we're before the first page, go to the last page instead.
  if (this.currentPage < 1) {
    this.currentPage = this.forms.length;
  }

  // Display the new current page and hide the other pages.
  this.setPage(this.currentPage);
};
```

Here is an example that implements a multipage form:

```
#include "Form.as"

// Create two input text fields.
_root.createTextField("name_txt",  1, 100, 100, 100, 20);
_root.createTextField("email_txt", 2, 100, 130, 100, 20);
name_txt.border  = true;
name_txt.type    = "input";
email_txt.border = true;
email_txt.type   = "input";

// Create a Form object and add the text fields to it. This is the first page.
myForm0 = new Form();
myForm0.addElement(name_txt);
myForm0.addElement(email_txt);

// Create two radio buttons and add them to a group.
_root.attachMovie("FRadioButtonSymbol", "myRadioButton0_rb", 3);
_root.attachMovie("FRadioButtonSymbol", "myRadioButton1_rb", 4);
myRadioButton0_rb.setGroupName("myRadioButtonGroup");
myRadioButton1_rb.setGroupName("myRadioButtonGroup");
myRadioButton0_rb.setLabel("item 1");
myRadioButton1_rb.setLabel("item 2");
myRadioButton0_rb.setData("label 1");
myRadioButton1_rb.setData("label 2");
myRadioButtonGroup.setPositions(100, 100);
```

```
// Create a Form object and add the radio button group (not the individual radio
// buttons) to it. This is the second page of the form.
myForm1 = new Form( );
myForm1.addElement(myRadioButtonGroup);

// Create a combo box and a Submit button.
_root.attachMovie("FComboBoxSymbol",   "myComboBox_cb", 5, {_x: 100, _y: 100});
_root.attachMovie("FPushButtonSymbol", "submitBtn_pb",  6, {_x: 100, _y: 130});
myComboBox_cb.setDataProvider(["a", "b", "c"]);

// Create a Form object and add the combo box and Submit button to it. This is the
// third page. The Submit button should be visible on the last page only.
myForm2 = new Form( );
myForm2.addElement(myComboBox_cb);
myForm2.addElement(submitBtn_pb);

// Create a MultiPageForm object and pass it the three Form pages.
myMultiForm = new MultiPageForm(myForm0, myForm1, myForm2);

// Display the first page of the form.
myMultiForm.setPage(1);

// Implement the Submit button as shown in Recipe 11.17.
submitBtn_pb.setLabel("submit");
submitBtn_pb.onRelease = function ( ) {
  // Submit form
};

// Create previous and next buttons to navigate the pages of the form.
_root.attachMovie("FPushButtonSymbol", "prevBtn_pb", 7, {_x: 100, _y: 160});
_root.attachMovie("FPushButtonSymbol", "nextBtn_pb", 8, {_x: 210, _y: 160});

prevBtn_pb.setLabel("previous page");
prevBtn_pb.onRelease = function ( ) {
  _root.myMultiForm.prevPage( );
};
nextBtn_pb.setLabel("next page");
nextBtn_pb.onRelease = function ( ) {
  _root.myMultiForm.nextPage( );
};
```

When you create a multipage form in this manner, you must ensure that all objects have unique depths. All the forms are really on the same frame but are hidden at different times. Therefore, if you create form elements with the same depths, the latter one will overwrite the former.

See Also

Recipe 11.17

11.17 Submitting a Multipage Form

Problem

You want to submit a multipage form to a URL.

Solution

Create and invoke a *submitToURL()* method for the custom *MultiPageForm* class.

Discussion

Once you have created the *getValues()* and *submitToURL()* methods of the *Form* class (see Recipe 11.13), you can leverage them to create versions of the same methods for the *MultiPageForm* class. Add the following code to your *Form.as* file for easy inclusion in other projects:

```
// The multipage version of submitToURL() is the same as the regular Form version.
MultiPageForm.prototype.submitToURL = function (url) {
  var lv = new LoadVars();
  var vals = this.getValues();
  for (var item in vals) {
    lv[item] = vals[item];
  }
  lv.send(url);
};

// MultiPageForm.getValues() uses Form.getValues() to create an object with the
// elements of all the form pages and their values.
MultiPageForm.prototype.getValues = function () {
  var obj = new Array();
  var formVals, elem;

  // Call the getValues() method of each form page and add those results to the
  // multipage values associative array.
  for (var i = 0; i < this.forms.length; i++) {
    formVals = this.forms[i].getValues();
    for (elem in formVals) {
      obj[elem] = formVals[elem];
    }
  }
  return obj;
};
```

The HTML paradigm for multipage forms requires server-side persistence (or client-side cookies) involving saving values to session or client variables. This is necessary with HTML because HTTP is a stateless environment. Flash, however, is stateful; ActionScript can remember values between pages, so there is no need to use session or client variables on the server when using Flash forms.

11.18 Validating a Multipage Form

Problem

You want to validate elements within a multipage form.

Solution

Create and invoke a *validate()* method for the custom *MultiPageForm* class.

Discussion

You can create a *MultiPageForm.validate()* method that leverages the *Form.validate()* method and works in much the same way. Add the following code to your *Form.as* file for easy inclusion in other projects:

```
MultiPageForm.prototype.validate = function () {
  var vRes;

  // Loop through all the form pages.
  for (var i = 0; i < this.forms.length; i++) {

    // Call the validate() method for each page of the form. If validate() returns
    // something other than true, some form element didn't validate. In that case,
    // display that page of the form and return the name of the offending element.
    vRes = this.forms[i].validate();
    if (!vRes) {
      this.setPage(i + 1);
      return vRes;
    }
  }
  return true;
};
```

You can use the *validate()* method for multipage forms as you did for single-page forms:

```
submitBtn_pb.onRelease = function () {
  // Call the validate() method of the multipage form.
  var valid = _root.myMultiForm.validate();

  // If the form validates, submit the form. Otherwise, display the name of the form
  // element that needs to be corrected. If an element fails to validate, the
  // multipage form automatically displays the page with the problem.
  if (valid) {
    // Submit form
  } else {
    trace(valid);
  }
};
```

Recipes 11.14 and 11.15

11.19 Transmitting Data Securely

Problem

You want to transmit data, such as credit card numbers, securely.

Solution

Use HTTPS to send the data over a secure channel or, if that is not possible, use a third-party encryption library for one-way data encryption.

Discussion

Flash can use the same protocols for data transmission—HTTP or HTTPS—as HTML pages. A great many servers are set up to accept communication over the insecure HTTP protocol only. Transmitting unencrypted data over HTTP is not secure and should be used only when the data is not sensitive. For example, if you are sending survey responses to the server, you might not care if that information can be seen by others. But insecure transmission compromises credit card numbers and other sensitive financial or personal information. Although a complete discussion of security is beyond the scope of this book, there are many good resources on security.

 If you are not using an off-the-shelf solution, such as SSL, there are many non-obvious pitfalls that can leave your data vulnerable. Leave the protocol design to the experts or consult a book that addresses secure cryptographic protocol design: *Secure Programming Cookbook for C and C++* by Viega and Messier (O'Reilly) or *Practical Cryptography* (not *Applied Cryptography*) by Schneier and Ferguson (Wiley).

Be aware that various encryption algorithms deemed secure today may be considered insecure in the near future due to advances in cryptanalysis and computer processor performance increases.

So what should you, as a Flash developer, do? First, you should recognize that Flash data transmission isn't secure if you are sending it over HTTP. Not only can your unsecured data be intercepted and decoded, but more nefariously, unauthenticated data can be forged. You should make sure that your e-commerce page doesn't accept bogus transactions, for example. There are two basic strategies you can use to secure Flash data transmissions. You can rely on the secure HTTPS protocol for transmission, or you can manually encrypt data (one-way encryption) with a third-party encryption library. If available, HTTPS is the simplest, fastest, and often the most secure to implement. So let's tackle that approach first.

When data is sent over HTTP, it is normally not encrypted in any way. This means that people with the known-how and resources can tap into that transmitted data and read it. However, when you use HTTPS, although the data sent between client and server might be intercepted, it likely cannot be decrypted by the eavesdropper. To use HTTPS from Flash, specify the *https* protocol as part of the URL when calling *LoadVars* or *XML* methods, or similar methods that accept a URL parameter. For example:

```
myLoadVars.send("https://www.myserver.com");
```

However, for this to work, two things have to be true:

- Your server has to actually support HTTPS. Otherwise, the URL will be unavailable. For your sever to support HTTPS it will need an SSL (Secure Socket Layer) certificate. If you use a shared host, contact the webmaster to see whether she already has something available for you. If you administer your own server, you will need to get a certificate from a certificate authority such as Verisign (*http://www.verisign.com*). You'll need to get a certificate to match the level of encryption (128-bit, 256-bit, etc.) that you want. Generally, the more bits, the stronger the encryption.

- The Flash movie needs to be playing in a web browser that supports encryption that matches the level of SSL encryption in use. For example, if using an encryption algorithm that requires 128-bit encryption (strong encryption), then you'll need to require that all users have a 128-bit-encryption-capable browser.

How does HTTPS/SSL work within Flash? When the Flash movie wants to send data to the server, it uses the browser's built-in HTTPS/SSL capabilities to request a *public key* from the server. A public key is exposed publicly by the server so the client-side data can be encrypted. Once the server returns the public key (and the key is validated), the data from Flash is encrypted in the browser and sent to the server. The data is then decrypted on the server (using a corresponding *private key*) before it is sent to any server-side scripts.

So how secure are HTTPS transactions? The answer depends on the level of security you demand and the capabilities of the browser. For example, modern browsers support at least 128-bit encryption, which is more secure than older 56-bit encryption. Although 56-bit encryption might appear better than nothing, a false sense of security is worse than no security; 56-bit encryption is considered vulnerable by modern standards and should not be used when true security is necessary. Many companies require 128-bit security because it is considerably less likely to be decrypted by a third party. Financial institutions, for example, almost always require 128-bit encryption. Although HTTPS/SSL is an industry standard for transmitting data securely, no encryption is perfect. That said, 256-bit encryption, when implemented on a properly secured system, is considered unbreakable by today's standards.

There is at least one additional issue of which you should be aware when working with HTTPS/SSL. Although data transmitted via HTTPS is encrypted during transmission, once the data has been received and decrypted by the server, it is again vulnerable to espionage. You must take precautions to secure the server and data sources. Implementing security measures to protect your server from crackers is arguably even more important than securing the data transmission. After all, you don't want to go to all the trouble to secure the data transmission but offer the cracker the convenience of being able to grab your entire database of credit card and social security numbers!

If you cannot use HTTPS/SSL (for example, if you don't have an SSL certificate or if your Flash movie plays as a Projector or is embedded in a Director application), you'll need another solution. Let's examine the third-party encryption options that are available.

There are three types of encryption we'll touch on: public key, symmetric, and one-way hash encryption. Each of these types of encryption is best suited to different types of scenarios. We've already seen an example of public key encryption when we looked at SSL. SSL certificates grant a server a public and private key. When a client wants to encrypt data to send to the server, it must first request the public key. It uses the public key to encrypt the data and then sends it to the server. The corresponding private key, which can be used to decrypt the data, is available only on the server with the SSL certificate. (Interestingly, data encrypted with the private key can be decrypted with the public key. What purpose does it serve to encrypt data that can be decrypted with a widely available public key? Although it doesn't offer privacy, encrypting data with a private key offers so-called *authentication*. If the public key can successfully decrypt the data, you are reasonably sure that it was encrypted by the entity to whom the corresponding private key belongs. Furthermore, you are assured that the data wasn't modified in transit.)

Symmetric encryption uses one key for both encryption and decryption. This means that the key must be known to both the encrypting and decrypting client and/or server (but not known to other parties). For this reason, symmetric encryption is best suited for scenarios in which the data is sent to the server in encrypted format for storage in encrypted format. The same client can later retrieve the data and decrypt it client-side with the same key.

One-way hash algorithms provide only one-way encryption—the data cannot be decrypted. This may seem like a strange idea. Why would you want to encrypt data if you can never decrypt it? The answer is that, in many cases, you would not. For example, you would not want to one-way encrypt text data such as an address or a name because chances are you'll want that data to be human-readable at some point. But one-way encryption is a great for things such as passwords. The data can be encrypted and stored on the server in encrypted format. When the user tries to log in, the password he enters is encrypted using the same algorithm, and the two encrypted passwords are compared. Since both values were encrypted using the same algorithm, the encrypted values match if the original, unencrypted values matched.

There are several third-party ActionScript libraries available for encrypting data. Most implement one-way encryption algorithms. So we'll look at those first.

Gerrit E.G. Hobbelt has ported a JavaScript MD5 encryption algorithm to Action-Script, and you can download the code from *http://flashexperiments.insh-allah.com/md5.zip*. Once you've downloaded the *.zip* file, extract the *md5.as* file using WinZip or another utility program. Save the *md5.as* file to your Flash *Include* directory. Once you extract the *.as* file, you can include it in any Flash movie and use the *calcMD5()* function to encrypt a string before sending it to the server.

When you use Hobbelt's MD5 library, you need to include the *md5.as* file in the scope where you want to invoke the *calcMD5()* function or provide a target path when invoking the function, as shown in the following example.

```
#include "md5.as"

send_btn.onRelease = function () {

    // Encode the value that the user enters into a text field.
    var encodedPasswordStr = _root.calcMD5(_root.password_txt.text);

    var lv = new LoadVars();
    lv.password = encodedPasswordStr;
    lv.send("loginScript.cgi");
}
```

Branden Hall also has a port of the MD5 algorithm as well as the SHA1 algorithm. These libraries are available for download at *http://www.waxpraxis.org/encryption/md5* and *http://www.waxpraxis.org/encryption/sha1*.

What if you need two-way encryption? The ActionCrypt project is an open source library that wraps well-known encryption library functions. So if you need additional encryption algorithms, consider ActionCrypt. At the time of this writing, ActionCrypt provides two-way encryption with the 56-bit blowfish algorithm. ActionCrypt also promises additional encryption algorithms, including other two-way as well as one-way and public key encryption. You can download ActionCrypt from *http://actioncrypt.sourceforge.net*.

See Also

For two good books on security, see the warning note earlier in this recipe. For more information on encryption, see *http://governmentsecurity.org/articles/AnOverviewofCryptography.php*. Also see *http://www.rsasecurity.com* for information related to Internet security in general. See *http://www.macromedia.com/devnet/*

mx/flash/whitepapers/security.pdf for more information regarding security in Flash. See *http://flashexperiments.insh-allah.com/#MD5* for information on Hobbelt's MD5 port. See *http://www.waxpraxis.org/encryption/md5* and *http://www.wax-praxis.org/encryption/sha1* for information on Branden Hall's MD5 and SHA1 ports. See *http://actioncrypt.sourceforge.net* for more information regarding the Action-Crypt project. Also refer to Recipe 8.6.

11.20 Prepopulating a Form

Problem

You want to programmatically fill in a form with defaults or a user's previous selections.

Solution

Use the methods and properties that allow you to set the values of each form element.

Discussion

Each type of form element has different ways of selecting the element or modifying its value. For example, you can set a text field's contents using the text property:

```
myTextField_txt.text = value;
```

You can set combo boxes and single-select list boxes using the *setSelectedIndex()* method. This method requires you to know the index of the item you wish to select programmatically (and not just its label or data value).

```
// Selects the third item from the menu
myComboBox_cb.setSelectedIndex(2);
```

You can programmatically select multiple items from a multiple-selection list box using the *setSelectedIndices()* method, which accepts an array of indexes to select:

```
// Selects the first three menu items from a multiple-selection list box
myListBox_lb.setSelectedIndices([0, 1, 2]);
```

To set a combo box or list box by its label or data property (rather than by its index), you can create a custom *setSelectedItem()* method for *FSelectableListClass* (the superclass of both combo boxes and list boxes). The method should accept a single parameter, which is the data value for the desired menu item. If the data properties of the menu items are all undefined, the *setSelectedItem()* method should try to match the value to a label instead. Additionally, you can create a *setSelectedItems()* method using the same basic process but you would set multiple items in a multiple-selection list box. The *setSelectedItems()* method should take an array of values (data values or labels to select).

Here is the custom *setSelectedItem()* method for list boxes and combo boxes. Make sure to add this code to your *Form.as* file, and remember that you can always download the completed version from *http://www.person13.com/ascb*.

```
FSelectableListClass.prototype.setSelectedItem = function (val) {
  var item, itemVal;

  // Loop through all the items in the menu. The getLength() method returns the
  // number of items in the menu.
  for (var i = 0; i < this.getLength(); i++) {

    // Get each item using the getItemAt() method.
    item = this.getItemAt(i);

    // If the data property is not undefined, use it for testing matches. Otherwise,
    // use the label property.
    if (item.data != undefined) {
      itemVal = item.data;
    } else {
      itemVal = item.label;
    }

    // If the data or label property matches the input val, call setSelectedIndex(),
    // passing it the current for loop index (i). Use a return statement to exit once
    // one item is found and selected.
    if (val == itemVal) {
      this.setSelectedIndex(i);
      return;
    }
  }
};
```

Here is the custom *setSelectedItems()* method for multiple-selection list boxes:

```
FSelectableListClass.prototype.setSelectedItems = function (vals) {
  var item, itemVal;

  // Create an array to holds the indexes of the items to select.
  var selectedIndices = new Array();

  // Loop through all the menu items. This uses similar logic as the
  // setSelectedItem() method.
  for (var i = 0; i < this.getLength(); i++) {
    item = this.getItemAt(i);
    if (item.data != undefined) {
      itemVal = item.data;
    } else {
      itemVal = item.label;
    }

    // The vals parameter is an array of values, so we loop through each element to
    // see if it matches with data or label. If so, it's a match, so add the current
    // for statement index (i) to the selectedIndices array.
    for (var j = 0; j < vals.length; j++) {
```

```
      if (vals[j] == itemVal) {
        selectedIndices.push(i);
      }
    }
  }
}

  // Call the setSelectedIndices() method for this list box and pass it the
  // selectedIndices array that was populated in the preceding for statement.
  this.setSelectedIndices(selectedIndices);
};
```

Here is an example of how to use these methods:

```
#include "Form.as"

// Create a combo box and populate it using a simple array. This means that each item
// has a label property but not a data property.
_root.attachMovie("FComboBoxSymbol", "myComboBox0_cb", 1);
myComboBox0_cb.setDataProvider(["a", "b", "c"]);

// Call setSelectedItem() with the label value "b" to select that item.
myComboBox0_cb.setSelectedItem("b");

// Create a combo box and populate it using a more complex data provider such that
// each menu item has both a label and a data property.
_root.attachMovie("FComboBoxSymbol", "myComboBox1_cb", 2, {_y: 40});
dp = new Array();
dp.push({label: "a", data: 24});
dp.push({label: "b", data: 33});
dp.push({label: "c", data: 42});
myComboBox1_cb.setDataProvider(dp);

// Call the setSelectedItem() method with a data value. This selects the menu item
// that corresponds (label "c").
myComboBox1_cb.setSelectedItem(42);

// Create a multiple-selection list box and populate it using the same data provider
// as the preceding combo box.
_root.attachMovie("FListBoxSymbol", "myListBox_lb", 3, {_y: 80});
myListBox_lb.setSelectMultiple(true);
myListBox_lb.setDataProvider(dp);

// Call setSelectedItems() with an array of data values. This selects the menu items
// with labels "a" and "c".
myListBox_lb.setSelectedItems([24, 42]);
```

11.21 Customizing the Tab Order

Problem

You want to specify the order in which form elements are chosen when the Tab key is pressed.

Solution

Use the `tabIndex` properties of the form elements to specify their sequence.

Discussion

Flash provides an automatic sequence through which items on the Stage are accessed when the Tab key is pressed. This automatic sequence includes all movie clips, buttons, and text fields, and is not necessarily in an order that makes sense for your application. This poses two challenges. First of all, only certain elements in the movie (such as form elements) should be selectable via the Tab key. Second, you want form elements to be accessed in a specific order. It can be frustrating for your application's users if pressing the Tab key after the first form element takes them to the last element instead of the next one.

Fortunately, you can specify a custom tab order for Flash to use and can include only those elements that you want to be selectable via the Tab key.

 The Tab key cannot be detected reliably in Test Movie mode unless you select the Control → Disable Keyboard Shortcuts option. Select Control → Test Movie, wait for the *.swf* file to appear, and then disable keyboard shortcuts from the Control menu.

To specify a custom tab order, assign an order (integer) value to each of the element's `tabIndex` properties. When a text field is selected and the user presses the Tab key, Flash looks at the text field's `tabIndex` value; it then looks for the element with the next highest value and switches to it. There is one caveat, however: although the user can switch out of text fields using the Tab key, other form elements can be switched to, but not out of, using the Tab key.

```
#include "Form.as"

/* Create the form elements. They appear on the Stage in this order:
    myTextField0_txt
    myComboBox0_cb
    myTextField1_txt
    myComboBox1_cb
    myTextField2_txt
    myCheckBox_ch
    myListBox_lb
    myRadioButton0_rb
    myRadioButton1_rb
    myRadioButton2_rb
*/
_root.createTextField("myTextField0_txt", 1, 0, 0, 100, 20);
myTextField0_txt.border = true;
myTextField0_txt.type = "input";
_root.attachMovie("FComboBoxSymbol", "myComboBox0_cb", 2, {_y: 30});
```

```
_root.createTextField("myTextField1_txt", 3, 0, 60, 100, 20);
myTextField1_txt.border = true;
myTextField1_txt.type = "input";
_root.attachMovie("FComboBoxSymbol", "myComboBox1_cb", 4, {_y: 90});
_root.createTextField("myTextField2_txt", 5, 0, 120, 100, 20);
myTextField2_txt.border = true;
myTextField2_txt.type = "input";
_root.attachMovie("FCheckBoxSymbol", "myCheckBox_ch", 6);
myCheckBox_ch.setGroupName("myCheckBoxGroup");
myCheckBoxGroup.setPositions(0, 150);
_root.attachMovie("FListBoxSymbol", "myListBox_lb", 7, {_y: 180});
_root.attachMovie("FRadioButtonSymbol", "myRadioButton0_rb", 8);
_root.attachMovie("FRadioButtonSymbol", "myRadioButton1_rb", 9);
_root.attachMovie("FRadioButtonSymbol", "myRadioButton2_rb", 10);
myRadioButton0_rb.setGroupName("myRadioButtonGroup");
myRadioButton1_rb.setGroupName("myRadioButtonGroup");
myRadioButton2_rb.setGroupName("myRadioButtonGroup");
myRadioButtonGroup.setPositions(0, (myListBox_lb._y + myListBox_lb._height + 10));

// Specify the desired tab order by assigning each element's tabIndex property.
myTextField0_txt.tabIndex = 1;
myComboBox0_cb.tabIndex   = 2;
myTextField1_txt.tabIndex = 3;
myComboBox1_cb.tabIndex   = 4;
myTextField2_txt.tabIndex = 5;
myCheckBox_ch.tabIndex    = 6;

// There is no real reason to include these last two because they can never be tabbed
// to or out of (it would require a text field to precede them to switch to them).
// However, as you can see by this example, it does no harm to also add them in the
// sequence.
myListBox_lb.tabIndex      = 7;
myRadioButton0_rb.tabIndex = 8;
```

11.22 Using Tables to Arrange Form Elements

Problem

You want to use ActionScript to arrange the elements of a form on the screen.

Solution

Create and use a custom *Table* class.

Discussion

You can use ActionScript to control the position of any graphical object such as a movie clip, a button, or a text field, using the _x and _y properties. Additionally, each graphical object has properties that return its height and width (_height and _width).

You can use these properties in concert to position instances on the Stage relative to one another.

For example, we can position a movie clip horizontally such that its x coordinate is five pixels to the right of a text field. The text field's _x property plus its _width property yields the x coordinate of the right edge of the text field. In this example, we add five pixels to allow for spacing between the movie clip and the text field. We also align the top of the movie clip with the top of the text field.

```
myMovieClip_mc._x = myTextField_txt._x + myTextField_txt._width + 5;
myMovieClip_mc._y = myTextField_txt._y;
```

In this example, we position the movie clip such that its y coordinate is five pixels below the bottom of the text field. This example is similar to the preceding one but uses the _y and _height properties to calculate the vertical position. We also align the left edges of the movie clip and the text field.

```
myMovieClip_mc._y = myTextField_txt._y + myTextField_txt._height + 5;
myMovieClip_mc._x = myTextField_txt._x;
```

The code we've looked at up to this point assumes that the movie clip we are positioning has its registration point in its upper-left corner. However, as you are likely aware, the registration point of a clip defaults to its center and can be placed at an arbitrary location. Fortunately, it is relatively simple to correct for this offset by subtracting the movie clip's minimum x and y values as obtained from the *getBounds()* method. Here, we revisit the two previous code examples, shown with offsets that accommodate movie clips with registration points of any kind.

This code positions a movie clip to the right of the text field:

```
bnds = myMovieClip_mc.getBounds();
myMovieClip_mc._x = myTextField_txt._x + myTextField_txt._width + 5 - bnds.xMin;
myMovieClip_mc._y = myTextField_txt._y - bnds.yMin;
```

This code positions the movie clip below the text field:

```
bnds = myMovieClip_mc.getBounds();
myMovieClip_mc._y = myTextField_txt._y + myTextField_txt._height + 5 - bnds.yMin;
myMovieClip_mc._x = myTextField_txt._x - bnds.xMin;
```

The preceding code examples show the logic that you can use to position instances relative to one another within a Flash movie. However, when you start working with more objects, your code can start to get long and confusing. To arrange 20 elements on a form requires at least 40 lines of code. A more effective way to approach this problem is to create a *Table* class that you can use to position any kind of graphical object on the Stage.

The following code creates a custom *Table* class that you can use to effectively arrange graphical objects. The *Table* class relies on two other custom classes—*TableColumn* and *TableRow*—that are also defined in the code that follows. Every table is composed of one or more rows, and every row is composed of one or more columns. The columns are, in turn, composed of elements. The elements can be any kind of graphical object (movie clip, button, or text field). A cell (the intersection of a row and a table) can contain a single table element. Alternatively, nested tables within tables allow a single cell to contain multiple elements, allowing for more advanced layouts.

Here is our code to define the *Table*, *TableColumn*, and *TableRow* classes. It should be placed in a *Table.as* file in your *Include* directory for future use. The *Table* class is designed so that the spacing works as it does in HTML tables—a single value is used for both the vertical and horizontal spacing applied around each element, column, and row. It is left as an exercise for you to redefine the class constructors to accept and implement separate horizontal and vertical spacing parameters.

```
// Define the TableColumn constructor. spacing defines the amount of space (in
// pixels) between elements in the column.
_global.TableColumn = function (spacing) {
  // Store the spacing parameter in an instance property of the same name. spacing
  // defaults to 5 if not otherwise specified.
  this.spacing = (spacing == undefined) ? 5 : spacing;

  // The _width and _height properties store the total width and height of the
  // column. Initialize them to 0.
  this._width  = 0;
  this._height = 0;

  // The elements array holds all the elements of the column.
  this.elements = new Array();

  // If any parameters are passed to the constructor, from the second position
  // onward, add these values (assumed to be references to graphical objects
  // or to a Table object) to the column using the addElement() method.
  for (var i = 1; i < arguments.length; i++) {
    this.addElement(arguments[i]);
  }
};

// The addElement() method adds elements to a column.
TableColumn.prototype.addElement = function (element) {

  if (element instanceof Table) {
    // If the element is a Table object, set the containsTable
    // property to true. Reinitialize elements to ensure that the table
    // is the only element in the column.
    this.containsTable = true;
    this.elements = new Array();
    this.elements.push(element);

    // Reset the width and height of the column.
    this._width  = 0;
    this._height = 0;
  }
  else {
```

```
  // Otherwise, the element is not a table. Reinitialize all the properties if the
  // column previously held a table.
  if (this.containsTable) {
    this.containsTable = false;
    this.elements = new Array( );
    this._width  = 0;
    this._height = 0;
  }

  // Add the element to the elements array.
  this.elements.push(element);
}

// Make sure the column's width reflects the width of the widest element.
this._width = Math.max(this._width, element._width);

// Increment the column's height by the height of the element plus the spacing.
this._height += element._height + this.spacing;
};

// TableColumn.render( ) positions the elements within the column relative to one
// another. The startx and starty parameters give the x and y coordinates for the
// first element in the column. The TableColumn.render( ) method is called by the
// render( ) method of the row in which the column is contained.
TableColumn.prototype.render = function (startx, starty) {

  // The startx and starty parameters default to 0 if not specified.
  if (startx == undefined) {
    startx = 0;
  }
  if (starty == undefined) {
    starty = 0;
  }

  // If the column contains a table, call the render( ) method of that table.
  // Otherwise, set the x and y coordinates for each element in the column.
  if (this.containsTable) {
    this.elements[0].render(true, startx, starty);
  }
  else {
    var bnds;
    for (var i = 0; i < this.elements.length; i++) {

      // Get the bounds of the elements in case the
      // registration point is not in the upper-left corner.
      bnds = this.elements[i].getBounds( );

      // The y coordinate of the element is given by starty plus the height of the
      // previous element in the column, plus the spacing between them. To
      // accommodate any offsets due to registration points, subtract the element's
      // minimum y coordinate.
      this.elements[i]._y = this.elements[i-1]._height + this.spacing +
                            starty - bnds.yMin;
```

```
        // The x coordinate of the element is given by startx plus spacing. To
        // accommodate any offsets due to registration points, subtract the element's
        // minimum x coordinate.
        this.elements[i]._x = startx + this.spacing - bnds.xMin;

        // Increment starty each time by the height of the previous element plus the
        // spacing between elements.
        starty += this.elements[i - 1]._height + this.spacing;
    }
  }
};

// removeElementAt( ) removes an element from a column at the given index. Note that
// the index is zero-relative (the first column is column 0).
TableColumn.prototype.removeElementAt = function (index) {
  this.elements.splice(index, 1);
};

// The TableColumn.resize( ) method recalculates the width and height of a column. It
// is called automatically by TableRow.resize( ) (which is, in turn, called by
// Table.resize( )).
TableColumn.prototype.resize = function ( ) {

  // Reset the width and height to 0.
  this._width  = 0;
  this._height = 0;

  // If the column contains a table, call the resize( ) method of the table to ensure
  // that the correct size of that table has been calculated.
  if (this.containsTable) {
    this.elements[0].resize( );
  }

  // Set the column width to the widest element and calculate the column height.
  for (var i = 0; i < this.elements.length; i++) {
    this._width = Math.max(this._width, this.elements[i]._width);
    this._height += this.elements[i]._height + this.spacing;
  }
};

// Define the TableRow constructor. The spacing parameter defines the number of
// pixels between columns in the row.
_global.TableRow = function (spacing) {
  // Store the spacing parameter in an instance property of the same name. spacing
  // defaults to 5 if not otherwise specified.
  this.spacing = (spacing == undefined) ? 5 : spacing;

  // The columns array contains all the columns in the row.
  this.columns = new Array( );

  // Initialize the width and height of the row.
  this._width  = 0;
  this._height = 0;
```

```
    // If any parameters are passed to the constructor, from the second position
    // onward, add these values (references to columns) to the row using the
    // addColumn() method.
    for (var i = 1; i < arguments.length; i++) {
      this.addColumn(arguments[i]);
    }
};

// The addColumn() method adds columns to the row.
TableRow.prototype.addColumn = function (column) {

    // Add the column to the columns array.
    this.columns.push(column);

    // Increase the row's width by the width of the column plus the spacing. Also, if
    // the column has a greater height than any of the existing columns, set the row's
    // height to the height of the column.
    this._width += column._width + this.spacing;
    this._height = Math.max(this._height, column._height);
};

// TableRow.render() positions the columns within a row relative to one another and
// relative to x and y coordinates given by startx and starty. TableRow.render() is
// called automatically by the render() method of the table that contains the row.
TableRow.prototype.render = function (startx, starty) {

    // Call each column's render() method. Position each column to the right of the
    // preceding one.
    for (var i = 0; i < this.columns.length; i++) {
      this.columns[i].render(startx, starty);
      startx += this.columns[i]._width + this.spacing;
    }
};

// removeColumnAt() removes a column from a row at the given index. Note that the
// index is zero-relative (the first row is row 0).
TableRow.prototype.removeColumnAt = function (index) {
    this.columns.splice(index, 1);
};

// TableRow.resize() recalculates the height and width of a row. It is called
// automatically by Table.resize().
TableRow.prototype.resize = function () {

    // Reset the width and height to 0.
    this._width  = 0;
    this._height = 0;

    for (var i = 0; i < this.columns.length; i++) {
      // Recalculate the size of each column and use those values to calculate the
      // height and width for the row.
      this.columns[i].resize();
```

```
    this._width += this.columns[i]._width;
    this._height = Math.max (this._height, this.columns[i]._height);
  }
};

// Define the Table constructor. spacing determines the number of pixels between
// rows. startx and starty define the position of the table's upper-left corner.
_global.Table = function (spacing, startx, starty) {

  // Store the spacing parameter in an instance property of the same name. spacing
  // defaults to 5 if not otherwise specified.
  this.spacing = (spacing == undefined) ? 5 : spacing;

  // Store the startx and starty parameters in instance properties of the same name.
  // Use Number() to convert undefined values to 0, if necessary.
  this.startx = Number(startx);
  this.starty = Number(starty);

  // The rows array contains the rows in the table.
  this.rows = new Array();

  // Initialize the height and width of the table.
  this._height = 0;
  this._width  = 0;

  // If any parameters are passed to the constructor, from the fourth position
  // onward, add these values (assumed to be references to rows)
  // to the table using addRows().
  for (var i = 3; i < arguments.length; i++) {
    this.addRow(arguments[i]);
  }

  // Render the table to start.
  this.render(false, this.startx, this.starty);
};

// addRow() adds a new row to the table and recalculates its height and width.
Table.prototype.addRow = function (row) {
  this.rows.push(row);
  this._height += row._height + this.spacing;
  this._width = Math.max(this._width, row._width);
};

// Table.render() positions the rows within the table. The doResize parameter
// determines whether it should call Table.resize(). The startx and starty parameters
// determine the position of the upper-left corner of the table.
Table.prototype.render = function (doResize, startx, starty) {

  // If doResize is true, call the table's resize() method. This is useful to update
  // the table size after something in the table changes.
  if (doResize) {
    this.resize();
  }
```

```
// Reposition the table at (startx,starty). Position defaults to previous position
// if a new position is not specified.
if (startx != undefined) {
  this.startx = startx;
}
if (starty != undefined) {
  this.starty = starty;
}
var x = this.startx;
var y = this.starty;

// Render the rows of the table (which in turn renders the columns).
for (var i = 0; i < this.rows.length; i++) {
  this.rows[i].render(x, y);
  y += this.rows[i]._height + this.spacing;
}
};

// removeRowAt() removes a row from the table at a given index. Note that the index
// is zero-relative (the first row is row 0).
Table.prototype.removeRowAt = function (index) {
  this.rows.splice(index, 1);
};

// The resize() method calculates the height and width for a table.
Table.prototype.resize = function () {
  this._width = 0;
  this._height = 0;
  for (var i = 0; i < this.rows.length; i++) {
    this.rows[i].resize();
    this._width = Math.max(this._width, this.rows[i]._width);
    this._height += this.rows[i]._height + this.spacing;
  }
};
```

Now that you have seen the code for the *Table* class (as well as the *TableColumn* and *TableRow* classes), let's look a little more closely at how it all works.

All three classes have the same basic functionality, so understanding one class helps to understand them all. Let's look at the *TableRow* class first.

Each constructor handles four basic setup tasks. First of all, the constructor records the spacing between the subunits. In the case of the *TableRow* class, the subunits are columns within the row. The constructor also creates an array property to store the subunits. Next, the constructor initializes the _width and _height properties. Using the names _width and _height for all subunits allows us to determine their width and height without having to know if the subunit is a table, row, column, movie clip, button, or text field. Finally, the constructor adds any subunits to the object that were passed to the constructor as parameters. This is accomplished using the arguments

array so that there is no predefined limit to the number of subunits that can be passed
to a constructor:

```
_global.TableRow = function (spacing) {
  this.spacing = spacing;
  if (spacing == undefined) {
    this.spacing = 5;
  }
  this.columns = new Array();
  this._width  = 0;
  this._height = 0;
  for (var i = 1; i < arguments.length; i++) {
    this.addColumn(arguments[i]);
  }
};
```

Next, each class defines a method to add subunits. In the case of the *TableRow* class
this method is named *addColumn()*. The method adds the subunit to the appropriate array and recalculates the height and width of the object. Using the *Math.max()*
method is a shorthand way of saying "store the largest value for this dimension." For
example, if an element's height is greater than that of any preceding element in the
row, this._height is updated to store the new maximum height of the row.

```
TableRow.prototype.addColumn = function (column) {
  this.columns.push(column);
  this._width += column._width + this.spacing;
  this._height = Math.max(this._height, column._height);
};
```

The *render()* method of both the *Table* and the *TableRow* classes works by calling
the *render()* method of each of the subunits of the object. The actual positioning of
the movie clips, buttons, and text fields occurs within the *TableColumn.render()*
method, so let's examine that method a little more closely. If the column contains a
nested table, we call the *render()* method to render it. Otherwise, the column contains graphical objects, and each of those objects needs to be positioned. This is
accomplished by looping through the elements array and setting the _x and _y properties of each element appropriately. The elements of a column should all appear one
below the other, spaced by the number of pixels specified by spacing. Therefore, the
_x properties are the same for all elements in a column, and the _y properties are
determined by the _y value of the previous element plus the height of the previous
element, plus the spacing between elements.

```
TableColumn.prototype.render = function (startx, starty) {
  if (startx == undefined) {
    startx = 0;
  }
  if (starty == undefined) {
    starty = 0;
  }
  if (this.containsTable) {
    this.elements[0].render(true, startx, starty);
```

```
      } else {
        for (var i = 0; i < this.elements.length; i++) {
          this.elements[i]._y = this.elements[i - 1]._height + this.spacing + starty;
          this.elements[i]._x = startx + this.spacing;
          starty += this.elements[i - 1]._height + this.spacing;
        }
      }
    };
```

The *resize()* method for each of the three classes is used when new subunits are added or existing subunits are removed or resized. The *resize()* method recalculates the height and width of an object based on the updated subunits. This is accomplished by resetting the _width and _height properties to 0, then looping through all the sub-units and incrementing the object's _width and _height properties appropriately:

```
    TableRow.prototype.resize = function () {
      this._width = 0;
      this._height = 0;
      for (var i = 0; i < this.columns.length; i++) {
        this.columns[i].resize();
        this._width += this.columns[i]._width;
        this._height = Math.max(this._height, this.columns[i]._height);
      }
    };
```

Next, let's look at some code that can help you get a sense of how to use table objects in your movies. This code creates 10 text fields to start. Additionally, a push button instance is created using *attachMovie()* (so you must make sure that the PushButton component symbol is included in your Library). The text fields and the button are added to the table in six rows. The first two rows have three columns of text fields, the third and fifth rows have a single column, and the fourth row has two columns. The push button instance is added to the sixth (final) row. An example of this is shown in Figure 11-1.

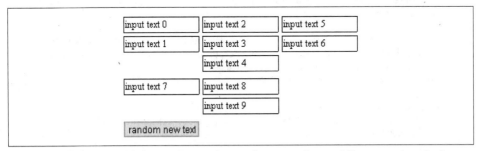

Figure 11-1. A sample table layout showing how each row can have a different number of columns

Finally, the button is assigned actions such that when it is pressed and released, a new text field is created and assigned to a random column, and the table is reren-dered to accommodate the new layout. This code is for demonstration purposes only and illustrates that the table can accommodate changes dynamically.

```
// Include TextField.as from Chapter 8.
#include "TextField.as"
// Include MovieClip.as from Chapter 7.
#include "MovieClip.as"
// Include the recipes needed from this chapter.
#include "Form.as"
#include "Table.as"
// Create 10 text fields with names text0_txt through text9_txt.
for (var i = 0; i < 10; i++) {
  _root.createInputTextField("text" + i + "_txt", _root.getNewDepth());
  _root["text" + i + "_txt"].text = "input text " + i;
}

// Create a push button instance.
_root.attachMovie("FPushButtonSymbol", "addBtn", _root.getNewDepth());
addBtn.setLabel("random new text");

// Create six table columns. Each column is assigned one or more text fields
// or the push button instance. The spacing is set to five pixels.
tc0 = new TableColumn(5, text0_txt, text1_txt);
tc1 = new TableColumn(5, text2_txt, text3_txt, text4_txt);
tc2 = new TableColumn(5, text5_txt, text6_txt);
tc3 = new TableColumn(5, text7_txt);
tc4 = new TableColumn(5, text8_txt, text9_txt);
tc5 = new TableColumn(5, addBtn);

// Create three table rows and add the table columns to them.
tr0 = new TableRow(5, tc0, tc1, tc2);
tr1 = new TableRow(5, tc3, tc4);
tr2 = new TableRow(5, tc5);

// Add a table with the table rows added to it. The table is positioned at (0,0).
myTable = new Table(5, 0, 0, tr0, tr1, tr2);

// Add the actions to the button such that, when it is pressed and released, a new
// text field is created and added to the table.
addBtn.onRelease = function () {

  // Randomly determine the column to which the text field should be added. We
  // introduce randomness here only for the purpose of demonstrating the table's
  // ability to dynamically accommodate changes.
  var rn = Math.round(Math.random() * 4);

  // Create the new text field.
  _root.createInputTextField("text" + _root.i, _root.getNewDepth());
  _root["text" + _root.i].text = "input text " + _root.i;

  // Select the random table column and add the text field to it.
  _root["tc" + rn].addElement(_root["text" + _root.i]);

  // Increment the i variable so that the next text field created will have a unique
  // name and depth.
  _root.i++;
```

```
    // Rerender the table. Specify true for the doResize parameter so that the table
    // automatically recalculates the size before rendering.
    _root.myTable.render(true);
};
```

Next, let's look at how a table is used to lay out a form. First, here is the code that creates a simple form and positions the elements using a table. (The result is shown in Figure 11-2.) Also, if you test this code in your own movie, make sure that you add all the necessary component symbols to the movie's Library.

```
#include "Form.as"
#include "Table.as"

// Create a list box, a combo box, a push button, and two text field labels.
this.attachMovie("FListBoxSymbol", "interests_lb", 1);
this.attachMovie("FComboBoxSymbol", "favUICmpnt_cb", 2);
this.attachMovie("FPushButtonSymbol", "submitBtn", 3);
this.createTextField("interestsLabel_txt", 4, 0, 0, 120, 20);
this.createTextField("favUICmpntLabel_txt", 5, 0, 0, 120, 20);

// Populate the list box and adjust its size to accommodate the values.
interests_lb.addItem("Flash", "flash");
interests_lb.addItem("ActionScript", "as");
interests_lb.addItem("More ActionScript", "as+");
interests_lb.setSelectMultiple(true);
interests_lb.adjustWidth();
interests_lb.setRowCount(interests_lb.getLength());

// Populate the combo box and adjust its size accordingly.
favUICmpnt_cb.addItem("Checkbox", "ch");
favUICmpnt_cb.addItem("Combo box", "cb");
favUICmpnt_cb.addItem("List box", "lb");
favUICmpnt_cb.addItem("Radio button", "rb");
favUICmpnt_cb.addItem("Push button", "pb");
favUICmpnt_cb.adjustWidth();

// Add a label to the push button.
submitBtn.setLabel("submit");

// Add text to the text fields.
interestsLabel_txt.text = "Interests:";
favUICmpntLabel_txt.text = "Favorite Component: ";

// Create three table rows. The first contains two columns: a label and the list box.
// The second row contains two columns: a label and the combo box.
// The third row contains the submit button.
tr0 = new TableRow(5, new TableColumn(0, interestsLabel_txt),
                      new TableColumn(0, interests_lb));
tr1 = new TableRow(5, new TableColumn(0, favUICmpntLabel_txt),
                      new TableColumn(0, favUICmpnt_cb));
tr2 = new TableRow(5, new TableColumn(0, submitBtn));

// Create the table. Position the table with the upper-left corner at (120,90) and
// add the three rows.
formTable = new Table(5, 120, 90, tr0, tr1, tr2);
```

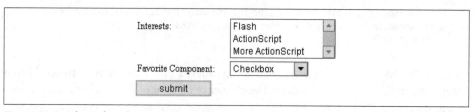

Figure 11-2. A basic form layout using a table

Next, let's enhance our example further. The following code block can be appended to the previous code block. In this example we add two radio buttons, another label, and a text area with a message to the user. We then add a new table that nests the previous table to create a complex layout. (The result is shown in Figure 11-3.) Since this code includes radio buttons, make sure that you add the radio button symbol to your movie's Library if you test this code.

```
// Add two radio buttons.
this.attachMovie("FRadioButtonSymbol", "asRating0_rb", 6);
this.attachMovie("FRadioButtonSymbol", "asRating1_rb", 7);

// Add two text fields. One is a label, the other is a text area.
this.createTextField("words_txt", 8, 0, 0, 120, 150);
this.createTextField("asRatingLabel_txt", 9, 0, 0, 120, 20);

// Add labels to the radio buttons and add them to a radio button group.
asRating0_rb.setLabel("ActionScript is fun.");
asRating1_rb.setLabel("ActionScript is REALLY fun.");
asRating0_rb.setGroupName("asRating");
asRating1_rb.setGroupName("asRating");

// Use the adjustWidth( ) method to make sure the radio button labels are visible.
asRating.adjustWidth( );

// Set the value for the text label.
asRatingLabel_txt.text = "Rate of ActionScript";

// Set the text area text field to word wrap and display multiple lines.
// Then set the text value.
words_txt.wordWrap = true;
words_txt.multiline = true;
words_txt.text = "We hope you have enjoyed this form. It was designed using" +
        "ActionScript and the custom Table class";

// Create a table row that includes two columns: one with the nested table, and the
// other with the new elements.
mainTr0 = new TableRow(5, new TableColumn(0, formTable), new TableColumn(5,
asRatingLabel_txt, asRating0_rb, asRating1_rb, words_txt));

// Create the new table. Position the table at (60,120). Notice that the position of
// the nested table is overwritten
mainTable = new Table(5, 60, 120, mainTr0);
```

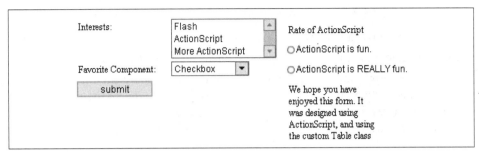

Figure 11-3. A form containing a complex table structure

11.23 Creating Auto-Complete Text Fields

Problem

You want to create auto-complete input text fields in which entering a few letters automatically fills in a previously entered value.

Solution

Use a shared object to store the previously entered values for a text field. Then use the *onChanged()*, *onSetFocus()*, and *onKillFocus()* methods of the text field to create, position, size, and populate a list box with possible values.

Discussion

Internet Explorer and similar browsers offer a feature that remembers values that users have previously entered for a text field in an HTML form. When a user brings focus to the text field, she can use the arrow keys or the mouse to select from a list of previously entered values. This feature can help the user save time typing if she wants to fill out the form with values similar to those entered previously. Flash text fields do not have this kind of functionality built into them, but with a little bit of work, you can add this feature to your forms.

You can use a local shared object to store previously entered values for text fields within a domain. Then you can use a list box to display those values to the user when she brings focus to a text field. As the user types into the text field, the values in the list box should be updated to partially match the string she has entered into the text field. For example, if the user types a "t" in the text field, the list box should display only those values that begin with "t." And if the user selects a value from the list box (either by mouse or by keyboard), that value should automatically be placed within the text field.

Follow these steps to create auto-completing text fields in your movie:

1. Create a new Flash document or open an existing one.

2. On the main timeline add a new layer named *AutoCompleteCode*.

3. Add a list box symbol to the movie's Library by dragging the ListBox component from the Components panel onto the Stage. Then delete the instance from the Stage (we will add the list box to the movie using ActionScript). The symbol will remain in the movie's Library. The ListBox symbol is automatically linked for export.

4. Open the Actions panel and add the following code to the first frame of the *AutoCompleteCode* layer.

5. Make sure you have assigned names to the input text fields in your movie and then test.

Here is the auto-complete code. Add it to an *AutoCompleteText.as* file. (And remember that you can find the completed *AutoCompleteText.as* file at *http://www.person13.com/ascb*.)

```
// Create the local shared object at the top level of the domain so that all text
// fields in all Flash movies in the domain can access it.
TextField.so = SharedObject.getLocal("textfieldAutoComplete", "/");

// When the user types into the text field or when she brings focus to it (either
// programmatically, by tab index, or by clicking with the  mouse) call the custom
// makeAutoCompleteOptions() method.
TextField.prototype.onChanged = function () {
  this.makeAutoCompleteOptions();
};

TextField.prototype.onSetFocus = function () {
  this.makeAutoCompleteOptions();
};

TextField.prototype.makeAutoCompleteOptions = function () {

  // Create a copy of the array stored in the shared object for the text field with
  // the current text field's name.
  var history = TextField.so.data[this._name].concat();

  // If the text is not empty, find any partial matches in the history array.
  if (this.text != "") {
    for (var i = 0; i < history.length; i++) {
      // Removes any elements that don't match from the history array.
      if (history[i].indexOf(this.text) != 0) {
        history.splice(i, 1);
        i--;
      }
    }
  }
}
```

```
// If the history array is undefined or has no elements, remove any existing list
// box and exit this method.
if (history.length == 0 || history.length == undefined) {
  this._parent.autoCompleteHistory.removeMovieClip( );
  return;
}

// Create a list box and position it just underneath the text field.
this._parent.attachMovie("FListBoxSymbol", "autoCompleteHistory", 100000);
this._parent.autoCompleteHistory._x = this._x;
this._parent.autoCompleteHistory._y = this._y + this._height;

// Resize the list box to fit the width of the text field.
this._parent.autoCompleteHistory.setSize(this._width, 50);

// If history has fewer than three elements, shorten the list box.
if (history.length < 3) {
  this._parent.autoCompleteHistory.setRowCount(history.length);
}

// Fill the list box with the elements from history and set the handler to call
// when any changes occur to the list box (via changes to the text field's
// contents).
this._parent.autoCompleteHistory.setDataProvider(history);
this._parent.autoCompleteHistory.setChangeHandler("setValue", this);
};

// The setValue( ) method is the change handler function for the list box.
TextField.prototype.setValue = function (lb) {

  // usingArrows indicates whether the method was called due to the user pressing the
  // arrow keys. If she used the arrow keys, exit the function because we don't want
  // to close the list box until she has actually selected a value.
  if (this.usingArrows) {
    this.usingArrows = false;
    return;
  }

  // Set the text field value to the selected value from the list box and then remove
  // the list box.
  this.text = lb.getSelectedItem( ).label;
  lb.removeMovieClip( );
};

TextField.prototype.onKillFocus = function ( ) {

  // Remove the list box when the text field loses focus.
  _root.autoCompletHistory.removeMovieClip( );

  // If the text field contains no text, exit the method.
  if (this.text == "") {
    return;
  }
```

```
// Get the array stored in the shared object for the text field. Exit this method
// if the array already contains the text field's text value.
var history = TextField.so.data[this._name];
for (var i = 0; i < history.length; i++) {
  if (this.text == history[i]) {
    return;
  }
}

// If the shared object doesn't already have an array
// for this text field, create one.
if (TextField.so.data[this._name] == undefined) {
  TextField.so.data[this._name] = new Array();
}

// Add the text field's text value to the shared object's array.
TextField.so.data[this._name].push(this.text);
};

// Create a key listener to respond whenever keys are pressed.
keyListener = new Object();

keyListener.onKeyDown = function () {

  // Get the current focus and create a reference to the list box.
  var focus = eval(Selection.getFocus());
  var ach = focus._parent.autoCompleteHistory;

  // Get the key code for the key that has been pressed.
  var keyCode = Key.getCode();

  if (keyCode == 40) {
    // If the key is the down arrow, set usingArrows to true and set the selected
    // index in the list box to the next value in the list.
    focus.usingArrows = true;
    var index = (ach.getSelectedIndex() == undefined) ?
                    0 : ach.getSelectedIndex() + 1;
    index = (index == ach.getLength()) ? 0 : index;
    ach.setSelectedIndex(index);

    // Scroll if the selected index is not visible in the list box.
    if (index > ach.getScrollPosition() + 2) {
      ach.setScrollPosition(index);
    } else if (index < ach.getScrollPosition()) {
      ach.setScrollPosition(index);
    }
  } else if (keyCode == 38) {
    // If the key is the up arrow, do a similar thing as when the down arrow is
    // pressed, but move the selected index up instead of down.
    focus.usingArrows = true;
    var index = (ach.getSelectedIndex() == undefined) ?
                    0 : ach.getSelectedIndex() - 1;
```

```
      index = (index == -1) ? ach.getLength( ) - 1 : index;
      ach.setSelectedIndex(index);
      if (index > ach.getScrollPosition( ) + 2) {
        ach.setScrollPosition(index);
      } else if (index < ach.getScrollPosition( )) {
        ach.setScrollPosition(index);
      }
    } else if (keyCode == Key.ENTER) {
      // If the user has pressed the Enter key, call setValue( ) to set the text field's
      // value and close the list box.
      focus.setValue(ach);
    } else {
      // Otherwise, if the user presses any other key, exit the function.
      return;
    }

    // Set the focus to the text field.
    Selection.setFocus(focus);
  };

  // Add the key listener to the Key object.
  Key.addListener(keyListener);
```

To use the auto-complete feature, you only need to include *AutoCompleteText.as* in a
Flash document that contains input text fields. Then test the movie. The text fields
will automatically remember any contents you entered into them.

```
  #include "AutoCompleteText.as"

  this.createTextField("myTextField0", 1, 100, 100, 100, 20);
  this.createTextField("myTextField1", 1, 100, 140, 100, 20);
```

11.24 Customizing a Component's Appearance

Problem

You want to customize the appearance of an instance of a UI component.

Solution

Use the *setStyleProperty()* method to set the colors for each of the style properties or
use a *FStyleFormat* object to apply changes to more than one component at a time.

Discussion

You can change the appearance of all Flash UI components using the
globalStyleFormat object, as detailed in Recipe 11.25. You can also modify the artwork in the Skins folders in the Library to change all instances of a particular type of

component. However, you can also modify the appearance of each instance individually using the *setStyleProperty()* method. The advantage of this technique is, of course, that you can modify each instance without affecting all other instances.

Each Flash UI component instance has the following style properties:

arrow
> Color of the arrow in the scrollbar and combo boxes

background
> Color of the background when the component is active

backgroundDisabled
> Color of the background when the component is disabled (dimmed)

check
> Color of the checkbox's check

darkshadow
> Color of the darkened inner shadow for a border

embedFonts
> Whether or not to embed fonts for text

face
> The main color of a component

focusRectInner
> Color of inner focus rectangle

focusRectOuter
> Color of outer focus rectangle

foregroundDisabled
> Color of a component's foreground when in a disabled state

highlight
> Color of the inner portion of the highlight

highlight3D
> Color of the outer portion of the highlight

radioDot
> Color of a radio button's dot

scrollTrack
> Color of a scroll track on a scrollbar

selection
> Color of the highlight for a selection, such as in a combo box or list box

selectionDisabled
> Color of the highlight for a selection in a component in a disabled state

selectionUnfocused
    Color of the highlight for a selection in a component when the instance does not
    have keyboard focus
shadow
    Color of the shadow
textAlign
    How to align the text ("right", "left", or "center")
textBold
    Either true (bolded) or false (regular)
textColor
    Color of text
textDisabled
    Color of text in a disabled component instance
textFont
    Name of the font to use
textIndent
    Number of pixels by which to indent the first line of text
textItalic
    Either true (italicized) or false (regular)
textLeftMargin
    Left margin in pixels
textRightMargin
    Right margin in pixels
textSelected
    Color of text in a selected item (such as in a combo box or list box)
textSize
    The size of the text font in points
textUnderline
    Either true (underlined) or false (regular)

You can set the style properties of an instance by using the *setStyleProperty()*
method. The method takes two parameters: the name of the style property as a string
and the value you want to assign to the property. For example:

```
myComboBox.setStyleProperty("arrow", 0x0000FF);
```

Notice that not all components support all styles. If you set a style that is not applicable for a component instance, Flash will simply ignore that style. For example, a
checkbox component uses the "check" style but ignores the "radioDot" style. Conversely, a radio button uses the "radioDot" style but ignores the "check" style.

You can also use an *FStyleFormat* object to affect the same types of changes. *FStyleFormat* is most useful when you want to apply the same color scheme to more than one (but not all) components in your movie. Here are the steps:

1. Create a new *FStyleFormat* object:

   ```
   fstyle = new FStyleFormat( );
   ```

2. Use the *addListener()* method to define the component or components that the object should affect:

   ```
   fstyle.addListener(myComboBox, myListBox, myCheckBox);
   ```

3. Set the values for the properties of the *FStyleFormat* object:

   ```
   fstyle.face       = 0x0000FF;
   fstyle.background = 0xFF0000;
   ```

4. Apply the changes with *applyChanges()*:

   ```
   fstyle.applyChanges( );
   ```

11.25 Customizing All Components' Appearances

Problem

You want to apply global style changes to all Flash UI Component instances.

Solution

Use the *globalStyleFormat* object. Assign values to the style properties you want to modify and then call the *applyChanges()* method.

Discussion

You can learn how to modify the style property settings for individual component instances in Recipe 11.24. This can be a useful technique when you want to adjust the appearance of each instance separately. However, to apply the same style changes to all instances of all UI components, you should use the *globalStyleFormat* object.

The *globalStyleFormat* object is available in your Flash movie whenever you have added at least one UI component to your movie. The *globalStyleFormat* object has properties corresponding to the same style properties listed in Recipe 11.24, but the values for the *globalStyleFormat* object apply to all instances of UI components instead of just one.

To apply changes to the global styles, you should set the values of the corresponding properties on the *globalStyleFormat* object itself. You can access the properties using dot notation:

```
// Apply a new value to the global face property.
globalStyleFormat.face = 0x97DE50;
```

Once you have changed a value, you need to tell Flash to update the view by calling the *applyChanges()* method from the *globalStyleFormat* object, as follows:

```
globalStyleFormat.applyChanges( );
```

You can change more than one property before applying changes. For example:

```
globalStyleFormat.face = 0x97DE50;
globalStyleFormat.highlight = 0xF5F538;
globalStyleFormat.highlight3D = 0xF33AEB;
globalStyleFormat.applyChanges( );
```

See Also

Recipe 11.24

CHAPTER 12

Objects and Custom Components

12.0 Introduction

ActionScript is an object-based language. The entire language is composed primarily of blueprints, called classes, for different types of objects. Based on these blueprints you, as the developer, can construct many instances of many types of objects, and each instance automatically inherits all the characteristics and functionality of its class. For example, all arrays are members of the *Array* class, which defines the length property as well as the methods (*concat()*, *sort()*, etc.) that all arrays inherit.

Therefore, whenever you are using ActionScript, you are inherently using objects and object-oriented programming. Understanding the inner workings of ActionScript classes and objects puts you well on your way to harnessing the true power of the language. This knowledge enables you to add properties and methods to individual instances (objects) and to the classes they inherit from.

Every class in ActionScript has a prototype property. The prototype property contains an object from which all instances of the class inherit properties and methods.

 If you add a property or method to a class's prototype, all instances of that class automatically inherit that custom property or method.

Here is an example:

```
// Add a property to the Array class.
Array.prototype.testProperty = "this is a test property";

// Create a new array. This array inherits, along with all of the other properties
// and methods of the Array class, the custom testProperty property.
myArray = new Array();
```

```
// Displays: "this is a test property"
trace(myArray.testProperty);
```

Here is another example in which we add a method to a class's prototype:

```
// Add the testMethod( ) method to the Array class.
Array.prototype.testMethod = function ( ) {
    trace("This is a test method.");
};

// Create a new array. All arrays now inherit the testMethod( ) method.
myArray = new Array( );

// Displays: "This is a test method."
myArray.testMethod( );
```

Prototype-based inheritance works as follows. When a property is accessed or a method is invoked from an object, the ActionScript interpreter checks if that property or method is explicitly defined for the object. If not, ActionScript looks for it on the object's class's prototype property. Classes can even inherit from other classes. This is known as *subclassing* or extending a *superclass*. Therefore, if ActionScript cannot find a method or property in the class's prototype property, it looks next in the superclass's prototype property. This same process is followed until ActionScript finds the method or property, or until it reaches the final superclass. The *Object* class is the superclass of all other classes, so any properties or methods added to the *Object* class are automatically inherited by every object of any type:

```
// Add a property to the Object class.
Object.prototype.objectTextProperty = "this is a property for all objects";
// Create a new Date object.
myDate = new Date( );
// Displays: "this is a property for all objects"
trace(myDate.objectTextProperty);
```

However, a subclass can implement a property or method of the same name, effectively obscuring the property or method found in the superclass. For example, although the *Object* class implements a *toString()* method, the *Date* class implements its own custom *toString()* method that is more appropriate for its needs:

```
// Displays: [object Object]
trace (new Object().toString( ));
// Displays: Mon May 26 14:17:26 GMT-0400 2003
trace (new Date().toString( ));
```

See Also

Recipes 12.8, 12.9, and 12.12

12.1 Using Methods and Properties of Built-in Objects

Problem

You want to use the properties and methods of a built-in object, such as the *Math* object, to perform a given operation.

Solution

Access the properties and methods of the built-in object directly, such as *Math. random()* or *Math.PI.*

Discussion

ActionScript includes several objects with methods and properties that you can access directly from the class (there is no need to construct an instance of the class). Methods and properties accessed in this manner are often referred to as *static* methods and properties. Static methods and properties are often defined for classes that do not get instantiated. For example, the built-in *Math*, *Key*, *Selection*, and *Stage* objects define multiple static methods and properties. However, there are also classes, from which objects are otherwise instantiated, that include one or more static methods or properties. For example, the *String* class is typically instantiated (meaning you normally create string objects) but it also includes the static method *String.fromCharCode()*. Likewise, the *Object* class is typically instantiated but it includes the static method *Object.registerClass()*. In these cases, the static methods or properties are associated with the class because they don't pertain to a specific instance of the class.

In any case, you can access static methods and properties by invoking them directly from the class using dot syntax. Here are two examples:

```
trace(Math.PI);
trace(String.fromCharCode(108));
```

See Also

Recipe 12.2. Also refer to the "Language Reference" section of *ActionScript for Flash MX: The Definitive Guide* (O'Reilly), which documents ActionScript's *Accessibility*, *Capabilities*, *Arguments*, *Key*, *Math*, *Mouse*, *Selection*, *SharedObject*, *Stage*, and *System* objects in detail.

12.2 Creating an Instance of a Class

Problem

You want to access the properties and methods of a class to achieve a particular goal, but those properties and methods are specific to a particular object (i.e., an instance of the class).

Solution

Create a instance of the class using the *new* operator and the constructor function for the class of interest. Then access the properties and methods of the instance, as returned by the constructor function.

Discussion

Many ActionScript classes must be *instantiated* before you can use them. This means that you must create an object that is based on the blueprint defined by the class. For example, the *Array* class defines the blueprint for all arrays. All arrays have the same kinds of properties and methods; however, each array instance is an individual object that merely *inherits* the common properties and methods from the class. It is important that each instance be individualized so that when you request the value for arrayA.length, you retrieve the length of arrayA and not the length of some other array, such as arrayB.

To create an instance of a class, you typically use the *new* operator with the appropriate *constructor function* for the class. The constructor function takes the same name as the class itself and is followed by the function operator (that is, parentheses). For example, the following creates a new generic instance of the *Object* class:

```
myObject = new Object( );
```

Note that the *new* statement returns an instance of the class, which you ordinarily store in a variable, in this case myObject.

Most classes allow you to construct objects in an analogous manner. For example, here is one way to create a new *Array* object:

```
myArray = new Array( );
```

As with all functions, constructor functions can accept parameters. In some cases, no parameters are accepted. In other cases, parameters are optional, and in still other cases, they are required. As you can see in the preceding example, you do not need to specify any parameters when constructing an array. However, the *Array()* constructor function accepts optional parameters of several varieties, as discussed in the Introduction to Chapter 6. This example constructs an array with two elements:

```
myArray = new Array("first element", "second element");
```

Once you have created an object (an instance), you can access the properties and methods of that object via dot syntax. For example, arrays have a `length` property that returns the number of elements:

```
trace(myArray.length);  // Displays: 2
```

Returning to the subject of specifying parameters when constructing an object, when you construct a *Color* object, you must provide the target movie clip as a parameter. For example:

```
myColor = new Color(myMovieClip);
```

See Recipe 3.1 for more details.

There are alternative ways to create certain types of objects without using the *new* operator. For example, using *object literal notation*, which employs curly braces, you can create a generic object. This example creates an object of the *Object* class:

```
myObj = {};
```

You can specify zero or more properties to add to the object within the curly braces. This example creates an object and adds two properties (x and y) to it:

```
myPoint = {x: 100, y: 50};
trace(myPoint.x);          // Displays: 100
```

Likewise, a new array can be created using *array literal notation*, which employs square brackets. This example creates an array with three elements:

```
myArray = ["a", "b", "c"];
```

There are other indirect ways to create objects. Most notably, some methods of existing objects return entirely new objects. For example, the *Array.splice()* method returns a new array (remember that arrays are one type of object). In this example, the call to *myArray.splice()* returns a second array containing the elements deleted from myArray, which we arbitrarily store in the variable `deletedElems`:

```
myArray = ["a", "b", "c", "d"];
// Remove two elements from myArray starting at index 0. The removed elements are
// stored in a new array, deletedElems.
deletedElems = myArray.splice(0, 2);
```

We've seen alternatives to using the *new* operator to construct an object. In fact, there are some classes that cannot be instantiated using a *new* operator, which necessitates an appropriate alternative. One alternative is to create an object in the authoring tool. For example, placing a movie clip on the Stage effectively creates an instance of the *MovieClip* class. Likewise, placing a text field on the Stage effectively creates an instance of the *TextField* class.

But what if you want to create a new text field object at authoring time? You might be tempted to use the following syntax, but it won't work:

```
myTextField = new TextField();  // This will not work!
```

Instead, you must invoke the *createTextField()* method on a movie clip object to create a new text field, as described in Recipe 8.2.

To create a new movie clip object, you might be tempted to use the following syntax:

```
myClip = new MovieClip( );  // This creates a subclass, not a new clip!
```

However, the preceding example won't have the intended effect. Instead of creating a new movie clip, it actually creates a subclass, as described in Recipe 12.12. To create new movie clips at runtime, use the *MovieClip.attachMovie()* method, or alternatives, as described in Recipe 7.19.

We've seen a variety of ways to construct new objects, including using the *new* operator and a constructor function. The exceptions and special cases are discussed in appropriate recipes throughout the book.

See Also

Recipes 7.1, 7.19, 8.1, 8.2, 12.12, 16.1, and 16.6. Recipe 12.5 discusses how to define your own custom classes rather than merely instantiating objects of an existing class. Recipe 12.1 explains how to access the properties and methods of any class, whether custom or built-in. See the "Language Reference" section of *ActionScript for Flash MX: The Definitive Guide*, which documents the properties and methods of ActionScript's *Array, Boolean, Button, Color, Date, Function, LocalConnection, LoadVars, MovieClip, Number, Object, Sound, String, TextField, TextFormat, XML, XMLnode,* and *XMLSocket* classes in detail.

12.3   Adding Properties to an Object Instance

Problem

You want to add custom properties (variables) to an object (an instance of a class).

Solution

Attach the new property to the object using an assignment statement and the dot operator.

Discussion

Objects derived from the built-in ActionScript classes have standard properties. For example, arrays have length properties, movie clips have _x and _y properties, and *Sound* objects have position and duration properties. But aside from these standard properties, you can add custom properties to any object in ActionScript. You can add new properties to an object (or change an existing property's value) by simply assigning the property a value. If the property does not yet exist, ActionScript creates it automatically.

```
myMovieClip.myProperty = "some value";
```

Custom properties of movie clip objects are sometimes referred to as *timeline variables*, as discussed in Recipe 1.12. However, you can apply the same principle not only to movie clip objects, but to any kind of object. For example, the following code adds a custom property to an array named myArray:

```
myArray.myProperty = "some value";
```

Attaching properties to objects is invaluable. For example, custom properties can store a value that is used internally within an event handler method (or any other method) of the object. You can initialize the property value outside any of the methods and then access it within a method. This technique creates a variable whose value persists between function invocations for the life of the object. For example:

```
// Initialize a clickedTimes property to 0. This happens only once.
myMovieClip.clickedTimes = 0;

// Increment the clickedTimes property whenever the movie clip is clicked.
myMovieClip.onPress = function () {
  this.clickedTimes++;
};
```

Another valuable reason for creating custom properties is to establish relationships between objects. Only movie clips can be targeted using relative paths. By creating a property of one object, objectA, that is a reference to another object, objectB, objectA can use or call objectB from within its methods in a relative fashion (without requiring the fully qualified target path). In this example, the targetArray property stored in the *LoadVars* object offers a convenient, relative way to access newArray:

```
// Create an array.
myArray = new Array();

// Create a LoadVars object.
lv = new LoadVars();

// Assign myArray to a custom property of the LoadVars object.
lv.targetArray = myArray;

// When the data from the server loads into the LoadVars object, use the targetArray
// property to add a value to myArray. (val is a variable returned from the server).
lv.onLoad = function () {
  this.targetArray.push(this.val);
};
```

It is important to understand the distinction between adding custom properties to objects (instances) and adding custom properties to classes. When you add a property to an object, it is available to that object only. In some situations, as discussed in this recipe, this is exactly what you want. If, however, you want to define a property that is accessible to all instances of a particular class, you should add that property to the class, as discussed in the Introduction and Recipe 12.5.

12.4 Adding Custom Methods to an Object Instance

Problem

You want to add custom methods to an object.

Solution

Assign a function definition (or a reference to one) to a custom property of an object that is already instantiated.

Discussion

You can add functionality to objects (instances of a class) by assigning new methods to them. First, define a function. Then store a reference to the function in a custom property of the object. That is, the definitions of an object's methods are stored as properties of the same object.

This example stores a function in the custom property `methodProp`:

```
myObject = new Object();
myObject.methodProp = function () {
  trace("Hello World");
};
```

The preceding example assigns a method to an object using an *anonymous function*. However, you can also use object properties to store references to *named functions*. The following example stores a reference to the named function, *myMethodFunction()*, in the property `myMethod`:

```
// Define a named function.
function myMethodFunction () {
  trace(this.myProperty);
}

// Create a new object. You can assign custom methods to any kind of object (movie
// clip, array, etc.), but this example uses a generic object of the Object class.
myObject = new Object();

// Create a custom property on the object. This is not necessary, per se, but we use
// it here to illustrate that when a function is called as a method of an object, the
// function has access to all the properties of that object by means of
// self-references (using the this keyword).
myObject.myProperty = "this is a custom property";
```

```
// Store a reference to myMethodFunction( ) in the property named myMethod. Note the
// lack of parentheses following myMethodFunction.
myObject.myMethod = myMethodFunction;

// Invoke the custom myMethodFunction( ) method by referring to the property that
// stores it. myMethod( ) is used to invoke myMethodFunction( ). Note the inclusion of
// the parentheses following myMethod.
myObject.myMethod( );  // Displays: "this is a custom property"
```

Once you have assigned a function to a property of an object, you can invoke that function as a method of the object, as shown in the preceding example.

 Do not include the parentheses after the function name when assigning it to the object's property. Without the parentheses, the function name is treated as a reference to the function definition, and the function is not invoked. However, use parentheses when invoking the function, as shown in the last line of the preceding example.

The preceding example shows how to store a named function in an object property. However, custom methods are commonly assigned using anonymous functions, as was briefly introduced earlier. An anonymous function is never given a name in its definition but is assigned directly to a variable (such as a custom property). Note that anonymous functions, also called *function literals*, should be followed by a semicolon after the closing curly brace. This technique results in slightly more compact code because the assignment and function definition all take place at once.

Here is the analog of the preceding example, implemented with an anonymous function instead of a named function:

```
myObject = new Object( );
myObject.myProperty = "this is a custom property";

// Assign an anonymous function to the custom myMethod property. The myMethod( )
// method is now a reference to an anonymous function.
myObject.myMethod = function ( ) {
  trace(this.myProperty);
};

// Invoke the custom method.
myObject.myMethod( );   // Displays: "this is a custom property"
```

Adding methods to objects is absolutely essential in many cases. For example, to use event handler methods for movie clips or *onLoad()* methods for *XML* objects or *LoadVars* objects, you have to define an appropriate method for that object, albeit with a specific name. For example, here we assign a custom function to the onEnterFrame property of a movie clip. This reserved property name holds the method to be invoked whenever the Flash Player triggers an *onEnterFrame* event, which occurs whenever the playhead reaches a frame.

```
myMovieClip.onEnterFrame = function () {
  trace("onEnterFrame() was reached");
};
```

In the preceding example, the *onEnterFrame()* method applies only to the movie clip to which it is attached. It has no effect on other movie clips. Because the Flash Player automatically generates *onEnterFrame* events during movie playback, our movie clip can respond to the event by simply defining a method (deemed an *event handler*) with the same name as the event. Although there may appear to be a difference between defining a custom method and defining an event handler, ActionScript makes no such distinction. Both are implemented by defining functions and storing the function reference in a property of the object. The only difference is that Flash movies automatically invoke the event handler methods when certain events occur, while custom methods are generally invoked manually by other ActionScript code written by you, the developer.

As seen in Chapter 7, you might want to define custom methods and make them available to all movie clips.

 Often, custom methods are defined for the entire class and not just an object (an instance of the class). To add a method to the class, assign it to the class's prototype property, rather than directly to an instance.

For example, Recipe 7.10 defines a new method that is made accessible to all movie clips by assigning it to the MovieClip.prototype property from which all movie clip instances inherit.

See Also

Recipe 12.5. Recipes throughout this book implement custom functions and attach them to the class's prototype property to enhance that class. Also refer to Chapters 7 and 9.

12.5 Creating a Custom Class

Problem

You want to create a custom ActionScript class to implement custom functionality or encapsulate related properties.

Solution

Create a constructor function and then assign properties and methods to its prototype.

Discussion

You might want to implement a custom class to encapsulate a series of methods and properties with related functionality. For example, you might implement a custom class that communicates with an external application. To create a custom class, first define a *constructor function*. The constructor function is defined in the typical fashion—either as a named function or as an anonymous function assigned to a variable. The latter technique is useful for creating globally accessible classes. Classes defined with named functions are accessible only within the scope of the timeline in which they are defined or by using the fully qualified target path.

Here are two degenerate examples. Obviously, constructor functions do not need to be empty; they can take parameters and they can have function bodies.

```
// Create a local class named MyClass.
function MyClass () {}

// Create a global class named MyClass.
_global.MyClass = function () {};
```

By convention, class names are capitalized. ActionScript is case-insensitive, so it is not technically an issue, but following this naming convention helps you easily distinguish classes from objects (instances of a class). Furthermore, the ECMA-262 standard, on which JavaScript is based, demands case-sensitivity. So by adopting the JavaScript convention, you make it easier for other developers to understand or port your code.

Typically, a constructor function's body initializes properties of that class. The this keyword, when used within a constructor (or any of the class methods), is a reference to the instance of the class from which it is invoked:

```
_global.MyClass = function (param1) {
    // Stored the passed-in parameter in a property of the object
    this.myProperty1 = param1;
};
```

You can add methods to a class using the same technique as shown in Recipe 12.4. However, assign the method to a property of the class's prototype so that the method is inherited by all instances of that class (i.e., all objects derived from the class).

```
MyClass.prototype.myMethod = function () {
    trace(this.myProperty1);
};
```

You can create instances of the class by calling the constructor function using the new keyword, as discussed in Recipe 12.2. For example:

```
// Define the class constructor for the MyClass class. It accepts one parameter and
// assigns its value to the myProperty1 property, which is unique for every instance.
_global.MyClass = function (param1) {
    this.myProperty1 = param1;
};
```

```
// Define a custom method for the class.
MyClass.prototype.myMethod = function () {
  trace(this.myProperty1);
};

// Create an instance of MyClass and pass a parameter to assign to myProperty1.
MyClassInstance0 = new MyClass("this is one instance");

// Invoke the myMethod( ) method of the object.
myClassInstance0.myMethod( );    // Displays: "this is one instance"

// Create a second instance of MyClass.
MyClassInstance1 = new MyClass("this is another instance");

// Invoke myMethod( ) on the second object. Note its unique value for myProperty1.
myClassInstance1.myMethod( );    // Displays: "this is another instance"
```

See Also

Recipe 12.2

12.6   Creating Smart Getter/Setter Properties

Problem

You want to create a class property on which you can perform calculations before setting or returning a value.

Solution

Use the *addProperty()* method.

Discussion

You can create what are called *getter/setter properties* for classes using the *addProperty()* method within the class's constructor. Getter/setter properties are accessed from object instances just like any other properties, but they secretly invoke methods rather than directly accessing an actual property of the same name. This allows your properties to be "smart"—you can perform calculations on the fly rather than just assigning or retrieving a simple value.

To create a getter/setter property, first create *getter* and *setter* methods for the class. The getter method should not require any parameters and should return a value. The setter method should take a single parameter and not return any value. By convention, the getter and setter methods are named *getPropertyName()* and *setPropertyName()*, where *PropertyName* is the name of the property name they control (with the first letter capitalized).

The *addProperty()* method creates a new property with the name you specify in the first parameter. The second and third parameters passed to *addProperty()* specify the getter and setter methods. It is important that you do not include the parentheses as part of the getter and setter method names when you pass them to the *addProperty()* method (i.e., *methodName()* is wrong, and methodName is correct). For example:

```
// Create a new Square class.
_global.Square = function (side) {

    // Assign the value passed to the constructor to the side property.
    this.side = side;

    // Create a getter/setter property named area that uses the getArea() and
    // setArea() methods. Qualify the references with the this keyword so that it
    // references the methods of the instance from which the area property is invoked,
    // not some other instance. Note the lack of parentheses.
    this.addProperty("area", this.getArea, this.setArea);
};

// Define the getter method, which should not take any parameters. It should return a
// value, in this case the area of the square (the side length squared).
Square.prototype.getArea = function () {
    return Math.pow(this.side, 2);
};

// Define the setter method, which should accept the new value to be assigned. It
// should not return a value, but it should set the hidden property. In this example,
// the value of side is calculated as the square root of the area.
Square.prototype.setArea = function (area) {
    this.side = Math.sqrt(area);
};

// Create a new square with a side of length 5.
sq = new Square(5);
trace(sq.area);  // Displays: 25

// Set the area to 36.
sq.area = 36;
trace(sq.area);   // Displays: 36
trace(sq.side);   // Displays: 6
```

Ideally, you should not read and write the hidden property directly from the object. Instead, use the setter method to set the property and the getter method to read it:

```
sq = new Square(5);
trace(sq.getArea());   // Displays: 25
```

You can use the setter method to impose restrictions or recalculate a value before assigning it to a property. For example, an area cannot be negative, and the square root of a negative number results in an imaginary number. This version of *setArea()* converts a negative number to its absolute value to avoid such problems:

```
Square.prototype.setArea = function (area) {
  this.side = Math.sqrt(Math.abs(area));
};
```

See Also

Recipe 12.7

12.7 Defining Read-Only Properties

Problem

You want to create a read-only property for a class.

Solution

Use the *addProperty()* method in the constructor and pass it a null value for the setter method.

Discussion

There are at least two good reasons to have read-only properties:

- You want to create constants for your class.
- You want to have a dependent property whose value depends on other properties/factors.

The *addProperty()* method creates getter/setter properties for a class. Passing *addProperty()* a null value for the setter method parameter effectively creates a read-only property.

See Recipe 12.6 for the initial implementation of the *Square* class. Here is a modified version:

```
_global.Square = function (side) {
  this.side = side;

  // Create a read-only property, version (effectively, a constant). The getter
  // method is getVersion(). The setter method is null.
  this.addProperty("version", this.getVersion, null);

  // Create a dependent property, area (its value changes, so it is not a constant,
  // but the value depends on other property values and can't be set directly). The
  // getter method is getArea(). The setter method is null.
  this.addProperty("area", this.getArea, null);
};
```

```
Square.prototype.getArea = function () {
  return Math.pow(this.side, 2);
};

Square.prototype.getVersion = function () {
  // Always returns the string "1.0". Therefore, it is a constant.
  return "1.0";
};

// Create a square with a side length of 5.
sq = new Square(5);
trace(sq.area);          // Displays: 25

// Try to set area directly. This is a read-only property. Though no error is
// displayed, it does not set the area.
sq.area = 36;

// Check the area again.
trace(sq.area);          // Displays: 25  (because area is not changed)

// Set the side property.
sq.side = 10;
trace(sq.area);          // Displays: 100 (dependent on the value of side)
trace(sq.version);       // Displays: 1.0

// Try to set version. It is a constant, so it will not be overwritten.
sq.version = "version 2.0";
trace(sq.version);       // Displays: 1.0
```

See Also

Recipe 12.6

12.8   Creating Subclasses

Problem

You want to create a subclass that inherits from a superclass.

Solution

Define a new class and set the new class's prototype property to an instance of the superclass.

Discussion

A *subclass* is a class that has its own methods and properties but also uses the methods and properties of another class (its *superclass*). For example, all the built-in Action-Script classes, such as the *Date* and *TextField* classes, are subclasses of the top-level

Object superclass. You can create a subclass that inherits all the properties and methods of a superclass by assigning a new instance of the superclass to the subclass's prototype property. For example:

```
MySubClass.prototype = new MySuperClass();
```

 Assigning a new instance of the superclass to the subclass's prototype wipes out any existing methods or properties of that prototype. You must assign the value to prototype before you add any methods or properties to the subclass.

This is the correct order in which to perform the actions:

1. Define the constructor method for the subclass.
2. Assign inheritance (i.e., the superclass) to the prototype property.
3. Add methods and properties to the prototype property.

Here is a example of the correct order in which to perform the actions:

```
_global.MySubClass = function () {};
MySubClass.prototype = new MySuperClass();
MySubClass.prototype.methodA = function () {};
MySubClass.prototype.myProperty = "some property value";
```

The following is incorrect! Because the inheritance is defined after the addition of *methodA()* and myProperty, those items are lost after the superclass assignment.

```
_global.MySubClass = function () {};
MySubClass.prototype.methodA = function () {};
MySubClass.prototype.myProperty = "some property value";
MySubClass.prototype = new MySuperClass();  // This should come earlier.
```

Here is a complete example with superclass and subclass definitions:

```
// Define a superclass.
_global.MySuperClass = function () {};

// Define a method for the superclass.
MySuperClass.prototype.myMethod = function () {
  return "MySuperClass.myMethod() called";
};

// Define the subclass.
_global.MySubClass = function () {};

// Define the inheritance such that MySubClass is a subclass of MySuperClass.
MySubClass.prototype = new MySuperClass();

// Define some methods and properties for the subclass, if desired.
MySubClass.prototype.methodA = function () {};
MySubClass.prototype.myProperty = "some property value";

// Create an instance of MySubClass.
sub = new MySubClass();
```

```
// Call myMethod( ) from the subclass instance. Even though myMethod is not explicitly
// defined for MySubClass, the subclass automatically inherits it from the
// superclass, MySuperClass.
trace(sub.myMethod( ));
```

Subclassing is essential to creating components (see Recipe 12.12). Additionally, it has practical applications in situations in which there is a natural relationship between two classes. In many cases, it makes sense for one class to inherit from another rather than to create redundancy. The following example with a *Rectangle* superclass and a *Square* subclass illustrates the point. Squares are a subset of rectangles—they are specialized rectangles in which all four sides are the same length. In this example, the *Rectangle* class defines the important functionality while the *Square* class inherits it without having to redefine it:

```
// Define the Rectangle class. The constructor accepts two parameters for the lengths
// of the sides (the height and width).
_global.Rectangle = function (sideA, sideB) {
  this.sideA = sideA;
  this.sideB = sideB;

  // Create a read-only area property.
  this.addProperty("area", this.getArea, null);
};

// Define the getArea( ) method for the area property.
Rectangle.prototype.getArea = function ( ) {
  return (this.sideA * this.sideB);
};

// Define a Square class. The constructor accepts one parameter only, since the width
// and height are always equal. Since the Square class subclasses Rectangle, it
// inherits the sideA and sideB properties. In the Square constructor, set both
// properties to the same value.
_global.Square = function (side) {
  this.sideA = this.sideB = side;
};

// Set Square to inherit from Rectangle.
Square.prototype = new Rectangle( );

// Create a new Square instance with a side of length 6.
sq = new Square(6);

// Display the value of the area property. Even though Square does not explicitly
// define an area property, it inherits it from Rectangle.
trace(sq.area);  // Displays: 36
```

See Also

Recipes 12.9 and 12.12. For a detailed discussion on an alternative, unsupported method of superclass assignment, refer to the discussion of so-called __*proto*__-*based* *inheritance* in the "Advanced Issues with Superclass Assignment" section of Chapter 12 in *ActionScript for Flash MX: The Definitive Guide*. That chapter is freely downloadable from *http://moock.org/asdg/samples*.

12.9 Implementing Subclass Versions of Superclass Methods

Problem

You want to write a subclass implementation of a superclass method (that is, you want a subclass to have a different implementation of a particular method than its superclass).

Solution

Add a method to the subclass with the same name as the superclass method. If you want to call the superclass method from within the subclass method, use the super keyword to reference the superclass.

Discussion

Although a subclass inherits all the methods and properties of a superclass, a subclass does not need to use the superclass implementations. Sometimes, a superclass method may be a generic implementation of particular functionality, and you want to create a more specific implementation within the subclass. When you explicitly define a method within the subclass, the ActionScript interpreter does not search up the *prototype chain* to find any other versions of that method (the prototype chain is the hierarchy of prototype properties from the subclass up to any superclasses that it inherits from). However, if you want a subclass implementation to call the superclass version of the method, use the super keyword to reference the superclass from within the subclass. For example:

```
// Define a superclass.
_global.MySuperClass = function () {};

// Create a superclass implementation of myMethod( ).
MySuperClass.prototype.myMethod = function () {
  return 12;
};

// Create a subclass.
_global.MySubClass = function () {};

// Define the inheritance for the subclass.
MySubClass.prototype = new MySuperClass();
```

```
// Define a subclass implementation of myMethod( ). This effectively obscures the
// inherited method of the same name (within the subclass only). However, you can
// have the subclass implementation call the superclass version of myMethod( ) using
// the super keyword.
MySubClass.prototype.myMethod = function ( ) {

    // Explicitly invoke the superclass implementation of myMethod( ). Invoking the
    // superclass implementation from within the subclass version of the method is
    // fairly typical.
    var superVal = super.myMethod( );

    // Return the superclass result plus three.
    return superVal + 3;
};

// Create an instance of MySubClass
sub = new MySubClass( );

// Displays: 15 (which is 12 from the superclass plus 3 from the subclass)
trace(sub.myMethod( ));
```

See Also

For a detailed discussion of the prototype chain, refer to the "The Almighty Proto-type Chain" section of Chapter 12 in *ActionScript for Flash MX: The Definitive Guide*. That chapter is freely downloadable from *http://moock.org/asdg/samples*.

12.10 Listening for Events

Problem

You want to perform an action in response to an event, such as when the Stage is resized, a text field's contents are scrolled, the mouse button is clicked, or a key is pressed.

Solution

Create a listener object that defines an appropriate listener event handler and add it as a listener using *addListener( )*.

Discussion

ActionScript's *listener events* allow one or more objects to respond to events that occur for other objects. A *listener object* (an object that has been added as a listener) is notified when one of the supported listener events occurs. For example, the built-in *Key*, *Mouse*, *Selection*, and *Stage* objects generate one or more listener events, as do instances of the *TextField* class, as shown in Table 12-1.

Table 12-1. Listener events for built-in objects and instances

Object	Built-in listener events
Key object	onKeyDown onKeyUp
Mouse object	onMouseDown onMouseMove onMouseUp
Selection object	onSetFocus
Stage object	onResize
TextField instance	onChanged onScroller

A listener object can be any kind of object, such as a text field, movie clip, or custom object. The listener object must define a listener event handler to respond to the event of interest, and it must be added as a listener using *addListener()*. For example, to respond to text-scrolling events, you can create an object that defines an *onScroller()* method and then register the object to the text field of interest using the *addListener()* method. Note that the *addListener()* method is called from the text field (or other object from Table 12-1) that is generating the listener events. The *addListener()* method accepts a parameter that is a reference to the listener object (in this case, the object that defines an *onScroller()* listener event handler).

You can register multiple listeners to a single object using separate calls to *addListener()*. For example, the following code adds two objects as listeners. The first listener object is a generic instance of the *Object* class that responds to any changes in the text field named myTextField. The second listener object is a movie clip named myMovieClip. It alters its own x coordinate in response to scroll events for myTextField.

```
// Create a new object and define an onChanged() listener event handler.
myListener = new Object();
myListener.onChanged = function (changedTextField) {
  // Actions go here.
  trace("The text field changed.");
};

// Define an onScroller() listener event handler for an existing movie clip.
myMovieClip.onScroller = function (scrolledTextField) {
  this._x = scrolledTextField.scroll * 10;
};

// Register the custom object and movie clip as listeners for the text field.
myTextField.addListener(myListener);
myTextField.addListener(myMovieClip);
```

When a listener object is added as a listener, it is eligible to receive all the listener events that the listened-to object generates. For example, an object registered as a listener using *Mouse.addListener()* can respond to *onMouseDown*, *onMouseMove*, and *onMouseUp* events by defining corresponding handlers for the events of interest. In the preceding example, note that both `myListener` and `myMovieClip` are eligible to receive *onChanged* and *onScroller* events from the text field. However, `myListener` implements an *onChanged()* event handler only, so it ignores *onScroller* events. Conversely, `myMovieClip` implements an *onScroller()* event handler but ignores *onChanged* events.

Furthermore, note that the *onChanged()* and *onScroller()* listener event handlers receive a parameter indicating which text field generated the event. This is handy when the listener object wants to access a property of the text field (for example, our movie clip listener sets its x location based on the text field's `scroll` property). It also allows a listener object to distinguish between multiple text fields, if it is receiving listener events from more than one.

Listener events are powerful because they allow you to define actions that should occur on multiple objects when another object is changed in some way. Likewise, listener events allow a single object to respond to changes that occur on multiple objects.

You can remove a listener by invoking the *removeListener()* method on the object that generates the events, passing it a reference to the listener object to remove. For example:

```
myTextField.removeListener(myListener);
```

All objects listed in Table 12-1 support both the *addListener()* and *removeListener()* methods.

See Also

Recipes 8.15, 8.27, and 12.11

12.11 Adding Listeners to Custom Classes

Problem

You want your objects of a custom class to generate listener events and support listener objects.

Solution

Write an *addListener()* method for your custom class. Use the *watch()* method to watch a property. When the property is modified, call all listeners.

Discussion

Listeners are a convenient way to automatically trigger methods on one or more objects when a property is modified within the object being listened to. Listeners are available for some classes of objects such as *Key*, *Mouse*, and *TextField* (see Table 12-1). Although ActionScript does not provide listeners for all objects, you can use the *watch()* method to generate listener events in response to property changes.

The *watch()* method requires at least two parameters: a string value that is the name of the property to watch and a reference to a *callback function* to call when the property is changed. (A callback function is simply a function that is called in response to a particular trigger.) The callback function is always automatically passed at least three values: the property name, the old value, and the new value. If the callback function returns true, the new value is assigned to the property, and if it returns false, the old value is assigned to the property. The *watch()* method can also be used for other purposes, such as implementing logic in the callback function to determine which value (old or new) should be assigned to the property. For the purposes of creating listener functionality, your callback function should always return true because you don't want to interfere with the setting of the property value (you only want to detect the change so that your code can trigger a method on the listener objects).

To add listener functionality to a class, you also need to create methods for adding and removing listeners. The *addListener()* method takes a reference to an object and adds it to an array property. The *removeListener()* method also takes a reference to an object, which it removes from the array, if found. Here is an example of how to create listener functionality for a custom class and how to use it:

```
// Create a constructor for a class, MyClass.
_global.MyClass = function (val) {

  // Store the value passed to the constructor in a property (myProperty).
  this.myProperty = val;

  // Tell the object to watch for any changes to myProperty. When a change occurs,
  // call the object's propSet() method.
  this.watch("myProperty", this.propSet);
};

// The propSet() method is the callback function invoked automatically when
// myProperty's value changes. The callback is passed the property name
// ('myProperty' in this case) plus the old value and the proposed new value.
MyClass.prototype.propSet = function (prop, oldVal, newVal) {

  // Call onMyPropertyChange(), if it exists, for each listener object. Pass that
  // method the old value and new value.
  for (var i = 0; i < this.listeners.length; i++) {
    this.listeners[i].onMyPropertyChange(oldVal, newVal);
  }
```

```
// Return the new value so that it is assigned to the property. This is very
// important. Without this line, myProperty becomes undefined.
return newVal;
};

// The addListener() method adds a listener object to an array of listeners.
MyClass.prototype.addListener = function (listener) {

  // If the listeners array property does not exist, create it.
  if (this.listeners == undefined) {
    this.listeners = new Array();
  }

  // Add the new listener to the existing array of listeners.
  this.listeners.push(listener);
};

// The removeListener() method removes a listener object from the listeners array.
MyClass.prototype.removeListener = function (listener) {

  // Remove the listener from the listeners array, if it is found.
  for (var i = 0; i < this.listeners.length; i++) {
    if (this.listeners[i] == listener) {
      this.listeners.splice(i, 1);
      break;
    }
  }
};

// Create a listener object. It must have a method named onMyPropertyChange() to
// listen effectively (because that's what the propSet() method tries to call).
obj = new Object();
obj.onMyPropertyChange = function (oldVal, newVal) {
  trace(oldVal + " " + newVal);
};

// Create a new instance of MyClass and add obj as a listener on the instance.
myClassInstance = new MyClass(6);
myClassInstance.addListener(obj);

// Each time myProperty is set, the callback function (propSet()) invokes the
// onMyPropertyChange() method of each listener object.
myClassInstance.myProperty = 24;
myClassInstance.myProperty = 42;
myClassInstance.myProperty = 36;
```

The preceding code gives you an idea of the process involved in adding listeners to objects. However, it is not as versatile as it could be. The primary issue is that it requires you to define the listener code for every class to which you want to add listeners. There is a better way.

All ActionScript classes inherit from the *Object* class. Therefore, if you add the listener code to the *Object* class, all classes automatically inherit it. The only real difference when you add the listener code to the *Object* class is that you cannot rely on having access to each class's constructor as you did in the preceding example. Therefore, you should create another method, *startListeners()*, that initiates the watch for a watched property. The *startListeners()* method should accept the name of the property to watch as a parameter. For future use, add the following code to an external *Object.as* file and include it in any project for which you want to implement custom listener functionality:

```
// The startListeners() method calls watch() to start watching
// a property. If you want an object to listen for multiple
// properties, call startListeners() for each property.
Object.prototype.startListeners = function (propName) {
  this.watch(propName, this.propSet);
};

// The addListener() and removeListener() methods are the same as the preceding
// example, except that they are applied to the Object class.
Object.prototype.addListener = function (listener) {
  if (this.listeners == undefined) {
    this.listeners = new Array();
  }
  this.listeners.push(listener);
};

Object.prototype.removeListener = function (listener) {
  for (var i = 0; i < this.listeners.length; i++) {
    if (this.listeners[i] == listener) {
      this.listeners.splice(i, 1);
      break;
    }
  }
};

// The propSet() method is the callback function for the watched properties. This
// method is slightly more generic than in the preceding example, insofar as it
// allows for any property to be watched.
Object.prototype.propSet = function (prop, oldVal, newVal) {

  // Loop through all the listeners.
  for (var i = 0; i < this.listeners.length; i++) {

    // This calls the onPropertyNameChange() method on each listener, where
    // PropertyName is given by the prop parameter.
    this.listeners[i]["on" + prop + "Change"](oldVal, newVal);
  }

  // Return the new value so it is properly assigned to the property.
  return newVal;
};
```

Here is an example that uses our new listener code:

```
#include "Object.as"

// Define a custom class. This time, the class does not need any of the listener code
// because it automatically inherits it from the Object class.
_global.MyClass = function (val0, val1) {
  this.myProperty0 = val0;
  this.myProperty1 = val1;
};

// Create a listener object. Define methods named onMyProperty0Change( ) and
// onMyProperty1Change( ) so the object can listen for changes to the watched
// properties named myProperty0 and myProperty1.
obj = new Object( );
obj.onMyProperty0Change = function (oldVal, newVal) {
  trace("myProperty0: " + oldVal + " " + newVal);
};
obj.onMyProperty1Change = function (oldVal, newVal) {
  trace("myProperty1: " + oldVal + " " + newVal);
};

// Create a new instance of MyClass.
myClassInstance = new MyClass(6, 9);

// Add obj as a listener. Start listeners for myProperty0 and myProperty1.
myClassInstance.addListener(obj);
myClassInstance.startListeners("myProperty0");
myClassInstance.startListeners("myProperty1");

// The following changes to the properties invoke the listener methods
// onMyProperty0Change( ) and onMyProperty1Change( ).
myClassInstance.myProperty0 = 24;
myClassInstance.myProperty0 = 42;
myClassInstance.myProperty1 = 36;

/* The results displayed in the Output window are as follows:
   myProperty0: 6 24
   myProperty0: 24 42
   myProperty1: 9 36
*/
```

Be aware that Flash cannot watch some properties, so you cannot add listeners in the following cases:

Legacy Flash 4 properties

Properties available in Flash 4, such as _x, _y, _width, _height, etc., cannot be watched. These properties are listed in the Actions Toolbox under the Properties folder.

Getter/setter properties

You cannot create custom listeners for any custom getter/setter properties you have defined (see Recipe 12.6). You cannot add listeners for any of the built-in getter/setter properties shown in Table 12-2.

Properties inherited from the object's prototype chain

A property must be defined on the object itself before you can watch it. For example, if you add a custom property, myCustomProperty, to the *Object* class, then that property cannot be watched for an instance of the *Object* class. In practice, this is generally a moot point. As soon as you assign a new value to the instance's property, you define the property for the instance, and it can be watched. If you have previously called the *watch()* method to watch the property, once you define the property for the actual instance, the callback function is invoked. For example:

```
// Add a custom property to the Object class.
Object.prototype.myCustomProperty = "This cannot be watched.";

// Create a new object.
myObject = new Object();

// Define a watch callback function.
myObject.myCustomPropertyCallback = function (prop, oldVal, newVal, useData) {
  trace(prop + " changed from " + oldVal + " to " + newVal);
};

// At first, Flash cannot watch myCustomProperty because it is inherited.
myObject.watch("myCustomProperty", this.myCustomPropertyCallback);

// Now, myCustomProperty can be watched, because it has been assigned on the
// object instance directly.
myObject.myCustomProperty = "This will be watched.";
```

Table 12-2 lists the getter/setter properties that cannot be watched, but it does not list all unwatchable properties. Note that Flash 4 legacy properties such as the _x, _y, _width, and _height movie clip properties also cannot be watched.

Table 12-2. Getter/setter properties, which cannot be watched

Object	Getter/setter properties
Button	tabIndex
Camera	All properties
Microphone	All properties
MovieClip	tabIndex
NetStream	All properties
Sound	duration position
Stage	All properties
TextField	All properties
TextFormat	All properties
Video	All properties

Table 12-2. Getter/setter properties, which cannot be watched (continued)

Object	Getter/setter properties
XML	contentType docTypeDecl ignoreWhite loaded status xmlDecl
XMLnode	attributes childNodes firstChild lastChild nextSibling nodeName nodeType nodeValue parentNode previousSibling

See Also

Recipe 12.10. Also refer to the *Object.watch()* entry in the "Language Reference" section of *ActionScript for Flash MX: The Definitive Guide*, from which Table 12-2 is reproduced.

12.12 Creating a Component That Subclasses MovieClip

Problem

You want to create a reusable component, such as an interface widget, or even a component without a UI.

Solution

Create a new movie clip symbol. On the first frame of the symbol's timeline define the component class (which must inherit from *MovieClip*). Then register the class using *Object.registerClass()*. All this code should be encapsulated between #initclip and #endinitclip pragmas.

Discussion

Components are a way of encapsulating movie clips so that the instances can be easily configured by setting parameters through a user interface at authoring time or through a programmatic interface at runtime. For those who prefer to use Flash as a design tool, many ready-made components (such as those included in the Flash UI Component sets) can be dragged into a movie, and parameters can be set via the Property inspector or Parameters panel. These components add functionality to the movie without the designer having to write all the code that is entailed. For our purposes, however, we will use the term "component" more specifically to refer to subclasses of *MovieClip*. In other words, we will be discussing components that are controlled programmatically instead of those that are controlled via an author-time user interface.

There are five (or six) basic steps to creating a component:

1. Create a new movie clip symbol and give it a name in the Symbol Property dialog box (accessed under Properties from the Library panel's pop-up Options menu). As a best practice, use the name you want to give to your component (such as `MyComponent`).

2. Export the movie clip symbol for ActionScript usage (using Linkage from the Library panel's pop-up Options menu). As a best practice, give the symbol a linkage identifier that follows the naming convention of `ComponentNameSymbol` (such as `MyComponentSymbol`).

3. Define the component class on the first frame of the component timeline. The class should follow these guidelines:

   a. As a best practice, name the class `ComponentNameClass` (such as `MyComponentClass`).

   b. The class constructor should not take any parameters.

   c. The class must inherit from *MovieClip* by assigning to the prototype property a new *MovieClip* instance. (Subclassing the *MovieClip* class is the only time you use a *MovieClip* constructor in a *new* statement.)

4. After defining the class, register it using *Object.registerClass( )*. The first parameter should be the symbol linkage identifier name specified as a string. The second parameter should be a reference to the class.

5. Place all the code for the component (the class definition and the registration code) between `#initclip` and `#endinitclip` pragmas so that the component class is defined and registered before it is called. This is essential. Without the `#initclip` pragma, the component class is loaded only after instances of the component are loaded into the movie.

6. The sixth step in creating a component is to specify the component definition for the symbol and optionally create a custom UI. You can read more about this process in the Macromedia technote, "Creating components in Macromedia Flash MX" at *http://www.macromedia.com/support/flash/applications/creating_comps*. For

our purposes, we will consider this step optional. Technically, a component is a component only if you have completed this step. But this step only enables an author-time interface for configuring the component instances—something we are not particularly interested in from an ActionScript standpoint.

Using our working definition, components are the only way to effectively subclass *MovieClip*, so they are the only way to create custom object classes with a visual aspect. Basic components can be created that do not subclass *MovieClip*. These types of components allow users to set values in the Component Parameters panel at authoring time but not via ActionScript. Basic components cannot be instantiated with ActionScript. In contrast, you can use ActionScript to control *MovieClip* subclass components and can even instantiate them using the *attachMovie()* method. Because a component class is registered to a particular linkage identifier name, Flash automatically knows to call the component class constructor function when a new instance of the symbol is created using *attachMovie()*.

Here is an example in which a component, *MyComponent*, is created and used within a movie. The component creates a text field within itself and has methods that allow it to move about the screen to random spots at a set interval.

1. Create a new movie clip symbol named *MyComponent*.

2. Open the Linkage properties for *MyComponent* using the Library panel's pop-up Options menu. Export the symbol for ActionScript and give it a linkage identifier of *MyComponentSymbol*.

3. On the first frame of the default layer of *MyComponent*, add the following code:

```
// Make sure everything is between the #initclip and #endinitclip pragmas.
#initclip

// The constructor function accepts no parameters.
function MyComponentClass () {

  // Create a text field that auto sizes. Set an initial text value.
  this.createTextField("myTextField", 1, 0, 0, 0, 0);
  this.myTextField.autoSize = true;
  this.myTextField.text = "init text value";
}

// MyComponentClass subclasses MovieClip, as must all scriptable components.
MyComponentClass.prototype = new MovieClip();

// Define a method that sets the text.
MyComponentClass.prototype.setText = function (val) {
  this.myTextField.text = val;
};
```

```
// The beginMove( ) method uses setInterval( ) to call the move( ) method of the
// component at the specified rate. The interval reference is stored in a
// property so that it can be removed later.
MyComponentClass.prototype.beginMove = function (rate) {
  this.moveInterval = setInterval(this, "move", rate);
};

// The endMove( ) method calls clearInterval( ) to stop the calls to move( ).
MyComponentClass.prototype.endMove = function ( ) {
  clearInterval(this.moveInterval);
};

// The move( ) method is called automatically at an interval when beginMove( ) is
// called. This method sets the _x and _y properties of the component to random
// values within the Stage.
MyComponentClass.prototype.move = function ( ) {
  this._x = Math.random( ) * 550;
  this._y = Math.random( ) * 400;
};

// Register the component class to the linkage identifier for the symbol.
Object.registerClass("MyComponentSymbol", MyComponentClass);

#endinitclip
```

4. Return to the first frame of the main timeline and add the following code to create an instance of the component:

```
// Create a new instance of the component. Because MyComponentClass is registered
// to the MyComponentSymbol linkage identifier, when this new instance is
// created, it will automatically call the MyComponentClass constructor.
_root.attachMovie("MyComponentSymbol", "myC", 1);

// Call the beginMove( ) method with a rate of 100. This causes the component to
// move approximately 10 times per second.
myC.beginMove(100);

// Define an interval callback function that calls the endMove( ) method for myC
// and clears the interval.
function doEndMove ( ) {
  myC.endMove( );
  clearInterval(cInterval);
}

// Set an interval at which doEndMove( ) is called after 10 seconds have elapsed.
cInterval = setInterval(doEndMove, 10000);
```

See Also

Chapters 14 and 16 of *ActionScript for Flash MX: The Definitive Guide* cover movie
clip subclasses and component development in detail.

12.13 Program: Color Selector Component

In this program, you create a color selector component similar to the one that is available from the Tools panel when you click on either the stroke or fill color. To do this, follow these steps:

1. Create a new movie clip symbol named *ColorSelector*.

2. Open the Linkage properties for *ColorSelector* using the Library panel's pop-up Options menu. Export the symbol for ActionScript and give it a linkage identifier of *ColorSelectorSymbol*.

3. On the first frame of the default layer of *ColorSelector*, add the following code:

```
#initclip

function ColorSelectorClass () {

  // Define color transform object properties. resetTransform resets a movie
  // clip's colors back to the symbol's original values. selectTransform sets the
  // movie clip's colors to white.
  this.resetTransform = {ra: 100, rb: 0, ga: 100, gb: 0, ba: 100, bb: 0, aa: 100,
                         ab: 0};
  this.selectTransform = {ra: 100, rb: 255, ga: 100, gb: 255, ba: 100, bb: 255,
                          aa: 100, ab: 0};

  // The num property is used to count the number of color swatches.
  this.num = 0;

  // The selectedColor property is the RGB value
  // of the color selected by the user.
  this.selectedColor = 0;

  // Call the startListeners() method to watch the selectedColor property. This
  // custom handler is implemented in Recipe 12.11.
  this.startListeners("selectedColor");

  // Create a movie clip to hold all the color swatches and initially set it to
  // be invisible. Set the y position of the swatches_mc movie clip to 15 so that
  // it appears below the button (see code that follows).
  this.createEmptyMovieClip("swatches_mc", 1);
  this.swatches_mc._visible = false;
  this.swatches_mc._y = 15;

  // Create the button movie clip that opens and closes the color selector. Draw
  // a square within it and add a text field with a c for color.
  this.createEmptyMovieClip("open_btn", 2);
  this.open_btn.lineStyle(0, 0x000000, 100);
  this.open_btn.beginFill(0xFFFFFF, 0);
  this.open_btn.drawRectangle(15, 15, 0, 0, 7.5, 7.5);
  this.open_btn.endFill();
  this.open_btn.createTextField("label_txt", 1, 0, 0, 0, 0);
  this.open_btn.label_txt.autoSize = true;
```

```
this.open_btn.label_txt.text = " c";
this.open_btn.label_txt.selectable = false;

// When the button is pressed, toggle the visibility of the swatches.
this.open_btn.onRelease = function () {
  this._parent.toggle();
};

var swatch, r, g, b, rgb;

// Create the swatches. There are 216 swatches total—six blocks of six-by-six
// swatches. Create three nested for loops to accomplish this.
for (var redModifier = 0; redModifier < 6; redModifier ++) {
  for (var blueModifier = 0; blueModifier < 6; blueModifier++) {
    for (var greenModifier = 0; greenModifier < 6; greenModifier++) {

      // The red, green, and blue values of each swatch follow a pattern that
      // you can see for yourself if you experiment with the color selector in
      // the Flash authoring environment. This code follows the same pattern.
      r = 0x33 * redModifier;
      g = 0x33 * greenModifier;
      b = 0x33 * blueModifier;
      rgb = (r << 16) | (g << 8) | b;

      // Create each swatch with the createSwatch()
      // method (see the following code).
      swatch_mc = this.createSwatch(rgb);

      // Move each swatch to its correct position.
      swatch_mc._y = 10*blueModifier;
      swatch_mc._x = 10*greenModifier + (redModifier*60);
      if (redModifier >= 3) {
        swatch_mc._y += 60;
        swatch_mc._x -= 180;
      }
    }
  }
}
}

// Component classes must inherit from MovieClip.
ColorSelectorClass.prototype = new MovieClip();

ColorSelectorClass.prototype.toggle = function () {
  this.swatches_mc._visible = !this.swatches_mc._visible;
};

ColorSelectorClass.prototype.createSwatch = function (rgb) {

  // Create the movie clips for the swatches. Each swatch name and depth must be
  // unique. Accomplish this by using the value of the num property, which is
  // incremented each time a new swatch is created.
  var swatch_mc = this.swatches_mc.createEmptyMovieClip(
              "swatch" + this.num + "_mc", this.num);
```

```
// Within the swatch_mc clip, create outline_mc and fill_mc movie clips so that
// the outline color can be controlled without affecting the fill color. This
// is important for the rollover effect.
swatch_mc.createEmptyMovieClip("outline_mc", 2);
swatch_mc.createEmptyMovieClip("fill_mc", 1);

// In the outline_mc clip, draw a square outline.
swatch_mc.outline_mc.lineStyle(0, 0x000000, 100);
swatch_mc.outline_mc.drawRectangle(9, 9, 0, 0, 5, 5);

// In the fill_mc clip, draw a filled square.
swatch_mc.fill_mc.lineStyle(0, 0x000000, 0);
swatch_mc.fill_mc.beginFill(rgb, 100);
swatch_mc.fill_mc.drawRectangle(10, 10, 0, 0, 5, 5);
swatch_mc.fill_mc.endFill();

// Set an rgb property for the swatch to be
// equal to the value of the fill color.
swatch_mc.rgb = rgb;

// Create a Color object to control the outline color.
// On rollover, set the color transform to the selectTransform
// object to turn the outline white. On rollout use the
// resetTransform object to set the color back to the original value.
swatch_mc.col = new Color(swatch_mc.outline_mc);
swatch_mc.onRollOver = function () {
  this.col.setTransform(this._parent._parent.selectTransform);
};
swatch_mc.onRollOut = function () {
  this.col.setTransform(this._parent._parent.resetTransform);
};

// When the swatch is clicked, set the selectColor property of the color
// selector component instance to the value of the swatch's rgb property. The
// selectColor property is listened to, so the onSelectedColorChange() method
// of any listener objects is automatically invoked.
swatch_mc.onRelease = function () {
  this._parent._parent.selectedColor = this.rgb;
  this._parent._parent.toggle();
};

// Increment num (used to generate unique names and depths).
this.num++;

// Return a reference to the swatch_mc clip.
return swatch_mc;
};

// Register the class to the ColorSelectorSymbol linkage identifier.
Object.registerClass("ColorSelectorSymbol", ColorSelectorClass);

#endinitclip
```

4. On the main timeline, add the following code to the first frame of the default layer. This code adds an instance of the component to the Stage.

```
// You must include DrawingMethods.as (from Chapter 4) and Object.as (from Recipe
// 12.11) in any movie in which you use the color selector component.
#include "DrawingMethods.as"
#include "Object.as"

// Add an instance of the component.
_root.attachMovie("ColorSelectorSymbol", "colorSelector", 1);

// Create a listener object with the onSelectedColorChange( ) method.
colorListener = new Object( );
colorListener.onSelectedColorChange = function (oldVal, newVal) {

  // When the color is selected, this method is called and the hexadecimal value
  // is displayed in the Output window.
  trace(newVal.toString(16));
};

// Add the listener to the color selector.
colorSelector.addListener(colorListener);
```

CHAPTER 13
Programming Sound

13.0   Introduction

You can add sound to your movie at authoring time by importing a sound into a layer of a timeline. Furthermore, you can set the volume and pan for that sound at authoring time. However, to control the sound during runtime, you must use a *Sound* object. With a *Sound* object, you can programmatically control sounds in ways that you cannot at authoring time, including:

- Attaching sounds from the library
- Loading external MP3s
- Starting and stopping playback based on user input, server responses, or other runtime events
- Adjusting the sound panning and volume based on user input, server responses, or other runtime events
- Controlling the playback position of a sound (such as user-controlled seek, fast-forward, and rewind)
- Accessing the sound's total duration
- Reading song data (artist name, title, etc.) from ID3 tags (for loaded MP3s only)

Sound objects control the sounds that exist within a movie clip—whether those sounds were placed within the movie clip at authoring time or attached or loaded into the movie clip at runtime using ActionScript. It is possible to place multiple sounds within a single movie clip; however, doing so is poor practice because it prevents you from controlling the sounds individually. Rather, in most cases, you should create separate movie clips for each sound and create a separate *Sound* object to target each movie clip.

The hierarchy of movie clip timelines also comes into play with sounds. The volume and panning for sounds in parent movie clips affect the perceived volume and panning of nested sounds. For example, if you set the volume to 50 for a *Sound* object targeting _root, the playback of all sounds in the movie will be at half their own volume settings.

There are a few things to keep in mind when using sounds in Flash. First of all, Flash can play only up to eight sounds simultaneously. So make sure you plan accordingly.

See Also

This chapter looks at sounds that are added to a movie programmatically. When you add sounds programmatically, Flash does not provide a way to automatically synchronize the animation to the sound. For basic information on using and synchronizing sound in Flash, see Help → Using Flash → Adding Sound. See Recipe 15.3 for loading an external MP3 sound. Also refer to Chapter 14 for recipes dealing with audio as it relates to the FlashCom server.

13.1   Creating an Object to Control Sound

Problem

You want to control sounds at runtime.

Solution

Create a new movie clip to serve as the sound's target and then pass a reference to that clip to the *Sound()* constructor function (to create a new *Sound* object). Alternatively, create and invoke a custom *createNewSound()* method that handles this process automatically.

Discussion

Sound objects enable you to load sounds, play sounds, and control the volume and panning of sounds within your Flash movies. A *Sound* object must target a movie clip (_root is also a valid target). The audio that is controlled must be placed in the movie clip's timeline at authoring time or loaded into the movie clip at runtime using *attachSound()* or *loadSound()*. In any case, it is possible for you to place/load multiple sounds into a single movie clip, but doing so is discouraged. The reason for this is that a *Sound* object controls the audio in the target movie clip as a whole, so it is not possible to control each of the sounds separately if they are all in the same movie clip. Therefore, it is better to place/load each sound into its own movie clip and create a separate *Sound* object to control each one.

When you create a new *Sound* object, specify a target movie clip. To control sounds in the current timeline, specify the keyword this as the target.

```
// Incorrect. This does not work properly.
mySound0_sound = new Sound( );
// Correct. This targets the current timeline.
mySound1_sound = new Sound(this);
// Correct. This targets mySoundHolder_mc.
mySound2_sound = new Sound(mySoundHolder_mc);
```

When you are using *attachSound()* or *loadSound()* to add audio to a movie clip, it is a good idea to use the *createEmptyMovieClip()* method to create the clip:

```
// Create a new movie clip to hold the audio. Then create a new Sound object and pass
// it a reference to the holder movie clip.
_root.createEmptyMovieClip("soundHolder0_mc", 1);
mySound0_sound = new Sound(soundHolder0_mc);

// To manage additional sounds, use the same process to create holder movie clips and
// Sound objects for each one.
_root.createEmptyMovieClip("soundHolder1_mc", 2);
mySound1_sound = new Sound(soundHolder1_mc);
```

As you can see, the preceding process is repetitive when creating multiple sounds in your movie. You have to create each holder movie clip and *Sound* object and keep track of numbers and depths. You can automate this process with a custom *createNewSound()* method. The *createNewSound()* method should be defined as a static method for the *Sound* class. (A static method is a method that is called directly from the class, rather than from an object instance of the class.)

The custom *createNewSound()* method returns a new *Sound* object, which targets an automatically generated holder movie clip. The movie clip is created within _root by default, but you can specify a parent movie clip as an optional parameter. Add the following *createNewSound()* method definition to an external *Sound.as* file for easy inclusion in other projects:

```
// This code requires getNewDepth( ) from Chapter 7, so include MovieClip.as.
#include "MovieClip.as"

Sound.createNewSound = function (parentClip) {

  // If parentClip is specified, create the sound holder movie clip in that timeline.
  // Otherwise, use _root as the parent clip.
  if (parentClip == undefined) {
    parentClip = _root;
  }

  // soundCount keeps track of the holder movie clips that are created.
  // It defaults to 0.
  if (parentClip.soundCount == undefined) {
    parentClip.soundCount = 0;
  }

  // Create a holder movie clip in parentClip using createEmptyMovieClip( ). Give it a
  // unique name by appending the value of soundCount to "soundHolderClip". Give each
  // clip a unique depth using getNewDepth( ).
```

```
var soundHolder_mc = parentClip.createEmptyMovieClip("soundHolderClip" +
                                            parentClip.soundCount + "_mc",
                                            parentClip.getNewDepth( ));

// Create the Sound object that targets the holder movie clip.
var soundObj_sound = new Sound(soundHolder_mc);

// Store a reference to the clip in the Sound
// object's mc property for later access.
soundObj_sound.mc = soundHolder_mc;

// Use soundHolder_mc.parent to establish a relationship between the sound
// holder movie clip and the Sound object. Use soundObj_sound.parent to establish
// a relationship between the Sound object and the parent clip. These
// relationships are important so that each object has a reference to one
// another, which they would not otherwise have. This enables communication
// between the objects for the purposes of creating fades (see Recipes 13.14
// and 13.15) and other functionality.
soundHolder_mc.parent = soundObj_sound;
soundObj_sound.parent = parentClip;

// Increment soundCount so that the next holder movie clip has a unique name.
parentClip.soundCount++;

// If an allSounds array doesn't already exist, create it. It contains references
// to all the sounds that have been created using createNewSound( ). This is useful
// when you want to perform an action on all the sounds.
if (_global.allSounds == undefined) {
  _global.allSounds = new Array( );
}

// Add the new sound to the array.
_global.allSounds.push(soundObj_sound);

// Return the Sound object.
return soundObj_sound;
};
```

Here is an example of how to use the *createNewSound()* method:

```
#include "Sound.as"

// Create a new Sound object named mySound_sound by calling the static method
// Sound.createNewSound( ). You do not need to create a holder movie clip because the
// method does it for you.
mySound_sound = Sound.createNewSound( );

// You can access the target holder movie clip via the Sound object's mc property.
// Assuming that mySound_sound was the first Sound object created in a movie, this
// trace( ) statement displays: _level0.soundHolderClip0
trace(mySound_sound.mc);
```

See Also

This recipe explained how to create a *Sound* object to control sounds, but not how to play a sound. Refer to subsequent recipes for details on using a *Sound* object's full capabilities. For details on attaching sounds at runtime using *attachSound()*, see Recipe 13.2. For tips on using *loadSound()*, see Recipe 15.5. See Recipe 2.7 to determine whether the device is capable of playing sounds.

13.2   Attaching Sounds at Runtime

Problem

You want to use ActionScript to attach a sound from the Library to your movie at runtime.

Solution

Use the *Sound.attachSound()* method.

Discussion

A sound must be attached to a movie clip before it can be played at runtime. You can programmatically attach sounds from the Library to *Sound* objects using the *attachSound()* method. To use this method properly, you must first do three things:

1. Create a *Sound* object (see Recipe 13.1).
2. Import a sound into the Library using File → Import to Library.
3. Set the sound symbol to export and set its linkage identifier using the Linkage option in the Library panel's pop-up Options menu.

After successfully completing these three steps, you can call the *attachSound()* method and pass it the linkage identifier of the sound symbol to attach:

```
// Include Sound.as to access the createNewSound() method from Recipe 13.1.
#include "Sound.as"

// Create a new Sound object.
mySound_sound = Sound.createNewSound( );

// Attach a sound to the Sound object. The Library sound symbol
// must be set to export and have a linkage identifier that matches
// the string passed to attachSound( ).
mySound_sound.attachSound("MySoundSymbol");
```

See Also

Attached sounds do not start playing until you tell them to do so. See Recipe 13.3 for more information about playing sounds. Recipe 14.5 demonstrates how to use *Microphone.attachAudio()* to attach audio data from the user's microphone.

13.3   Playing and Stopping a Sound

Problem

You want to play a sound or stop one from playing.

Solution

Use the *start()* and *stop()* methods of the *Sound* object that controls the sound.

Discussion

Sounds added to timelines at authoring time begin playback as soon as the playhead enters the frame containing the sound. In contrast, sounds that are added programmatically (see Recipes 13.2 and 15.5) do not begin playing until they are started with the *Sound.start()* method:

```
mySound_sound.start( );
```

You can also specify the number of seconds into the audio track at which to begin playback by passing the *start()* method an optional *offset* parameter. For example, if you pass the *start()* method a value of 6, the audio will begin playing six seconds into the sound clip:

```
mySound_sound.start(6);
```

Unless directed otherwise, a sound plays once (until it reaches its end). You can stop a sound prematurely with the *stop()* method:

```
mySound_sound.stop( );
```

You can also stop all sounds in a movie using the *stopAllSounds()* global function:

```
stopAllSounds( );
```

When you stop a sound and then restart it, Flash automatically restarts the sound at the beginning.

See Also

To pause and resume sounds, see Recipe 13.7. See Recipe 13.6 for setting in and out points.

13.4   Getting Playback Time

Problem

You want to determine the time of the current playback position of a sound.

Solution

Use the `position` property. To get the total time of a sound, use the `duration` property.

Discussion

Flash offers a convenient way to access information about the playback time for a sound. All *Sound* objects have `position` and `duration` properties (both are read-only), which reflect the current playback position and the total duration of a sound. Both values are given in milliseconds.

```
trace(mySound_sound.position);
trace(mySound_sound.duration);
```

The position property updates automatically during playback. You can get the percentage that corresponds to the current playback position by dividing `position` by `duration` and multiplying the result by 100:

```
trace(mySound_sound.position/mySound_sound.duration * 100);
```

13.5   Looping a Sound

Problem

You want to loop a sound so that it plays repeatedly.

Solution

Use the *start()* method of the *Sound* object that controls the sound and pass it a *looping* parameter.

Discussion

The *start()* method tells a sound to begin playing. The optional first parameter indicates how far into the sound (in seconds) to begin playing it. You also can specify a second parameter (*looping*) that instructs the sound to loop the playback a certain number of times. (If you omit the second parameter, the sound plays once.)

```
// Play the sound six times in a row.
mySound_sound.start(0, 6);
```

If you want the entire sound to loop, you should pass the *start()* method the value 0 for the first parameter (the *offset*) as shown in the preceding example. (To specify the *looping* parameter, you must specify an *offset*, even if it is 0.) If you pass the method a nonzero *offset* parameter value, the sound loop begins that many seconds into the audio with each pass. There is no pause between the loops even when you specify a nonzero *offset*.

```
// Play the sound six times, each time starting the audio three seconds from the
// beginning of the sound clip. There is no pause between each playback.
mySound_sound.start(3, 6);
```

See Also

Recipe 13.6 explains how to set an out point for the sound.

13.6   Setting In and Out Points

Problem

You want to play a sound with start and stop (in and out) points other than the beginning or end of the sound.

Solution

Create and invoke a custom *play()* method.

Discussion

The *start()* method plays and optionally loops a sound with a configurable starting offset. You can define a custom method that also allows you to stop the sound after an elapsed period of time. We can achieve this by using an empty movie clip to poll the sound's elapsed time and telling Flash to stop the sound when the maximum time is exceeded.

Our custom *play()* method works with *Sound* objects created using the custom *createNewSound()* method from Recipe 13.1. If you don't want to use the *createNewSound()* method, you must create an empty movie clip and store a reference to that movie clip in a property named mc within the *Sound* object (*createNewSound()* does this automatically).

Here is our custom *play()* method, which accepts up to three parameters: the starting offset (in seconds), the number of loops, and the maximum playing time (in milliseconds). We'll also define another method that allows us to add a callback function that is invoked when the sound stops. Make sure you add these methods to your *Sound.as* file for easy inclusion in other projects.

```
Sound.prototype.play = function (startOffset, loops, maxTime) {

  // Call the start( ) method with the values for offset and loops.
  this.start(startOffset, loops);

  // If maxTime is undefined, then don't do anything else.
  if (maxTime == undefined) {
    return;
  }
  // Otherwise, we have to detect the elapsed playing time. Record the time when the
  // sound started.
  var startTime = getTimer( );

  // Use an interval to monitor the sound by calling the custom monitorPlayback
  // method every 100 ms. Pass the method the values for startTime and maxTime.
  this.monitorPlaybackInterval = setInterval(this, "monitorPlayback",
                                 100, startTime, maxTime);
};

// Here is the function invoked at each interval.
Sound.prototype.monitorPlayback = function (startTime, maxTime) {

  // If the elapsed time exceeds the maxTime, stop the sound, clear the interval, and
  // invoke the callback function.
  if (getTimer( ) - startTime >= maxTime) {
    this.stop( );
    clearInterval(this.monitorPlaybackInterval);
    this.onStopPath[this.onStopCB]( );
  }
};

// The setOnStop( ) method allows you to define a callback function to invoke when the
// sound stops. The parameters are a string specifying the function name and an
// optional path to the function. If path is undefined, the Sound object's parent
// property is used instead. The parent property is defined only if you use the
// custom createNewSound( ) method to create the sound.
Sound.prototype.setOnStop = function (functionName, path) {
  this.onStopPath = (path == undefined) ? this.parent : path;
  this.onStopCB = functionName;
};
```

Here is an example of how to use the *play()* method:

```
#include "Sound.as"

// Create the sound.
mySound_sound = Sound.createNewSound( );

// Attach a sound from the Library. Alternatively, you can load the sound from an
// external source (see Recipe 15.5).
mySound_sound.attachSound("MySoundSymbol");

// Define a callback function.
function onSoundStop ( ) {
```

```
    trace("Sound has stopped.");
}

// Play the sound from the beginning. Loop it (up to) six times and stop the sound
// after 15 seconds.
mySound_sound.play(0, 6, 15000);

// Set the callback function.
mySound_sound.setOnStop("onSoundStop");
```

Note that the starting offset is measured in seconds, but the maximum playing time is measured in milliseconds (and the timing is accurate only to within about 100 milliseconds). You can modify the *play()* method to use seconds or milliseconds for both values. Also note that the *play()* method does not check the current time of the sound. Instead, it tracks the total amount of time that the sound has been playing. Depending on the duration of the sound and the specified inputs, the sound may not complete, or it may loop multiple times before the maximum elapsed time is reached. In either case, *maxTime* is not a true out point, but simply an elapsed time limit.

Here is a modified version, *playToPoint()*, that accepts a true out point as the third parameter. The out point is relative to the sound's beginning, in milliseconds, regardless of the starting offset. Add the following code to your *Sound.as* file for easy inclusion in other projects:

```
Sound.prototype.playToPoint = function (startOffset, loops, outPoint) {
  // If loops is invalid, play the sound once from startOffset to outPoint.
  if (loops <= 1) {
    loops = 1;
  }
  // Store the input parameters in object properties of the same name.
  this.loops = loops;
  this.startOffset = startOffset;

  // If outPoint is undefined or 0, then just play the sound as usual.
  if (outPoint == undefined || outPoint == 0) {
    // Call the start() method with the values for startOffset and loops.
    this.start(startOffset, loops);
    return;
  }

  // Call the start() method with a starting offset (startOffset) only.
  // We'll manually loop the sound the specified number of times
  // from within onSoundComplete(), each time restarting the sound
  // at startOffset once it reaches outPoint.
  this.start(startOffset);

  // Initialize the loopCount to 0.
  this.loopCount = 0;
```

```
    // Use onSoundComplete() to catch when the sound completes after each loop if the
    // specified outPoint happens to be past the duration of the sound.
    this.onSoundComplete = function () {
      this.loopCount++;
      if (this.loopCount < this.loops) {
        this.start(this.startOffSet);
      }
    };

    // Monitor the sound status every 50 ms and pass the interval callback method the
    // values for startOffset, loops, and outPoint.
    this.monitorOutpointInterval = setInterval(this, "monitorOutpoint",
                                  50, startOffset, loops, outPoint);
  };

// Here is the function invoked at each interval.
Sound.prototype.monitorOutpoint = function (startOffset, loops, outPoint) {

  // If the sound's current time exceeds the outPoint, stop the sound and increment
  // the loopCount.
  if (this.position >= outPoint) {
    this.stop();
    this.loopCount++;

    // If the total number of loops is reached, stop the sound, clear the interval,
    // and invoke the callback function.
    if (this.loopCount > loops) {
      this.stop();
      clearInterval(this.monitorOutpointInterval);
      this.onStopPath[this.onStopCB]();
    } else {
      // Otherwise, restart the sound from startOffset and wait for it to reach
      // outPoint again.
      this.start(startOffset);
    }
  }
};

// Our setOnStop() method, which defines a callback function to invoke when the sound
// stops, is the same as in the previous example.
Sound.prototype.setOnStop = function (functionName, path) {
  this.onStopPath = (path == undefined) ? this.parent : path;
  this.onStopCB = functionName;
};
```

Here is an example of how to use the *playToPoint()* method:

```
#include "Sound.as"

// Create the sound.
mySound_sound = Sound.createNewSound();

// Attach a sound from the Library.
mySound_sound.attachSound("MySoundSymbol");
```

```
// Define a callback function.
function onSoundStop () {
  trace("Sound has stopped.");
}

// Play the sound from two seconds in. Loop it three times and stop the sound each
// time it reaches the out point six seconds into the sound.
mySound_sound.play(2, 3, 6000);

// Set the callback function.
mySound_sound.setOnStop("onSoundStop");
```

13.7   Pausing and Resuming a Sound

Problem

You want to pause and then resume a sound.

Solution

To pause a sound, store the sound's current position and call the *stop()* method. To resume the sound, call the *start()* method, passing it the value of the sound's stopping position. Alternatively, you can create custom *pause()* and *resume()* methods to automate this process.

Discussion

The *Sound* class does not provide built-in methods to pause and resume a sound. However, with a little bit of code, you can achieve the same result. The key is to store the sound's position property before stopping (pausing) the sound and then use that value to tell Flash at what point to resume playback.

Therefore, to pause a sound:

1. Get the value of the sound's position property and store it in a variable:

   ```
   pauseTime = mySound_sound.position;
   ```

2. Call the *stop()* method:

   ```
   mySound_sound.stop();
   ```

And when you want to resume the sound, simply do the following:

1. Convert the stored position, in milliseconds, into a starting offset, in seconds, by dividing by 1000.

2. Call the *start()* method and pass it the appropriate value for the offset:

   ```
   mySound_sound.start(pauseTime/1000);
   ```

You can automate the preceding process by creating two custom methods: *pause()* and *resume()*. Add the following code to your *Sound.as* file for easy inclusion in other projects:

```
Sound.prototype.pause = function () {
  // Get the current position and then stop the sound.
  this.pauseTime = this.position;
  this.stop();
};

Sound.prototype.resume = function () {
  // Start the sound at the point at which it was previously stopped.
  this.start(this.pauseTime/1000);
};
```

Here is an example that uses the custom *pause()* and *resume()* methods:

```
// Attach a push button from the Library. You must first drag a push button from the
// Components panel to the Stage to create the Library symbol.
this.attachMovie("FPushButtonSymbol", "myPushButton", 1);

// Create a sound holder movie clip.
this.createEmptyMovieClip("soundHolder_mc", 2);

// Create the Sound object.
mySound_sound = new Sound(soundHolder_mc);

// Attach the sound from the Library. You must have a sound with the linkage
// identifier of MySoundSymbol for this to work.
mySound_sound.attachSound("MySoundSymbol");

// Define two callback functions. One resumes the sound, and the other pauses the
// sound. When each is called, it toggles the click handler for the push button to
// the other function.
function resumeSound () {
  mySound_sound.resume();
  myPushButton.setClickHandler("pauseSound");
  myPushButton.setLabel("Pause Sound");
}

function pauseSound () {
  mySound_sound.pause();
  myPushButton.setClickHandler("resumeSound");
  myPushButton.setLabel("Resume Sound");
}

// Define the initial click handler and label for the push button.
myPushButton.setClickHandler("pauseSound");
myPushButton.setLabel("Pause Sound");

// Tell the sound to start.
mySound_sound.start();
```

13.8 Performing Actions When a Sound Ends

Problem

You want to perform certain actions when a sound finishes playing.

Solution

Define an *onSoundComplete()* method for the *Sound* object.

Discussion

The *Sound* class has a built-in event that triggers the *onSoundComplete()* method for a *Sound* object when the sound finishes playing. This is a convenient place to perform actions when the sound ends. All you need to do is define the *onSoundComplete()* method and Flash will automatically invoke it at the correct time:

```
mySound_sound.onSoundComplete = function () {
  trace("The sound has finished playing.");
};
```

The *onSoundComplete()* method is invoked only when the end of the sound is reached. It is not invoked when the sound is stopped by way of ActionScript. Also, *onSoundComplete()* is invoked only when the last loop completes, not each time the sound loops, when a sound's playback is looped.

See Also

Recipes 13.6 and 13.9

13.9 Queuing Sounds

Problem

You want to play multiple sounds in series (one after another).

Solution

Create an array of *Sound* objects and use an *onSoundComplete()* method to play the next sound in the array when the preceding sound ends.

Discussion

You can queue sounds rather easily by using an *onSoundComplete()* method to start the next sound when the preceding one finishes. The most convenient way to keep track of the order of sounds is to place the *Sound* objects in an array.

The following example creates a queue of three sounds (all songs judging by the names), which play one after another:

```
// Create an array of Sound objects. This example assume that the Sound objects
// already exist.
_global.soundQueue_array = new Array(song0_sound, song1_sound, song2_sound);

// Use a custom property to track the current sound
// element index. Initialize it to 0.
_global.soundQueue_array.currentIndex = 0;

// Define the function that we assign to the onSoundComplete() method for each of the
// Sound objects. This function starts the next sound in the array.
function startNextInQueue () {
  _global.soundQueue_array[++_global.soundQueue_array.currentIndex].start( );
}

// Assign the startNextInQueue() function as the onSoundComplete() handler for each
// of the elements of the array.
for (var i = 0; i < soundQueue_array.length; i++) {
  startNextInQueue[i].onSoundComplete = startNextInQueue;
}

// Start the first sound. The remaining sounds play after it finishes.
_global.soundQueue_array[0].start( );
```

See Also

Recipes 13.6 and 13.8

13.10 Adding Sounds to Buttons and UI Components

Problem

You want to add sounds that play when the user clicks a button or when a UI component selection is made.

Solution

Add the sound to the movie by attaching it from the Library or by loading an external MP3. Create a *Sound* object to target the sound. Then add a call to *start()* within the button's or component's handler function.

Discussion

You can use sounds in conjunction with buttons and UI components to alert the user that something has happened (i.e., a selection has been made, a button has been pressed, etc.). To accomplish this, you need to complete the following three steps:

1. Add the sound to the movie, either programmatically by attaching the sound from the Library or by loading the sound from an external MP3. If you are loading the sound, be sure to do so on a keyframe of a timeline prior to when you want to use the sound. You should make sure you give Flash enough time to download the sound.

   ```
   // Create a sound holder movie clip.
   this.createEmptyMovieClip("soundHolder_mc", 1);

   // Create the Sound object.
   click_sound = new Sound(soundHolder_mc);

   // Attach a sound from the library.
   click_sound.attachSound("MySoundSymbol");
   ```

2. Call the *Sound.start()* method from within the handler function or method for the button or UI component. For example, if you want the sound to play when a push button is clicked, place the call to *start()* inside the click handler function:

   ```
   function onClick () {
     click_sound.start();
   }

   myPushButton.setClickHandler("onClick");
   ```

   Alternatively, if you are using a standard button or a movie clip as a button, you can place the call to *start()* inside the *onPress()* or *onRelease()* event handler method:

   ```
   myButton_mc.onRelease = function () {
     _root. click_sound.start();
   };
   ```

   Or, if you are using another type of UI component, you can add the call to *start()* to the appropriate handler function. For example, you can play a sound when a selection is made in a combo box by adding the call to *start()* in the change handler function:

```
function onChange ( ) {
  click_sound.start( );
}

myComboBox.setChangeHandler("onChange");
```

If you want to play a sound when a message box opens, you cannot use this exact technique because there is no open handler function available. Instead, place the call to *start()* on the line before or after the line of code in which you open the message box. (For more information on using message boxes, see Recipe 11.15.)

```
myMessageBox._visible = true;
click_sound.start( );
```

You can use these techniques to play short sounds such as clicks or beeps when buttons are pressed or selections are made, as in the preceding snippets of code. Here is a complete example:

```
// Attach a push button from the Library. You must first drag a push button from the
// Components panel to the Stage to create the Library symbol.
this.attachMovie("FPushButtonSymbol", "myPushButton", 1);

// Create a sound holder movie clip.
this.createEmptyMovieClip("soundHolder_mc", 2);

// Create the Sound object.
click_sound = new Sound(soundHolder_mc);

// Load a sound from an external MP3. You can use this URL as long as you are playing
// the movie in the test Player or standalone Player.
click_sound.loadSound("http://www.person13.com/ascb/sounds/click.mp3");

// Define the click handler function.
function onClick ( ) {
  click_sound.start( );
}

// Set the click handler function and label for the push button.
myPushButton.setClickHandler("onClick");
myPushButton.setLabel("Click!");
```

You can also use the same technique to play longer sounds. The following example shows how you can use a push button to toggle between playing and stopping an attached sound:

```
// Attach a push button from the Library. You must first drag a push button from the
// Components panel to the Stage to create the Library symbol.
this.attachMovie("FPushButtonSymbol", "myPushButton", 1);

// Create a sound holder movie clip.
this.createEmptyMovieClip("soundHolder_mc", 2);
```

```
// Create the Sound object.
click_sound = new Sound(soundHolder_mc);

// Attach the sound from the library. You must have a sound symbol with a linkage
// identifier of MySoundSymbol for this to work.
click_sound.attachSound("MySoundSymbol");

// Create two click handler functions: one to start the sound and one to stop the
// sound. When one is called, it switches the push button's click handler and label
// so that the sound alternately plays and stops.
function startSound () {
  click_sound.start();
  myPushButton.setClickHandler("stopSound");
  myPushButton.setLabel("Stop Sound");
}

function stopSound () {
  click_sound.stop();
  myPushButton.setClickHandler("startSound");
  myPushButton.setLabel("Start Sound");
}

myPushButton.setClickHandler("startSound");
myPushButton.setLabel("Start Sound");
```

See Also

For basic information on using sounds in Flash, see Help → Using Flash → Adding Sound. Also refer to Recipes 13.2, 13.3, and 15.5.

13.11 Setting the Volume of a Sound

Problem

You want to set the volume of a sound.

Solution

Use the *setVolume()* method of the *Sound* object that controls the sound.

Discussion

You can use *Sound.setVolume()* to set the volume on a scale of 0 to 100, in which 0 is mute and 100 is the loudest:

```
mySound_sound.setVolume(50);
```

It *is* possible to set the volume beyond the range of 0 to 100. If you set the volume to less than 0, Flash converts the volume setting to its absolute value. For example, if you set the volume to –50, Flash plays the sound at 50% volume (+50). If you exceed the value of 100, the sound gets increasingly distorted. The exception to this is if you are setting the volume of a parent *Sound* object in which the nested *Sound* objects' volumes are less than 100. For example, if your nested *Sound* object has a volume of 50 and you set the parent *Sound* object to a volume of 200, the result is that the nested sound seems to play at full (100 percent) volume.

```
// Create two Sound objects. One targets the current timeline, and the other targets
// a nested timeline.
parent_sound = new Sound(this);
nested_sound = new Sound(this.soundHolder_mc);

// Attach a sound to the nested Sound object.
nested_sound.attachSound("MySoundSymbol");

// Play the nested sound.
nested_sound.start();

// Set the volume of the nested sound to 50 and the volume of the parent sound to
// 200. The result is that the nested sound seems to play at full volume.
nested_sound.setVolume(50);
parent_sound.setVolume(200);
```

Sound.setVolume() sets the volume to an absolute value. Regardless of the previous volume setting, the preceding example sets the volume to an absolute value of 50. You can use *getVolume()* in conjunction with *setVolume()* to set the volume relative to the current value.

The *getVolume()* method returns the sound's current volume level. You can add or subtract a number to or from the current value to increment or decrement the sound's volume relatively:

```
// Increment the current volume by 6.
mySound_sound.setVolume(mySound_sound.getVolume() + 6);
```

The volume value is given in percentage of perceived loudness. This means that 100 sounds twice as loud as 50.

It is also important to note that ActionScript controls only the volume of sounds within the Flash Player. It cannot control the user's system volume or speaker volume. This means that if the user has his system volume or speaker volume turned all the way down, he will not hear any sounds. There is also no way to detect the user's current system or speaker volume settings.

Because each *Sound* object targets a movie clip, there exists a parent/child relationship between *Sound* objects that corresponds to the parent/child relationship of the target movie clips. This does not mean that one *Sound* object can target another using _parent, but the volume (or panning) settings applied to a "parent" *Sound* object affect the resultant volumes (or panning) of "child" sounds. For example, if you set the volume of a *Sound* object targeting _root to 50, all nested sounds play at half their own volume settings. Therefore, you can easily adjust the volume of all sounds in your movie by creating a *Sound* object that targets _root and setting that object's volume. For example:

```
master_sound = new Sound(_root);

// Mute all sounds.
master_sound.setVolume(0);
```

See Also

Recipe 13.16

13.12 Controlling the Panning of a Sound

Problem

You want to control the panning of a sound.

Solution

Use the *setPan()* method of the *Sound* object that controls the sound.

Discussion

You can use *Sound.setPan()* to programmatically control the panning of a sound between the left and right channels. A value of −100 plays the sound entirely in the left channel, and a value of 100 plays the sound entirely in the right channel. A value of 0 plays the sound equally between the two channels.

```
// Set the panning of a sound to 100, meaning that the sound is played completely in
// the right channel and not in the left.
mySound_sound.setPan(100);
```

You can use *getPan()* in conjunction with *setPan()* to set the panning relative to its current value:

```
// Set the panning of a sound 15% to the left of the previous setting.
mySound_sound.setPan(mySound_sound.getPan( ) - 15);
```

You can use *setPan()* over time to create the effect of a sound moving from one side to the other:

```
#include "Sound.as"

mySound_sound = Sound.createNewSound( );

// Attach a sound from the Library.
mySound_sound.attachSound("MySoundSymbol");
```

```
// Start the playback of the sound.
mySound_sound.start( );

// Define a function to call on an interval.
function moveLeftToRight ( ) {

  // Get the current position and the total duration of the sound.
  var pos = mySound_sound.position;
  var dur = mySound_sound.duration;

  // Determine the panning for the current position. At the beginning of the sound,
  // the panning should be to the left, and at the end of the sound the panning
  // should be to the right.
  var pan = (pos - dur/2)/(dur/2) * 100;

  // Set the panning.
  mySound_sound.setPan(pan)
}

// Create an interval on which to call the sound panning function.
panInterval = setInterval(moveLeftToRight, 100);
```

Here's another example in which the sound's panning follows the mouse. When the mouse moves to the left, the panning moves to the left. When the mouse moves to the right, the panning moves to the right.

```
#include "Sound.as"

mySound_sound = Sound.createNewSound( );
mySound_sound.attachSound("MySoundSymbol");
mySound_sound.start( );

// Create a mouse listener object. Add a property to
// the object that references the sound.
mouseListener = new Object( );
mouseListener.snd = mySound_sound;

// Define an onMouseMove( ) method for the listener so that it is called every time
// the mouse moves.
mouseListener.onMouseMove = function ( ) {
  // Set the panning of the sound so that it follows the mouse.
  var x = _root._xmouse;
  var w = Stage.width;
  this.snd.setPan((x - w/2)/(w/2) * 100);
};

// Add the listener to the Mouse object.
Mouse.addListener(mouseListener);
```

See Also

Recipe 13.13

13.13 Creating Advanced Stereo Panning Effects

Problem

You want to be able to modify the panning of both the right and left channels of a stereo sound.

Solution

Use the *setTransform()* method.

Discussion

When working with monaural sounds, the basic *getPan()* and *setPan()* methods suffice. However, when dealing with stereo sounds, you can use the *getTransform()* and *setTransform()* methods to control the panning of each channel.

The *setTransform()* method takes a single parameter: a sound transform object. You can create a sound transform object by creating a generic instance of the *Object* class with the following properties:

ll   Percentage of the left channel playing through the left speaker

lr   Percentage of the left channel playing through the right speaker

rl   Percentage of the right channel playing through the left speaker

rr   Percentage of the right channel playing through the right speaker

Here is an example in which the right channel is played through the left speaker and the left channel is played through the right speaker:

```
soundTransform = {ll: 0, lr: 100, rl: 100, rr: 0};
mySound_sound.setTransform(soundTransform);
```

You can also use *getTransform()* in conjunction with *setTransform()* to perform changes relative to the current settings:

```
// Get the current transform object.
soundTransform = mySound_sound.getTransform( );

// Add 50 to the current ll property.
soundTransform.ll += 50;

// Set the new transform object.
mySound_sound.setTransform(soundTransform);
```

See Also

Recipe 13.12

13.14 Fading In a Sound

Problem

You want to fade in a sound from the beginning of playback over a span of a number of milliseconds.

Solution

Create and invoke a custom *fadeIn()* method.

Discussion

Although there is no built-in method for fading in sounds, you can create a custom method for the *Sound* class to handle this task. Our custom *fadeIn()* method, shown in the following code, accomplishes this by using an *onEnterFrame()* event handler method to monitor the position of the sound's playback and to set the volume accordingly. The *fadeIn()* method requires that the *Sound* object is created using our custom *createNewSound()* method from Recipe 13.1 because it uses the sound holder movie clip.

The *fadeIn()* method accepts up to six parameters:

millis
> The number of milliseconds over which the sound should fade in

minVol
> The volume percentage from which the sound should start to fade (defaults to the current volume or 0 if the current volume is 100)

maxVol
> The volume percentage at which the sound fade should end (defaults to 100)

startFadeTime
> The number of milliseconds from the beginning of the sound at which to begin the fade (defaults to 0)

startSound
> A Boolean value that indicates whether to start the playback of the sound automatically

startPlayOffset
> The number of milliseconds from the beginning of the sound at which to begin playback

Add the following custom *fadeIn()* method to an external *Sound.as* file for easy inclusion in other projects:

```
Sound.prototype.fadeIn = function (millis, minVol, maxVol, startFadeTime,
                                   startSound, startPlayOffset) {
```

```
  // If the sound is already at 100% volume, set the volume to 0. That is, because
  // sounds default to 100% volume, we want to fade from 0 (unless minVol specifies
  // otherwise). By default, if the volume is not already 100%, fade up from the
  // current volume.
  if (this.getVolume() == 100) {
    this.setVolume(0);
  }

  minVol = (minVol == undefined) ? this.getVolume() : minVol;
  maxVol = (maxVol == undefined) ? 100 : maxVol;
  startFadeTime = (startFadeTime == undefined) ? 0 : startFadeTime;

  // If startSound is true, start the playback of the sound.
  if (startSound) {
    this.start(startPlayOffset/1000);
  }

  // Invoke the custom monitorFadeIn() method every 100 ms. Pass it the parameters
  // needed to make the sound fade calculations.
  this.monitorFadeInInterval = setInterval(this, "monitorFadeIn",
                     100, millis, minVol, maxVol, startFadeTime);
};

// Invoke this function periodically to monitor the sound fade.
Sound.prototype.monitorFadeIn = function (fadeInMillis, minVol, maxVol,
                                 startFadeTime) {
  // Once the fade-in time is exceeded, make sure the maximum volume is reached and
  // clear the interval to end the fade.
  var pos = this.position;
  if (pos > fadeInMillis + startFadeTime) {

    // Make sure the volume is set to maximum before terminating the fade.
    this.setVolume(maxVol);
    clearInterval(this.monitorFadeInInterval);

    // Call the onFadeInStop() callback function if one is defined.
    this.onFadeInStopPath[this.onFadeInStopCB]();
  }

  // Set the volume based on the current sound position, fading from minVol to maxVol
  // over the specified time duration. Make sure the volume doesn't exceed maxVol
  // accidentally.
  var volumePercent = Math.min(minVol + (pos - startFadeTime) / fadeInMillis *
                     (maxVol - minVol), maxVol);
  volumePercent = (volumePercent < 0) ? 0 : volumePercent;

  // Set the volume of the sound repeatedly to simulate a sound fade.
  this.setVolume(volumePercent);
};

// The setOnFadeInStop() method allows you to define a callback function to invoke
// when the sound finishing fading in. The parameters are a string specifying the
// function name and an optional path to the function. If path is undefined, the
```

```
// Sound object's parent property is used instead. The parent property is defined
// only if you use the custom createNewSound() method to create the sound.
Sound.prototype.setOnFadeInStop = function (functionName, path) {
  this.onFadeInStopPath = (path == undefined) ? this.parent : path;
  this.onFadeInStopCB = functionName;
};
```

Once defined, the *fadeIn()* method can be used to fade in any sound created using our custom *createNewSound()* method. You can use the *fadeIn()* method with sounds that were not created using the *createNewSound()* method, as long as you add a property named mc that is a reference to an empty movie clip. Also, notice that we've created a way to define a callback function for when the fade in stops (reaches the maximum volume).

Here is an example of how to use the *fadeIn()* method. Notice that the sound begins playback only if you start the sound with the *start()* method or pass the *fadeIn()* method a value of true for the startSound parameter.

```
#include "Sound.as"

mySound_sound = Sound.createNewSound( );

// Attach a sound from the Library.
mySound_sound.attachSound("MySoundSymbol");

// Tell the sound to fade in over 5,000 milliseconds (5 seconds), starting from zero
// volume and going to 100%. Also, start the playback of the sound at three seconds
// into the sound and begin the fade at six seconds in.
mySound_sound.fadeIn(10000, 0, 100, 6000, true, 3000);
```

Optionally, you can also define a callback function for the fade in:

```
function onFadeInStop () {
  trace("Sounded has faded in.");
}

mySound_sound.setOnFadeInStop("onFadeInStop");
```

See Also

Recipe 13.15

13.15 Fading Out a Sound

Problem

You want to fade out a sound over a span of a number of milliseconds.

Solution

Create and invoke a *fadeOut()* method.

Discussion

As with fading in a sound, there is no built-in functionality for fading out a sound. However, you can create a custom *fadeOut()* method to handle this task. Our custom *fadeOut()* method is slightly longer than the *fadeIn()* method, but it utilizes similar logic. In addition, the *fadeOut()* method allows you to use two callback functions: one that is called when the sound begins to fade out, and another that is called when the fade out has completed. This can be useful in situations in which you want a particular action or actions to occur when the fade out begins and/or ends. For example, you may want to begin the playback of a second sound when the first begins to fade out. As the second sound fades in, you achieve a cross-fade effect.

As with the *fadeIn()* method, the *fadeOut()* method works only with sounds that are created using our custom *createNewSound()* method.

The *fadeOut()* method accepts up to five parameters:

millis
> The number of milliseconds over which the sound should fade out.

minVol
> The volume percentage to which the sound should fade (default is 0).

maxVol
> The volume percentage from which the sound should start fading (default is current volume).

startTime
> The point (in milliseconds) in the sound that the fade out should begin. If no value is specified, the fade out begins *millis* milliseconds before the end of the sound (so that it completes when the sound ends).

stopSound
> A Boolean indicating whether the sound should stop when the fade is done (default is false).

Add the following custom *fadeOut()* method to your external *Sound.as* file for easy inclusion in other projects:

```
Sound.prototype.fadeOut = function (millis, minVol, maxVol, startTime, stopSound) {

    // If startTime is undefined, fade the sound out at the very end.
    startFadePos = (startTime == undefined) ? this.duration - millis : startTime;

    minVol = (minVol == undefined) ? 0 : minVol;
    maxVol = (maxVol == undefined) ? this.getVolume( ) : maxVol;
```

```
// The madeCallback property is initialized to false. This property is set to true
// when the fade-out-start callback function has been invoked. It ensures that the
// callback is called once and only once, when the fade out begins.
this.madeCallback = false;

// Invoke the custom monitorFadeOut() method every 100 milliseconds.
this.monitorFadeOutInterval = setInterval(this, "monitorFadeOut", 100, millis,
                                         startFadePos, minVol, maxVol, stopSound);
};

Sound.prototype.monitorFadeOut = function (fadeOutMillis, startFadePos, minVol,
                                           maxVol, stopSound) {
    var pos = this.position;
    var dur = this.duration;

    // Execute the fade out once the desired point in the sound is reached.
    if (pos >= startFadePos) {

        // Call the fade-out-start callback function if it has not been called yet.
        if (!this.madeCallback) {
            this.madeCallback = true;
            this.onFadeOutStartPath[this.onFadeOutStartCB]();
        }

        // If the ending fade out position has been reached, clear the interval so as
        // not to needlessly monitor the sound anymore.
        if (pos >= dur || pos >= startFadePos + fadeOutMillis) {

            // Make sure the volume is set to the minVol before terminating the fade.
            this.setVolume(minVol);
            clearInterval(this.monitorFadeOutInterval);
        }

        // Set the volume based on the current sound position, fading to minVol over the
        // specified time span. The fade occurs relative to maxVol.
        var volumePercent = ((startFadePos + fadeOutMillis) - pos) /
                            fadeOutMillis * maxVol;

        // If the volume reaches minVol, call the fade-out-stop callback, clear the
        // interval, and, if appropriate, stop the sound.
        if (volumePercent <= minVol) {
            volumePercent = minVol;
            this.onFadeOutStopPath[this.onFadeOutStopCB]();
            clearInterval(this.monitorFadeOutInterval);
            if (stopSound) {
                this.stop();
            }
        }

        // Set the volume of the sound.
        this.setVolume(volumePercent);
    }
};
```

```
// The setOnFadeOutStop() and setOnFadeOutStart() methods allow you to define
// callback functions to invoke when the fade starts and stops. The parameters are a
// string specifying the function name and an optional path to the function. If path
// is undefined, the Sound object's parent property is used instead. The parent
// property is defined only if you use the custom createNewSound() method to create
// the sound.
Sound.prototype.setOnFadeOutStop = function (functionName, path) {
  this.onFadeOutStopPath = (path == undefined) ? this.parent : path;
  this.onFadeOutStopCB = functionName;
};

Sound.prototype.setOnFadeOutStart = function (functionName, path) {
  this.onFadeOutStartPath = (path == undefined) ? this.parent : path;
  this.onFadeOutStartCB = functionName;
};
```

You can use the *fadeOut()* method to fade out any sound created using our custom *createNewSound()* method. Note that the *fadeOut()* method merely queues the sound to fade. You must start the sound using *Sound.start()*.

```
#include "Sound.as"

mySound_sound = Sound.createNewSound();

// Attach a sound from the Library.
mySound_sound.attachSound("MySoundSymbol");

// Fade out the sound over 5,000 milliseconds (5 seconds) at the end of the sound.
mySound_sound.fadeOut(5000);

// Start the playback of the sound.
mySound_sound.start();
```

The preceding example does not use the callback functions. Here is an example that uses callbacks, which will be notified when the sound fade out begins and ends:

```
#include "Sound.as"

mySound_sound = Sound.createNewSound();

mySound_sound.attachSound("MySoundSymbol");

// Tell the sound to fade out over 5000 milliseconds (5 seconds) starting when the
// sound's playback position is at 20,000 milliseconds (20 seconds).
mySound_sound.fadeOut(5000, 0, 100, 20000);

// Define callback functions.
function doWhenFadeOutStart() {
  trace("Sound fade out has begun");
}

function doWhenFadeOutStop() {
  trace("Sound fade out has completed");
}
```

```
// Set the callback functions for the sound.
mySound_sound.setOnFadeOutStart("doWhenFadeOutStart");
mySound_sound.setOnFadeOutStop("doWhenFadeOutStop");

// Start the playback of the sound.
mySound_sound.start( );
```

See Also

Recipe 13.14

13.16 Program: A Sound Controller Component

This example program implements a sound controller component that creates a controller for the playback of sounds. The entire component is created using Action-Script, including the drawing of the buttons and sliders.

In this example, you'll learn how to create, package, install, and use the component.

To create the component, do the following:

1. Open a new Flash document and save it as *Sound Controller.fla*. Normally, it is not good practice to include spaces in the names of your Flash documents. However, components that are installed using the Extensions Manager show up in the Components panel under a menu selection with the same name as the *.fla* from which the components were installed. So we want to use a readable, user-friendly name.

2. Create a new movie clip symbol named *Slider*. This movie clip will be a component used by the sound controller component. It creates a slider controller.

3. Although it is usually considered a best practice not to attach code directly to a symbol, creating a reusable component mandates an exception to the rule. Therefore, attach the following code directly to the first frame of the *Slider* symbol:

   ```
   #initclip

   // Include the .as files for getNewDepth( ), drawRectangle( ), and drawCircle( ).
   // MoveClip.as is from Chapter 7, and DrawingMethods.as is from Chapter 4.
   #include "MovieClip.as"
   #include "DrawingMethods.as"

   // The constructor does not need to do anything, but it does need to exist.
   function SliderClass( ) {}

   // The SliderClass class is a subclass of MovieClip.
   SliderClass.prototype = new MovieClip( );
   ```

```
/*
  The create() method draws the slider and adds its functionality.
  Parameters:
    size - The length of the slider in pixels
    fill - true applies a fill to the slider and false does not
    fillColor - A color for the fill, in 0xRRGGBB format (applies if fill is
                true)
    horizontal - true creates a horizontal slider (otherwise vertical)
*/
SliderClass.prototype.create = function (size, fill, fillColor, horizontal) {

  this.size = size;

  // Create the track_mc movie clip to act as the path along which the slider can
  // be moved. Draw a rectangle at the specified size (minus two because the
  // drawing API adds on a pixel at either end).
  this.createEmptyMovieClip("track_mc", this.getNewDepth());
  this.track_mc.lineStyle(1, 0x000000, 100);
  this.track_mc.drawRectangle(size - 2, 3, 0, 0, size/2);

  // If fill is true, create a trackFill_mc movie clip and draw a filled
  // rectangle, filled with the color specified by fillColor.
  if (fill) {
    this.createEmptyMovieClip("trackFill_mc", this.getNewDepth());
    this.trackFill_mc.lineStyle(0, 0x000000, 0);
    this.trackFill_mc.beginFill(fillColor, 100);
    this.trackFill_mc.drawRectangle(size - 2, 3, 0, 0, size/2);
    this.trackFill_mc.endFill();
  }

  // Create a thumbSlide_mc clip to be moved by the user along the track_mc clip.
  // Use built-in and custom drawing methods to create a white circle.
  this.createEmptyMovieClip("thumbSlide_mc", this.getNewDepth());
  this.thumbSlide_mc.lineStyle(1, 0x000000, 100);
  this.thumbSlide_mc.beginFill(0xFFFFFF, 100);
  this.thumbSlide_mc.drawCircle(5);
  this.thumbSlide_mc.endFill();

  // Allow the thumbSlide_mc clip to be dragged between 0 and the size of the
  // track while the mouse is depressed.
  this.thumbSlide_mc.onPress = function () {
    this._parent.isDragging = true;
    this.startDrag(false, 0, 0, this._parent.size, 0);
  };

  this.thumbSlide_mc.onRelease = function () {
    this._parent.isDragging = false;
    this.stopDrag();

    // Search for and invoke a function, on the same timeline as the slider
    // instance, with the name that was passed to the setOnRelease() method.
    this._parent._parent[this.onReleaseFunctionName]();
  };
```

```
    // If horizontal is not true, rotate the clip to the vertical.
    if (!horizontal) {
      this._rotation = -90;
    }
};

    // The setOnReleaes() method allows for a callback function
    // to be automatically called when the thumb slide is released.
    // The method is passed a function name as a string. The function
    // must reside on the same timeline as the slider instance.
    SliderClass.prototype.setOnRelease = function (functionName) {
      this.thumbSlide_mc.onReleaseFunctionName = functionName;
    };

    // Set the position of the thumb slide from 0 to 100%.
    SliderClass.prototype.setPosition = function (percent) {
      this.thumbSlide_mc._x = (this.size * percent) / 100;
    };

    // Get the percentage (0 to 100) to which the
    // current thumb slide position corresponds.
    SliderClass.prototype.getPercent = function () {
      return (this.thumbSlide_mc._x / this.size) * 100;
    };

    // Register the class to the linkage identifier name of SliderSymbol.
    Object.registerClass("SliderSymbol", SliderClass);

    #endinitclip
```

4. Open the Linkage properties of the *Slider* symbol using the Library panel's pop-up Options menu. Select the Export for ActionScript and Export in First Frame checkboxes and specify a symbol linkage identifier of *SliderSymbol*. Click OK.

5. Create a new Font symbol by choosing New Font from the Library panel's pop-up Options menu.

6. In the Font Symbol Properties dialog box, enter Verdana in the Name field and choose Verdana from the drop-down Font list. Leave the checkboxes unchecked. Click OK.

7. Select the Verdana font symbol in the Library and open its linkage properties, again using the Library panel's pop-up Options menu. Select the Export for ActionScript and Export in First Frame checkboxes and specify a symbol linkage identifier of *VerdanaFontSymbol*. Click OK.

8. Create a new movie clip symbol named *Sound Controller* using Insert → New Symbol. This is the main sound controller component.

9. Again, following the recommended approach to create reusable components, edit the *Sound Controller* symbol and attach the following code directly to its first frame:

```
#initclip

// Include the custom Table class from Chapter 11 and the custom Date class
// methods from Chapter 10.
#include "Table.as"
#include "Date.as"

// The SoundControllerClass constructor
function SoundControllerClass( ) {

    // The creation of the buttons, sliders, and text fields is divided among three
    // methods that are defined later in this class. Call these methods here to
    // create the controller elements.
    this.createButtons( );
    this.createSliders( );
    this.createTextFields( );

    // Create a table that positions the elements of the controller using custom
    // methods from our Table class, which is defined in Chapter 11.
    var tc0 = new TableColumn(5, this.rwBtn);
    var tc1 = new TableColumn(5, this.playBtn);
    var tc2 = new TableColumn(5, this.pauseBtn);
    var tc3 = new TableColumn(5, this.ffBtn);
    var tc4 = new TableColumn(5, this.volumeBtn);
    var tc5 = new TableColumn(5, this.positionSlider);
    var tr0 = new TableRow(2, tc0, tc1, tc2, tc3, tc4, tc5);
    var t = new Table(5, tc0._width/2, this.volumeSlider._height, tr0);

    // The volumeSlider and time elements overlay other parts of the controller, so
    // they must be positioned without the use of the table.
    this.volumeSlider._x = this.volumeBtn._x;
    this.volumeSlider._y = this.volumeBtn._y;
    this.time._y += this.positionSlider._y;
    this.time._x = this.positionSlider._x + (this.positionSlider._width/2) -
                 (this.time._width/2);
}

// The SoundControllerClass class is a subclass of MovieClip.
SoundControllerClass.prototype = new MovieClip( );

SoundControllerClass.prototype.createButtons = function ( ) {

    // The makeButton( ) method is defined later in this class. It creates a movie
    // clip of the specified name to use as a button. "Btn" is appended to the
    // specified name, so the first clip created here is named rwBtn.
    this.makeButton("rw");
    this.makeButton("play");
    this.makeButton("pause");
    this.makeButton("ff");
    this.makeButton("volume");
```

```
// When the play button is clicked, call the controller's start( ) method.
this.playBtn.onRelease = function ( ) {
  this._parent.start( );
};

// When the pause button is clicked, call the stop( ) method of the Sound
// object that the controller targets.
this.pauseBtn.onRelease = function ( ) {
  this._parent.snd.stop( );
};

// The fast-forward and rewind buttons work similarly. When they are pressed,
// an interval is defined that continually increments or decrements the
// currentPosition property of the controller and then tells the controller to
// begin playing the sound. This creates a fast-forward or rewind effect. When
// the buttons are released, the interval is deleted to stop the action.
this.ffBtn.onPress = function ( ) {
  this.ffInterval = setInterval(this._parent, "fastForward", 100);
};
this.ffBtn.onRelease = function ( ) {
  clearInterval(this.ffInterval);
};
this.rwBtn.onPress = function ( ) {
  this.rwInterval = setInterval(this._parent, "rewind", 100);
};
this.rwBtn.onRelease = function ( ) {
  clearInterval(this.rwInterval);
};
};

SoundControllerClass.prototype.fastForward = function ( ) {
// Fast-forward 500 milliseconds at a time
this.currentPosition += 500;
this.start( );
};

SoundControllerClass.prototype.rewind = function ( ) {
// Rewind 500 milliseconds at a time
this.currentPosition -= 500;
this.start( );
};

SoundControllerClass.prototype.createSliders = function ( ) {

// Create an instance of the slider component to control the volume. This
// slider is 75 pixels high, and the initial volume position is 100%.
this.attachMovie("SliderSymbol", "volumeSlider", this.getNewDepth( ));
this.volumeSlider.create(75);
this.volumeSlider.setPosition(100);

// The volume slider is invisible until the volume button is pressed.
this.volumeSlider._visible = false;
```

```
// When the volume button is pressed, make the button semi-transparent and make
// the volume slider visible.
this.volumeBtn.onPress = function () {
  this._alpha = 42;
  this._parent.volumeSlider._visible = true;
};

// Set the onRelease callback for the volume slider to the volumeOnRelease()
// method defined within this class.
this.volumeSlider.setOnRelease("volumeOnRelease");

// Create the position slider. This slider controls the playback of the sound.
// Make the slider 150 pixels wide and give it a blue fill, which is used to
// display the load progress when a sound is loaded from an external MP3.
this.attachMovie("SliderSymbol", "positionSlider", this.getNewDepth());
this.positionSlider.create(150, true, 0x0000FF, true);

// Set the onRelease callback for the volume slider to the positionOnRelease()
// method defined within this class.
this.positionSlider.setOnRelease("positionOnRelease");
};

// This method is called automatically when the volume slider is released. It
// sets the volume slider to be invisible, makes the volume button fully opaque,
// and sets the volume of the sound appropriately.
SoundControllerClass.prototype.volumeOnRelease = function () {
  this.volumeSlider._visible = false;
  this.volumeBtn._alpha = 100;
  this.snd.setVolume(this.volumeSlider.getPercent());
};

// This method is called automatically when the position slider is released. It
// sets the current position within the sound based on the slider position.
SoundControllerClass.prototype.positionOnRelease = function () {
  this.moveSoundPosition(this.positionSlider.getPercent()/100);
};

SoundControllerClass.prototype.createTextFields = function () {

  // This creates a text field to contain the time value for the sound in the
  // format of "current position/total duration". For the sound controller to be
  // semi-transparent, the text field must use an embedded font.
  this.createAutoTextField("time", this.getNewDepth(), 0, 0, 0, 0);
  var tf = new TextFormat();
  tf.font = "VerdanaFontSymbol";
  tf.size = 9;
  this.time.embedFonts = true;
  this.time.setNewTextFormat(tf);
  this.time.text = "00:00 / 00:00";
  this.time.selectable = false;
};

// This method starts the sound.
SoundControllerClass.prototype.start = function () {
```

```
  // If the sound is already playing, stop it.
  this.snd.stop();

  // Start the sound at the position that is currently stored in the controller.
  // This enables a sound to be paused and then started again from the same
  // position. Sound.start() accepts the start position in seconds, but the
  // current position is stored in milliseconds, so divide by 1000.
  this.snd.start(this.currentPosition/1000);

  // Call the monitorPosition() method (defined later in this class) to begin
  // watching the position of the sound.
  this.monitorPosition();
};

// This method stops a sound, as opposed to just pausing it. It stops the sound
// from playing, stops monitoring the sound position, and resets the current
// position to 0.
SoundControllerClass.prototype.stop = function () {
  this.snd.stop();
  clearInterval(this.monitorPositionInterval);
  this.currentPosition = 0;
};

// The moveSoundPosition() method starts playing a sound at a new point
// determined by ratio, which should be between 0 and 1.
SoundControllerClass.prototype.moveSoundPosition = function (ratio) {
  this.snd.stop();
  this.snd.start((ratio * this.snd.duration)/ 1000);
};

// The setTarget() method sets the sound to be controlled by the component. If
// autoPlay is true, the sound plays automatically once it is loaded.
SoundControllerClass.prototype.setTarget = function (snd, autoPlay) {
  this.snd = snd;

  // If the sound is loaded and autoPlay is true, start the sound.
  // Otherwise, if the sound is not loaded, call monitorLoad()
  // to watch the sound until it is loaded.
  if (snd.isLoaded && autoPlay) {
    this.start();
  } else if (!snd.isLoaded) {
    this.monitorLoad(autoPlay);
  }
};

// The setPositionSlider() method sets the position of the slider to correspond
// to the position of the playback of the sound.
SoundControllerClass.prototype.setPositionSlider = function () {

  // If the slider is not being dragged, set _x of the position slider's slide.
  if (!this.positionSlider.isDragging) {
    var positionRatio = this.snd.position / this.snd.duration;
    this.positionSlider.slide._x = positionRatio * this.positionSlider.size;
  }
};
```

```
// Monitor the sound position, and update the position slider and time display.
SoundControllerClass.prototype.monitorPosition = function () {
  this.monitorPositionInterval = setInterval(this,
                                    "monitorPositionActions", 100);
};

SoundControllerClass.prototype.monitorPositionActions = function () {
  var pos = this.snd.position;
  var dur = this.snd.duration;

  // Set the time display.
  this.time.text = Date.formatMilliseconds(pos) + " / " +
                 Date.formatMilliseconds(dur);

  // Set the currentPosition property of the sound controller and set the
  // position of the position slider.
  this.currentPosition = pos;
  this.setPositionSlider();

  // If the position is greater than or equal to the duration of the sound, set
  // the current position back to 0.
  if (pos >= dur) {
    this._parent.currentPosition = 0;
    this.positionSlider.setPosition (0);
  }
};

// The monitorLoad() method monitors the load progress of a
// sound loaded from an external MP3.
SoundControllerClass.prototype.monitorLoad = function (autoPlay) {
  this.autoPlay = autoPlay;
  this.monitorLoadInterval = setInterval(this, "monitorLoadActions", 100);
};

SoundControllerClass.prototype.monitorLoadActions = function () {

  var pLded = this.snd.percentLoaded;

  // Display the percentage of the sound that has loaded using a fill.
  this.positionSlider.trackFill_mc._xscale = pLded;

  // Once the sound finishes loading, play it if autoPlay is true.
  if (this.snd.isLoaded) {
    if (this.autoPlay) {
      this.start();
    }
    clearInterval(this.monitorLoadInterval);
  }
};

// The makeButton() method is attached to the MovieClip class so that it can be
// called from a movie clip such as the sound controller. It automatically
// generates a new movie clip of the name nameBtn.
MovieClip.prototype.makeButton = function (name) {
  this.createEmptyMovieClip(name + "Btn", this.getNewDepth());
```

```
// The button is composed of two parts: a circle created with drawButton() and
// a symbol, such as an arrow, created with drawSymbol().
this[name + "Btn"].drawButton();
this[name + "Btn"].drawSymbol(name);
};

// The drawButton() method draws a filled and outlined circle within a clip.
MovieClip.prototype.drawButton = function () {
  this.createEmptyMovieClip("btn", this.getNewDepth());
  this.btn.lineStyle(0, 0x000000, 100);
  this.btn.beginFill(0xFFFFFF, 100);
  this.btn.drawCircle(10);
  this.btn.endFill();
};

// The drawSymbol() method draws the requested shape within a clip.
MovieClip.prototype.drawSymbol = function (shape) {
  this.createEmptyMovieClip("symbol", this.getNewDepth());
  this.symbol.lineStyle(0, 0x000000, 100);
  this.symbol.beginFill(0x000000, 100);

  // Use a switch statement to determine the shape to draw (play, rewind, etc.).
  switch (shape) {
    case "play":
      this.symbol.drawTriangle(10, 10, 60);
      this.symbol.endFill();
      this.symbol._rotation = 30;
      break;
    case "pause":
      this.symbol.drawRectangle(9, 3);
      this.symbol.drawRectangle(9, 3, 0, 0, 0, 6);
      this.symbol.endFill();
      this.symbol._rotation = 90;
      this.symbol._x += 3;
      break;
    case "ff":
      this.symbol.drawTriangle(7, 7, 60, 30);
      this.symbol.drawTriangle(7, 7, 60, 30, 6);
      this.symbol.endFill();
      this.symbol._rotation = 180;
      this.symbol._x += 3;
      break;
    case "rw":
      this.symbol.drawTriangle(7, 7, 60, 30);
      this.symbol.drawTriangle(7, 7, 60, 30, 6);
      this.symbol.endFill();
      this.symbol._x -= 3;
      break;
    case "volume":
      this.symbol.drawrectangle(3, 5);
      this.symbol.drawTriangle(9, 9, 60, 30, 4);
      this.symbol.endFill();
      this.symbol.moveTo(8, 3);
      this.symbol.curveTo(10, 0, 8, -3);
```

```
            this.symbol.moveTo(8, 6);
            this.symbol.curveTo(15, 0, 8, -6);
            this.symbol._x -= 5;
        }
    this.symbol.endFill();
    };

    Object.registerClass("SoundControllerSymbol", SoundControllerClass);

    #endinitclip
```

10. Drag an instance of the *Slider* symbol onto the Stage within the *Sound Controller* component symbol. The *Slider* symbol is never used, and it does not have a visual appearance within the component. The purpose of this is to establish a nested relationship between the two symbols so that when the *Sound Controller* component is copied into a movie's Library, the *Slider* symbol is as well.

11. Open the Linkage properties of the *Sound Controller* symbol using the Library panel's pop-up Options menu. Select the Export for ActionScript and Export in First Frame checkboxes and specify a symbol linkage identifier of *SoundControllerSymbol*. Click OK.

12. Select the *Sound Controller* symbol in the Library and choose Component Definition from the pop-up Options menu. Select the Display in Components Panel checkbox and click OK.

13. Save the *Sound Controller.fla* document and close it.

14. Open a new text document and add the following code to it:

```
<macromedia-extension name="Sound Controller Component" version="1.0.0"
  type="flash component">
  <description>
    <![CDATA[The sound controller component]]>
  </description>
  <ui-access>
    <![CDATA[This component is installed in the Components panel]]>
  </ui-access>
  <author name="Your Name" />
  <products>
    <product name="Flash" version="6" required="true" />
  </products>
  <files>
    <file source="Sound Controller.fla" destination="$flash/components/" />
  </files>
</macromedia-extension>
```

15. Save this document as *soundController.mxi* in the same directory as the *Sound Controller.fla* document.

16. Open the Macromedia Extensions Manager (using Help → Manage Extensions) and choose the Package Extension option from the Extension Manager's File menu.

17. Browse to and select the *soundController.mxi* document in the window that appears. Click OK.

18. Save the package as *soundController.mxp*.

19. Once you have successfully completed the packaging of the component, choose Install Extension from the Extension Manager's File menu, and choose the *soundController.mxp* file as the package to install.

20. The component should successfully install. Once this is done, close Flash if it is open.

21. Open Flash, and open a new document within the application.

22. Open the Components panel and select Sound Controller from the drop-down menu.

23. Copy an instance of the Sound Controller component into the new Flash movie's Library by dragging an instance onto the Stage (after doing so, you can delete the instance from the Stage).

24. Open the Library and make sure it shows three symbols: Sound Controller, Slider, and Verdana.

25. On the first frame of the main timeline, add the following code:

```
#include "Sound.as"

// Create the new Sound object and load a sound into it from an external source.
// (See Recipe 15.5 for more information about loading external MP3s.) Replace
// urlToMp3 with a valid URL to an MP3 for the sound controller to play.
mySound_sound = Sound.createNewSound( );
mySound_sound.loadSound(urlToMp3);

// Create an instance of the sound controller and set its target to mySound_sound
// with autoPlay set to true.
_root.attachMovie("SoundControllerSymbol", "sc", 1);
sc.setTarget(mySound_sound, true);
```

See Also

Recipe 15.5 and Chapter 26

## PART II

Remote Recipes

## CHAPTER 14

FlashCom Server

14.0 Introduction

Flash Communication Server MX (FlashCom) is a technology that enables your Flash movies (which are referred to as *clients* in the context of FlashCom) to communicate in real time with the server. FlashCom enables clients to communicate using text-based commands and enables Flash clients to record, stream live, and play back video and audio. The applications of using FlashCom are vast. You can:

- Create text-based chat rooms
- Create video conferencing applications
- Broadcast live events, conferences, and seminars, and archive the audio and video streams for future playback
- Create interactive education systems

This chapter addresses many problems specific to publishing and subscribing to audio and video content. Additionally, we'll take a look at the server-side aspects of FlashCom. See Recipes 16.6, 17.5, and 17.6 for applications using FlashCom remote shared objects.

Here is some of the terminology used throughout this chapter. Note that our conventions are not used universally by the developer community.

Stream
> A *stream* is used to control the flow of data—be it text, audio, video, or other media—to, from, and within a Flash movie. A *net stream*, which takes its name from ActionScript's *NetStream* class, is any audio or video content that is sent to a FlashCom server from the client (publishing stream) or from the server to the client (subscribing stream).

FlashCom

> We use the term *FlashCom* to refer to the software that enables realtime communication (including the server software and the client components), or as an adjective to modify other words, as in "FlashCom audio" or "FlashCom application."

FlashCom server

> The term *FlashCom server* refers to the computer running FlashCom or the address at which such a device can be found.

Full coverage of FlashCom is beyond the scope of this book. For basic information about FlashCom, refer to the list of online documentation at:

> *http://www.macromedia.com/support/flashcom/documentation.html*

For a list of online articles, tutorials, and more, see:

> *http://www.macromedia.com/support/flashcom/tutorial_index.html*

Macromedia has a free developer edition of FlashCom to get you started. You can download the software from:

> *http://www.macromedia.com/software/flashcom/*

14.1   Creating a New FlashCom Application

Problem

You want to create a new FlashCom application.

Solution

Create a new subdirectory in the FlashCom server's *applications* directory, which automatically creates a FlashCom application of the same name.

Discussion

To create a new FlashCom application you need to create a new subdirectory (officially called a *registered application directory*) within the FlashCom server's *applications* directory. Of course, a complete, working application requires additional elements, such as one or more Flash movies, but creating the application's subdirectory is the first step.

As of FlashCom version 1.5, the default location of the *applications* directory is *Program Files\Macromedia\Flash Communication Server MX\applications* in a Windows environment and */opt/macromedia/fcs/applications/* in Linux. The name of the new FlashCom application is automatically determined by the name you give the new subdirectory you create. This is also the name you use to connect Flash to the intended FlashCom application. For example, you can create a new FlashCom application named *myNewApplication* by creating a new subdirectory called *myNewApplication* within the FlashCom server's *applications* directory.

See Also

Once you have created the new FlashCom application, you need to connect to an instance of that application. The connection is initiated by the client-side Flash movie, as discussed in Recipe 14.2. For an example of a full-blown FlashCom server application, see the video chat application implemented in Chapter 24.

14.2   Connecting to the FlashCom Server

Problem

You want to connect to a FlashCom server application.

Solution

nection object and invoke the *connect()* method from it. To detect ...tus, add an *onStatus()* method to the *NetConnection* object.

...on class enables you to connect your Flash movies to a FlashCom ...n. You first need to create a *NetConnection* object and then invoke ...thod from that instance. The *connect()* method requires the Univer- ...entifier (URI) to the FlashCom server application to which you wish to connect.

```
// Create the NetConnection object.
myConnection = new NetConnection( );

// Call the connect( ) method to connect to an application named myApplication, where
// the FlashCom server is on the same machine as the .swf file.
myConnection.connect("rtmp:/myApplication/");
```

The URI must always be in one of two formats (the items in brackets are optional):

```
rtmp://host[:port]/applicationName[/instanceName]
```

or:

```
rtmp:[:port]/applicationName[/instanceName]
```

You should use the first URI format when the FlashCom server and the *.swf* file are not on the same machine (as is the case in most production environments). The second URI format is acceptable when the FlashCom server and the *.swf* file are on the same machine (which is typically the case in a development environment). In either case, you need to supply the port number only if the FlashCom server is running on a port other than the default FlashCom port (1935). The *applicationName* portion of a URI must match the name of a subdirectory in the FlashCom *applications* directory (see Recipe 14.1). Finally, the optional *instanceName* allows you to create unique instances of an application. Each instance shares the common functionality of the application but manages clients and other values separately. The common example is that of a chat room application in which all rooms share the same basic functionality of the main application, but each room (instance) has its own list of users (clients). If you don't specify an instance name, then your Flash movie will connect to the default instance, _definst_.

Here's an example of a URI for an application named *myVideoChatApp* that resides on *www.myflashcomsever.com*. The server is running FlashCom on the default port, so there is no need to specify the port. Notice that when you specify a URI that includes the host portion, you must follow *rtmp:* with two forward slashes (//).

```
rtmp://www.myflashcomserver.com/myVideoChatApp
```

If *www.myflashcomserver.com* is running FlashCom on a port other than 1935, such as port 1940, then you would need to use the following URI:

```
rtmp://www.myflashcomserver.com:1940/myVideoChatApp
```

Next, here is an example of a URI that connects to *myGroupPaintApp*, which resides on the same host as the *.swf* file. Because they are on the same host, there is no need to specify the host as part of the URI. Notice that when you don't specify the host, the *rtmp:* is followed by only one forward slash (/).

```
rtmp:/myGroupPaintApp
```

If the localhost is running FlashCom on a nondefault port, you should specify the port in the URI, as shown here (note the two colons):

```
rtmp::1940/myGroupPaintApp
```

You can monitor the connection status by adding an *onStatus()* method to the net connection instance. The *onStatus()* method is automatically invoked every time there is a change in connection status. Each time the *onStatus()* method is invoked, it is automatically passed an info object whose code property indicates the change in status. For example, when the connection is successfully made, the *onStatus()* method is invoked and passed an info object with a code property of "NetConnection.Connect.Success". Any other value indicates that the connection has either been lost or rejected.

Here is an example *onStatus()* handler that detects the code property of the info object:

```
myConnection.onStatus = function (infoObj) {
  if (infoObj.code == "NetConnection.Connect.Success") {
    trace("connection made successfully");
  }
};
```

The *onStatus()* method is invoked both when there is a connection attempt and when the connection is closed. You can use the *onStatus()* method to:

- Perform proper initialization when a connection is made
- Perform necessary actions when a connection is closed (i.e., try to reestablish a connection or tell the user that the application has closed)
- Perform error handling when a connection fails or is closed unexpectedly

Here is an example *onStatus()* handler that deals with various status conditions:

```
myConnection.onStatus = function (infoObj) {
  switch (infoObj.code) {
    case "NetConnection.Connect.Success":
      // Perhaps initialize necessary elements in the movie, such as video objects.
      break;
    case "NetConnection.Connect.Failed":
      // The connection failed because the server is unreachable. Perhaps try again
      // or simply tell the user that the server cannot be reached.
      break;
    case "NetConnection.Connect.Rejected":
      // The connection was rejected because of invalid credentials or parameters.
      // Perhaps prompt the user for valid information.
      break;
    case "NetConnection.Connect.InvalidApp":
      // The connection failed because no application by the specified name exists.
      break;
    case "NetConnection.Connect.Closed":
      // The connection was closed successfully by a command issued from the client.
      // Use the opportunity to remove any elements, such as video objects; go to
      // another screen; or otherwise inform the user of the closure.
      break;
    case "NetConnection.Connect.AppShutDown":
      // The application was shut down by an administrator or because the server is
      // being shut down or restarted.
  }
};
```

14.3 Adding a Video Object at Runtime

Problem

You want to add video (and audio) to a Flash movie at runtime.

Solution

Create a movie clip symbol with an embedded *Video* object and set it to export for ActionScript.

Discussion

Although there is no way to create a *Video* object at runtime, you can create a movie clip with an embedded video at authoring time. If you set the movie clip symbol to export for ActionScript, you can add instances of the movie clip (including the embedded video) to your Flash movie at runtime with an *attachMovie()* method, as you would with any other exported movie clip. Here are the steps you should follow:

1. Open the Library and choose New Video from the Library's pop-up Options menu to create a new video symbol.

2. Create a new movie clip symbol (using New → Symbol) and drag an instance of the video symbol into it, positioning the video at (0,0).

3. Name the instance of the video symbol my_video.

4. Open the linkage settings for the movie clip symbol (by choosing Linkage from the Library's pop-up Options menu) and select the Export for ActionScript and Export in First Frame checkboxes. Enter a linkage identifier of *VideoMcSymbol*.

5. At the point in your ActionScript code where you wish to add a video, use the *attachMovie()* method to attach an instance of *VideoMcSymbol*, as follows:

```
// Create an instance of the video movie clip symbol.
_root.attachMovie("VideoMcSymbol", "myVideo_mc", 1);
```

6. When you want to target the video (to attach a net stream, for example), you should use the path to the wrapper movie clip instance followed by my_video (to target the nested video object), as follows:

```
// Invoke the attachVideo( ) method of the nested video object.
_root.myVideo_mc.my_video.attachVideo(myNetStream);
```

There are occasions when it is appropriate to create all the video instances at authoring time. However, in other cases it may be desirable or even imperative to add video instances dynamically at runtime. For example, to create a video conferencing application that can accept any number of clients, you must add video instances using the technique discussed in this recipe.

See Also

Recipe 7.19. Note that adding the video symbol to the movie doesn't play any content. To play a video, you must add video content, as shown in step 6. For information on adding local video content to a video object, see Recipe 14.4. For information on adding video content from a net stream (content from the FlashCom server), see Recipe 14.7.

14.4 Capturing and Displaying Video from a Web Cam

Problem

You want to display the video from a user's web cam within a Flash movie, or you want to capture the data in order to publish it to a FlashCom application. (See Recipe 14.9.)

Solution

Use the *Camera.get()* method.

Discussion

The *Camera.get()* method returns a stream of (video-only) data from the camera attached to the user's computer. For example:

```
myCam_cam = Camera.get( );
```

If there are multiple cameras, Flash defaults to the camera that is selected under the Camera tab of the Player Settings dialog box. Flash also assigns each recognized camera an index, starting from 0 and incrementing by 1. For example, if there are three cameras attached to the computer, Flash identifies them by the indexes 0, 1, and 2. You can pass the index to the *Camera.get()* method to open a data stream from that camera:

```
// Open a stream from the second camera.
myCam_cam = Camera.get(1);
```

In practice, developers ordinarily use one of two strategies:

- Allow the user to select a camera before opening the camera stream.
- Open the camera stream to the default camera, and then allow the user to choose a different camera.

You can allow a user to choose a camera in at least two ways:

- Open the Player Settings dialog box to the Camera tab using the following code:

    ```
    System.showSettings(3);
    ```

    However, this technique is intrusive because it confronts the user with the Player Settings dialog box. Therefore, you should provide a button to open the Player Settings dialog box, which offers the user more control. For example:

    ```
    openSettings_btn.onRelease = function ( ) {
      System.showSettings(3);
    };
    ```

- Create a custom UI, such as combo box, to allow the user to select his camera. You can populate the combo box using the Camera.names array, which contains the names of the available cameras.

```
// Include Form.as from Chapter 11 to access its custom adjustWidth( ) method.
// This is optional, as it is for formatting purposes only.
#include "Form.as"

// For this example to work, you must add a combo box named cameraSelector_cb to
// your movie.

// Define a change handler function for the combo box.
function selectCamera (cb) {
  // Create a camera object using the index of the camera the user has selected.
  selected_cam = Camera.get(cb.getValue( ));
}

// Loop through all the elements of the Camera.names array.
for (var i = 0; i < Camera.names.length; i++) {
  // Add the camera names to the combo box.
  cameraSelector_cb.addItem(Camera.names[i], i);
}

// Adjust the width of the combo box to accommodate the contents.
cameraSelector_cb.adjustWidth( );

// Set the change handler function to selectCamera( )
cameraSelector_cb.setChangeHandler("selectCamera");
```

In isolation, the *Camera.get()* method is not very useful. You need to apply the camera data to a net stream for publishing to a FlashCom application (see Recipe 14.9) or to a video object within the same Flash movie. To apply the camera data to a video object, use the *attachVideo()* method. This is useful for allowing a user to see what his camera is displaying (perhaps while simultaneously publishing that same data to a FlashCom server).

 The video displayed from a local web cam is, in most cases, of higher quality than the video published to the FlashCom server. Although the aforementioned technique of monitoring local web cam data is useful, the user should be warned that subscribers to the published stream will not necessarily see video of the same quality.

Some users might not have *any* camera connected to their computer. Therefore, you should test to see whether a camera exists before trying to get the camera stream. A simple way to check for a camera is to make sure that the Camera.names array has at least one element.

This example checks whether a camera exists before attempting to display the video:

```
// Make sure that the user has a camera.
if (Camera.names.length > 0) {
```

```
// The user has a camera, so let's get and use the camera data source.
myCam = Camera.get( );

// Apply the data to a video object, my_video, which is nested within myVideo_mc,
// as covered in Recipe 14.3. This code displays the user's video output in a Video
// object within the same Flash movie.
myVideo_mc.my_video.attachVideo(myCam);
} else {
// The user doesn't have a video camera.
// Display an alert using a message box named alertBox.
alertBox.setMessage("This application requires that you have a camera.");
alertBox._visible = true;
}
```

Although it is possible to attach camera data to a video object (or a net stream) with an anonymous reference, it is usually better to first create a variable to which you assign the camera stream, and then pass that variable to the *attachVideo()* method. The reason for this is that sometimes, even after a stream has been removed from the embedded video or the net stream has stopped publishing, the camera might not be released properly by Flash. This is not necessarily a problem in terms of the functioning of the FlashCom application, but it can be a little strange when a user's web cam light is still on even after a FlashCom application has stopped using it. You can set the camera stream variable to null at any point to release the camera. If you have used an anonymous reference to the camera stream, this option isn't open to you.

This example passes an anonymous reference to a camera stream to *attachVideo()*:

```
myVideo_mc.my_video.attachVideo(Camera.get( ));
```

This example assigns a variable to the camera reference before passing it to *attachVideo()*:

```
myCam = Camera.get( );
myVideo_mc.my_video.attachVideo(myCam);
// At a later point, setting myCam (the camera stream variable)
// to null releases the camera.
myCam = null;
```

If you are not concerned with Flash properly releasing the camera, there is nothing wrong with passing *attachVideo()* an anonymous reference to the camera.

See Also

Recipe 14.5, Recipe 14.9, and the video chat application in Chapter 24

14.5   Capturing and Playing Audio from a Microphone

Problem

You want to get audio from a user's microphone to add it to a movie clip within the Flash movie or publish it to a FlashCom application. (See Recipe 14.9.)

Solution

Use the *Microphone.get()* method.

Discussion

The *Microphone.get()* method is analogous to the *Camera.get()* method, but it gets audio data from a user's microphone instead of video from his camera. For example:

```
myMic_mic = Microphone.get();
```

The *Microphone.get()* method gets the data for the default microphone (as set in the Microphone tab of the Player Settings dialog box) if you do not specify any parameters. However, if the user has multiple microphones, you can use the Microphone.names array to offer the user a choice among them. See Recipe 14.4, which demonstrates the analogous technique for multiple video cameras.

There is the possibility that the user does not have any microphone. The elements in the Microphone.names array correspond to the recording devices reported by the user's operating system. In most cases the devices are sound cards, and the existence of a sound card does not necessarily mean there is a microphone. Therefore, there is no definitive way to determine whether a user has a microphone (although if the Microphone.names array is empty, he does not).

```
if (Microphone.names.length > 0) {
    // Place code here for getting and using a microphone stream. The user may, in
    // fact, have only a sound card and no microphone.
} else {
    // Place code here to handle the case in which the user has no microphone.
}
```

Like the *Camera.get()* method, *Microphone.get()* is not useful in isolation. You need to actually do something with the data it returns. You can apply that data to a net stream, in order to publish it to a FlashCom application (see Recipe 14.9), or you can apply it to a movie clip within the same Flash movie. Applying the microphone audio to a movie clip allows a user to hear his microphone output locally (generally, at the same time it is being published to a FlashCom application). You can attach the microphone output to a movie clip using the *attachAudio()* method, as follows:

```
mySoundHolderMc.attachAudio(myMic_mic);
```

Attaching the audio to a movie clip automatically plays the audio that is being retrieved from the microphone. You do not need to tell it to start, and you cannot tell the sound to stop. You can, however, set the *Microphone* object to null, which closes the stream, effectively stopping the sound. Alternatively, you can use a *Sound* object to control the volume, as discussed in Recipe 14.6. You cannot rewind or otherwise seek through microphone output.

If you are allowing a user to monitor both his microphone and camera output, and you have created the video object using the technique from Recipe 14.3, then it is convenient to attach the microphone audio to the video object's wrapper movie clip:

```
// Attach the camera video to the nested video object (my_video).
myVideo_mc.my_video.attachVideo(Camera.get( ));

// Attach the microphone audio to the wrapper movie clip (myVideo_mc).
myVideo_mc.attachAudio(Microphone.get( ));
```

See Also

Recipes 13.2, 14.3, 14.4, 14.6, and 14.9

14.6   Controlling FlashCom Audio

Problem

You want to control the volume and pan of audio attached to a movie clip with the *attachAudio( )* method.

Solution

Create a *Sound* object that targets the movie clip to which the sound is attached and use the pan and volume methods of the *Sound* class.

Discussion

FlashCom audio (meaning audio coming from either a microphone stream or from a net stream) can be heard once it has been attached to a movie clip using the *attachAudio( )* method. However, the volume and panning levels play at the default settings. But don't fret. There is a solution.

Although you cannot use a *Sound* object to control the playback (stopping, starting, or seeking) of an attached FlashCom sound, you can control the volume and panning with a *Sound* object that targets the movie clip to which the sound has been attached:

```
// Attach audio (which can be either local microphone data or a net stream) to a
// movie clip.
mySoundHolderMc.attachAudio(Microphone.get( ));
```

```
// Create a Sound object that targets the movie clip to
// which the sound has been attached.
mySound = new Sound(mySoundHolderMc);

// Control the sound using the Sound class's get/set methods as you would normally.
// Shown here is an example that sets the volume.
mySound.setVolume(60);
```

 Early revisions of Flash Player 6 had a bug that prevented you from controlling attached sounds in this way. This technique requires Flash Player 6.0.60.0 or later. Not only should you update your plugin Player but also the Test Player, which is used during authoring. Go to *http://www.macromedia.com/support/flash/downloads.html* for more information and to download the latest players.

See Also

Recipes 13.2, 13.11, and 13.12

14.7   Subscribing to Audio/Video Content

Problem

You want to subscribe a Flash movie to audio and/or video content from a Flash-Com server.

Solution

Create a net stream that uses an existing net connection to the FlashCom server and invoke the *NetStream.play()* method.

Discussion

FlashCom audio and video are transferred between the client and server using net streams. When a Flash movie accesses a net stream of a FlashCom application, it is said to be *subscribed* to that net stream.

The *NetStream* class, from which you can create net stream objects, facilitates the sending and receiving of audio and video. You should use a net stream object to subscribe to any audio or video content from a FlashCom server. The same code is used to receive the stream whether that content has been previously recorded or whether it is live. When you create a net stream object, you must specify the net connection object (see Recipe 14.2) over which the stream should be sent. For example:

```
// Create the NetConnection object.
myConnection = new NetConnection();
```

```
// Call the NetConnection.connect( ) method to connect to an application.
myConnection.connect("rtmp:/myApplication/");

// Create a net stream that uses the net connection myConnection.
subscribe_ns = new NetStream(myConnection);
```

Once you have created a net stream object, you can use the *NetStream.play()* method to subscribe to any available audio and/or video content on the server. The *play()* method requires you to specify the name of the stream as it was published to the FlashCom application. It is your responsibility to know the name of the stream. Presumably, you either created the movie that published the stream in the first place, or you can discover the information from the developer who did.

```
subscribe_ns.play("myAVStream");
```

The preceding example is the simplest form of the *play()* method. When you provide only the name of the stream to play, Flash automatically does the following:

- Attempts to locate a live stream of the specified name. If the live stream is found, Flash opens the live stream and plays it until it is no longer available.
- If no live stream is found, Flash looks for a recorded stream of the specified name. If a recorded stream is found, Flash opens the recorded stream and plays it until it ends.
- If no existing live or recorded stream is found, Flash opens a live stream with the specified name and waits for someone to publish to it.

You can also specify *start* and *length* parameters to wield more control over how Flash looks for and plays streams. The *start* parameter is an optional second parameter with the following possible values:

0 or greater
Looks for a recorded stream only. If no such stream is found, Flash plays the next stream in the playlist, if applicable. If found, Flash begins playback at the specified number of seconds from the beginning of the stream.

–1 Looks for a live stream only. If no live stream is found, the behavior depends on the value for the *length* parameter. If *length* is negative, Flash waits indefinitely for someone to publish to the stream. Otherwise, Flash times out after the number of seconds specified by *length* and moves to the next stream in the playlist, if applicable.

Numbers less than or equal to –2
Same as the default behavior described earlier: looks for a live stream first. If no live stream is found, it looks for a recorded stream. If no recorded stream is found, it opens a live stream and waits for someone to publish to it.

The *length* parameter is an optional third parameter with the following possible values:

Any negative number
> Plays the stream until it ends (for a recorded stream) or until it is no longer available (for a live stream).

0   Plays a single frame at the time specified by the *start* parameter. This is useful for showing stills from a stream.

Any positive number
> Plays the stream for the specified number of seconds or until the stream ends.

If the net stream content includes video content, you must use the *attachVideo()* method to attach the net stream to a video object in order to display the video. Again, it is your responsibility to know whether or not the stream contains video.

```
myVideo_mc.my_video.attachVideo(subscribe_ns);
```

You do not need to attach the audio portion of a net stream to a movie clip using *attachAudio()* in order to hear it. However, if you want to be able to control the sound, you must attach it to a movie clip (see Recipe 14.6).

The video and/or audio from a subscribed net stream begins playback as soon as enough has buffered into the Player. The default buffer time for a stream is 0. This means that the stream begins playing immediately (technically, the Flash Player still buffers approximately 10 milliseconds). However, if there is any lag in the connection, unbuffered content is interrupted. To help ensure smooth playback, use the *setBufferTime()* method to specify the number of seconds to buffer before playing the stream. The buffer is ignored for live streams.

```
// Set the buffer time to 30 seconds.
subscribe_ns.setBufferTime(30);
```

See Also

Recipe 13.2, and Recipe 14.6 for information on controlling attached audio

14.8   Creating Playlists

Problem

You want to create a playlist in which streams are queued and played one after another.

Solution

Use the *NetStream.play()* method to add streams to the playlist. Specify `false` for the *flushPlaylists* parameter.

Discussion

You can create playlists for net streams relatively quickly and easily with built-in functionality. The *NetStream.play()* method allows you to create playlists by simply appending new streams with each subsequent *play()* invocation. However, the default behavior is for *play()* to flush the current playlist. To avoid flushing the existing playlist, specify `false` for the optional fourth parameter, *flushPlaylists*. You can use −2 and −1 as placeholders for the intervening *start* and *length* parameters to maintain the default behavior:

```
    // Add three streams to a net stream object's playlist.
    mySubscribe_ns.play("stream0", -2, -1, false);
    mySubscribe_ns.play("stream1", -2, -1, false);
    mySubscribe_ns.play("stream2", -2, -1, false);
```

Flash automatically begins playback of the next stream in the playlist when the current stream stops, which depends on the values specified for the *start* and *length* parameters. These parameters are discussed in Recipe 14.7.

You can create a new playlist at any time by calling *play()* with a value of true for the *flushPlaylists* parameter. This flushes the current playlist, stops the current stream, and plays the new stream.

```
    mySubscribe_ns.play("stream3", -2, -1, true);
```

Omitting the fourth parameter performs the same operation:

```
    mySubscribe_ns.play("stream3", -2, -1);
```

14.9 Recording and Publishing Video and Audio

Problem

You want to record video and/or audio from a Flash movie and publish it to a Flash-Com server.

Solution

Create a net stream, attach the video using *attachVideo()*, and attach the audio using *attachAudio()*. Then call the *NetStream.publish()* method and specify "record" or "append" as the recording mode.

Discussion

To use a net stream object to record and publish video and/or audio to a FlashCom server, follow these steps:

1. Establish a net connection:

   ```
   myConnection = new NetConnection( );
   ```

2. Connect to the FlashCom server:

   ```
   myConnection.connect("rtmp:/myApplication/");
   ```

3. Create the net stream:

   ```
   publishRecorded_ns = new NetStream(myConnection);
   ```

4. Attach the audio and/or video to the net stream using the *attachAudio()* and/or *attachVideo()* method:

   ```
   myMic_mic = Microphone.get( );
   myCam_cam = Camera.get( );
   publishRecorded_ns.attachAudio(myMic_mic);
   publishRecorded_ns.attachVideo(myCam_cam);
   ```

5. Use *NetStream.publish()* to record the stream on the server. The first parameter is the name by which the stream should be known by the FlashCom application (when a client wants to subscribe to it, for example). The second parameter is the recording mode. If you specify "record" as the recording mode, any existing stream of the same name (within the FlashCom application) is overwritten. If you specify "append" as the recording mode, the new stream data is appended to any existing stream of the same name (a new stream is created on the server if none exists).

   ```
   publishRecorded_ns.publish("myFirstStream", "record");
   ```

6. Call *NetStream.publish()* again with the value false when you want to stop recording the stream:

   ```
   publishRecorded_ns.publish(false);
   ```

Even if your FlashCom application permits multiple people to record to a single stream, only one user at a time can record to that stream. Additionally, if a recorded stream is being played by a subscribing client, FlashCom locks the stream, preventing you from recording to it. In both of these scenarios, you can catch these errors with an *onStatus()* method. The net stream's *onStatus()* method is invoked whenever there is a status update related to the stream. Flash passes an info object parameter containing information about the status update to the *onStatus()* handler. When another user is recording to a stream, the code property of the info object has the value "NetStream.Publish.BadName"; when the stream is being played, the code property has the value "NetStream.Record.NoAccess".

Here is an example with an *onStatus()* handler that detects these error codes:

```
myConnection = new NetConnection( );
myConnection.connect("rtmp:/myApplication/");
publishRecorded_ns = new NetStream(myConnection);
```

```
publishRecorded_ns.onStatus = function (infoObj) {
  if (infoObj.code == "NetStream.Publish.BadName") {
    trace("Someone is already recording to this stream");
  } else if (infoObj.code == "NetStream.Record.NoAccess") {
    trace("Someone is playing this stream");
  } else {
    trace("Stream accessed successfully.");
  }
};

myMic_mic = Microphone.get( );
myCam_cam = Camera.get( );
publishRecorded_ns.attachAudio(myMic_mic);
publishRecorded_ns.attachVideo(myCam_cam);
publishRecorded_ns.publish("myFirstStream", "record");
```

See Also

Recipe 14.10. For more information on client-side *NetStream* info object codes, see
http://download.macromedia.com/pub/flashcom/documentation/FlashCom_CS_ASD.pdf.

14.10 Publishing Live Content

Problem

You want to publish a live stream without recording it.

Solution

Create a net stream, attach the audio and/or video to the stream using *attachAudio( )*
and/or *attachVideo( )*, then call the *NetStream.publish( )* method and specify "live" as
the recording mode.

Discussion

The procedure to publish a live stream is the same as that of publishing a recorded
stream (see Recipe 14.9) except that you specify the mode as "live" when you call the
publish( ) method. Live streams are not recorded and are available only as they are
being published.

Here is an example that publishes a live stream called "livePresentation":

```
// Establish the net connection.
myConnection = new NetConnection( );
myConnection.connect("rtmp:/myApplication/");

// Create a net stream using a net connection named myConnection.
publishLive_ns = new NetStream(myConnection);
```

```
// Attach the camera and microphone data to the net stream.
publishLive_ns.attachAudio(Microphone.get());
publishLive_ns.attachVideo(Camera.get());

// Publish the stream as live content.
publishLive_ns.publish("livePresentation", "live");
```

If not specified, the recording mode defaults to "live". Therefore, the last line of the example could also be written as:

```
publishLive_ns.publish("livePresentation");
```

See Also

To publish a live stream and archive it for subsequent playback, see Recipe 14.9.

14.11 Pausing and Resuming a Net Stream

Problem

You want to control the playback (pause or resume) of audio and/or video that is being played from a net stream.

Solution

Use the *NetStream.pause()* method.

Discussion

You can use the *NetStream.pause()* method to pause the playback of a net stream. For example, if a net stream is playing, the following line of code pauses its playback:

```
myNetStream.pause();
```

However, the *pause()* method, when used without a parameter, acts as a toggle between pausing and resuming playback. If the net stream in the preceding example is already paused at the time that the *pause()* method is invoked, the stream begins playing again at the point where it left off.

Alternatively, you can specify a Boolean parameter to indicate whether the net stream should pause or resume, regardless of its current state. A value of true causes a net stream to pause if it is playing or to remain paused if it is already paused. On the other hand, a value of false causes the net stream to resume playing if it is paused or to continue playing if it is already playing. For example:

```
// Cause a net stream to pause.
myNetStream.pause(true);

// Cause a net stream to play.
myNetStream.pause(false);
```

The *play()* method should not be used to resume the playback of a net stream, nor should it be used to fast-forward or rewind (see Recipe 14.12). The *play()* method retrieves a stream from the FlashCom server and adds it to a client's net stream for playback. If you call *play()* more than once, one of two things can happen:

- If you specify false for the *flushPlayLists* parameter, the stream is added to the playlist, and it begins playing only after any existing streams in the playlist have finished.
- If *flushPlayLists* is undefined or true, the stream begins playing again from the specified starting point. Technically, you could use this to try to seek the stream. However, this would be very inefficient because each time *play()* is called, the stream is requested from the server.

You can pause and resume any stream, even live streams. However, when you pause a live stream, it resumes at the current (realtime) position, not at the point where the stream was paused.

See Also

Recipes 13.3, 14.8, and 14.12

14.12 Fast-Forwarding and Rewinding a Net Stream

Problem

You want to fast-forward or rewind (also called *seeking*) a net stream.

Solution

Use the *NetStream.seek()* method.

Discussion

You can fast-forward or rewind to any point within a net stream using the *NetStream.seek()* method. This method requires you to specify the number of seconds from the beginning of the net stream to which to seek. For example, to return to the beginning of a net stream, you can use the value 0:

```
// Return to the beginning of a net stream.
myNetStream.seek(0);
```

The preceding technique seeks to an absolute position within the stream. However, if you want to seek to a position relative to the current playback position, such as five seconds forward or backward, add or subtract the number of seconds from the net stream's `time` property (which returns the current playback time in seconds from the beginning of the net stream):

```
// Seek six seconds ahead of the current time.
myNetStream.seek(myNetStream.time + 6);
```

Also, stream data may not contain keyframes at every frame, and the *seek()* method can seek only to a keyframe. Therefore, by default, the *seek()* method moves to the keyframe that is nearest to the frame you specify. For example, if you instruct a net stream to seek to 12 seconds, but the two nearest keyframes are at 10 and 15 seconds, the net stream seeks to 10 seconds. If you need more precision, you can adjust the *Application.xml* file, which is found in a subdirectory of the FlashCom installation (such as *C:\Program Files\Macromedia\Flash Communication Server MX\ conf_defaultRoot__defaultVHost_*). You can change the `EnhancedSeek` value to true to increase the seeking precision for all net streams. Here is the snippet from the *Application.xml* file that you should change:

```
...
    <StreamManager>
        <EnhancedSeek>true</EnhancedSeek>
    </StreamManager>
...
```

With enhanced seeking, you can seek to any whole second within the stream. Be aware, however, that this greatly increases the processing load on the server, so it should be used only when necessary.

See Also

Recipes 14.11 and 14.13

14.13 Seeking Relative to the Total Stream Length

Problem

You want to seek a stream based on the total length of the stream.

Solution

Get the stream length from the server and then use the *seek()* method.

Discussion

A problem arises when you want to seek within a stream relative to the total length of the stream. For example, if you want to create a slider that a user can move to seek through a stream, you must determine the total length of a stream. There is no client-side property or method that returns that information. However, you can write a server-side function to return a stream's length using the *Stream.length()* method. Here are the steps to return a stream's length from the server:

1. In the server-side *.asc* file (either the *main.asc* file or another *.asc* file that is loaded by *main.asc*) create a method for client objects that takes the name of a stream and returns the length of that stream (see Recipe 14.4). Most often, you assign methods to a client in the *application.onConnect()* method.

   ```
   // The application.onConnect() method is invoked automatically whenever a new
   // client connects to the FlashCom application. The client object is created and
   // passed as a parameter to the method.
   application.onConnect = function (newClient) {

     // Create a custom getStreamLength() method for each client. The method takes
     // the name of a stream as a parameter.
     newClient.getStreamLength = function (streamName) {
       // Return the length of the requested stream.
       return Stream.length(streamName);
     };
   };
   ```

2. In the client-side ActionScript, connect to the FlashCom application:

   ```
   myConnection = new NetConnection();
   myConnection.connect("rtmp:/myApp");
   ```

3. Create a *response object* to handle the result from the call to *getStreamLength()*. A response object is an object created from the *Object* class, for which you have defined an *onResult()* method. When the *onResult()* method is invoked by a response from the FlashCom server, a result is returned from FlashCom and passed to the method as a parameter:

   ```
   myResponse = new Object();
   myResponse.onResult = function (result) {
     _root.streamLength = result;
     trace("the stream length is: " + result);
   };
   ```

4. Once a connection is established and a response object is defined, call the server-side *getStreamLength()* method using the *call()* method of the client-side connection object. Specify that any response should be handled by the response object you created in the previous step and pass along the name of the stream as a parameter.

   ```
   myConnection.call("getStreamLength", myResponse, "myStreamName");
   ```

Once you have retrieved the total length of the stream, you can use that value in conjunction with a slider controller to determine values to pass to the *seek()* method. Here is an example:

```
// Create the connection.
myConnection = new NetConnection();
myConnection.connect("rtmp:/myApp");
```

```
// Create the net stream. This example assumes that the stream is an audio-only
// stream for which we don't want to control the volume or panning, so we don't need
// to attach any audio or video.
subscribe_ns = new NetStream(myConnection);

// Create the response object.
myResponse = new Object( );
myResponse.onResult = function (result) {

  // Assign the stream length to a variable on _root.
  _root.streamLength = result;

  // Begin the playback of the stream.
  _root.subscribe_ns.play("myStreamName");

  // Use an interval to call updateScroll( ) to continually update the scroll position
  // so that it corresponds to the stream position.
  setInterval(_root, "updateScroll", 100);
};

// Call the server-side getStreamLength( ) method. We're assuming you created this
// already in your main.asc file (or other loaded .asc).
myConnection.call("getStreamLength", myResponse, "myStreamName");

// Create an isMouseDown variable, and toggle its value depending on the mouse state.
// We use this to determine whether the user is scrolling or if the scrollbar is
// being updated by the sound playback progress.
_root.onMouseDown = function ( ) {
  _root.isMouseDown = true;
};
_root.onMouseUp = function ( ) {
  _root.isMouseDown = false;
};

// Create a callback function for the scrollbar.
function onScroll (sb) {
  // Perform the enclosed actions only if the user is scrolling, not if the scrollbar
  // position is being updated due to the progress of sound playback.
  if (_root.isMouseDown && scrollBar_sb.hitTest(_root._xmouse, _root._ymouse)) {

    // Get the current scroll position of the scrollbar (from 0 to 100).
    var percent = sb.getScrollPosition( );

    // Calculate the seconds value that correspond to the percentage based on the
    // total stream length.
    var seconds = percent * streamLength / 100;

    // Seek to the appropriate point in the stream.
    subscribe_ns.seek(seconds);
  }
}

// This function updates the position of the scrollbar based on the current playback
// position of the stream.
function updateScroll ( ) {
```

```
    if (!_root.isMouseDown && !scrollBar_sb.hitTest(_root._xmouse, _root._ymouse)) {
      var position = subscribe_ns.duration / streamLength * 100;
      scrollBar_sb.setScrollPosition(position);
    }
  }
}

// Set the scrollbar properties and assign the change handler callback function. This
// example assumes that you have created a scrollbar instance on the Stage with a
// name of scrollBar_sb.
scrollBar_sb.setScrollProperties(10, 0, 100);
scrollBar_sb.setChangeHandler("onScroll");
```

See Also

Recipes 14.12, 14.14, and 14.16

14.14 Implementing Server-Side ActionScript

Problem

You want to handle advanced FlashCom application needs with server-side functionality.

Solution

Place the server-side code in a *main.asc* or *[registered_app_name].asc* file in the Flash-Com application's root directory.

Discussion

Server-Side ActionScript must be placed within *.asc* files in the FlashCom application directory. FlashCom always looks for an *.asc* file named *main.asc* or *[registered_app_name].asc* (such as *myApplication.asc*) in the application's root directory. FlashCom also detects files named *main.js* or *[registered_app_name].js* as alternatives to the files with *.asc* file extensions.

If none of these files exist, there is no custom server-side functionality. On the other hand, if FlashCom does find one of these files, it automatically looks for special application event handler methods when the corresponding events occur. Of these event handler methods, here are three of the most common:

application.onAppStart( )
> This method is automatically called when the application first starts. You should place all your application initialization code within this method.

application.onConnect( )
> This method is automatically called when a client connects to the application. FlashCom creates a new client object on the server and passes a reference to that

object to the *onConnect()* method. Additionally, if the client-side *connect()* method includes any extra parameters, those values are also passed to *onConnect()*. The *onConnect()* method is the place to do any client initialization, such as adding methods to the client object that can be invoked from the client-side movie. Also, you must either accept or reject connecting clients with the *application.acceptConnection()* or *application.rejectConnection()* methods.

application.onDisconnect()

This method is automatically called when a client disconnects from the application. FlashCom passes to this method a reference to the client object corresponding to the user who has disconnected from the application. This is the place to clean up anything that needs to be taken care of when a client disconnects. For example, you might want to remove the client from the list of connected users in a chat room.

Here is an example of a *main.asc* file, which can be placed in the FlashCom application's directory. It defines the three most common handlers you'll use to detect FlashCom events.

```
application.onAppStart = function () {

  // When the application starts up, create a server-side remote shared object and
  // save it to an application-wide property named mySsRso.
  application.mySsRso = SharedObject.get("mySharedObject");

  // Create an application-wide property to keep track of the total number of users
  // that have connected since the application started.
  application.usersConnectedFromAppStart = 0;

  // Create an application-wide property to keep track of the total number of users
  // that have disconnected since the application started.
  application.usersDisconnectedFromAppStart = 0;
};

application.onConnect = function (newClient) {

  // Accept the connection to the new client.
  application.acceptConnection(newClient);

  // Increment the number of connected users.
  application.usersConnectedFromAppStart += 1;
};

application.onDisconnect = function (disconnectClient) {

  // Increment the number of disconnected users.
  application.usersDisconnectedFromAppStart += 1;
};
```

See Also

Recipe 14.16. For more information about Server-Side ActionScript for FlashCom, see:

http://download.macromedia.com/pub/flashcom/documentation/FlashCom_SS_ASD.pdf

14.15 Tracking Clients Connected to the Application

Problem

You want to keep track of all the clients connected to the FlashCom application.

Solution

Use the server-side `application.clients` property.

Discussion

Server-Side ActionScript (for FlashCom) includes a built-in, application-wide property named `application.clients`, which is an array of all the connected client objects.

This example defines a custom *getUserInfo()* method, for each client, which returns information about the clients connected to the application:

```
// Create an application.onConnect() method. This example assume that when the client
// connects, a username parameter is passed along.
application.onConnect = function (newClient, username) {

  // Accept the connection to the new client.
  application.acceptConnection(newClient);

  // Add the username to the client object as a custom property.
  newClient.username = username;

  // Define a custom getUserInfo() method for the client object. This method can then
  // be called from the client.
  newClient.getUserInfo = function () {

    // Create a new array, loop through all the connected clients in
    // application.clients and add the usernames to the array.
    var clients_ar = new Array();
    for (var i = 0; i < application.clients.length; i++) {
      clients_ar.push(application.clients[i].username);
    }
```

```
      // Return the array of usernames.
      return clients_ar;
    };
  };
```

See Also

Recipe 14.14

14.16 Invoking Server-Side Functions from the Client Movie

Problem

You want to invoke a server-side function from a client movie.

Solution

In the *.asc* file (*main.asc* or another *.asc* file included in *main.asc*), define the server-side function as a method of the client object. Then, from the client, invoke the *call()* method from the net connection object.

Discussion

To invoke a server-side function from a client, you must first associate the server-side function with the connected client object. You can do this by assigning the function as a method of the client object. Generally, this is done within the *onConnect()* method, as follows:

```
application.onConnect = function (newClient) {
  application.acceptConnection(newClient);
  newClient.ssFunction = function () {
    // Do something here.
  };
};
```

Then, from the client movie you can use the *call()* method to invoke the server-side client method:

```
// Invoke the server-side ssFunction() method from a net connection object.
myConnection.call("ssFunction");
```

If you want the server-side method to return a value to the client, you must define a response object on the client. A response object is an object derived from the *Object* class for which you have defined an *onResult()* method. The value returned from the server-side method is passed to the client-side *onResult()* method as a parameter.

```
myResponse = new Object( );
myResponse.onResult = function (result) {
  // Do something with result here.
};
```

Once you have defined the response object on the client, you need to tell Flash to associate it with the response for a given call to a server-side function. To do this, you should modify your *call()* invocation by passing it a reference to the response object:

```
myConnection.call("ssFunction", myResponse);
```

Let's look at an example of how you might use this. First, in the *.asc* file you should define a custom method for each of the connecting clients:

```
application.onConnect = function (newClient) {

  // Accept the connection to the new client.
  application.acceptConnection(newClient);

  // Define a custom getUserCount( ) method for the client object.
  newClient.getUserCount = function ( ) {

    // Return the number of connected clients.
    return application.clients.length;
  };
};
```

Then, from within the client code you can invoke the server-side *getUserCount()* method. Don't forget to create a response object as well.

```
myResponse = new Object( );
myResponse.onResult = function (result) {
  _root.numberOfUsers_txt.text = result;
};
myConnection.call("getUserCount", myResponse);
```

See Also

Recipes 14.14 and 14.17

14.17 Invoking Client-Side Functions from the Server

Problem

You want to invoke a client-side function from Server-Side ActionScript.

Solution

Define the client-side function as a method of the client-side net connection object, and then, on the server, invoke the *call()* method on the client object.

Discussion

To invoke client-side functionality from the FlashCom server, you must first define the client-side functionality within a method of the net connection object. Then you can invoke that method from the FlashCom server using the *call()* method of the corresponding client object.

For example, here is a snippet of client-side code (meaning it should be in your Flash movie) that defines a custom method for a net connection object:

```
myConnection.myCsFunction = function () {
  trace("Method called from server!");
};
```

Then, in the Server-Side ActionScript (in the *main.asc* file or other *.asc* included in *main.asc*), you can invoke the server-side function, in this case *myCsFunction()*, using the *call()* method. You should invoke the *call()* method on the client object that corresponds to the client on which you want to invoke the function. For example, you can invoke the same method in all connected clients using a *for* statement, as shown here:

```
for (var i = 0; i < application.clients.length; i++) {
  application.clients[i].call("myCsFunction");
}
```

See Also

Recipes 14.16 and 17.6. This chapter has barely scratched the surface of what can be done with FlashCom server and Server-Side ActionScript. For more information on these topics, see *http://www.macromedia.com/support/flashcom/documentation.html* for a list of online documentation and *http://www.macromedia.com/support/flashcom/tutorial_index.html* for a list of online articles and tutorials.

## CHAPTER 15

Loading Assets

15.0   Introduction

Loading external *.swf* files into a Flash movie has long been a part of ActionScript. Beginning with Flash Player 6 it is also possible to load JPEG and MP3 files into a Flash movie at runtime. The implications of this are rather important. There are many good reasons for loading external content into your Flash movies at runtime, such as:

- It is easier and more convenient to manage external assets than to have to open the Flash document, import new or modified assets, and re-export the *.swf* file each time you want to make a change.

- In larger applications it makes sense to have different *.swf* files that are authored by different people or teams that can be assembled at runtime by a main, loading movie. This solves the bottleneck problems that can occur when trying to author a single *.swf* file (since only one person at a time can edit a Flash document).

- By loading external assets, you can create applications in which users can load their own assets into the Flash movie (for an example, see the jukebox application in Chapter 26).

- Loading external assets at runtime enables you to download assets to the client's computer as they are requested. This is important for large applications. For example, consider an application that allows a user to view photographs of a room in order to select a paint color. The application might allow a user to select from 90 colors, and each color selection might display a different version of the same photograph in which the walls have been painted that color. It is likely that most users will not view all 90 images, so it makes sense to avoid downloading all the images (which could create a significant increase in initial download time). Instead, the appropriate images can be downloaded as they are requested.

The preceding list includes just a few of the many benefits of loading external assets. Undoubtedly, you can discover more as you create your own application.

In the recipes throughout this chapter, you can find solutions to all kinds of problems related to loading external, *binary assets* at runtime. Binary assets include SWFs, JPEGs, and MP3s. For more information about loading textual data see the recipes dealing with the *LoadVars* and *XML* classes in Chapters 18 and 19.

15.1   Loading an External SWF

Problem

You want to load an external SWF into your Flash movie.

Solution

Use the *loadMovie()* method.

Discussion

The *loadMovie()* method is the preferred technique for loading external *.swf* files into a Flash movie. You should call this method from the movie clip into which you want to load the *.swf* file and pass it the URL at which the *.swf* file can be found:

```
// Load a .swf file into myMovieClip using a relative URL to a file in the same
// directory as the loading Flash movie.
myMovieClip.loadMovie("mySWF.swf");

// Load a .swf file into myMovieClip using a full URL to a file within the same
// domain as the loading Flash movie.
myMovieClip.loadMovie("http://www.mydomain.com/path/mySWF.swf");
```

Flash's security sandbox prevents Flash movies from loading assets from different domains. In other words, a Flash movie being served from *www.mydomain.com* can load a *.swf* file from *www.mydomain.com* or any other server in the same domain (such as *www2.mydomain.com*), but it cannot load a *.swf* file from *www.yourdomain.com*. Recipe 15.2 describes how you can create trusted relationships between domains using *allowDomain()*. Recipe 15.6 shows a different approach that uses a proxy script to load content from any domain.

The *loadMovie()* method replaces the timeline of the movie clip from which it is called with the timeline of the specified *.swf*. All existing content within the movie clip is wiped out when *loadMovie()* is called. Therefore, it is convenient to use the *createEmptyMovieClip()* method to create a container movie clip into which you load the *.swf* file (as opposed to creating instances at authoring time). For example:

```
// Create myMovieClip using createEmptyMovieClip().
_root.createEmptyMovieClip("myMovieClip", 1);

// Load the .swf file into myMovieClip.
myMovieClip.loadMovie("mySWF.swf");
```

The *loadMovie()* method works asynchronously. This means that when the Action-Script interpreter encounters a *loadMovie()* call, it initiates the request to load the external content, but it does not wait for the content to load before proceeding to the next line of code. This can have very important ramifications. For example, if you want to resize a movie clip into which you have loaded a new *.swf* file, you have to wait until the file has fully loaded. Here is some sample code to illustrate the problem:

```
// Create myMovieClip using createEmptyMovieClip().
_root.createEmptyMovieClip("myMovieClip", 1);

// Load the .swf file into myMovieClip.
myMovieClip.loadMovie("mySWF.swf");

// This displays 0 even if the width of the loaded .swf is greater than 0 because the
// width of the movie clip is not properly set until the .swf file has fully loaded.
trace(myMovieClip._width);
```

To solve this problem you should monitor the loading progress, as shown in Recipes 15.7 and 15.8.

Although it is recommended that you use *loadMovie()* to load content into movie clips when loading external *.swf* files, there is an exception in which it is preferable to use a different technique. When you load content using *loadMovie()*, the content must be fully loaded before it can be viewed. Therefore, in situations in which you want to stream the loaded *.swf* file you need to use a different technique. For loading streaming content you must load the *.swf* file into a *level* instead of a movie clip.

The Flash Player can contain more than one level. The default level is level 0, and you can target it in ActionScript using _level0. In fact, you may have noticed that in your movies, _root and _level0 are often synonymous (this is not necessarily the case when you start adding more levels). Additional levels can be created, and they are simply named level 1 (_level1), level 2 (_level2), etc. As the level number increases, so does the stacking order. In other words, content in level 1 will appear in front of content in level 0. You can treat each level in the same way you treat _root. This means you can move the contents of a level using the _x and _y properties, change the size using the _height and _width properties, etc.

You can load content into levels by using the *loadMovieNum()* global function. All you need to do is tell Flash the URL of the content and the level into which you want to load the content.

```
// Load someSWF.swf into _level1.
loadMovieNum("someSWF.swf", 1);
```

If the level does not yet exist, Flash first creates it, and then loads the content. If the level already exists, Flash replaces the existing content with the loaded content.

If you load a new *.swf* file into _level0, you will lose all the contents of the original movie as well as any other contents that have been loaded into other levels. Likewise, be careful when using the global *loadMovie()* function. If you specify a nonexistent path for the target, such as specifying _level1 when no _level1 object exists, *loadMovie()* replaces the current timeline with the newly loaded movie. To avoid the problem altogether, specify the target clip as a string, such as "_level1", or use the *MovieClip.loadMovie()* method instead.

If you want to hide the contents of level 0 it is better to set the level's visibility to false:

```
_level0._visible = false;
```

You can unload levels (remove the contents and the level itself) using the *unloadMovieNum()* global function:

```
// Unload level 2.
unloadMovieNum(2);
```

The *getURL()* method is also worth noticing. It is useful (aside from opening new browser windows) when you have a Flash movie being played from an HTML page and you want to replace both the *.swf* contents and the entire HTML page. This is important if, for example, you want to load a new *.swf* file with different dimensions. You can call the *getURL()* method from any movie clip as well. To replace the contents of the existing HTML page, use the value "_self" for the *window* parameter, as follows.

```
_root.getURL("newHTMLPage.html", "_self");
```

See Also

For a detailed discussion of document levels within the Player, see the section "The .swf Document '_level' Stack" in Chapter 13 of *ActionScript for Flash MX: The Definitive Guide*. This chapter is freely downloadable from *http://www.oreilly.com/catalog/actscript2/chapter/index.html*.

15.2 Loading an External SWF from a Trusting Domain

Problem

You want to load an external *.swf* file into your Flash movie, but the *.swf* file resides within a different domain.

Solution

Use the *allowDomain( )* method from within the *.swf* file you want to load to create a trusting relationship between the domains.

Discussion

The *System.security.allowDomain( )* method allows you to create trusting relationships between *.swf* files in different domains. The *allowDomain( )* method must be called from within the *.swf* file you wish to load. Therefore, this technique is applicable only if you want to load *.swf* files to which you can add the *allowDomain( )* method call. Otherwise, see Recipe 15.6 to load content by a proxy script.

Here is a scenario in which you can use *allowDomain( )* to create a trusting relationship: you have two *.swf* files, *my.swf* and *your.swf*. The *my.swf* movie is on *www.mydomain.com*, and *your.swf* is on *www.yourdomain.com*. If you want *my.swf* to be able to load *your.swf*, add the following line to *your.swf*:

```
System.security.allowDomain("mydomain.com");
```

This line of code tells *your.swf* to allow itself to be loaded by any movies in the *mydomain.com* domain. The *my.swf* movie can then load *your.swf* using a standard *loadMovie( )* method call:

```
// Create myMovieClip using createEmptyMovieClip( ).
_root.createEmptyMovieClip("myMovieClip", 1);

// Load the trusting .swf file into myMovieClip.
myMovieClip.loadMovie("http://www.yourdomain.com/your.swf");
```

If you want to allow *your.swf* to be loaded from more than one domain, you can specify them as a series of parameters passed to the *allowDomain( )* method. For example:

```
System.security.allowDomain("mydomain.com", "anotherdomain.org", "yetanother.net");
```

The parameters of the *allowDomain( )* method can be in any of the following formats:

```
"mydomain.com"
"http://mydomain.com"
"http://ipaddress"
```

See Also

Recipes 15.6 and 17.4

15.3   Loading an External JPEG Image

Problem

You want to load a standard JPEG graphic into your Flash movie from a remote URL.

Solution

Use the *MovieClip.loadMovie()* method.

Discussion

The *loadMovie()* method allows you to load not only *.swf* files but also JPEG images (*.jpg* or *.jpeg* files) into your Flash movie. The syntax and usage of the method is similar whether you are loading a *.swf* file or a JPEG:

```
// Load a JPEG into myMovieClip.
myMovieClip.loadMovie("myImage.jpg");
```

You should load external JPEGs into a holder movie clip nested within another movie clip because when you load any content into a movie clip using *loadMovie()*, the movie clip's timeline is replaced by that content. When you load a JPEG into a movie clip, therefore, the movie clip's timeline is replaced by the image, and you can no longer control that object with the properties and methods of a movie clip. However, if the movie clip into which you load the JPEG is nested within a parent movie clip, then the parent can still be controlled as a movie clip (and the nested image is controlled correspondingly).

Here is a good methodology to follow when loading JPEGs into Flash movies:

1. Begin with an existing movie clip or create a new movie clip using *createEmptyMovieClip()*. This clip will act as the parent clip.
2. Create a nested movie clip within the parent using *createEmptyMovieClip()*. This is the movie clip into which the JPEG should be loaded.
3. Call the *loadMovie()* method from the nested movie clip (not the parent clip).
4. Once the JPEG has loaded, control the image using the parent movie clip.

For example:

```
// Create a parent movie clip.
_root.createEmptyMovieClip("myMovieClip", 1);

// Create a nested movie clip.
myMovieClip.createEmptyMovieClip("imageHolder", 1);
```

```
// Load the JPEG into the nested movie clip.
myMovieClip.imageHolder.loadMovie("myImage.jpg");
```

JPEGs, like *.swf* files, are loaded into Flash movies asynchronously (see Recipe 15.1 for an explanation). Therefore, the same need to monitor load progress applies. Furthermore, *loadMovie()* loads only nonprogressive JPEG files; other formats are not directly supported.

See Also

The global *loadMovie()* and *loadMovieNum()* functions can also load JPEG files. See Recipe 15.4 for information on loading files in other image formats. See Recipe 15.1 for more information on how to use the *loadMovie()* method. See Recipes 15.7 and 15.8 for more information on monitoring load progress.

15.4 Loading an External Image (All Formats)

Problem

You want to load image formats such as BMP, GIF, PNG, or progressive JPEG files into your Flash movie.

Solution

Because *MovieClip.loadMovie()* supports only nonprogressive JPEG files, convert the image into the proper JPEG format before calling *loadMovie()*.

Discussion

The Flash Player supports runtime loading of only nonprogressive JPEG images. If you want to load images of another format, you have two basic options:

- Convert the image to JPEG format and save it to the server during authoring time.
- Use a server-side script to convert the image from the original format to a JPEG on the fly.

This recipe provides several different scripts depending on the server platform you are using. ColdFusion, Perl, .NET, and PHP scripts are included.

The ColdFusion version of the script is Java-based, so it requires ColdFusion MX. Additionally, this script requires that the <cfcontent> tag is enabled on the server.

Some server administrators disable this tag for security reasons. You can download the necessary files, already compiled, from *http://www.person13.com/ascb/*.

Alternatively, if you want to write the code yourself, follow these steps:

1. To compile the Java classes, you need the Java 2 Standard Development Kit (J2SDK), available from *http://java.sun.com/j2se/downloads.html*.

2. Download and install the Java Advanced Imaging (JAI) API on your local computer. You need this so that you can compile the Java class. You can download the API from *http://java.sun.com/products/java-media/jai/*.

3. Make sure to include the JAI JAR files in your system's classpath.

4. Upload the *jai_codec.jar* and *jai_core.jar* files to the *WEB-INF/lib/* directory on your ColdFusion server under the web root.

5. Create a new Java document and save it as *ImageConverter.java* to your local computer.

6. Add the following code to the *ImageConverter.java* document:

```
package imaging;

import java.net.*;
import javax.media.jai.*;

public class ImageConverter {

  private RenderedOp image = null;

  // This method accepts the location of the image to convert and the location
  // where to save the new image file locally.
  public void convertImage(String location, String fileSaveLocation)
  throws Exception{
    URL url = new URL(location);
    image = JAI.create("url", url);
    JAI.create("fileStore", image, fileSaveLocation, "JPEG", null);
  }
}
```

7. Once you have added the code to the file, save it and compile it into *ImageConverter.class*. Keep the *.class* file in the same directory as the source.

8. Create a new directory named *imaging* within the *WEB-INF/classes/* directory on your ColdFusion server under the web root.

9. Upload *ImageConverter.class* to the *imaging* directory on the server.

10. Create a new ColdFusion page and name it *getMyImage.cfm*.

11. Add the following code to *getMyImage.cfm*:

```
<cfobject type="java" name="ic" class="imaging.ImageConverter" action="create">
<cflock type="exclusive" timeout="5">
  <cfscript>
```

```
      tempImage = "#ExpandPath('./')#" & "myCFImage.jpg";
      ic.convertImage(URL.url, tempImage);
    </cfscript>
  </cflock>
  <cfcontent deletefile="yes" file="#tempImage#" type="image/jpeg">
```

12. Upload *getMyImage.cfm* to your ColdFusion web root.

13. Refer to the testing instructions at the end of this recipe, following the alternative language implementations.

If your server uses Perl, then follow these steps.

1. Make sure that the ImageMagick Perl module is installed. (This module is fairly common but not ubiquitous; ask your webmaster to install it if necessary.) ImageMagick is available from *http://www.imagemagick.com*.

2. Create a new document named *getMyImage.cgi*. (Some servers use *.pl* in place of the *.cgi* extension. If you are unsure, contact your webmaster.)

3. Add the following code to *getMyImage.cgi*:

```
#!/usr/bin/perl

use CGI;
use HTTP::Request;
use LWP::UserAgent;
use Image::Magick;

my $cgi = CGI->new( );

# Get the image from the URL.
my $ua = LWP::UserAgent->new;
my $request = HTTP::Request->new(GET => $cgi->param('url'));
my $response = $ua->request($request);

# Read the image into ImageMagick.
my $image = Image::Magick->new( );
$image->BlobToImage($response->content);

# Print the header and JPEG image to STDOUT.
print $cgi->header(-type=>'image/jpeg');
$image->Write('jpg:-');
```

4. Save the document and upload it to your server in the directory for CGI scripts (usually *cgi* or *cgi-bin*).

5. Make sure to correctly set the permissions on the file so that it can be executed (this applies to Unix servers only). The correct permissions value is 755. You can set the permissions from most FTP programs or use *chmod*.

6. Refer to the testing instructions at the end of this recipe, following the alternative language implementations.

If you are using a server that supports ASP.NET, you can write an ASPX page that can convert images to JPEGs on the fly. The .NET framework includes all the classes necessary to accomplish this, and therefore you do not need to concern yourself with adding any additional assemblies. Follow these steps to create the ASP.NET script:

1. Create a new ASPX document and name it *getMyImage.aspx*.

2. Add the following code to the document:

```
<!-- set the content type for the page to image/jpeg so that the
    correct data format is returned -->
<%@ Page Language="C#" ContentType="image/jpeg" %>

<%
// Get the image from the URL passed to this ASPX page.
System.Net.HttpWebRequest webRequest =
        (System.Net.HttpWebRequest)System.Net.WebRequest.Create(
          (string)Request.QueryString["url"]);
System.Net.HttpWebResponse webResponse =
        (System.Net.HttpWebResponse)webRequest.GetResponse( );
System.IO.Stream inStream = webResponse.GetResponseStream( );

// Create an Image object using the stream obtained from the image URL.
System.Drawing.Image img = System.Drawing.Image.FromStream(inStream);

// Save the output the image in JPEG format to the output stream.
img.Save(Response.OutputStream, System.Drawing.Imaging.ImageFormat.Jpeg);
%>
```

3. Save the document and upload it to your server.

4. Refer to the testing instructions at the end of this recipe, following the alternative language implementations.

If you want to use PHP to convert images on the fly, then you can use PHP's image functions. However, be aware that the image functions require you to have the GD library installed for PHP. Most web hosts that offer PHP have this library installed, but if not, ask for it to be installed. Complete the following steps to create a PHP script that converts JPEG, GIF, PNG, and BMP images to a JPEG format that Flash can read:

1. Create a new PHP document and name it *getMyImage.php*.

2. Add the following code to the document:

```
<?php
// The following line is needed only if gd wasn't compiled in.
if (!extension_loaded('php_gd.so')) exit; // Change to php_gd.dll on Windows.
header('Content-type: image/jpeg');
$imgname = $_GET['url'];
switch(substr($imagename, -3)) {
  case 'jpg':
  case 'jpeg':
    $im = imagecreatefromjpeg($imgname);
    break;
  case 'gif':
    // This option is only available in gd1 or in the bundled gd library.
    $im = imagecreatefromgif($imgname);
```

```
            break;
        case 'png':
            $im = imagecreatefrompng($imgname);
            break;
        case 'bmp':
            $im = imagecreatefromwbmp($imgname);
            break;
    }
    imagejpeg($im, '', 100);
    ?>
```

3. Save the document and upload it to your server.

4. See the following testing instructions.

To test the script in your chosen language, run it from a web browser. Regardless of the language implementation, the script expects a parameter named *url* that specifies the location of the image to convert. Each implementation should display the image (as a JPEG) in the browser window.

For example, if the CFML script is being served at *http://www.mydomain.com/getMyImage.cfm* and the image that you want to convert is at *http://www.mydomain.com/myImage.png*, you can test the script in a browser using *http://www.mydomain.com/getMyImage.cfm?url=http://www.mydomain.com/myImage.png*.

Similarly, you can test the Perl script in a browser using the following URL syntax:

> *http://www.mydomain.com/cgi-bin/getMyImage.cgi?url=http://www.mydomain.com/myImage.png*

You can test the ASP.NET script in a browser using:

> *http://www.mydomain.com/getMyImage.aspx?url=http://www.mydomain.com/myImage.png*

You can test the PHP script in a browser using:

> *http://www.mydomain.com/getMyImage.php?url=http://www.mydomain.com/myImage.png*

Regardless of which language implementation you choose, you use it in the same manner. Once you have one of the server-side scripts in place, you can call it from a Flash movie with *MovieClip.loadMovie()*. For example, you can load a converted PNG into a movie with the following code:

```
myMovieClip.imageHolder.loadMovie(
    "http://www.mydomain.com/getMyImage.cfm?url=http://www.mydomain.com/myImage.png");
```

As an additional benefit, each of the conversion scripts also overcomes Flash's sandbox security restrictions. This means that you can load images of any format from any domain.

See Also

Recipes 15.3 and 15.6

15.5 Loading an External MP3 Sound

Problem

You want to load an MP3 sound file into your Flash movie at runtime.

Solution

Use the *Sound.loadSound()* method.

Discussion

You can use the *Sound.loadSound()* method to load MP3 sound files into your Flash movie at runtime. The first step is to create a *Sound* object. For this purpose, use the custom *createNewSound()* method from Recipe 13.1:

```
// Include the Sound.as file from Chapter 13.
#include "Sound.as"
mySound = Sound.createNewSound( );
```

Next, call the *loadSound()* method from the *Sound* object. You should pass the *loadSound()* method two parameters: the URL where the MP3 can be found and a Boolean value indicating whether the sound should be streamed. Be careful to select the correct option for streaming because there is a major difference between streamed and nonstreamed sounds. Streaming sounds begin playing automatically as soon as enough data has been buffered (i.e., enough of the sound has loaded into the Flash movie). Nonstreamed sounds, on the other hand, must load completely into the movie before you can instruct them to start playing. You can control a non-streamed sound using all the methods and properties of a *Sound* object. Streaming sounds, however, cannot be controlled other than by stopping the playback:

```
// Load an MP3 from the same directory as the Flash movie. Set streaming to false.
mySound.loadSound("myMP3.mp3", false);
```

You cannot start the playback of a nonstreamed sound until it has loaded completely, nor can you retrieve any information about the sound (duration, position, etc.) until after the loading is finalized. Therefore, you should monitor the loading of a sound and define a callback function to be called once loading is complete. You can use the same techniques to monitor the loading of an MP3 that you use to monitor the loading of a JPEG or SWF. See Recipes 15.7 and 15.8 for more information on these techniques.

See Also

Recipes 2.7, 13.2, and 14.5

15.6 Loading Remote Content by Proxy

Problem

You want to load content into your Flash movie from another domain and are prevented from doing so by Flash's security sandbox.

Solution

Use a proxy script on the server to overcome the domain restrictions.

Discussion

Flash's security sandbox prevents you from loading content into your Flash movies from other domains indiscriminately. You can load *.swf* files, JPEGs, and MP3s from the same domain (or subdomain), and you can also load *.swf* files from a trusting domain. However, if you need to load content that is not in the same domain, and it is not a trusted *.swf* file, you have at least three options:

- Copy the content to the same domain. This is the simplest solution if it is possible for you to implement.
- Create a DNS entry within your own domain such that the remote server is mapped to a machine name within the same domain. For example, you can create a DNS entry such that *www.remotedomain.com* maps to *remotedomain.localdomain.com* within your own domain. This solution requires that you have administrator access and DNS knowledge.
- Create and use a proxy script that downloads the remote content to the local server (either in memory or to disk) on the fly and then returns the local copy to the Flash movie.

Included in this recipe are instructions for creating proxy scripts for ColdFusion, Perl, .NET, and PHP.

If you use ColdFusion, you can write a proxy script with just a few lines of code. Be aware that for this to work, the <cfcontent> tag must be enabled on the server. Some web hosts disable this tag for security purposes. To create a ColdFusion proxy script, complete the following steps:

1. Create a new CFML document named *getMyContent.cfm*.

2. Add the following code to the document:

```
<!--- Make sure the code is single-threaded so that the requested content
      from one client doesn't get sent to another by mistake. --->
<cflock timeout="10" type="exclusive">

    <!--- Get the remote content and save it to the server --->
    <cfhttp url="#URL.url#" method="get" path="#ExpandPath("./")#"></cfhttp>

    <!--- Display the content that has been saved. Delete the file afterward. --->
    <cfcontent file="#ExpandPath(GetFileFromPath(Url.url))#" deletefile="yes"
type="#cfhttp.mimetype#">
</cflock>
```

3. Save the document and upload it to your server.

4. Refer to the testing instructions at the end of this recipe, following the alternative language implementations.

If Perl is your choice for server-side scripting, you can create a proxy script by completing the following steps:

1. Create a new Perl script document named *getMyContent.cgi*.

2. Add the following code to the document:

```
#!/usr/bin/perl

# Proxy for Flash to bypass sandbox security limitations
# Supports GET and POST CGI methods
# Arun Bhalla (bhalla@arun.groogroo.com) 2002.07.15

use CGI qw/-oldstyle_urls/;
use HTTP::Request::Common;
use LWP::UserAgent;

my $cgi = new CGI;
my $ua  = new LWP::UserAgent;
my $location;
my $method;

if ($cgi->param()) {
    # extract the location (URL) and method values from the parameter list
    $location = $cgi->param('location');
    $method = $cgi->param('method');
    $cgi->delete('location');
    $cgi->delete('method');
}

$method = uc($method) || 'GET';
my $res;
```

```perl
if ($method eq 'GET') {
    if ($location =~ /\?/) {
        $location .= '&' . $cgi->query_string;
    } else {
        $location .= '?' . $cgi->query_string;
    }

    $req = HTTP::Request->new(GET => $location);
} elsif ($method eq 'POST') {
    $req = HTTP::Request->new(POST => $location);
    $req->content_type($cgi->content_type() ||
            'application/x-www-form-urlencoded');
    $req->content($cgi->query_string);
}

my $res = $ua->request($req);
print $res->headers_as_string, "\n", $res->content;(
```

3. Save the document and upload it to your server.

4. Refer to the testing instructions at the end of this recipe, following the alternative language implementations.

If you are using ASP.NET, follow these steps:

1. Create a new ASPX document named *getMyContent.aspx*.

2. Add the following code to the document:

```
<%@ Page Language="C#" %>
<%

// First, get the content from the remote domain.
System.Net.HttpWebRequest webRequest =
        (System.Net.HttpWebRequest)System.Net.WebRequest.Create(
         (string)Request.QueryString["url"]);
System.Net.HttpWebResponse webResponse =
        (System.Net.HttpWebResponse)webRequest.GetResponse();
System.IO.Stream inStream = webResponse.GetResponseStream();

// Next, read the content into an array of bytes.
byte[] buffer = new byte[(int)webResponse.ContentLength];
inStream.Read(buffer, 0, (int)webResponse.ContentLength);

// Next, set the appropriate content type and write the data as binary output.
Response.ContentType = webResponse.ContentType;
Response.BinaryWrite(buffer);

// Finally, close everything that is still open.
inStream.Close();
webResponse.Close();
%>
```

3. Save the document and upload it to your server.

4. Refer to the testing instructions at the end of this recipe, following the alternative language implementations.

If you are using PHP, follow these steps:

1. Create a new PHP document named *getMyContent.php*.

2. Add the following code to the document:

```php
<?php
  // Stop Script from Timing Out.
  set_time_limit(0);

  // Check for variable "url" in querystring.
  if ($_GET['url']) {
    $fp = fopen ($_GET['url'], "r");
    $file = "";
    while (!feof($fp)) {

      // Read Target File in chunks of 4 KB (4096 bytes).
      $file .= fgets($fp, 4096);
    }
    fclose($fp);

    // Send File Data to Flash
    echo $file;
  }
?>
```

3. See the following testing instructions.

To test the script in your chosen language, run it from a web browser. Regardless of the language implementation, the script expects a parameter named *url* that specifies the location of the data to copy to the proxy server.

For example, if the CFML script is being served at *http://www.mydomain.com/getMyContent.cfm* and the content that you want to retrieve is at *http://www.remotedomain.com/sound.mp3*, you can test the script in the browser using:

> *http://www.mydomain.com/getMyContent.cfm?url=http://www.remotedomain.com/sound.mp3*

This should retrieve the MP3 and play it in the browser window (if you have the appropriate player).

Similarly, you can test the Perl script in a browser using the following URL syntax:

> *http://www.mydomain.com/cgi-bin/getMyContent.cgi?url=http://www.remotedomain.com/sound.mp3*.

You can test the ASP.NET script in a browser using the following URL syntax:

> *http://www.mydomain.com/getMyContent.aspx?url=http://www.remotedomain.com/sound.mp3*.

You can test the PHP script in a browser using the following URL syntax:

> *http://www.mydomain.com/getMyContent.php?url=http://www.remotedomain.com/sound.mp3*.

Regardless of which language implementation you choose, you use it in the same manner. When you invoke the *loadMovie()* or *loadSound()* method from your Flash movie, instead of passing the URL to the remote asset, pass the URL to the proxy script that is running on the same domain and append the URL of the remote asset as a query string. For example:

```
myMovieClip.loadMovie("http://localhost/getMyContent.aspx?
url=http://www.remotedomain.com/someSwf.swf");
```

When you use a proxy script, be aware that the content can take even longer to load into the Player than it would if the content is loaded directly. The reason is that the asset has to first download to the proxy server, then to the Player.

See Also

Recipes 15.2, 15.4, and 17.4

15.7   Determining if an Asset Is Loaded

Problem

You want to know if an asset has completed loading into the Player.

Solution

Use the *getBytesLoaded()* and *getBytesTotal()* methods. Alternatively, define a custom isLoaded property for the *Sound* and *MovieClip* classes.

Discussion

There are three kinds of assets that can be loaded into a Flash movie using Action-Script: *.swf* files, JPEGs, and MP3s. The first two types are loaded into movie clips, and MP3s are loaded into *Sound* objects. Both the *MovieClip* and *Sound* classes have methods named *getBytesLoaded()* and *getBytesTotal()*, which you can use to determine whether the asset is loaded. So, no matter which type of asset you are loading, the ActionScript is essentially the same.

The *getBytesLoaded()* method returns the number of bytes that are currently loaded into a movie clip or *Sound* object, and the *getBytesTotal()* method returns the number of bytes that will be loaded when the asset has been completely received. You know that the asset is completely loaded into the Player once the values returned by the two methods are equal.

The *getBytesLoaded()* and *getBytesTotal()* methods use uncompressed file sizes and thus are not necessarily accurate measurements of the compressed asset sizes. However, their ratio yields a reasonable estimate of what percentage of the asset has loaded.

There is a caveat when comparing the values returned by *getBytesLoaded()* and *getBytesTotal()*. Before an object retrieves the information about the file it is loading (such as the total file size), both *getBytesLoaded()* and *getBytesTotal()* return 0. Thus, there is always a moment during which the two values are equal to 0, but the asset has not been loaded. You can address this problem by also checking whether the total bytes is also greater than zero. Therefore, we have:

```
if ( (myObj.getBytesLoaded() == myObj.getBytesTotal()) &&
     (myObj.getBytesTotal() > 0) ) {
  trace("The asset has completed loading");
}
```

If you load many assets into your Flash movies, consider adding a custom property to the *Sound* and *MovieClip* classes that handles all this logic for you. The following code should be added to the *Sound.as* file created in Chapter 13:

```
// The getIsLoaded() method returns true if the asset has loaded completely;
// otherwise, it returns false.
Sound.prototype.getIsLoaded = function () {
  return ( (this.getBytesLoaded() == this.getBytesTotal()) &&
           (this.getBytesTotal() > 0) );
};

// The isLoaded property is created for all Sound objects by calling the
// addProperty() method from the Sound class's prototype. This code configures the
// isLoaded property to automatically call the getIsLoaded() method.
Sound.prototype.addProperty("isLoaded", Sound.prototype.getIsLoaded, null);
```

You should add the following code to the *MovieClip.as* file created in Chapter 7. This code is exactly the same as the preceding code, except that it is applied to the *MovieClip* class instead of the *Sound* class.

```
MovieClip.prototype.getIsLoaded = function () {
  return ( (this.getBytesLoaded() == this.getBytesTotal()) &&
           (this.getBytesTotal() > 0) );
};
MovieClip.prototype.addProperty("isLoaded", MovieClip.prototype.getIsLoaded, null);
```

Once you have defined the isLoaded property, you can check to see if an asset has loaded, as follows:

```
if (myObj.isLoaded) {
  trace("The asset has completed loading");
}
```

In real-life scenarios, you monitor the load status repeatedly rather than simply checking it once. Monitoring the load status is demonstrated in Recipes 15.9 and 15.10.

See Also

Recipe 15.8. Also refer to Recipe 12.6 for an explanation of the techniques used in this recipe with regard to the *addProperty()* method and the isLoaded property. See Recipe 18.3 for details on detecting the loading of text variables using the *LoadVars* class. See Recipe 19.11 for details on monitoring XML loading progress.

15.8 Getting the Percentage of an Asset That Has Loaded

Problem

You want to determine what percentage of an asset has loaded.

Solution

Use the *getBytesLoaded()* and *getBytesTotal()* methods. Alternatively, you can create a custom percentLoaded property for the *Sound* and *MovieClip* classes.

Discussion

You can use the *getBytesLoaded()* and *getBytesTotal()* methods to determine the percentage of an asset that has loaded. The percentage is calculated by determining the ratio of the bytes loaded to the total bytes:

```
ratio = myObj.getBytesLoaded() / myObj.getBytesTotal();
```

The ratio is always between 0 and 1. Therefore, to format the percentage for display, you can multiply the ratio by 100. If you want the percentage to be a whole number, you can round the result as well:

```
percentLoaded = Math.round(ratio * 100);
```

The only caveat is that before any information about the asset has been retrieved (such as its file size), the *getBytesLoaded()* and *getBytesTotal()* methods both return 0, and 0 divided by 0 does not yield a valid number. Therefore, you should also use the *isNaN()* (is Not-a-Number) function to catch if the percentage is not a valid number and set it to 0 instead:

```
if (isNaN(percentLoaded)) {
  percentLoaded = 0;
}
```

You can encapsulate this process by defining a custom percentLoaded property for the *Sound* and *MovieClip* classes. The following code should be added to the *Sound.as* file created in Chapter 13:

```
// The getPercentLoaded( ) method returns the percent that has loaded as a whole
// number. It also makes sure that the returned value is always a valid number.
Sound.prototype.getPercentLoaded = function ( ) {
  var pLoaded = Math.round((this.getBytesLoaded() / this.getBytesTotal( )) * 100);
  if (isNaN(pLoaded)) {
    pLoaded = 0;
  }
  return pLoaded;
};

// The percentLoaded property is created for all Sound objects using the
// addProperty( ) method. This code configures the Sound class so that whenever the
// percentLoaded property is accessed, the getPercentLoaded( ) method is called
// automatically.
Sound.prototype.addProperty("percentLoaded",
                            Sound.prototype.getPercentLoaded, null);
```

You should add the following code to the *MovieClip.as* file created in Chapter 7:

```
MovieClip.prototype.getPercentLoaded = function ( ) {
  var pLoaded = Math.round((this.getBytesLoaded() / this.getBytesTotal( )) * 100);
  if (isNaN(pLoaded)) {
    pLoaded = 0;
  }
  return pLoaded;
};
MovieClip.prototype.addProperty("percentLoaded",
                                MovieClip.prototype.getPercentLoaded, null);
```

Once you have defined the percentLoaded property for the *Sound* and *MovieClip* classes, you can get the percentage that has loaded using a single call to the property:

```
trace(myObj.percentLoaded);
```

In real-life scenarios, you monitor the load status repeatedly, rather than simply checking it once. Monitoring the load status is demonstrated in Recipes 15.9 and 15.10.

See Also

Recipe 15.7. Also refer to Recipe 12.6 for an explanation of the techniques used in this recipe with regard to the *addProperty()* method and the percentLoaded property. See Recipe 18.3 for details on detecting the loading of text variables using the *LoadVars* class. See Recipe 19.11 for details on monitoring XML loading progress.

15.9 Monitoring Load Progress Using a Progress Bar Component

Problem

You want to display the progress of an asset-loading operation using a progress bar.

Solution

Use the Progress Bar component.

Discussion

The Progress Bar component is included in the Flash UI Components Set 2. You can download this components set for free from the Macromedia Flash Exchange at *http:// www.macromedia.com/exchange/flash/*. The full URL is:

http://www.macromedia.com/cfusion/exchange/index.cfm?view=sn110#loc=en_ us&view=sn111&viewName=Flash%20Extension&extID=365880&lc_id=55920

After downloading the components set, install it using the Macromedia Extension Manager (also a free download from the Flash Exchange). You have to restart Flash to see the new components. Once you restart Flash, you should see the Flash UI Components Set 2 option in the Components panel menu.

You can add a progress bar to a movie manually at authoring time, or you can add the Progress Bar component to the movie's Library and use the *attachMovie()* method to add the component to the movie at runtime:

```
_root.attachMovie("FProgressBarSymbol", "pBar", 1);
```

You should use the *setLoadTarget()* method of a progress bar instance to specify a movie clip or a sound that the component should monitor:

```
// This code configures a progress bar named soundPBar to monitor the load progress
// of a sound named mySound_sound.
soundPBar.setLoadTarget(mySound_sound);

// This code configures a progress bar named jpegPBar to monitor the load progress of
// a JPEG into a movie clip named myMovieClip_mc.imageHolder_mc.
jpegPBar.setLoadTarget(myMovieClip_mc.imageHolder_mc);
```

Here is a complete example showing how to monitor the loading of an MP3:

```
// Include the Sound.as file from Chapter 13.
#include "Sound.as"

// Create the Sound object.
mySound_sound = Sound.createNewSound( );
```

```
// Load an MP3 from the same directory as the Flash movie. Set streaming to false.
mySound_sound.loadSound("myMP3.mp3", false);

// Add the progress bar.
_root.attachMovie("FProgressBarSymbol", "pBar", 1);

// Set the progress bar to monitor the sound.
pBar.setLoadTarget(mySound_sound);
```

The progress bar indicates the load progress each time a new chuck of data is received. The perceived smoothness of this depends on the connection speed and latency.

See Also

Recipes 15.11 and 15.12. See Recipe 15.10 for an alternative approach. You can also find other third-party progress bars by going to the Macromedia Flash Exchange (*http://www.macromedia.com/exchange/flash*) and searching for "Progress Bar."

15.10 Monitoring Load Progress Without a Progress Bar Component

Problem

You want to monitor the load progress of an asset without having to use the Progress Bar component.

Solution

Create a movie clip and define an *onEnterFrame()* method that monitors the load progress of the asset, or use an interval function. Alternatively, you can create a custom *LoadMonitor* class.

Discussion

The Progress Bar component is a handy, pre-built resource for graphically representing the progress of an operation, such as asset loading. However, the Progress Bar component is overkill if you merely want to monitor the download progress in the background in order to trigger other actions when appropriate.

You can use a movie clip with an *onEnterFrame()* method to monitor the load progress of an asset. Within the *onEnterFrame()* method, you should continually check the percentage of the asset that has loaded.

```
// Create a movie clip and begin loading a .swf file into it.
_root.createEmptyMovieClip("swfHolder", 1);
swfHolder.loadMovie("externalSWF.swf");
```

```
// Create a movie clip to monitor the load progress.
_root.createEmptyMovieClip("loadMonitorMc", 2);

// Define an onEnterFrame() method for the monitor movie clip.
loadMonitorMc.onEnterFrame = function () {

  // Execute trace() once the .swf file has finished loading.
  if (_root.swfHolder.isLoaded) {
    trace("SWF has loaded");
  }
};
```

Or, you can achieve similar results using an interval function instead of a movie clip:

```
// Create a movie clip and begin loading a .swf file into it.
_root.createEmptyMovieClip("swfHolder", 1);
swfHolder.loadMovie("externalSWF.swf");

// Define a function to call at an interval.
function monitor () {
  // Execute trace() once the .swf file has finished loading.
  if (swfHolder.isLoaded) {
    trace("SWF has loaded");
  }
};

// Invoke monitor() every 100 milliseconds to update the load status.
monitorInterval = setInterval("monitor", 100);
```

You can also write a custom *LoadMonitor* class that you can reuse in multiple movies. You can add the following code to a *LoadMonitor.as* file in your Flash *Include* directory for easy inclusion in other projects:

```
// The LoadMonitor constructor accepts a reference to the object it should monitor.
// This object can be a Sound object or a movie clip.
_global.LoadMonitor = function (obj) {

  // Create a property with the value of the monitored object.
  this.monitored = obj;

  // Set the interval.
  this.interval = setInterval(this, "monitor", 100);
};

// The setChangeHandler() method allows you to define a callback function that is
// invoked automatically each time there is load progress. The method accepts a
// reference to the callback function.
LoadMonitor.prototype.setChangeHandler = function (callback) {
  this.callback = callback;
};

LoadMonitor.prototype.monitor = function () {

  // If the percent loaded is greater than the last time monitor() was called, invoke
  // the callback function, passing it a reference to the monitored object. The
```

```
    // parameter makes it convenient to reference the monitored object within the
    // callback function.
    var pLoaded = this.monitored.percentLoaded;
    if (pLoaded != this.percent) {
      this.callback(this.monitored);
    }
    this.percent = pLoaded;

    // If the monitored object is fully loaded, delete the interval so as to avoid
    // unnecessarily calling this method again.
    if (this.loadingObj.isLoaded) {
      clearInterval(this.interval);
    }
};
```

You can use the custom *LoadMonitor* class as follows:

```
#include "LoadMonitor.as"

// Include the Sound.as file from Chapter 13 for its createNewSound( ) method.
#include "Sound.as"

// Define the callback function.
function playSound (obj) {
  if (obj.isLoaded) {
    obj.start( );
  }
}

// Create the Sound object.
mySound_sound = Sound.createNewSound( );

// Load an MP3 from the same directory as the Flash movie. Set streaming to false.
mySound_sound.loadSound("myMP3.mp3", false);

// Create the LoadMonitor object to monitor the progress of mySound_sound and set the
// callback function.
lm = new LoadMonitor(mySound_sound);
lm.setChangeHandler(playSound);
```

Consider using the *LoadMonitor* class in situations in which you want to monitor the load progress of assets, but you don't want to visually represent this to the user. The resulting *.swf* will have a slightly smaller file size, and you can include the *LoadMonitor* class without having to add a component to your library or attach a movie clip to your movie.

See Also

Recipes 15.9 and 15.11

15.11 Performing Actions When the Asset Is Loaded

Problem

You want to define actions to occur when an asset has loaded completely.

Solution

For sounds, use the *onLoad()* event handler method. For all other datatypes, set a callback function using the *setChangeHandler()* of the *FProgressBar* class or the custom *LoadMonitor* class (depending on which technique you are using).

Discussion

The *Sound* class provides a convenient way to perform actions when the sound has loaded. Simply define an *onLoad()* method for the *Sound* object and Flash automatically invokes that method once the sound has loaded:

```
mySound_sound.onLoad = function () {
  // When the sound loads, tell it to start.
  this.start();
};
```

Other types of assets require another way of determining when the asset has loaded. When using the Progress Bar component, you can define a callback function that is called each time there is progress in the loading of the asset. The *setChangeHandler()* method accepts the name of a callback function as a string. It also accepts an optional, second parameter specifying a reference to the object in which the function can be found. If the second parameter is omitted, the timeline in which the Progress Bar component exists is assumed. The callback function is automatically passed a reference to the Progress Bar component.

```
// Define the callback function.
function onProgress (cmpt) {
  trace("onProgress() called for the progress bar " + cmpt);
}

// Set the callback function for updates on the progress bar named pBar.
pBar.setChangeHandler("onProgress");
```

Note that the callback function is called every time there is an update in the load progress for the asset being monitored. If you want to perform certain actions only when the loading has completed, use the *FProgressBar.getPercentComplete()* method to check whether the loading progress has reached 100%. For example:

```
function onProgress (cmpt) {
  // Ensure that the asset has completed loading before performing the actions.
```

```
    if (cmpt.getPercentComplete( ) == 100) {
      trace("Loading complete");
    }
  }
}
```

If you are using the custom *LoadMonitor* class (see Recipe 15.10), you can set a call-back function for the *LoadMonitor* object using the *setChangeHandler()* method. Like the change handler callback function for *FProgressBar*, the callback function for *LoadMonitor* is called each time load progress is made. Therefore, within the callback function, you should first determine whether the asset has completely loaded before performing any actions.

```
// Include the custom LoadMonitor class.
#include "LoadMonitor.as"

// Define the callback function.
function resize (obj) {
  if (obj.isLoaded) {
    obj._xscale = 50;
    obj._yscale = 50;
  }
}

// Create a movie clip and load an external .swf file.
this.createEmptyMovieClip("myMovieClip_mc", 1);
myMovieClip_mc.loadMovie("mySWF.swf");

// Create the LoadMonitor object to monitor the progress of myMovieClip_mc and set
// the callback function.
lm = new LoadMonitor(myMovieClip_mc);
lm.setChangeHandler(resize);
```

See Also

Recipes 15.9 and 15.10

15.12 Hiding the Graphics and Text for a Progress Bar

Problem

You want to hide the graphics and/or text for a progress bar.

Solution

Set the _visible property of the progress bar instance to false, or use the *setDisplayGraphics()* and/or *setDisplayText()* methods of the progress bar.

Discussion

Progress bars display the loading progress using both graphical and textual means. Although you may want to show both at times, you may want to use the component to monitor the load progress silently—that is, without displaying anything on the screen. Even if you want to display the progress to the user, once the asset has loaded, you generally should turn off the display of the progress bar. In either case, you can easily hide the visual components of the progress bar by setting its _visible property to false:

```
pBar._visible = false;
```

Here is some sample code that hides a progress bar once the asset has completed loading:

```
function onProgress (cmpt) {
  if (cmpt.getPercentComplete( ) == 100) {
    cmpt._visible = false;
  }
}
```

You can hide the graphics and text of the progress bar separately using the *setDisplayGraphics()* and *setDisplayText()* methods. Both methods accept a Boolean parameter, in which true shows the graphics or text and false hides them.

```
// Add the progress bar. (You must have already added the symbol to your library.)
_root.attachMovie("FProgressBarSymbol", "pBar", 1);

// Hide the graphics.
pBar.setDisplayGraphics(false);

// Hide the text.
pBar.setDisplayText(false);
```

See Also

Recipe 15.9

## CHAPTER 16

Storing Persistent Information

16.0 Introduction

You already know how to work with data that is stored in memory as long as a Flash movie is open. In fact, almost all data you work with in ActionScript is of this type. But what if you want to be able to store data between Flash movie sessions? Or what if you want to be able to share data between Flash movies running on the same client, or even on different clients? To accomplish these feats, we'll need to look at how we can store and transmit data outside of the Flash Player.

This chapter addresses both client-side and server-side data. First, we'll examine client-side data. Prior to Flash 6, the only way to store persistent data on the client was with complex techniques that invoked external JavaScript functions to read and write cookies. However, Flash 6 introduced *local shared objects* to ActionScript, making it possible to store and retrieve persistent data on the client without the use of these other, complicated techniques.

We'll also take a closer look at server-side data. Prior to Flash 6, server-side data manipulation was limited to invoking server-side scripts (using *loadVariables()* or an *XML* object) to read and write data to text files and/or databases on the server. The problem was, of course, that this functionality required that you had the necessary scripts on the server. While this kind of functionality still has its place (although the *LoadVars* class supercedes the older *loadVariables()* method), this chapter examines how *remote shared objects*, used in conjunction with FlashCom, allow us to work with server-side data in a different way.

Shared objects come in several varieties. Local shared objects (LSOs) are similar to browser cookies in that they are stored on the client's machine. Local shared objects are useful for storing the same kinds of information for which cookies have traditionally been used, such as the capability for a web site to remember a user so that the user does not have to manually log in during each visit. But LSOs are more powerful than cookies because they can store more data than cookies and store native ActionScript datatypes. Local shared objects are available to any Flash 6 movie, and they do not require any additional software on the client or on the server.

In contrast with local shared objects, remote shared objects (RSOs) are available only for movies that are clients of a Flash Communication Server MX (FlashCom) application (see Chapter 14). Remote shared objects allow you to store persistent data that is accessible by all clients of that application. Remote shared objects can also be used for nonpersistent data sharing between clients (see Recipe 16.5).

Local shared objects exist on the client only. On the other hand, remote shared objects must be opened on both the client and the server. Throughout this chapter, we refer to shared objects that are opened on the client (whether local or remote shared objects) as *client-side shared objects*, and we refer to shared objects opened on the server (using code within an *.asc* file) as *server-side shared objects*. This is an important distinction because the ActionScript that you use in each case is different.

16.1 Storing and Retrieving Locally Persistent Information

Problem

You want to store information on a client's computer that persists between movies and sessions.

Solution

Use a local shared object (LSO).

Discussion

Local shared objects are to Flash what cookies are to web browsers—but more so. They are called "super cookies" by some developers because they allow you to store potentially large amounts of data (if the user allows) and because they also allow you to store and retrieve many native ActionScript datatypes (as well as objects created from custom classes). Local shared object files are saved to the client computer. Flash movies within the same domain can write to and read from these files by means of ActionScript's *SharedObject* class.

The static *getLocal()* method is the mechanism by which LSOs are both created and opened for reading. The method requires at least one parameter—a string that specifies the name of the shared object to create or open:

```
my_l_so = SharedObject.getLocal("myFirstLSO");
```

The *getLocal()* method attempts to first locate an existing LSO by the specified name stored on the client computer. If none is found, Flash creates a new LSO with that name. In either case, the existing or new LSO is opened. The *getLocal()* method returns a *SharedObject* instance. It is used instead of the *new* operator to instantiate a new local shared object.

For a complete example of how to create, write to, and save a local shared object, see Recipe 16.4.

See Also

Recipe 16.5 discusses sharing data between movies. Also refer to Recipe 2.8 for details on opening the Flash Player Settings dialog box to the Local Storage tab. See Recipe 16.2 for important information on how to store data in a local shared object. See Recipe 16.3 for important information on how to retrieve data from a local shared object. See Recipe 16.4 for information on the *SharedObject.flush()* method, which is used to manually save data to a shared object.

16.2   Adding Data to a Client-Side Shared Object

Problem

You want to add data to a client-side shared object (whether it be a remote or local shared object).

Solution

Add the values as properties of the shared object's data object.

Discussion

Shared objects have a special built-in property named data. The data property is an object to which you should add any information that you want to save to the shared object:

```
// Store a username value to the shared object.
mySO.data.username = "Joey";
```

Properties attached directly to the shared object, rather than to its data property, are not written to the shared object. Thus, attaching properties directly to the shared object is useful only for data that does not need to persist between sessions. Therefore, the following code is potentially an erroneous attempt to save data:

```
mySO.someVal = "this value is lost when the movie closes";
```

The correct approach is to attach the value to the data property, as follows:

```
mySO.data.someVal = "this value is stored in the shared object";
```

You can store several native ActionScript datatypes to the shared object's data property, as follows.

```
mySO.data.myArray = new Array("a", "b", "c");
mySO.data.myDate = new Date( );
```

However, you cannot store movie clips, buttons, text fields, or shared objects themselves to a shared object's data property such that the data persists correctly between sessions.

You can also store objects created from custom classes to a shared object's data property. However, for the object to be properly cast (interpreted as the intended datatype) when it is retrieved in the next session, you must use the *Object.registerClass()* method. If you do not register your custom class, ActionScript won't know what to do with the data retrieved from the shared object.

The conventional use of the *registerClass()* method is to associate a class to a symbol in the Library. You should do this when you want to develop components with class definitions. However, you can also use the *registerClass()* method to register a class to an arbitrary identifier:

```
function MyClass ( ) {}
```

```
Object.registerClass("MyClassID", MyClass);
```

This code tricks the object into storing information about the class that created it. Therefore, when the data is retrieved from the shared object, Flash knows what kind of object it is.

The custom class must be defined and registered in all movies that retrieve the custom object data from a shared object.

There is one additional consideration you must address to successfully recast custom datatypes when they are retrieved from a shared object. When an object is retrieved from a shared object, all the properties are set and then the constructor for the class is called. This process will likely wipe out some, if not all, of the properties of the object if your constructor includes any initialization functionality. To understand this potential problem, consider the following example:

```
// Define a custom class. The constructor sets a property in the new object.
function MyClass(val) {
  this.val = val;
}

// Register the class.
Object.registerClass("MyClassID", MyClass);

// Create or open a local shared object.
my_l_so = SharedObject.getLocal("myFirstLSO");
```

```
// If the shared object doesn't already have an objA object, create a new MyClass
// object and assign it to the shared object. Otherwise, if objA already exists
// (meaning that it was saved from a previous session), display the value of its val
// property in the Output window.
if (my_l_so.data.objA == undefined) {
  my_l_so.data.objA = new MyClass("yay");
  my_l_so.flush( );
} else {
  trace(my_l_so.data.objA.val);
}
```

In this example, the value of the object's val property is always undefined. The reason is that even though the object was initially saved with the value "yay", the constructor is called with an undefined value each time the shared object data is retrieved. You can solve this problem by enclosing all the initialization code within the constructor in an *if* statement, as follows, which prevents the property from being erroneously reinitialized:

```
function MyClass(val) {
  if (!this.inited) {
    this.inited = true;
    this.val = val;
  }
}
```

When you change the constructor in this way, the original value for val is retained. When the *MyClass* object is first created, the inited property does not exist. Therefore, the *if* statement's condition is true. However, when the object is retrieved from the shared object, the inited property is true, and the initialization code does not execute. In this way the val property is not overwritten.

See Also

Recipes 16.3, 16.10, and 17.2

16.3 Reading Values from a Client-Side Shared Object

Problem

You want to read values from a client-side shared object (either a remote or local shared object).

Solution

Read the values from the properties of the shared object's data property.

Discussion

There is nothing difficult about reading the values from a client-side shared object. All persistent values are stored in the shared object's data property, so you simply read the values from the data property, as follows:

```
// Read the value of myProperty from the shared object, mySO, and write it to the
// Output window.
trace(mySO.data.myProperty);
```

See Also

Recipe 16.2. Also refer to Recipe 16.9 for important differences when reading data from a remote shared object.

16.4   Saving a Local Shared Object

Problem

You want to save local shared object data to the client computer.

Solution

Use the *SharedObject.flush()* method in the Flash movie.

Discussion

Flash automatically attempts to save local shared object data to disk when the movie is unloaded from the Player (such as when the Player closes). However, it is not a good practice to rely on the automatic save functionality, as there are several reasons why the data might not save successfully. Instead, you should explicitly instruct the local shared object to write the data to disk using the *SharedObject.flush()* method:

```
flushResult = my_l_so.flush();
```

When the *flush()* method is invoked, it attempts to write the data to the client computer. The result of a *flush()* invocation can be one of three possibilities:

- If the user set the local storage for the domain to "Never", the data is not saved and the method returns false.

- If the amount of disk space required to save the local shared object's data is less than the local storage setting for the domain, the data is written to disk and the method returns true.

- If the user has not allotted as much space as the shared object data requires, he is prompted to allow enough space or to deny access to save the data. When this happens, the method returns "pending". If the user chooses to grant access, the extra space is automatically allotted and the data is saved.

In the third case, in which the *flush()* method returns "pending", there is an additional step you can take to determine whether the user grants or denies access to save the data. When the user makes a selection from the automatic prompt, the *onStatus()* method of the shared object is automatically invoked. It is up to you to define the method to handle the results in the way that is appropriate for your application. When the callback method is invoked, it is passed a parameter. The parameter is an object with a code property that is set to "SharedObject.Flush.Success" if the user granted access or "SharedObject.Flush.Failed" if the user denied access.

Here is an example that invokes *flush()* to save the data explicitly and then handles the possible responses:

```
my_l_so = SharedObject.getLocal("myFirstLSO");
my_l_so.data.val = "a value";
result = my_l_so.flush();
// If the flush operation completes, check the result.
// If the operation is pending, the onStatus() method of the
// shared object is invoked before any result is returned.
if (result) {
    // Saved successfully. Place any code here that you want to execute after the data
    // was successfully saved.
}
else if (!result) {
    // This means the user has the local storage settings to 'Never.' If it is
    // important to save your data, you may want to alert the user here. Also, if you
    // want to make it easy for the user to change his settings, you can open the local
    // storage tab of the Player Settings dialog box with the following code:
    // System.showSettings(1);.
}

// Define the onStatus() method for the shared object.
// It is invoked automatically after the user makes a selection
// from the prompt that occurs when flush() returns "pending."
my_l_so.onStatus = function (infoObj) {
    if (infoObj.code == "SharedObject.Flush.Success") {
        // If the infoObj.code property is "SharedObject.Flush.Success", it means the
        // user granted access. Place any code here that you want to execute when the
        // user grants access.
    } else if (infoObj.code == "SharedObject.Flush.Failed") {
        // If the infoObj.code property is "SharedObject.Flush.Failed", it means the user
        // denied access. Place any code here that you want to execute when the user
        // denies access.
    }
};
```

If you know in advance that a shared object is likely to continue to increase in size with each session, it is prudent to request a larger amount of local storage space when the shared object is created. Otherwise, each time the current allotted space is exceeded, the user is prompted again to accept or deny the storage request. Setting aside extra space avoids repeatedly asking the user for permission to store incrementally more data. You can request a specific amount of space when you call the *flush()* method by passing it a number of bytes to set aside for the shared object:

```
// Request 500 KB of space for the shared object.
result = mySO.flush(1024 * 500);
```

16.5 Sharing Information Between Movies Within the Same Domain

Problem

You want two movies within the same domain to have access to the same local shared object.

Solution

Specify a local path parameter when creating and opening the local shared object.

Discussion

By default, local shared objects are saved to a path on the client computer that is unique to the domain, path, and name of the *.swf* file that is calling the *getLocal()* method. This prevents name conflicts between local shared objects from different domains or even different movies on the same domain. For example, on a system running Windows XP, if a movie named *myMovie.swf* served from *www.person13.com/ascb/* writes a local shared object named *myFirstLSO*, the data is saved to the following location:

> *D:\Documents and Settings\[UserName]\Application Data\Macromedia\Flash Player\person13.com\ascb\myMovie.swf\myFirstLSO.sol*

The name of the *.swf* file is included in the path to which the LSO is saved so that it will not conflict with an LSO named *myFirstLSO* created by another movie served from the same domain and path. However, in some cases, you want two movies on the same domain to have access to the same LSO. In these cases, you should use the optional local path parameter when creating and opening the LSO using *getLocal()*.

The local path parameter (the second parameter passed to *getLocal()*) must be a string that specifies the full or partial path to the *.swf* file that created the LSO. For example:

```
my_l_so = SharedObject.getLocal("myFirstLSO", "/");
```

If the preceding code exists in *myMovie.swf*, which is served from *www.person13.com/ascb/*, the local shared object is stored at the following location:

> *D:\Documents and Settings\[UserName]\Application Data\Macromedia\Flash Player\person13.com\myFirstLSO.sol*

An LSO created in this way can be opened by any other Flash movie in the same domain with the following line of ActionScript:

```
my_l_so = SharedObject.getLocal("myFirstLSO", "/");
```

It is important to understand that a movie can only create and/or open an LSO within the same full or partial path. To understand this, consider an example with two Flash movies: *movieOne.swf* and *movieTwo.swf*. Both movies are served from the same domain—*www.person13.com*—but at different paths. *movieOne.swf* is served from *www.person13.com/ascb/firstGroup/*, and *movieTwo.swf* is served from *www.person13.com/ascb/secondGroup/*. In this scenario, *movieOne.swf* can create and read LSOs with any of the following local path values:

```
/
/ascb
/ascb/firstGroup
```

and *movieTwo.swf* can create and read LSOs with any of the following local path values:

```
/
/ascb
/ascb/secondGroup
```

Therefore, if you want both movies to be able to access a common LSO, you must specify one of the two local paths that the movies share (/ or /ascb) when you invoke the *getLocal()* method.

To illustrate how you can share data between two (or more) Flash movies within the same domain, let's take a look at an example. If the movies don't exist within the same directory, we must specify a local path that is common to both of them in the directory hierarchy. Let's start by looking at what happens if we fail to specify a common local path:

1. Create a new Flash document, and on the first frame of the main timeline add the following code:

   ```
   this.createTextField("message_txt", 1, 100, 100, 100, 20);
   message_l_so = SharedObject.getLocal("messageLSO");
   val = (message_l_so.data.val == undefined) ? 0 : message_l_so.data.val;
   message_l_so.data.val = val;
   message_txt.text = "movie A value: " + val;
   ```

2. Create a new directory somewhere on your computer. Name this directory *LSOTest*.

3. Create two subdirectories within *LSOTest*. Name these subdirectories *movieAPath* and *movieBPath*.

4. Save the document as *movieA.fla* to the *LSOTest/movieAPath* directory.

5. Export the movie as *movieA.swf* to the *LSOTest/movieAPath* directory.

6. Create a new Flash document, and on the first frame of the main timeline add the following code (it's almost identical to the code in *movieA.fla*):

```
this.createTextField("message_txt", 1, 100, 100, 100, 20);
message_1_so = SharedObject.getLocal("messageLSO");
val = (message_1_so.data.val == undefined) ? 0 : message_1_so.data.val;
message_1_so.data.val = val;
message_txt.text = "movie B value: " + val;
```

7. Save the document as *movieB.fla* to the *LSOTest/movieBPath* directory.

8. Export the movie as *movieB.swf* to the *LSOTest/movieBPath* directory.

9. Open *movieA.swf* in a web browser and reload the page several times. Each time you reload, you should see the number increment by one.

10. Test *movieB.swf* in the same way you tested *movieA.swf*. You should see the number increment by one with each reload as well. However, notice that the number starts at 0. This is because, as it stands, *movieA.swf* and *movieB.swf* use different shared objects. Even though the shared objects have the same name, they have different paths.

11. To cause both movies to use the same shared object, we must tell them to look in the same path. Modify the line of code that opens the shared object so that it reads as follows in both *movieA.fla* and *movieB.fla*:

```
message_1_so = SharedObject.getLocal("messageLSO", "/");
```

This causes both movies to look to a common path for the shared object, and hence use the same file.

12. Save the Flash documents and re-export the *.swf* files.

13. Test the movies again as in steps 9 and 10. This time, notice that each update to one movie also increments the value used by the other movie. This is because they are now using the same shared object.

See Also

Chapter 17

16.6 Storing Persistent Data on the Server

Problem

You want to store persistent data on the FlashCom server.

Solution

Use a remote shared object to store persistent data on the server and access it from one or more clients. Use the *SharedObject.get()* method in the Server-Side Action-Script to create the shared object, and then connect the client(s) to the shared object using the *SharedObject.getRemote()* and *connect()* methods in the client-side Action-Script. Or, you can create the RSO entirely from the client using the *SharedObject. getRemote()* method.

Discussion

To create persistent remote shared objects, you can use one of two approaches. Either you can create the server-side shared object using the *SharedObject.get()* method in an *.asc* file and then connect to it from the Flash clients, or you can handle everything from the client. Creating the shared object on the server side is preferable in most scenarios because it allows you to do more things with the data on the server. (The server-side *.asc* file must exist within the FlashCom application. See Recipes 14.1 and 14.14.) The *get()* method requires you to specify the name of the shared object as well as a Boolean value indicating whether the shared object should be persistent (true) or not (false). (In this case, you want to create a persistent object. See Recipe 17.5 for information about creating nonpersistent shared objects.) If a shared object with the same name already exists on the server, then it is opened; otherwise, a new shared object is created.

```
// Create a new persistent shared object named myFirstRSO and
// assign that reference to a variable named myServer_r_so.
// This code belongs in an .asc file on the FlashCom server.
myServer_r_so = SharedObject.get("myFirstRSO", true);
```

Once a shared object has been created on the server, you can connect Flash movie clients to it using the client-side *SharedObject.getRemote()* and *SharedObject.connect()* methods. The *getRemote()* method requires three pieces of information: the name of the shared object (which must match the name of the shared object that was created using the Server-Side ActionScript), the URI for the net connection to the FlashCom server (which can be retrieved using the uri property of the net connection object), and a Boolean indicating whether the shared object is persistent (true) or not (false). The *getRemote()* method returns a *SharedObject* instance. It is used instead of the *new* operator to instantiate a new remote shared object.

Additionally, you must also instruct the client-side shared object to connect to the FlashCom server to synchronize with the server-side object by using the *connect()* method. The *connect()* method requires that you specify which connection object to use to make the connection.

```
// Create a new, client-side, persistent RSO in the Flash movie. This code looks for
// a server-side shared object named myFirstRSO on the server and application
// specified by the URI (returned by the myConnection.uri property).
myClient_r_so = SharedObject.getRemote("myFirstRSO", myConnection.uri, true);
myClient_r_so.connect(myConnection);
```

When any changes are made to a remote shared object, the server automatically synchronizes the client-side data and invokes the *onSync()* method of the client-side shared object for all clients. Therefore, to catch any synchronization events, you should define an *onSync()* method for the client-side shared object. For example:

```
myClient_r_so.onSync = function () {
  trace("RSO data has been updated/retrieved.");
};
```

It is important to understand that there will always be some degree of latency between the creation and connection of the remote shared object and the retrieval of the data from the server-side object. Therefore, you cannot rely on the data being available within the client immediately following the calls to *getRemote()* and *connect()*. Consider, for example, that you want to use data from a remote shared object to initialize a list box in a client movie. It might seem natural enough to try something like this:

```
myClient_r_so = SharedObject.getRemote("myFirstRSO", myConnection.uri, true);
myClient_r_so.connect(myConnection);

// Try to set the data provider of the list box to an array stored in the shared
// object (it doesn't work).
myListBox.setDataProvider(myClient_r_so.data.anArray);
```

However, this will not work! The problem is that, most likely, the remote data has not yet been loaded into the client. This is why it is important that you use the *onSync()* method to catch any updates to the client-side data (which includes the initial retrieval of the server-side data). Here is the correct way to implement the preceding example:

```
myClient_r_so = SharedObject.getRemote("myFirstRSO", myConnection.uri, true);
myClient_r_so.connect(myConnection);

// Place the setDataProvider( ) call inside the onSync( ) method to ensure that the
// server-side data has been retrieved before trying to use it.
myClient_r_so.onSync = function () {
  _root.myListBox.setDataProvider(this.data.anArray);
};
```

See Also

See Recipe 16.10 for important information on how to store data in the remote shared object. Also refer to Recipe 17.5.

16.7   Saving Remote Shared Object Data

Problem

You want to save the data stored in a remote shared object.

Solution

Define an *onAppStop()* callback handler or use the *SharedObject.flush()* method on the server.

Discussion

When you are working with RSOs, there are really two shared objects: the object as it exists on the server and the object as it exists on the client. And in a scenario in which the shared objects are persistent, there is both a persistent, disk-based version and a working version stored in memory. As the client makes changes to the data in the client-side, memory-based shared object, it is automatically sent to the server, and the data in the server-side, memory-based shared object is synchronized with the client-side data. And once the server data is updated, the *onSync()* method is invoked for all clients connected to the RSO.

```
// Create or open an RSO and connect to it.
my_r_so = SharedObject.getRemote("myFirstRSO", myConnection.uri);
my_r_so.connect(myConnection);

// Add data to the RSO. The data is automatically sent to the server.
my_r_so.data.myData = "Your Value Here.";
```

However, even though the memory-based shared objects are kept in synch with one another, the persistent, disk-based shared objects are not always kept in synch with the current data. This is because file access is a relatively "expensive" task. It requires more time to read and write to disk than to read and write to memory. As such, the default behavior for shared objects is that the data is not written to disk until the memory-based object is about to be deleted. This occurs on the client when the Flash movie is being closed, and it occurs on the server when the application is being shut down. You can read more about how to save the client-side data to disk in Recipe 16.4. For more information on storing server-side data to disk, keep reading.

The RSO data should need to be written to disk only if and when the FlashCom application stops. To tell FlashCom server to write the RSO data to disk when the application stops, define an *application.onAppStop()* method that returns true in your *main.asc* file on the server, as follows:

```
application.onAppStop = function () {
  return true;
};
```

You can also invoke the *flush()* method on the server-side shared object (from the .asc file) at any point to explicitly write the data to disk:

```
// Place this in your main.asc file or other included .asc file.
ssSo.flush();
```

See Also

Recipe 16.6

16.8   Checking for Updates to Remote Shared Objects

Problem

You want to be able to efficiently check to see what data has changed when a remote shared object is synchronized.

Solution

Use the *list* parameter that is automatically passed to the *onSync()* method. Loop through the parameter to locate all the elements in which the code property has the value indicating the type of update you are interested in.

Discussion

When the *onSync()* method is invoked (see Recipe 16.6), it is automatically passed a parameter that contains information about how the data has changed. The parameter is an array of objects, one for each property of the remote shared object. For example, if a remote shared object has two properties named myDate and myArray (meaning my_r_so.data.myDate and my_r_so.data.myArray), then the *list* parameter passed to the *onSync()* method will have two elements. In turn, each element contains three properties: code, name, and oldVal. One element will have its name property set to "myDate", and the other will have its name property set to "myArray". The code property can have the following values for persistent shared objects:

"success"
     The server-side value was successfully updated from a change made by this client.

"reject"
     The client tried to make a change to the value, but it was rejected by the server—usually because the same object was being updated by another client.

"change"
     The client-side value has been updated based on a new value from the server.

"delete"
     The property has been deleted.

"clear"
     Either the object is not persistent on the server or on the client, or all the properties have been deleted.

This change information is useful when you want to make changes in the client movie following a synchronization event, and you need to determine what data changed and how. For example, in a whiteboard application, you might use an RSO to store the positions of various movie clips that can be controlled by multiple users. Each movie clip's data can be stored as a different element in the RSO. When one client updates the position of a movie clip, you want to update that movie clip's position in all other connected clients. However, you don't want to unnecessarily update the positions of other movie clips that have not been moved. The following client-side code defines an *onSync()* method that determines which movie clips moved and updates their positions accordingly:

```
myClient_r_so = SharedObject.getRemote("myFirstRSO", myConnection.uri, true);
myClient_r_so.connect(myConnection);

myClient_r_so.onSync = function (list) {
  for (var i = 0; i < list.length; i++) {
    // Synchronize changes to a movie clip's position across all connected clients.
    // Check only for elements marked as "change" because the movie clip's properties
    // will be changed locally already for those marked "success".
    if (list[i].code == "change") {
      // This code assumes that the name of the elements in the shared object
      // correspond to the names of movie clips in _root.
      _root[list[i].name]._x = this.data[list[i].name]._x;
      _root[list[i].name]._y = this.data[list[i].name]._y;
    }
  }
};
```

Of course, the preceding code does not work in isolation. It requires that the client also contain code that writes to the RSO each time a client moves a movie clip. For example:

```
myMovieClip_mc.onPress = function () {
  this.startDrag();
};

myMovieClip_mc.onRelease = function () {
  this.stopDrag();

  // Create a new property in the RSO with the same name as the movie clip. Set that
  // property's value equal to an object with _x and _y properties.
  _root.myClient_r_so.data["myMovieClip_mc"] = {_x: this._x, _y: this._y};

};
```

See Also

See Recipe 16.10 for important information on how to store data in the remote shared object. Also refer to Recipe 17.6.

16.9 Reading Values from a Server-Side Shared Object

Problem

You want to read values from a server-side shared object.

Solution

Use the *SharedObject.getProperty()* method.

Discussion

You cannot read from a server-side shared object the same way you can from a client-side shared object. Use the *SharedObject.getProperty()* method to read from a server-side shared object. This method requires that you specify the name of the property to read, and it returns the value of that property.

```
// This code should be within an .asc file. It retrieves the value of myProperty and
// assigns that value to the variable myPropertyVar.
myPropertyVar = my_r_so.getProperty("myProperty");
```

See Also

Recipes 16.3, 16.8, and 16.10

16.10 Adding Data to a Server-Side Shared Object

Problem

You want to add values to a server-side shared object.

Solution

Use the *SharedObject.setProperty()* method.

Discussion

If you try to add values to a server-side shared object in the same way that you add values to a client-side shared object, you will receive an error. The correct way to add values (or modify existing values) to a server-side shared object is to use the *SharedObject.setProperty()* method. The *setProperty()* method requires that you specify both the name of the property and the value to assign to the property.

```
// This example code should appear in an .asc file. It adds a property named
// myProperty to a shared object and assigns the property the value of 6.
my_r_so.setProperty("myProperty", 6);
```

If you want to modify an existing property relative to its current value, you can use
the *getProperty()* method in conjunction with *setProperty()*:

```
// Set the myProperty property to one more than its current value.
my_r_so.setProperty("myProperty", my_r_so.getProperty("myProperty") + 1);
```

See Also

See Recipe 16.9 for details on *SharedObject.getProperty()*. See Recipe 16.2 for important differences when setting data for a local shared object.

Communicating with Other Movies

17.0 Introduction

When we speak of Flash movies interacting with one another, there are two types of interactions. First, there are interactions between movies that are running on the same computer. And second, there are interactions between movies on different computers.

Prior to Flash MX, the only way to communicate between movies on the same computer (without using server-side functionality) was to use the *fscommand()* global function, which executes JavaScript methods. Unfortunately, these methods were both cumbersome to use and not always reliable (due to lack of support in various browsers). Also, these methods worked only with Flash movies running in web browsers in which the browser windows had references to one another. However, Flash MX introduced *local connections*—a means by which any Flash movie can broadcast to and listen for broadcasts from any other movie on the same computer. The advantages of local connections are:

- They are relatively simple to use.
- They are implemented entirely in ActionScript, and they work for movies running in Flash Player 6 or later.

Additionally, prior to Flash MX, the only way to communicate between movies on different clients was to use a socket connection via the *XMLSocket* class. While the *XMLSocket* class is still a valuable and powerful technology, it has its disadvantages:

- Using sockets requires a server-side socket server. Although creating your own socket server requires proficiency in a server-side programming, third-party socket servers, such as Unity (*http://moock.org/unity*) are widely available and make working with the socket server considerably easier.
- The *XMLSocket* class does not have a very robust feature set. *XMLSocket* objects allow users to send data to a socket server and listen for data from a socket server. Additional code is necessary to handle that data in a meaningful way.

Using Flash Player 6 in conjunction with Flash Communication Server MX (Flash-Com), it is possible to create communication between client movies without relying on the *XMLSocket* class. The advantages of FlashCom are:

- It provides a standardized way of implementing communication between clients.
- It provides a rich API, and it automatically serializes and deserializes datatypes.
- It is capable of much more than just creating channels of communication between client movies. You can also use FlashCom for audio and video recording, playback, and live broadcasts. Socket servers don't offer this kind of functionality.

At the same time, you should take into consideration that there are possible disadvantages to FlashCom:

- FlashCom costs money; however so do many professional socket servers. Furthermore, a developer version of FlashCom server is freely available for testing, and the personal edition of FlashCom server is bundled with Director MX.
- FlashCom may not perform as well as socket servers when it comes to a large number of connections or high volumes of data transfer. Do some research and testing to determine whether FlashCom's performance characteristics meet the needs of your application.

See Also

See Chapter 14 for FlashCom recipes. See *http://www.macromedia.com/software/flashcom* for more information on FlashCom and its pricing. Third-party socket servers of varying price and capability include moockComm (*http://www.moock.org/chat/moockComm.zip*), Unity (*http://moock.org/unity*), aquaServer (*http://www.figleaf.com/development/flash5/aquaserver.zip*), Fortress (*http://www.xadra.com/products/fortress/fortress_faqs.html*), and ElectroServer (*http://www.electrotank.com/ElectroServer*).

17.1 Communicating with Other Movies on the Same Computer

Problem

You want to communicate from one Flash movie to one or more Flash movies playing on the same client computer.

Solution

Use a *LocalConnection* object to invoke a function in the receiving movie from the sending movie. Use *LocalConnection.connect()* to listen for messages in the receiving movie and define the function that will be invoked. Use *LocalConnection.send()* from the sending movie to invoke a function on the remote computer. Both the sending and receiving movies must specify the same named channel for communication.

Discussion

When two or more Flash movies are playing on the same client computer, they can communicate with each other via a local connection created with the *LocalConnection* class. As long as the movies are playing on the same computer, a connection can be made regardless of the domains from which the movies are being served.

 By default, movies accept communications from movies on the same domain only. However, you can configure them to receive from other domains as well. See Recipe 17.4.

To successfully communicate between multiple movies on the same computer you must do three things:

1. Configure the receiving movie(s) to listen for communications.
2. Tell the receiving movie(s) what to do when messages are received.
3. Send messages to the receiving movie(s) from the sending movie.

A receiving movie must listen for messages over a specific, named local connection. To establish this communication channel, you should create a local connection object in the receiving movie and tell it to listen to a named connection using the *connect()* method:

```
// Create the local connection object in the receiving movie.
receiving_lc = new LocalConnection( );

// Instruct the local connection object to listen for messages sent over the
// "_myConnection" channel.
receiving_lc.connect("_myConnection");
```

As shown in the preceding example, the best practice is to name your communication channel (not the local connection object) with an initial underscore (_). Naming your connections in this way also simplifies communicating across domains.

All communications are targeted to specific, custom methods of the receiving local connection object. For example, if the sending movie sends a communication that looks for a method named *myMethod()*, you should define *myMethod()* on the receiving movie's local connection object, as follows:

```
receiving_lc.myMethod = function () {
  _root.output_txt.text = "communication received!";
};
```

To set up the sending movie, you must first create a local connection object:

```
// Create the local connection object in the sending movie.
sending_lc = new LocalConnection();
```

Then use the *LocalConection.send()* method to send a communication. The first parameter of the *send()* method is a string that specifies the name of a connection over which to send the communication, enabling you to create multiple discrete connections. The second parameter of the *send()* method is a string specifying the name of the method to call in the receiving movie. When a movie receives a message, it invokes the method of the same name on the receiving local connection object. This example invokes a remote method:

```
// Send a communication across the "_myConnection" channel that invokes a method
// named myMethod() in the receiving movie.
sending_lc.send("_myConnection", "myMethod");
```

When a sending movie sends a communication over a connection, any movie listening to that connection receives the communication. Therefore, you can have more than one receiving movie for a single sending movie. Conversely, multiple movies can send messages to a single receiving movie over a single named connection.

Note that both the sending and receiving movies have to be playing on the same computer at the same time. To communicate between movies that play on the same computer at different times, use a local shared object. See Recipes 16.1 and 16.5.

See Also

To send data over a local connection, see Recipes 17.2 and 17.5.

17.2   Sending Data Using Local Connections

Problem

You want to send data to one or more movies playing on the same computer.

Solution

Pass the data as additional parameters to the *send()* method of the sending local connection object.

Discussion

You can send data to another movie using a local connection by passing the data as additional parameters to the *send()* method of the sending local connection object. The *send()* method requires at least two parameters: the name of the connection and the name of the method to invoke on the receiving movie. Any additional parameters passed to the *send()* method are automatically passed as parameters to the receiving movie's method. Note that the name of the method you are invoking on the receiving movie cannot be one of the built-in methods of the *LocalConnection* class, such as *send*, *connect*, etc. For a complete list of the built-in methods of a local connection, see the "Language Reference" section of *ActionScript for Flash MX: The Definitive Guide*, or the Reference panel (Window → Reference) in Flash.

You should define the receiving method so it accepts the parameters sent to it. In this example, the receiving movie contains a local connection with a method named *myMethod()*. The method expects three parameters: str, num, and bool.

```
receiving_lc = new LocalConnection();
receiving_lc.connect("_myConnection");
receiving_lc.myMethod = function (str, num, bool) {
  _root.output_txt.text = "The parameters are: " +
                          str + newline +
                          num + newline +
                          bool;
};
```

Here is a code snippet from a sending movie that calls *myMethod()* in the receiving movie and passes it parameters, similar to invoking it as follows: *myMethod("a string", 6, true)*.

```
// Send three parameters to a receiving movie's local connection method named
// myMethod(). The parameters happen to be a string, a number, and a Boolean.
sending_lc = new LocalConnection();
sending_lc.send("_myConnection", "myMethod", "a string", 6, true);
```

You are not limited to sending primitive datatypes only. Specifically, you can send data of the following complex types: *Object, Array, Date, TextFormat*, and *XML*.

Additionally, you can send objects of custom types. The process for doing so involves many of the same steps as storing and retrieving custom object types from a shared object. You can find more details about the theory behind this in Recipe 16.2, but the required steps are:

1. Define the custom class in both the sending and receiving movies.
2. Register the class in the sending and receiving movies using the *Object. registerClass()* method.
3. Define the constructor of the class such that any initialization code is enclosed in an *if* statement that is executed only once.

The following is an example of the code in a sending movie and a receiving movie that passes data of a custom object type from one to the other.

First, let's define the custom class in its own *.as* file so that we can easily include it in both the sending and receiving movies. For the purposes of this example, name the file *MyClass.as*.

```
// Define the custom class, MyClass.
function MyClass(val) {
```

```
    // Since the constructor contains initialization code, enclose it in an if
    // statement so that it is executed only when the object is first created and not
    // on subsequent deserializations. The inited property is used to track whether the
    // data has been initialized.
    if (!this.inited) {
      this.inited = true;
      this.val = val;
    }
  }
}

// Let's define a method for the class so that we can show that Flash allows us to
// invoke the method in the receiving movie.
MyClass.prototype.getVal = function () {
  return this.val;
};

// Register the class to an arbitrary ID.
Object.registerClass("MyClassID", MyClass);
```

Here's the receiving movie code:

```
#include "MyClass.as"

// Define the local connection object to listen over "_myConnection".
receiving_lc = new LocalConnection();
receiving_lc.connect("_myConnection");

receiving_lc.myMethod = function (param) {
  // If the parameter is an instance of MyClass, display its val property by the
  // getVal() method.
  if (param instanceof MyClass) {
    trace("Parameter value is " + param.getVal());
  } else {
    trace("Param is not of the expected type.");
  }
};
```

and here's the sending movie code:

```
#include "MyClass.as"

// Create the local connection and send a MyClass object to the receiving movie.
sending_lc = new LocalConnection();
sending_lc.send("_myConnection", "myMethod", new MyClass("test"));
```

Regardless of what type of data is being sent, the same rules apply to any type of local connection communication. Both movies must be running on the same computer at the same time, and the receiving movie must be listening on the same channel that the sending movie uses to send. Also, it is worth noting that once you have defined a custom datatype in both the sending and receiving movies, you can send that type of data in both directions (although you should use two separate channels for bidirectional communication, as discussed in Recipe 17.3).

See Also

Recipe 17.1

17.3 Validating Receipt of Communication Over a Local Connection

Problem

You want a sending movie to receive confirmation that the communication was successfully received.

Solution

Configure the receiving movie to return a receipt to the sending movie.

Discussion

If you need to confirm that a communication was received, you can have the receiving movie send a message back to the original sending movie. Here are the steps for confirming receipt of a communication:

1. Set up the sending and receiving movies, as described in Recipe 17.1.

2. In addition to whatever code you include in the method that is invoked on the receiving movie, write code to send a receipt over a new channel (e.g., "_myConnectionReceipt"). You can use *this.send()* within the local connection's method to send a receipt back to the original sender.

3. In the sending movie, call the *connect()* method, passing it the name of the channel over which the receiving movie sends the receipt (again, "_myConnectionReceipt").

4. In the sending movie, create a method on the local connection object to handle the receipt communication. Make sure this method name matches the name of the method that the receiving movie invokes when sending the receipt.

The following is an example of some code from a sending movie and a receiving movie.

First, the receiving movie code:

```
// Create the receiving code to listen on the "_myConnection" channel.
lc = new LocalConnection();
lc.connect("_myConnection");
lc.myMethod = function () {
  // In addition to whatever other code goes in the
  // receiving method, add this code to issue a receipt
```

```
    // back to the sending movie over the "myConnectionReceipt" channel.
    // The this keyword refers to the current local connection object.
    this.send("_myConnectionReceipt", "onReceipt");
  };
```

Then, the sending movie code:

```
    // Create the local connection object for sending over the "_myConnection" channel.
    sending_lc = new LocalConnection();
    sending_lc.send("_myConnection", "myMethod");

    // Tell the local connection to listen on the "_myConnectionReceipt" channel for the
    // receipt broadcast by the receiving movie.
    sending_lc.connect("_myConnectionReceipt");

    // Define the onReceipt() method that gets called from the receiving movie.
    sending_lc.onReceipt = function () {
      _root.output_txt.text = "received";
    };
```

The key point is that the name of the channel on which a local connection object listens (using *connect()*) must be the same as the name of the channel over which another movie's local connection object sends a message (using *send()*). Also, notice that the two movies do not communicate back and forth over the same channel. This is because a movie ignores any broadcasts over any channel to which it is also listening. So we establish two one-way channels because a single channel is not two-way in practice.

See Also

Recipe 17.1

17.4 Accepting Communications from Other Domains

Problem

You want a movie to accept local connection communications from movies served from other domains.

Solution

Use the *allowDomain()* method of the receiving local connection object.

Discussion

By default, receiving movies accept communications from sending movies on the same domain only. However, you can use the *allowDomain()* method of a local connection object to allow or disallow communications from any domains. You need to define the *allowDomain()* method for each receiving local connection object for which you wish to define a custom list of domains to accept or deny.

If present, the *allowDomain()* method is automatically invoked when a local connection object receives a communication. If *allowDomain()* returns true, the communication is accepted; if it returns false, the communication is denied. Therefore, you can configure a local connection object to receive communications from any domain by having its *allowDomain()* method return true in all cases:

```
// Define the receiving local connection, and instruct it to listen to communications
// over the "_myConnection" channel.
receiving_lc = new LocalConnection();
receiving_lc.connect("_myConnection");

// Define the allowDomain() method for the receiving local connection object, which
// is invoked automatically whenever a communication is received. This example always
// returns true, so all communications are accepted.
receiving_lc.allowDomain = function (domain) {
  return true;
};
```

However, it is generally not a good practice to allow communications from all domains, because doing so allows any other movie to invoke an arbitrary method on your movie. It is better to specify trusted domains from which to accept connections. The domain of the sending movie is passed to the *allowDomain()* method as a parameter, and you can use this to determine whether the sending domain should be trusted. For example:

```
receiving_lc.allowDomain = function (domain) {
  // If the domain of the sending movie is person13.com, allow the communication.
  // Otherwise, disallow it.
  if (domain == "person13.com") {
    return true;
  } else {
    return false;
  }
};
```

Local connection objects also provide a convenient means of determining the domain of the receiving movie. The *domain()* method can be invoked from any local connection object to reveal the domain from which the movie is being served. You can use this method within the *allowDomain()* method to allow communications from the same domain. For example:

```
receiving_lc.allowDomain = function (domain) {
  // If the domain of the sending movie is the same as that of the receiving movie,
  // allow the communication. Otherwise, disallow it.
```

```
      if (domain == this.domain()) {
        return true;
      } else {
        return false;
      }
    };
```

The preceding example accomplishes exactly the same thing as though you had not defined the *allowDomain()* method at all—it allows communications from the same domain only. Normally, therefore, you use *domain()* to allow communications from the same domain as well as communications from other domains:

```
    receiving_lc.allowDomain = function (domain) {
      // If the domain of the sending movie is person13.com or the same domain as the
      // receiving movie, allow the communication. Otherwise, disallow it.
      if ( (domain == "person13.com") || (domain == this.domain()) ) {
        return true;
      } else {
        return false;
      }
    };
```

See Also

Recipes 15.2 and 15.6

17.5 Communicating Between Movies on Different Computers

Problem

You want to create a channel of communication between two or more movies on different computers.

Solution

Create a remote shared object and connect each of the clients to it.

Discussion

LocalConnection objects can be used to communicate between movies on the same computer but not on different computers. Remote shared objects offer a way to create channels of communication between multiple computers acting as clients of a FlashCom application. Remote shared objects can be either persistent or nonpersistent. In most cases where you simply want to create a channel of communication between FlashCom clients, there is no need to create a persistent shared object (in which the data is stored to disk). On the other hand, if you want to save the data between sessions or restarts of the FlashCom application, you should make the shared object persistent, as discussed in Recipe 16.6.

Each client must create a client-side remote shared object using the *SharedObject.getRemote()* method and connect using the *connect()* method:

```
// Create a nonpersistent client-side RSO and connect it to the server. This example
// assumes that you have an existing net connection object named myConnection.
myClient_r_so = SharedObject.getRemote("clientComRSO", myConnection.uri, false);
myClient_r_so.connect(myConnection);
```

See Also

See the Introduction to Chapter 16 as well as Recipe 16.6 for more information regarding remote shared objects and the details of the *get()*, *getRemote()*, and *connect()* methods. See Recipe 17.6 for further information on using an RSO to communicate between connected FlashCom clients. Also refer to Recipes 14.15 and 17.1.

17.6   Broadcasting Data to Remote Shared Object Clients

Problem

You want to send data to all the clients of a FlashCom application that are connected to a remote shared object.

Solution

Use the *SharedObject.onSync()* method to catch synchronization events, and use the *SharedObject.send()* method to broadcast messages without writing to the RSO.

Discussion

Every time the server-side data for a remote shared object changes, FlashCom attempts to synchronize the client-side data for all clients connected to that RSO. The *SharedObject.onSync()* method for a client-side remote shared object is automatically invoked whenever a synchronization attempt has occurred, so you can monitor all synchronization events. (See more on this in Recipe 16.8.) This is useful in situations in which a relatively small amount of data is shared among multiple clients. Whenever one client makes a change, all the other clients are automatically notified. The *onSync()* method works the same regardless of whether the remote shared object is persistent.

You can also manually invoke a client-side method on all clients connected to a remote shared object by using the *SharedObject.send()* method, and you can call the *send()* method from either a server-side or client-side remote shared object. In either case, the *send()* method requires that you specify the name of the method to invoke on the client(s). You should then ensure that the client movies have a method with that same name defined for the client-side remote shared object.

```
// Use send() to invoke a method named clientMethod() on all connected clients. The
// send() method can be used on either a server-side or client-side RSO.
my_r_so.send("clientMethod");

// The following code should exist within the client movie. It defines a method named
// clientMethod() for the client-side RSO named my_r_so.
my_r_so.clientMethod = function () {
  trace("clientMethod() called");
};
```

Additionally, you can pass parameters to the client-side method, as follows:

```
// Invoke a method named clientMethod() on all connected clients and pass the method
// two parameters: 6 and six.
my_r_so.send("clientMethod", 6, "six");

// The following code should exist within the client movie. This time, the
// clientMethod() method expects two parameters.
my_r_so.clientMethod = function (numNum, numStr) {
  trace("clientMethod() called with parameters: " + numNum + " " + numStr);
};
```

We've seen two ways to broadcast messages to connected clients using RSOs: either explicitly calling the *send()* method or implicitly relying on the *onSync()* method. It is important to determine when to use which technique.

Generally, it is not a good idea to write a lot of data to a single property of a remote shared object. As the amount of data saved to a property of the RSO grows, so does the latency in the application. For example, in a chat application it is not a good idea to write all the chat messages to a property of an RSO and rely on the *onSync()* method to update the clients. At first this will appear to work fine, but after a few users have joined the chat room and more messages are sent, things will get slower and slower because the entire chat history is synchronized each time someone sends a new message. Instead, you should use the *send()* method to broadcast each new message to all the connected clients. In that case, the new message is sent to all connected clients, but the chat history is not. The only drawback is that the chat history is not available to new, connecting clients. What you can do to remedy this is to also use a *call()* method to send each new message to the server and append each new message to a chat history application variable. This way, the information is available when you want to use it, but it is not automatically sent with each new message.

See Also

Recipes 14.15, 14.17, 16.6, and 16.8

## CHAPTER 18

Sending and Loading Variables

18.0 Introduction

There are many reasons why you may want to send and load values from and to your Flash movies. Here is a brief list of some of the possibilities:

- Send form values to a server-side script to store in a database
- Send values from an email form to a server-side script to send the email
- Load values from a text file (appropriate when the values are subject to change, such as for the current weather or for a links page)
- Load values from a server-side script where the values are drawn from a database, such as categories in an e-commerce application
- Send values to a server-side script for processing, and return a value to the Flash movie, such as for a login process

When you are loading variables into Flash, it is important that you correctly format the values to load. Flash can interpret data in URL-encoded format. URL-encoded variables follow these rules:

- Each variable name is associated with a value using an equals sign, without spaces on either side of the equals sign.
- Values loaded into Flash movies are always treated as strings; therefore, you should not enclose any values in quotes, as you would within ActionScript. A proper example of this is artist=Picasso.
- When there is more than one name/value pair, each pair is separated by an ampersand. For example, artist=Picasso&type=painting.
- Spaces within the values should be replaced by plus signs, not %20, as in: title=The+Old+Guitarist. (Spaces and %20 may also work, but stick with plus signs for the greatest compatibility.)
- Any character that is not a digit, a Latin 1 letter (non-accented), or a space should be converted to the hexadecimal escape sequence. For example, the value

"L'Atelier" should be encoded as L%27Atelier (%27 is the escape sequence for an apostrophe).

Here is an example of variables in URL-encoded format:

```
artist=Picasso&type=painting&title=Guernica&seller=Joey+Lott&room=L%27Atelier
```

Flash 6 introduced the *LoadVars* class, which provides a much more robust means of sending and loading variables than the *loadVariables()* method, which was available previously. Therefore, *LoadVars* is the preferred means of performing these actions, and it is used for the recipes in this chapter. Refer to Recipes 11.13, 11.17, and 11. 19, which demonstrate how to transmit data associated with a form. There are, of course, other ways to send and receive data in Flash. Chapter 19 covers data transmission using XML. Chapter 20 covers data transmission using Flash Remoting (see also Chapter 21 with regard to recordsets).

Loading values using a *LoadVars* object is subject to Flash's standard security sandbox. That is, you can load variables from a text file or script only if it is within the same domain as the Flash movie. For ways around the domain security limitation, see Recipes 17.4, 15.2, and 15.6.

18.1 Loading Variables from a Text File

Problem

You want to load variables into your Flash movie from an external text file.

Solution

Use the *LoadVars.load()* method.

Discussion

You should use the *LoadVars.load()* method when you want to load URL-encoded data into your Flash movie from a text file. This technique allows your Flash movie to access values that change frequently without modifying the Flash movie itself.

The *load()* method requires a URL where it can find the text file. The URL can be an absolute or relative address.

```
// You must first create the LoadVars object.
myLoadVars = new LoadVars( );

// This example loads values from a text file at an absolute URL.
myLoadVars.load("http://www.person13.com/myText.txt");

// This example loads values from a text file located at a relative URL, in this
// case, in the same directory as the Flash .swf file.
myLoadVars.load("myText.txt");
```

Here is an example of what the text file might contain:

```
someText=testing&myVariable=123
```

Once you invoke the *load()* method of a *LoadVars* object, Flash attempts to load the values from that URL into the same *LoadVars* object. After the data loads, Flash attempts to decode the values and invokes the object's *onLoad()* method. It is up to you to define the *onLoad()* method so that the object can do something useful once the data is loaded and decoded.

You should define an *onLoad()* method that expects a Boolean parameter indicating whether Flash was able to load the values. If Flash cannot load the values, such as if the file (or script) is unreachable, the *onLoad()* method is passed a value of false.

 When playing the movie in the Test Player, you will also receive an error message in the Output window if the specified URL is unreachable.

Here is an example *onLoad()* handler:

```
myLoadVars.onLoad = function (success) {
  // If the data didn't load, write a message to a text field and assign some default
  // values to the variables that would otherwise have been loaded.
  if (!success) {
    _root.output_txt.text = "Flash is using the default values.";
    this.title = "Loading Variables For Fun and Profit";
    this.author = "Anonymous";
    this.articleBody = "You too can enjoy the fun of loading variables.";
  } else {
    // Process the loaded variables.
  }
};
```

If loading is successful, Flash stores the loaded variables as properties of the *LoadVars* object and invokes *onLoad()*, passing it the value true. Here is an example that accesses a known property. It assumes that there was a variable named title in the text file from which the data was loaded.

```
myLoadVars.onLoad = function (success) {
  // If the loaded data was decoded, display the title property.
  if (success) {
    trace(this.title);
  } else {
    trace("Unable to load the title.");
  }
};
```

Here is what the text file might look like:

```
title=ActionScript+Cookbook
```

In most cases, you already know the names of the variables that are loaded from the external file or script. For example, you might use a *LoadVars* object to load a daily article from a server-side script or file, and regardless of the article's content, you expect three variables—title, author, and articleBody—to be loaded. You know which variables to expect because you wrote the server-side script, work with the person who wrote the script, or have access to documentation on the script. However, there are some situations in which you might not know all the variables that are being loaded. In such cases, you can use a *for…in* statement to enumerate all the variables that have loaded. Remember that a *for…in* statement loops through all the custom properties and methods of an object, including the variables loaded from the script or file; the built-in methods and properties of the *LoadVars* class don't show up. Since your *onLoad()* method is stored as a custom property, that method shows up in a *for…in* statement. You can use an *if* statement to filter out *onLoad()* from the display. This principle also holds true for other custom properties or methods you might have defined for the object that you don't want to appear (in order to display the loaded variables only). For example:

```
myLoadVars.onLoad = function (success) {
  if (success) {
    // Use a for...in statement to enumerate the elements of this, which is the
    // LoadVars object, myLoadVars.
    for (var prop in this) {
      // Display the property only if it is not "onLoad". To omit other properties or
      // methods, add them to the conditional expression with &&'s. For example:
      // (prop != "onLoad" && prop != "aCustomProperty")
      if (prop != "onLoad") {
        _root.output_txt.text += prop + ": " + this[prop] + newline;
      }
    }
  }
};
```

If the *LoadVars* object already has properties with the same names as any of the loaded variables, those properties are overwritten. Therefore, avoid variables with the same names as any of the properties or methods of the *LoadVars* class (including the undocumented *onData()* and *decode()* methods). Here is an example of a text file that includes a variable named onLoad:

```
onLoad=test&myVariable=abc
```

If you load these values into a Flash movie, the *onLoad()* method is never invoked because once the data is loaded and decoded, the *onLoad()* method is overwritten with the value "test".

See Also

Recipe 18.2. See Recipe 6.13 for details on *for…in* loops.

18.2 Loading Variables from a Server-Side Script

Problem

You want to load variables into a Flash movie from a server-side script (ColdFusion, Perl, PHP, etc.).

Solution

Use the *LoadVars.load()* method.

Discussion

The ActionScript to load variables from a server-side script is exactly the same as that used to load variables from a text file. When you call the *load()* method you should pass it the URL of the script from which you want to load the variables, then handle the results with an *onLoad()* method, as shown in Recipe 18.1.

You should use server-side scripts as the source for variables loaded into Flash when the values for the variables are generated from a database or another resource accessible only to the server. The script that you use must output URL-encoded data only, beginning from the first character. If you are writing a CGI script in Perl, the result is URL-encoded, so you do not need to make any special adjustments. For example:

```perl
#!/usr/bin/perl

# In a more practical example this value would be retrieved
# from a database or other server-side resource.
$myVar = "test";

# Define the Content-Type header.
print "Content-Type: text/plain\n\n";

# Output the name-value pair.
print "myVar=$myVar";
```

However, when you use a ColdFusion page to load variables into Flash, you need to take steps to ensure that it outputs URL-encoded data and that the output begins from the first character. Otherwise, extra whitespace characters may precede the output of the URL-encoded data, in which case Flash cannot properly decode the values.

Here is what you should do:

1. Include the `<cfsetting enablecfoutputonly="yes">` tag at the beginning of the document.
2. Make sure to enclose any values you want to output within a `<cfoutput>` element.

3. Place the whole document in a `<cfprocessingdirective suppresswhitespace="yes">` tag. This ensures that no extra whitespace characters are output.

For example:

```
<cfsetting enablecfoutputonly="yes">
<cfprocessingdirective suppresswhitespace="yes">
  <cfset myVar="test">
  <cfoutput>
    myVar=#myVar#
  </cfoutput>
</cfprocessingdirective>
```

If you use PHP, perform output using echo or print from within a processing directive, such as:

```
<?php
$myVar = "test";
echo "myVar=$myVar";
?>
```

Other preprocessor markup languages may or may not require additional steps to ensure proper output. JSP and ASP (.NET and classic) do not require any special considerations. One trick that seems to work in most cases is to simply surround each name/value pair with ampersands. This helps Flash know where to begin and end each variable pair. This solution should work regardless of the language/platform you are using (ASP, JSP, CFML, etc.). For example, if you don't want to use the `<cfprocessingdirective>` and `<cfsetting>` tags in your ColdFusion page, you should be able to rewrite the preceding ColdFusion example as follows (note the ampersands in bold):

```
<cfset myVar="test">
<cfoutput>&myVar=#myVar#&</cfoutput>
```

In each of the preceding examples, the server-side script returns a single variable, myVar, to Flash. Here is an example of the ActionScript code that loads the variable from a script and displays it in the movie:

```
// You must first create the LoadVars object.
myLoadVars = new LoadVars();

// Then load the variable from the server-side script. This example
// uses the loadVarsScript.cgi script, which is assumed to be in
// the /cgi-bin directory on the same server. To test this code,
// change the URL to point to an actual script on your server.
myLoadVars.load("/cgi-bin/loadVarsScript.cgi");

myLoadVars.onLoad = function (success) {
  // If the data loads, display the variable in a
  // text field named output_txt on _root.
  if (success) {
    _root.output_txt.text = this.myVar;
```

```
  }
};
```

Of course, many of the same things apply to loading variables from a script as when loading from a file. For example, if you don't know all the variable names, you can use a *for...in* statement to list them and their values, as shown in Recipe 18.1.

See Also

Recipes 18.1 and 19.11

18.3   Checking Load Progress

Problem

You want to know how much of the data has loaded.

Solution

Use the *LoadVars.getBytesLoaded()* and *LoadVars.getBytesTotal()* methods. Alternatively, use a progress bar (see Recipe 15.9).

Discussion

The *LoadVars* class's *getBytesLoaded()* and *getBytesTotal()* methods work in the same way as the methods of the same name from the *MovieClip*, *Sound*, and *XML* classes. Prior to a request to load external data, both methods return 0. Once Flash determines information about the requested data, *getBytesTotal()* returns the total number of bytes to load. The value of *getBytesLoaded()* changes each time there is load progress. All the data is loaded when *getBytesLoaded()* is equal to *getBytesTotal()*, provided they're not both 0. Typically, you should use a movie clip with an *onEnterFrame()* method or an interval function to monitor the load progress. For example:

```
myLoadVars = new LoadVars( );
myLoadVars.load("myText.txt");
myLoadVars.onLoad = function (success) {
  // Process loaded data here
};

function monitorLV ( ) {

  // Get the percentage by multiplying the loaded-to-total bytes ratio by 100.
  var percent = Math.round(myLoadVars.getBytesLoaded( ) /
               myLoadVars.getBytesTotal( ) * 100);

  // If the percentage is not a number (no bytes have loaded), set it to 0.
```

```
    percent = (isNaN(percent)) ? 0 : percent;

    // Display the load percentage in the Output window.
    trace(percent);
}
```

You can use a Progress Bar component to monitor the progress of data loaded with a *LoadVars* object, just as you can monitor the progress of data loaded into a movie clip or *Sound* object. You should set the progress bar's load target to the *LoadVars* object, as follows:.

```
_root.attachMovie("FProgressBarSymbol", "pBar", 1);
pBar.setLoadTarget(myLoadVars);
```

See Also

Recipe 15.9 offers more details on how to use the Progress Bar component. See Recipes 15.8, 15.10, 15.11, and 19.11.

18.4   Sending Data to a Server-Side Script

Problem

You want to send data from a Flash movie to a server-side script.

Solution

Use the *LoadVars.send()* method. Use *LoadVars.sendAndLoad()* if you expect a response.

Discussion

Use the *LoadVars.send()* method to send data to a server-side script if there is no need to process the result. For example, you might want to submit a web form's data to a server-side script without displaying any result from the server-side processing. However, the *send()* method does not return any confirmation that the data was received, so it isn't practical in most cases. Even if you just want to display a static message such as "Thank you for submitting the form," you need confirmation that the variables were successfully received on the server. Therefore, if you want confirmation of receipt, use the *sendAndLoad()* method instead (see Recipe 18.5).

The *send()* method sends all the enumerable properties of a *LoadVars* object to the specified URL. Enumerable properties are any properties that show up in a *for...in* statement for that object. The built-in methods and properties of the *LoadVars* class do not show up in a *for...in* statement, but custom properties do:

```
myLoadVars = new LoadVars();
```

```
// Nothing is displayed in this example.
for (var prop in myLoadVars) {
  trace(prop);
}

myLoadVars.myVar = "test";

// Now the myVar property shows up. When send( ) is invoked
// from myLoadVars, the myVar variable is sent to the specified URL.
for (var prop in myLoadVars) {
  trace(prop);
}
```

The *send()* method requires at least one parameter: the URL to which to send the variables. The URL can be absolute or relative:

```
// Send variables to a CGI script with an absolute URL.
myLoadVars.send("http://www.person13.com/cgi-bin/submitVars.cgi");

// Send variables to a CGI script relative to the location of the Flash .swf file.
myLoadVars.send("cgi-bin/submitVars.cgi");
```

The server's response to a *send()* method is disregarded by the Flash movie but can be sent to a browser window. If you want the response to be displayed in a web browser, specify a target browser window as the second parameter. Use the target of "_blank" to display the response in a new browser window, or you can display the result in another, named window or frame that is already open if you know the correct target name. Neither of these two options have any effect on the browser window containing the Flash movie. However, specifying the target as "_self" or "_parent" replaces the page contained the Flash movie.

```
// Send variables to a CGI script and display the script's output in a new browser
// window.
myLoadVars.send("cgi-bin/submitVars.cgi", "_blank");
```

If you want the response to be returned to the Flash movie, use the *sendAndLoad()* method, as discussed in Recipe 18.5.

By default, the *send()* method uses the HTTP POST method to send data to the specified script. If the server-side script handles data sent using GET only, you can specify "GET" as the *method* parameter (the third parameter) when calling *send()*:

```
// Send variables to a CGI script using the GET method. The null value is specified
// for the target parameter so that the response is disregarded.
myLoadVars.send("cgi-bin/submitVars.cgi", null, "GET");
```

Note that the *method* parameter must be the literal "GET" or "POST". Variables or expressions are not allowed for the *method*.

See Also

Recipe 18.5. See Recipe 6.13 for details on *for...in* loops. See Recipes 11.13, 11.17, and 11.19 for ways to transmit data associated with a form.

18.5 Sending Variables and Handling a Returned Result

Problem

You want to send variables to a server-side script and handle the results of the server-side processing.

Solution

Use the *LoadVars.sendAndLoad()* method.

Discussion

You should use the *sendAndLoad()* method when you want to send variables to a server-side script and have the results returned to Flash. An example of such a scenario is a Flash storefront for a product catalog that is stored in a database. Typically, items are categorized. When a user selects a category, the Flash movie might send the selected category ID to a server-side script and expect the script to return all the items in the category.

The *sendAndLoad()* method sends variables to a server-side script in the same way that the *send()* method does. Any enumerable properties of the *LoadVars* object are automatically sent to the script at the specified URL. The difference between *send()* and *sendAndLoad()* is that with the latter you must also provide a reference to a *LoadVars* object that handles the loading of the results. You can use the same *LoadVars* object to load the returned data as you used to send the variables. However, it is a best practice to specify a different object for loading the data. Using two *LoadVars* objects avoids conflicts with variable names. Otherwise, if the sending object has a property with the same name as one of the loaded variables, the loaded variable overwrites the sending object's property. Here is an example using two separate *LoadVars* objects (one for sending and one for receiving):

```
// Create an object to handle the data loading. Define an onLoad( ) method.
loadLV = new LoadVars( );
loadLV.onLoad = function (success) {
  if (success) {
    trace("loaded results");
  }
};
```

```
// Create an object to send the variables to the script.
sendLV = new LoadVars( );

// Define at least one variable to send.
sendLV.categoryID = 42;

// Invoke the sendAndLoad( ) method specifying loadLV as the object that handles the
// loading of the returned data.
sendLV.sendAndLoad("cgi-bin/getCategoryItems.cgi", loadLV);
```

See Also

Recipe 18.4. Recipe 19.14 covers analogous functionality using XML. Also refer to Recipe 17.3.

CHAPTER 19

XML

19.0 Introduction

The capability to load, parse, and send XML data was added to Flash in version 5, and it marked a significant advance in the ease of communicating complex data to and from a server script. Prior to the introduction of the *XML* class to Flash, the only way to load and send text data was to use URL-encoded values, as discussed in Chapter 18. XML is a superior alternative in many cases because, unlike URL-encoded data, XML data is *structured*. URL encoding is fine for passing simple data between Flash and server-side scripts, but for complex data or Unicode characters, XML generally works much better. For example, if you want to load data from a text file that represents a simple datatype such as a string, URL-encoded data, such as the following, can be loaded using a *LoadVars* object:

```
myString=a+string+value
```

However, when you want to load data from an external source and use that data to create an ActionScript object, you are presented with the problem of how to represent that data as a URL-encoded string. You might try something like the following, in which each property-value pair is separated by an asterisk (*), and each property is separated from its corresponding value by a vertical pipe (|):

```
myObject=prop0|val0*prop1|val1*prop2|val2
```

Once the string value is returned for myObject, you could use *String.split()* to recreate the elements that make up the object. Although you can get by with this approach, it is often much easier to represent complex values in XML. For example, the same object can be represented by the following XML snippet:

```
<myObject>
  <prop0>val0</prop0>
  <prop1>val1</prop1>
  <prop2>val2</prop2>
</myObject>
```

XML data offers several advantages over URL-encoded data, including:

- When creating XML manually (for a static XML document) or programmatically (from a ColdFusion script, PHP script, etc.), it is much easier to represent complex data.

- Most server-side scripting languages offer built-in functionality for reading and generating XML data.

- XML is a standard used for the transfer and storage of data across all kinds of applications and platforms.

There are, of course, other ways to send and receive data in Flash. Chapter 17 covers ways to transmit data using the *LocalConnection* and *SharedObject* classes. Chapter 20 covers data transmission using Flash Remoting. However, this chapter focuses on XML, which doesn't require a server-side installation (as does Flash Remoting) and works in Flash Player 5, unlike the *LocalConnection* and *SharedObject* classes.

An XML tree generally has an object of the *XML* class as its top node and objects of the *XMLnode* class as nodes below it. Many of the methods and properties discussed in this chapter work with both *XML* and *XMLNode* objects, but some apply to objects of the *XML* class only. This is because the *XML* class is a subclass of the *XMLNode* class.

The following methods and properties apply to all instances of the *XMLNode* and *XML* classes:

appendChild( )
attributes
childNodes
cloneNode( )
firstChild
hasChildNodes( )
insertBefore( )
lastChild
nextSibling
nodeName
nodeType
nodeValue
parentNode
previousSibling
removeNode( )
toString( )

The following methods, properties, and event handlers apply to instances of the *XML* class but not to *XMLNode* instances:

```
contentType
createElement()
createTextNode()
docTypeDecl
getBytesTotal()
getBytesLoaded()
ignoreWhite
load()
loaded
onData()
onLoad()
parseXML()
send()
sendAndLoad()
status
xmlDecl
```

In this chapter, the following terminology is used:

XML document
> A file containing XML, or the contents of that file. We also use this term to refer to XML data that is being loaded or sent.

XML packet
> An XML packet can be any snippet of XML—from an entire XML document to just a single node—as long as it is represents a complete, well-formed piece of information in XML.

XML node
> A node is the basic building block for XML. Nodes can be elements, text nodes, attributes, and so on. We refer to elements and text nodes collectively as "nodes" when talking in general terms.

XML element
> The term "element" is often used interchangeably with the term "tag." More accurately, however, an element contains tags. Elements must have an opening and closing tag (`<myElement></myElement>`), or the opening and closing tags can be combined into one when the element has no nested elements (`<myElement />`).

Root node
> The root node is an element that is at the top of the XML hierarchy of elements.

Text node
> A node containing text. Text nodes are generally nested within elements.

Attribute

An attribute is a node that is part of an element. Attributes are placed within the tags of elements in name/value pair format, such as `<myElement name="value">`.

XML declaration

The declaration typically looks like this: `<?xml version="1.0" ?>`. It is a special tag that the XML parser recognizes as containing information about the XML document, and it is not parsed as an element.

XML tree

Also sometimes called the "data tree," an XML tree is the hierarchy of nodes in XML data.

19.1 Understanding XML Structure (Reading and Writing XML)

Problem

You want to understand how to read or write XML.

Solution

XML is tag-based and hierarchical. If you are familiar with HTML, learning the basics of XML isn't very difficult.

Discussion

Although reading and writing good XML is not a skill that is specific to Action-Script, it is, nonetheless, a skill from which your ActionScript can benefit. If you are not yet familiar with XML, don't worry. This is going to be painless.

XML is a way of representing structured data. This means that you explicitly define the context for the data. For example, without XML you might have a string of data such as:

```
Jerry,Carolyn,Laura
```

You can use XML to tell us *who* these people are:

```
<family>
  <father>Jerry</father>
  <mother>Carolyn</mother>
  <sister>Laura</sister>
</family>
```

Now, as you can see, the XML tells us a lot more about the data. Here are a few other points to notice about XML:

- XML is composed mainly of nodes. A node is a general term that can refer to many parts within the XML. For example, `<family>` is a node in the preceding XML snippet. These kinds of nodes are called *elements*. Also, the values such as Jerry, Carolyn, and Laura are nodes. These kinds of nodes are called *text nodes*.

- Every XML element must have a matching opening and closing tag. The opening tag might look like `<family>`, and the closing tag is identical except that it uses a forward slash to indicate it is closing the element, as in `</family>`. The opening and closing tags can be combined if the element does not contain any nested nodes. For example, `<emptyElement />` is an element that combines the opening and closing tags. Notice that there is a space between the element name, `emptyElement`, and the forward slash.

- Elements can contain nested nodes (be they other elements or text nodes). There are several examples of this in the `<family>` XML document shown earlier. The `<family>` element, which is the *root node* in this example, contains three nested elements: `<father>`, `<mother>`, and `<sister>`. These nested nodes are also called *child nodes*. Each of these child nodes also contains a nested node. However, their nested nodes are text nodes, and not elements. In either case, they are still treated as child nodes.

There is one other type of node that we want to look at here. An *attribute* is a special kind of node that can be assigned to an element, and in many cases it can even be used as an alternative to a nested node. If you've ever worked with HTML, you are already familiar with attributes. Some common attributes in HTML include the `href` attribute of the `<a>` element and the `colspan` attribute of the `<td>` element. Here is how we can rewrite the same XML document we examined previously using attributes instead of nested nodes:

```
<family father="Jerry" mother="Carolyn" sister="Laura" />
```

Notice that we were able to eliminate the nested elements and write the same data all in one element. Also notice that since `<family>` no longer contains any nested nodes, we can combine the opening and closing tags.

You may be wondering when and why to use attributes versus nested nodes. This is often a matter of preference. Sometimes it may appear easier or clearer to you to write the XML data using attributes. Generally, attributes are a good idea when you want to represent a fairly small number of values and when those values are relatively short. Also, the attributes' names need to be unique within the element. When you want to represent larger quantities of data, when the data is long (more than a few words), or when the names of the attributes would not be unique within the element, use nested elements instead.

Also, you can use a combination of both attributes and nested nodes. Here is an example of an <article> element that includes attributes for the title and author but uses a nested text node to represent the article text. This is a good example of when one of the values (the article text) is simply too long to reasonably be an attribute.

```
<article title="XML: It's Not Just for Geeks" author="Samuel R. Shimowitz">
My friends couldn't believe it when I started working with XML. I became an
outcast, confined to my dark office illuminated only by the glow of my trusty CRT.
Blah blah blah.
</article>
```

You can create XML strings right in Flash for cases in which you are constructing XML data to send to an external script. For example:

```
xmlStr = "<feedback name='Aham' comments='nice'>";
```

To construct a static XML document outside of Flash, use a simple text editor and save it as plain text. To create an XML document dynamically using a server-side script, consult the appropriate reference for the language you are using.

See Also

The preceding examples are very simple cases. XML can get much more complex, including namespaces, document type declarations, etc. Most of these details are well beyond the scope of this book and beyond what you need to know to work with XML and Flash. For more information on XML in general, see *http://www.xml.com*. For more information on XML data structures and how to access them in Flash, refer to the *XML*, *XMLnode*, and *XMLSocket* classes in the "Language Reference" section of *ActionScript for Flash MX: The Definitive Guide*.

19.2   Creating an XML Object

Problem

You want to create an XML object complete with a tree structure and data.

Solution

A *populated* XML object contains data, just as a populated city contains people.

Use one of the following to create a populated XML object:

- Populate the XML object tree by passing an XML string to the constructor.
- Create a blank object and use the *parseXML()* method to populate the XML tree with an XML string.

- Create a blank object and use the *XML* class's properties and methods to populate the XML tree one node at a time.

- Create a blank object and load the XML data from an external source.

Discussion

There are many possibilities for creating a populated XML object in Flash. Each technique offers its own advantages, and you should base your decision on the needs of your project.

The simplest way to create a populated XML object is to pass an XML string to the constructor:

```
my_xml = new XML("<abc><a>eh</a><b>bee</b><c>see</c>");
```

This first technique is appropriate when you already know the complete XML string before you want to create the object. For example, if you want to create a simple XML object to send a user's name and score to the server, you could easily construct the XML string using known data and then construct the XML object, as follows:

```
xmlStr = "<gamescore><username>" + username +
         "</username><score>" + score + "</score></gamescore>";
score_xml = new XML(xmlStr);
```

You can also use the *parseXML()* method to populate an XML object using an XML string. This is useful in situations in which you already have an existing XML object, but you want to populate it with new data. For example, you might already have an existing score_xml object in which you stored the name and score of the last player. Instead of creating a new object, you can simply repopulate the existing object using *parseXML()*. For example:

```
xmlStr = "<gamescore><username>" + username + "</username><score>" +
         score + "</score></gamescore>";
score_xml.parseXML(xmlStr);
```

There are other cases, however, in which you don't necessarily know all the data at one time. You might want to build the XML object's tree over time. For example, if you use an XML object to store a user's shopping cart information, you need to modify the object's data each time the user modifies her shopping cart. In such cases, you should use the built-in properties and methods that allow you to add and remove nodes, as described in Recipes 19.3 and 19.4.

And let's not forget about populating XML objects with data retrieved from an external source, such as a static XML document or a script that generates dynamic XML. Up to this point we've looked only at constructing XML objects send data to a server. But you can load data from the server for all kinds of reasons—retrieving user data, catalog information, or movie initialization information, just to name a few. For these scenarios, you should use either the *load()* or the *sendAndLoad()* method, as discussed in Recipes 19.11 and 19.14.

See Also

See Recipes 19.3, 19.4, 19.5, and 19.6 for more information on constructing an XML tree using the built-in properties and methods of the *XML* class. For more information on loading information from external sources, see Recipes 19.11 and 19.14. Also refer to Recipe 19.16 for an example of how to use loaded data to initialize a movie.

19.3   Adding Elements to an XML Object

Problem

You want to construct an *XML* object and add elements to it.

Solution

Use the *createElement()* method to create the element, and then use the *appendChild()* or *insertBefore()* method to add the element to the XML tree.

Discussion

You might want to add elements to an XML object to construct an XML data structure to pass to another application. There are several ways to accomplish this, as discussed in Recipe 19.2.

You can create XML elements using the *createElement()* method of any *XML* object. You should specify the element name as a string parameter passed to the *createElement()* method. The method returns a reference to the new element (an *XMLnode* object).

```
my_xml = new XML( );

// Create a new element, <myFirstElement />.
myElement = my_xml.createElement("myFirstElement");
```

Although the *createElement()* method creates the new element, it doesn't insert it into the XML tree hierarchy. Instead, you have to instruct Flash where to insert the new element using either the *appendChild()* or *insertBefore()* method. The *appendChild()* method adds the element to the end of the children elements of the *XML* object (or *XMLNode* object) from which the method is called:

```
// Adds the myElement element to the my_xml object.
my_xml.appendChild(myElement);

trace(my_xml);   // Displays: <myFirstElement />

// Create another element, <myFirstNestedElement />.
myNestedElement0 = my_xml.createElement("myFirstNestedElement");
```

```
// Add the new element as a child of myElement.
myElement.appendChild(myNestedElement0);

// Displays: <myFirstElement><myFirstNestedElement /></myFirstElement>
trace(my_xml);
```

If you want to insert an element before another child element (instead of simply appending it to the end of the list of child nodes), use the *insertBefore()* method. This method works just like the *appendChild()* method except that you also need to supply a reference to the element before which the new element is inserted.

```
// Create and append a third nested element (before adding the second).
myNestedElement2 = my_xml.createElement("myThirdNestedElement");
myElement.appendChild(myNestedElement2);

// Displays: <myFirstElement><myFirstNestedElement />
//           <myThirdNestedElement /></myFirstElement>
trace(my_xml);

// Create the second element and insert it before the third element.
myNestedElement1 = my_xml.createElement("mySecondNestedElement");
myElement.insertBefore(myNestedElement1, myNestedElement2);

// Displays: <myFirstElement><myFirstNestedElement />
//           <mySecondNestedElement /><myThirdNestedElement /></myFirstElement>
trace(my_xml);
```

See Also

Recipe 19.4

19.4 Adding Text Nodes to an XML Object

Problem

You want to add text nodes to an *XML* object.

Solution

Use the *createTextNode()* and *appendChild()* methods.

Discussion

The *createTextNode()* method is very similar to the *createElement()* method discussed in Recipe 19.3, except that it creates a new text node instead of an XML element. As with the *createElement()* method, the *createTextNode()* method does not insert the node into the XML object hierarchy but returns a reference to the newly created node. You are responsible for inserting the text node into the XML object using the *appendChild()* or *insertBefore()* method.

```
// Create an XML object.
my_xml = new XML( );

// Create an element to which to add the text node.
myElement = my_xml.createElement("myFirstElement");

// Create the next node with the value "this is some text".
myTextNode = my_xml.createTextNode("this is some text");

// Add the text node to the element.
myElement.appendChild(myTextNode);

// Add the element to the XML object
my_xml.appendChild(myElement);

// Displays: <myFirstElement>this is some text</myFirstElement>
trace(my_xml);
```

Generally, text nodes are not of much use in isolation. Remember, XML data is structured. That means that your text nodes should always be nested in XML elements such as the <myFirstElement> node in the preceding example. Therefore, we first create the element using the *createElement()* method (see Recipe 19.3). We then create the text node and assign it a value of "this is some text"—both accomplished using the *createTextNode()* method. Neither of the two nodes (the element nor the text node) has been added to the XML object, so we use the *appendChild()* method to nest these nodes. We nest the text node in the element, and we nest the element in the XML object as the root node.

 The *appendChild()* method is valid for all *XMLNode* objects, including text nodes. However, text nodes cannot contain nested nodes; therefore, calling *appendChild()* from a text node has no effect.

It might seem strange to have to create a text node as a separate node from its parent element. After all, you may wonder why we don't just assign the text value to a property of the element instead. The answer is that XML can be more complex than that solution would allow. Consider, for a moment, a *mixed element*, which is an element that contains not only a child text node or child elements, but both. For example:

```
<article>
<title>XML: It's Not Just for Geeks</title>
<author>Samuel R. Shimowitz</author>
My friends couldn't believe it when I started working with XML. I became an
outcast, confined to my dark office illuminated only by the glow of my trusty CRT.
Blah blah blah.
</article>
```

In this example, <article> is a mixed element because it contains not only nested elements (<title> and <author>) but also a nested text node. This is perfectly valid XML, and for this reason, we want to be able to treat each nested item as its own node.

When working with text nodes, it can be convenient to create the text node and the parent element all in one step. You can automate this process with a short and simple custom method, *createElementWithText()*. Add this method to the *XMLNode* class by placing the following code in a custom *XML.as* file that you place in your Flash *Include* directory for easy inclusion in future projects. The method accepts two parameters: the name of the element and the value to add to the nested text node.

```
XMLNode.prototype.createElementWithText = function (name, text) {

  // Create the element.
  var elem = this.createElement(name);

  // Create the text node.
  var txtNode = this.createTextNode(text);

  // Add the text node to the element.
  elem.appendChild(txtNode);

  // Return the element.
  return elem;
};
```

Here is an example of the *createElementWithText()* method in use:

```
#include "XML.as"

my_xml = new XML();
myElement = my_xml.createElementWithText("where", "here");
my_xml.appendChild(myElement);
trace(my_xml);  // Displays: <where>here</where>
```

Notice that the *createElementWithText()* method returns a new *XMLNode* object just like the *createElement()* and *createTextNode()* methods. This means that you need to add it to an *XML* object using a method such as *appendChild()*.

See Also

Recipe 19.3

19.5 Creating an XML Object from an Array

Problem

You want to create an *XML* object using an array to populate it.

Solution

Use a *for* statement to create and insert the elements and text nodes.

Discussion

Generating an XML object, especially a large one, can be somewhat tedious. In some cases you can make your job a little easier by storing the text node values in an array and inserting them into the XML object using a *for* loop.

Let's take a look at an example in which you want to create an *XML* object to represent a menu and the menu items. This might be a useful example if, say, you are creating a Flash movie that allows the user to configure a menu's items and save them to the server so he can retrieve them later on.

```
// Include XML.as for the custom createElementWithText( ) method from Recipe 19.4.
#include "XML.as"

// Create the array of text node values.
menuItems = new Array("Springs", "Cogs", "Widgets", "Gizmos");

my_xml = new XML( );

// Create the root element for the XML object.
rootElement = my_xml.createElement("menu")

// Use a for statement to loop through all the elements in the array.
for (var i = 0; i < menuItems.length; i++) {

  // Create an XML element for each arrangement.
  menuItemElement = my_xml.createElementWithText("menuItem", menuItems[i]);
  rootElement.appendChild(menuItemElement);
}

// Add the root element to the XML object.
my_xml.appendChild(rootElement);

// Displays: <menu><menuItem>Springs</menuItem><menuItem>Cogs</menuItem>
//           <menuItem>Widgets</menuItem><menuItem>Gizmos</menuItem></menu>
trace(my_xml);
```

The first thing we did in this example was to create an array of options we'll add to the XML object. Each element represents a menu item. In a real-world example the elements of the array might be added one at a time by the user, but in our code snippet we're creating the array all at once for the sake of demonstration. Next, we create a new XML object and a root element. Then, using a *for* statement, we loop through all the items in the array, create new elements and text nodes one by one, and append them to the root element.

We can also create a custom method, *populateFromArray()*, and add it to the *XMLNode* class. This custom method automates the same process, so you can use it in many different situations, not just when creating an XML packet to represent a menu. Add the following code to your custom *XML.as* file in your Flash *Include* directory. The method accepts two parameters: the array of values to add and the name of each nested element.

```
XMLNode.prototype.populateFromArray = function (items_ar, elementName) {
  for (var i = 0; i < items_ar.length; i++) {
    // Create an element.
    itemElement = my_xml.createElementWithText(elementName, items_ar[i]);
    this.appendChild(itemElement);
  }
};
```

Next, we'll use the method to accomplish the same thing we did earlier with the menu XML. The uncommented lines of code are the same as before. The new code is shown in bold.

```
#include "XML.as"

menuItems = new Array("Springs", "Cogs", "Widgets", "Gizmos");
my_xml = new XML();
rootElement = my_xml.createElement("menu")

// Populate the rootElement node with the contents of menuItems.
rootElement.populateFromArray(menuItems, "menuItem");

my_xml.appendChild(rootElement);

// Displays: <menu><menuItem>Springs</menuItem><menuItem>Cogs</menuItem>
//           <menuItem>Widgets</menuItem><menuItem>Gizmos</menuItem></menu>
trace(my_xml);
```

19.6   Adding Attributes to an XML Element

Problem

You want to add attributes to an XML element.

Solution

Assign properties to the attributes property of an *XMLNode* object representing an element.

Discussion

Every *XMLNode* object has a read/write attributes object that determines the attributes of the element. You can assign properties to the attributes object, and those properties are automatically added to the element's attributes. For example:

```
my_xml = new XML();
myElement = my_xml.createElement("myFirstElement");
```

```
// Create attributes a, b, and c for myElement.
myElement.attributes.a = "eh";
myElement.attributes.b = "bee";
myElement.attributes.c = "see";

my_xml.appendChild(myElement);

// Displays: <myFirstElement c="see" b="bee" a="eh" />
trace(my_xml);
```

When you assign values to the attributes object, be careful not to overwrite the entire object, as in:

```
myElement.attributes = {a: "eh", b: "bee", c: "see"};
```

Using an object literal to add multiple properties will add extra, undesired attributes since the new object also includes two hidden properties, __proto__ and constructor.

Now, let's talk briefly about some of the things you can and cannot do with attributes in Flash. First of all, even though XML allows for attribute values containing newline characters, Flash does not. Therefore, if your attribute will contain a newline, be sure to use a nested node instead. Also, if you access attributes using dot syntax, as shown in the preceding example, you must use valid Flash variable names for the names of the attributes. This means that the attributes must have names consisting of numbers, letters, and underscores, and the first character cannot be a number. However, XML attribute names can sometimes contain other characters for good reasons. For example, though a full discussion of namespaces is beyond the scope of this book, XML namespaces can require that an attribute's name contain characters such as a colon (:). You can use array-access notation to create or read attributes whose names contain invalid variable name characters. For example:

```
myElement.attributes["xmlns:soap"] = "http://schemas.xmlsoap.org/wsdl/soap";
```

See Also

For more information on using attributes in XML, see Recipes 19.2 and 19.10.

19.7   Reading Elements in an XML Tree

Problem

You want to extract the child elements of an *XML* or *XMLnode* object.

Solution

Use the firstChild, lastChild, nextSibling, and previousSibling properties to read the elements one at a time. Alternatively, use the childNodes property to extract all the child elements as an array.

Discussion

You'll often want to "walk" (traverse) an XML tree to extract or examine one or more elements. This is convenient for searching for a given element or processing elements in which you know (or don't care about) their precise order.

All the child elements of an *XML* or *XMLnode* object fall into one of three possible categories: the first child, the last child, or some other sibling. Working from this premise, you can extract the child elements of a node using the firstChild, lastChild, nextSibling, and previousSibling properties. The firstChild and lastChild properties return the first and last child elements of an *XML* or *XMLnode* object, respectively. Assuming that there are no whitespace nodes in an *XML* object, the root element is returned by the firstChild property of that object.

```
my_xml = new XML("<sections><a /><b /><c /><d /></sections>");

// Extract the root element (<sections>).
rootElement = my_xml.firstChild;

// Extract the first child element of the root element (<a>).
aElement = rootElement.firstChild;

// Extract the last child element of the root element (<d>).
dElement = rootElement.lastChild;
```

You can access a child element's sibling nodes using the nextSibling and previousSibling properties:

```
// Extract the next sibling to the <a> element (<b>).
bElement = aElement.nextSibling;

// Extract the previous sibling to the <d> element (<c>).
cElement = dElement.previousSibling;
```

Another way to extract the child elements of an *XML* or *XMLnode* object is to work with them as elements of an array. The childNodes property returns such an array:

```
children = rootElement.childNodes;

// Displays:
// <a />
// <b />
// <c />
// <d />
for (var i = 0; i < children.length; i++) {
  trace(children[i]);
}
```

Using the aforementioned properties, you can walk through an XML tree structure recursively, as shown in the following example. The *search()* method we create here can be useful in simple situations in which you want to find all the elements with a particular name regardless of their contents or location in the tree's hierarchy. For more advanced and complex searches, use XPath (see Recipe 19.15).

We'll add the *search()* method to the *XMLNode* class, and the method should accept a single parameter: the node name for which to search. You can add this custom function to your *XML.as* file for easy inclusion in other projects:

```
XMLNode.prototype.search = function (searchName) {

  // Create an array in which to store the matching elements.
  var matches = new Array( );

  // If the current node has children, loop through all elements to find matches.
  if (this.hasChildNodes( )) {
    for (var i = 0; i < this.childNodes.length; i++) {
      // For each child node, invoke the search( ) method recursively. Concatenate the
      // results with the current matches array.
      matches = matches.concat(this.childNodes[i].search(searchName));
    }
  }

  // If the current node is a match, add it to the matches array. For more
  // information on the nodeName property, see Recipe 19.8.
  if (this.nodeName == searchName) {
    matches.push(this);
  }

  // Return the matches.
  return matches;
};
```

Here is an example of how you might use this method:

```
#include "XML.as"

// Set ignoreWhite to true for the XML class. See Recipe 19.12 for more information
// on the ignoreWhite property.
XML.prototype.ignoreWhite = true;

// Create an XML object and load data from an external document named books.xml.
my_xml = new XML( );
my_xml.load("books.xml");
my_xml.onLoad = function (success) {
  if (success) {
    // When the document loads, use the search( ) method to find all the <author>
    // elements. Display the results in the Output window. We join all the elements
    // of the resulting array together with a newline so that each one appears on its
    // own line.
    trace(this.search("author").join("\n"));
  }
};
```

See Also

Recipes 19.15, 19.12, and 19.8

19.8 Finding Elements by Name

Problem

You want to identify an element by name rather than by its position in the XML hierarchy.

Solution

Use the nodeName property.

Discussion

You can use the nodeName property to make sure you are properly processing an XML object when the exact order of elements is not known. The nodeName property returns the element name:

```
// Create an XML object with a single element.
my_xml = new XML("<root />");

// Extract the root element.
rootElement = my_xml.firstChild;

// Displays: root
trace(rootElement.nodeName);
```

This example extracts elements based on their names. Note that it walks the XML tree using the childNodes array to examine each element in sequence:

```
my_xml = new XML("<elements><a /><d /><b /><c /></element>");
rootElement = my_xml.firstChild;
children = rootElement.childNodes;

for (var i = 0; i < children.length; i++) {
  // Set the value of the proper variable depending on the value of nodeName. This
  // technique works regardless of the order of the child elements.
  switch (children[i].nodeName) {
    case "a":
      aElement = children[i];
      break;
    case "b":
      bElement = children[i];
      break;
    case "c":
      cElement = children[i];
      break;
```

```
    case "d":
      dElement = children[i];
      break;
  }
}
```

See Also

For a more complex example using nodeName, see the *search()* method in Recipe 19.7.

19.9   Reading Text Nodes and Their Values

Problem

You want to extract the value from a text node.

Solution

Extract the text node from its parent using the firstChild property. Then get the text node's value using the nodeValue property.

Discussion

In Recipe 19.4 we looked at text nodes and how to create them in your XML objects. Now we want to look at how to extract the value from a text node. You can use the firstChild, lastChild, nextSibling, previousSibling, and childNodes properties discussed in Recipe 19.7 to get a reference to a text node the same way you would get a reference to any other node (such as an element). Then, once you have a reference to the text node, use the nodeValue property to retrieve that node's text value.

An example will help illustrate. Let's consider the following XML packet:

```
<book>
  <title>ActionScript Cookbook</title>
</book>
```

In this XML packet, the root node is <book>, which contains a child element, <title>. The <title> element, in turn, contains a nested node—a text node with a value of "ActionScript Cookbook".

If we parse this XML packet into an *XML* object, we can get the root node by using the firstChild property. Then we can get the <title> element with the firstChild property of the root node. And finally, we can get the text node with the firstChild property of the <title> element.

```
my_xml = new XML("<book><title>ActionScript Cookbook</title></book>");

// Extract the root node (<book>).
bookElement = my_xml.firstChild;
```

```
// Extract the <title> element.
titleElement = bookElement.firstChild;

// Extract the text node (ActionScript Cookbook).
titleTextNode = titleElement.firstChild;
```

Once you have extracted a text node, you can read its value using the nodeValue property:

```
value = titleTextNode.nodeValue;

trace(value); // Displays: ActionScript Cookbook
```

See Also

Recipe 19.4

19.10 Reading an Element's Attributes

Problem

You want to extract the attributes of an element.

Solution

Use the attributes property.

Discussion

You should use the attributes property to return an associative array of an element's attributes. The keys of the associative array are the names of the attributes, and the values corresponding to those keys match up with the attribute values:

```
my_xml = new XML("<myElement a='eh' b='bee' c='see' />");
attribs = my_xml.firstChild.attributes;

// Use a for...in statement to loop through the
// keys and values of the associative array. This displays:
// a = eh
// b = bee
// c = see
for (var key in attribs) {
  trace(key + " = " + attribs[key]);
}
```

The attributes property is very important in any situation in which you want to retrieve XML data stored in attributes. For example, suppose you want to display information about an article to the user, including the title and author, both of which are stored in an element as attributes. Here is an example of such an XML packet:

```
<article title="XML: It's Not Just for Geeks" author="Samuel R. Shimowitz" />
```

Once you have loaded this content into an XML object, you can display the values to the user with just a few lines of code:

```
// Create the XML object and set ignoreWhite to true since we're loading the data
// from an external source.
article_xml = new XML( );
article_xml.ignoreWhite = true;

// Define the onLoad( ) method. When the data is loaded, display the title and author
// data in their respective text fields on the main timeline.
article_xml.onLoad = function ( ) {
  var articleElement = this.firstChild;
  _root.title_txt.text = articleElement.attributes.title;
  _root.author_txt.text = articleElement.attributes.author;
};

// Load the external data from a file named article.xml.
article_xml.load("article.xml");
```

See Also

For more information on the attributes property, see Recipe 19.6.

19.11 Loading XML

Problem

You want to load XML data from an XML document or a server-side script that generates XML.

Solution

Use the *XML.load( )* method to load the data. Define an *onLoad( )* method to handle the results.

Discussion

The *load( )* method loads XML data from the URL that you specify:

```
my_xml = new XML( );

// Initiate the loading of an XML document in the same directory as the .swf file.
my_xml.load("myXMLDoc.xml");
```

To meaningfully process the XML data that loads, you must define an *onLoad( )* method for the *XML* object on which you called *load( )*. The *onLoad( )* method is automatically invoked when the data loads, and it is passed a Boolean value indicating whether the XML data was successfully parsed. It is up to you to define the *onLoad( )* method so that it processes the XML data in the way that you want it to.

```
my_xml.onLoad = function (success) {
  if (success) {
    trace("The XML was successfully parsed. Here are the contents: ");
    trace(this);
  } else {
    trace("There was an error parsing the XML data");
  }
};
```

You should, almost without exception, set the XML object's `ignoreWhite` property to true before you load any XML data into a Flash movie. Otherwise, the ActionScript XML parser creates whitespace nodes for any space, tab, carriage return, newline, or form feed character. The resulting data is much more difficult to handle because you have to contend with excess whitespace nodes. Setting the `ignoreWhite` property to true causes the parser to automatically ignore whitespace and not create separate whitespace elements in the data. You must set the property to true prior to the parsing of the data. In practical terms this means you should set the property to true before you call the *load()* method. See a more detailed discussion in Recipe 19.12.

```
my_xml.ignoreWhite = true;
```

Setting ignoreWhite on the prototype sets it for all XML objects:

```
XML.prototype.ignoreWhite = true;
```

See Also

Recipe 19.12

19.12 Removing Extra Whitespace from XML Objects

Problem

You want to remove whitespace nodes from your *XML* object because they are interfering with your ability to programmatically extract the values you want.

Solution

Set the ignoreWhite property to true before loading external data into an *XML* object or before parsing any string into an *XML* object, or use a custom *removeWhitespace()* method to remove whitespace nodes after loading data or for legacy purposes.

Discussion

XML documents are often written with extra whitespace characters for the purposes of formatting so that it is easier for humans to read. Most of the time, each element

---

appears on its own line (meaning that newline, carriage return, or form feed characters have been added), and child nodes are sometimes indented using tabs or spaces. In what follows, you can see the same XML data formatted in two ways. The first is the data formatted without the whitespace characters, and the second is the same data with formatting. Which is easier to read?

```
<book><title>ActionScript Cookbook</title><authors><author name="Joey Lott" /></
authors></book>
```

or:

```
<book>
  <title>ActionScript Cookbook</title>
  <authors>
    <author name="Joey Lott" />
  </authors>
</book>
```

While the formatted XML data may be easier for you, as a human, to read, the unformatted XML data is better suited for Flash. Flash counts all of the whitespaces as their own text nodes, which means that Flash parses every newline or tab character into its own node. The result is that you might have a more difficult time trying to accurately locate the data you want.

Fortunately, when you load data from an external source, such as a static file or a server-side script, or when you parse any string into an *XML* object, you can tell Flash to ignore whitespace nodes when parsing the data. The ignoreWhite property is set to false by default, which means that Flash parses whitespace nodes. However, if you set the ignoreWhite property to true prior to parsing any data into the object, Flash will not create whitespace nodes. This means that you should set the ignoreWhite property for an XML object to true before calling the *load()* method or *sendAndLoad()* method, or before using the *parseXML()* method to parse a string:

```
// Create the XML object.
my_xml = new XML();

// Set ignoreWhite to true to ignore whitespace during parsing.
my_xml.ignoreWhite = true;

// Define an onLoad() method and then load the data. (See Recipe 19.11.)
my_xml.onLoad = function (success) {
    // Actions to perform on load
};
my_xml.load("externalDoc.xml");
```

Since, in most cases, you want to set ignoreWhite to true, you can set the value of the ignoreWhite property for the entire *XML* class. This means that you only have to set the property once and all *XML* objects will inherit that value. For most Flash developers, this is a common practice.

```
XML.prototype.ignoreWhite = true;
```

You can even add the preceding line to your *XML.as* file. Just be aware that you've effectively changed the default behavior for all XML parsing operations.

Now, if you want to remove whitespace nodes from an XML document after the data has been loaded and/or parsed, you need to create a custom method. Such a method is necessarily recursive, meaning that it calls itself to make sure that all the nodes are checked. Here, then, is our recursive whitespace-stripping function, suitable for inclusion in your *XML.as* file, if not for framing:

```
XMLNode.prototype.removeWhitespace = function () {
    var cNode, hasNonWhitespace;

    // Loop through all the child nodes.
    for (var i = 0; i < this.childNodes.length; i++) {
      cNode = this.childNodes[i];

      // If the node is a text node...
      if (cNode.nodeType == 3) {

        // Check to see if any of the characters it contains are non-whitespace
        // characters. If so, set hasNonWhitespace to true and break out of the for
        // loop since all it takes is one non-whitespace character to mean the node is
        // a non-whitespace node.
        for (var j = 0; j < cNode.nodeValue.length; j++) {
          if (cNode.nodeValue.charCodeAt(j) > 32) {
            hasNonWhitespace = true;
            break;
          }
        }

        // If the node is a whitespace node, remove it with the removeNode() method and
        // decrement i so that we don't skip over a node now that we've removed one.
        if (!hasNonWhitespace) {
          cNode.removeNode();
          i--;
        }
      } else {
        // Otherwise, it is not a text node; invoke removeWhitespace() recursively.
        cNode.removeWhitespace();
      }
    }
};
```

Here is an example in which we use the *removeWhitespace()* method to remove whitespace after having loaded the data:

```
#include "XML.as"
my_xml = new XML();
my_xml.load("books.xml");
my_xml.onLoad = function (success) {
  if (success) {
```

```
  // Run the removeWhitespace( ) method and display the results.
  this.removeWhitespace( );
  trace(this);
  }
};
```

19.13 Sending XML

Problem

You want to send XML data to a server-side script.

Solution

In almost all cases, use *XML.sendAndLoad()*, as discussed in Recipe 19.14. In some isolated cases, use the *XML.send()* method.

Discussion

XML is normally used to transfer data to and from applications, and in this case, Flash movies. Therefore, it is quite unusual that you would want to create XML objects in your Flash movies for use within Flash alone. Instead, you generally load XML data from another source, create XML data in Flash for the purposes of sending to another application, or both. In this recipe, we want to look at sending XML data from Flash to another application. There are lots of reasons to do this. For example, in a Flash game you might want to use XML to send the user's name and score to the server. At other times, you might want to send XML packets to a server-side script to invoke server-side functionality. This is a process that is sometimes called a remote procedure call (RPC), and it can use XML to send the function invocation information (function name, parameters, etc.) to the server. So as you can see, the possibilities for sending XML to the server are quite diverse.

ActionScript actually includes two methods for sending XML data: *send()* and *sendAndLoad()*. The original idea was that *send()* would be for sending data in which no response was necessarily expected or in which the response would be opened in a new browser window. The *sendAndLoad()* method was intended for those times when you wanted to send data and also receive a response from the server. However, the *send()* method seems to function other than expected. The *send()* method relies on a mechanism in the web browser to work. However, only one browser supports that functionality. Therefore, the *send()* method will not work in the Test Player, the Standalone Player, Projectors, or in many web browsers. For these reasons, it is suggested that you use the *sendAndLoad()* method even when you don't expect a server response.

See Also

Recipe 19.14

19.14 Sending XML Data and Receiving a Response

Problem

You want to send XML data to a server-side script and load the response into the same Flash movie.

Solution

Use the *XML.sendAndLoad( )* method.

Discussion

The *sendAndLoad( )* method does just what its name suggests—it sends XML data to a server-side script and loads the response back into Flash. It is ideal when you want to send data to the server for processing and then receive the results back in the Flash movie. Additionally, since there are limitations in the *XML.send( )* method, the *sendAndLoad( )* method is the best choice even in situations in which you don't expect any response from the server.

The *sendAndLoad( )* method sends the XML data from the object on which it is called. You must specify a target XML object into which the response is loaded. You can use the same *XML* object to load the data as you use to send it, but generally it is better to create a separate *XML* object for the loaded data, since the loaded response replaces any existing data in the target *XML* object. Therefore, in most cases, you should create two XML objects—one for sending and one for loading. For example:

```
// Create the loading object.
myLoadXML = new XML( );

// As when loading data using the load( ) method, set ignoreWhite to true.
myLoadXML.ignoreWhite = true;

// Define the onLoad( ) method. (See Recipe 19.11.)
myLoadXML.onLoad = function (success) {
  if (success) {
    trace("The XML was successfully parsed. Here are the contents: ");
    trace(this);
  } else {
    trace("There was an error parsing the XML data");
  }
};
```

```
// Create the sending object.
mySendXML = new XML("<sendingData>this is some data</sendingData>");

// Set the content type and XML declaration. See the Discussion for details.
mySendXML.contentType = "text/xml";
mySendXML.xmlDecl = "<?xml version=\"1.0\" ?>";

// Call the sendAndLoad( ) method. This sends the data to a script and tells Flash to
// load the server response into myLoadXML.
mySendXML.sendAndLoad("cgi-bin/processXML.cgi", myLoadXML);
```

In the preceding example, you may notice that we also set the contentType and xmlDecl properties of the sending *XML* object. Though not always necessary, it is a good idea to set these properties before sending the data. Some scripts/languages require them, but defining them doesn't hurt even if they are not required. By default, the contentType property is set to "application/x-www-form-urlencoded", and the xmlDecl property has no defined value. In most cases you'll want to set contentType to "text/xml" and set xmlDecl to "<?xml version=\"1.0\" ?>".

Now let's take a look at a complete working example. In what follows, we'll first create the necessary client-side ActionScript code, and then you should choose from one of the server-side solutions. Choose the one that is supported by your server (or your personal computer if you use that as your server). There are server-side scripts in Perl, PHP, and ColdFusion.

The first thing you should do is create a Flash movie and add the PushButton component to the Library by dragging an instance from the Components panel to the Stage. Then add the following code on the first frame of the main timeline:

```
function init( ) {

  // Create an XML object to handle the response from the server.
  result_xml = new XML( );
  result_xml.onLoad = function ( ) {
    if (this.firstChild.firstChild.nodeValue == "1") {
      _root.message_txt.text = "Saved successfully."
    } else {
      _root.message_txt.text = "Error.";
    }
  };

  // Create two text fields. One for messages to the user, one for the username.
  this.createTextField("message_txt", 1, 100, 100, 100, 20);
  this.createTextField("username_txt", 2, 100, 150, 100, 20);

  // Create a push button instance.
  this.attachMovie("FPushButtonSymbol", "saveScore_pb", 3, {_x: 100, _y: 180});

  message_txt.text = "Enter a username and click the button";
  message_txt.autoSize = true;
  username_txt.border = true;
  username_txt.type = "input";
```

```
    saveScore_pb.setClickHandler("saveScore");
    saveScore_pb.setLabel("Save");
}

// A function to generate a random score from 500 to 1000
function generateScore () {
    return Math.round(Math.random( ) * 500) + 500;
}

function saveScore () {

    // Create a score.
    var score = generateScore( );

    // Create the XML packet string.
    var xmlStr = "<gamescore><username>" + username_txt.text +
                 "</username><score>" + score + "</score></gamescore>";

    // Create an XML object using the XML string.
    var score_xml = new XML(xmlStr);

    // Set the content type and XML declaration. Then send the XML data to the server
    // script. This example uses a URL for a ColdFusion page on the localhost. Use the
    // correct URL for your script. Also, when invoking the sendAndLoad( ) method, tell
    // Flash to return the results to the result_xml object.
    score_xml.contentType = "text/xml";
    score_xml.xmlDecl = "<?xml version=\"1.0\" ?>";
    score_xml.sendAndLoad("http://localhost/gamescores.cfm", result_xml);

    // Tell the user that the score is being sent to the server.
    message_txt.text = "Score (" + score + ") sent!";
}

// Call the init( ) function to get things started.
init( );
```

Obviously, in a real-world example the user's score would be generated based on his performance in a game. In this example we just want to demonstrate sending and receiving XML, so we generate the score randomly.

The next step is to create the server-side script. First, here's the Perl option. If you use this option, place the following code in a text file named *gamescores.cgi* (or *gamescores.pl*) in a directory on your web server that has CGI access enabled (usually *cgi* or *cgi-bin*).

```
#!/usr/bin/perl

# Flash/Perl+CGI XML interaction demo
# Arun Bhalla (arun@groogroo.com)

use strict;
use XML::Simple;
use CGI;
```

```
my $ScoreFile = "scores.txt";

# Here we assume that this CGI script is receiving XML in text/xml form
# via POST.  Because of this, the XML will appear to the script via STDIN.
my $input = XMLin(join('',<STDIN>));

# Write out the HTTP header
print CGI::header('text/xml');

# Try to open score file for writing, or return an error message.
open(SCORES, ">> $ScoreFile") || (printMessage(0) &&
                die "Error opening $ScoreFile");

# Save the score in a pipe-delimited text file.
print SCORES join('|', $input->{username}, $input->{score}), "\n";

# Return the result in XML.
printMessage(1);

# Subroutine to output the result in XML.
sub printMessage {
  my $value = shift;
  my $message = {};
  $message->{success} = $value;
  print XMLout($message, keeproot => 1, rootname => 'result');
}
```

If you are using ColdFusion, a sample ColdFusion script is provided in the following code block. Place this code in a ColdFusion page named *gamescores.cfm* within a directory on your web server that can run ColdFusion pages.

```
<cfsilent>
<cfsetting enablecfoutputonly="Yes">
<cfset success = 0>
<cftry>
  <!--- XML packet sent by Flash MX. // --->
  <cfset scores_xml = XmlParse( getHTTPRequestData( ).content ) >

  <!--- Parse out the XML packet sent from Flash MX. // --->

  <!--- Grab the username and score from the XML document and save as
        local variables so they are easier to work with. // --->
  <cfset username = scores_xml.gamescore.username.XmlText >
  <cfset score = scores_xml.gamescore.score.XmlText >

  <!--- Append the latest score to our scores file. This could also be
        stored in the database or another XML document. // --->
  <cffile action="APPEND" file="#ExpandPath( 'scores.txt' )#"
  output="#username#|#score#|#getHTTPRequestData( ).content#" addnewline="Yes">
  <cfset success = 1 >
  <cfcatch type="Any">
    <cfset success = 0 >
    <cffile action="APPEND" file="#ExpandPath( 'attempts.txt' )#" output="ERROR"
    addnewline="Yes">
```

```
      </cfcatch>
    </cftry>
  </cfsilent>
  <cfcontent type="text/xml">
  <cfoutput><?xml version="1.0" ?><success>#success#</success></cfoutput>
  <cfsetting showdebugoutput="no" enablecfoutputonly="No">
```

If you are using PHP on your server, a sample PHP script follows. Place this code in a PHP page named *gamescores.php* on your web server in a directory that allows PHP access.

```php
<?php

// Read In XML from Raw Post Data.
$xml = $GLOBALS['HTTP_RAW_POST_DATA'];

// Process XML using DOM PHP extension.
$document = xmldoc($xml);

// Read root element <gameinfo>.
$rootElement = $document->root();

// Read child nodes <username> and <score>.
$childNodes = $rootElement->children();

$data = "";

// Loop through child nodes and place in array.
foreach($childNodes as $childNode){
  // Add data to array;
  $name = $childNode->tagName();
  $value = $childNode->get_content();
  $data[$name] = $value;
}

// Append data to scores.txt ( format: username|score )
$fp = fopen("scores.txt","a+");
$dataString = $data['username'] . "|" . $data['score'] . "\n";
fputs($fp,$dataString,strlen($dataString));
fclose($fp);

// Return success code to Flash
echo "<success>1</success>";
?>
```

Once you have the Flash movie and the server-side script in place, you need only to run the movie and click on the button to test it. The movie should get a successful response, and if you check in the directory on the server in which the script has been created, you should find a *scores.txt* file containing the data you just entered via the Flash movie.

19.15 Searching XML

Problem

You want to search an *XML* object for nodes based on keywords and other criteria such as node hierarchy.

Solution

Use the third-party *XPath* class from XFactorStudio.com.

Discussion

Thus far in this chapter you've read recipes on how to work with *XML* objects using the DOM, or Document Object Model. This means that if you want to locate a particular node in the XML tree, you need to know the relationship of that node to the whole (i.e., first child, next sibling, etc.). However, when you want a more flexible way of looking for nodes, the DOM can become tedious.

XPath is a language that allows you a much more intuitive and flexible way to find nodes within an *XML* object. XPath is a W3C standard (see *http://www.w3c.org/TR/ xpath*) that is supported on many platforms, but it is not natively supported in Flash. However, Neeld Tanksley of XFactorStudio.com has created an ActionScript *XPath* class that you can download from *http://www.xfactorstudio.com/projects/XPath/ index.php*. You should download the *.zip* file and extract all the *.as* files into your Flash *Include* directory (make sure they are extracted into the *Include* directory, and not into subdirectories).

Once you have downloaded and installed the custom *XPath* class, you can include it in your Flash movies and begin using *XPath* to work with XML, as follows:

```
#include "XPath.as"
```

XPath uses path expressions to denote the node or nodes you want to find. For example, if the root node in your XML object is named *books*, then you can find that root node using:

```
/books
```

If *books* contains child nodes named *book*, then you can return all the *book* nodes using:

```
/books/book
```

If you don't know or care about the full path from the root node to the node or nodes for which you are searching, you can use a double slash to indicate that you want to locate all matching nodes at any level in the XML tree. For example, the following returns all *author* nodes regardless of their hierarchy:

```
//author
```

An asterisk (*) is a wildcard. For example, the following matches all *author* nodes that are children of any nodes that are, in turn, children of the *books* node:

```
/books/*/author
```

You can also use square brackets ([]) to indicate criteria that the nodes must match. For example, you can match all *book* nodes that contain *author* nodes with the following:

```
//book[author]
```

Notice that the preceding is different from *//book/author* in that the former returns *book* nodes and the latter returns *author* nodes.

You can also use expressions with equality operators such as the following, which returns all *book* nodes containing a child *title* node with a text value of "ActionScript Cookbook":

```
//book[title='ActionScript Cookbook']
```

The @ sign can be used to signify an attribute. The following example matches all *author* nodes containing a name attribute:

```
//author[@name]
```

There are also many other built-in functions, operators, and keywords in XPath that you can read about in the documentation.

The *XPath* class has one method that we are interested in for this recipe. The *XPath.selectNodes()* method is a static method, which means you invoke it from the class itself, not from an instance of *XPath*. The method takes two parameters—the *XMLNode* object to search and the XPath expression to use—and returns an array of matching nodes:

```
matches = XPath.selectNodes(my_xml, "/books/book");
```

Now let's take a look at an example of XPath in use. For this example you should make sure that you have installed all the *.as* files for the *XPath* class.

1. Create an XML document using a simple text editor such as WordPad. Add the following XML code to the document, and then save it as *books.xml*:

```
<books>
  <book>
    <title>ActionScript Cookbook</title>
    <authors>
      <author name="Joey Lott" />
    </authors>
  </book>
  <book>
    <title>Flash Cookbook</title>
    <authors>
      <author name="Joey Lott" />
      <author name="Jeffrey Bardzell" />
    </authors>
  </book>
```

```xml
    <book>
      <title>Flash Remoting: The Definitive Guide</title>
      <authors>
        <author name="Tom Muck" />
      </authors>
    </book>
    <book>
      <title>ActionScript for Flash MX: The Definitive Guide</title>
      <authors>
        <author name="Colin Moock" />
      </authors>
    </book>
  </books>
```

2. Open a new Flash document. Copy the PushButton component symbol into the Library by dragging an instance from the Components panel onto the Stage and then deleting the instance. The symbol remains in the Library. Then add the following code to the first frame of the main timeline:

```
#include "XPath.as"

function doSearch () {
  // Use the selectNodes() method to find all matches to the XPath expression
  the
  // user has entered into xpath_txt. Display the results in output_txt. Use a
  // newline character between each match.
  var results = XPath.selectNodes(my_xml, xpath_txt.text);
  output_txt.text = results.join("\n");
}

// Create the input text field for the user to enter the XPath expression.
this.createTextField("xpath_txt", 1, 20, 20, 300, 20);
xpath_txt.border = true;
xpath_txt.type = "input";

// Create the text field for the output of the results.
this.createTextField("output_txt", 2, 20, 70, 300, 300);
output_txt.border = true;
output_txt.multiline = true;
output_txt.wordWrap = true;

// Add the push button instance so the user can perform the search.
this.attachMovie("FPushButtonSymbol", "search_pb", 3, {_x: 20, _y: 45});
search_pb.setClickHandler("doSearch");
search_pb.setLabel("Find Matches");

// Set the ignoreWhite property to true for all XML objects.
XML.prototype.ignoreWhite = true;

// Create an XML object and load books.xml into it.
my_xml = new XML();
my_xml.load("books.xml");
```

3. Save the Flash document to the same directory as the *books.xml* file. Test the movie. Try entering the following XPath expressions, and you should get the results as shown:

//book/title

    \<title>ActionScript Cookbook\</title>

    \<title>Flash Cookbook\</title>

    \<title>Flash Remoting: The Definitive Guide\</title>

    \<title>ActionScript for Flash MX: The Definitive Guide\</title>

//book[contains(title, 'ActionScript')]/title

    \<title>ActionScript Cookbook\</title>

    \<title>ActionScript for Flash MX: The Definitive Guide\</title>

//book[authors[author[@name='Joey Lott']]]/title

    \<title>ActionScript Cookbook\</title>

    \<title>Flash Cookbook\</title>

See Also

XPath is too large a subject to cover in detail in this book. For more information, refer to the online tutorial at *http://www.w3schools.com/xpath/default.asp* or check out the book *XPath and XPointer* by John E. Simpson (O'Reilly).

19.16 Using XML Data to Initialize a Movie

Problem

You want to use XML data from an external source to initialize certain elements of your Flash movie.

Solution

Use the *XML.load()* method to load the XML data, and then initialize the movie's elements within the *onLoad()* method.

Discussion

One of the many uses for XML within your Flash movie is initializing elements such as menus, navigation elements, news, headlines, and so on. By loading the data from an external source, you can more easily update the values or even generate them from a database. This is extremely important for applications in which the content changes frequently, such as product catalogs, news sites, and message boards. To initialize your movie using XML data, load the data using the *XML.load()* method, and then perform the initialization within the *onLoad()* method (or within a function called by *onLoad()*):

```
my_xml = new XML( );
my_xml.load("myAppValues.xml");
my_xml.onLoad = function ( ) {

  /* This example populates a list box with message titles and
     IDs from XML data that might look something like this:
     <messages>
      <message>
        <title>XML fun</title>
        <id>0</id>
      </message>
      <message>
        <title>more XML fun</title>
        <id>1</id>
      </message>
      <message>
        <title>XML fun yet</title>
        <id>2</id>
      </message>
     </messages>
  */
  var messages = this.firstChild.childNodes;
  for (var i = 0; i < messages.length; i++) {
    _root.messagesLB.addItem(messages[i].firstChild.firstChild.nodeValue,
                       messages[i].lastChild.firstChild.nodeValue);
  }
};
```

See Also

See Recipe 16.1 for information on using local shared objects to store client-side information between sessions.

CHAPTER 20
Flash Remoting

20.0 Introduction

Flash Remoting is a technology that enables you to easily connect your Flash movie to a server-side back end. Prior to Flash Remoting, the only options for transferring data were through XML or URL-encoded data strings, both of which require you, the developer, to *serialize* and *deserialize* the data on both the client and server. The terms serialize and deserialize refer to the process of formatting complex data so that it can be transferred between programs, and then translating the serialized data back into the appropriate datatype. For example, consider the scenario in which you want to pass an ActionScript array from Flash to a server-side script using *LoadVars*. To do this, you have to first convert the array into a string (serialization). Here is an example of a serialized array in which vertical pipes are used as delimiters between elements:

```
myArray=val0|val1|val2
```

Not only do you have to serialize the data before sending it, but you have to deserialize it in the server-side script to convert it back into an array. Furthermore, the data may not be correctly interpreted when it is deserialized. XML and URL-encoded strings allow you to send string data only. So, for example, if your array has Boolean values and you serialize it as follows:

```
myArray=true|false|true
```

when you deserialize it, the resulting array will be an array of strings with the values "true", "false", and "true". Furthermore, although arrays are fairly simple to serialize, other datatypes, such as recordsets, can become much more complex.

The problem of transferring data between applications is not unique to Flash, and many different solutions exist. One such solution is WDDX, an XML-based language that describes both simple and complex datatypes. WDDX is supported in many programming languages, including ActionScript (if you download Branden Hall's WDDX ActionScript file available from *http://chattyfig.figleaf.com/~bhall/code/*

wddx_mx.as). However, the downside with WDDX is that, although it handles the nitty-gritty details of serialization/deserialization, you still have to manually instruct your application to perform these tasks.

Flash Remoting is Macromedia's answer to this dilemma. Flash Remoting is supported for ColdFusion MX, .NET, and J2EE. For details, see *http://www.macromedia.com/ software/flashremoting*. Additionally, there are third-party implementations: AMFPHP for PHP (*http://amfphp.org*), FLAP for Perl (*http://www.simonf.com/flap*), and OpenAMF for Java (*http://www.openamf.org*). Whatever the server-side implementation, I refer to it as the Flash Remoting gateway, or simply the gateway.

Flash Remoting uses a proprietary message format called action message format (AMF) for sending data between Flash movies and server-side applications. As a developer, you never have to see the AMF messages, since the Flash Player (on the client) and the Flash Remoting gateway (on the server) perform the serialization and deserialization for you, automatically and transparently. Flash Remoting knows how to convert between ActionScript datatypes and the appropriate server-side datatypes. This chapter necessarily assumes you have some familiarity with the server-side platform on which you intend to use Flash Remoting. For more information, refer to the resources cited in appropriate recipes.

In addition to the server-side implementation of Flash Remoting, you'll also want to download and install the free Flash Remoting Components available from Macromedia at *http://www.macromedia.com/software/flashremoting/downloads/components*. The term "Components" is slightly misleading. You will not be installing any Flash components, but rather a handful of *.as* files in the Flash *Include* directory. These files define important ActionScript classes you'll need to harness the power of Flash Remoting. Simply download the file appropriate for your platform and unzip it. You should automatically be prompted to save the *.as* files to the correct directory (the *Include* directory in the Flash installation).

 Whenever you use Flash Remoting, you must include the *NetServices.as* library file, which contains the code necessary to connect to a Flash Remoting–enabled server from Flash. If you do not include *NetServices.as*, the example does not work; however, you do not receive any errors within the authoring environment.

Once you have the server-side software (a valid gateway) and client-side software (the Flash Remoting Components) set up, you are ready to get started with Flash Remoting. Of course, you'll also want to have a general idea of how Flash Remoting works. The Flash Player has a built-in class called *NetConnection*, which enables the Flash Player to send and receive AMF messages. Therefore, it is possible for the Flash Player to send messages to a server-side script that is configured to listen for and accept messages (the gateway) and for the server to send messages back to Flash. Using AMF messages, you can actually instruct the gateway to invoke server-side functions and return the value (if any) to Flash. When invoking server-side function-ality with Flash Remoting, there are two terms you should be aware of:

Service
> A service contains the functionality you want to invoke. For example, a ColdFu-sion Component (CFC), a JavaBean, or a .NET assembly can contain methods that you want to invoke from Flash Remoting. Therefore, these constructs are referred to as services.

Service function
> A service function is the remote function that you want to invoke from Flash. For example, the methods within a CFC, a JavaBean, or a .NET assembly are all service functions.

Table 20-1 shows the types of services and corresponding service functions for Cold-Fusion, J2EE, and .NET.

Table 20-1. Flash Remoting services and service functions

Server	Service	Service function
ColdFusion	Directory	ColdFusion page
ColdFusion	CFC	CFC method
ColdFusion	Web service	Web method
J2EE	Context	JSP or servlet
J2EE	Java class	Public method
J2EE	JNDI for EJB	Public method
J2EE	MBean	MBean method
.NET	Directory	ASP.NET page
.NET	Assembly	Public method
.NET	Web service	Web method

20.1 Establishing a Connection via Flash Remoting

Problem

You want to establish a connection to the Flash Remoting gateway on your chosen server.

Solution

Pass the URL of the Flash Remoting gateway to *NetServices.createGatewayConnection()*. Alternatively, set a default gateway URL using *NetServices.setDefaultGatewayURL()*. As an optional, additional step, specify the gateway URL in the `FlashVars` attribute within the HTML page in which the Flash movie is embedded (when applicable).

Discussion

A Flash movie accesses Flash Remoting functionality on a sever via a *connection object* that communicates via a *gateway*. A connection object is obtained by invoking *NetServices.createGatewayConnection()*. A gateway is simply specified as a URL to the appropriate server.

Within ActionScript, you have two options for setting the Flash Remoting gateway URL that a connection object uses. The exact URL varies depending on the location of your remote application and the server model in use, as described in Recipes 20.2, 20.3, 20.4, and 20.5. The most direct route is to specify the URL as a parameter when you invoke the *NetServices.createGatewayConnection()* method. For example:

```
#include "NetServices.as"

myConnection =
    NetServices.createGatewayConnection("http://localhost/flashservices/gateway/");
```

There is technically nothing wrong with this direct approach. However, a better, more flexible approach is to set a default gateway URL with *NetServices. setDefaultGatewayURL()* and not specify any parameter when creating the connection object. For example:

```
#include "NetServices.as"

// First, set the default gateway URL.
NetServices.setDefaultGatewayURL("http://localhost/flashservices/gateway/");

// Then, create the connection object without passing a parameter to the method.
myConnection = NetServices.createGatewayConnection();
```

This technique may not seem advantageous, because it requires two lines of code to do what can essentially be accomplished in one line. However, to understand the benefit of this technique, it is helpful to know how Flash decides which gateway URL to use. Flash determines the gateway as follows:

1. If a value is passed to *createGatewayConnection()*, Flash uses that gateway, no matter what.
2. Otherwise, if the variable `gatewayUrl` was passed to the Flash movie by way of the `FlashVars` attribute, Flash uses the `gatewayUrl` variable's value.
3. Otherwise, Flash uses the default gateway specified via *setDefaultGatewayURL()*.

Using *setDefaultGatewayURL()* is particularly valuable when, as in most scenarios, the gateway URL changes between the development phase and the release of your application. If you hardcode the gateway URL into your Flash movie (by specifying the value in the *createGatewayConnection()* method), you must change that value and reexport the Flash movie before publishing it to the production environment.

The recommended scenario is to set the default gateway URL in your Flash movie to the server that you use for development and/or testing, and do not specify a URL parameter for the *createGatewayConnection()* method. This way, you can easily test your movie during development. For example:

```
#include "NetServices.as"

NetServices.setDefaultGatewayURL(
    "http://development.server.com/flashservices/gateway/");
myConnection = NetServices.createGatewayConnection();
```

Then, in the HTML page in which the Flash movie is embedded for production, set a gatewayUrl variable with the production server's URL. Use the FlashVars attribute to accomplish this (shown in bold in the following code listing). In this way, you do not have to make changes to the Flash movie between the development and production environments.

```
<OBJECT
    classid="clsid:D27CDB6E-AE6D-11cf-96B8-444553540000"
    codebase="http://download.macromedia.com/pub/shockwave/
cabs/flash/swflash.cab#version=6,0,0,0"
    WIDTH="100%"
    HEIGHT="100%"
    id="myMovie">
<PARAM
  NAME=flashvars
  VALUE="gatewayUrl=http://localhost/flashservices/gateway">
<PARAM NAME=movie VALUE="myMovie.swf">
<PARAM NAME=quality VALUE=high>
<PARAM NAME=bgcolor VALUE=#FFFFFF>
<EMBED src="myMovie.swf"
  FLASHVARS="gatewayUrl=http://localhost/flashservices/gateway"
    quality=high
  bgcolor=#FFFFFF
  WIDTH="100%"
  HEIGHT="100%"
  NAME="myMovie"
  TYPE="application/x-shockwave-flash"
  PLUGINSPAGE="http://www.macromedia.com/go/getflashplayer">
</EMBED>
</OBJECT>
```

See Also

Recipe 20.2 discusses the proper gateway URL for ColdFusion applications. Recipe 20.3 discusses the proper gateway URL for .NET applications. Recipe 20.4 discusses the proper gateway URL for J2EE applications. Recipe 20.5 gives pointers to resources for using Flash Remoting with PHP and Perl.

20.2 Configuring Flash Remoting for ColdFusion

Problem

You want to configure Flash Remoting for ColdFusion MX.

Solution

Flash Remoting comes preinstalled as part of ColdFusion MX.

Discussion

Flash Remoting comes preinstalled and preconfigured for ColdFusion MX. You do not need to make any modifications. If you are using CFMX with Updater 3, you must configure your *web.xml* file to turn on access for Flash Remoting to work with web services. Prior to Updater 3, this feature was on by default.

When you use Flash Remoting for ColdFusion MX, the gateway URL, as discussed in Recipe 20.1, should be of the form:

```
http://coldFusionServerNameOrIP[:port]/flashservices/gateway
```

in which *coldFusionServerNameOrIP* is the domain name or IP address to the ColdFusion MX server. If the ColdFusion MX server is running on a port other than 80, then you also need to specify the port. For example, if the ColdFusion server is running on *localhost* at port 8500, then the correct gateway URL is:

```
http://localhost:8500/flashservices/gateway
```

See Also

Recipes 20.1, 20.10, 20.11, 20.12, 20.15, 20.18, and 20.24

20.3 Configuring Flash Remoting for .NET

Problem

You want to configure Flash Remoting for .NET.

Solution

Add the *flashgateway.dll* file to the .NET web application's *bin* directory and create a blank *gateway.aspx* file in the web application's root directory. The file and folder permissions must be set to allow access to .NET web services. For example, web services won't work if the ASP.NET user doesn't have permission to run *wsdl.exe*. To support all Flash Remoting features, install the entire .NET SDK on the server, and not just the limited .NET Framework.

Discussion

Flash Remoting for .NET allows Flash clients to communicate with Windows .NET applications. The Flash Remoting for .NET gateway is sold separately by Macromedia (see *http://www.macromedia.com/software/flashremoting/productinfo/versions_pricing*). You must download and install either the trial version or full version before proceeding.

To use Flash Remoting for .NET, two things must be properly configured on the server: the Flash Remoting assembly (*flashgateway.dll*), which implements Flash Remoting support on the server, and an ASPX page, which is used as the Flash Remoting gateway. If you have installed Flash Remoting for .NET, the default installation creates a *flashremoting* directory within the IIS web root (usually *C:\Inetput\wwwroot*). The *flashgateway.dll* assembly file can be found within the *bin* directory of that directory, and you should copy it to the *bin* directory of your own .NET web application. Additionally, you should create a blank ASPX page within your web application's root directory. For Flash to connect to the Flash Remoting gateway, it needs a URL to a valid ASPX page in the web application's root. While it is not absolutely necessary that you create an ASPX page specifically for this purpose (since any ASPX page will do), it is generally a good idea to keep things simple and standardized. Likewise, it is a good idea to name the ASPX file *gateway.aspx*, although it is not absolutely necessary.

The gateway URL that you should use in your Flash movies to connect to the Flash Remoting gateway for .NET applications (as discussed in Recipe 20.1) should be of the form:

```
http://dotNetServerNameOrIP/applicationContext/gateway.aspx
```

in which *dotNetServerNameOrIP* is the domain name or IP address of the .NET server. *applicationContext* should be the context of the .NET web application as it has been set in the IIS snap-in. For example, the correct gateway URL for a web application on *localhost* with a context of */myApplication* is:

```
http://localhost/myApplication/gateway.aspx
```

See Also

Recipes 20.1, 20.9, 20.16, 20.19, and 20.24

20.4 Configuring Flash Remoting for J2EE

Problem

You want to configure Flash Remoting for J2EE.

Solution

Copy the *flashgateway.jar* file into the web application's *WEB-INF/lib* directory and configure a servlet and servlet-mapping in the *web.xml* file. If you use JRun 4 as your J2EE server, Flash Remoting comes preinstalled.

Discussion

If you are using JRun 4 as your J2EE server, Flash Remoting comes preinstalled and you do not need to purchase or configure any additional software. If you use a third-party J2EE server, such as IBM WebSphere or BEA Weblogic, the Flash Remoting for J2EE gateway, sold separately by Macromedia, allows Flash clients to communicate with Enterprise Java applications (see *http://www.macromedia.com/software/flashremoting/ productinfo/versions_pricing*). If you are not using JRun 4, you must download and install either the trial version or full version before proceeding. (As an open source alternative, see the OpenAMF project at *http://www.openamf.org*.)

All the necessary code for Flash Remoting for J2EE is contained within the *flashgateway.jar* file. You can find this file in the Flash Remoting installation (on Windows machines this is typically under *C:\Program Files\Macromedia\Flash Remoting MX*). You can either extract the *.jar* file from the *.war* file (*flashgateway-samples.war*) or copy it from the sample application (within the *sample\WEB-INF\lib* subdirectory). You should copy this *.jar* file to the *WEB-INF/lib* directory of your own J2EE web application.

Once you have copied the *.jar* file into your web application, you only need to configure a servlet and servlet-mapping for the J2EE Flash Remoting gateway servlet that is contained within the *.jar* file. You should map the servlet to the URL pattern */gateway* (the name */gateway* is not required, but it is a logical choice). The following shows an example *web.xml* file with the necessary <servlet> and <servlet-mapping> tags:

```
<?xml version="1.0" encoding="UTF-8"?>
<!DOCTYPE web-app PUBLIC "-//Sun Microsystems, Inc.//DTD Web Application 2.2//EN"
  "http://java.sun.com/j2ee/dtds/web-app_2_2.dtd">
<web-app>
  <display-name>My Application</display-name>
  <servlet>
    <servlet-name>FlashGatewayServlet</servlet-name>
    <servlet-class>
      flashgateway.controller.GatewayServlet
```

```
      </servlet-class>
      <init-param>
        <param-name>LOG_LEVEL</param-name>
        <param-value>Error</param-value>
      </init-param>
      <init-param>
        <param-name>DISABLE_JAVA_ADAPTERS</param-name>
        <param-value>false</param-value>
      </init-param>
      <load-on-startup>1</load-on-startup>
    </servlet>
    <servlet-mapping>
      <servlet-name>FlashGatewayServlet</servlet-name>
      <url-pattern>/gateway</url-pattern>
    </servlet-mapping>
  </web-app>
```

The correct gateway URL to use within your Flash movies to connect to Flash Remoting for J2EE (as discussed in Recipe 20.1) should be of the form:

```
http://j2eeServerNameOrIP[:port]/applicationContext/gateway
```

in which *j2eeServerNameOrIP* is the domain name or IP address of the J2EE application server, and *applicationContext* is the context for the web application as it is configured by the application server. For example, the correct gateway URL for web application on *localhost* (port 80) with a context of */myApplication* is:

```
http://localhost/myApplication/gateway
```

See Also

Recipes 20.1, 20.13, 20.17, and 20.20. "Flash Remoting for J2EE Developers" at *http://www.onjava.com/pub/a/onjava/2003/02/26/flash_remoting.html* and The OpenAMF Java Flash Remoting project (*http://www.openamf.org*), a free, open source alternative to Macromedia's Flash Remoting for J2EE. Information on JRun can be found at *http://www.macromedia.com/software/jrun*.

20.5   Configuring Flash Remoting for PHP or Perl

Problem

You want to use Flash Remoting with something other than ColdFusion MX, .NET, or J2EE, which are the only three server-side platforms officially supported by Macromedia.

Solution

Use a third-party solution such as AMFPHP (*http://amfphp.org*), which offers PHP support, or FLAP (*http://www.simonf.com/flap*), which offers Perl support.

Discussion

Although the AMF format is not open or documented, it turns out that it is the same format used by remote shared objects. An enterprising individual, Wolfgang Hamann, reverse-engineered the AMF format, allowing developers to build open source libraries to support Flash Remoting in server-side languages not supported by Macromedia.

The AMFPHP project implements a Flash Remoting library for PHP. The Flash Remoting in Perl project (FLAP) implements a Flash Remoting library for Perl. Refer to their web sites (*http://amfphp.org* and *http://www.simonf.com/flap*, respectively) for installation, configuration, and support information.

See Also

OpenAMF for Java (*http://www.openamf.org*)

20.6 Invoking a Remote Function on a Service

Problem

You want to call a service function from a Flash movie (see Table 20-1 for Flash Remoting service function types).

Solution

Create a *service object* by invoking the *getService()* method from the connection object returned by *createGatewayConnection()*. The service object is the object returned by *getService()*. Then call the *service function* (any function defined for the service) as a method of the service object.

Discussion

The first step in calling a service function from a Flash movie is to create a connection object (see the Introduction and Recipe 20.1 for more information about this). For example:

```
#include "NetServices.as"
NetServices.setDefaultGatewayURL("http://localhost/flashservices/gateway");
myConnection = NetServices.createGatewayConnection( );
```

Once you have created the connection object, you can create an object that maps to any service available through the specified gateway using the *getService()* method. There are two variations when using the *getService()* method. In the first variation, you specify a single response object to handle responses from all functions invoked on the object. In the second variation, instead of specifying the response object when invoking *getService()*, you specify it as the first parameter each time you invoke a service function.

Both variations require that you provide the name of the service as it is known to the Flash Remoting gateway. A service is known by the URL that accesses the service. See the Introduction and Recipes 20.2, 20.3, and 20.4 for more details on determining the correct service name.

In the first variation, you also need to provide a reference to an object that will handle the response by default (called the *response object*). In this variation, the response object should be an object with named result functions (see Recipe 20.7 for details on how to handle results using named result functions). By convention, the object is the same object within which the service object is defined (see also Recipe 20.7 for more details on service objects).

```
// Create a service object that maps to a service named serviceName and set this (the
// same object within which the service object is defined) to handle the response.
myService = myConnection.getService("serviceName", this);
```

Notice that the service object is returned by *getService()*, and the response object is optionally passed to *getService()* to handle the response. After obtaining the service object with *getService()*, based on the service name, you can invoke any service function as a method of the service object. If the service function expects parameters, you can pass the parameters to it just as with any other method invocation.

```
// Call a service function named serviceFunction0 with no parameters.
myService.serviceFunction0( );
```

```
// Call a service function named serviceFunction1 with
// two parameters: a string and a Boolean.
myService.serviceFuncton1("param value", true);
```

In the alternative approach, when calling the *getService()* method, you don't specify a response object to handle the response. Instead, with this variation, you specify the response object as the first parameter when invoking a service function. However, the response object parameter is not sent to the service function.

```
// Create the service object without specifying the response object.
myService = myConnection.getService("serviceName");
```

```
// Call serviceFunction0, specifying that myResponseObject should handle the results,
// but do not pass any additional parameters. myResponseObject is not sent to the
// service function.
myService.serviceFunction0(myResponseObject);
```

```
// Call serviceFunction1, specifying that myResponseObject should handle the results,
// and pass two additional parameters. myResponseObject is not sent to the service
// function, but the string and Boolean values are sent.
myService.serviceFunction1(myResponseObject, "param value", true);
```

In this variation, the response object should contain an *onResult()* method, as described in Recipe 20.7.

In most cases, the second variation—in which the response object is specified as the first parameter when calling a service function—is the better choice. This option enables you to specify different response objects for each service function call (something you cannot do using the first variation, in which the service object is set when calling *getService()*).

It is worth noting that you must always declare a response object, either when calling the *getService()* method or in the service function invocation. This is true even if the service function does not return any result. Also, you should never try to define a response object in both places. Doing so will only create errors.

See Also

Recipes 20.7, 20.9, 20.10, and 20.13

20.7   Handling Flash Remoting Results

Problem

You want to handle the results from calling a service function using Flash Remoting.

Solution

Use a named result function or, as a better alternative, use a response object.

Discussion

Unlike invocations of functions and methods that are defined within the Flash movie, Flash Remoting service function invocations are asynchronous. This means that when the ActionScript interpreter encounters a remote service function call within the code, it initiates the call but does not wait for a response before continuing to the next line of ActionScript code. The same thing is true when loading any external content, be it by means of an *XML* object, a *LoadVars* object, or a movie clip using *loadMovie()*. This asynchronous behavior allows the Flash movie to continue to run without waiting on something that has the potential for high latency. Therefore, if a remote service function returns a value, you cannot use that value within your ActionScript code immediately, as you would the return value of a native ActionScript function or method.

```
// myVariable is undefined because the service function
// does not return a value immediately.
myVariable = myService.myServiceFunction(responseObject);
```

Instead, you have to use a response object with callback functions or methods to obtain the result. There are two ways to handle results from a Flash Remoting service function, and they correspond to the two variations of invoking the service function (see Recipe 20.6).

The first technique, *named result functions*, is used, by convention, when you have specified a default response object for a service object (that is, when you've passed a response object to the *getService()* method). Named result functions are functions that must be named with the pattern *serviceFunctionName_Result()*. For example, if the service function is named *getUserList()*, then the named result function should be named *getUserList_Result()*. The Flash Remoting gateway automatically passes any returned value to the result function as a parameter. For example:

```
// Define the named result function getUserList_Result( ) to handle the result from
// the service function getUserList( ).
function getUserList_Result (result) {
  trace(result);
}

// Create a service object from a connection object. Define the default response
// object as this, since this is where the result function is defined.
myService = myConnection.getService("serviceName", this);

// Invoke getUserList( ).
myService.getUserList( );
```

The second technique is to use a response object that declares an *onResult()* method. By convention, you should use this technique when you are defining a response object for each service function invocation. This technique is much more flexible than the first, in that you can define different response objects for each service function invocation, or you can share a single response object among multiple service function invocations. Note that this, which represents the current object, is passed as the response object in the preceding example.

To create a response object, define an *onResult()* method on it. The *onResult()* method is automatically invoked when a result is returned to the Flash movie from the service function, and any returned value is passed to the *onResult()* method as a parameter. For example:

```
// Create an object and define an onResult( ) method for it.
myResponseObject = new Object( );
myResponseObject.onResult = function (result) {
  trace(result);
};

// Create the service object from a connection object. Do not set
// a default response object.
myService = myConnection.getService("serviceName");

// Call the getUserList( ) service function and specify that the response should be
// handled by the myResponseObject response object.
myService.getUserList(myResponseObject);
```

See Also

Recipes 20.6 and 20.8

20.8 Distinguishing Among Results from Multiple Calls to a Single Service

Problem

You want to be able to distinguish among results from multiple calls to a single service function.

Solution

Use instances of a custom response class for each response object.

Discussion

When a result is returned from a Flash Remoting service function, Flash doesn't automatically tell you which service function invocation generated the result. Furthermore, due to the asynchronous nature of Flash Remoting, you cannot rely on results being returned to Flash in the same order in which the functions were invoked. However, you can distinguish between the results from calls to multiple service functions by using a separate instance of a custom class for each response object. Simply attach a custom property to each response object instance and check its value when the result from the service function is returned.

This solution uses a custom response class that takes an id parameter in the constructor. This allows you to create multiple instances of the class—one for each function invocation—and assign each one a unique id. Then, when the result comes back, you can distinguish between the results using the id property of the response object. For example:

```
// Define a constructor for a custom response object class that assigns an id
// property to each instance.
function MyResponseObject(id) {
  this.id = id;
}

// Define the onResult( ) method for the response object class.
MyResponseObject.prototype.onResult = function (result) {
  // Process the result differently depending on the value of the id property.
  trace("The response came from the call with id " + this.id);
};

// Call the same service function multiple times. In this example the service
// function, getUserInfo( ), which is not shown, retrieves user information for
```

```
// different users based on a username parameter. In each case, use an instance of
// the MyResponseObject class as the response object. Assign each instance an id
// corresponding to the username so that you can distinguish between them when the
// results are returned.
myService.getUserInfo(new MyResponseObject("Heather"), "Heather");
myService.getUserInfo(new MyResponseObject("Julie"), "Julie");
myService.getUserInfo(new MyResponseObject("Sarah"), "Sarah");
```

See Also

Recipe 20.7

20.9   Calling ASP.NET Functions from Flash

Problem

You want to call ASP.NET service functions using Flash Remoting.

Solution

Use ASP.NET pages (which requires modifying the code) or, preferably, use public DLL methods (which requires no modification).

Discussion

You can call ASP.NET pages or public DLL methods as service functions from a Flash movie using Flash Remoting.

Ideally, DLL methods should be used in place of ASP.NET pages when it comes to Flash Remoting. Although some people may have hesitancy about writing/using DLLs because they require compilation, they are far more advantageous than using ASP.NET pages. Any public method of an ASP.NET DLL can be called using Flash Remoting without any modification to the DLL code. Furthermore, using DLLs allows you to separate your business logic from your presentation logic, so the same DLL can be used by multiple interfaces (Flash movies, ASP.NET pages, Windows Forms, etc.). Using DLLs for your business logic is a best practice regardless of whether you are using Flash Remoting.

To call a DLL method from a Flash movie, you should place that DLL in the web application's *bin* directory and create a service object that maps to the class within it. The correct service name to use is the fully qualified class name, which must include the namespace. For example:

```
// Create a service object that maps to the Book class in the OReilly.ASCB namespace.
myService = myConnection.getService("OReilly.ASCB.Book");
```

```
// Call the getTitle() method of the Book class and specify a response object, as
// shown in Recipe 20.7, to handle the results.
myService.getTitle(myResponseObject);
```

If you must use an ASP.NET page, there are several modifications you must make to access it via Flash Remoting.

You must create a *FlashGateway.Flash* object in the page. By convention, this object is named flash. You can accomplish this one of two ways:

Tag-based

Use the Register directive to register a tag prefix to the *FlashGateway* namespace and the *flashgateway* assembly. Then create an instance of the Flash class with a <Macromedia:Flash> tag. The ID attribute should be the name of the object, and the runat attribute should always be "server". For example:

```
<%@ Register TagPrefix="Macromedia" Namespace="FlashGateway"
Assembly="flashgateway" %>
<Macromedia:Flash ID="flash" runat="server" />
```

Code block

Whether in a render block in the ASP.NET page or in a code-behind class, you can create an instance of the *FlashGateway.Flash* class using the constructor. The following example is in C#:

```
FlashGateway.Flash flash = new FlashGateway.Flash();
```

If you want to accept parameters, you must extract them from the *FlashGateway.Flash* object's Params property. Params implements *IList,* and the parameters are stored as elements with integer indexes.

```
string myFirstParam  = flash.Params[0];
string mySecondParam = flash.Params[1];
```

If you want to return a value to the Flash movie, you must assign that value to the *FlashGateway.Flash* object's Result property. The standard output of the ASP.NET page is disregarded by Flash Remoting. Only the value of the Result property is returned to Flash.

When you want to call an ASP.NET page as a service function, the service name is the path to that page within the web application's hierarchy. Slashes should be replaced by dots. For example:

```
// Create a service object that maps to the /aspx/users directory
// of the web application.
myService = myConnection.getService("aspx.users");

// Create a service object that maps to the root directory of the web application.
myService = myConnection.getService("");
```

The service function name should be the same as the filename of the ASP.NET page. For example:

```
// Invoke the page called getUserInfo.aspx.
myService.getUserInfo(myResponseObject);
```

20.10 Calling ColdFusion Functions from Flash

Problem

You want to invoke ColdFusion service functions using Flash Remoting.

Solution

Preferably use a ColdFusion Component (CFC). Alternatively, you can invoke a ColdFusion page, with some modifications.

Discussion

When you are using ColdFusion, there are two types of Flash Remoting service functions: ColdFusion pages and CFC methods.

Preferably, you should use CFC methods instead of ColdFusion pages for all of your Flash Remoting needs. Calling a CFC method from Flash Remoting does not require any special code changes to the CFC. The only consideration is that you must make sure that the CFC method can be accessed remotely by setting the `<cffunction>` tag's access attribute to "remote", as follows:

```
<cffunction name="myCFCMethod" access="remote">
    <!--- method body --->
</cffunction>
```

When you want to call a CFC method from a Flash movie, you should create a service object that maps to the CFC by specifying the fully qualified CFC name in the *getService()* method. The fully qualified CFC name includes any packages in which the CFC has been placed. For example:

```
// Create a service object that maps to a CFC named MyCFC in the root of the
// ColdFusion application.
myService = myConnection.getService("MyCFC");

// Or, if the CFC is in a package, create a service object including the package
// name. This example maps to a CFC named MyCFC in the OReilly.ASCB package.
myService = myConnection.getService("OReilly.ASCB.MyCFC");
```

If you must use a ColdFusion page with Flash Remoting, you must make changes to the code within the page. Any values that the page receives or returns are contained within the ColdFusion FLASH scope. All parameters that you send to the ColdFusion page via the service function invocation are stored in the params array within the FLASH scope. If you want to return a value to the Flash movie from the ColdFusion page, you should assign that value to the result variable within the FLASH scope. You can return only one value per ColdFusion page. The last value assigned to the FLASH.result variable when the page has been processed is the value that is returned.

```
<!--- Set two variables within the ColdFusion page to the values of the first
      two parameters passed to the page from the Flash movie that called it --->
```

```
<CFSET myFirstParam = FLASH.params[1]>
<CFSET mySecondParam = FLASH.params[2]>

<!--- Return a value to the Flash movie --->
<CFSET FLASH.result = "a return value">
```

See Also

Recipe 20.11

20.11 Passing Named Parameters to ColdFusion Component Methods

Problem

You want to pass named parameters to a ColdFusion Component (CFC) method using Flash Remoting.

Solution

Create an ActionScript object with properties corresponding to the expected CFC method parameters, and pass that object as a single parameter to the CFC method.

Discussion

You can pass named parameters (as opposed to positional parameters) to a CFC method from a Flash movie. To accomplish this, you should pass a single object parameter to the CFC method in which the property names correspond to the names you have given to the parameters in the CFC method. ColdFusion automatically matches up the object's property values to the CFC method's parameters with the same names. For example:

```
<!--- A sample CFC method definition --->
<cffunction name="getCarInfo" access="remote">
  <cfargument name="make" type="string">
  <cfargument name="model" type="string">
  <!--- rest of method body --->
<cffunction>

// The corresponding ActionScript snippet...

// Create an object with properties named make and model.
params = new Object();
params.make = "Honda";
params.model = "Accord";

// Call the getCarInfo() service function and pass it the params object.
myService.getCarInfo(myResponseObject, params);
```

See Also

Recipe 20.12

20.12 Passing Complex Parameters to ColdFusion Component Methods

Problem

You want to pass an object parameter to a ColdFusion Component (CFC) method using Flash Remoting.

Solution

Pass the value as a named parameter.

Discussion

ColdFusion automatically attempts to convert object parameters into named parameters (see Recipe 20.11). This is problematic if you want to pass an ActionScript object to a CFC method as a parameter. Consider the following example:

```
<!--- A sample CFC method definition --->
<cffunction name="insertCatalogItem" access="remote">
  <cfargument name="catalogItem" type="struct">
  <!--- rest of method body --->
<cffunction>

// The corresponding ActionScript snippet...

// Create an item object with name, price, and description properties.
item = new Object();
item.name = "Widget";
item.price = 9.99;
item.description = "Widgets available in green, blue, and gold";

// Call the insertCatalogItem( ) service function and pass it the item object.
myService.insertCatalogItem(myResponseObject, item);
```

In the preceding example, we want to pass the item object from Flash to the CFC method as a parameter that should be converted into a struct (a complex datatype). However, ColdFusion attempts to convert the properties of the item object into named parameters, and it tries to match up the name, price, and description properties to corresponding parameters within the CFC method. This prevents it from successfully passing a complex parameter, such as an object datatype.

You should pass the object parameter as a named parameter instead of as a positional parameter. Here, the item object is passed as the named parameter catalogItem:

```
MyService.insertCatalogItem(myResponseObject, {catalogItem: item});
```

Note that using named parameters prevents ColdFusion from trying to convert the subitems into individual parameters within the CFC method, thus allowing complex datatypes to be passed.

See Also

Recipe 20.11

20.13 Calling Java or JSP Functions from Flash

Problem

You want to invoke J2EE service functions using Flash Remoting.

Solution

Use public Java class methods. Alternatively, use servlets/JSPs that have been modified to work with Flash Remoting.

Discussion

Although Flash Remoting for J2EE enables you to invoke public methods of Java classes or servlets/JSPs, invoking Jave class methods is the preferable option. You can invoke any public method of a Java class without having to modify the Java code at all. This is an obvious advantage. To access the methods of a Java class from Flash Remoting, you should create an ActionScript service object that maps to the fully qualified Java class name:

```
// Create a service that maps to the Book class in the oreilly.ascb package.
myService = myConnection.getService("oreilly.ascb.Book");
```

If you must use servlets/JSPs instead of invoking Java class methods, you need to modify the servlet/JSP code for it to work properly with Flash Remoting. Values are passed to and from the servlet/JSP by way of attributes of the request object. Parameters are passed from Flash to the servlet/JSP using the attribute named FLASH.PARAMS. You can retrieve the attribute value using the *getAttribute()* method of the request object. For example:

```
Object myFlashParams = request.getAttribute("FLASH.PARAMS");
```

The value of the FLASH.PARAMS attribute is a *List* object. However, if you want the servlet/JSP to be accessible from a web browser as well as from Flash Remoting, you should cast the value only after checking to make sure it actually is an instance of *List*. Otherwise, when the servlet/JSP is accessed from a web browser (and no FLASH.PARAMS attribute exists), the attempt to cast the object to *List* will cause an error. Therefore, you should use:

```
if (myFlashParams instanceof List) {
    List myParamsList = (List) myFlashParams;
    // Process the parameters here.
}
```

You can return a value to a Flash movie from a servlet/JSP using the FLASH.RESULT attribute of the request object. Assign the value you want to return to Flash to the attribute using the *setAttribute()* method. The *setAttribute()* method accepts complex datatypes only. You cannot set the attribute value to a primitive datatype such as float. If you want to return a primitive datatype, use a wrapper class instead, such as:

```
// Return a floating-point number to Flash using the Float class.
request.setAttribute("FLASH.RESULT", new Float(6.6));
```

20.14 Transmitting Custom Datatypes to a Flash Remoting Back End

Problem

You want to create an object of a custom type to send to a Flash Remoting back end.

Solution

On the client-side, create a custom class in the ActionScript code, and then use *Object.registerClass()* to register it.

Discussion

Flash Remoting enables you to send and receive many different kinds of data—even custom datatypes—to and from a Flash Remoting back end. However, Flash has to know about the datatype for it to be properly transmitted. The *Object.registerClass()* method takes care of registering custom classes with the Flash movie so that it knows how to handle objects of those types when sending and receiving them via Flash Remoting. When you use the *registerClass()* method for this purpose, the first parameter should be an arbitrary name by which Flash should know the datatype, and the second parameter should be a reference to the class that you want to register. Conventionally, the name to which you register the class should match the class name.

```
// Create a custom class.
function MyClass( ){}
```

```
// Register the class so that Flash knows it by the ID MyClass.
Object.registerClass("MyClass", MyClass);
```

Note that for the properties of a custom class to be correctly interpreted by Flash, when using this technique, you must declare the properties as members of the class's prototype:

```
// Create a custom class. The constructor accepts two parameters and sets two
// properties. Normally this would be all that is necessary.
function MyClass(a, b) {
  this.a = a;
  this.b = b;
}

// When you want to register a custom class you should also declare the properties as
// members of the class's prototype.
MyClass.prototype.a;
MyClass.prototype.b;
```

20.15 Receiving Typed Objects with ColdFusion

Problem

You want to be able to handle typed object parameters (i.e., properties of an object that store data of a custom type) sent to a ColdFusion back end (a CFC function or a CFM page).

Solution

Work with the parameter as an *ASObject*. Use the *get()* method to get the values for the properties, and use the *getType()* method to get the registered class name.

Discussion

Typed objects are automatically converted to *ASObject* datatypes in ColdFusion. *ASObject* is a Java class that extends the *java.util.HashMap* class (meaning all the properties and methods of a *HashMap* will also work for an *ASObject*) that also adds the *getType()* and *setType()* methods. If you are not yet familiar with how to work with Java objects in ColdFusion, you can read more about this in the ColdFusion documentation here:

http://livedocs.macromedia.com/cfmxdocs/Developing_ColdFusion_MX_Applications_with_CFML/Java5.jsp#1134356

Here is an example of a snippet of ActionScript code that creates a typed object and sends it to a ColdFusion service function:

```
function MyClass(a, b) {
  this.a = a;
```

```
    this.b = b;
  }
MyClass.prototype.a;
MyClass.prototype.b;

Object.registerClass("MyClass", MyClass);

// Send a new MyClass object to a ColdFusion service function.
myCFService.serviceFunction(myResponseObj, {param: new MyClass("eh", "bee")});
```

Here is an example of a ColdFusion snippet that extracts the values from properties named a and b from an *ASObject* named param and also retrieves the object's type:

```
<!--- aVal = eh, bVal = bee, objTypeName = MyClass --->
<cfset aVal = param.get("a")>
<cfset bVal = param.get("b")>
<cfset objTypeName = param.getType()>
```

See Also

Recipes 20.14 and 20.18

20.16 Receiving Typed Objects with ASP.NET

Problem

You want to be able to handle typed object parameters sent to a .NET back end (an ASPX page, DLL method, or web service method).

Solution

Create a .NET class with the same name as the name to which the ActionScript class is registered. The .NET Flash Remoting gateway automatically converts the Action-Script typed object to an object of the corresponding .NET type.

Discussion

When you pass a typed object to a .NET back end from a Flash movie, the .NET Flash Remoting gateway looks for a .NET class with the same name as the registered class name of the ActionScript object and tries to convert the ActionScript object to that .NET type. Therefore, you need to create a .NET type to correspond to each of the registered ActionScript classes.

For example, in the Flash movie, define the following ActionScript class and register it using the name "MyClass":

```
function MyClass(a, b) {
  this.a = a;
  this.b = b;
```

```
    }
MyClass.prototype.a;
MyClass.prototype.b;

Object.registerClass("MyClass", MyClass);
```

Then create a .NET class with the same name and the same properties. The .NET class should have a constructor that requires no parameters.

```
public class MyClass {

    public string a;
    public string b;

    public MyClass(){}
}
```

Then, so long as the .NET *MyClass* is accessible to the .NET service function (be it a DLL method, an ASPX page, or a web service method), the service function can accept a parameter of type *MyClass*. Here is an example of a DLL method that accepts a *MyClass* parameter:

```
public string returnPropertiesString(MyClass myCls) {
    return myCls.a + " " + myCls.b;
}
```

See Also

Recipe 20.19

20.17 Receiving Typed Objects with Java

Problem

You want to handle typed objects using a J2EE service function.

Solution

Use JavaBean classes that correspond to the ActionScript classes, and use the third-party *ASTranslator* class to perform conversions between datatypes.

Discussion

Unlike the .NET version, Flash Remoting for J2EE does not automatically convert typed ActionScript objects into corresponding custom Java types. Instead, the gateway converts the ActionScript objects into *ASObject* types. The *flashgateway.io.ASObject* class (included in *flashgateway.jar*) is a subclass of *java.util.HashMap* to which two additional methods (*getType()* and *setType()*) have been added. The properties of the

ActionScript object are stored as key/value pairs in the *ASObject*. You can create your own proprietary code to convert between an *ASObject* and the appropriate Java datatype. However, Carbon Five has already created an excellent utility named ASTranslator to do this for you.

ASTranslator is freely available for download from *http://www.carbonfive.com/opensource-main-1.html*. It converts between *ASObject* and custom Java datatypes using JavaBean-style introspection. Therefore, it requires that your custom Java datatypes adhere to the JavaBean rules (namely, they must implement *java.io. Serializable*, use get/set methods for all publicly accessible properties, and have a constructor that requires no parameters).

Here is how to use ASTranslator to receive typed objects and convert them to custom Java types:

1. Download the *ASTranslator.jar* file and place it in your web application's *WEB-INF/lib* directory.

2. Create a JavaBean class that corresponds to the registered ActionScript class. The JavaBean class should have the same name as the name to which the Action-Script class is registered. Also, the JavaBean class should have get and set methods for each property in the ActionScript class. Here is an example ActionScript class:

```
function MyClass(a, b) {
  this.a = a;
  this.b = b;
}
MyClass.prototype.a;
MyClass.prototype.b;

Object.registerClass("MyClass", MyClass);
```

Here is a the code for the corresponding JavaBean class:

```
public class MyClass implements java.io.Serializable{

  private string _a;
  private string _b;

  public MyClass() {}

  public void setA(string a) {
    this._a = a;
  }

  public void setB(string b) {
    this._b = b;
  }

  public string getA() {
    return this._a;
  }
}
```

```
      public string getB( ) {
        return this._b;
      }

    }
```

3. The Flash Remoting service function (servlet/JSP, Java class, etc.) should accept a parameter of type *ASObject*. Then you can convert the *ASObject* into a JavaBean using the *fromActionScript()* method of an *ASTranslator* object. Here is an example of a Java class method that does this:

```
    public void myMethod(ASObject aso) {

      // Create the ASTranslator instance.
      com.carbonfive.flash.ASTranslator ast = new
                                      com.carbonfive.flash.ASTranslator( );

      // Convert and cast the ASObject to a MyClass object using the
      // fromActionScript( ) method.
      MyClass myCls = (MyClass) ast.fromActionScript(aso);

      // Now you can do something with the properly cast Java object.
    }
```

See Also

Recipe 20.20

20.18 Returning Typed Objects from ColdFusion

Problem

You want to return a typed object from ColdFusion to a Flash movie.

Solution

Create an *ASObject* and set the type to match the name of a registered ActionScript class.

Discussion

When an *ASObject* is returned to a Flash movie, Flash attempts to find a registered class in which the registered name matches the name of the type that has been set for the *ASObject* via the *setType()* method. You can create an *ASObject* within ColdFusion using the ColdFusion techniques for creating Java objects. If you are not familiar with how to do this, you can read more about it in the ColdFusion documentation available here:

> http://livedocs.macromedia.com/cfmxdocs/Developing_ColdFusion_MX_
> Applications_with_CFML/Java5.jsp#1134356

Here is an example of a ColdFusion Component method that creates and returns an *ASObject*:

```
<cffunction name="getTypedObject" access="remote">

    <!--- Create a Java object from the flashgateway.io.ASObject class.
          Add the name attribute with the arbitrary name ASObjectClass so
          that you can initialize the object properly. --->
    <cfobject type="Java" class="flashgateway.io.ASObject"
            name="ASObjectClass"
            action="create" >

    <!--- The init() method returns a proper ASObject. --->
    <cfset aso = ASObjectClass.init()>

    <!--- Set the type of the ASObject to match the name
          of a registered ActionScript class --->
    <cfset aso.setType("MyClass")>
    <cfset aso.put("a", "eh")>
    <cfset aso.put("b", "bee")>
    <cfreturn aso>
</cffunction>
```

Here is an example snippet of ActionScript code that corresponds to the preceding ColdFusion method:

```
function MyClass(a, b) {
   this.a = a;
   this.b = b;
}
MyClass.prototype.a;
MyClass.prototype.b;

// Add a method that just writes all the properties to the Output window. This
// example simply illustrates that the ASObject is correctly converted into a MyClass
// object when returned to Flash.
MyClass.prototype.traceProperties = function () {
   for (var prop in this) {
      trace(prop + " = " + this[prop]);
   }
};

Object.registerClass("MyClass", MyClass);

// Create a response object.
myResponse = new Object();
myResponse.onResult = function (result) {
   // The result parameter is correctly converted to a MyClass object. You can prove
   // this because the traceProperties() method gets called.
   result.traceProperties();
};

// Call the service function.
myCFCService.getTypedObject(myResponse);
```

See Also

Recipe 20.15

20.19 Returning Typed Objects from ASP.NET

Problem

You want to return a typed object to Flash from a .NET back end.

Solution

Use an *ASObject* and set the ASType property to match the name of the ActionScript class as it is registered in Flash.

Discussion

Flash automatically attempts to convert any returned *ASObject* values into Action-Script datatypes. It tries to find an ActionScript class that is registered within Flash with the same name as the value of the *ASObject*'s ASType property. Therefore, you can return a typed object to a Flash movie from a .NET back end by using an *ASObject* and setting its ASType property to the name of an ActionScript class as it is registered in the Flash movie. Use the *Add()* method to add properties to the *ASObject*. Here is an example of a .NET DLL method that returns an *ASObject*:

```
public FlashGateway.IO.ASObject getTypedObject( ) {

    // Create an ASObject.
    FlashGateway.IO.ASObject aso = new FlashGateway.IO.ASObject( );

    // Add properties to the object.
    aso.Add("a", "eh");
    aso.Add("b", "bee");

    // Set the ASType of the ASObject to match the name
    // of a registered ActionScript class.
    aso.ASType = "MyClass";

    // Return the ASObject.
    return aso;
}
```

Here is an example snippet of ActionScript code that handles the *ASObject* that the preceding code returns:

```
function MyClass(a, b) {
    this.a = a;
    this.b = b;
}
```

```
MyClass.prototype.a;
MyClass.prototype.b;

// Add a method that just writes all the properties to the Output window.
// This example simply illustrates that the ASObject is correctly converted into a
// MyClass object when returned to Flash.
MyClass.prototype.traceProperties = function () {
  for (var prop in this) {
    trace(prop + " = " + this[prop];
  }
};

Object.registerClass("MyClass", MyClass);

// Create a response object.
myResponse = new Object( );
myResponse.onResult = function (result) {
  // The result parameter is correctly converted to a MyClass object.
  // You can prove this because the traceProperties( ) method iss called.
  result.traceProperties( );
};

// Call the service function.
myNETService.getTypedObject(myResponse);
```

 .NET web services do not allow you to return *ASObject* data. This is a limitation of .NET web services, and it prevents you from returning typed objects from them.

See Also

Recipe 20.16

20.20 Returning Typed Objects from Java

Problem

You want to return a typed object from a J2EE back end.

Solution

Use the third-party *ASTranslator* class to convert a JavaBean object to an *ASObject*, and return the *ASObject*.

Discussion

For details on obtaining ASTranslator, see Recipe 20.17.

Once you have ASTranslator included in your web application, you can use the *toActionScript()* method of an *ASTranslator* object to convert a JavaBean object into an *ASObject* that can be returned to Flash. Here is an example of a Java method that creates a JavaBean object, converts it into an *ASObject*, and returns the *ASObject*:

```
public flashgateway.io.ASObject getTypedObject( ) {

    // Create a MyClass JavaBean object. See Recipe 20.14 for the MyClass code.
    MyClass myCls = new MyClass( );

    // Set the properties of the object.
    myCls.setA("eh");
    myCls.setB("bee");

    // Create an ASTranslator object.
    com.carbonfive.flash.ASTranslator ast = new com.carbonfive.flash.ASTranslator( );

    // Convert the MyClass object to an ASObject.
    flashgateway.io.ASObject aso = ast.toActionScript(myCls);

    // Return the ASObject.
    return aso;

}
```

Here is an example ActionScript snippet that handles the returned *ASObject*:

```
function MyClass(a, b) {
    this.a = a;
    this.b = b;
}
MyClass.prototype.a;
MyClass.prototype.b;

// Add a method that just writes all the properties to the Output window. This
// example illustrates that the ASObject is correctly converted into a MyClass object
// when returned to Flash.
MyClass.prototype.traceProperties = function ( ) {
    for (var prop in this) {
        trace(prop + " = " + this[prop]);
    }
};

Object.registerClass("MyClass", MyClass);

// Create a response object.
myResponse = new Object( );
myResponse.onResult = function (result) {
    // The result parameter is correctly converted to a MyClass object. You can prove
    // this because the traceProperties() method is called.
    result.traceProperties( );
};

// Call the service function.
myJ2EEService.getTypedObject(myResponse);
```

See Also

Recipes 20.14 and 20.17

20.21 Writing Server-Side Functions in ActionScript

Problem

You want to write Sever-Side ActionScript (SSAS) that you can call from a Flash Remoting movie.

Solution

Create an ASR file as part of your ColdFusion or JRun web application.

Discussion

SSAS is available only for ColdFusion and JRun, and it allows you to create server-side functions that you can call from Flash Remoting. The advantage is that with SSAS, you can perform some basic server-side functionality (such as database queries and HTTP requests) using familiar ActionScript syntax. The disadvantage of SSAS is that it is quite limited in its (documented) functionality.

 Flash Remoting SSAS (as opposed to the FlashCom SSAS in Recipe 14.14) is based on Java, and the standard Java API is available in a modified, ActionScript-like form. This might hold some appeal to Java developers. The syntax is entirely ActionScript-like, and it also allows for the less strict declaration and typing of ActionScript variables. However, you can create objects of all Java types. For example:

```
myFile = new File("test.txt");
```

To write SSAS, all you need to do is create an ASR file within the web application. The file must end with the *.asr* extension and should contain functions, which can be written with any plain-text editor. For example, an ASR file could contain the following:

```
function mySSASFunction () {
  return "This is a value from SSAS";
}
```

Within your Flash movie, you can create a service object that maps to an ASR file using the *getService()* method and specifying the fully qualified path and name of the ASR file (minus the *.asr* extension):

```
// Create a service object that maps to mySSAS.asr where the ASR file is within a
// directory called ssasFiles.
mySSASSrv = myConnection.getService("ssasFiles.mySSAS");
```

See Also

Recipes 20.22 and 20.23

20.22 Querying a Database with Server-Side ActionScript

Problem

You want to use Server-Side ActionScript (SSAS) to query a database.

Solution

Make sure the database is registered as a datasource with ColdFusion or JRun, and then use the *query()* method of the SSAS CF object.

Discussion

Server-Side ActionScript allows you to query any registered datasource by way of the *CF.query()* method. The first step is to make sure that your database has been properly registered with ColdFusion or JRun. If you are not sure how to do this, then you should consult your ColdFusion or JRun documentation.

The *CF.query()* method allows you to pass it the following arguments as either positional or named parameters:

datasource
    The name of the datasource as registered with ColdFusion or JRun.

sql
    The SQL command.

username
    If the datasource requires a username, you can specify it with this parameter.

password
    If the datasource requires a password, you can specify it with this parameter.

maxrows
    You can optionally specify the maximum number of records to return.

timeout
    An optional number of milliseconds to wait before timing out.

When you use the *CF.query()* method with positional parameters, you can specify one or more optional parameters in the following orders:

```
CF.query(datasource, sql);
CF.query(datasource, sql, maxrows);
```

```
CF.query(datasource, sql, username, password);
CF.query(datasource, sql, username, password, maxrows);
```

You can use the *timeout* parameter only if you used named parameters. Otherwise, you can use named parameters by passing the method an object in which the properties match the parameter names. For example:

```
CF.query({datasource: "myDatabase", sql: "SELECT * FROM MyTable"});
```

The *CF.query()* method returns a recordset that you can return to the Flash movie. For example, here is an SSAS function that accepts a parameter and performs a database query to find records containing that value. The function then returns the recordset to the Flash movie.

```
function getUsers (city) {
    return CF.query("MyDatabase", "SELECT * FROM UsersTable WHERE city = " + city);
}
```

However, the recordset that the *CF.query()* method returns is not an ActionScript *RecordSet* object in SSAS (although it is converted into a *RecordSet* object in the Flash movie). This is because the ActionScript *RecordSet* class is available only in client-side ActionScript, not in SSAS. The object that *CF.query()* returns is actually a *coldfusion.sql.QueryTable* object. The *coldfusion.sql.QueryTable* class subclasses *javax.sql.RowSet*, so if you absolutely want to work with the recordset on the server before returning the data to Flash, you can use the methods of the *RowSet* class.

See Also

Recipe 20.21. Also, Chapter 21 covers recordsets in detail. For more information on *RowSet* objects, see the Java API at *http://java.sun.com/j2ee/sdk_1.3/techdocs/api/javax/sql/RowSet.html*.

20.23 Making HTTP Requests with Server-Side ActionScript

Problem

You want to make HTTP requests using Server-Side ActionScript (SSAS).

Solution

Use the *CF.http()* method.

Discussion

The Server-Side ActionScript *CF.http()* method enables you to make HTTP requests to any resource available on the Web. This is a convenient way to run server-side scripts on remote domains and return those values to Flash.

The *CF.http()* method accepts the following parameters:

url

> The URL to the requested resource (e.g., "http://www.remotedomain.com/logical-Path/page.cfm") or the protocol and server address/domain name (e.g., "http://www.remotedomain.com/"). You may also need to specify values for the *path* and *file* parameters when you use the second format.

method

> Either "post" or "get", corresponding to the HTTP method (POST or GET) used to send any parameters.

path

> If you do not include the logical path and filename in the *url* parameter, then you should indicate the logical path with the *path* parameter. For example, if the resource is "http://www.remotedomain.com/logicalPath/page.cfm", and you use the value "http://www.remotedomain.com" for the *url* parameter, then you should set *path* to "/logicalPath".

file

> The filename of the requested resource when you do not include it in the *url* parameter. For example, if the resource is "http://www.remotedomain.com/logicalPath/page.cfm", and you use the value "http://www.remotedomain.com/" for the *url* parameter, then you should set *file* to "path.cfm".

username

> The username, if required.

password

> The password, if required.

resolveurl

> A value of either "yes" or "no". If "yes", then relative links and references within the remote document are converted to absolute references. The values of the *url* and *path* parameters are used for this purpose. For example, if the *url* parameter is "http://www.remotedomain.com", and the *path* parameter is "/logicalPath", then an HTML tag in the remote document such as `<a href="pages/myPage.cfm">` is converted to `<a href="http://www.remotedomain.com/logicalPath/pages/myPage.cfm">` in the returned value.

params

> The *params* parameter contains the values (if any) that are sent to the resource, and it should be in the form of an indexed array of objects with the following properties:

name

> The variable name.

value

> The variable value.

type

> The scope for the variable. The possible values for *type* are "URL", "Form-Field", "Cookie", and "CGI".

You can pass the arguments to *CF.http()* as either positional or named parameters. If you use positional parameters, the following is a list of possible parameter orders:

```
CF.http(url);
CF.http(method, url);
CF.http(method, url, username, password);
CF.http(method, url, params, username, password);
```

Notice that *path*, *file*, and *resolveurl* are not available when using positional parameters. If you want to use these parameters, you must use named parameters.

The *CF.http()* method returns an associative array with the following properties:

Header

> The raw response header.

Charset

> The character the requested resource uses.

Mimetype

> The mime type of the requested resource.

Statuscode

> The status code, such as "200 OK" or "500 Internal Server Error".

Responseheader

> The response header as an associative array. Each response header key (such as Date, Server, etc.) is an element of the associative array.

Text

> A Boolean value. The value is true if the requested resource contains text, and false otherwise.

FileContent

> The contents of the requested resource.

Most of the time, you should return the result of a *CF.http()* to the Flash movie, and you can process the result as a normal ActionScript associative array within the client movie. However, if you want to process the result using SSAS, be aware that on the server, the object is actually an *ASObject*. Therefore, you must use the *ASObject* methods (*ASObject* subclasses *java.util.HashMap*) to process the result of a *CF.http()* method invocation within SSAS:

```
// Get the contents of http://www.person13.com and assign the result to httpResult.
var httpResult = CF.http("http://www.person13.com");

// Extract the value of the FileContent element using the get( ) method.
var fContent = httpResult.get("FileContent");
```

See Also

Recipe 20.21

20.24 Consuming Web Services with Flash Remoting for .NET or ColdFusion

Problem

You want to consume a web service using Flash Remoting for .NET or ColdFusion.

Solution

Use a Flash Remoting service object that maps to the *.wsdl* file for the web service and invoke the web service method from the service object.

Discussion

One of the great features of Flash Remoting for .NET and ColdFusion is that you can use it to invoke web service methods directly from the Flash movie. You don't have to create any server-side scripts to consume the web service and return the results to Flash.

The process for calling a web service method from a Flash movie is the same as calling any service function using Flash Remoting. You need to create a connection object, a service object, and a response object. Then, you only need to invoke the service function from the service object and tell it to return the results to the response object. The only change when working with web services (versus service functions) is that you should map the service object to the web service's WSDL (Web Services Description Language) document. You should still use your local application server as the Flash Remoting gateway, regardless of the domain of the web service. Your local application server actually proxies the request for you. For example:

```
// Create a connection object that uses your local application server
// as the Flash Remoting gateway.
gwURL = "http://localhost:8500/flashservices/gateway";
```

```
NetServices.setDefaultGatewayUrl(gwURL);
myConnection = NetServices.createGatewayConnection();

// Create a service object that maps to the WSDL document for the web service. In
// this example it exists at http://www.somedomain.com/wsdls/myWebService.wsdl.
wsSrv = myConnection.getService(
    "http://www.somedomain.com/wsdls/myWebService.wsdl");

// Create a response object.
myResponse = new Object();
myResponse.onResult = function (result) {
  // Do something with the result here.
};

// Invoke a web service method named myWebMethod( ).
wsSrv.myWebMethod(myResponse);
```

See Also

See Recipes 20.2 and 20.3 for important configuration information to allow Flash Remoting access to web services with ColdFusion MX Updater 3 and ASP.NET. For more information, see *http://www.flash-remoting.com/notablog/home.cfm?newsid=21*.

## CHAPTER 21

Recordsets

21.0 Introduction

Databases are an integral part of many applications, and Flash Remoting helps to integrate databases into your Flash applications easily. Data in a database is stored in tables as records. You can think of a database table as a grid and a record as being a single row in that table containing data for each column. When data is retrieved from a database it is stored as a recordset. ColdFusion recordsets are called *Query* objects, Java recordsets are called *ResultSet* objects, and .NET recordsets are called *DataTable* objects. But regardless of what the datatype is called in the server-side application, when it is returned to your Flash movie by way of Flash Remoting it is automatically converted into a *RecordSet* object. See Recipe 20.22 for more information on retrieving a recordset.

The *RecordSet* class is part of the Flash Remoting Components installation. To include the class in your Flash movies, you should include the *NetServices.as* file:

```
#include "NetServices.as"
```

If you are using client-side recordsets only, it is sufficient to include *RecordSet.as* instead of *NetServices.as*.

21.1 Creating Recordsets

Problem

You want to create and populate a recordset.

Solution

Return a recordset from Flash Remoting, or create a recordset using the constructor and populate it using the *RecordSet.addItem()* or *RecordSet.addItemAt()* methods.

Discussion

Most often, recordsets are returned to Flash movies from Flash Remoting. Recordsets cannot be meaningfully passed back to an application server portion of a Flash Remoting application. Therefore, it is rarely necessary to create recordsets with ActionScript. However, recordsets can be a convenient way of storing data, and with the *DataGlue* class, the data within a recordset can be used to populate many UI components.

The constructor function for recordsets requires an array of column names as a parameter, as follows:

```
// Make sure to include NetServices.as whenever you work with recordsets, although
// for this simple example, including RecordSet.as would suffice.
#include "NetServices.as"

// Create a new recordset with three columns: COL0, COL1, and COL2.
rs = new RecordSet(["COL0", "COL1", "COL2"]);
```

Once you have created a recordset using the constructor, you can add records to it using the *addItem()* and *addItemAt()* methods. Both methods require a *record object* parameter. A record object is merely an object (an instance of the *Object* class) in which the property names match the column names of the recordset. The *addItemAt()* method differs from the *addItem()* method in that *addItemAt()* inserts a new record at a specific index within the recordset, while *addItem()* appends a record to the end of the recordset. Note that recordset indexes are zero-relative.

```
// Appends a record to the recordset.
rs.addItem({COL0: "val0", COL1: "val1", COL2: "val2"});

// Adds a record to the recordset at index 5.
rs.addItemAt(5, {COL0: "val0", COL1: "val1", COL2: "val2"});
```

Additionally, you can use the *RecordSet.setField()* method to alter a single column of an existing record within a recordset. The method takes three parameters: the index of the record, the column name, and the new value to assign.

```
#include "NetServices.as"

// Create a new recordset and fill it with three records.
rs = new RecordSet(["SHAPE", "COLOR"]);
rs.addItem({SHAPE: "square", COLOR: 0x00FF00});
rs.addItem({SHAPE: "circle", COLOR: 0xFF00FF});
rs.addItem({SHAPE: "triangle", COLOR: 0x0000FF});

// Change the COLOR column to 0x000000 in the record with index 2 (the third record).
rs.setField(2, "COLOR", 0x000000);
```

21.2   Reading Recordsets

Problem

You want to read the data from a recordset.

Solution

Use the *RecordSet.getItemAt()* method to get a record at a particular index. Use *RecordSet.getColumnNames()* to get an array of the column names.

Discussion

You can think of recordsets as being composed of rows and columns, like a grid. Each row represents a single record, and each column represents a field within each record. All recordsets have a *getItemAt()* method that returns a record object at a given row index.

```
#include "NetServices.as"

// Create a recordset and populate it using addItem( ) (see Recipe 21.1).
rs = new RecordSet(["COL0", "COL1", "COL2"]);
rs.addItem({COL0: "a", COL1: "b", COL2: "c"});
rs.addItem({COL0: "d", COL1: "e", COL2: "f"});
rs.addItem({COL0: "g", COL1: "h", COL2: "i"});

// Get a single record from the recordset using getItemAt( ).
record1 = rs.getItemAt(1);

// Output the values from the record object. Displays: d e f
trace(record1.COL0 + " " + record1.COL1 + " " + record1.COL2);
```

The *getItemAt()* method is all you need, as long as you know the column names. However, if you do not already know the column names (remember, recordsets are often retrieved from the server), use the *getColumnNames()* method to get an array of the recordset's column names. You can then use that array to loop through all the columns of a given recordset.

```
// Get a record from the recordset.
record1 = rs.getItemAt(1);

// Retrieve the column names.
columnNames = rs.getColumnNames( );

/* Loop through all the columns and output the values for the record. Outputs:
   COL0: d
   COL1: e
   COL2: f
*/
```

```
  for (var i = 0; i < columnNames.length; i++) {
    trace(columnNames[i] + ": " + record1[columnNames[i]]);
  }
```

You can also use the *RecordSet.getLength()* method to determine the number of
records that a recordset contains. Using this value, you can loop through all the
records.

```
// Get the column names.
columnNames = rs.getColumnNames();

// Loop through each record in the recordset from 0 to the length, as returned by
// getLength().
for (var i = 0; i < rs.getLength(); i++) {

  // Display the record number.
  trace("record " + i);

  /* Loop through each column for each record and output the values. Displays:
      record 0
        COL0: a
        COL1: b
        COL2: c
      record 1
        COL0: d
        COL1: e
        COL2: f
      record 2
        COL0: g
        COL1: h
        COL2: i
  */
  for (var j = 0; j < columnNames.length; j++) {
    trace("   " + columnNames[j] + ": " + rs.getItemAt(i)[columnNames[j]]);
  }
}
```

You can create a custom method that allows you to write the recordset data to the
Output window during testing. The *RecordSet.trace()* method, as shown in the following code block, uses the same logic as the preceding code:

```
RecordSet.prototype.trace = function () {
  var columnNames = this.getColumnNames();
  for (var i = 0; i < this.getLength(); i++) {
    trace("record " + i);
    for (var j = 0; j < columnNames.length; j++) {
      trace("   " + columnNames[j] + ": " + this.getItemAt(i)[columnNames[j]]);
    }
  }
};
// Example usage (if rs contains a recordset):
rs.trace();
```

21.3   Filtering Recordsets

Problem

You want to create a new recordset that contains a subset of the original.

Solution

Use the *RecordSet.filter()* method.

Discussion

You can manually create a new *RecordSet* object by reading the records from a recordset and writing selected ones to a new recordset. However, this is unnecessarily laborious. Instead, you should use the *filter()* method, which handles almost all of the processing for you. Simply provide a filter function that contains the logic to decide which records to use. The *filter()* method expects a reference to a filter function as a parameter, and it accepts a second parameter that is automatically passed to the filter function. The second parameter lets you filter records based on different criteria. The *filter()* method returns a new *RecordSet* object.

```
filteredRs = rs.filter(filterFunction, context);
```

The filter function is called once for each record. Each time it is called, it is passed the next record object, and if a context parameter was specified in the *filter()* method call, that value is also passed along to the filter function. Within the filter function you should place the logic to determine whether the record should be included in the filtered recordset. The optional context parameter, if used, lets the filter function filter based on different criteria. If the filter function returns true, then the record is included in the filtered recordset; if it returns false, the record is not included.

```
function filterFunction (record, context) {
  // Determine whether to include the record and return true or false.
}
```

Here is an example in which a recordset is filtered twice to create two new recordsets, filteredRs0 and filteredRs1, based on different criteria:

```
#include "NetServices.as"

// Create and populate a new recordset.
rs = new RecordSet(["ID", "NAME"]);
rs.addItem({ID: 24, NAME: "a"});
rs.addItem({ID: 42, NAME: "b"});
rs.addItem({ID: 66, NAME: "c"});
rs.addItem({ID: 93, NAME: "d"});
rs.addItem({ID: 33, NAME: "e"});

// Define the filter function.
function filterer (record, context) {
```

```
    // If the record's ID value is greater than the context value, return true to
    // include the record. Otherwise, return false and exclude the record.
    if (record.ID > context) {
      return true;
    }
    return false;
}


// Use the filter() method to create two new recordsets. The first one is populated
// with all records in which the ID is greater than 51. The second is populated with
// all records in which the ID is greater than 36.
filteredRs0 = rs.filter(filterer, 51);
filteredRs1 = rs.filter(filterer, 36);

/* Output the values in filteredRs0. Displays:
   record 0
     ID: 66
     NAME: c
   record 1
     ID: 93
     NAME: d
*/
filteredRs0.trace();


/* Output the values in filteredRs1. Displays:
   record 0
     ID: 42
     NAME: b
   record 1
     ID: 66
     NAME: c
   record 2
     ID: 93
     NAME: d
*/
filteredRs1.trace();
```

It is not necessary to use the context parameter with the *filter()* method. You can also define a very specific filter function without it:

```
// Use a filter function that does not require a context parameter. Filter for
// records with ID values between 39 and 72.
function filterer (record) {
  if (record.ID > 39 && record.ID < 72) {
    return true;
  }
  return false;
}

filteredRs = rs.filter(filterer);

/* Output the values from filteredRs:
   record 0
```

```
        ID: 42
        NAME: b
    record 1
        ID: 66
        NAME: c
*/
filteredRs.trace();
```

 Filtered recordsets contain references to the records of the original
recordset. This is important to keep in mind because it means that if
you make changes to a record in a filtered recordset, the same change is
reflected in the original as well as in any filtered versions of the original.

See Also

See Recipe 6.8 for a discussion of complex datatypes and copying them by reference.
To create an independent copy of one or more records in a recordset, copy data manually into a new recordset using the methods of the *RecordSet* class, as described in
Recipes 21.1 and 21.2.

21.4   Sorting Recordsets by a Single Column

Problem

You want to sort the records in a recordset, ordering them by the values in a single
column.

Solution

Use the *RecordSet.sortItemsBy()* method.

Discussion

If you want to do a simple sort (sorting according to one column) on a recordset, use
the *sortItemsBy()* method. This method takes the name of the column on which to
sort as a parameter, and it sorts the records within the original recordset (no copy is
made). Passing the value "DESC" to the method as a second parameter sorts the
records in descending order. Otherwise, the sort order is ascending.

```
#include "NetServices.as"

rs = new RecordSet(["ID", "NAME"]);
rs.addItem({ID: 24, NAME: "a"});
rs.addItem({ID: 42, NAME: "b"});
rs.addItem({ID: 66, NAME: "c"});
rs.addItem({ID: 93, NAME: "d"});
rs.addItem({ID: 33, NAME: "e"});
```

```
// Sort the recordset by ID values in ascending order.
rs.sortItemsBy("ID");

/* Outputs:
   record 0
     ID: 24
     NAME: a
    record 1
     ID: 33
     NAME: e
   record 2
     ID: 42
     NAME: b
   record 3
     ID: 66
     NAME: c
   record 4
     ID: 93
     NAME: d
*/
rs.trace();

// Sort the recordset by the NAME column in descending order.
rs.sortItemsBy("NAME", "DESC");

/* Outputs:
   record 0
     ID: 33
     NAME: e
   record 1
     ID: 93
     NAME: d
   record 2
     ID: 66
     NAME: c
   record 3
     ID: 42
     NAME: b
   record 4
     ID: 24
     NAME: a
*/
rs.trace();
```

21.5 Populating Menu Components

Problem

You want to use a recordset to populate a menu component instance.

Solution

Use the *setDataProvider()* method for the menu component of interest. For more complex scenarios, use the *DataGlue* class.

Discussion

List boxes and combo boxes can both be populated by recordsets without much effort by employing one of two techniques. The first technique is to use the *setDataProvider()* method of the list box or combo box. You can pass a recordset reference to the *setDataProvider()* method, and it will know how to process it. The result is that the menu displays one item per record, with each item showing the record's column values in a comma-delimited list. The order in which the column values appear within each item is determined by the order of the columns within the recordset column names array.

```
#include "NetServices.as"

rs = new RecordSet(["ID", "NAME"]);
rs.addItem({ID: 24, NAME: "a"});
rs.addItem({ID: 42, NAME: "b"});
rs.addItem({ID: 66, NAME: "c"});
rs.addItem({ID: 93, NAME: "d"});
rs.addItem({ID: 33, NAME: "e"});

// Populate a list box and a combo box with the values from the recordset.
myListBox.setDataProvider(rs);
myComboBox.setDataProvider(rs);
```

Additionally, when you use a recordset as a data provider for a menu, the object(s) returned by the *getItemAt()*, *getSelectedItem()*, and *getSelectedItems()* methods are record objects instead of the conventional objects with data and label properties. This also means that the *getValue()* method of a menu populated by a recordset returns undefined. Another interesting effect of populating a menu with a recordset as a data provider is that changes made to the recordset cause the menu to be automatically updated.

```
#include "NetServices.as"

rs = new RecordSet(["ID", "NAME"]);
rs.addItem({ID: 24, NAME: "a"});

// Populate the list box with the recordset.
myListBox.setDataProvider(rs);

// Add an item to the recordset after having already set the data provider for the
// list box. The list box is automatically updated!
rs.addItem({ID: 99, NAME: "z"});
```

While using a recordset with the *setDataProvider()* method offers certain advantages, such as ease of use and automatic updating of menus, it also has its disadvantages. The main disadvantage of the technique is that you can't control the display of the data within the menu to any great degree. The other problem is that it doesn't conform to the standard way in which menus work—namely, using objects with data and label properties. The *DataGlue* class offers functionality that solves both of these problems.

The *DataGlue* class has two static methods for populating UI components with recordset data. Let's look at the first of these, the *bindFormatStrings()* method. This method requires four parameters:

dataConsumer
> A reference to the UI component, such as a combo box or a list box.

dataProvider
> A reference to the recordset.

labelString
> A string that is used for the menu labels. Any values in the string between pound signs (#) are dynamically evaluated as column names from the recordset.

dataString
> A string that is used for the menu items' data properties. Any values in the string between pound signs (#) are dynamically evaluated as column names from the recordset.

The *bindFormatStrings()* method populates the UI component with the values from the recordset and allows you to control the label and data values. By placing column names within pound signs (#) in the label and data string parameters, those values are evaluated when the menu is populated. For example, #COL0# is evaluated for the value of column COL0 for each record.

```
#include "NetServices.as"

// You must include the DataGlue.as file whenever you use DataGlue methods.
#include "DataGlue.as"

rs = new RecordSet(["ID", "NAME"]);
rs.addItem({ID: 24, NAME: "a"});
rs.addItem({ID: 42, NAME: "b"});
rs.addItem({ID: 66, NAME: "c"});
rs.addItem({ID: 93, NAME: "d"});
rs.addItem({ID: 33, NAME: "e"});

// Populate a combo box with the records from rs. The labels of each item are in the
// format NAME (ID). For example, a (24). The data properties for each item are the
// string equivalents of the ID values.
DataGlue.bindFormatStrings(myComboBox, rs, "#NAME# (#ID#)", "#ID#");

// Components populated using DataGlue methods are automatically updated as well!
rs.addItem({ID: 99, NAME: "f"});
```

The *bindFormatStrings()* method has a few shortcomings. One limitation is that it populates components only with strings, although you may want to populate menus in which the data property is a number, Boolean, or object. Another limitation is that it doesn't let you manipulate the column values. For example, if a recordset has a column PERSON_NAME with values that are in the format FirstName LastName, you might want to display that in the menu as LastName, FirstName. With *bindFormatStrings()*, this is not possible. However, the *bindFormatFunction()* method takes care of both of these problems.

The *bindFormatFunction()* method functions similarly to the *bindFormatStrings()* method. It takes the same first two parameters—the data consumer and data provider—but the third parameter for *bindFormatFunction()* is a reference to a format function. The format function is automatically passed a record, and it should return an object with data and label properties.

```
#include "DataGlue.as"

// Define the format function. The function should expect a record object.
function formatter (record) {

    // Create the object to which the label and data properties are added.
    var obj = new Object( );

    // Define the label property. This example displays the NAME column of each record
    // in uppercase, demonstrating the flexibility of the format function technique.
    obj.label = record.NAME.toUpperCase( ) + " (" + record.ID + ")";

    // Define the data property. This example assigns the value of the record itself to
    // the data property. This is useful in many cases.
    obj.data = record;

    // Return the object with label and data properties defined.
    return obj;
}

// Populate a combo box with the values from a recordset (rs).
DataGlue.bindFormatFunction(myComboBox, rs, formatter);
```

21.6   Using Recordsets with DataGrids

Problem

You want to display recordset data in a grid.

Solution

Use the DataGrid component.

Discussion

The DataGrid component is available for purchase from Macromedia as part of the DevNet Resource Kit (DRK) Volume 1, available from *http://www.macromedia.com/ software/drk/productinfo/product_overview/volume1*. It is invaluable for displaying complex data sets such as recordsets. Normal menus, such as list boxes, work great for showing one-dimensional lists of values, but when it comes to displaying two-dimensional (row and column) data, they are not up to par. The DataGrid component allows you to display data as rows and columns, and with the *DataGrid.setDataProvider()* method or the *DataGlue* class, you can populate a data grid with recordset data in short order.

The *setDataProvider()* method populates the data grid with data from a recordset. If the data grid has no defined columns, columns that match the columns of the recordset in name and order are automatically created.

```
#include "NetServices.as"

// Create a new recordset with columns ID, FIRST, LAST.
rs = new RecordSet(["ID", "FIRST", "LAST"]);
rs.addItem({ID: 24, FIRST: "Bob", LAST: "Bobson"});
rs.addItem({ID: 42, FIRST: "Sarah", LAST: "Littlefoot"});
rs.addItem({ID: 66, FIRST: "George", LAST: "Georgeman"});

// Set the data grid to alternate row colors between white and light blue.
myDataGrid.alternateRowColors(0xFFFFFF, 0xC1E0FD);

// Populate the data grid with the recordset data. It creates
// three columns: ID, FIRST, and LAST, in that order, which is the
// same order as the columns from the recordset.
myDataGrid.setDataProvider(rs);
```

If you want to change the order of the columns as they are displayed in the data grid, add columns to the data grid before calling the *setDataProvider()* method. The easiest way to add columns to the data grid is with the *setColumns()* method. You should call this method and pass it the names of the columns to add in the order you want them to be displayed. When you use this technique with *setDataProvider()*, you must make sure the columns you add to the data grid match the column names of the recordset.

```
myDataGrid.setColumns("ID", "LAST", "FIRST");
myDataGrid.setDataProvider(rs);
```

The *setDataProvider()* method works in many cases—especially when you want to display the raw data from a recordset without modification, except, perhaps, the column order. If you want to have more control over how the recordset data is displayed, use the *DataGlue* class.

The *DataGlue* class has two static methods, as described in Recipe 21.5. The *bindFormatStrings()* method is not of much use with data grids, but you can use the

---

bindFormatFunction() method with a format function to preprocess the recordset data and populate the data grid with custom objects. The format function should create and return objects with properties corresponding to the columns you want to display in the data grid. For example:

```
#include "DataGlue.as"

// Define the format function.
function formatter (record) {

    // Define the object that is used to populate a row of the data grid.
    var obj = new Object( );

    // Add a Name property to the object that is in the format of LAST, FIRST.
    obj.Name = record.LAST + ", " + record.FIRST;

    // Add an ID property to the object with the value of the record's ID column.
    obj.ID = record.ID;

    // Return the object.
    return obj;
}

// Populate the data grid with the recordset using the format function. The result is
// a data grid that has columns Name and ID.
DataGlue.bindFormatFunction(myDataGrid, rs, formatter);
```

Remember that you must always include the *DataGlue.as* file when you use the *DataGlue* class.

When you use the format function technique and you have not previously defined the columns within the data grid, the order of the columns is not under your control. However, if you add columns to the data grid before populating it, you can control the order in which they display. The column names you add to the data grid and the properties of the object returned by the format function must match.

```
#include "DataGlue.as"

function formatter (record) {
  var obj = new Object( );
  obj.Name = record.LAST + ", " + record.FIRST;
  obj.ID = record.ID;
  return obj;
}

// Set the column names and order within the data grid before
// populating it. The column names match those of the properties
// of the object returned by the format function.
myDataGrid.setColumns("Name", "ID");
DataGlue.bindFormatFunction(myDataGrid, rs, formatter);
```

See Also

Macromedia sells additional components as part of the DRKs available at *http://www.macromedia.com/software/drk/*. Third-party vendors also sell components. For example, B-Line Express (*http://www.blinex.com*) sells a package of charting components that provide a flexible and extensible library of charting and graphics functions for displaying data as pie charts, bar charts, and much, much more.

## PART III

Applications

## CHAPTER 22

Building a Flash Paint Application

Flash MX offers many possibilities for dynamically generating vector graphics and text using ActionScript. In this chapter, you will create a Flash Paint application. This application builds on many of the recipes from earlier chapters. Specifically, this application utilizes the following skills:

- Drawing and filling shapes with the Drawing API
- Developing and using custom components
- Extending classes
- Swapping depths of movie clips and text fields
- Using mouse and key listeners
- Changing colors of movie clips
- Getting and setting the current focus and selection

The Flash Paint application is designed to allow for the following functionality:

- Drawing lines, rectangles, and ellipses
- Adding text fields
- Rearranging existing shapes and text
- Moving existing shapes and text forward or backward to adjust the overlap with other objects
- Selecting a color to apply to new text and with which to draw shapes
- Filling existing shapes with solid color and applying color to existing text
- Deleting existing shapes and text

Planning the Application

You should begin designing the Flash Paint application by determining the necessary elements and mapping out how they should work together. The list of desired functionality in the previous section gives you a good idea of which elements you will need to develop. Essentially, there are four basic elements:

Toolbar buttons
> These are the buttons that allow the user to select which type of action to take, be it selecting items, drawing shapes, colorizing shapes, etc.

Color selector
> The color selector is the means by which a user can select the current color to use for drawing shapes, adding text, or filling or colorizing shapes or text.

Shapes
> Shapes can be drawn by the user. A shape can be a line, a rectangle, or an ellipse.

Text
> Text items, like shapes, are units that are added and modified by the user.

All of these elements can be contained within a single Flash document. At this point you should open a new Flash document and save it as *flashPaint.fla*. This is the document to which you should add all of the code and other modifications that are contained within the following sections. The final version is available at *http://www.person13.com/ascb*.

Building the Components

The four elements described in the previous section are all good candidates for components. In each case, the elements are discrete constituents that can be abstracted. For example, the toolbar is composed of multiple buttons that are responsible for different tasks. However, each of the buttons shares basic, core functionality. Likewise, each of the shape units that are drawn by the user may look different—different outline shapes, sizes, and fill colors—but the basic functionality of all shapes is the same. And it is the same with the text units as well. While there is only one color selector instance in the application, it is nonetheless a good candidate for a component because it is a distinct unit that can likely be reused in another application.

Creating the Superclass for the Components

The toolbar buttons, shape units, and text units all share some common functionality. Each of these three types of components needs to have the capability to define callback methods, including callback methods for when the component is selected, deselected, pressed, and released. While it is certainly possible to define the same methods individually in each of the component classes, you can also define a single superclass from which the component classes can inherit. This is advantageous because you can define the methods in one location.

Complete the following steps to define the custom *PaintBase* class from which three of the components inherit their methods:

1. In your *flashPaint.fla* document, create a new movie clip symbol named *PaintBaseClass*.

2. On the first frame of the default layer of the *PaintBaseClass* symbol, add the following code:

```
// Enclose the code using #initclip so that it executes before the rest of the
// code in the movie.
#initclip 0

function PaintBase () {}

// PaintBase needs to inherit from MovieClip because the classes that extend
// PaintBase are all component classes.
PaintBase.prototype = new MovieClip();

// The following four methods define callback functions for instances of the
// class. Each method requires at least one parameter: the name of the callback
// function as a string. Also, each accepts a second, optional parameter
// indicating the path to the function. If no path is supplied, the timeline on
// which the component instance exists is used.
PaintBase.prototype.setOnPress = function (functionName, path) {
  if (path == undefined) {
    path = this._parent;
  }
  this.onPressCB = functionName;
  this.onPressPath = path;
};

PaintBase.prototype.setOnRelease = function (functionName, path) {
  if (path == undefined) {
    path = this._parent;
  }
  this.onReleaseCB = functionName;
  this.onReleasePath = path;
};

PaintBase.prototype.setOnSelect = function (functionName, path) {
  if (path == undefined) {
    path = this._parent;
  }
  this.onSelectCB = functionName;
  this.onSelectPath = path;
};

PaintBase.prototype.setOnDeselect = function (functionName, path) {
  if (path == undefined) {
    path = this._parent;
  }
```

```
    this.onDeselectCB = functionName;
    this.onDeselectPath = path;
  };

  // Several of the components should automatically call the onPress() callback
  // function when a press event occurs.
  PaintBase.prototype.onPress = function () {
    this.onPressPath[this.onPressCB](this);
  };

  // Likewise, several of the components should automatically call the onRelease()
  // and onSelect() callback methods when the release event occurs. Additionally,
  // a selected property is set to true so that the component can keep track of its
  // current state.
  PaintBase.prototype.onRelease = function () {
    this.onReleasePath[this.onReleaseCB](this);
    this.selected = true;
    this.onSelectPath[this.onSelectCB](this);
  };

  // Several of the components include a deselect() method that calls the
  // onDeselect() callback function.
  PaintBase.prototype.deselect = function () {
    this.onDeselectPath[this.onDeselectCB](this);
  };

  #endinitclip
```

Congratulations! You have just created a superclass that defines some common functionality for any class that extends it. Now, perhaps a little explanation is due.

A class such as *PaintBase* is sometimes referred to as an *abstract class* because it contains abstract functionality that can be used by any class that extends it. By itself, *PaintBase* doesn't do very much. But it does save you from having to define the same methods in multiple classes later on. Instead, each of the component classes inherits from *PaintBase* in the following way:

```
    ComponentClassName.prototype = new PaintBase();
```

When you create a class that inherits from *PaintBase*, all the methods of *PaintBase* are available from instances of that class. For example, if myObj is an instance of *MyComponentClass*, and *MyComponentClass* inherits from *PaintBase*, then you can call any of the *PaintBase* methods from myObj:

```
    // Define an onRelease() callback function for myObj. Now,
    // whenever myObj is clicked and released the function
    // myOnReleaseCallback() defined on _root is invoked automatically.
    myObj.setOnRelease("myOnReleaseCallback", _root);
```

Now, let's look a little more closely at each of the methods of the *PaintBase* class.

The first line of code is an #initclip directive. In this case, you should follow the directive with the value 0, which instructs the Flash movie to execute all the code contained between the #initclip and #endinitclip directives before anything else, even before other code within #initclip directives. Flash processes all #initclip code before any code on the frame in which the component first exists. If the component is an exported symbol, the #initclip code is processed before the first frame of the main timeline. However, in this case you need to ensure that *PaintBase* is defined before any of the component classes are defined. You can specify the precedence for processing the #initclip code using the optional order parameter. Code with lower order parameters is processed first, and code with order parameters is processed before code without order parameters. Therefore, we use:

```
#initclip 0
```

The *PaintBase* class is an abstract class for component classes. All components must extend *MovieClip* directly or indirectly. Therefore, *PaintBase* must extend *MovieClip* (which is not to say that all abstract classes must extend *MovieClip*):

```
PaintBase.prototype = new MovieClip( );
```

The *setOnPress()*, *setOnRelease()*, *setOnSelect()*, and *setOnDeselect()* methods all work in the same manner. The concept is to closely mimic the functionality of the callback-setting methods of many of the predefined ActionScript classes and the UI components. Each of these four methods, therefore, accepts a string specifying the name of the callback function. Additionally, you can specify a path to the function. If no path is specified (that is, if the path parameter is undefined), the value of the timeline on which the component instance resides (given by this._parent) is used. In each case, the function name and path to the function are stored in unique properties, such as onPressCB and onPressPath:

```
PaintBase.prototype.setOnPress = function (functionName, path) {
  if (path == undefined) {
    path = this._parent;
  }
  this.onPressCB = functionName;
  this.onPressPath = path;
};
```

There is a very good reason to use callback functions instead of allowing each component to define *onPress()* and *onRelease()* methods directly. If *onPress()* or *onRelease()* methods were to be defined for the component instances, the prototype methods would be wiped out. Working with callback functions allows you to define actions to occur on these events for the instances while not overwriting the functionality defined for the prototype. The *PaintBase* class's *onPress()* and *onRelease()* methods demonstrate how the callback function is invoked without wiping out any functionality that is already defined within the prototype. ActionScript treats functions as properties (*Function* datatypes) of the timeline in which they are defined. You can use this fact to invoke the callback functions using array-access notation. In each case, the callback function is passed a reference to the component doing the callback. This is both convenient and in keeping with the conventions of callback functions as they are used throughout ActionScript.

```
PaintBase.prototype.onPress = function () {
  this.onPressPath[this.onPressCB](this);
};

PaintBase.prototype.onRelease = function () {
  this.onReleasePath[this.onReleaseCB](this);
  this.selected = true;
  this.onSelectPath[this.onSelectCB](this);
};
```

Creating the Toolbar Button Component

The toolbar comprises eight tools/buttons:

Select
> Allows existing shape and text items to be selected and moved.

Line
> Allows the user to draw a line.

Rectangle
> Allows the user to draw a rectangular outline.

Ellipse
> Allows the user to draw an elliptical outline.

Text
> Lets the user add text.

Fill
> Adds a fill to any shape that is clicked or applies a new color to any text that is clicked. The current color from the color selector is used in both cases.

Back
> Moves the selected shape or text back by one depth.

Forward
> Moves the selected shape or text forward by one depth.

Each of the toolbar buttons shares common functionality with every other toolbar button, namely:

- The buttons are drawn using the Drawing API. Each toolbar button is composed of the same basic button that is labeled with a symbol or text (a line on the line tool, "abc" on the text tool, etc.).
- Each button has a selected and deselected state. When the button is selected, it appears to be pressed in. When the button is deselected, it appears to be raised.

Additionally, there are two kinds of toolbar buttons. The first six buttons are called "stick" buttons because when they are pressed, they remain selected until otherwise deselected. The remaining two buttons (the back and forward buttons) are called "spring" buttons because they spring back after they have been clicked and released.

Perform the following steps to construct the ToolbarButton component:

1. Create a new movie clip symbol named *ToolbarButton*.
2. Edit the linkage properties of the symbol.
3. Select the Export for ActionScript and Export in First Frame checkboxes.
4. Set the linkage identifier to *ToolbarButtonSymbol*.
5. Click OK.
6. Edit the new symbol.
7. Rename the default layer as *superclass* and add a new layer named *toolbarButtonClass*.
8. On the *superclass* layer, drag an instance of the *PaintBaseClass* symbol. This ensures that the superclass is defined so that *ToolbarButtonClass* can extend it.
9. On the *toolbarButtonClass* layer, add the following code to the first frame:

```
#initclip

// Initialize the component instance to its unselected state.
function ToolbarButtonClass( ) {
  this.selected = false;
}

// This class extends PaintBase. Because PaintBase extends MovieClip,
// ToolbarButtonClass is still a valid component class.
ToolbarButtonClass.prototype = new PaintBase( );

// The create( ) method draws the button. The method requires a name that
// indicates what kind of symbol to draw (line, rectangle, etc.). It also
// requires a type parameter specifying if the button is a "stick" or "spring"
// button type.
ToolbarButtonClass.prototype.create = function (name, type) {

  // Set the type as a property. This is used later to determine how the button
  // responds to presses and releases.
  this.type = type;

  // Create a movie clip in which the button is drawn. Within this movie clip are
  // three nested movie clips: one for the highlight, one for the button's
  // center, and one for the shadow.
  this.createEmptyMovieClip("btn", this.getNewDepth( ));
  this.btn.createEmptyMovieClip("btnHighlight", this.btn.getNewDepth( ));
  this.btn.createEmptyMovieClip("btnShadow", this.btn.getNewDepth( ));
  this.btn.createEmptyMovieClip("btnCenter", this.btn.getNewDepth( ));

  // The width and height value of 42 and 21 are hardcoded for this application.
  // You could also choose to make this more abstract.
  var w = 42;
  var h = 21;
```

```
// Draw the button highlight, center, and shadow.
with (this.btn.btnHighlight) {
  lineStyle(0, 0x000000, 0);
  beginFill(0xECECEC, 100);
  drawRectangle(w + 2, h + 2);
  endFill();
}
with (this.btn.btnShadow) {
  lineStyle(0, 0x000000, 0);
  beginFill(0, 100);
  drawRectangle(w + 2, h + 2);
  endFill();
  _x += 1;
  _y += 1;
}
with (this.btn.btnCenter) {
  lineStyle(0, 0x000000, 0);
  beginFill(0xDFDFDF, 100);
  drawRectangle(w, h);
  endFill();
}

// Create the movie clip into which the button's symbol or label is added.
this.createEmptyMovieClip("symbol", this.getNewDepth());

// Add the appropriate symbol based on the name value. If "select", draw an
// arrow. If "line", draw a line. If "rectangle", draw a rectangle. If
// "ellipse", draw an ellipse. If "text", label the button "abc". If "fill",
// "back", or "forward", label the button with "fill", "back", or "forward".
switch (name) {
  case "select":
    with (this.symbol) {
      lineStyle(0, 0x000000, 100);
      beginFill(0, 100);
      drawRectangle(w/4, h/9);
      drawTriangle(2 * h/3, 2 * h/3, 60, 30, -w/4);
      endFill();
      _rotation += 30;
      _x += w/8;
      _y += h/8;
    }
    break;
  case "line":
    with (this.symbol) {
      lineStyle(1, 0x000000, 100);
      moveTo(-(w/2) + 6, -(h/2) + 6);
      lineTo((w/2) - 6, (h/2) - 6);
    }
    break;
  case "rectangle":
    with (this.symbol) {
      lineStyle(0, 0x000000, 100);
      drawRectangle(w - 12, h - 6);
    }
```

```
      break;
    case "ellipse":
      with (this.symbol) {
        lineStyle(0, 0x000000, 100);
        drawEllipse((w - 12)/2, (h - 6)/2);
      }
      break;
    case "text":
      this.symbol.createTextField("label", this.symbol.getNewDepth( ),
            -w/2, -h/2, w, h);
      this.symbol.label.text = "abc";
      var tf = new TextFormat( );
      tf.align = "center";
      this.symbol.label.setTextFormat(tf);
      break;
    case "fill":
      this.symbol.createTextField("label", this.symbol.getNewDepth( ),
            -w/2, -h/2, w, h);
      this.symbol.label.text = "fill";
      var tf = new TextFormat( );
      tf.align = "center";
      this.symbol.label.setTextFormat(tf);
      break;
    case "back":
      this.symbol.createTextField("label", this.symbol.getNewDepth( ),
            -w/2, -h/2, w, h);
      this.symbol.label.text = "back";
      var tf = new TextFormat( );
      tf.align = "center";
      this.symbol.label.setTextFormat(tf);
      break;
    case "forward":
      this.symbol.createTextField("label", this.symbol.getNewDepth( ),
            -w/2, -h/2, w, h);
      this.symbol.label.text = "forward";
      var tf = new TextFormat( );
      tf.align = "center";
      this.symbol.label.setTextFormat(tf);
  }

  // The drawing methods draw the buttons with the registration point at the
  // center of the shapes. To move the shapes so that the registration point of
  // the component is at the upper-left corner, adjust everything down and to the
  // right by half.
  var shiftx = this._height / 2;
  var shifty = this._width / 2;
  this.btn._y += shiftx;
  this.btn._x += shifty;
  this.symbol._y += shiftx;
  this.symbol._x += shifty;
};
```

```
// The select() method adjusts the elements of the button to give the effect of
// the button being pushed in.
ToolbarButtonClass.prototype.select = function () {
  this.btn._width += 1;
  this.btn._height += 1;
  this.symbol._width -= 1;
  this.symbol._height -= 1;
  this._x += 1;
  this._y += 1;
  this.btn.btnHighlight._visible = false;
  this.btn.btnShadow._visible = false;
};

// The deselect() method reverses the effects of the select() method.
ToolbarButtonClass.prototype.deselect = function () {
  this.btn._width -= 1;
  this.btn._height -= 1;
  this.symbol._width += 1;
  this.symbol._height += 1;
  this._x -= 1;
  this._y -= 1;
  this.btn.btnHighlight._visible = true;
  this.btn.btnShadow._visible = true;
};

// The toggleDeslect() method deselects the button if it is selected.
ToolbarButtonClass.prototype.toggleDeselect = function () {
  if (this.selected) {
    this.deSelect();
    this.selected = !this.selected;
  }
};

// When the button is pressed, if it is not already selected, call the select()
// method and the onSelect() callback function.
ToolbarButtonClass.prototype.onPress = function () {
  if (!this.selected) {
    this.select();
    this.onSelectPath[this.onSelectCB](this);
  }
};

// When the button is released, call the deselect() method if the
// button is already selected or if it is a "spring" button. Whenever
// a "spring" button is released, it automatically springs back to the
// original position. "Stick" buttons are deselected only if they had
// previously been selected. Additionally, toggle the selected status of
// the button if it is a "stick" button.
ToolbarButtonClass.prototype.onRelease = function () {
  if (this.selected || this.type == "spring") {
    this.deselect();
  }
```

```
      if (this.type == "stick") {
        this.selected = !this.selected;
      }
    };

    // You should register the component class to the name that you gave to the
    // component symbol.
    Object.registerClass("ToolbarButtonSymbol", ToolbarButtonClass);

    #endinitclip
```

The *ToolbarButtonClass* class is not an overly complex class, yet there are still some parts of it that warrant further examination. Let's take a closer look at parts of the class.

The *create()* method is a long method, but it doesn't need to be intimidating. Most of the code in this method is comprised of drawing methods. First, you create a movie clip for the basic button portion of the component. This movie clip contains three nested movie clips for the button's highlight, center, and shadow. Generally, it is a good idea to create different movie clips for any parts that you draw using the drawing API. Additionally, you should group together any related movie clips into a parent clip, as is done here:

```
this.createEmptyMovieClip("btn", this.getNewDepth());
this.btn.createEmptyMovieClip("btnHighlight", this.btn.getNewDepth());
this.btn.createEmptyMovieClip("btnShadow", this.btn.getNewDepth());
this.btn.createEmptyMovieClip("btnCenter", this.btn.getNewDepth());
```

Next, the highlight, shadow, and center of the button are drawn using the *drawRectangle()* method from Recipe 4.4. The center of the button is a gray rectangle. This movie clip has a greater depth than the other two, and so it appears above them. The other two movie clips are also rectangles. Each is drawn slightly larger than the button's center, and the shadow is offset by one pixel in the x and y directions. The size, positioning, and depths of the three movie clips give the illusion of three dimensions to the button.

```
with (this.btn.btnHighlight) {
  lineStyle(0, 0x000000, 0);
  beginFill(0xECECEC, 100);
  drawRectangle(w + 2, h + 2);
  endFill();
}
with (this.btn.btnShadow) {
  lineStyle(0, 0x000000, 0);
  beginFill(0, 100);
  drawRectangle(w + 2, h + 2);
  endFill();
  _x += 1;
  _y += 1;
}
with (this.btn.btnCenter) {
  lineStyle(0, 0x000000, 0);
```

```
    beginFill(0xDFDFDF, 100);
    drawRectangle(w, h);
    endFill();
}
```

You create the symbol movie clip above the basic button clip and add the appropriate symbol or label to it. You use a *switch* statement to determine which symbol or label to add, depending on the value of the name parameter that is passed to the *create()* method. If the value is "select", you should draw an arrow (for the selection tool). You can draw an arrow by placing a rectangle and a triangle end to end. Then, in this example, the entire symbol movie clip is rotated 30 degrees so that the arrow is angled.

```
case "select":
  with (this.symbol) {
    lineStyle(0, 0x000000, 100);
    beginFill(0, 100);
    drawRectangle(w/4, h/9);
    drawTriangle(2 * h/3, 2 * h/3, 60, 30, -w/4);
    endFill();
    _rotation += 30;
    _x += w/8;
    _y += h/8;
  }
  break;
```

You can draw a line, rectangle, or ellipse using the basic drawing techniques covered in Chapter 4.

When the value of name is "text", "fill", "back", or "forward", you should add a text field to the symbol movie clip instead of drawing anything in it. If you create the text field with the width and height of the button, you can format the text so that it is aligned to the center of the button.

```
case "text":
  this.symbol.createTextField("label", this.symbol.getNewDepth(),
          -w/2, -h/2, w, h);
  this.symbol.label.text = "abc";
  var tf = new TextFormat();
  tf.align = "center";
  this.symbol.label.setTextFormat(tf);
  break;
```

Finally, because the custom drawing methods such as *drawRectangle()* and *drawEllipse()* draw shapes with the registration point at the center, you should shift everything in the toolbar button down and to the right by half the height and half the width such that the component's registration point is in the upper-left corner:

```
var shiftx = this._height / 2;
var shifty = this._width / 2;
this.btn._y += shiftx;
this.btn._x += shifty;
this.symbol._y += shiftx;
this.symbol._x += shifty;
```

The *select()* and *deselect()* methods do the reverse of one another. The *select()* method gives the appearance of the button being in a pressed state. You accomplish this by increasing the dimensions of the basic button movie clip while hiding the highlight and shadow. Additionally, the width and height of the symbol are decreased (since we want to give the appearance of it being slightly further away). Then, when *deselect()* is called, these actions are all reversed.

```
ToolbarButtonClass.prototype.select = function () {
  this.btn._width += 1;
  this.btn._height += 1;
  this.symbol._width -= 1;
  this.symbol._height -= 1;
  this._x += 1;
  this._y += 1;
  this.btn.btnHighlight._visible = false;
  this.btn.btnShadow._visible = false;
};

ToolbarButtonClass.prototype.deselect = function () {
  this.btn._width -= 1;
  this.btn._height -= 1;
  this.symbol._width += 1;
  this.symbol._height += 1;
  this._x -= 1;
  this._y -= 1;
  this.btn.btnHighlight._visible = true;
  this.btn.btnShadow._visible = true;
};
```

The *onPress()* method needs to check to make sure the button is not selected. If it is selected, then nothing needs to be done. But if the button is not already selected, the *select()* method needs to be called (to make the button look like it is being pressed), and the *onSelect()* callback method should be called as well:

```
ToolbarButtonClass.prototype.onPress = function () {
  if (!this.selected) {
    this.select();
    this.onSelectPath[this.onSelectCB](this);
  }
};
```

When the button is released, the type of actions depends on the type of button—"stick" or "spring". A spring button should always appear deselected once it is released. Therefore, if the button is a spring button, call the *deselect()* method. On the other hand, if the button is a stick button, there are more decisions that need to be made. If the button had been previously selected, then the *deselect()* method should be called. Also, spring buttons cannot maintain a selected/deselected state—they are selected only when pressed—but stick buttons maintain a selected/deselected state. Therefore, each time a release event occurs on a stick button, the selected state should be toggled:

```
ToolbarButtonClass.prototype.onRelease = function () {
  if (this.selected || this.type == "spring") {
```

```
      this.deselect();
    }
    if (this.type == "stick") {
      this.selected = !this.selected;
    }
  };
```

Creating the Shape Component

The Flash Paint application uses shapes as one of the two kinds of units that can be drawn by the user (the other being text units). Here is a list of some of the basic characteristics of a shape:

- A shape can be a line, a rectangle, or an ellipse.
- Shapes can be drawn given a width and a height.
- Once a shape exists, it can be moved.
- Shapes can be filled (applies to rectangles and ellipses only).

Complete the following steps to create the shape component:

1. Create a new movie clip symbol named *Shape*.
2. Edit the linkage properties of the symbol.
3. Select the Export for ActionScript and Export in First Frame checkboxes.
4. Set the linkage identifier to *ShapeSymbol*.
5. Click OK.
6. Edit the new symbol.
7. Rename the default layer as *superclass* and add a new layer named *shapeClass*.
8. On the *superclass* layer, drag an instance of the *PaintBaseClass* symbol. This ensures that the superclass is defined so that *ShapeClass* can extend it.
9. On the *shapeClass* layer, add the following code to the first frame:

```
#initclip

// When the component is first instantiated, add fill_mc and outline_mc movie
// clips to it. Also, create Color objects to target each movie clip.
function ShapeClass() {
  this.createEmptyMovieClip("fill_mc", this.getNewDepth());
  this.createEmptyMovieClip("outline_mc", this.getNewDepth());
  this.outline_mc.col = new Color(this.outline_mc);
  this.fill_mc.col = new Color(this.fill_mc);
}

// ShapeClass extends PaintBase.
ShapeClass.prototype = new PaintBase();

// The create() method creates the shape. The method requires a width and
// height, plus an RGB value for the outline and the name of the shape to draw.
ShapeClass.prototype.create = function (w, h, outlineRGB, shape) {
```

```
    this.shape = shape;
    this.w = w;
    this.h = h;
    this.outline_mc.rgb = outlineRGB;

    // Draw the outline without a fill.
    this.draw(this.outline_mc, false);

    // If the shape is not a line, then also add a fill. If no color has been
    // assigned to the fill, it is made transparent.
    if (this.shape != "line") {
      this.draw(this.fill_mc, true);
    }
};

// The draw( ) method draws the shape within the specified movie clip (either
// outline_mc or fill_mc).
ShapeClass.prototype.draw = function (mc, doFill) {

  // Make sure to clear anything that might already be drawn in the movie clip.
  mc.clear( );

  // If doFill is true, set the outline to be transparent. If the fill color has
  // been assigned, then use that color; otherwise, make the fill transparent as
  // well. If doFill is not true, then set the outline to the color that has been
  // assigned to the outline.
  if (doFill) {
    mc.lineStyle(0, 0x000000, 0);
    if (this.fill_mc.rgb == undefined) {
      mc.beginFill(0, 0);
    } else {
      mc.beginFill(this.fill_mc.rgb, 100);
    }
  } else {
    mc.lineStyle(0, this.outline_mc.rgb, 100);
  }

  // If the shape is a line, just draw a line and break out of the method.
  if (this.shape == "line") {
    mc.lineTo(this.w, this.h);
    return;
  }

  // The drawEllipse( ) and drawRectangle( ) methods don't handle negative
  // numbers. So if the width and height are negative, use the absolute value.
  drawW = Math.abs(this.w);
  drawH = Math.abs(this.h);

  // Draw the appropriate shape. These require the DrawingMethods.as methods
  // defined in Chapter 4.
  switch (this.shape) {
    case "ellipse":
      mc.drawEllipse(drawW/2, drawH/2);
      break;
```

```
        case "rectangle":
            mc.drawRectangle(drawW, drawH);
    }

    // If the method was drawing a fill, make sure to end the fill.
    if (doFill) {
        mc.endFill();
    }

    // Offset the shape by half the width and height since the custom drawing
    // methods place the registration point at the center. Also, if the width
    // and/or height were negative, this corrects the offset as necessary.
    mc._x = this.w/2;
    mc._y = this.h/2;
};

// The toggleShowOutline() method reverses the visibility of the outline.
ShapeClass.prototype.toggleShowOutline = function () {
    this.outline_mc._visible = !this.outline_mc._visible;
};

// The doFill() method assigns a value to the RGB color for the
// fill movie clips. Then, when the draw() method is called, the
// fill is drawn with that color.
ShapeClass.prototype.doFill = function (rgb) {
    this.fill_mc.rgb = rgb;
    this.draw(this.fill_mc, true);
};

// When the component is deselected, set the outline color back to the original
// (the color is highlighted blue when it is selected.) Also, set selected to
// false so the component knows about its current state, and call the deselect()
// method of the superclass, PaintBase.
ShapeClass.prototype.deselect = function () {
    this.outline_mc.col.setRGB(this.outline_mc.rgb);
    this.selected = false;
    super.deselect();
};

// When the user mouses over the component, set the outline color to blue.
ShapeClass.prototype.onRollOver = function () {
    this.outline_mc.col.setRGB(0x0000FF);
};

// When the user mouses out of the component, reset the outline color to the
// original value if the component instance is not selected.
ShapeClass.prototype.onRollOut = function () {
    if (!this.selected) {
        this.outline_mc.col.setRGB(this.outline_mc.rgb);
    }
};
```

```
// When the component is pressed, call the onPress() method of the superclass
// and highlight the outline blue if it is not already.
ShapeClass.prototype.onPress = function () {
  super.onPress();
  if (!this.selected) {
    this.outline_mc.col.setRGB(0x0000FF);
  }
};

// Register the class to the linkage identifier for the symbol.
Object.registerClass("ShapeSymbol", ShapeClass);

#endinitclip
```

Now that you've had a chance to see the *ShapeClass* component class, let's delve into it a little more closely.

The *create()* method directs the drawing of a new shape. To create the shape, the method requires the width and height of the shape, the color to use for the outline, and the type of shape to draw. The possible values for the shape parameter are "line", "rectangle", and "ellipse". The method then proceeds to call the *draw()* method to draw the outline of the shape. If the shape is not a line, the *draw()* method is also called to draw a fill. At this point, no color has been defined for the fill, so the fill is transparent. This might seem to be a bit pointless, but a shape filled with a transparent fill is much easier to select than a shape that is only an outline.

```
ShapeClass.prototype.create = function (w, h, outlineRGB, shape) {
  this.shape = shape;
  this.w = w;
  this.h = h;
  this.outline_mc.rgb = outlineRGB;
  this.draw(this.outline_mc, false);
  if (this.shape != "line") {
    this.draw(this.fill_mc, true);
  }
};
```

The *draw()* method contains the core drawing functionality for the shape component. Before the *draw()* method is invoked, the component should already have at least three properties defined by the call to *create()*: shape ("line", "rectangle", or "ellipse"), w (the width), and h (the height). Therefore, the *draw()* method does not require any of these values to be passed to it as parameters. However, the *draw()* method does need to know into which movie clip it should draw (outline_mc or fill_mc) and whether to apply a fill:

```
ShapeClass.prototype.draw = function (mc, doFill) {
  ...
};
```

The *draw()* method can be invoked multiple times for each shape, so it is important that any existing contents in the movie clip are cleared:

```
mc.clear();
```

Next, the method needs to determine what line styles and what kind of fill (if any) to apply. If the doFill parameter is true, then the outline should be transparent. If the fill color has been defined, it should be used for the fill. Otherwise, the fill should be transparent. On the other hand, if doFill is not true, the outline should be the color that has been set for the rgb property of the outline movie clip.

```
if (doFill) {
  mc.lineStyle(0, 0x000000, 0);
  if (this.fill_mc.rgb == undefined) {
    mc.beginFill(0, 0);
  } else {
    mc.beginFill(this.fill_mc.rgb, 100);
  }
} else {
  mc.lineStyle(0, this.outline_mc.rgb, 100);
}
```

The next part of the *draw()* method uses a little programming trick with a *return* statement. If the shape is a line, then all you need to do is call *lineTo()* once. Therefore, you can use a *return* statement immediately following that to end the processing of the method.

```
if (this.shape == "line") {
  mc.lineTo(this.w, this.h);
  return;
}
```

Finally, if the shape is an ellipse or rectangle, the appropriate drawing method is called. These methods don't accept negative values, so it is important that you convert the width and height of the shape to their absolute values.

```
drawW = Math.abs(this.w);
drawH = Math.abs(this.h);
switch (this.shape) {
  case "ellipse":
    mc.drawEllipse(drawW/2, drawH/2);
    break;
  case "rectangle":
    mc.drawRectangle(drawW, drawH);
}
```

The *doFill()* method accomplishes a fill by defining the rgb property of the fill_mc movie clip and then calling the *draw()* method. Once the rgb property is defined, the *draw()* method draws the shape with that fill color.

```
ShapeClass.prototype.doFill = function (rgb) {
  this.fill_mc.rgb = rgb;
  this.draw(this.fill_mc, true);
};
```

Creating the Text Component

Text units are the other kind of unit (in addition to shapes) that users can create using Flash Paint. Text units behave similarly to shape units in many ways. Here is a list of the functionality of the text component:

- Text units can be drawn given a width and a height.
- Existing text units can be moved.
- You can apply a new color to existing text.

Complete the following steps to create the text component:

1. Create a new movie clip symbol named *Text*.
2. Edit the linkage properties of the symbol.
3. Select the Export for ActionScript and Export in First Frame checkboxes.
4. Set the linkage identifier to *TextSymbol*.
5. Click OK.
6. Edit the new symbol.
7. Rename the default layer as *superclass* and add a new layer named *textClass*.
8. On the *superclass* layer, drag an instance of the *PaintBaseClass* symbol. This ensures that the superclass is defined so that *TextClass* can extend it.
9. On the *textClass* layer, add the following code to the first frame:

```
#initclip

function TextClass () {}

// TextClass extends PaintBase.
TextClass.prototype = new PaintBase();

// The create() method creates the text field within the component instance. The
// method takes three parameters: the width, height, and color of the text.
TextClass.prototype.create = function (w, h, rgb) {

  // Create the text field. The text field should be a multiline, input text
  // field with a white background and a blue border.
  this.createTextField("input_txt", 1, 0, 0, w, h);
  this.input_txt.type = "input";
  this.input_txt.multiline = true;
  this.input_txt.textColor = rgb;
  this.input_txt.border = true;
  this.input_txt.background = true;
  this.input_txt.borderColor = 0x0000FF;

  // When the user adds new text for the first time, set the text to autosize.
  this.input_txt.onChanged = function () {
    this.autoSize = true;
    delete this.onChanged;
  }
```

```
// Call the deselect() method of the component whenever focus is lost (meaning
// the user clicked outside of the text field).
this.input_txt.onKillFocus = function () {
  if (this.text != "") {
    this._parent.deselect();
  }
}

// Set the focus to the text field.
Selection.setFocus(this.input_txt);
this.selected = true;

// Invoke the checkEditing() method at an interval to constantly see if the
// text is being edited.
this.checkInterval = setInterval(this, "checkEditing", 100);
};

// The deselect() method first calls the superclass's deselect() method. It then
// sets other properties of the component so it can keep track of its state.
// Additionally, the border and background of the text field are turned off.
TextClass.prototype.deselect = function () {
  super.deselect();
  this.editing = false;
  this.input_txt.background = false;
  this.input_txt.border = false;
  this.selected = false;
};

// The doFill() method sets the text color.
TextClass.prototype.doFill = function (rgb) {
  this.input_txt.textColor = rgb;
};

// When the component instance is moused over,
// turn on the border only (not the background).
TextClass.prototype.onRollOver = function () {
  if (!this.selected) {
    this.input_txt.border = true;
  }
};

// When the user mouses out of the component instance, if it is not otherwise
// selected, turn off the border.
TextClass.prototype.onRollOut = function () {
  if (!this.selected) {
    this.input_txt.border = false;
  }
};

// When the component instance is pressed, check whether the component has been
// double-clicked. If so, turn on editing and set the focus to the text field.
// Otherwise, call the onPress() method of the superclass.
TextClass.prototype.onPress = function () {
  this.input_txt.border = true;
```

```
      this.currentTime = getTimer();
      if (this.currentTime - this.previousTime < 500) {
        this.editing = true;
        this.input_txt.background = true;
        super.deselect();
        Selection.setFocus(this.input_txt);
        Selection.setSelection(this.input_txt.length, this.input_txt.length);
      } else {
        super.onPress();
      }
      this.previousTime = this.currentTime;
    };

    // The checkEditing() method continually checks to see if the text field is
    // being edited. If so, and if the focus of the text field has been lost, then
    // reset the focus to the text field.
    TextClass.prototype.checkEditing = function () {
      if (this.editing && !(Selection.getFocus() != String(this.input_txt))) {
        Selection.setFocus(this.input_txt);
        Selection.setSelection(this.input_txt.text.length,
                               this.input_txt.text.length);
      }
    };

    // Call the superclass's onRelease() method if the user is not editing the text.
    TextClass.prototype.onRelease = function () {
      if (!this.editing) {
        super.onRelease();
      }
    };

    // Register the class to the symbol's linkage identifier.
    Object.registerClass("TextSymbol", TextClass);

    #endinitclip
```

The *TextClass* component class is not overly complex, but it is also not without its own intricacies that are worth exploring in a little more depth.

First of all, notice that both the *ShapeClass* and the *TextClass* classes have *create()* methods. Furthermore, the *create()* method of each class accepts similar parameters in a similar order (although *ShapeClass.create()* accepts one additional parameter). This similarity is intentional and allows for text and shape components to be treated more or less identically by the Flash Paint application.

The *TextClass.create()* method includes several points of interest. First of all, notice that the text field is always created with a depth of 1. The *create()* method can be called multiple times for the same text unit, and creating the text field with the same depth each time ensures that any previous text fields are overwritten:

```
this.createTextField("input_txt", 1, 0, 0, w, h);
```

Additionally, the *create()* method employs an interesting technique using the *onChanged()* event handler method for the text field. When the text field is first created, it is designed to have a specified width and height. The width and height are maintained until the user first enters text into the text field. At that point the *onChanged()* method is automatically invoked, and the text field is set to autosize. The *onChanged()* method has done its job at that point, so it can delete itself:

```
this.input_txt.onChanged = function () {
  this.autoSize = true;
  delete this.onChanged;
};
```

The *onKillFocus()* event handler method of the text field is also used. This method calls the *deselect()* method of the component instance. The purpose of this is to deselect the unit when the user clicks outside of the text field.

```
this.input_txt.onKillFocus = function () {
  if (this.text != "") {
    this._parent.deselect();
  }
};
```

When a text unit is deselected, set the self-describing `editing` and `selected` properties to false. Additionally, the border and background of the text field should be hidden. The *TextClass.descelect()* method calls the *deselect()* method of the superclass, which ultimately invokes the *onDeselect()* callback function to perform necessary housekeeping, such as recording which tool is selected:

```
TextClass.prototype.deselect = function () {
  super.deselect();
  this.editing = false;
  this.input_txt.background = false;
  this.input_txt.border = false;
  this.selected = false;
};
```

The *TextClass.doFill()* method shares its name with the *ShapeClass.doFill()* method for the same reasons that the *create()* methods are named the same. The *doFill()* method of the *TextClass* class assigns the new color to the text field:

```
TextClass.prototype.doFill = function (rgb) {
  this.input_txt.textColor = rgb;
};
```

The *onPress()* and *checkEditing()* methods are designed to overcome a specific problem that can occur when you place a text field within a movie clip. Normally, when you use the mouse to click on an input text field, Flash brings focus to that text field, and you can type in it. However, if the text field is nested within a movie clip, and the movie clip handles button events (press, release, etc.), the movie clip's event handling takes precedence over the event handling of the nested text field. Therefore, there is not a convenient way to select a text field when it is nested within a movie clip that handles button events (such as with the *TextClass* component class). To work around this issue, the *onPress()* method checks for double-clicks versus single-clicks. When the component is clicked, the value returned by *getTimer()* is recorded. Then that time is compared with the value of the previous click. If the difference is less than half a second, it constitutes a double-click. Otherwise, it is a single-click. When a double-click occurs, the *Selection.setFocus()* and *Selection.setSelection()* methods are used to bring focus to the text field and to move the cursor to the end of the existing text. When a single-click occurs, the *onPress()* method of the superclass is invoked to allow the default handling for single-clicks, namely dragging the item on the paint canvas.

```
TextClass.prototype.onPress = function () {
  this.input_txt.border = true;
  this.currentTime = getTimer();
  if (this.currentTime - this.previousTime < 500) {
    this.editing = true;
    this.input_txt.background = true;
    super.deselect();
    Selection.setFocus(this.input_txt);
    Selection.setSelection(this.input_txt.length, this.input_txt.length);
  } else {
    super.onPress();
  }
  this.previousTime = this.currentTime;
};
```

You might think that the code in the *onPress()* method should be enough to successfully keep the focus on the text field when it is double-clicked. However, the button events keep causing the text field to lose focus. As a workaround for this, the *checkEditing()* method continually brings focus back to the text field if editing is on. You'll need to refer back to the *create()* method to see where we set the interval on which this method is called. The only drawback to this technique is that it does not allow you to do any kind of editing to the text field other than append text or delete text from the end.

```
Text.prototype.checkEditing = function () {
  if (this.editing && !(Selection.getFocus() != String(this.input_txt))) {
    Selection.setFocus(this.input_txt);
    Selection.setSelection(this.input_txt.text.length, this.input_txt.text.length);
  }
};
```

Creating the Color Selector Component

You should use the color selector component that you created in Recipe 12.13. If you followed the complete instructions for that program, then the color selector component should be available from the Components panel. If not, download the code from *http://www.person13.com/ascb* and install it according to the instructions in Chapter 12.

When you have created or installed the color selector, create a copy of the component symbol in the *flashPaint.fla* Library. You can do this by dragging an instance of the component from the Components panel onto the Stage. Then delete the instance from the Stage. The symbol remains in the Library.

Assembling the Flash Paint Application

You have now created all the necessary components for the Flash Paint application. The only remaining step is to create the main routine that puts them all together. To accomplish this, add the following code to the first frame of the main timeline of the *flashPaint.fla* document:

```
// Include MovieClip.as from Chapter 7, DrawingMethods.as from Chapter 4, and
// Table.as from Chapter 11 for their custom methods.
#include "MovieClip.as"
#include "DrawingMethods.as"
#include "Table.as"

// Initialize the movie.
function init( ) {
  selectedShape = null;
  selectedTool = null;
  shapes = new Array( );
  makeTools( );
}

// The makeTools( ) method creates the toolbar buttons.
function makeTools ( ) {

  // Define an array of the first six tool names. These names match the accepted
  // values within the toolbar button component.
  toolbarBtnNames = ["select", "line", "rectangle", "ellipse", "text", "fill"];

  // Create an array to hold references to the "stick" toolbar button instances.
  toolbarBtns = new Array( );

  // Create a toolbar movie clip to contain all the tools (including
  // the color selector) and a nested btns movie clip to specifically
  // contain the toolbar buttons.
  _root.createEmptyMovieClip("toolbar", _root.getNewDepth( ));
  toolbar.createEmptyMovieClip("btns", toolbar.getNewDepth( ));
  var name, btn;

  // Create a table for holding the buttons. Set the row spacing to three pixels.
  t = new Table(3);

  // Loop through all the names of the buttons.
  for (var i = 0; i < toolbarBtnNames.length; i++) {
    name = toolbarBtnNames[i];
```

```
    // Create the toolbar button instance.
    btn = toolbar.btns.attachMovie("ToolbarButtonSymbol",
                                   name + "Btn",
                                   toolbar.getNewDepth( ),
                                   {val: name});
    // Call the create( ) method for each of the "stick" buttons. Set the onSelect( )
    // callback function for each.
    btn.create(name, "stick");
    btn.setOnSelect("onSelectTool", _root);

    // Add the button to the array and to a table column and row.
    toolbarBtns.push(btn);
    t.addRow(new TableRow(0, new TableColumn(0, btn)));
  }

  // Create the back and forward buttons, which are "spring" buttons.
  toolbar.btns.attachMovie("ToolbarButtonSymbol", "backBtn",
                           toolbar.getNewDepth( ), {val: name});
  toolbar.btns.attachMovie("ToolbarButtonSymbol", "forwardBtn",
                           toolbar.getNewDepth( ), {val: name});
  toolbar.btns.backBtn.create("back", "spring");
  toolbar.btns.backBtn.setOnSelect("moveBack", _root);
  toolbar.btns.forwardBtn.create("forward", "spring");
  toolbar.btns.forwardBtn.setOnSelect("bringForward", _root);

  // Add the two buttons to the table.
  t.addRow(new TableRow(0, new TableColumn(0, toolbar.btns.backBtn)));
  t.addRow(new TableRow(0, new TableColumn(0, toolbar.btns.forwardBtn)));

  // Add the color selector to the toolbar and to the table. Then render the table.
  toolbar.attachMovie("ColorSelectorSymbol", "colSelect", toolbar.getNewDepth( ));
  t.addRow(new TableRow(0, new TableColumn(0, toolbar.colSelect)));
  t.render(true);
}

// This function is called when one of the first six tools is selected.
// The function loops through the toolbarBtns array elements and deselects
// any other buttons in case they are selected. It also sets the selectedTool
// variable to the current tool.
function onSelectTool (cmpt) {
  for (var i = 0; i < toolbarBtns.length; i++) {
    if (toolbarBtns[i] != cmpt) {
      toolbarBtns[i].toggleDeselect( );
    }
  }
  _root.selectedTool = cmpt.val;
}

// bringForward( ) moves the selected shape or text forward by one depth.
function bringForward ( ) {

  // Loop through the existing shapes to find the index of the selected shape.
  for (var i = 0; i < shapes.length; i++) {
```

```
    if (shapes[i] == selectedShape) {
      break;
    }
  }

  // If the shape is already at the front, then exit the function.
  if (i == shapes.length - 1) {
    return;
  }

  // Swap the depths and positions of the shape (or text unit) with the shape (or
  // text unit) that has a index within the array that is one greater than the
  // selected shape (or text unit).
  selectedShape.swapDepths(shapes[i + 1]);
  shapes[i] = shapes[i + 1];
  shapes[i + 1] = selectedShape;
}

// The moveBack( ) function moves the selected shape or text back by one depth. The
// function uses the same logic as the bringForward( ) function.
function moveBack ( ) {
  for (var i = 0; i < shapes.length; i++) {
    if (shapes[i] == selectedShape) {
      break;
    }
  }
  if (i == 0) {
    return;
  }
  selectedShape.swapDepths(shapes[i - 1]);
  shapes[i] = shapes[i - 1];
  shapes[i - 1] = selectedShape;
}

// If the mouse is currently over any shapes or text units, the isMouseOverShapes( )
// method returns true. Otherwise, it returns false.
function isMouseOverShapes ( ) {
  var isOver = false;

  // Loop through all the existing shapes (or text units) and use hitTest( ) to
  // determine if the mouse is currently over any of them.
  for (var i = 0; i < shapes.length; i++) {
    if (shapes[i].hitTest(_root._xmouse, _root._ymouse, true)) {
      isOver = true;
      break;
    }
  }
  return isOver;
}

// This function deselects all the existing shapes except for the one specified by
// the keepSelectedShape parameter (if any).
function deselectShapes (keepSelectedShape) {
  for (var i = 0; i < shapes.length; i++) {
```

```
      if (shapes[i] != keepSelectedShape) {
        shapes[i].deselect( );
      }
    }
  }
  selectedShape = keepSelectedShape;
}

// The removeSelected( ) function removes the selected shape (or text unit) from the
// movie and from the shapes array.
function removeSelected ( ) {
  for (var i = 0; i < shapes.length; i++) {
    if (shapes[i] == selectedShape) {
      shapes.splice(i, 1);
      break;
    }
  }
  selectedShape.removeMovieClip( );
}

// When the shape or text unit is pressed, this callback function is invoked
// automatically. Check to see which tool is selected. If it is the select tool, make
// the unit draggable. If it is the fill tool, call the doFill( ) method of the shape
// with the selected color.
function onPressShape (cmpt) {
  if (selectedTool == "select") {
    cmpt.startDrag( );
  }
  if (selectedTool == "fill") {
    cmpt.doFill(toolbar.colSelect.getSelectedColor( ));
  }
}

// When the shape or text unit is released, this callback function is invoked
// automatically. Make sure the unit is no longer being dragged.
function onReleaseShape (cmpt) {
  cmpt.stopDrag( );
}

// When a shape or text unit is selected, this callback function is invoked
// automatically. Deselect any other shapes that are already selected and set the
// selected shape to current shape or text unit.
function onSelectShape (cmpt) {
  if (selectedShape != undefined) {
    deselectShapes(cmpt);
  }
  selectedShape = cmpt;
}

// When a shape is deselected, set the selected shape to null.
function onDeselectShape (cmpt) {
  selectedShape = null;
}
```

```
// The checkIfMouseDown() function continually checks to see if the mouseDown
// variable is true. If so, and if the selected tool is a rectangle, ellipse, line,
// or text, the doShapeDraw() function is called.
function checkIfMouseDown () {
  if (mouseDown) {
    switch(selectedTool) {
      case "rectangle":
      case "ellipse":
      case "line":
      case "text":
        doShapeDraw();
    }
  }
}

mouseCheckIntervalID = setInterval(checkIfMouseDown, 100);

// The doShapeDraw() function calculates the width and height of the shape to draw
// based on the difference between the starting coordinates and the current
// coordinates of the mouse. It then calls the create() method of the current shape.
function doShapeDraw () {
  var w = _root._xmouse - startX;
  var h = _root._ymouse - startY;
  newShape.create(w, h, toolbar.colSelect.getSelectedColor(), selectedTool);
}

// The mouseListener object is a listener object applied to the mouse to listen for
// mouseDown and mouseUp events.
mouseListener = new Object();

mouseListener.onMouseDown = function () {

  // Perform the following actions only if the mouse is not over the toolbar buttons.
  // This prevents the user from accidentally drawing shapes when trying to select
  // buttons on the toolbar.
  if (!_root.toolbar.btns.hitTest(_root._xmouse, _root._ymouse)) {

    // Set the mouseDown variable to true. This alerts the code in the
    // checkIfMouseDown() function to be processed.
    _root.mouseDown = true;

    // Set the starting coordinates of the shape/text unit
    // to the current mouse position.
    _root.startX = _root._xmouse;
    _root.startY = _root._ymouse;

    // Get a new unique depth and name of the shape or text unit.
    var uniqueVal = _root.getNewDepth();

    // Perform the correct actions depending on the selected tool.
    switch (_root.selectedTool) {
      case "select":
        // If the mouse is clicked, but not over an existing shape/text unit,
        // deselect any selected units and set selectedShape to null.
        if (!_root.isMouseOverShapes()) {
```

```
            _root.deSelectShapes( );
            root.selectedShape = null;
          }
          break;
        case "line":
        case "rectangle":
        case "ellipse":
          // If the line, rectangle, or ellipse tools are selected, create a new shape
          // component instance and set the callback functions for each.
          _root.newShape = _root.attachMovie("ShapeSymbol", "shape" + uniqueVal,
                          uniqueVal, {_x: _root.startX, _y: _root.startY});
          _root.newShape.setOnPress("onPressShape", _root);
          _root.newShape.setOnRelease("onReleaseShape", _root);
          _root.newShape.setOnSelect("onSelectShape", _root);
          _root.newShape.setOnDeselect("onDeselectShape", _root);
          _root.shapes.push(_root.newShape);
          break;
        case "text":
          // If the text tool is selected, create a new text component and set the
          // callback functions for each.
          _root.newShape = _root.attachMovie("TextSymbol", "shape" + uniqueVal,
                          uniqueVal, {_x: _root.startX, _y: _root.startY});
          _root.newShape.setOnPress("onPressShape", _root);
          _root.newShape.setOnRelease("onReleaseShape", _root);
          _root.newShape.setOnSelect("onSelectShape", _root);
          _root.newShape.setOnDeselect("onDeselectShape", _root);
          _root.shapes.push(_root.newShape);
    }
  }
};

// When the mouse is released, set mouseDown to false so the checkIfMouseDown( ) code
// stops executing.
mouseListener.onMouseUp = function ( ) {
  _root.mouseDown = false;
};

Mouse.addListener(mouseListener);

// The key listener checks to see if the delete key is pressed. If so, call the
// removeSelected( ) function. Note: The delete key has a special meaning when you use
// the "Test Movie" feature in Flash. If you want to test your movie in this way,
// make sure you select the Disable Keyboard Shortcuts option from the Control menu
// in the Test Player.
keyListener = new Object( );
keyListener.onKeyDown = function ( ) {
  if (Key.getCode( ) == Key.DELETEKEY) {
    _root.removeSelected( );
  }
};

Key.addListener(keyListener);

// Call the init( ) function to get everything started.
init( );
```

The main routine of the Flash Paint application is a long one, but don't let that intimidate you. It really is not that scary. Let's take a closer look at some of the code.

The *init()* function is pretty straightforward. The selectedShape variable is used throughout the application to keep track of the shape (or text) unit that is currently selected. Because no shape is selected (or yet created) at the beginning of the application, initialize this variable to null. Likewise, the selectedTool variable is used to keep track of the tool that is selected. The shapes array is used to keep track of which shapes have been created, and the relative depths of each of them.

```
function init( ) {
  selectedShape = null;
  selectedTool = null;
  shapes = new Array( );
  makeTools( );
}
```

The *makeTools()* function creates all the toolbar elements. There are two types of buttons: "stick" buttons and "spring" buttons. The stick buttons need to be associated with one another because only one can be selected at a time. Therefore, create an array into which the buttons are stored:

```
toolbarBtns = new Array( );
```

To create the stick buttons, for each element of the toolbarBtnNames array the function creates a toolbar button component instance and attaches it to the toolbar.btns movie clip. Using the toolbarBtnNames array is not essential, but it is a convenient way to create the component instances. By using the array of names, you can create all the component instances within a single *for* statement instead of having to type the *attachMovie()*, *create()*, *setOnSelect()*, *push()*, and *addRow()* methods separately for each toolbar button:

```
for (var i = 0; i < toolbarBtnNames.length; i++) {
  name = toolbarBtnNames[i];
  btn = toolbar.btns.attachMovie("ToolbarButtonSymbol",
                                 name + "Btn",
                                 toolbar.getNewDepth( ),
                                 {val: name});
  btn.create(name, "stick");
  btn.setOnSelect("onSelectTool", _root);
  toolbarBtns.push(btn);
  t.addRow(new TableRow(0, new TableColumn(0, btn)));
}
```

Next, we want to create the Back and Forward buttons. Each of these buttons are spring buttons, and they invoke different callback functions from the stick buttons, so we create these instances separately from the stick buttons:

```
toolbar.btns.attachMovie("ToolbarButtonSymbol", "backBtn",
                         toolbar.getNewDepth( ), {val: name});
toolbar.btns.attachMovie("ToolbarButtonSymbol", "forwardBtn",
                         toolbar.getNewDepth( ), {val: name});
```

```
toolbar.btns.backBtn.create("back", "spring");
toolbar.btns.backBtn.setOnSelect("moveBack", _root);
toolbar.btns.forwardBtn.create("forward", "spring");
toolbar.btns.forwardBtn.setOnSelect("bringForward", _root);
```

The *bringForward()* and *moveBack()* functions are almost identical. The difference is in which shapes are swapped. All the shapes and text units are stored in the shapes array in the order of their depths. The higher the index of an element in the shapes array, the higher it appears in the stacking order. Therefore, to bring a shape forward, you should swap its depth with the element in the shapes array that has an index that is one higher. Then, to keep the order of the elements in the shapes array corresponding to the order of depths, also switch the positions of the two elements in the array. The process for the *moveBack()* function works the same, except the shape swaps depths with the element that has an index of one less.

```
function bringForward( ) {
  for (var i = 0; i < shapes.length; i++) {
    if (shapes[i] == selectedShape) {
      break;
    }
  }
  if (i == shapes.length - 1) {
    return;
  }
  selectedShape.swapDepths(shapes[i + 1]);
  shapes[i] = shapes[i + 1];
  shapes[i + 1] = selectedShape;
}

function moveBack( ) {
  for (var i = 0; i < shapes.length; i++) {
    if (shapes[i] == selectedShape) {
      break;
    }
  }
  if (i == 0) {
    return;
  }
  selectedShape.swapDepths(shapes[i - 1]);
  shapes[i] = shapes[i - 1];
  shapes[i - 1] = selectedShape;
}
```

The *removeSelected()* function removes the selected shape or text unit from the movie, with the *removeMovieClip()* method, and it updates the shapes array so that the array contains existing shapes only. Therefore, the function loops through all of the elements of the shapes array until it finds the selected shape. It then calls the *splice()* method to remove that item from the array.

```
function removeSelected( ) {
  for (var i = 0; i < shapes.length; i++) {
```

```
      if (shapes[i] == selectedShape) {
        shapes.splice(i, 1);
        break;
      }
    }
  }
  selectedShape.removeMovieClip( );
}
```

The *checkIfMouseDown()* interval function continually checks to see if the mouseDown variable is true. (The variable is set to true in the *onMouseDown()* method applied to the mouse listener.) Then, if the selected tool is a rectangle, ellipse, line, or text, the application draws a shape or text unit using the *doShapeDraw()* function. As long as the mouse is down, the mouseDown variable is set to true. Therefore, the *doShapeDraw()* method is called continuously to draw, and redraw, a shape.

```
function checkIfMouseDown ( ) {
  if (mouseDown) {
    switch(selectedTool) {
      case "rectangle":
      case "ellipse":
      case "line":
      case "text":
        doShapeDraw( );
    }
  }
}

mouseCheckIntervalID = setInterval(checkIfMouseDown, 100);
```

The *doShapeDraw()* method calls the *create()* method of the newly created shape (or text) unit. The width and height are calculated based on the x and y coordinates of the mouse when it was first clicked and the current x and y coordinates of the mouse. Therefore, when the user presses the mouse button, holds it, and drags the mouse, the width and height change. The *create()* method is also supplied with the color value that is selected from the color selector and the name of the current tool. The name of the tool is either "line", "rectangle", "ellipse", or "text". The *ShapeClass* component class's *create()* method uses this value to determine which shape to draw. The *TextClass* component class's *create()* method does not need this parameter, so it is extraneous when the new shape happens to be a text unit.

```
function doShapeDraw ( ) {
  var w = _root._xmouse - startX;
  var h = _root._ymouse - startY;
  newShape.create(w, h, toolbar.colSelect.getSelectedColor( ), selectedTool);
}
```

The *onMouseDown()* method of the mouse listener does several very important things. First, the method sets the `mouseDown` variable to `true`, which activates the *checkIfMouseDown()* code that starts calling *doShapeDraw()*:

```
_root.mouseDown = true;
```

The *onMouseDown()* method also sets the `startX` and `startY` variables to the position of the mouse at the time the mouse button is pressed:

```
_root.startX = _root._xmouse;
_root.startY = _root._ymouse;
```

Next, the method determines the appropriate course of action depending on the selected tool. If the selected tool is a line, rectangle, ellipse, or text, the method creates a new component instance positioned at the mouse pointer and adds that component to the shapes array. The new component instance is assigned to the `newShape` variable so that regardless of the instance name, the *doShapeDraw()* method always calls the *create()* method from the newly created component instance.

```
switch (_root.selectedTool) {
  case "select":
    if (!_root.isMouseOverShapes()) {
      _root.deSelectShapes();
      root.selectedShape = null;
    }
    break;
  case "line":
  case "rectangle":
  case "ellipse":
    _root.newShape = _root.attachMovie("ShapeSymbol", "shape" + uniqueVal,
                     uniqueVal, {_x: _root.startX, _y: _root.startY});
    _root.newShape.setOnPress("onPressShape", _root);
    _root.newShape.setOnRelease("onReleaseShape", _root);
    _root.newShape.setOnSelect("onSelectShape", _root);
    _root.newShape.setOnDeselect("onDeselectShape", _root);
    _root.shapes.push(_root.newShape);
    break;
  case "text":
    _root.newShape = _root.attachMovie("TextSymbol", "shape" + uniqueVal,
                     uniqueVal, {_x: _root.startX, _y: _root.startY});
    _root.newShape.setOnPress("onPressShape", _root);
    _root.newShape.setOnRelease("onReleaseShape", _root);
    _root.newShape.setOnSelect("onSelectShape", _root);
    _root.newShape.setOnDeselect("onDeselectShape", _root);
    _root.shapes.push(_root.newShape);
}
```

Using Flash Paint

Once you have completed the Flash Paint application you will undoubtedly want to impress your friends and enemies with your mighty design prowess. However, while

Flash Paint is not without its charm, it is possible that you may want to do more with it. While I won't go into any more detail in this chapter, here are some suggestions for how to extend this application:

- Add more types of shapes that can be drawn (stars, triangles, etc.).

- Use a *SharedObject* to store the shapes, including their colors, positions, sizes, and any text content. Then retrieve the *SharedObject* data when the application is re-opened and lay out the contents as they existed when the application was last run.

- Use FlashCom to enable multiple users to interact with Flash Paint so that all connected users can see the same thing. Flash Paint then resembles a whiteboard application.

## CHAPTER 23

Creating a Simple Animation
in Stages

Although some ActionScript projects may appear a bit daunting at first glance, each one is quite manageable when you can break it down into parts. While it is true that applications must function as a whole, it is also true that a well-designed application can be developed in stages and in discrete units. The creative spark that sets a project in motion is typically in the form of a gestalt—a unified vision or idea for the entire application. However, the execution of the idea generally involves analysis—breaking apart the whole into smaller, more manageable parts.

In this chapter, you will create a simple Flash movie using ActionScript alone to create all the elements (in other words, no author-time movie clips or buttons are placed on the Stage). To get a feel for how to analyze a task, you will create this movie in five stages:

1. Create a single circle that moves around and bounces off the sides of a rectangle.

2. Use the same algorithms from the first stage, but create a component that bounces around within a rectangle.

3. Create a movie clip on the main timeline and fill that movie clip with multiple instances of the circle component. Also, modify the circle component so that the circles bounce not only off the sides of the rectangle but also off each other.

4. Create a button component and add instances of the button component to the movie so that the user can control the position, scale, and rotation of the movie clip containing the circle component instances. Use a table to position the buttons.

5. Create an XML document and load that document into the Flash movie. Use the data from the XML document to determine the movie's parameters, such as the number of circles; the size, color, and velocity of the circles; and the size of the rectangle within which the circles bounce.

Admittedly, it is unlikely that you will add this Flash movie to your own web site to show off your ActionScript prowess. However, in this chapter, you get the opportunity to become familiar with some of the concepts and techniques that are used throughout some of the recipes in the rest of this book, including:

- Creating custom components
- Using the *getNewDepth()* method to ensure that graphical object instances have unique depths
- Working with the custom drawing methods
- Using runtime-generated text
- Loading XML data

The completed files can be downloaded from *http://www.person13.com/ascb*.

Stage One

In the first stage of the application, begin with the most fundamental and central task of the application. In an application that involves bouncing circles, the most natural place to begin is to create a single circle that bounces within the boundaries of a rectangle. Here are the steps to complete this stage of the application:

1. Create a new Flash document named *stage1.fla* and open it.
2. Add the following code to the first frame of the default layer of the main timeline:

```
// Include DrawingMethods.as from Chapter 4 for its custom drawing methods.
#include "DrawingMethods.as"

// Include MovieClip.as from Chapter 7 for its getNewDepth( ) method.
#include "MovieClip.as"

// Create the circle movie clip and draw a circle of radius 10 within it.
_root.createEmptyMovieClip("circle", _root.getNewDepth( ));
with (circle) {
  lineStyle(0, 0x000000, 0);
  beginFill(0, 100);
  drawCircle(10);
  endFill( );
}

// Create a movie clip for the box and draw a rectangular outline within it.
_root.createEmptyMovieClip("border", _root.getNewDepth( ));
with (border) {
  lineStyle(0, 0, 100);

  // Draw a 200 × 200 rectangle.
  drawRectangle(200, 200);
  _x += 100;
  _y += 100;
}
```

```
// Create some properties for the circle that define the area within which its
// movement should be constrained.
circle.minX = 0;
circle.minY = 0;
circle.maxX = 200;
circle.maxY = 200;

// Initialize the circle at a random coordinate within the acceptable range.
circle._x = Math.random( ) * circle.maxX;
circle._y = Math.random( ) * circle.maxY;

// Set the velocity of the circle to six pixels per frame.
circle.vel = 6;

// Set a property that determines the direction or angle of the initial movement
// of the circle. The value needs to be in radians, so generate a random value
// between 0 and 2π (which is 360 in degrees).
circle.dir = Math.random( ) * Math.PI * 2;

// Define an onEnterFrame( ) method for the circle so that it continually updates
// its position.
circle.onEnterFrame = function ( ) {

  // Calculate the new x and y coordinates for the circle.
  // Using basic trigonometric formulas, we can derive the x
  // and y components of a vector, a line that has both direction
  // (an angle) and velocity. See Recipes 5.12 and 5.14.
  this._x += Math.cos(this.dir) * this.vel;
  this._y += Math.sin(this.dir) * this.vel;

  // If the circle is touching the rectangle or is outside its boundaries, change
  // the direction of the circle.
  if ((this._x + this._width/2) >= this.maxX) {
    this._x = this.maxX - this._width/2 - 1;
    this.dir += 2 * (Math.PI/2 - this.dir);
  }
  else if ((this._x - this._width/2)<= this.minX) {
    this._x = this.minX + this._width/2 + 1;
    this.dir += 2 * (Math.PI/2 - this.dir);
  }
  if ((this._y + this._height/2) >= this.maxY) {
    this._y = this.maxY - this._height/2 - 1;
    this.dir -= 2*this.dir;
  }
  else if ((this._y - this._height/2) <= this.minY) {
    this._y = this.minY + this._height/2 + 1;
    this.dir -= 2*this.dir;
  }
};
```

That is all there is to stage one of the application. If you save and test your movie, you should see a single circle that bounces around within the boundaries of a rectangle. The majority of the code in this stage is nothing new or complicated. Some of the mathematics involved in the calculations might be new to you, but the ActionScript syntax is familiar. The only portion of the code that really needs some further explanation is a snippet from the *onEnterFrame()* method. Within this method you want to update the position of the circle according to the direction and velocity for the circle. There are two basic trigonometric formulas that you can employ here to find the new x and y coordinates based on the information you do know (the direction/angle and the velocity).

Trigonometry says that the x coordinate can be found by multiplying the cosine of the angle by the velocity, and the y coordinate can be found by multiplying the sine of the angle by the velocity. Now, if the circle was only going to move along a straight line forever, then this would be all that is needed. However, you want the circle to bounce when it hits the sides of the rectangle. Therefore, you need to use a series of *if* statements. In each case, you must calculate whether the edge of the circle is touching or outside of the rectangle. You can find the edge of the circle by adding or subtracting the radius from the center of the circle (the radius is half of either the width or the height). When the circle needs to bounce, you must do two things. First, set the circle so that it is within the boundaries of the rectangle by at least one pixel. Otherwise, the circle can get trapped along the side of the rectangle. The other thing you should do is assign the circle a new direction. The new direction is determined either by adding twice the difference between $\pi/2$ and the current direction (in the case of the circle bouncing off the left or right walls) or by subtracting twice the current direction (in the case of the circle bouncing off the top or bottom walls), as shown in the preceding *onEnterFrame()* handler.

Stage Two

In stage two, we want to use the calculations that were worked out in the first stage to create a component. The advantage of a component, in this case, is that you can create the component code once and then create as many instances as you want. Here are the steps you should complete to create the second stage of the application:

1. Open *stage1.fla* and save it as *stage2.fla*.
2. Delete all the code from the first frame of the main timeline. You may want to select it and cut it because you will use much of the same code within the component.
3. Create a new movie clip symbol named *Circle*.
4. Open the linkage properties for the *Circle* movie clip symbol.
5. Select the Export for ActionScript and Export on First Frame options and give the symbol a linkage identifier of *CircleSymbol*.
6. Click OK to close the linkage properties dialog box.
7. Edit *Circle*.

8. On the first frame of the default layer within the *Circle* symbol, add the following code:

```
// Component class code should always be enclosed within #initclip/#endinitclip.
#initclip

function CircleClass () {}

CircleClass.prototype = new MovieClip();

CircleClass.prototype.init = function (minX, minY, maxX, maxY, vel,
                                       col, radius) {

  // Draw the circle with radius specified by the radius parameter.
  with (this) {
    lineStyle(0, 0x000000, 0);
    beginFill(0, 100);
    drawCircle(radius);
    endFill();
  }

  // Define the area within which the circle moves.
  this.minX = minX;
  this.minY = minY;
  this.maxX = maxX;
  this.maxY = maxY;

  // Assign a random coordinate at which the circle initializes.
  this._x = Math.random() * this.maxX;
  this._y = Math.random() * this.maxY;

  // If the string "random" is passed to the method as the vel parameter,
  // generate a random velocity between 3 and 9. Otherwise, use the value of vel.
  if (vel == "random") {
    this.vel = Math.random() * 6 + 3;
  } else {
    this.vel = vel;
  }

  // Generate a random direction in which the circle should initially move.
  this.dir = Math.random() * Math.PI * 2;

  // Create a color object to control the color of the circle.
  this.colObj = new Color(this);

  // If the col parameter is "random", generate a random color value.
  if (col == "random") {
    col = Math.random() * 255 * 255 * 255;
  }

  // Set the color.
  colObj.setRGB(col);
};
```

```
// The onEnterFrame( ) method here is the same as from stage one.
CircleClass.prototype.onEnterFrame = function () {
  this._x += Math.cos(this.dir) * this.vel;
  this._y += Math.sin(this.dir) * this.vel;
  if ((this._x + this._width/2) >= this.maxX) {
    this._x = this.maxX - this._width/2 - 1;
    this.dir += 2 * (Math.PI/2 - this.dir);
  }
  else if ((this._x - this._width/2)<= this.minX) {
    this._x = this.minX + this._width/2 + 1;
    this.dir += 2 * (Math.PI/2 - this.dir);
  }
  if ((this._y + this._height/2) >= this.maxY) {
    this._y = this.maxY - this._height/2 - 1;
    this.dir -= 2*this.dir;
  }
  else if ((this._y - this._height/2) <= this.minY) {
    this._y = this.minY + this._height/2 + 1;
    this.dir -= 2*this.dir;
  }
};

// Register the class to the linkage identifier CircleSymbol.
Object.registerClass("CircleSymbol", CircleClass);

#endinitclip
```

9. On the first frame of the default layer of the main timeline, add the following code:

```
// Include DrawingMethods.as from Chapter 4 and MovieClip.as from Chapter 7.
#include "DrawingMethods.as"
#include "MovieClip.as"

// Create an instance of the circle component. Call the init( ) method to define
// the initialization parameters.
_root.attachMovie("CircleSymbol", "circle" + i, 1);
circle.init(0, 0, 200, 200, "random", "random", 10);

_root.createEmptyMovieClip("border", 2);
with (border) {
  lineStyle(0, 0, 100);
  drawRectangle(200, 200, 0, 0, 100, 100);
}
```

When you save and test your movie in stage two, you should see pretty much the same thing you saw in stage one. The only apparent difference is that the color and velocity are randomized. But you have accomplished much more than just what is apparent from this simple example. You have successfully created a component that can be used to make more circle instances, as you will see in the next stage.

Most of the code in stage two of this application is the same as the code from stage one. However, there is one thing that is worth mentioning with regards to the colorization. In this example you have created a color object to control the color of the circle.

Technically, this is not necessary since you could easily set the color in the *beginFill()* method when drawing the circle. However, if at a later point you want to alter the color of the circle, it is much simpler to use a color object. For example, you could extend this application a little by assigning a new, random color to the circle every time it bounces.

Stage Three

In the third stage you want to add more circle instances to the movie. In and of itself, this is quite easy now that you have created a component. However, adding more circles adds another level of complexity. The circles should bounce off each other as well as the sides of the rectangle. To accomplish this, you need to devise a way in which each circle knows about all the other circles. This is not as difficult as it may sound. Here are the steps to complete the third stage of the application:

1. Open *stage2.fla* and save it as *stage3.fla*.
2. Open the *Circle* symbol and modify the code as follows (changes are in bold):

```
#initclip

function CircleClass( ) {}

CircleClass.prototype = new MovieClip( );

CircleClass.prototype.init = function (minX, minY, maxX, maxY, vel, col, radius)
{
  with (this) {
    lineStyle(0, 0x000000, 0);
    beginFill(0, 100);
    drawCircle(radius);
    endFill( );
  }
  this.minX = minX;
  this.minY = minY;
  this.maxX = maxX;
  this.maxY = maxY;
  this._x = Math.random( ) * this.maxX;
  this._y = Math.random( ) * this.maxY;
  if (vel == "random") {
    this.vel = Math.random( ) * 6 + 3;
  } else {
    this.vel = vel;
  }
  this.dir = Math.random( ) * Math.PI * 2;
  this.colObj = new Color(this);
  if (col == "random") {
    col = Math.random( ) * 255 * 255 * 255;
  }
  colObj.setRGB(col);
};
```

```
// The setCircleArray( ) method allows you to define an array of references to
// all the circle instances.
CircleClass.prototype.setCircleArray = function (cirAr) {
  this.circleArray = cirAr;
};

CircleClass.prototype.onEnterFrame = function ( ) {
  this._x += Math.cos(this.dir) * this.vel;
  this._y += Math.sin(this.dir) * this.vel;
  if ((this._x + this._width/2) >= this.maxX) {
    this._x = this.maxX - this._width/2 - 1;
    this.dir += 2 * (Math.PI/2 - this.dir);
  }
  else if ((this._x - this._width/2)<= this.minX) {
    this._x = this.minX + this._width/2 + 1;
    this.dir += 2 * (Math.PI/2 - this.dir);
  }
  if ((this._y + this._height/2) >= this.maxY) {
    this._y = this.maxY - this._height/2 - 1;
    this.dir -= 2*this.dir;
  }
  else if ((this._y - this._height/2) <= this.minY) {
    this._y = this.minY + this._height/2 + 1;
    this.dir -= 2*this.dir;
  }

  // Loop through all the elements in the circle array and determine if the
  // circle has collided with any of them.
  for (var i = 0; i < this.circleArray.length; i++) {
    cirB = this.circleArray[i];

    // Get the distance between the two circles using the Pythagorean theorem
    // (see Recipe 5.13).
    var dx = Math.abs(this._x - cirB._x);
    var dy = Math.abs(this._y - cirB._y);
    var dist = Math.sqrt(Math.pow(dx, 2) + Math.pow(dy, 2));

    // If the distance between the two circles is less than the sum of their
    // radii, they have collided. Also, make sure the current circle is not this
    // because you don't want to detect a circle's collision with itself!
    if(dist <= (this._width/2 + cirB._width/2) && cirB != this) {

      // This code sets the new directions for the colliding circles.
      var circlesAngle = Math.atan2(this._y - cirB._y, this._x - cirB._x) +
                              Math.PI/2;
      this.dir = (circlesAngle + this.dir)/2;
      cirB.dir = (-circlesAngle + cirB.dir)/2;
    }
  }
};

Object.registerClass("CircleSymbol", CircleClass);

#endinitclip
```

3. Modify the code on the first frame of the main timeline as follows (changes in bold):

```
#include "DrawingMethods.as"

// Place the code in a function to keep things organized as you add more
// functionality in the subsequent stages.
function initCircles() {

    // Create a movie clip to contain all the circle instances.
    _root.createEmptyMovieClip("circleHolder", _root.getNewDepth());

    // Create an array to hold the references to all the circles.
    circles = new Array();

    // Create 10 circle instances. For each circle, store a reference to the circle
    // array and then add the circle instance to the array. This enables each
    // circle to reference all the other circles.
    for (i = 0; i < 10; i++) {
        cir = _root. CircleHolder.attachMovie("CircleSymbol", "circle" + i, i);
        cir.init(0, 0, 200, 200, "random", "random", 10);
        cir.setCircleArray(circles);
        circles.push(cir);
    }

    // Draw the border within the circle holder movie clip instead of on _root.
    circleHolder.createEmptyMovieClip("border", i);
    with (circleHolder.border) {
        lineStyle(0, 0, 100);
        drawRectangle(200, 200, 0, 0, 100, 100);
    }
}

initCircles();
```

The additional code in this stage of the application is rather straightforward. By creating an array of references to all of the circle instances, and assigning that array as a property of each circle, each circle can know about all the other instances. Then, within the *onEnterFrame()* method, you check whether the circle has collided with the rectangle boundaries or with any of the other circles. The only thing that might be unclear in this new code is the mathematics involved. Refer to Chapters 4 and 5, and draw a diagram of two colliding circles, and that will help to clarify the math. Save and test your movie to see how it works.

Stage Four

In the fourth stage of the application we want to add some buttons that allow the user to move the circles, as a group, as they bounce around. Also, we'll let the user scale and rotate the circles as a group. Here are the steps to follow to complete stage four:

1. Open *stage3.fla* and save it as *stage4.fla*.
2. Create a new movie clip symbol named *RectangleButton*.
3. Open the linkage properties for *RectangleButton*.
4. Check the Export for ActionScript and Export in First Frame options and add a linkage identifier of *RectangleButtonSymbol*.
5. Click OK to close the linkage properties.
6. Edit *RectangleButtonSymbol*.
7. Add the following code to the first frame of the default layer:

```
#initclip

function RectangleButtonClass () {}

RectangleButtonClass.prototype = new MovieClip();

RectangleButtonClass.prototype.init = function (label, col, w, h) {

  // If w (width) is undefined, default to 100; if h (height) is undefined,
  // default to 30; if col (for color) is undefined, default to 0xDFDFDF (light
  // gray); and if label is undefined default to "submit".
  w = (w == undefined) ? 100 : w;
  h = (h == undefined) ? 30 : h;
  col = (col == undefined) ? 0xDFDFDF : col;
  label = (label == undefined) ? "submit" : label;

  // Create a movie clip into which to draw the rectangle button.
  this.createEmptyMovieClip("btn", 1);

  // Create a label text field. Use createAutoTextField() to make the text field
  // autosize. (You will include TextField.as from Chapter 8 on the main
  // timeline.)
  this.createAutoTextField("label", 2);

  // Make the text field nonselectable so it doesn't interfere with the button.
  this.label.selectable = false;
  this.label.text = label;

  // If the label text field's width is greater than w, reassign a value to w to
  // accommodate the text field.
  w = (this.label._width > w) ? this.label._width + 6 : w;

  // Draw a rectangle in the btn movie clip. (You will include MovieClip.as from
  // Chapter 7 on the main timeline.)
  with (this.btn) {
    lineStyle(0, 0x000000, 0);
    beginFill(col);
    drawRectangle(w, h);
    endFill();
```

```
      _x += w/2;
      _y += h/2;
    }

    // Center the label within the button.
    this.label._x = this._width/2 - this.label._width/2;
    this.label._y = this._height/2 - this.label._height/2;

    // When the btn clip is pressed and released, scale it to create an effect.
    this.btn.onPress = function () {
      this._xscale = 96;
      this._yscale = 96;
    }
    this.btn.onRelease = function () {
      this._xscale = 100;
      this._yscale = 100;
    }
  };

  Object.registerClass("RectangleButtonSymbol", RectangleButtonClass);

  #endinitclip
```

8. Edit the code on the first frame of the main timeline and make the modifications shown here (changes are in bold):

```
// Include DrawingMethods.as from Chapter 4 and MovieClip.as from Chapter 7.
#include "DrawingMethods.as"
#include "MovieClip.as"

// Include the libraries for the table and text field custom methods.
// TextField.as is from Chapter 8, and Table.as is from Chapter 11.
#include "TextField.as"
#include "Table.as"

function initCircles () {
  circles = new Array();
  _root.createEmptyMovieClip("circleHolder", _root.getNewDepth());
  for (var i = 0; i < 10; i++) {
    cir = circleHolder.attachMovie("CircleSymbol", "circle" + i,
                        circleHolder.getNewDepth());
    cir.init(0, 0, 200, 200, Math.random() * 3 + 3, "random", 10);
    cir.setCircleArray(circles);
    circles.push(cir);
  }
  circleHolder.createEmptyMovieClip("border", circleHolder.getNewDepth());
  with (circleHolder.border) {
    lineStyle(0, 0x000000, 100);
    drawRectangle(200, 200, 0, 0, 100, 100);
  }

  // Add an onEnterFrame() method to circleHolder that makes changes to the
  // movie clip's properties depending on what button has been pressed.
  circleHolder.onEnterFrame = function () {
    var vel = 5;
```

```
      switch (this.action) {
        case "up":
          this._y -= vel;
          break;
        case "down":
          this._y += vel;
          break;
        case "left":
          this._x -= vel;
          break;
        case "right":
          this._x += vel;
          break;
        case "rotateCW":
          this._rotation += vel;
          break;
        case "rotateCCW":
          this._rotation -= vel;
          break;
        case "scaleUp":
          this._xscale += vel;
          this._yscale += vel;
          break;
        case "scaleDown":
          this._xscale -= vel;
          this._yscale -= vel;
      }
    };
}


function initButtons () {

  // Create an array of names for the buttons.
  btnNamesAr = new Array("left", "right", "up", "down",
                        "scaleUp", "scaleDown", "rotateCW", "rotateCCW");

  // For each button in the array, create instances of the button component.
  for (var i = 0; i < btnNamesAr.length; i++) {
    btn = _root.attachMovie("RectangleButtonSymbol", btnNamesAr[i] + "Btn",
                        _root.getNewDepth( ));
    btn.init(btnNamesAr[i]);

    // Assign the button name to the action property for that button. This value
    // corresponds to the possible action values for the circleHolder within the
    // switch statement in its onEnterFrame( ) method.
    btn.action = btnNamesAr[i];

    // Assign onPress( ) and onRelease( ) functions for each button.
    btn.onPress = pressBtn;
    btn.onRelease = releaseBtn;
  }
}
```

```
// This function is assigned to the onPress() event handler method for all the
// buttons; it sets the action property of the circleHolder to the action
// property value for the button being pressed. This causes the corresponding
// action to take place for circleHolder.
function pressBtn () {
  _root.circleHolder.action = this.action;
}

// When a button is released, set the circleHolder's action property to null to
// stop the current action.
function releaseBtn () {
  _root.circleHolder.action = null;
}

// Create a table to position all the elements on the stage.
function createTable () {
  tr0 = new TableRow(5, new TableColumn(5, circleHolder));
  tr1 = new TableRow(5, new TableColumn(5, leftBtn, rightBtn, upBtn, downBtn),
                        new TableColumn(5, scaleUpBtn, scaleDownBtn),
                        new TableColumn(5, rotateCWBtn, rotateCCWBtn));
  t = new Table(5, 0, 0, tr0, tr1);
}

initCircles();
initButtons();
createTable();
```

There is a lot of new code added in stage four. Save the file, and let's take a look at some of the snippets that could use a little more explanation.

Within the *initCircles()* function, we added an *onEnterFrame()* method for the circleHolder movie clip. This is a technique you can use to create continuous changes to the movie clip's properties when a button is pressed. When you assign actions to an *onPress()* method for a button (or button movie clip in this case), that action occurs only once each time the button is pressed. For example, if you place code to increment a movie clip's _x property within the *onPress()* method, you have to click the button repeatedly to move the movie clip. If you want to use the button to continuously change some object's properties, then you need to come up with a different solution. In this case, you can use an *onEnterFrame()* method on circleHolder (the movie clip whose properties you want to change). Each button assigns a different value to the circleHolder's action property; using a *switch* statement, you can determine which property or properties to update for the movie clip.

```
circleHolder.onEnterFrame = function () {
  var vel = 5;
  switch (this.action) {
    case "up":
      this._y -= vel;
      break;
    case "down":
      this._y += vel;
      break;
```

```
      case "left":
        this._x -= vel;
        break;
      case "right":
        this._x += vel;
        break;
      case "rotateCW":
        this._rotation += vel;
        break;
      case "rotateCCW":
        this._rotation -= vel;
        break;
      case "scaleUp":
        this._xscale += vel;
        this._yscale += vel;
        break;
      case "scaleDown":
        this._xscale -= vel;
        this._yscale -= vel;
    }
  };
```

Next, you should create all the buttons. You can create the rectangle button component instances one at a time, or, more conveniently, you can use a *for* statement to
take care of this for you. In this example, we use an array to store all the button
names and then loop through that array and create a component instance for each
element. We pass the *init()* method the button name as a parameter so that its value
shows up in the button's label. You also should assign the name to the action
parameter of the component instance. You use this property value in the *onPress()*
method to determine which value to assign to the action property of the
circleHolder movie clip:

```
function initButtons( ) {
  btnNamesAr = new Array("left", "right", "up", "down",
                          "scaleUp", "scaleDown", "rotateCW", "rotateCCW");
  for (var i = 0; i < btnNamesAr.length; i++) {
    btn = _root.attachMovie("RectangleButtonSymbol", btnNamesAr[i] + "Btn",
                            _root.getNewDepth( ));
    btn.init(btnNamesAr[i]);
    btn.action = btnNamesAr[i];
    btn.onPress = pressBtn;
    btn.onRelease = releaseBtn;
  }
}
```

When a button is pressed, assign that button's action property value to the
circleHolder movie clip's action property. This sets into motion the corresponding
actions. On the other hand, when the button is released, set the circleHolder movie
clip's action property to null to stop the actions.

```
function pressBtn ( ) {
  _root.circleHolder.action = this.action;
```

```
}
function releaseBtn () {
  _root.circleHolder.action = null;
}
```

Stage Five

The final stage in this application is to use an XML file to load initialization data. Up to this point, we have hardcoded the number of circles as well as their properties (color, radius, and velocity) into the Flash document. However, you can create an XML document from which you can load all that data at runtime so that you can make changes to the movie without having to reexport the *.swf* file. Here are the steps you should complete to finish the fifth stage of the application:

1. Open a new text document and save it as *circles.xml* in the same directory as where you are saving your Flash documents.

2. Add the following content to your XML document and save it:
   ```xml
   <collisionMovieData>
     <!-- Define the dimensions of the rectangle within which circles can move. -->
     <bounceArea width="200" height="200" />

     <!-- Define the circles that should be created. In this example you create four
          circles with random velocities and colors and with various radii. -->
     <circles>
       <circle radius="30" vel="random" col="random" />
       <circle radius="5" vel="random" col="random" />
       <circle radius="24" vel="random" col="random" />
       <circle radius="10" vel="random" col="random" />
     </circles>
   </collisionMovieData>
   ```

3. Open *stage4.fla* and save it as *stage5.fla*.

4. Modify the code on the main timeline, as shown here (changes are in bold):
   ```
   #include "DrawingMethods.as"
   #include "MovieClip.as"
   #include "TextField.as"
   #include "Table.as"

   function loadData () {
     var myXML = new XML();
     myXML.ignoreWhite = true;

     // Load the XML data from the XML document.
     myXML.load("circles.xml");
     myXML.onLoad = function () {

       // Get the width and height attribute values from the <bounceArea> element.
       var bounceAreaWidth = this.firstChild.firstChild.attributes.width;
       var bounceAreaHeight = this.firstChild.firstChild.attributes.height;
   ```

```
    // Create an array to hold the values for each of the circles.
    var circlesInfo = new Array();

    // Get the array of the <circle> elements.
    var circlesNodes = this.firstChild.lastChild.childNodes;
    var atr;

    // Loop through all the <circle> elements, and add the
    // attributes object for each to the circlesInfo array.
    // The properties of the attributes object are vel, col, and dir.
    for (var i = 0; i < circlesNodes.length; i++) {
      circlesInfo.push(circlesNodes[i].attributes);
    }

    // Call the initCircles(), initButtons(), and createTable() functions only
    // once the data has loaded. Pass initCircles() the width and height for the
    // bounce area, and also pass it the circlesInfo array.
    _root.initCircles(bounceAreaWidth, bounceAreaHeight, circlesInfo);
    _root.initButtons();
    _root.createTable();
  };
}

// Modify initCircles() to accept parameters that define the width and height
// of the rectangle as well as an array of circle information objects.
function initCircles(baW, baH, circlesInfo) {
  circles = new Array();
  _root.createEmptyMovieClip("circleHolder", _root.getNewDepth());
  var cInfo;

  // Loop through all the circle information objects, and use those
  // values to create the circle component instances.
  for (var i = 0; i < circlesInfo.length; i++) {
    cInfo = circlesInfo[i];
    cir = circleHolder.attachMovie("CircleSymbol", "circle" + i,
                                   circleHolder.getNewDepth());
    cir.init(0, 0, baW, baH, cInfo.vel, cInfo.col, cInfo.radius);
    cir.setCircleArray(circles);
    circles.push(cir);
  }
  circleHolder.createEmptyMovieClip("border", circleHolder.getNewDepth());
  with (circleHolder.border) {
    lineStyle(0, 0x000000, 100);
    drawRectangle(baW, baH, 0, 0, baW/2, baH/2);
  }
  circleHolder.onEnterFrame = function () {
    var vel = 5;
    switch (this.action) {
      case "up":
        this._y -= vel;
        break;
      case "down":
        this._y += vel;
        break;
      case "left":
```

```
            this._x -= vel;
            break;
          case "right":
            this._x += vel;
            break;
          case "rotateCW":
            this._rotation += vel;
            break;
          case "rotateCCW":
            this._rotation -= vel;
            break;
          case "scaleUp":
            this._xscale += vel;
            this._yscale += vel;
            break;
          case "scaleDown":
            this._xscale -= vel;
            this._yscale -= vel;
        }
    };
}

function initButtons () {
  btnNamesAr = new Array("left", "right", "up", "down",
                         "scaleUp", "scaleDown", "rotateCW", "rotateCCW");
  for (var i = 0; i < btnNamesAr.length; i++) {
    btn = _root.attachMovie("RectangleButtonSymbol", btnNamesAr[i] + "Btn",
                            _root.getNewDepth( ));
    btn.init(btnNamesAr[i]);
    btn.action = btnNamesAr[i];
    btn.onPress = pressBtn;
    btn.onRelease = releaseBtn;
  }
}


function pressBtn () {
  _root.circleHolder.action = this.action;
}

function releaseBtn () {
  _root.circleHolder.action = null;
}


function createTable () {
  tr0 = new TableRow(5, new TableColumn(5, circleHolder));
  tr1 = new TableRow(5, new TableColumn(5, leftBtn, rightBtn, upBtn, downBtn),
                        new TableColumn(5, scaleUpBtn, scaleDownBtn),
                        new TableColumn(5, rotateCWBtn, rotateCCWBtn));
  t = new Table(5, 0, 0, tr0, tr1);
}
```

```
// Call loadData( ) instead of the other three functions. The other
// functions are now called once the data has loaded.
loadData( );
```

Save the file and test it. There are really only two changes that we have made in this
stage of the application. First of all, rather than hardcode the data into the Flash document, we use an XML object to load the data into the movie at runtime. You don't
want to initialize the movie until after the data has loaded, so you should invoke the
initCircles(), *initButtons()*, and *createTable()* functions from within the *XML* object's
onLoad() method. Additionally, you want to extract values from the XML data and
pass those values along to the *initCircles()* function. The bounceAreaWidth and
bounceAreaHeight values are rather self-evident. The circlesInfo array, on the other
hand, might not be immediately clear. You want to construct an array in which each
element represents the properties (color, velocity, and radius) of the circles that are
defined in the XML document. This is rather convenient because each of the
<circle> elements contains an associative array with those three properties (the
attributes of the XML element). So you can use the *push()* method to append the
value of each <circle> element's attributes property to the circlesInfo array.

```
myXML.onLoad = function ( ) {
  var bounceAreaWidth = this.firstChild.firstChild.attributes.width;
  var bounceAreaHeight = this.firstChild.firstChild.attributes.height;
  var circlesInfo = new Array( );
  var circlesNodes = this.firstChild.lastChild.childNodes;
  var atr;
  for (var i = 0; i < circlesNodes.length; i++) {
    circlesInfo.push(circlesNodes[i].attributes);
  }
  _root.initCircles(bounceAreaWidth, bounceAreaHeight, circlesInfo);
  _root.initButtons( );
  _root.createTable( );
};
```

Then you need to make a small modification to the *initCircles()* function so that it
accepts and uses the parameters loaded from the XML data. Not much needs to
change. The hardcoded values for each circle's color, velocity, and radius should be
replaced by the values from the circlesInfo array, and the hardcoded values that
previously defined the width and height of the bounce area rectangle should be
replaced by the parameters baW and baH:

```
for (var i = 0; i < circlesInfo.length; i++) {
  cInfo = circlesInfo[i];
  cir = circleHolder.attachMovie("CircleSymbol", "circle" + i,
      circleHolder.getNewDepth( ));
  cir.init(0, 0, baW, baH, cInfo.vel, cInfo.col, cInfo.radius);
  cir.setCircleArray(circles);
  circles.push(cir);
}
```

```
circleHolder.createEmptyMovieClip("border", circleHolder.getNewDepth());
with (circleHolder.border) {
  lineStyle(0, 0x000000, 100);
  drawRectangle(baW, baH, 0, 0, baW/2, baH/2);
}
```

Conclusion

We've seen a realistic example of the multistage process characteristic of software development. At each stage, we added features and refined existing features, building on our prior work. As we developed the application, you may have identified features you'd like to add or other applications in which you can use similar techniques. This chapter introduced you to an approach that can serve you well in future software development, which is usually an iterative process. Think of it as an example of how to break down a large problem into smaller problems. Practice the techniques the chapter demonstrates, such as the ability to create components, reuse code, etc.

## CHAPTER 24

Video Chat/Message Center

Flash Communication Server MX is a technology that enables real-time communication between Flash clients and the FlashCom server. Equally important is that FlashCom enables Flash clients to publish (record or send a live stream) and subscribe to audio and video streams. The video chat/message center application in this chapter takes advantage of a wide range of FlashCom functionality. It builds on the FlashCom-related recipes of Chapter 14.

The video chat/message center application is a video version of a telephone/voice mail system. In this application a user (the administrator) can open up a client to the FlashCom application and receive live video calls from calling clients. Additionally, if the administrator is offline, currently on another call, or otherwise unavailable, the calling client has the option to record a video message, which the administrator can retrieve and play back at a later time.

The completes files can be downloaded from *http://www.person13.com/ascb*.

Developing the Application Overview

The video chat/message center application, perhaps more than any of the others in this book, requires good planning. This is because this application requires three parts that must work in tight coordination:

The administrator client
> The administrator is the person who receives incoming calls and can listen to messages that callers have left. You need to create a client that can accept incoming calls and retrieve messages from the FlashCom server.

The caller 4client
> Many callers can attempt to call the one administrator. The caller client should enable a caller to place a call to the administrator. If the administrator is not logged in, is on another call, or simply doesn't accept the incoming call, the caller should be able to leave a video message.

The server-side application file

The server-side part of the FlashCom application has a lot of work to do as well. It is responsible for keeping track of who is connected, who is calling, who is leaving messages, etc. This portion of the application is the main switchboard that keeps everything in order. In this application, we keep all the server-side code in a single ASC file.

Creating the Server-Side Application

The server-side portion of the video chat/message center application is contained within a single ASC file, *main.asc*. Here are the steps necessary to create the server-side part of this application:

1. Create a new FlashCom application named *CommunicationCenterApp*. You can do this by making a new directory with this name inside of the FlashCom server's *applications* directory.

2. Create a new file inside of the *CommunicationCenterApp* directory. Name the file *main.asc*.

3. Add the following code to *main.asc*:

```
// The application.onConnect( ) method is invoked each time a new client connects
// to the application. The newClient parameter is a FlashCom-generated reference
// to the new client. The username parameter is a value passed to the method by
// the Flash client.
application.onConnect = function (newClient, username, password) {

    newClient.username = username;
    newClient.password = password;

    // The acceptClient( ) function accepts the client and assigns methods to the
    // client object according to the user type.
    acceptClient(newClient);
};

// The application.onDisconnect( ) method is automatically invoked whenever a
// client disconnects from the application.
application.onDisconnect = function (disconnectClient) {

    // If the client who has disconnected was on a call with the administrator,
    // release that connection by setting the callingClient property to null. Also,
    // if the administrator is still online, invoke the incomingCallEnd( ) method
    // in the administrator client to clean up things on that end.
    if (application.callingClient == disconnectClient) {
        application.callingClient = null;
        if (application.admin != undefined) {
            application.admin.call("incomingCallEnd", null);
        }
    }
}
```

```
// If the client who has disconnected happens to be the administrator, take
// care of the necessary loose ends.
if (application.admin = disconnectClient) {

  // If the administrator was on a call, alert the calling client that the call
  // has ended.
  if (application.callingClient != null) {
    application.callingClient.call("adminEndCall", null);
  }

  // Set callingClient to null and delete the admin property since there are no
  // more active calls and no administrator logged in.
  application.callingClient = null;
  delete application.admin;
  }
};

// When the application first starts, this method is invoked automatically to
// initialize necessary application properties.
application.onAppStart = function () {

  // The callingClient property is assigned a reference to the client object when
  // a client is on a call with the administrator.
  application.callingClient = null;

  // The messages shared object is a remote shared object (RSO) that contains all
  // the messages that have been left for the administrator.
  application.messagesSO = SharedObject.get("messages", true);

  // The messageNum property of the shared object is used to guarantee unique
  // message numbers. If the property doesn't exist, initialize it to 0.
  if (application.messagesSO.getProperty("messageNum") == undefined) {
    application.messagesSO.setProperty("messageNum", 0);
  }
};

// The acceptClient() function is invoked from
// the application.onConnect() method.
function acceptClient(newClient) {

  // Make sure a calling client doesn't try to log in with the username "admin".
  if (newClient.username == "admin" && newClient.password != "adminPass") {
    application.rejectConnection(newClient);
    return;
  }

  // Accept all other client connections.
  application.acceptConnection(newClient);

  // Set the methods available to the client objects.
  newClient.recordMessageInfo = recordMessageInfo;
  newClient.getMessageID = getMessageID;
  newClient.placeCall = placeCall;
  newClient.endCall = endCall;
```

```
    // If the client is the administrator client,
    // then take care of a few other tasks.
    if (newClient.username == "admin") {
      // Set the admin property to a reference to the connecting client object.
      application.admin = newClient;

      // Set a few administrator-only client methods.
      newClient.acceptIncomingCall = acceptIncomingCall;
      newClient.sendToLeaveMessage = sendToLeaveMessage;
      newClient.removeMessage = removeMessage;
    }
}

// This function is a method assigned to the administrator client. When this
// method is invoked, the administrator has accepted an incoming call, and the
// acceptCall() method on the calling client is invoked.
function acceptIncomingCall () {
  application.callingClient.call("acceptCall", null);
}

// This function is a method assigned to the administrator client. It is invoked
// when the administrator does not answer an incoming call.
function sendToLeaveMessage () {
  application.callingClient.call("notAvailable", null);
  application.callingClient = null;
}

// The placeCall() function is assigned to clients as a method. This method is
// invoked when a client attempts to call the administrator.
function placeCall () {

  // If the administrator is logged in and if there is not already another call
  // in place, invoke the onIncomingCall() method on the administrator client to
  // alert the user that there is an incoming call. Otherwise, alert the calling
  // client that the administrator is not available for a call right now.
  if (application.admin != undefined && application.callingClient == null) {
    application.admin.call("onIncomingCall", null, this.username);
    application.callingClient = this;
  } else {
    this.call("notAvailable", null);
  }
}

// The endCall() function is a method of all clients,
// and it ends the current call by invoking methods on
// both the calling client and the administrator client.
function endCall () {
  application.callingClient("adminEndCall", null);
  application.callingClient = null;
  application.admin.call("incomingCallEnd", null);
}
```

```
// The recordMessageInfo( ) function is a method of the calling clients, and it
// is invoked when the user records a new message so that the information about
// the message (such as username and time and date) can be stored as well.
function recordMessageInfo(id) {

  // Get the messages array property of the messages shared object. If the
  // property is undefined, create the array.
  var messages = application.messagesSO.getProperty("messages");
  if (messages == undefined) {
    messages = new Array( );
  }

  // Create an object that contains the message id, username, and the date when
  // the message was recorded. Add this object to the messages array.
  var infoObj = {id: id, username: this.username, dateTime: new Date( )};
  messages.push(infoObj);

  // Add the updated info back to the shared object and write the data to disk.
  application.messagesSO.setProperty("messages", messages);
  application.messagesSO.flush( );
}

// The removeMessage( ) function is a method of the administrator client, and it
// allows the administrator to remove recorded messages.
function removeMessage(streamName) {

  // Use the Stream.get( ) method to get a reference to the stream on the server.
  var messageStream = Stream.get(streamName);

  // Use the clear( ) method to delete the stream.
  messageStream.clear( );

  // Get the messages property of the shared object, and loop through it to find
  // the information for the stream that has been deleted. When the message
  // information is found, delete it with a splice( ) method.
  var messages = application.messagesSO.getProperty("messages");
  for (var i = 0; i < messages.length; i++) {
    if ("message" + messages[i].id == streamName) {
      messages.splice(i, 1);
      break;
    }
  }

  // Update the shared object and write it to disk.
  application.messagesSO.setProperty("messages", messages);
  application.messagesSO.flush( );
}

// The getMessageID( ) function returns a unique message number.
function getMessageID ( ) {
  // Get the messageNum property from the shared object and increment the value
  // stored in the shared object.
  var messageNum = application.messagesSO.getProperty("messageNum");
```

```
      application.messagesSO.setProperty("messageNum", messageNum + 1);
      application.messagesSO.flush( );
      return messageNum;
   }
```

The ASC file contains a lot of code, but fortunately, most of it is not very complex once you familiarize yourself with it. Let's look at some of the code with a little more explanation as to what is going on and why.

The *onConnect()* method is a method that FlashCom automatically invokes when a new client connects to the application. FlashCom creates a new client object and passes a reference to the object as a parameter to the *onConnect()* method. In addition, we pass two custom parameters: a username and a password. The username is important because it helps the application keep track of what kinds of users are logged in (calling clients or an administrator). The password is null in the case of all calling clients, but it has the value of "adminPass" in the case of the administrator (this is something you will hardcode into the administrator client movie). The password is important because it helps to prevent a calling client from logging in with the username of "admin" (which is the username we use for the administrator).

```
   application.onConnect = function (newClient, username, password) {
      newClient.username = username;
      newClient.password = password;
      acceptClient(newClient);
   };
```

Analogous to the *onConnect()* method, the *onDisconnect()* method is invoked each time a client disconnects from the application. As with the *onConnect()* method, FlashCom passes a parameter to *onDisconnect()* that references the client who has just disconnected. The *onDisconnect()* method is important in this application only when the disconnecting client was on a live call. The server needs to know that the call has ended so it can alert the other client that the call has ended and can set the correct values for properties it uses to track the call status. When the administrator is online, the application keeps track of the administrator using a property named admin. And when a call is in progress, the calling client object is stored as a property named callingClient. See the *acceptClient()* function for more on these two properties.

Therefore, if the disconnecting client happens to be the same client that is stored as the calling client, set the calling client to null (since there is no longer a calling client connected) and invoke a method on the administrator client to tell it that the call has ended. Alternatively, if the disconnecting client is the administrator, invoke a method on any calling client to let it know that the call has ended. Also, it is important to set callingClient to null and delete the admin property so that the application knows who is logged in and what the call status is.

```
   application.onDisconnect = function (disconnectClient) {
      if (application.callingClient == disconnectClient) {
         application.callingClient = null;
```

```
      if (application.admin != undefined) {
        application.admin.call("incomingCallEnd", null);
      }
    }
    if (application.admin = disconnectClient) {
      if (application.callingClient != null) {
        application.callingClient.call("adminEndCall", null);
      }
      application.callingClient = null;
      delete application.admin;
    }
};
```

The *onAppStart()* method is automatically invoked once when the application starts. So this is where you should place actions that should occur only once. Initialize the callingClient property to null (since there is no call in progress when the application is first started) and get a remote shared object for the application to store information about messages left for the administrator. If the shared object has not been created (the first time the application runs), initialize a messageNum property, which the application uses to make sure each message is assigned a unique ID.

```
application.onAppStart = function () {
  application.callingClient = null;
  application.messagesSO = SharedObject.get("messages", true);
  if (application.messagesSO.getProperty("messageNum") == undefined) {
    application.messagesSO.setProperty("messageNum", 0);
  }
};
```

The *acceptClient()* function is invoked by the *onConnect()* method every time a new client connects to the application. You should make sure that the client has not tried to log in with the username "admin", unless it is accompanied by the password "adminPass". The calling clients are not asked for a password when they log in, so the password will be undefined. The administrator password is hardcoded into the administrator client movie. So if a calling client tries to log in with the username "admin", reject the connection and exit from the function. Otherwise, accept the connection and assign methods to the client object. If the client is the administrator, also assign some administrator-only methods to the object and assign the client object reference to the admin property. The admin property does two things. First, it lets the application know that the administrator is online (so users can place calls). Second, it gives you a convenient way to invoke methods on the administrator client throughout the server-side code.

```
function acceptClient (newClient) {
  if (newClient.username == "admin" && newClient.password != "adminPass") {
    application.rejectConnection(newClient);
    return;
  }
  application.acceptConnection(newClient);
  newClient.recordMessageInfo = recordMessageInfo;
  newClient.getMessageID = getMessageID;
```

```
newClient.placeCall = placeCall;
newClient.endCall = endCall;
if (newClient.username == "admin") {
  application.admin = newClient;
  newClient.acceptIncomingCall = acceptIncomingCall;
  newClient.sendToLeaveMessage = sendToLeaveMessage;
  newClient.removeMessage = removeMessage;
}
}
```

The *recordMessageInfo()* function is assigned as a method of client objects, and it is
invoked when the calling client leaves a message. Although the video and audio portion of the message is published completely from the client, this server-side function
records information about the message into a remote shared object. This is important because it allows the administrator to retrieve a list of messages. Each entry in
the shared object contains the unique message ID, the username of the client leaving
the message, and the date and time when the message was recorded.

```
function recordMessageInfo (id) {
  var messages = application.messagesSO.getProperty("messages");
  if (messages == undefined) {
    messages = new Array();
  }
  var infoObj = {id: id, username: this.username, dateTime: new Date()};
  messages.push(infoObj);
  application.messagesSO.setProperty("messages", messages);
  application.messagesSO.flush();
}
```

The *removeMessage()* function is a method of the administrator client object, and it
removes a data stream (the FLV file) from the server when the administrator chooses
that option. The client passes the name of the stream to this method and, using the
Stream.get() method, retrieves a server-side reference to the stream. Then the *clear()*
method removes the stream from the server. However, you also need to remove the
message information from the shared object so that it no longer appears in the
administrator's list of messages. Do this by looping through all the elements of the
messages array until you find the matching entry. Then use the *splice()* method to
remove that element, break out of the *for* loop, and save the updated information
back to the shared object.

```
function removeMessage (streamName) {
  var messageStream = Stream.get(streamName);
  messageStream.clear();
  var messages = application.messagesSO.getProperty("messages");
  for (var i = 0; i < messages.length; i++) {
    if ("message" + messages[i].id == streamName) {
      messages.splice(i, 1);
      break;
    }
  }
  application.messagesSO.setProperty("messages", messages);
  application.messagesSO.flush();
}
```

Creating the Calling Client

The calling client should include the following functionality:

- The user should be asked to log in before connecting to the FlashCom application and being allowed to place a call.
- When the client first connects, the user should be presented with a button that enables him to place a call.
- If the administrator is not online or otherwise cannot accept the call, the Place Call button should change to a Record button to allow the user to record a message.
- If the user's call is accepted by the administrator, the client should display the video from both the calling client and the administrator client. Additionally, the client should play the audio from the administrator. The button should change to an End Call button, so the user can end the call.

Here are the steps to follow to create the calling client:

1. Create a new Flash document named *callingClient.fla* and open it.
2. Add the PushButton component symbol to the Library. You can do this by dragging an instance of the push button to the Stage and then deleting it.
3. Add a new video symbol by choosing New Video from the Library panel's pop-up Options menu.
4. Create a new movie clip symbol named *videoMc*.
5. Edit *videoMc*, and create an instance of the video symbol within it so that the video symbol instance is placed at (0,0).
6. Name the video symbol instance vid.
7. Open the linkage properties for *videoMc*.
8. Select the Export for ActionScript and Export on First Frame options and set the linkage identifier to *VideoMcSymbol*.
9. Add the following code to the first frame of the main timeline:

```
// NetDebug.as is part of Flash Remoting.
#include "NetDebug.as"

// Include MovieClip.as from Chapter 7 and TextField.as from Chapter 8.
#include "MovieClip.as"
#include "TextField.as"

// Include Table.as and Forms.as from Chapter 11.
#include "Table.as"
#include "Forms.as"

// Create the login form.
function createLoginForm () {
```

```
// Create a login button.
_root.attachMovie("FPushButtonSymbol", "loginBtn", _root.getNewDepth( ));
loginBtn.setLabel("login");

// When the user clicks the button to log in, connect the user to the FlashCom
// application.
loginBtn.onRelease = function ( ) {
  var un = _root.usernameField.text;
  _root.username = un;

  // Connect the user only if she has entered a username.
  if (un != "") {
    myConnection.connect("rtmp:/communicationCenterApp/", un);
  }
};

// Create a label for the input text field.
_root.createAutoTextField("usernameLabel", _root.getNewDepth( ));
usernameLabel.text = "username: ";

// Create the input text field for the user to enter a username.
_root.createInputTextField("usernameField", _root.getNewDepth( ));

// Use a table to position the elements.
f0tr0 = new TableRow(5, new TableColumn(5, usernameLabel),
                        new TableColumn(5, usernameField));
f0tr1 = new TableRow(5, new TableColumn(5, loginBtn));
form0Table = new Table(5, 100, 100, f0tr0, f0tr1);

// Add the elements to a form.
form0 = new Form( );
form0.addElement(usernameLabel);
form0.addElement(usernameField);
form0.addElement(loginBtn);
}

// Create the form for the main screen.
function createMainForm ( ) {

  // Create clips for displaying the calling client's and administrator's videos.
  _root.attachMovie("videoMcSymbol", "localVideoMc", _root.getNewDepth( ));
  _root.attachMovie("videoMcSymbol", "remoteVideoMc", _root.getNewDepth( ));

  // Create a button so the user can place a call.
  _root.attachMovie("FPushButtonSymbol", "makeCallBtn", _root.getNewDepth( ));
  makeCallBtn.setLabel("place call");
  makeCallBtn.setClickHandler("placeCall");

  // Position the items using a table.
  f1tr0 = new TableRow(5, new TableColumn(5, makeCallBtn));
  f1tr1 = new TableRow(5, new TableColumn(5, localVideoMc),
                          new TableColumn(5, remoteVideoMc));
  form1Table = new Table(5, 100, 100, f1tr0, f1tr1);
```

```
  // Add the elements to a form.
  form1 = new Form( );
  form1.addElement(makeCallBtn);
  form1.addElement(localVideoMc);
  form1.addElement(remoteVideoMc);
}

// Create a multipage form so that only the login screen or the main application
// screen is visible at once.
function createMultiForm ( ) {
  mForm = new MultiPageForm(form0, form1);
  mForm.setPage(1);
}

myConnection = new NetConnection( );

// When the user successfully connects to the FlashCom application, display the
// main application form.
myConnection.onStatus = function (infoObject) {
  if (infoObject.code == "NetConnection.Connect.Success") {
    _root.mForm.setPage(2);
  }
};

// The acceptCall( ) method is invoked by the FlashCom application when the
// administrator accepts a call.
myConnection.acceptCall = function ( ) {
  _root.doLiveCall( );
};

// The adminEndCall( ) method is invoked when the administrator disconnects or
// otherwise ends the call.
myConnection.adminEndCall = function ( ) {
  _root.endCall( );
};

// The notAvailable( ) method is invoked when the
// administrator does not accept the call. When this occurs,
// modify the button so that the user can record a message.
myConnection.notAvailable = function ( ) {
  _root.makeCallBtn.setLabel("start recording");
  _root.makeCallBtn.setClickHandler("startRecord");
};

// The placeCall( ) function is one of the
// button's callback functions. It invokes the
// server-side placeCall( ) method to place a call to the administrator.
function placeCall ( ) {
  myConnection.call("placeCall", null);
}
```

```
// The response object for when the FlashCom application returns a message ID.
messageIDRes = new Object( );
messageIDRes.onResult = function (result) {
  _root.doRecord(result);
};

// The startRecord( ) function is one of the callback functions for the button,
// and it initiates the process for recording a message. The getMessageID( )
// method on the server is invoked to get a new message ID, and the result is
// returned to the messageIDRes response object.
function startRecord(pb) {
  pb.setLabel("stop recording");
  pb.setClickHandler("stopRecord");
  myConnection.call("getMessageID", messageIDRes);
}

// The doLiveCall( ) function is invoked when the administrator accepts a call.
function doLiveCall ( ) {

  // Create the net stream to publish the calling client's video and audio.
  livePublishNs = new NetStream(myConnection);
  livePublishNs.attachVideo(Camera.get( ));
  livePublishNs.attachAudio(Microphone.get( ));
  livePublishNs.publish(username + "live", "live");

  // Create the net stream to subscribe to the administrator's video and audio.
  liveSubscribeNs = new NetStream(myConnection);
  liveSubscribeNs.play("adminLive");

  // Add the local video to the local video object and add the administrator's
  // video to the remote video object.
  localVideoMc.vid.attachVideo(Camera.get( ));
  remoteVideoMc.vid.attachVideo(liveSubscribeNs);

  // Modify the button behavior to allow the user to end the call.
  makeCallBtn.setLabel("end call");
  makeCallBtn.setClickHandler("endCall");
}

// The endCall( ) function is invoked when a call is ended by either the calling
// client or the administrator.
function endCall ( ) {

  // Reset the button so the user can place another call.
  makeCallBtn.setLabel("place call");
  makeCallBtn.setClickHandler("placeCall");

  // Clear all the videos and net streams.
  livePublishNs.publish(false);
  livePublishNs.close( );
  liveSubscribeNs.close( );
  localVideoMc.vid.attachVideo(null);
  localVideoMc.vid.attachVideo(null);
```

```
    remoteVideoMc.vid.clear();
    localVideoMc.vid.clear();

    // Call the endCall() method on the server.
    myConnection.call("endCall", null);
}

// The doRecord() function is invoked after a new message ID is returned from
// the server.
function doRecord(id) {

    // Create a net stream and attach the audio and video to it.
    publishNs = new NetStream(myConnection);
    publishNs.attachVideo(Camera.get());
    publishNs.attachAudio(Microphone.get());

    // Publish a recorded stream.
    publishNs.publish("message" + id, "record");

    // Invoke the recordMessageInfo() method on the server.
    myConnection.call("recordMessageInfo", null, id);

    // Display the camera locally so the user can see what is being recorded.
    localVideoMc.vid.attachVideo(Camera.get());
}

// The stopRecord() function is invoked when the user clicks on the button to
// stop recording a message.
function stopRecord(pb) {

    // Clear the video and net stream.
    publishNs.attachVideo(null);
    publishNs.publish(false);
    publishNs.close();
    pb.setLabel("placeCall");
    pb.setClickHandler("placeCall");
    localVideoMc.vid.attachVideo(null);
    localVideoMc.vid.clear();
}

createLoginForm();
createMainForm();
createMultiForm();
```

Although there is a lot of code in the client, most of it is nothing you haven't seen before. There are two forms that you create and between which you can switch using a multipage form object. The remainder of the code is primarily user-initiated invocations of server-side functions.

Creating the Administrator Client

The administrator client should include the following functionality:

- The administrator should be able to view a list of available messages that have been left.
- The administrator should be able to play and/or delete messages.
- The administrator should be alerted when there is an incoming call and should be able to accept or ignore the call.
- If the administrator accepts a call, she should be able to end the call by clicking on a button.

Complete the following steps to make the administrator client movie:

1. Create a new Flash document named *adminClient.fla* and open it.
2. Add the PushButton and ListBox component symbols to the Library by creating an instance of each on the Stage and then deleting them.
3. Add a new video symbol by choosing New Video from the Library panel's pop-up Options menu.
4. Create a new movie clip symbol named *videoMc*.
5. Edit *videoMc* and create an instance of the video symbol within it so that the video symbol instance is placed at (0,0).
6. Name the video symbol instance vid.
7. Open the linkage properties for *videoMc*.
8. Select the Export for ActionScript and Export on First Frame options and set the linkage identifier to *VideoMcSymbol*.
9. Add the following code to the first frame of the main timeline:

```
// NetDebug.as is part of Flash Remoting.
#include "NetDebug.as"

// Include MovieClip.as from Chapter 7 and Date.as from Chapter 10.
#include "MovieClip.as"
#include "Date.as"

// Include Table.as and Forms.as from Chapter 11.
#include "Table.as"
#include "Forms.as"

// Include DrawingMethods.as from Chapter 4.
#include "DrawingMethods.as"

function init () {
    // Create a net connection and connect to the FlashCom application as the
    // administrator (username = "admin", password = "adminPass").
    myConnection = new NetConnection();
    myConnection.connect("rtmp:/communicationCenterApp/", "admin", "adminPass");
```

```
    // Once the connection has been made successfully, invoke initMessagesList().
    myConnection.onStatus = function (infoObject) {
      if (infoObject.code == "NetConnection.Connect.Success") {
        _root.initMessagesList(this);
      }
    };

    // The onIncomingCall() method is invoked from the server when a calling
    // client places a call to the administrator.
    myConnection.onIncomingCall = function (username) {
      _root.incomingCallUser = username;

      // Make the incoming call button visible.
      _root.incomingCallBtn._visible = true;

      // Create an interval on which the notifyIncomingCall() function is called.
      _root.incomingCallInterval = setInterval(_root, "notifyIncomingCall",
                                        1000, getTimer());
    }

    // This method is invoked when a call is ended.
    myConnection.incomingCallEnd = function () {
      // Delete the incoming caller name and clear the videos and net streams.
      delete _root.incomingCallUser;
      _root.livePublishNs.publish(false);
      _root.livePublishNs.close();
      _root.liveSubscribeNs.close();
      _root.incomingVideoMc.vid.attachVideo(null);
      _root.localVideoMc.vid.attachVideo(null);
      _root.imcomingVideoMc.vid.clear();
      _root.localVideoMc.vid.clear();
    };

  createForm();
}

// The createForm() function creates all the movie clip/component/symbol
// instances and positions them.
function createForm () {

  // Add the list box to display the list of available messages.
  _root.attachMovie("FListBoxSymbol", "messageList", _root.getNewDepth());

  // Create the video instance for the incoming calls.
  _root.attachMovie("videoMcSymbol", "incomingVideoMc", _root.getNewDepth());

  // Add a push button instance that enables the administrator to accept an
  // incoming call.
  _root.attachMovie("FPushButtonSymbol", "incomingCallBtn",
                  _root.getNewDepth());

  // Create a movie clip containing a small, green circle used to alert the
  // administrator of an incoming call.
  _root.createEmptyMovieClip("callLight", _root.getNewDepth());
```

```
with (callLight) {
  lineStyle(0, 0, 0);
  beginFill(0x00FF00, 100);
  drawCircle(5);
  endFill( );
}
callLight._visible = false;

incomingCallBtn.setLabel("incoming call");
incomingCallBtn._visible = false;
incomingCallBtn.setClickHandler("acceptCall");

// Create the videos for displaying the messages
// and for monitoring the local camera stream during calls.
_root.attachMovie("videoMcSymbol", "messageVideoMc", _root.getNewDepth( ));
_root.attachMovie("videoMcSymbol", "localVideoMc", _root.getNewDepth( ));

// Create buttons for playing and removing messages.
_root.attachMovie("FPushButtonSymbol", "playBtn", _root.getNewDepth( ));
_root.attachMovie("FPushButtonSymbol", "removeBtn", _root.getNewDepth( ));
playBtn.setClickHandler("viewMessage");
playBtn.setLabel("play message");
removeBtn.setClickHandler("removeMessage");
removeBtn.setLabel("remove message");

// Use a table to position all the elements.
tr0 = new TableRow(5, new TableColumn(5, messagelist, playBtn, removeBtn),
                   new TableColumn(5, messageVideoMc));
tr1 = new TableRow(5, new TableColumn(5, incomingVideoMc),
                   new TableColumn(5, localVideoMc));
tr2 = new TableRow(5, new TableColumn(0, callLight, incomingCallBtn));
t = new Table(5, 0, 0, tr0, tr1, tr2);
}

// The startLiveCall( ) function is invoked when the administrator accepts an
// incoming call.
function startLiveCall ( ) {

  // Create a net stream for subscribing to the calling client's audio and video.
  liveSubscribeNs = new NetStream(myConnection);
  liveSubscribeNs.play(incomingCallUser + "live");

  // Attach the local and remote video streams to the respective video instances.
  localVideoMc.vid.attachVideo(Camera.get( ));
  incomingVideoMc.vid.attachVideo(liveSubscribeNs);

  // Create a net stream for publishing the administrator's audio and video.
  livePublishNs = new NetStream(myConnection);
  livePublishNs.attachVideo(Camera.get( ));
  livePublishNs.attachAudio(Microphone.get( ));
  livePublishNs.publish("adminLive", "live");
}
```

```
// The notifyIncomingCall() function is invoked at
// one-second intervals when an incoming call is being placed.
function notifyIncomingCall(startTime) {

  // Toggle the visibility of the call light. This creates a blinking effect.
  callLight._visible = !callLight._visible;

  // If the user has been trying to place the call for more than ten seconds,
  // clear the interval, make the call button and call light invisible, and send
  // the incoming caller to record a message instead.
  if (getTimer() - startTime > 10000) {
    clearInterval(incomingCallInterval);
    callLight._visible = false;
    incomingCallBtn._visible = false;
    myConnection.call("sendToLeaveMessage", null, incomingUser);
    delete incomingCallUser;
  }
}


// The acceptCall() function is invoked when the administrator accepts an
// incoming call.
function acceptCall() {

  // Once the call is accepted, turn off the call light.
  callLight._visible = false;

  // Modify the button so that it allows the administrator to end the call.
  incomingCallBtn.setLabel("end call");
  incomingCallBtn.setClickHandler("endCall");

  // If there is an incoming caller, clear the interval that blinks the call
  // light and call the server-side acceptIncomingCall() method.
  if (incomingCallUser != undefined) {
    clearInterval(incomingCallInterval);
    myConnection.call("acceptIncomingCall", null);
    startLiveCall();
  }
}

// The endCall() function is invoked when
// the administrator clicks the End Call button.
function endCall () {

  // Reset the button behavior so that when another call comes in, the
  // administrator can accept it.
  incomingCallBtn.setLabel("incoming call");
  incomingCallBtn._visible = false;
  incomingCallBtn.setClickHandler("acceptCall");

  // Invoke the endCall() method on the server
  // to take care of all the loose ends.
  myConnection.call("endCall", null);
}
```

```
// The viewMessage() function is invoked when the
// administrator clicks on the button to play a message.
function viewMessage () {
   subscribeNs.play("message" + messageList.getSelectedItem().data);
   _root.messageVideoMc.vid.attachVideo(subscribeNs);
}

// The initMessagesList() function is invoked when the administrator has
// connected to the FlashCom application. It retrieves the list of messages from
// the server and populates the list box.
function initMessagesList () {

   // Create a remote shared object to retrieve the message data from the server.
   messagesSO = SharedObject.getRemote("messages", myConnection.uri, true);
   messagesSO.connect(myConnection);

   // When there is an update to the messages
   // information, repopulate the list box.
   messagesSO.onSync = function () {

      // First, remove all existing items from the list box.
      _root.messageList.removeAll();
      var mssg, un, dt;

      // Loop through all the items in the messages list from the server and add an
      // item to the list box for each.
      for (var i = 0; i < this.data.messages.length; i++) {
         mssg = this.data.messages[i];
         un = mssg.username;
         dt = mssg.dateTime;
         _root.messageList.addItem(un + " " + dt.format("MM-dd-yyyy") + " " +
                                   dt.format("hh:mm a"), mssg.id);
         _root.messageList.adjustWidth();
         _root.t.render(true);
      }
   };

   // Create the net stream over which each video message can be retrieved.
   subscribeNs = new NetStream(myConnection);
}

// The removeMessage() function is invoked when the administrator clicks the
// Remove Message button. It invokes the removeMessage() method on the server.
function removeMessage() {
   var messageName = "message" + messageList.getSelectedItem().data;
   myConnection.call("removeMessage", null, messageName);
}

init();
```

Now that you have completed the administrator client, save the file, and let's take a closer look at some elements of the code.

The *init()* function creates the net connection and connects the administrator to the FlashCom application. Notice that the username and password are hardcoded into the *connect()* method invocation. This is not a secure approach, although for this example application it should not pose a problem. If you need to ensure security, the username and password should be entered by the administrator via a login screen.

```
myConnection = new NetConnection( );
myConnection.connect("rtmp:/communicationCenterApp/", "admin", "adminPass");
```

You want to invoke the *initMessagesList()* function once the connection is completed. Do this by invoking it from within the connection object's *onStatus()* method:

```
myConnection.onStatus = function (infoObject) {
  if (infoObject.code == "NetConnection.Connect.Success") {
    _root.initMessagesList(this);
  }
};
```

When the administrator accepts an incoming call, you want to start a live call. To do this, follow these steps:

1. Create a net stream, subscribe to the stream that the calling client is publishing, and display that video.

2. Display the video that the administrator is publishing so that she can monitor what the calling client is seeing.

3. Publish the camera and microphone data so that the calling client can subscribe to it.

For example:

```
function startLiveCall ( ) {
  liveSubscribeNs = new NetStream(myConnection);
  liveSubscribeNs.play(incomingCallUser + "live");
  localVideoMc.vid.attachVideo(Camera.get( ));
  incomingVideoMc.vid.attachVideo(liveSubscribeNs);
  livePublishNs = new NetStream(myConnection);
  livePublishNs.attachVideo(Camera.get( ));
  livePublishNs.attachAudio(Microphone.get( ));
  livePublishNs.publish("adminLive", "live");
}
```

When a calling client places a call to the administrator, blink the call light by creating an interval that invokes *notifyIncomingCall()* once per second. Each time the function is invoked, the visibility of the call light is toggled. Additionally, you want the call to time out after 10 seconds. To do this, compare the current timer value with the timer value from when the interval began (which is passed to the function as the startTime parameter). Once the call request has timed out, clear the interval and reset the rest of the values that changed when the call request came in.

```
function notifyIncomingCall(startTime) {
  callLight._visible = !callLight._visible;
```

```
    if (getTimer( ) - startTime > 10000) {
      clearInterval(incomingCallInterval);
      callLight._visible = false;
      incomingCallBtn._visible = false;
      myConnection.call("sendToLeaveMessage", null, incomingUser);
      delete incomingCallUser;
    }
  }
```

The *initMessagesList()* function is invoked when the connection to the FlashCom application is made successfully. This function creates a remote shared object and uses it to populate the list box with the available messages. By placing the code to populate the list box within the *onSync()* method, the list box is updated every time a new message is left.

```
  function initMessagesList ( ) {
    messagesSO = SharedObject.getRemote("messages", myConnection.uri, true);
    messagesSO.connect(myConnection);
    messagesSO.onSync = function ( ) {
      _root.messageList.removeAll( );
      var mssg, un, dt;
      for (var i = 0; i < this.data.messages.length; i++) {
        mssg = this.data.messages[i];
        un = mssg.username;
        dt = mssg.dateTime;
        _root.messageList.addItem(un + " " + dt.format("MM-dd-yyyy") + " " +
                                  dt.format("hh:mm a"), mssg.id);
        _root.messageList.adjustWidth( );
        _root.t.render(true);
      }
    };
    subscribeNs = new NetStream(myConnection);
  }
```

Putting It All Together

You have now completed the entire video chat/message center application. The only thing that remains is to test it. To do this, you will need to enlist the help of friends. You need to publish your application to a publicly accessible FlashCom server so that others can connect to it. You can publish the calling client movie to an HTML page on the server as well, and send that URL to your friends. Then simply open the administrator client movie in the Standalone Player on your own computer and wait for incoming calls and messages. Refer to Chapter 14 for more information on FlashCom.

CHAPTER 25

Image Viewer/Slideshow

Loading images at runtime is a powerful feature of Flash, and it is not a particularly difficult skill to acquire. However, there remain several subtleties that practice and experience will help you to master. This chapter is devoted to the creation of an image viewer/slideshow application that highlights some of the following key skills:

- Loading JPEG content at runtime
- Monitoring the download of the content using a progress bar
- Loading XML data and using it to populate a UI component
- Extensive use of the drawing API
- Creating drag-and-drop functionality within a menu
- Using intervals to automate timed tasks
- Watching for keyboard activity

The application that you create in this chapter includes the following features:

- URLs to available images are loaded from an XML document.
- Each image has a title as well as a thumbnail, low resolution, and full image URL.
- The titles of available images are used to populate a list box.
- Users can preview the low-resolution images in a preview pane. Each preview image opens up in its own window that can be moved and resized within the preview pane.
- Users can add images to a sequence of thumbnails, the order of which can be rearranged by dragging and dropping the thumbnail images.
- The full versions of the images can be played back in the same order as the thumbnails.

Planning the Application Design

The first thing you should do when developing any application is formulate a blue-print. That is, you should decide what elements you need, and how those elements fit together to make a whole. There is never only one correct way to create an application, so creating a plan helps you ensure that the way you are approaching the development includes the necessary features and that everything fits together.

The image viewer/slideshow application has four main parts:

Low-resolution preview pane
> This portion of the application allows the user to view the low-resolution versions of the images. Each image is loaded into its own viewer that can be resized and moved.

Sequencer
> The user can add thumbnails to the sequencer. Dragging and dropping the images into different positions changes the order of the thumbnails.

Sequence viewer
> The full images can be played back in the same order as the thumbnails in the sequencer.

Menu
> The menu consists of a list box of available images as well as buttons for previewing the images, adding images to the sequencer, and starting the sequence playback.

Beginning the Application

The image viewer/slideshow application should be created using a single FLA document. Therefore, you should create a new Flash document named *imageViewer.fla* and use it for all of the subsequent steps in this chapter. The final version of the application is available at *http://www.person13.com/ascb*.

Additionally, the application relies on several UI components, so make sure you include the following components in the Library of the Flash document:

> ListBox
> ProgressBar (Flash UI Components Set 2)
> PushButton
> ScrollBar
> ScrollPane

You also need to make sure that you have the following ActionScript library files (also available from the preceding URL) available to the Flash document:

> *MovieClip.as* (from Chapter 7)
> *DrawingMethods.as* (from Chapter 4)

Table.as (from Chapter 11)
Forms.as (from Chapter 11)
TextField.as (from Chapter 8)

Creating the Components

Components are incredibly useful for developing well-constructed, object-oriented Flash applications. You should consider making elements of a movie into components when they meet either of these criteria:

- The same elements, or similar elements, are used multiple times throughout a movie.

- The element has complex behaviors and can be treated as a discrete unit.

For the image viewer/slideshow application, we will make seven components:

Image
> A component that loads images given a URL

ImageViewPane
> A component that allows an image to be moved and resized

PreviewPane
> A component into which image view panes are added

SequenceViewer
> The viewer for the full image slideshow sequence

SequencerItem
> One of the thumbnail items that can be added to the sequencer

Sequencer
> The component into which thumbnails are added and ordered

Menu
> The menu for the application

Designing the Image Element

The preview pane, sequencer, and sequence viewer all include elements that load images. Rather than reinvent the wheel with each, it makes sense to create a single Image component that can be utilized in each case. The Image component should have basic functionality that includes:

- Loading an image from a given URL

- Monitoring load progress with a progress bar

- Invoking a callback function when loading is complete

- Resizing itself to scale (maintaining the aspect ratio) to fit within specific dimensions

To create the Image component, complete the following steps:

1. Create a new movie clip symbol named *Image*.
2. Edit the linkage properties of the symbol.
3. Select the Export for ActionScript and Export in First Frame checkboxes.
4. Set the linkage identifier to *ImageSymbol*.
5. Click OK.
6. Edit the new symbol.
7. On the default layer, add the following code to the first frame:

```
#initclip 0

// The constructor creates a new movie clip into which the image is loaded.
function Image () {
  this.createEmptyMovieClip("imageHolder", this.getNewDepth());
}

Image.prototype = new MovieClip();

// The load() method loads an image from a URL into the image holder.
Image.prototype.load = function (url, w, h) {

  // Attach an instance of the progress bar, which monitors the load progress.
  this.attachMovie("FProgressBarSymbol", "pBar", this.getNewDepth());

  // Load the image into imageHolder.
  this.imageHolder.loadMovie(url);

  // Set the target for the progress bar and specify
  // the load progress callback method.
  this.pBar.setLoadTarget(this.imageHolder);
  this.pBar.setChangeHandler("onLoadProgress", this);

  // Center the progress bar.
  this.pBar._x = w/2 - this.pBar._width/2;
  this.pBar._y = h/2 - this.pBar._height/2;
};

// The onLoadProgress() method is invoked automatically by the progress bar each
// time there is some load progress.
Image.prototype.onLoadProgress = function () {

  // Check to see if the progress is 100%.
  if (this.pBar.getPercentComplete() == 100) {

    // Make the progress bar invisible.
    this.pBar._visible = false;

    // Get the height and width of the image as it is when it is originally
    // loaded. This is used to properly scale the image later.
    this.origHeight = this._height;
    this.origWidth = this._width;
```

```
    // If an onLoad callback is defined for the image component, invoke it.
    this.onLoadPath[this.onLoadCB](this);
  }
};

// The scale() method resizes the image to fit within a specified width and
// height while maintaining the aspect ratio. If fill is true, the image fills
// the specified area even at the expense of cutting off one of the sides.
//  Otherwise, the image is resized to fit entirely within the boundaries,
// leaving space on the sides if necessary.
Image.prototype.scale = function (w, h, fill) {
  var iw = this.origWidth;
  var ih = this.origHeight;
  var scale = 1;

  // The scale ratios in the x and y directions are obtained
  // by dividing the width and height of the boundaries by the
  // width and height of the original image.
  var xscale = w/iw;
  var yscale = h/ih;

  if (fill) {
    // Set scale to the larger of xscale and yscale.
    scale = (xscale > yscale) ? xscale : yscale;
  } else {
    // set scale to the smaller of xscale and yscale.
    scale = (xscale > yscale) ? yscale : xscale;
  }

  // Set the _xscale and _yscale values of the component to the value of scale
  // times 100 (which converts the scale ratio to a percentage).
  this._xscale = scale * 100;
  this._yscale = scale * 100;
};

// Set the onLoad callback where the function name is given as a string and the
// path is an optional parameter indicating the path to the callback function.
Image.prototype.setOnLoad = function (functionName, path) {
  if (path == undefined) {
    path = this._parent;
  }
  this.onLoadCB = functionName;
  this.onLoadPath = path;
};

Object.registerClass("ImageSymbol", Image);

#endinitclip
```

The Image component is short and uncomplicated. Each of the methods is straight-forward. Let's look at each of them more closely to review what each one does and how.

The *load()* method initiates the loading of the image into the image holder movie clip with the *loadMovie()* method. Additionally, the *load()* method creates a progress bar and sets it to monitor the load progress of the image using the *setLoadTarget()* method. Also, using the *setChangeHandler()* method, we tell the progress bar to call the *onLoadProgress()* method of the image component whenever there is any load progress. We refer to the Image component using the keyword this, which refers to the component from which the *load()* method was invoked in the first place.

```
Image.prototype.load = function (url, w, h) {
    this.attachMovie("FProgressBarSymbol", "pBar", this.getNewDepth());
    this.imageHolder.loadMovie(url);
    this.pBar.setLoadTarget(this.imageHolder);
    this.pBar.setChangeHandler("onLoadProgress", this);
    this.pBar._x = w/2 - this.pBar._width/2;
    this.pBar._y = h/2 - this.pBar._height/2;
};
```

The *onLoadProgress()* method is invoked automatically by the progress bar whenever there is any progress made with the loading image. We want to wait until the image is completely loaded, so we use the *getPercentComplete()* method to check whether the percentage loaded is equal to 100. If it is, then we make the progress bar invisible (the loaded image is visible, and we don't want the progress bar to obscure it). Additionally, we get the original height and width of the image, which is necessary for proper scaling. And finally, if there is an *onLoad* callback defined for the component, we invoke it.

```
Image.prototype.onLoadProgress = function () {
    if (this.pBar.getPercentComplete() == 100) {
        this.pBar._visible = false;
        this.origHeight = this._height;
        this.origWidth = this._width;
        this.onLoadPath[this.onLoadCB](this);
    }
};
```

The *scale()* method is the most complex of all the methods of the Image component. But even so, it probably looks scarier than it really is. The *w* and *h* parameters tell the method the dimensions of the area into which we want the image to fit. Given these dimensions, and the dimensions of the original image size, we can find the scale ratios in the x and y directions by dividing the width and height of the new area by the width and height of the original image size.

For example, if the new area's dimensions are 120 × 60, and the original image size is 240 × 120, the xscale and yscale ratios are both 1/2. In other words, we want to scale the image to 50% of the original size. Now, if we didn't care about the aspect ratio of the image, we wouldn't need to perform any further calculations. However, we want to make sure that the image doesn't end up looking squished. For example, if the original image dimensions are 240 × 120, but the new area's dimensions are 120 × 90, the xscale and yscale ratios are not equal, and the image would be squished.

We want to use the same ratio to set the scale properties in both the x and y directions. Therefore, we need to determine which of the ratios to use. If the `fill` parameter is true, we want use the larger of the two ratios so that the image fills the entire area, even though some of the image might extend beyond the boundaries. Otherwise, we use the smaller ratio, since that will ensure that the entire image fits within the boundaries. Then, once we have determined the correct ratio, we set the _xscale and _yscale properties of the component to the ratio times 100 to create a percentage.

```
Image.prototype.scale = function (w, h, fill) {
  var iw = this.origWidth;
  var ih = this.origHeight;
  var scale = 1;
  var xscale = w/iw;
  var yscale = h/ih;
  if (fill) {
    scale = (xscale > yscale) ? xscale : yscale;
  } else {
    scale = (xscale > yscale) ? yscale : xscale;
  }
  this._xscale = scale * 100;
  this._yscale = scale * 100;
};
```

The *setOnLoad()* method enables you to specify an *onLoad* callback function. When you call this method you must provide it a string name of a function. Optionally, you can also specify the path in which the function can be found. If no path is specified, the component looks to the parent timeline.

```
Image.prototype.setOnLoad = function (functionName, path) {
  if (path == undefined) {
    path = this._parent;
  }
  this.onLoadCB = functionName;
  this.onLoadPath = path;
};
```

Designing the Image View Pane

Before we get to the preview pane, we need to first look at its subelements, the Image View Pane components. The image view panes load the low-resolution images so that they can be viewed, dragged, resized, collapsed/expanded, and closed. Figure 25-1 shows an example of a preview pane with two opened image viewers.

The Image Viewer component includes a title bar, a close button, a frame/outline, a resize button, and an Image component. The image viewer should have the following functionality:

- Loading an image using the Image component
- Automatically sizing itself to match the dimensions of the loaded image
- Displaying the image title in the title bar

Figure 25-1. A preview pane with two opened image viewers

- Becoming draggable when the title bar is clicked
- Collapsing/expanding when the title bar is double-clicked
- Closing when the close button is clicked
- Resizing when the resize button is dragged

Follow these steps to create the image view pane component:

1. Create a new movie clip symbol named *ImageViewPane*.
2. Edit the linkage properties of the symbol.
3. Select the Export for ActionScript and Export in First Frame checkboxes.
4. Set the linkage identifier to *ImageViewPaneSymbol*.
5. Click OK.
6. Edit the new symbol.
7. On the default layer, add the following code to the first frame:

```
#initclip 1

// The constructor creates title bar and view pane movie clips, and within
// the view pane movie clip, it loads an instance of the image component.
function ImageViewPane () {
  this.createEmptyMovieClip("titleBar", this.getNewDepth());
  this.createEmptyMovieClip("viewPane", this.getNewDepth());
  this.viewPane.attachMovie("ImageSymbol", "img", this.viewPane.getNewDepth());
}

ImageViewPane.prototype = new MovieClip();
```

```
// The load() method loads the image from the specified
// URL and sets the title text.
ImageViewPane.prototype.load = function (url, title) {

    // Draw the title bar and the view pane.
    this.makeTitleBar(title, 200, 20);
    this.makeViewPane(200, 100);

    // Call the load() method of the image component.
    this.viewPane.img.load(url, 200, 100);

    // Set the onLoad callback function of the Image component to the
    // onImageLoad() method of the image view pane.
    this.viewPane.img.setOnLoad("onImageLoad", this);
};

// The open() method opens the component if it has otherwise been closed.
ImageViewPane.prototype.open = function () {

    // Make sure everything is visible.
    this.viewPane._visible = true;
    this._visible = true;

    // Call the onSelect callback if it is defined.
    this.onSelectPath[this.onSelectCB](this);
};

// The makeViewPane() method draws the view pane portion of the component, given
// the width and height.
ImageViewPane.prototype.makeViewPane = function (w, h) {

    // If the view pane frame is undefined, create the movie clip. If the frame has
    // a greater depth than the Image component instance, swap depths so that the
    // image is not hidden.
    if (this.viewPane.frame == undefined) {
        this.viewPane.createEmptyMovieClip("frame", this.viewPane.getNewDepth());
        if (this.viewPane.frame.getDepth() > this.viewPane.img.getDepth()) {
            this.viewPane.frame.swapDepths(this.viewPane.img);
        }
    }

    // Clear any existing frame and draw a rectangle to the specified dimensions.
    with (this.viewPane.frame) {
        clear();
        lineStyle(0, 0x000000, 100);
        beginFill(0xFFFFFF, 100);
        drawRectangle(w, h);
        endFill();
        _x = w/2;
        _y = h/2 + 21;
    }

    // If the resize button is undefined, create it.
    if (this.viewPane.resizeBtn == undefined) {
```

```
      this.viewPane.createEmptyMovieClip("resizeBtn",
                                          this.viewPane.getNewDepth());

    // Draw a triangle.
    with (this.viewPane.resizeBtn) {
      lineStyle(0, 0x000000, 100);
      beginFill(0xFFFFFF, 100);
      drawTriangle(10, 10, 90, 180, -5, 15);
      endFill();
    }

    // When the resize button is pressed, make it draggable and set the
    // isBeingResized property of the image view pane instance to true.
    this.viewPane.resizeBtn.onPress = function () {
      var viewer = this._parent._parent;
      viewer.isBeingResized = true;
      this.startDrag();
    };

    // When the resize button is released, do the opposite of onPress().
    this.viewPane.resizeBtn.onRelease = function () {
      var viewer = this._parent._parent;
      viewer.isBeingResized = false;
      this.stopDrag();
    };
  }

  // Position the resize button in the lower-right corner of the image view pane.
  this.viewPane.resizeBtn._x = w;
  this.viewPane.resizeBtn._y = h;
};

// Create the title bar, given the title and the width and height.
ImageViewPane.prototype.makeTitleBar = function (title, w, h) {

  // If the bar portion of the title bar is undefined, create it.
  if (this.titleBar.bar == undefined) {
    this.titleBar.createEmptyMovieClip("bar", this.titleBar.getNewDepth());

    this.titleBar.bar.onPress = function () {
      var viewer = this._parent._parent;

      // Invoke the onSelect callback function.
      viewer.onSelectPath[viewer.onSelectCB](viewer);

      // If the user double-clicked the title bar, expand/collapse the view pane.
      // Otherwise, it's a single click, so make the image view pane draggable.
      var currentTime = getTimer();
      if (currentTime - this.previousTime < 500) {
        viewer.viewPane._visible = !viewer.viewPane._visible;
      } else {
        viewer.startDrag();
      }
      this.previousTime = currentTime;
    };
```

```
    // When the bar is released, stop dragging the image view pane and invoke the
    // onUpdate() callback function.
    this.titleBar.bar.onRelease = function () {
      viewer = this._parent._parent;
      viewer.stopDrag();
      viewer.onUpdatePath[viewer.onUpdateCB](viewer);
    }
  }

  // Draw (or redraw) the rectangle.
  with (this.titleBar.bar) {
    clear();
    lineStyle(0, 0, 100);
    beginFill(0xDFDFDF, 100);
    drawRectangle(w, h);
    endFill();
    _x = w/2;
    _y = h/2;
  }

  // If the title text field is not yet defined, create it.
  if (this.titleBar.title == undefined) {
    this.titleBar.createTextField("title", this.titleBar.getNewDepth(),
                                  0, 0, 0, 0);
    this.titleBar.title.selectable = false;
  }

  // Set the width of the title to the width of the image view pane.
  this.titleBar.title._width = w;
  this.titleBar.title._height = h;

  // Assign the title to the title text field.
  this.titleBar.title.text = title;

  // If the close button is not yet defined, create it.
  if (this.titleBar.closeBtn == undefined) {
    this.titleBar.createEmptyMovieClip("closeBtn", this.titleBar.getNewDepth());

    // Draw a 10 × 10 square.
    with (this.titleBar.closeBtn) {
      lineStyle(0, 0x000000, 100);
      beginFill(0xE7E7E7, 100);
      drawRectangle(10, 10);
      endFill();
    }

    // When the close button is released, hide the entire image view pane.
    this.titleBar.closeBtn.onRelease = function () {
      this._parent._parent._visible = false;
    };
  }

  // Position the close button at the upper-right corner of the image view pane.
  this.titleBar.closeBtn._x = w - 10;
```

```
    this.titleBar.closeBtn._y = 10;
};

// The onImageLoad( ) method is invoked automatically when the image has
// completed loading.
ImageViewPane.prototype.onImageLoad = function ( ) {
  var img = this.viewPane.img;

  // Create the title bar and view pane to fit the loaded image.
  this.makeTitleBar(this.titleBar.title.text, img._width, 20);
  this.makeViewPane(img._width, img._height);

  // Move the image down by 21 pixels so it does not cover the title bar.
  img._y += 21;

  // Call the onUpdate callback function.
  this.onUpdatePath[this.onUpdateCB](this);
};

// The onEnterFrame( ) method continually checks to see if the view pane is being
// resized. If so, it calls the resize( ) method with the coordinates of the
// resize button.
ImageViewPane.prototype.onEnterFrame = function ( ) {
  if (this.isBeingResized) {
    this.resize(this.viewPane.resizeBtn._x, this.viewPane.resizeBtn._y);
  }
};

// The resize( ) method resizes the image, the view pane, and the title bar to
// the specified width and height.
ImageViewPane.prototype.resize = function (w, h) {

  // Call makeViewPane( ) and makeTitleBar( ) to
  // redraw the view pane and title bar.
  this.makeViewPane(w, h);
  this.makeTitleBar(this.titleBar.title.text, w, 20);

  // Call the scale( ) method of the image component to resize the loaded image.
  this.viewPane.img.scale(w, h);

  // Reposition the Image component so that it is centered in the view pane.
  this.viewPane.img._x = w/2 - this.viewPane.img._width/2;
  this.viewPane.img._y = h/2 - this.viewPane.img._height/2 + 21;
};

// Set the onSelect and onUpdate callback functions.
ImageViewPane.prototype.setOnSelect = function (functionName, path) {
  if (path == undefined) {
    path = this._parent;
  }
  this.onSelectCB = functionName;
  this.onSelectPath = path;
};
```

```
ImageViewPane.prototype.setOnUpdate = function (functionName, path) {
  if (path == undefined) {
    path = this._parent;
  }
  this.onUpdateCB = functionName;
  this.onUpdatePath = path;
};

Object.registerClass("ImageViewPaneSymbol", ImageViewPane);

#endinitclip
```

Much of the Image View Pane component is quite straightforward. However, there are some parts that deserve closer examination. Undoubtedly, it will be much clearer once we look at what is going on.

The constructor instantiates several of the main parts of the component. The title bar movie clip is the rectangle that appears at the top of the image and displays the title. The view pane is the remaining portion of the image view pane that appears below the title bar and contains the image itself.

```
function ImageViewPane () {
  this.createEmptyMovieClip("titleBar", this.getNewDepth());
  this.createEmptyMovieClip("viewPane", this.getNewDepth());
  this.viewPane.attachMovie("ImageSymbol", "img", this.viewPane.getNewDepth());
}
```

To avoid unnecessarily reloading images, the close button merely makes the image view pane invisible. Therefore, the *open()* method can open a closed image view pane by setting the _visible properties to true. Additionally, the *open()* method invokes the *onSelect* callback function because when an image view pane is opened, it should be selected as well.

```
ImageViewPane.prototype.open = function () {
  this.viewPane._visible = true;
  this._visible = true;
  this.onSelectPath[this.onSelectCB](this);
};
```

The *makeViewPane()* method is long, but it is not very complicated when you look at it more closely.

First, we create the frame movie clip if it has not been created. The frame is the outline and background in which the image appears. Therefore, if the frame is created such that the depth is greater than the Image component, we swap their depths so that the image is not hidden behind the frame:

```
if (this.viewPane.frame == undefined) {
  this.viewPane.createEmptyMovieClip("frame", this.viewPane.getNewDepth());
  if (this.viewPane.frame.getDepth() > this.viewPane.img.getDepth()) {
    this.viewPane.frame.swapDepths(this.viewPane.img);
  }
}
```

Once we are sure the frame exists, we draw a filled rectangle within it. The *clear()* method clears out any content that might have previously existed within the movie clip. Then we position the frame correctly. Since the *drawRectangle()* method draws a rectangle with its center at (0,0), we move the rectangle down and to the right by half its height and width. The frame is moved down another 21 pixels to accommodate the title bar (which is 20 pixels high).

```
with (this.viewPane.frame) {
  clear();
  lineStyle(0, 0x000000, 100);
  beginFill(0xFFFFFF, 100);
  drawRectangle(w, h);
  endFill();
  _x = w/2;
  _y = h/2 + 21;
}
```

Next, we create the resize button and draw a triangle in it, if it doesn't exist. Also, we assign event handler methods to the button so that it is draggable when pressed. The isBeingResized property tells the image view pane whether the image is being resized.

```
if (this.viewPane.resizeBtn == undefined) {
  this.viewPane.createEmptyMovieClip("resizeBtn", this.viewPane.getNewDepth());
  with (this.viewPane.resizeBtn) {
    lineStyle(0, 0x000000, 100);
    beginFill(0xFFFFFF, 100);
    drawTriangle(10, 10, 90, 180, -5, 15);
    endFill();
  }
  this.viewPane.resizeBtn.onPress = function () {
    var viewer = this._parent._parent;
    viewer.isBeingResized = true;
    this.startDrag();
  };
  this.viewPane.resizeBtn.onRelease = function () {
    var viewer = this._parent._parent;
    viewer.isBeingResized = false;
    this.stopDrag();
  };
}
```

The resize button should always appear in the lower-right corner of the image view pane:

```
this.viewPane.resizeBtn._x = w;
this.viewPane.resizeBtn._y = h;
```

Like the *makeViewPane()* method, the *makeTitleBar()* method is long but not overly complex. Let's take a closer look at some of the code.

First, we create the bar portion of the title bar if it doesn't exist. We also assign *onPress()* and *onRelease()* methods to it. When the bar is pressed, the *onPress()*

method determines if the click was a single-click or a double-click. A single-click initiates a *startDrag()* action. A double-click toggles the view pane's visibility, creating the effect of collapsing and expanding the view pane. We check for double-clicks by recording the time (using *getTimer()*) of each press. If two presses occur within 500 milliseconds, it constitutes a double-click.

```
if (this.titleBar.bar == undefined) {
  this.titleBar.createEmptyMovieClip("bar", this.titleBar.getNewDepth());

  this.titleBar.bar.onPress = function () {
    var viewer = this._parent._parent;
    viewer.onSelectPath[viewer.onSelectCB](viewer);
    var currentTime = getTimer();
    if (currentTime - this.previousTime < 500) {
      viewer.viewPane._visible = !viewer.viewPane._visible;
    } else {
      viewer.startDrag();
    }
    this.previousTime = currentTime;
  };

  this.titleBar.bar.onRelease = function () {
    viewer = this._parent._parent;
    viewer.stopDrag();
    viewer.onUpdatePath[viewer.onUpdateCB](viewer);
  };
}
```

Once we know the bar exists, we want to draw a rectangle with the specified dimensions. The *clear()* method makes sure that the previous content is cleared out first:

```
with (this.titleBar.bar) {
  clear();
  lineStyle(0, 0x000000, 100);
  beginFill(0xDFDFDF, 100);
  drawRectangle(w, h);
  endFill();
  _x = w/2;
  _y = h/2;
}
```

If the title text field is undefined, we create it. Also, the text field should be nonselectable. This is important because otherwise it could interfere with the events of the bar portion of the title bar.

```
if (this.titleBar.title == undefined) {
  this.titleBar.createTextField("title", this.titleBar.getNewDepth(),
                    0, 0, 0, 0);
  this.titleBar.title.selectable = false;
}
```

If the close button is not yet defined, we create it and draw a square within it. When the close button is released, the visibility of the image view pane is set to false. This creates the effect of closing the image view pane. However, since the component is still on the Stage, it can later be reopened without having the reload the image.

```
if (this.titleBar.closeBtn == undefined) {
  this.titleBar.createEmptyMovieClip("closeBtn", this.titleBar.getNewDepth());
  with (this.titleBar.closeBtn) {
    lineStyle(0, 0x000000, 100);
    beginFill(0xE7E7E7, 100);
    drawRectangle(10, 10);
    endFill();
  }
  this.titleBar.closeBtn.onRelease = function () {
    this._parent._parent._visible = false;
  };
}
```

When the image is loaded, the *onImageLoad()* method is invoked automatically. This is important because once the image is loaded, we want to correctly size the image view pane to accommodate the image.

```
ImageViewPane.prototype.onImageLoad = function () {
  var img = this.viewPane.img;
  this.makeTitleBar(this.titleBar.title.text, img._width, 20);
  this.makeViewPane(img._width, img._height);
  img._y += 21;
  this.onUpdatePath[this.onUpdateCB](this);
};
```

The isBeingResized property is set to true only when the resize button is being pressed. When this occurs, we invoke the *resize()* method and give it the coordinates of the resize button (which is always in the lower-right corner of the image, at the maximum width and height).

```
ImageViewPane.prototype.onEnterFrame = function () {
  if (this.isBeingResized) {
    this.resize(this.viewPane.resizeBtn._x, this.viewPane.resizeBtn._y);
  }
};
```

Designing the Preview Pane

The Preview Pane component serves as a scrolling container for the image view panes for the low-resolution images.

Complete the following steps to create the Preview Pane component:

1. Create a new movie clip symbol named *PreviewPane*.
2. Edit the linkage properties of the symbol.
3. Select the Export for ActionScript and Export in First Frame checkboxes.
4. Set the linkage identifier to *PreviewPaneSymbol*.
5. Click OK.

6. Edit the new symbol.

7. On the default layer, add the following code to the first frame:

```
#initclip

function PreviewPane () {

    // Add a scroll pane to the component, within which
    // the preview images are contained.
    this.attachMovie("FScrollPaneSymbol", "sp", this.getNewDepth());

    // Create a movie clip for the scroll content.
    this.createEmptyMovieClip("content", _root.getNewDepth());

    // Create a movie clip within the scroll content and draw a rectangle in it.
    // The background movie clip is used to properly align the scroll contents to
    // the scroll pane.
    this.content.createEmptyMovieClip("background", this.content.getNewDepth());
    with (this.content.background) {
        lineStyle(0, 0x000000, 0);
        drawRectangle(320, 240, 0, 0, 160, 120);
    }

    // Call updateViewer() to set the scroll pane to target the scroll content.
    this.updateViewer();

    // Create arrays to keep track of the images that are currently opened and the
    // images that have been loaded (whether open or not).
    this.currentViewAr = new Array();
    this.loadedAr = new Array();
}

PreviewPane.prototype = new MovieClip();

// Return a reference to an Image View Pane component if one already exists for
// the specified URL. Image view panes may be within the preview pane but may not
// be visible if they were closed.
PreviewPane.prototype.isURLLoaded = function (url) {
    for (var i = 0; i < this.loadedAr.length; i++) {
        if (this.loadedAr[i].url == url) {
            return this.loadedAr[i].vp;
        }
    }
    return false;
};

PreviewPane.prototype.setSize = function (w, h) {
    this.sp.setSize(w, h);
};

// The updateViewer() method adjusts the scroll content. This method is invoked
// every time there is a change made to the scroll content.
PreviewPane.prototype.updateViewer = function () {
    this.content.background._width = this.content._width;
```

```
    this.content.background._height = this.content._height;
    this.sp.setScrollContent(this.content);
    if (this.content._width > this.sp._width - 10) {
      this.sp.setHScroll(true);
    }
};

// The bringToFront( ) method brings the
// specified image view pane to the foreground
PreviewPane.prototype.bringToFront = function (viewer) {

  // Remove and return the last value in the currentViewAr array (the image view
  // pane with the greatest depth).
  var topViewer = this.currentViewAr.pop( );

  // If the specified image view pane is not already on top...
  if (viewer != topViewer) {

    // Swap the depths of the selected view pane with the top view pane, bringing
    // the selected view pane to the foreground.
    viewer.swapDepths(topViewer);

    // Search through the currentViewAr array for the index of the selected image
    // view pane and assign the value of the (previously) top view pane to that
    // index in the array.
    for (var i = 0; i < this.currentViewAr.length; i++) {
      if (this.currentViewAr[i] == viewer) {
        break;
      }
    }
    this.currentViewAr[i] = topViewer;
  }

  // Append the selected viewer to the end of the currentViewAr array.
  this.currentViewAr.push(viewer);
};

// The open( ) method opens an image view pane given a URL and a title.
PreviewPane.prototype.open = function (url, title) {
  var uniqueVal = this.content.getNewDepth( );

  // If an image view pane with the same URL is already loaded, isURLLoaded( )
  // returns a reference to it. Otherwise, it returns false.
  var loaded = this.isURLLoaded(url);

  // If loaded is...
  if (loaded == false) {
    // ...false, then create a new image view pane and load the image into it.
    var vp = this.content.attachMovie("ImageViewPaneSymbol", "vp" + uniqueVal,
                                      uniqueVal);
    vp.load(url, title);
```

```
    // Set the onSelect callback function to the bringToFront() method
    // so that when the image view pane is selected, it is always
    // brought to the foreground.
    vp.setOnSelect("bringToFront", this);

    // Set the onUpdate callback function to the updateViewer()
    // method so that when the image view pane is updated in any way,
    // the preview pane is also updated.
    vp.setOnUpdate("updateViewer", this);

    // Add the image view pane to the currentViewAr and loadedAr arrays.
    this.currentViewAr.push(vp);
    this.loadedAr.push({url: url, vp: vp});
  } else {
    // If loaded is true, call the open() method of the image pane.
    loaded.open();
  }
};

Object.registerClass("PreviewPaneSymbol", PreviewPane);

#endinitclip
```

The Preview Pane component is not very long, nor does it introduce too many new concepts. However, there are a few areas that could use a little further study.

The constructor creates a scroll pane and a movie clip for the scroll content. This part is standard. However, we use a little trick to keep the scroll content correctly positioned within the scroll pane. We create the background movie clip within the scroll content clip. We then draw a rectangle within the background with an invisible outline! This may seem a little confusing at first, but there is a good reason why we do it this way. A scroll pane always aligns the scroll content so that the upper-left corner of the actual content is in the upper-left corner of the scroll pane. The scroll pane doesn't align the scroll content relative to the registration point of the scroll content movie clip. The problem is that if the user opens one image view pane in the preview pane, that one image view pane is aligned such that the upper-left corner is in the upper-left corner of the preview pane. If the user then drags the image view pane, the scroll pane will realign the scroll content such that the image view pane appears in the same position as it did previously. By adding a background movie clip to the scroll content that is aligned with the upper-left corner at the scroll content's registration point, we force the scroll pane to align the scroll content to the registration point (in most cases).

```
function PreviewPane () {
  this.attachMovie("FScrollPaneSymbol", "sp", this.getNewDepth());
  this.createEmptyMovieClip("content", _root.getNewDepth());
  this.content.createEmptyMovieClip("background", this.content.getNewDepth());
  with (this.content.background) {
    lineStyle(0, 0x000000, 0);
    drawRectangle(320, 240, 0, 0, 160, 120);
  }
```

```
      this.updateViewer();
      this.currentViewAr = new Array();
      this.loadedAr = new Array();
    }
```

To close an image view pane we just make it invisible. This saves the user from having to reload the image if he decides to open it again. The *isURLLoaded()* method searches through the loadedAr array to find any image view pane (even an invisible one) that has already been loaded for the specified URL. If none is found, the method returns false.

```
PreviewPane.prototype.isURLLoaded = function (url) {
  for (var i = 0; i < this.loadedAr.length; i++) {
    if (this.loadedAr[i].url == url) {
      return this.loadedAr[i].vp;
    }
  }
  return false;
};
```

We need to create the *updateViewer()* method to update the scroll pane when the scroll content changes. First, we resize the background movie clip so that its dimensions match the rest of the content. This helps to ensure that the content remains properly aligned. Then, the *setScrollContent()* method resets the scroll content for the scroll pane with the updated info. Finally, if the scroll pane has a vertical scrollbar, it is possible that part of the scroll contents can be hidden without the possibility of scrolling horizontally. Therefore, if the scroll content's width is greater than the width of the scroll pane minus the width of a scroll bar, we tell the scroll pane to display a horizontal scroll bar.

```
PreviewPane.prototype.updateViewer = function () {
  this.content.background._width = this.content._width;
  this.content.background._height = this.content._height;
  this.sp.setScrollContent(this.content);
  if (this.content._width > this.sp._width - 10) {
    this.sp.setHScroll(true);
  }
};
```

When an image view pane is selected, it should be brought in front of the rest of the content. The currentViewAr array contains references to all the opened image view panes; the elements are in the order of depth, with the greatest depth at the end of the array. Therefore, we can get a reference to the image view pane that is currently on top by calling the *pop()* method of the currentViewAr array, which also removes the element from the end of the array and returns its value. If the top view pane and the selected view pane are not the same, we swap their depths and swap the positions of the elements in the array.

```
PreviewPane.prototype.bringToFront = function (viewer) {
  var topViewer = this.currentViewAr.pop();
  if (viewer != topViewer) {
```

```
      viewer.swapDepths(topViewer);
      for (var i = 0; i < this.currentViewAr.length; i++) {
        if (this.currentViewAr[i] == viewer) {
          break;
        }
      }
      this.currentViewAr[i] = topViewer;
    }
    this.currentViewAr.push(viewer);
  };
```

The *open()* method opens an image, given a URL and a title, and is designed such
that it can determine whether to make an existing image view pane visible or create a
new image view pane:

```
  PreviewPane.prototype.open = function (url, title) {
    var uniqueVal = this.content.getNewDepth( );
    var loaded = this.isURLLoaded(url);
    if (loaded == false) {
      var vp = this.content.attachMovie("ImageViewPaneSymbol", "vp" + uniqueVal,
                                        uniqueVal);
      vp.load(url, title);
      vp.setOnSelect("bringToFront", this);
      vp.setOnUpdate("updateViewer", this);
      this.currentViewAr.push(vp);
      this.loadedAr.push({url: url, vp: vp});
    } else {
      loaded.open( );
    }
  };
```

Designing the Sequence Viewer

The sequence viewer component is the portion of the application that plays back the
images as a slide show. The component should fill the Flash Player with a black
background and play the full images in sequence using *setInterval()* to determine
when to change images.

Follow these steps to create the Sequence Viewer component:

1. Create a new movie clip symbol named *SequenceViewer*.
2. Edit the linkage properties of the symbol.
3. Select the Export for ActionScript and Export in First Frame checkboxes.
4. Set the linkage identifier to *SequenceViewerSymbol*.
5. Click OK.
6. Edit the new symbol.
7. On the default layer, add the following code to the first frame:

    ```
    #initclip

    function SequenceViewer ( ) {
    ```

```
  // The array of image items.
  this.items = new Array( );

  // Create the black rectangle to fill the background of the Player.
  this.createEmptyMovieClip("background", this.getNewDepth( ));
  with (this.background) {
    lineStyle(0, 0x000000, 0);
    beginFill(0, 100);
    drawRectangle(Stage.width, Stage.height);
    endFill( );
    _x = Stage.width/2;
    _y = Stage.height/2;
  }

  // Make the viewer invisible to start.
  this._visible = false;
}

// SequenceViewer subclasses MovieClip.
SequenceViewer.prototype = new MovieClip( );

// Add an image to the sequence viewer by URL.
SequenceViewer.prototype.addItem = function (url) {
  var uniqueVal = this.getNewDepth( );

  // Add an image component and load the image into it.
  var img = this.attachMovie("ImageSymbol", "image" + uniqueVal, uniqueVal);
  img.load(url);

  // Set the onLoad callback for the image component
  // to the onImageLoad( ) method.
  img.setOnLoad("onImageLoad", this);

  // Add the image to the items array.
  this.items.push(img);

  // Make the image invisible to start.
  img._visible = false;
};

// When the image loads, scale it to fill in the Player.
SequenceViewer.prototype.onImageLoad = function (img) {
  img.scale(Stage.width, Stage.height, true);
};

// Change the order of an image in the sequence.
SequenceViewer.prototype.changeOrder = function (prevIndex, newIndex) {
  var img = this.items[prevIndex];
  this.items.splice(prevIndex, 1);
  this.items.splice(newIndex, 0, img);
};

// Start the playback of the images.
SequenceViewer.prototype.play = function (intervalm randomize) {
```

```
  // Make the viewer visible.
  this._visible = true;

  // Set the itemIndex property to -1 so that the first image shown is index 0.
  this.itemIndex = -1;

  // Call the nextImage( ) method at the specified interval. Also, pass it the
  // value of the randomize parameter.
  this.playInterval = setInterval(this, "nextImage", interval, randomize);
};

// The stop( ) method stops the playback of the images.
SequenceViewer.prototype.stop = function ( ) {

  // Clear the interval.
  clearInterval(this.playInterval);

  // Make the viewer invisible.
  this._visible = false;

  // Set the current image to be invisible. Otherwise, when the sequence is
  // played again, this image will still be visible.
  this.items[this.itemIndex]._visible = false;
  this.itemIndex = 0;
};

// The nextImage( ) method is called at the specified
// interval when the sequence is played.
SequenceViewer.prototype.nextImage = function (randomize) {

  // The previous image is made invisible and the index is incremented.
  this.items[this.itemIndex++]._visible = false;

  // If we're at the last image, start over at the first image.
  if (this.itemIndex > this.items.length - 1) {
    this.itemIndex = 0;
  }

  // If randomize is true, create a random index.
  if (randomize) {
    this.itemIndex = Math.round(Math.random( ) * (this.items.length - 1));
  }

  // Make the item with the specified index visible.
  this.items[this.itemIndex]._visible = true;
};

// The removeItem( ) method removes the item with the specified index from the
// movie and from the array.
SequenceViewer.prototype.removeItem = function (index) {
  this.items[index].removeMovieClip( );
  this.items.splice(index, 1);
};
```

```
Object.registerClass("SequenceViewerSymbol", SequenceViewer);

#endinitclip
```

The Sequence Viewer component is not very complicated. Let's shed some light on the parts that might appear to be more complicated than they really are.

The constructor does three things. First of all, it creates the `items` array property, which is used to hold references to all the Image components. Next, it creates the background movie clip, which is a black rectangle that fills the Player while the sequence viewer is playing. And finally, the constructor initializes the viewer as invisible because we don't want to see the sequence viewer until the user selects the option to play the sequence.

```
function SequenceViewer () {
  this.items = new Array();
  this.createEmptyMovieClip("background", this.getNewDepth());
  with (this.background) {
    lineStyle(0, 0x000000, 0);
    beginFill(0, 100);
    drawRectangle(Stage.width, Stage.height);
    endFill();
    _x = Stage.width/2;
    _y = Stage.height/2;
  }
  this._visible = false;
}
```

The *addItem()* method is a straightforward method that adds a new Image component to the viewer. When the image is added, we also append it to the `items` array. The `items` array is what determines the order in which the sequence plays back, so each new image is added to the end of the sequence. Additionally, we want to make each new image invisible, because the playback works by turning on and off the visibility of the images in sequence.

```
SequenceViewer.prototype.addItem = function (url) {
  var uniqueVal = this.getNewDepth();
  var img = this.attachMovie("ImageSymbol", "image" + uniqueVal, uniqueVal);
  img.load(url);
  img.setOnLoad("onImageLoad", this);
  this.items.push(img);
  img._visible = false;
};
```

The *changeOrder()* method changes the order of an element in the sequence, given the original index and the new index. We accomplish this by first deleting the element at the old index and then inserting it into the array at the new index.

```
SequenceViewer.prototype.changeOrder = function (prevIndex, newIndex) {
  var img = this.items[prevIndex];
  this.items.splice(prevIndex, 1);
  this.items.splice(newIndex, 0, img);
};
```

We want to play back the images, one at a time, at a set interval. Therefore, we use the *setInterval()* function to repeatedly call a method that updates the image display. In this case, we save the interval ID to a property (playInterval) so that we can clear the interval when the user stops the playback:

```
SequenceViewer.prototype.play = function (interval, randomize) {
    this._visible = true;
    this.itemIndex = -1;
    this.playInterval = setInterval(this, "nextImage", interval, randomize);
};
```

The *stop()* method clears the play interval, first and foremost. This stops the images from being played. We also want to make the viewer invisible again. Additionally, it is important that we reset the last image that was visible to be invisible again. If we didn't do this, there could be problems with overlapping images when the sequence is played again.

```
SequenceViewer.prototype.stop = function ( ) {
    clearInterval(this.playInterval);
    this._visible = false;
    this.items[this.itemIndex]._visible = false;
    this.itemIndex = 0;
};
```

The *nextImage()* method is called at the interval when the sequence is played. Each time the method is called, we make the previous image invisible and make the current image visible. In this case, we increment the itemIndex value within the first line. Because the increment operator (++) appears at the end of the variable, the value is incremented after the previous value is used in the first line. This saves a line of code, although you could insert another line after the first and increment the value there instead.

```
SequenceViewer.prototype.nextImage = function (randomize) {
    this.items[this.itemIndex++]._visible = false;
    if (this.itemIndex > this.items.length - 1) {
        this.itemIndex = 0;
    }
    if (randomize) {
        this.itemIndex = Math.round(Math.random( ) * (this.items.length - 1));
    }
    this.items[this.itemIndex]._visible = true;
};
```

Designing the Sequencer Item Component

The sequencer is composed of *sequence items*. The items are rectangles into which thumbnails are loaded. Figure 25-2 shows an example of the sequencer with two sequence items in it.

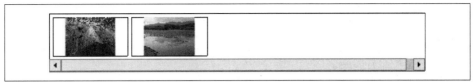

Figure 25-2. The sequencer with two sequence items

The Sequence Item component should have the following functionality:

- Loads a thumbnail from a URL
- Is selectable (outline highlights blue to indicate selection)
- Can be dragged and dropped within the constraints of the sequencer

Complete the following steps to create the Sequence Item component:

1. Create a new movie clip symbol named *SequenceItem*.
2. Edit the linkage properties of the symbol.
3. Select the Export for ActionScript and Export in First Frame checkboxes.
4. Set the linkage identifier to *SequenceItemSymbol*.
5. Click OK.
6. Edit the new symbol.
7. On the default layer, add the following code to the first frame:

```
#initclip 1

function SequencerItem () {

    // Create the background movie clip (the rectangular frame). Add a fill and a
    // outline to the background and draw a filled rectangle and an outline in
    // them.
    this.createEmptyMovieClip("background", this.getNewDepth());
    this.background.createEmptyMovieClip("fill", this.background.getNewDepth());
    this.background.createEmptyMovieClip("outline",
                                         this.background.getNewDepth());
    with (this.background.fill) {
      lineStyle(0, 0x000000, 0);
      beginFill(0xFFFFFF, 100);
      drawRectangle(100, 50);
      endFill();
      _x = 50;
      _y = 25;
    }
    with (this.background.outline) {
      lineStyle(0, 0x000000, 100);
      drawRectangle(100, 50);
      _x = 50;
      _y = 25;
    }
```

```
  // Create a color object to target the outline.
  this.background.outline.col = new Color(this.background.outline);
};


SequencerItem.prototype = new MovieClip();

// The loadImage() method adds an image component and loads an image from a URL.
SequencerItem.prototype.loadImage = function (url) {
  this.url = url;
  this.attachMovie("ImageSymbol", "img", this.getNewDepth());
  this.img.load(url, 100, 50);
  this.img.setOnLoad("onImageLoad", this);
};

// The onImageLoad() method is the callback function that is invoked
// automatically when the image has completed loading. At that point, it scales
// the image to fit within the sequence item frame and moves it to the center.
SequencerItem.prototype.onImageLoad = function (imageHolder) {
  this.img.scale(100, 50);
  this.img._x = this.background._width/2 - this.img._width/2;
  this.img._y = this.background._height/2 - this.img._height/2;
};

// The onEnterFrame() method continually checks to see if the component is being
// dragged (dragging is set to true when the component is pressed). If it is, the
// method performs a series of actions.
SequencerItem.prototype.onEnterFrame = function () {
  if (this.dragging) {

    // Loop through all the other sequence items in the sequencer (this._parent),
    // and if the item that is being dragged has a lower depth than another item
    // that it is being dragged over, swap depths.
    for (var mc in this._parent) {
      if (this.hitTest(this._parent[mc]) && this.getDepth() <
                            this._parent[mc].getDepth()) {
        this.swapDepths(this._parent[mc]);
      }
    }

    // Get a reference to the sequencer's scroll pane and its scroll content.
    var sp = this._parent._parent.sp;
    var sc = sp.getScrollContent();

    // If the mouse is outside the scroll pane, increment or decrement the scroll
    // position accordingly. Also, move the sequencer item accordingly.
    if (sp._xmouse > sp._width) {
      sp.setScrollPosition(sp.getScrollPosition().x + 5, 0);
    } else if (sp._xmouse < 0) {
      sp.setScrollPosition(sp.getScrollPosition().x - 5, 0);
    }
    this._x = sc._xmouse - this.clickPosition;
  }
};
```

```
SequencerItem.prototype.onPress = function () {

  // Get the x coordinate of the mouse within the item's coordinate system at the
  // time the mouse was pressed.
  this.clickPosition = this._xmouse;

  // Get the x coordinate of the item before it is moved. This is used to snap
  // items to the correct positions.
  this.startPosition = this._x;

  // Set dragging to true so that the actions in
  // the onEnterFrame( ) method are activated.
  this.dragging = true;

  // Make the item draggable along the X axis within the sequencer.
  this.startDrag(false, 0, this._y, this._parent._width, this._y);

  // Toggle the selected state.
  this.selected = !this.selected;
  if (this.selected) {
    this.background.outline.col.setRGB(0xFF);
    this.onSelectPath[this.onSelectCB](this);
  }
};

SequencerItem.prototype.onRelease = function () {

  // Set dragging to false so the onEnterFrame( ) actions
  // stop executing and stop the draggability.
  this.dragging = false;
  this.stopDrag( );

  // Get the drop target and split it into an array using a slash as the
  // delimiter. The value of the drop target is given in Flash 4 syntax, so the
  // slashes are used where dots are used in Flash 5+ syntax.
  var itemBAr = this._droptarget.split("/");

  // Remove the end items from the array until
  // the last element contains the value "item".
  while(itemBAr[itemBAr.length - 1].indexOf("item") == -1) {
    itemBAr.pop( );
  }

  // Call the onDrop( ) callback function, and pass it the reference to this item
  // and the drop target item.
  This.onDropPath[this.onDropCB](this, eval(itemBAr.join("/")));

  if (!this.selected) {
    this.deselect( );
  }
};

// Set the onReleaseOutside( ) method to do the same thing as onRelease( ).
SequencerItem.prototype.onReleaseOutside = SliderMenuItem.prototype.onRelease;
```

```
SequencerItem.prototype.deselect = function () {
  this.selected = false;
  this.background.outline.col.setRGB(0);
};

SequencerItem.prototype.setOnSelect = function (functionName, path) {
  if (path == undefined) {
    path = this._parent;
  }
  this.onSelectCB = functionName;
  this.onSelectPath = path;
};

SequencerItem.prototype.setOnDrop = function (functionName, path) {
  if (path == undefined) {
    path = this._parent;
  }
  this.onDropCB = functionName;
  this.onDropPath = path;
};

Object.registerClass("SequencerItemSymbol", SequencerItem);

#endinitclip
```

The Sequencer Item component contains many code elements that are similar to the other components that we have already created throughout this chapter. However, there are a few parts of the code that involve techniques that are unique to the Sequence Item component, and they bear further discussion.

In the *onEnterFrame()* method, the component continually checks to see if the property named dragging is true. The dragging property is true when, and only when, the user is pressing the component. This technique is nothing new, as we have used it throughout several of the other components. What is new is the rest of the code.

First of all, when the sequencer item is being dragged, we want to make sure that it appears above all the other sequence items that might be in the sequencer. We achieve this by performing a hit test on every other sequencer item and swapping depths with any item that the selected component is obscured by (overlapping and beneath). Sequencer items are contained within a scroll content movie clip within the sequencer, so we can loop through all the elements of the parent movie clip using a *for...in* statement. Then, we check to see if the selected item is touching another sequencer item with a *hitTest()* method. If the selected item is beneath an item for which the hit test is true, we use *swapDepths()* to bring the selected item forward.

```
for (var mc in this._parent) {
  if (this.hitTest(this._parent[mc]) && this.getDepth() <
                        this._parent[mc].getDepth()) {
    this.swapDepths(this._parent[mc]);
  }
}
```

The next part of the *onEnterFrame()* method code may look like the most challenging thus far, but it is not so bad once you understand the problem we are trying to solve. When the user clicks on the sequencer item and then drags the mouse pointer beyond the sequencer scroll pane, the scroll pane does not scroll. This is not the desired behavior. We want the scroll pane to automatically scroll in the same direction as the mouse pointer. To accomplish this, we continually compare the position of the mouse pointer to the boundaries of the scroll pane (given by 0 on the left and _ width on the right). If the mouse position is greater than the width of the scroll pane, we increment the scroll pane's scroll position by five. On the other hand, if the mouse position is less than zero (meaning it is to the left of the scroll pane), we decrement the scroll position by five. In addition to this, we move the sequencer item; otherwise, the sequencer item and the scroll pane content would be out of synch. In the *onPress()* method, we recorded the value of the x coordinate where the mouse clicked on the item to begin with. We then set the x coordinate of the item to the x coordinate of the mouse pointer minus the offset at which the user clicked on the item.

```
var sp = this._parent._parent.sp;
var sc = sp.getScrollContent();
if (sp._xmouse > sp._width) {
  sp.setScrollPosition(sp.getScrollPosition().x + 5, 0);
} else if (sp._xmouse < 0) {
  sp.setScrollPosition(sp.getScrollPosition().x - 5, 0);
}
this._x = sc._xmouse - this.clickPosition;
```

The *onPress()* method contains only a few things that need to be mentioned here. The x coordinate of the sequencer item at the time it is clicked is saved in the startPosition property. This value is used later, when the item is released (and the *dropItem()* method is called), to determine where to place the item. Also, the *startDrag()* method constrains the area in which the item can be moved to a horizontal line spanning the width of the sequencer scroll pane's contents.

```
SequencerItem.prototype.onPress = function () {
  this.clickPosition = this._xmouse;
  this.startPosition = this._x;
  this.dragging = true;
  this.startDrag(false, 0, this._y, this._parent._width, this._y);
  this.selected = !this.selected;
  if (this.selected) {
    this.background.outline.col.setRGB(0xFF);
    this.onSelectPath[this.onSelectCB](this);
  }
};
```

The *onRelease()* method involves some code that might appear confusing until we look at it in a little more detail. This method attempts to get a reference to a sequencer item onto which the selected sequencer item is dropped. We then call the *dropItem()* method of the sequencer with both a reference to the selected item and the drop target item.

This is relatively simple, except for the fact that Flash reports the innermost nested movie clip as the drop target. This means that if, for example, the selected sequencer item is dragged over and dropped onto the sequencer item instance named item3, the value returned by the _droptarget property might be "/seqncr/sc/item3/img/image-Holder" or "/seqncr/sc/item3/background/fill" (in which *seqncr* is the instance name of the sequencer on the main timeline). The reason for this is that the _droptarget property reports the nested movie clips of img.imageHolder and background.fill instead of the parent movie clip, item3.

This is the expected behavior. However, we want to extract the portion of the path that resolves to the sequencer item instance, such as "/seqncr/sc/item3". Since the parts of the path returned by _droptarget are separated by slashes (since it is given in Flash 4 syntax), it is convenient to use the *split()* method to split the string into an array using a slash as the delimiter. At that point, we use a *while* loop to remove elements from the end of the array until the last element contains the substring "item". Then, we call the *onDrop()* callback function with a reference to the selected sequencer item (this), and a reference to the drop target item. To get an actual reference to the drop target item, we have to use *join()* to reassemble the path as a Flash 4–syntax string and use *eval()* to convert that string to a movie clip reference.

```
SequencerItem.prototype.onRelease = function () {
  this.dragging = false;
  this.stopDrag();
  var itemBAr = this._droptarget.split("/");
  while(itemBAr[itemBAr.length - 1].indexOf("item") == -1) {
    itemBAr.pop();
  }
  this.onDropPath[this.onDropCB](this, eval(itemBAr.join("/")));
  if (!this.selected) {
    this.deselect();
  }
};
```

Designing the Sequencer Component

The sequencer is the part of the application in which the thumbnails are loaded and can be ordered by the user. The sequencer itself is composed of a scroll pane and sequencer item components. The sequencer must:

- Add new sequencer items when the user chooses to add an image to the sequencer
- Remove a selected sequencer item
- Reorder sequencer items when they are dragged and dropped by the user
- Target a sequence viewer

Complete these steps to create the Sequencer component:

1. Create a new movie clip symbol named *Sequencer*.
2. Edit the linkage properties of the symbol.
3. Select the Export for ActionScript and Export in First Frame checkboxes.
4. Set the linkage identifier to *SequencerSymbol*.
5. Click OK.
6. Edit the new symbol.
7. On the default layer, add the following code to the first frame:

```
#initclip

function Sequencer () {

    // Define the sequencer to have a width of 500 and a height of 75.
    var w = 500;
    var h = 75;

    // Define the width and height for each sequencer item.
    this.itemWidth = 100;
    this.itemHeight = 50;

    // Add a scroll pane and set the size of it to the width and height.
    this.attachMovie("FScrollPaneSymbol", "sp", this.getNewDepth());
    this.sp.setSize(w, h);

    // Create a scroll content movie clip and create a background in it. The
    // background serves a similar purpose to the background for the scroll content
    // in the Preview Pane component.
    this.createEmptyMovieClip("sc", this.getNewDepth());
    this.sc.createEmptyMovieClip("background", 0);
    with (this.sc.background) {
      lineStyle(0, 0x000000, 100);
      beginFill(0xFFFFFF, 100);
      drawRectangle(w, h);
      endFill();
      _x += w/2;
      _y += h/2;
    }

    // Create the array that is used to store the order of the sequencer items.
    this.items = new Array();
}

Sequencer.prototype = new MovieClip();

Sequencer.prototype.getItems = function () {
  return this.items;
};
```

```
// Add an item to the sequencer with a URL to an image.
Sequencer.prototype.addItem = function (url) {
  var uniqueVal = this.sc.getNewDepth( );

  // Add a Sequencer Item component and load the image into it.
  var item = this.sc.attachMovie("SequencerItemSymbol", "item" + uniqueVal,
                                 uniqueVal);
  item.loadImage(url);

  // Position the sequencer item such that it is to the right of any other items
  // in the sequencer.
  item._x += (this.items.length * 105) + 5;
  item._y += 5;

  item.setOnDrop("dropItem", this);
  item.setOnSelect("setSelected", this);

  // Set the background of the scroll content to match the width of the scroll
  // content plus five (so that there is a five-pixel margin on the right side of
  // the scroll content).
  this.sc.background._width = this.sc._width + 5;
  this.sc.background._x = this.sc.background._width/2;

  // Update the scroll pane view.
  this.sp.setScrollContent(this.sc);

  // Add the sequencer item to the items array.
  this.items.push(item);
};

// The dropItem( ) method is invoked any time one of the sequencer items is
// released by the user. It is passed a reference to the item that was dropped
// and a reference to the drop target.
Sequencer.prototype.dropItem = function (itemA, itemB) {

  // If the drop target (itemB) is either undefined or is the scroll content
  // background, reset itemA back to the starting position.
  if (itemB == undefined || itemB == this.sc.background) {
    itemA._x = itemA.startPosition;
  } else {
    // ...Otherwise, set itemA to the same position as the drop target.
    itemA._x = itemB._x;
    var aIndex = 0;
    var bIndex = 0;
    var aSet = false;
    var bSet = false;

    // Loop through the sequencer items and find the indexes of itemA and itemB.
    for (var i = 0; i < this.items.length; i++) {
      if (this.items[i] == itemA) {
        aIndex = i;
        aSet = true;
      } else if (this.items[i] == itemB) {
        bIndex = i;
```

```
      bSet = true;
    }
    if (aSet && bSet) {
      break;
    }
  }
}

// Shift the rest of the items appropriately.
if (aIndex < bIndex) {
  for (var i = aIndex + 1; i <= bIndex; i++) {
    this.items[i]._x -= (this.itemWidth + 5);
  }
} else {
  for (var i = bIndex; i < aIndex; i++) {
    this.items[i]._x += (this.itemWidth + 5);
  }
}

// Change the order of the items.
this.items.splice(aIndex, 1);
this.items.splice(bIndex, 0, itemA);

// Call the changeOrder( ) method of the targeted sequence viewer so that the
// order of the images during playback is correct.
this.sequenceVwr.changeOrder(aIndex, bIndex);
  }
};

// Set an item to be selected, and deselect the rest of the items.
Sequencer.prototype.setSelected = function (item) {
  for (var i = 0; i < this.items.length; i++) {
    if (this.items[i] == item) {
      this.selectedItemIndex = i;
    } else {
      this.items[i].deselect( );
    }
  }
};

// The removeSelected( ) method removes the selected item from the sequencer.
Sequencer.prototype.removeSelected = function ( ) {

  // Shift all the items after the removed item.
  for (var i = this.selectedItemIndex + 1; i < this.items.length; i++) {
    this.items[i]._x -= 105;
  }

  // Remove the selected Sequencer Item component.
  this.items[this.selectedItemIndex].removeMovieClip( );

  // Remove the item from the items array.
  this.items.splice(this.selectedItemIndex, 1);
```

```
    // Remove the item from the sequence viewer as well.
    this.sequenceVwr.removeItem(this.selectedItemIndex);
  };

  // Set the targeted sequence viewer.
  Sequencer.prototype.setSequenceViewer = function (sequenceVwr) {
    this.sequenceVwr = sequenceVwr;
  };

  Object.registerClass("SequencerSymbol", Sequencer);

  #endinitclip
```

The sequencer component employs many of the same techniques as several of the other components throughout this chapter, so much of the code should be quite familiar to you. However, there are a few code snippets that do require a little further illumination.

The *dropItem()* method is, perhaps, the most intimidating of the methods in this component class. However, upon closer examination you will see that it is not difficult to understand. The method is set to be the *onDrop* callback function for each of the sequencer items. This means that each time a sequencer item is dropped, the *dropItem()* method is called and passed a reference to the item that was dropped, as well as the drop target item. We first determine whether the drop target is another sequencer item. If the drop target item (itemB) is undefined or the scroll content background, we know that the item was not dropped on another sequencer item. Therefore, we want to reset the position of the dropped item to its starting position, which is recorded in the item's startPosition property:

```
if (itemB == undefined || itemB == this.sc.background) {
  itemA._x = itemA.startPosition;
}
```

Otherwise, if the drop target is a sequencer item, we rearrange all the sequencer items appropriately. The first thing to do, therefore, is to set the position of itemA to the position of itemB. This snaps itemA to the correct slot in the sequencer.

```
itemA._x = itemB._x;
```

Once itemA is in place, we still need to accomplish several remaining tasks, for which we need to know the indexes of itemA and itemB within the items array. Therefore, we use a *for* loop to search for itemA and itemB in the items array. When we find a match, we set the appropriate variable (either aIndex or bIndex) to the value of the looping index (i). To make the loop more efficient, we use two Boolean variables to keep track of whether itemA and itemB have been located. Once both indexes have been located, we break out of the *for* loop.

```
var aIndex = 0;
var bIndex = 0;
var aSet = false;
var bSet = false;
```

```
for (var i = 0; i < this.items.length; i++) {
  if (this.items[i] == itemA) {
    aIndex = i;
    aSet = true;
  } else if (this.items[i] == itemB) {
    bIndex = i;
    bSet = true;
  }
  if (aSet && bSet) {
    break;
  }
}
```

Once the indexes are known, we can reposition the appropriate items. If itemA was originally positioned to the left of itemB, we shift all the elements from (but not including) itemA through (and including) itemB to the left by the width of a single item plus the 5-pixel buffer. Otherwise, if itemA was originally to the right of itemB, we shift everything from (and including) itemB up to (but not including) itemA to the right by the width of a single item plus the 5-pixel buffer.

```
if (aIndex < bIndex) {
  for (var i = aIndex + 1; i <= bIndex; i++) {
    this.items[i]._x -= (this.itemWidth + 5);
  }
} else {
  for (var i = bIndex; i < aIndex; i++) {
    this.items[i]._x += (this.itemWidth + 5);
  }
}
```

Finally, we adjust the order of the items in the items array as well as the targeted sequence viewer. We use the *splice()* method to first remove itemA from the items array. Then, we use the *splice()* method to insert itemA back into the array at the index that was previously assigned to itemB.

```
this.items.splice(aIndex, 1);
this.items.splice(bIndex, 0, itemA);
this.sequenceVwr.changeOrder(aIndex, bIndex);
```

Designing the Menu Component

The Menu component is the part of the application that does the following:

- Reads an XML document and populates a list box with available images
- Allows users to preview low-resolution images
- Allows users to add images to the sequencer
- Allows users to start the playback of the sequence of images

The first step in designing the Menu component is to create the XML document that the menu uses to populate itself. We won't actually load the XML directly from the Menu component (we do that in the main application routine), but you need to be familiar with the structure of the document to understand parts of the Menu component code. Follow these steps:

1. Open a new text document in an external text editor.

2. Add code with the following structure to your document. You can use the URLs that are in this sample document (if you will play the Flash movie in the Standalone Player), or you can replace them with your own valid URLs to images on your own computer or the server on which you will be serving the Flash movie. This example document includes two <image> elements. If you want to add more images to your application, you can add more <image> elements to your XML document.

```
<images>
  <image>
    <title>Waterfall</title>
    <thumbnail>http://www.person13.com/ascb/images/image1_thumbnail.jpg
              </thumbnail>
    <lowRes>http://www.person13.com/ascb/images/image1_lowRes.jpg</lowRes>
    <full>http://www.person13.com/ascb/images/image1.jpg</full>
  </image>
  <image>
    <title>Lake</title>
    <thumbnail>http://www.person13.com/ascb/images/image2_thumbnail.jpg
              </thumbnail>
    <lowRes>http://www.person13.com/ascb/images/image2_lowRes.jpg</lowRes>
    <full>http://www.person13.com/ascb/images/image2.jpg</full>
  </image>
</images>
```

3. Save the document as *images.xml* to the same directory as your Flash document.

The root element of the XML document is <images>, and the root element contains <image> child nodes for each image that should appear in the menu. Each <image> element, in turn, has four child nodes: <title>, <thumbnail>, <lowRes>, and <full>. The title is the name of the image that appears both in the list box and in the title bar of the preview image. If you do not have a low-resolution and/or thumbnail version of an image, you can use the same URL for two or all three of the image variations. The application automatically resizes the thumbnails, and the preview images can be of any size. The only purpose in having variations for each of the images is because the low-resolution and thumbnail versions can have smaller file sizes (and therefore take less time to load).

To create the Menu component, complete the following steps:

1. Create a new movie clip symbol named *Menu*.

2. Edit the linkage properties of the symbol.

3. Select the Export for ActionScript and Export in First Frame checkboxes.

4. Set the linkage identifier to *MenuSymbol*.

5. Click OK.

6. Edit the new symbol.

7. On the default layer, add the following code to the first frame:

```
#initclip

function Menu () {

    // Create the list box to list the available images and add a value to it that
    // says "loading..." to initialize it.
    this.attachMovie("FListBoxSymbol", "imagesMenu", this.getNewDepth());
    this.imagesMenu.addItem("loading...");

    // Add the preview, sequencer add, and play buttons.
    this.attachMovie("FPushButtonSymbol", "previewBtn", this.getNewDepth());
    this.attachMovie("FPushButtonSymbol", "addBtn", this.getNewDepth());
    this.attachMovie("FPushButtonSymbol", "playBtn", this.getNewDepth());

    // Create a table to organize the menu elements.
    var tr0 = new TableRow(0, new TableColumn(0, this.imagesMenu));
    var tr1 = new TableRow(0, new TableColumn(0, this.previewBtn));
    var tr2 = new TableRow(0, new TableColumn(0, this.addBtn));
    var tr3 = new TableRow(0, new TableColumn(0, this.playBtn));
    var t = new Table(3, 0, 0, tr0, tr1, tr2, tr3);
}

Menu.prototype = new MovieClip();

// The setValues() method takes an XML object parameter and populates the menu.
Menu.prototype.setValues = function (xmlData) {

    // Remove the "loading..." message from the list box.
    this.imagesMenu.removeItemAt(0);

    var imageNodes = xmlData.firstChild.childNodes;
    var imageNode, title, thumbnail, full;

    // Loop through all the <image> nodes.
    for (var i = 0; i < imageNodes.length; i++) {
      imageNode = imageNodes[i];

        // Get the title, thumbnail URL, low-resolution URL, and full image URL.
        title = imageNode.firstChild.firstChild.nodeValue;
        thumbnail = imageNode.firstChild.nextSibling.firstChild.nodeValue;
        lowRes = imageNode.firstChild.nextSibling.nextSibling.firstChild.nodeValue;
        full = imageNode.lastChild.firstChild.nodeValue;

        // Add an item to the list box. The item should display the image title and
        // the data for the item should be an object with thumbnail, full, lowRes,
        // and title properties.
        this.imagesMenu.addItem(title, {thumbnail: thumbnail, full: full,
                                        lowRes: lowRes, title: title});
    }

    // Adjust the width of the list box to accommodate the titles.
    this.imagesMenu.adjustWidth();
```

```
    this.previewBtn.setLabel("preview image");
    this.addBtn.setLabel("add to sequence");
    this.playBtn.setLabel("start sequence");
    this.playBtn.setClickHandler("startSequence", this);
    this.previewBtn.setClickHandler("previewImage", this);
    this.addBtn.setClickHandler("addImageToSequence", this);
};

// Set the reference to the preview pane.
Menu.prototype.setPreviewPane = function (previewPn) {
  this.previewPn = previewPn;
};

// This is the callback function for the preview button. It calls the open()
// method of the preview pane with the selected low-resolution URL and title.
Menu.prototype.previewImage = function () {
  var selected = this.imagesMenu.getValue();
  var lrURL = selected.lowRes;
  var title = selected.title;
  this.previewPn.open(lrURL, title);
};

// Set the reference to the sequencer and sequence viewer.
Menu.prototype.setSequencer = function (sqncr, seqViewer) {
  this.sqncr = sqncr;
  this.seqViewer = seqViewer;
};

// This is the callback function for the sequencer add button. It calls the
// addItem() methods of both the sequencer and the sequence viewer with the
// appropriate URLs.
Menu.prototype.addImageToSequence = function () {
  var selected = this.imagesMenu.getValue();
  var tnURL = selected.thumbnail;
  var fullURL = selected.full;
  this.sqncr.addItem(tnURL);
  this.seqViewer.addItem(fullURL);
};

// This is the callback function for the start sequence playback button. It calls
// the play() method of the sequence viewer with an interval of 3000
// milliseconds (3 seconds) per image.
Menu.prototype.startSequence = function () {
  this.seqViewer.play(3000);
};

Object.registerClass("MenuSymbol", Menu);

#endinitclip
```

The Menu component class is fairly straightforward. The *setValues()* method is the only portion of it that may potentially be a little confusing at first. The method is passed an *XML* object parameter. The *XML* object should be in the same format as the *images.xml* document, and it should not have any extra whitespace nodes (we take care of all of this in the main routine of the application). Then, inside the *setValues()* method, we extract the values for each image's title and the three URLs. We then assign those values to items within the list box. The label for each list box item should be the title, but the data should be an object that contains all the values for that image. This is important because it then gives us access to all that information for an image when it is selected from the menu.

```
for (var i = 0; i < imageNodes.length; i++) {
  imageNode = imageNodes[i];
  title = imageNode.firstChild.firstChild.nodeValue;
  thumbnail = imageNode.firstChild.nextSibling.firstChild.nodeValue;
  lowRes = imageNode.firstChild.nextSibling.nextSibling.firstChild.nodeValue;
  full = imageNode.lastChild.firstChild.nodeValue;
  this.imagesMenu.addItem(title, {thumbnail: thumbnail, full: full,
                                  lowRes: lowRes, title: title});
}
```

Putting Together the Application

Once you have created all the components, you can breathe a sigh of relief knowing that you have completed all the difficult work. All that remains is to put the components together so they work in conjunction with one another to produce a complete, working application.

The main routine of the application is responsible for the following:

- Adding all the necessary components to the movie at runtime
- Loading the XML data
- Listening for keypresses

To complete the main routine of the image viewer application, add the following code to the first frame of the default layer of the main timeline:

```
// Include the necessary libraries in the document. MovieClip.as is from Chapter 7,
// and DrawingMethods.as is from Chapter 4.
#include "MovieClip.as"
#include "DrawingMethods.as"
// Table.as and Forms.as are from Chapter 11.
#include "Table.as"
#include "Forms.as"
// TextField.as is from Chapter 8.
#include "TextField.as"

function init () {
  draw();

  // Create the XML object and load the images.xml document. Be sure to set
  // ignoreWhite to true so that the extra whitespace nodes are eliminated.
  imagesXML = new XML();
```

```
  imagesXML.ignoreWhite = true;
  imagesXML.load("images.xml");
  imagesXML.onLoad = XMLOnLoad;
}

function draw () {

  // Create the Menu component and the Preview Pane component.
  _root.attachMovie("MenuSymbol", "imagesMenu", _root.getNewDepth());
  _root.attachMovie("PreviewPaneSymbol", "previewPn", _root.getNewDepth());
  imagesMenu.setPreviewPane(previewPn);

  // Add the menu and preview pane to a table row.
  tr0 = new TableRow(3, new TableColumn(3, imagesMenu),
                        new TableColumn(3, previewPn));

  // Create the Sequencer component and add it to a table row.
  _root.attachMovie("SequencerSymbol", "seqncr", _root.getNewDepth());
  tr1 = new TableRow(3, new TableColumn(3, seqncr));

  // Create the table to position the elements on the Stage.
  appTable = new Table(3, 0, 0, tr0, tr1);

  // Create the sequence viewer and set the proper references in the Sequencer and
  // Menu components.
  _root.attachMovie("SequenceViewerSymbol", "seqViewer", _root.getNewDepth());
  seqncr.setSequenceViewer(seqViewer);
  imagesMenu.setSequencer(seqncr, seqViewer);
}

// This is the onLoad method for the XML object.
function XMLOnLoad () {

  // Call the setValues() method of the Menu component and
  // pass it a reference to the XML object.
  _root.imagesMenu.setValues(this);

  // Calculate the dimensions of the preview pane according to the new width of the
  // menu, then set the size of the preview pane and render the table.
  var menuW = _root.imagesMenu._width;
  var pvW = Stage.width - menuW - 12;
  var pvH = Stage.height - _root.seqncr._height - 12;
  _root.previewPn.setSize(pvW, pvH);
  _root.appTable.render(true);
}

// Create a listener object to detect keypresses. If the delete key is pressed, call
// the removeSelected() method of the sequencer to remove the selected sequencer
// item. Otherwise, call the stop() method of the sequence viewer to stop the
// playback (if it is playing).
keyListener = new Object();
keyListener.onKeyDown = function () {
  if (Key.getCode() == Key.DELETEKEY) {
    _root.seqncr.removeSelected();
```

```
    } else {
        _root.seqViewer.stop( );
    }
};
Key.addListener(keyListener);

init( );
```

Wrapping It Up

Congratulations. You have completed the image viewer/slideshow application. We've applied many of the techniques from recipes throughout the book. We've also seen how to create an application from a series of custom components. And we've explored real-world techniques to address operational requirements such as synchronization, performance, and dynamic interaction. The remaining chapters explore additional applications that apply and extend what you've learned.

CHAPTER 26

Creating an MP3 Jukebox

One of the exciting features introduced in Flash MX was the ability to load MP3s at runtime using the *Sound* class. In this chapter, we create an MP3 jukebox application that enables users to load MP3 files from various locations. The user can create a playlist of songs and play them back. To make things extra saucy, we also add a five-second cross-fade between songs. Refer to Chapter 13 for basic recipes regarding sound playback. Refer to Chapter 14 for information on recording and publishing audio with FlashCom.

Creating an Application Overview

The MP3 player that you create in this chapter is composed of several parts, so the first step is to determine what these pieces are and how they work together to create an entire application. The final files are available for download from *http://www.person13.com/ascb*. Here is a brief synopsis of each part of this application:

Local MP3 selector
> Combines HTML, JavaScript, and a Flash movie using a local connection to select MP3 files from the hard drive of the client computer so that they can be played in the jukebox.

Server MP3 selector
> Allows users to select an MP3 from the server from which the jukebox is being served so that it can be played. This feature uses Flash Remoting.

Jukebox controller component
> A custom component used to control the playback of the songs in the jukebox playlist. The jukebox controller is composed of two instances of the Sound Controller component from Recipe 13.16.

Main jukebox Flash movie
> Ties everything else together.

Developing the MP3 Selectors

In the following sections, we create both the local and server MP3 selectors. These are the parts of the jukebox application that enable a user to select MP3s from both her own hard drive and from the server by using a graphical user interface instead of having to type in a URL or path to the file.

Creating a Local MP3 Selector

For a user to be able to add an MP3 to her jukebox playlist from her local hard drive, she needs to know the path to that file. This process can be simplified for the user if we can provide her with a way of browsing her hard drive graphically and selecting a file with her mouse. This is the idea behind the local MP3 selector feature.

HTML allows you to create forms with elements of type "file". File form fields include a Browse button that opens a dialog box so that users can select files from their local hard drives. Flash does not natively support a local browse feature; however, we can devise a workaround using HTML, JavaScript, and a Flash movie with a local connection. There are three files necessary for the local MP3 selector functionality—two HTML pages and one Flash movie. Let's look at each of these files individually.

Making the Form page

We will use a standard HTML file form field in a small pop-up browser window to allow the user to select a file from her hard drive. Create a new HTML document named *localFileForm.html* and add the following code to it:

```
<!-- Create a form (must be multipart/form-data in order for the file field
     type to work properly). The form should submit to submitFileForm.html
     (an HTML page we'll create next) using the GET method. -->
<form enctype="multipart/form-data" method="get" action="submitFileForm.html">

<!-- Create a file input field named path. -->
<input type="file" name="path">
<br>

<!-- Create a Submit button. -->
<input type="submit">
</form>
```

As you can see, *localFileForm.html* is not very complicated. If you test the page in a web browser, you can see that a Browse button is created automatically as part of the file input field. Clicking the Browse button opens a dialog box that allows you to select a local file.

Making the Submit page

Once a user has selected a file using the *localFileForm.html* page and clicked the Submit button, the form data is sent to another HTML page named *submitFileForm.html*. We want this HTML page to take the form data (specifically, the value from the file field) and pass it to a Flash movie, which we will create next. You can use the FLASHVARS attribute of the <OBJECT> and <EMBED> tags to pass a value to the movie loaded into the HTML page. Normally, if the values you want to pass to a Flash movie are static, you can hardcode them into the HTML code, as shown in this example (FLASHVARS attributes are shown in bold):

```
<OBJECT classid="clsid:D27CDB6E-AE6D-11cf-96B8-444553540000"
codebase="http://download.macromedia.com/pub/shockwave/cabs/flash/
swflash.cab#version=6,0,0,0"
        WIDTH="550" HEIGHT="400" id="myMovie" ALIGN="">
  <PARAM NAME=movie VALUE="myMovie.swf">
  <PARAM NAME=quality VALUE=high>
  <PARAM NAME=bgcolor VALUE=#FFFFFF>
  <PARAM NAME=FLASHVARS VALUE="param1=value1&param2=value2">
  <EMBED src="myMovie.swf" quality=high bgcolor=#FFFFFF
        WIDTH="550" HEIGHT="400" NAME="myMovie" ALIGN=""
        TYPE="application/x-shockwave-flash"
        PLUGINSPAGE="http://www.macromedia.com/go/getflashplayer"
        FLASHVARS ="param1=value1&param2=value2">
  </EMBED>
</OBJECT>
```

However, we want to obtain the file value dynamically from the HTML form. One option is to use JavaScript to extract the value from the URL—the form values are appended to the URL since we used the GET method to submit the form—and then use the JavaScript *write()* method to generate the <OBJECT> and <EMBED> tags within the HTML page. This solution offers several advantages. First of all, because JavaScript is run on the client and understood by almost all web browsers, you don't have to worry about any server-side language. Furthermore, JavaScript shares the same syntax and many core classes with ActionScript, so it is approachable for most ActionScript developers.

In the following code block, you can see the HTML and JavaScript code that extracts the form value from the URL and passes it a Flash movie using the FLASHVARS attribute. Add this code to an HTML document named *submitFileForm.html* and save it to the same directory as *localFileForm.html*.

```
<HTML>
<HEAD>
<TITLE>Get Path</TITLE>
</HEAD>
<BODY bgColor=#FFFFFF leftmargin="0" marginheight="0" marginwidth="0" topmargin="0">
<SCRIPT language=JavaScript>
<!--
```

```
var path = location.search.split("=")[1];
var swfCode = "<OBJECT classid=\'clsid:D27CDB6E-AE6D-11cf-96B8-444553540000\' ";
swfCode += " codebase=\'http://download.macromedia.com/pub/shockwave/cabs/flash/
swflash.cab#version=6,0,0,0\'";
swfCode += " WIDTH=300 HEIGHT=150>";
swfCode += " <PARAM NAME=movie  VALUE='pathUploader.swf'>";
swfCode += " <PARAM NAME=quality VALUE=best> ";
swfCode += " <PARAM NAME=FlashVars VALUE='path=" + path + "'>";
swfCode += " <EMBED src='pathUploader.swf'";
swfCode += " FLASHVARS ='path=" + path + "'";
swfCode += " quality=best WIDTH=300 HEIGHT=150 ";
swfCode += " TYPE=\'application/x-shockwave-flash\' ";
swfCode += "PLUGINSPAGE=\'http://www.macromedia.com/shockwave/download/
index.cgi?P1_Prod_Version=ShockwaveFlash\'> ";
swfCode += " </EMBED> </OBJECT> ";

document.write(swfCode);
//-->
</SCRIPT>

</BODY>
</HTML>
```

Let's take a closer look at some of the JavaScript code. First of all, we want to get the value that was submitted by the form. In JavaScript the query string portion of the URL (everything following the ?) can be referenced by location.search. In this case, the value of location.search is of the form path=*userSelectedPath*. You can use the *split()* method to split the value into an array using the equals sign as the delimiter; the chosen file path is stored in the array's second element. Hence, we use:

```
var path = location.search.split("=")[1];
```

Next, we want to construct the <OBJECT> and <EMBED> tags. Most of the string defining the tags is hardcoded to contain the necessary attributes. The name of our Flash movie, *pathUploader.swf*, is specified as the movie parameter for the <OBJECT> tag and the src attribute for the <EMBED> tag. Notice that the FLASHVARS attribute is set to include the file path obtained from the form.

```
var swfCode = "<OBJECT classid=\'clsid:D27CDB6E-AE6D-11cf-96B8-444553540000\' ";
swfCode += " codebase=\'http://download.macromedia.com/pub/shockwave/cabs/flash/
swflash.cab#version=6,0,0,0\'";
swfCode += " WIDTH=300 HEIGHT=150>";
swfCode += " <PARAM NAME=movie  VALUE='pathUploader.swf'>";
swfCode += " <PARAM NAME=quality VALUE=best> ";
swfCode += " <PARAM NAME=FLASHVARS  VALUE='path=" + path + "'>";
swfCode += " <EMBED src='pathUploader.swf'";
swfCode += " FLASHVARS ='path=" + path + "'";
swfCode += " quality=best WIDTH=300 HEIGHT=150 ";
swfCode += " TYPE=\'application/x-shockwave-flash\' ";
swfCode += "PLUGINSPAGE=\'http://www.macromedia.com/shockwave/download/
index.cgi?P1_Prod_Version=ShockwaveFlash\'> ";
swfCode += " </EMBED> </OBJECT> ";
```

Once the string is constructed, we use the *document.write()* method to output the value in the HTML page.

```
document.write(swfCode);
```

Making the local connection Flash movie

To finish the local MP3 selector, we must create a Flash movie that takes the value passed to it via FLASHVARS and sends it to the main jukebox movie. You can enable movie-to-movie communication with two Flash movies running on the same computer using a *LocalConnection* object.

We'll name our Flash movie *pathUploader.swf*, as per the movie and src attributes in the preceding *submitFileForm.html* page. This movie should do the following:

- Send the local MP3 file path to the main jukebox movie using a local connection
- Display the selected MP3 file path to the user
- Include a button that allows the user to close the pop-up window

Here are the steps involved in creating this Flash movie:

1. Create a new Flash document named *pathUploader.fla* in the same directory as the HTML files you have already created.
2. Adjust the document settings (under Modify → Document) so that the movie has dimensions of 300 × 150 pixels, which are the dimensions of the browser window that we will open for displaying this movie.
3. Add the PushButton component to the document's Library by dragging an instance from the Components panel onto the Stage and then deleting the instance. (The symbol is copied to the Library.)
4. Add the following code to the first frame of the default layer of the main timeline:

```
// Include MovieClip.as from Chapter 7 and TextField.as from Chapter 8.
#include "MovieClip.as"
#include "TextField.as"

// Create a text field to display the path.
_root.createTextFieldAuto("pathUploadConfirm", _root.getNewDepth());
pathUploadConfirm.multiline = true;
pathUploadConfirm.text = "the file: \n" + path +
                         "\n has been added to the playlist";

// Format the text so it is centered.
tf = new TextFormat();
tf.align = "center";
pathUploadConfirm.setTextFormat(tf);
pathUploadConfirm._y = Stage.height/2 - pathUploadConfirm._height/2;
pathUploadConfirm._x = Stage.width/2  - pathUploadConfirm._width/2;

// Create a Close button so the user can close the pop-up window.
_root.attachMovie("FPushButtonSymbol", "closeBtn", _root.getNewDepth());
```

```
closeBtn._y = pathUploadConfirm._y + pathUploadConfirm._height + 5;
closeBtn._x = Stage.width/2 - closeBtn._width/2;
closeBtn.setLabel("close window");

// When the Close button is released, call the window.close() method for the
// HTML page using the getURL("javascript: void( );") technique.
closeBtn.onRelease = function () {
  this.getURL("javascript: void(window.close( ));");
};

// Create a local connection and send the MP3 path over a connection named
// "pathSendConnection". The listening movie (the main jukebox movie) needs to
// have a receivePathInfo( ) method to receive this value.
sender = new LocalConnection( );
sender.send("pathSendConnection", "receivePathInfo", path);
```

5. Save the document and export the movie as *pathUploader.swf*.

Creating the Server MP3 Selector

In the preceding section, we developed a mechanism by which the user can select an
MP3 from her local hard drive. In this section, we create a similar mechanism that
allows the user to select an MP3 from a server. This portion of the application
requires the use of Flash Remoting. Moreover, the example shown here uses ColdFusion to browse the contents of the server directory. However, this feature is not
essential to the overall functioning of the application, and if you do not use Flash
Remoting or ColdFusion, you can skip over this portion.

The server MP3 selector involves three basic parts:

- A ColdFusion Component (CFC) that retrieves directory and file information
  and returns it to the Flash movie that calls it
- A Flash movie that calls the CFC function via Flash Remoting and displays the
  results in a Tree component
- An HTML page for the Flash movie

The server MP3 selector opens up in a new browser window, as does the local MP3
selector. The server MP3 selector should allow a user to browse the directory in
which the CFC is saved, as well as any of the subdirectories. The user can select a file
and add it to the playlist in the main jukebox movie by way of a local connection.

Making the CFC

The first step in creating the server MP3 selector is to make the CFC that retrieves
the directory and file information. The CFC needs only one method, which takes a
parameter specifying the name of the directory about which to return information.
The method returns an object with the information about that directory, including
the directory name and the files and subdirectories it contains.

To make the CFC, do the following:

1. Create a new file named *DirectoryBrowser.cfc* in the ColdFusion web root (for example, *C:\CfusionMX\wwwroot*).

2. Add the following code to the CFC:

```
<cfcomponent>
  <cffunction name="getDirectoryInfo" access="remote" returntype="struct">

    <!--- Tell the method to expect a string parameter named dir --->
    <cfargument name="dir" type="string" required="false">

    <cfscript>
      // Use the path of the CFC on the server as the default path in case the
      // dir parameter is undefined.
      getdir = #GetDirectoryFromPath(GetCurrentTemplatePath( ))#;
      if (isDefined("arguments.dir")){
        getdir = arguments.dir;
      }
    </cfscript>

    <!--- Use the <cfdirectory> tag to get a directory listing for the specified
          path. Sort the directory contents first by type, then by name. --->
    <cfdirectory directory="#getdir#" name="dirListing" sort="type ASC, name
ASC">

    <cfscript>
      // Create a Struct to return the directory information. Add to this a dir
      // property that contains the value of the current directory as well as a
      // dirListing property that contains the results of <cfdirectory>.
      res = StructNew( );
      res.dir = getdir;
      res.dirListing = dirListing;

      // Return the Struct.
      return res;
    </cfscript>
  </cffunction>
</cfcomponent>
```

3. Save the CFC.

In the first part of the CFC method, we determine the path to the directory for which we should get the information. The first time the method is called, we don't know the path to the directory, but on subsequent calls (i.e., calls to retrieve subdirectory information) we do. For this reason, the dir parameter should not be required. Also, the directory path value that we use (getdir) should default to the path to the directory containing the CFC, but if a parameter is passed to the CFC method, that value should be used instead.

```
<cfargument name="dir" type="string" required="false">
<cfscript>
  getdir = #GetDirectoryFromPath(GetCurrentTemplatePath( ))#;
```

```
  if (isDefined("arguments.dir")){
    getdir = arguments.dir;
  }
</cfscript>
```

The <cfdirectory> tag returns an array of Structs that provide information about all the files and subdirectories within a given directory. Each of the Structs has both a type and a name property, in which type can be either "Dir" or "File" and name is the name of the file or subdirectory. We sort the results first by type and then by name, yielding a listing in which the subdirectories are grouped together and alphabetized, as are the files.

```
<cfdirectory directory="#getdir#" name="dirListing" sort="type ASC, name ASC">
```

Making the server MP3 selector Flash movie

The next part of the server MP3 selector is the Flash movie that interfaces with the CFC via Flash Remoting. The Flash movie is opened in its own pop-up browser window, and it displays the directory listing using a Tree component. Once the user selects a file, the path is sent to the main jukebox movie using a local connection, just as with the local MP3 selector.

Here are the steps to complete to make the MP3 selector Flash movie:

1. Create a new Flash document named *directoryBrowser.fla*.
2. Create an instance of the Tree component in the document's Library. You can do this by dragging an instance of the component from the Components panel onto the Stage and then deleting it. The Tree component is part of the Flash UI Components Set 2 available for free from the Flash Exchange (*http://www.macromedia.com/exchange/flash*).

```
// Include NetServices.as for Flash Remoting support.
#include "NetServices.as"

// Include MovieClip.as from Chapter 7 and TextField.as from Chapter 8.
#include "MovieClip.as"
#include "TextField.as"
// Include Forms.as and Table.as from Chapter 11.
#include "Forms.as"
#include "Table.as"

function init () {

    // Create a Flash Remoting connection. If necessary, adjust the example gateway
    // URL to match your server configuration.
    var gwURL = "http://localhost:8500/flashservices/gateway";
    NetServices.setDefaultGatewayURL(gwURL);
    var conn = NetServices.createGatewayConnection();

    // Create a service object that maps to the DirectoryBrowser CFC.
    dirBrowserSrvc = conn.getService("DirectoryBrowser");
```

```
// Create a response object. When a result is returned to this response object,
// call the addNodes() function (defined next) with the result returned from
// the service function.
dirInfoRes = new Object();
dirInfoRes.onResult = function (result) {
  _root.addNodes(result);
};

// Call the getDirectoryInfo() service function to initialize the movie with
// the contents of the ColdFusion web root (where the CFC is stored). Tell
// Flash to send any responses to the dirInfoRes response object.
dirBrowserSrvc.getDirectoryInfo(dirInfoRes);

// Create a local connection for sending the path to the main jukebox movie.
sender = new LocalConnection();

// The currentNode variable is used to keep track of the tree node that is
// being viewed. Initially no node is being viewed, so set it to null.
currentNode = null;
}

// Create the form in which the user can browse the directory and subdirectories
// using a Tree component.
function createTreeForm () {

  // Create the Tree component instance as well as a text field to display the
  // name of the selected file and a Submit button.
  _root.attachMovie("FTreeSymbol", "tree", _root.getNewDepth());
  _root.createInputTextField("path", _root.getNewDepth(), 0, 0, 150, 20);
  _root.attachMovie("FPushButtonSymbol", "submitBtn", _root.getNewDepth());

  // When a node is selected in the Tree component,
  // call the doSelect() function.
  tree.setChangeHandler("doSelect");

  submitBtn.setClickHandler("submitSelected");
  submitBtn.setLabel("submit");

  // Create a table for positioning the tree, text field, and button.
  treeTr0 = new TableRow(5, new TableColumn(5, tree));
  treeTr1 = new TableRow(5, new TableColumn(5, path));
  treeTr2 = new TableRow(5, new TableColumn(5, submitBtn));
  treeTable = new Table(5, 0, 0, treeTr0, treeTr1, treeTr2);

  // Create a form and add the elements to the form.
  treeForm = new Form();
  treeForm.addElement(tree);
  treeForm.addElement(path);
  treeForm.addElement(submitBtn);
}

// Create a form that displays the path of the selected file and allows the user
// to close the window with a button after the file has been submitted. This code
// is almost identical to the code contained within pathUploader.fla.
function createConfirmForm () {
```

```
_root.createAutoTextField("pathUploadConfirm", _root.getNewDepth( ));
pathUploadConfirm.multiline = true;
pathUploadConfirm.text = "the file: \n\n\n has been added to the playlist";
tf = new TextFormat( );
tf.align = "center";
pathUploadConfirm.setNewTextFormat(tf);
pathUploadConfirm._y = Stage.height/2 - pathUploadConfirm._height/2;
pathUploadConfirm._x = Stage.width/2 - pathUploadConfirm._width/2;
_root.attachMovie("FPushButtonSymbol", "closeBtn", _root.getNewDepth( ));
closeBtn._y = pathUploadConfirm._y + pathUploadConfirm._height + 5;
closeBtn._x = Stage.width/2 - closeBtn._width/2;
closeBtn.setLabel("close window");
closeBtn.onRelease = function ( ) {
  this.getURL("javascript: void(window.close( ));");
};

  // Add the elements to a form.
  confirmForm = new Form( );
  confirmForm.addElement(pathUploadConfirm);
  confirmForm.addElement(closeBtn);
}

// Create a multipage form so that treeForm and confirmForm can occupy the same
// space and only one is visible at a time.
function createMultiForm ( ) {
  myMPForm = new MultiPageForm( );
  myMPForm.addForm(treeForm);
  myMPForm.addForm(confirmForm);
  myMPForm.setPage(1);
}

// This function is invoked automatically every time a value is returned from the
// service function (and it is passed that value in dlInfo).
function addNodes(dlInfo) {

  // If currentNode is null, it was the first call to the service function.
  // Therefore, create a root node for the Tree component and populate it with
  // the data for the web root directory listing.
  if (currentNode == null) {

    // The dir property is the full path to the directory that is being browsed.
    // To get the name of that directory, split the path into an array using "\"
    // as a delimiter for Windows systems. Don't forget to escape the backslash.
    // If you are using a Unix-based server, use "/" as the delimiter instead.
    var dirNameAr = dlInfo.dir.split("\\");

    // The directory name is mostly like the last element of the array.
    var dirName = dirNameAr[dirNameAr.length - 1];

    // If the directory path has a trailing slash, the last element of the array
    // is an empty string, so the directory name is the second-to-last element.
    if (dirName == "") {
      dirName = dirNameAr[dirNameAr.length - 2];
    }
```

```
    // Create the root node.
    var node = new FTreeNode();
    node.setLabel(dirName);
    node.setData(dlInfo.dir);
    tree.setRootNode(node);
    currentNode = node;
  }

  // The currentNode is the one being browsed. Set a custom property for the
  // current node that contains the full path on the server of the directory the
  // node represents.
  currentNode.baseDir = dlInfo.dir;

  // Add a trailing slash to baseDir, if necessary, so that you can safely append
  // a subdirectory name to it.
  if (currentNode.baseDir.lastIndexOf("\\") != currentNode.baseDir.length - 1) {
    currentNode.baseDir += "\\";
  }

  // The custom hasContents property indicates whether the contents of the
  // directory the node represents have already been loaded.
  currentNode.hasContents = true;

  var dl = dlInfo.dirListing;

  // Loop through all the directory listing's elements, and add nodes to the
  // current node for each of the subdirectories and files.
  for (var i = 0; i < dl.getLength(); i++) {
    var tmpNode = new FTreeNode();
    tmpNode.setLabel(dl.getItemAt(i).name);
    tmpNode.setData(currentNode.baseDir + dl.getItemAt(i).name);
    tmpNode.type = dl.getItemAt(i).type;
    if (dl.getItemAt(i).type.toLowerCase() == "dir") {
      tmpNode.setIsBranch(true);
    }
    tree.addNode(currentNode, tmpNode);
  }
}

// The doSelect() function is the callback function for when a node is selected.
// It is automatically passed a reference to the Tree component.
function doSelect (tr) {

  // Get the selected node.
  var sn = tr.getSelectedNode();

  // If the selected node is not a branch node (meaning it does not have any
  // child nodes), it represents a file; otherwise, it represents a directory.
  // Display the file name in the path text field and store the full path
  // information in a custom property of the text field so that if the user
  // clicks the Submit button, the full path can be located easily.
  if (!sn.isBranch()) {
    path.text = sn.getLabel();
    path.data = sn.getData().substr(tree.getRootNode().baseDir.length);
```

```
            pathUploadConfirm.text = "the file: \n" + path.data +
                                "\n has been added to the playlist";
        }

        // Since a new node has been selected, set the
        // currentNode to the selected node.
        currentNode = sn;

        // If the directory listing hasn't already been downloaded, retrieve it from
        // the server by passing the service function the full path to the directory
        // represented by the selected node
        if (!sn.hasContents) {
            dirBrowserSrvc.getDirectoryInfo(dirInfoRes, sn.getData());
        }
    }

    // The submitSelected() function is invoked when the Submit button is clicked.
    function submitSelected () {

        // If the data property of the text field is defined (meaning a file has been
        // selected) send the filename to the main jukebox movie using a local
        // connection (sender). Set the multipage form to the second page.
        if (path.data != undefined) {
            sender.send("pathSendConnection", "receivePathInfo", path.data);
            myMPForm.setPage(2);
        }
    }

    init();
    createTreeForm();
    createConfirmForm();
    createMultiForm();
```

3. Save the Flash document. We export the movie in the next section.

Now let's look at some of the ActionScript code in this document a little more closely. Much of the code is quite straightforward, but some sections involve techniques with which you might not be familiar.

The *init()* function does not do much that is unusual. It creates a connection object and a service object that maps to the *DirectoryBrowser.cfc* file. In addition, it creates a response object for handling the results from the service function. This uses standard Flash Remoting techniques, as discussed in Chapter 20. The call to the service function is standard as well, but notice that we don't pass any parameters to the function. The first time this service function is called, we don't yet know the path to the directory to list. Remember that you designed the CFC function such that if it receives no parameter, it uses the directory in which the CFC is stored.

```
function init () {
    var gwURL = "http://localhost:8500/flashservices/gateway";
    NetServices.setDefaultGatewayURL(gwURL);
    var conn = NetServices.createGatewayConnection();
    dirBrowserSrvc = conn.getService("DirectoryBrowser");
```

```
    dirInfoRes = new Object( );
    dirInfoRes.onResult = function (result) {
      _root.addNodes(result);
    };
    dirBrowserSrvc.getDirectoryInfo(dirInfoRes);
    sender = new LocalConnection( );
    currentNode = null;
}
```

The *createTreeForm()* and *createCofirmForm()* functions are very straightforward.
They each create form elements, position them, and add them to forms. Then, the
createMultiForm() function adds both forms to a multipage form and sets it to display the first page. This allows the two forms to occupy the same space while only
one is visible.

```
function createMultiForm ( ) {
  myMPForm = new MultiPageForm( );
  myMPForm.addForm(treeForm);
  myMPForm.addForm(confirmForm);
  myMPForm.setPage(1);
}
```

The *addNodes()* function is called whenever a result is returned from the service
function, which we use to populate the selected node in the Tree component. The
first time this function is called, the currentNode variable is null, and the function
must create the root node of the Tree component. In this case, it needs to get the
directory name from the full path. One convenient way to do this is to split the path
into an array using the slash as a delimiter. For example, if the path value is "C:\
CFusionMX\wwwroot\", you can create an array with values "C:", "CFusionMX",
"wwwroot", and an empty string (because of the trailing slash). The directory name
is always either the last element of the array (in the case of no trailing slash) or the
second-to-last element (in the case of a trailing slash). This code finds the directory
name in either case:

```
if (currentNode == null) {
  var dirNameAr = dlInfo.dir.split("\\");
  var dirName = dirNameAr[dirNameAr.length - 1];
  if (dirName == "") {
    dirName = dirNameAr[dirNameAr.length - 2];
  }
  var node = new FTreeNode( );
  node.setLabel(dirName);
  node.setData(dlInfo.dir);
  tree.setRootNode(node);
  currentNode = node;
}
```

When the user selects a file element from a tree node, you need to know the
path to that file on the server. For this purpose, you should store the directory
path (dlInfo.dir) as a property of the node that is currently being populated.

Additionally, to append the filename to the path, the path must end in a trailing slash, so we add a trailing slash, if necessary:

```
currentNode.baseDir = dlInfo.dir;
if (currentNode.baseDir.lastIndexOf("\\") != currentNode.baseDir.length - 1) {
  currentNode.baseDir += "\\";
}
```

The custom hasContents property tells Flash if a node already has contents loaded into it:

```
currentNode.hasContents = true;
```

Once the contents have been retrieved from the server, it would be wasteful to request that information again, so we'll make future Flash Remoting requests only if hasContents is not true.

The last part of the *addNodes()* function populates the selected node with the contents. The dirListing property of the object that is returned from the service function is an array of objects in which each object has a name and type property (this is the value that the <cfdirectory> returns). To populate the selected node, use a *for* statement to loop through all the elements of the object array. For each element, create a tree node in which the label is the name of the file or subdirectory, and the data is the full path to the file or subdirectory. Furthermore, if the element is a subdirectory, use the *setIsBranch()* method to configure the node so that it can be opened (expanded into a subdirectory listing).

```
var dl = dlInfo.dirListing;
for (var i = 0; i < dl.getLength( ); i++) {
  var tmpNode = new FTreeNode( );
  tmpNode.setLabel(dl.getItemAt(i).name);
  tmpNode.setData(currentNode.baseDir + dl.getItemAt(i).name);
  tmpNode.type = dl.getItemAt(i).type;
  if (dl.getItemAt(i).type.toLowerCase( ) == "dir") {
    tmpNode.setIsBranch(true);
  }
  tree.addNode(currentNode, tmpNode);
}
```

The *doSelect()* callback function is invoked whenever a tree node is selected. To process the node, you must determine its type. Nodes that represent files are not branch nodes, as detected with the *isBranch()* method.

When a user selects a file from the Tree component, you should:

1. Display the filename in the path text field

2. Store the file's path so that you can access it easily, if and when the user chooses to submit that file to the jukebox

3. Display the path in the pathUploadConfirm text field so that the user gets the confirmation that she has added the correct file before clicking Submit

Notice that the path.data value is a substring of the selected node's data value. The jukebox movie needs to know only the relative path to the file and not the full path. Since the CFC and the jukebox *.swf* file are stored in the same directory, the relative path to the selected file is the difference between the full path to the file and the full path to the application's root directory (which is stored in the baseDir property of the Tree component's root node object). For example, if the full path to the selected file is *C:\CFusionMX\wwwroot\myMp3.mp3* and the full path to the application's root directory is *C:\CFusionMX\wwwroot*, then the relative path to the file is simply *myMp3.mp3*. You can employ a little trick to determine the relative path: start with the file's full path, and then extract the substring starting from the length of the root's path and spanning to the end of the string. Additionally, set the currentNode variable to reference the selected node. If the contents of the node have not been downloaded, call the service function to retrieve the data, passing it the path to the directory that the node represents.

```
function doSelect (tr) {
  var sn = tr.getSelectedNode();
  if (!sn.isBranch()) {
    path.text = sn.getLabel();
    path.data = sn.getData().substr(tree.getRootNode().baseDir.length);
    pathUploadConfirm.text = "the file: \n" + path.data +
                             "\n has been added to the playlist";
  }
  currentNode = sn;
  if (!sn.hasContents) {
    dirBrowserSrvc.getDirectoryInfo(dirInfoRes, sn.getData());
  }
}
```

When the user clicks the Submit button, send the relative path of the selected file to the main jukebox using a local connection. Additionally, display the next page of the multipage form (the confirmation screen).

```
function submitSelected () {
  if (path.data != undefined) {
    sender.send("pathSendConnection", "receivePathInfo", path.data);
    myMPForm.setPage(2);
  }
}
```

Making the HTML page for the server MP3 selector

The last step in making the server MP3 selector is to export the *.swf* file and create the HTML page in which to embed it. Flash's Publish feature creates both the *.swf* and *.html* files. Afterwards, we modify the *.html* file to set the margins to 0 so that the Flash movie is flush with the top-left corner of the browser window.

Here are the steps to create the *.swf* file and HTML page:

1. With the *directoryBrowser.fla* open in Flash, choose File → Publish Settings, which opens the Publish Settings dialog box.

2. Under the Formats tab, select the Flash and HTML checkboxes. Also, select the Use Default Names checkbox so that Flash generates files named *directoryBrowser.swf* and *directoryBrowser.html*.

3. Click the Publish button to generate the *.swf* and *.html* files.

4. Click OK to close the Publish Settings dialog box.

5. Close the Flash document.

6. Open *directoryBrowser.html* in a text editor or web page editor. If you use a WYSIWYG editor such as Dreamweaver, switch to Code view mode to modify the code directly.

7. Modify the <body> tag so that it reads:

   ```
   <BODY bgcolor="#FFFFFF" leftmargin="0" topmargin="0">
   ```

8. Save *directoryBrowser.html* and close it.

Notes on the server MP3 selector

Note the following when implementing the server MP3 selector:

- The server MP3 selector allows the user to browse the directory (and its subdirectories) in which the CFC is stored on the server. Therefore, to let the user select MP3 files from the server, place them within that directory or one of its subdirectories.

- The Tree component distinguishes between selecting a node and opening/expanding a node, but our select handler function is not called only when a node is selected. When the user clicks on a node icon to highlight it, our *doSelect()* handler function is triggered. However, a branch node can be opened/expanded by clicking on the plus sign next to the node icon. This does not automatically select the node, and there is no simple way to detect this event. The problem is that nodes aren't populated until they are selected. Therefore, a node that has been opened but not selected does not display its contents. There are at least two possible solutions:

  — Leave things as they are, and require the user to both select and expand a node to view the contents.

  — Revise the code so that it recursively populates all the subdirectories from the beginning.

- As designed, the main jukebox movie must be served from a web server (as opposed to running from a local file) to work correctly with the server MP3 selector. Furthermore, the CFC, the Flash movies, and the HTML files must be in the same directory. This ensures that the paths returned from the CFC match up relative to the location of the Flash movie.

Developing the Jukebox Application

In the next sections, you will create both the SoundController component and the main jukebox movie code that is responsible for making this application work. All the subsequent code is contained within a single Flash document. Therefore, the first step in this process is to create a new Flash document named *jukebox.fla* and save it.

Adding the Sound Controller

The JukeboxController component is an essential part of the jukebox application. It is required to play the songs. The component uses two SoundController components so that one song can be queued while another is playing. Here are the steps to follow to complete the component:

1. The jukebox controller requires the SoundController component from Recipe 13.16. If you completed that exercise, you should have a Sound Controller menu option in the Components panel, which contains a SoundController component. Otherwise, you can download and install the completed SoundController component from *http://www.person13.com/ascb/components/soundController.zip*.

2. Once you have the SoundController component installed, create a copy of it in your jukebox movie's Library by dragging an instance onto the Stage and deleting the instance. The symbol remains in the Library, even after the instance is deleted.

3. Create a new movie clip symbol named *JukeboxController*.

4. Open the linkage properties for the *JukeboxController* symbol using the Library panel's pop-up Options menu.

5. Select the Export for ActionScript and Export on First Frame checkboxes.

6. Give the symbol a linkage identifier of *JukeboxControllerSymbol*.

7. Click OK to close the Linkage Properties dialog box.

8. Edit the *JukeboxController* symbol.

9. Add the following code to the first frame of the default layer:

```
// Make sure to enclose the code in #initclip/#endinitclip so that this code
// executes before any code on the main timeline.
#initclip

// In the JukeboxController constructor, create two SoundController instances and
// store references to them in the currentPlayer and queuePlayer properties. Hide
// the second player instance by setting its _alpha to 0.
function JukeboxController () {
  this.attachMovie("SoundControllerSymbol", "player2", _root.getNewDepth());
```

```
    this.attachMovie("SoundControllerSymbol", "player1", _root.getNewDepth());
    this.player2._alpha = 0;
    this.currentPlayer = this.player1;
    this.queuePlayer = this.player2;
}

// Make sure that JukeboxController subclasses MovieClip.
JukeboxController.prototype = new MovieClip();

// The loadSong() method uses the SoundController's setTarget() method to set
// currentPlayer's target sound and tell it to play once it is loaded.
JukeboxController.prototype.loadSong = function (snd) {
  this.currentPlayer.setTarget(snd, true);
};

// The loadQueue() method sets the target sound for queuePlayer without playing
// the sound immediately.
JukeboxController.prototype.loadQueue = function (snd) {
  this.queuePlayer.setTarget(snd);
};

// The startNext() method starts the next song.
JukeboxController.prototype.startNext = function () {
  // Use the custom fade() method (from MovieClip.as in Chapter 7) to fade
  // the currentPlayer sound down and the queuePlayer sound up.
  this.currentPlayer.fade(5);
  this.queuePlayer.fade(5, true);

  // Swap the references for currentPlayer and queuePlayer. If currentPlayer was
  // player1, it becomes player2 and queuePlayer becomes player1.
  var tmp = this.currentPlayer;
  this.currentPlayer = this.queuePlayer;
  this.queuePlayer = tmp;

  // Swap the sound controllers' depths so that
  // currentPlayer has the greater depth.
  this.currentPlayer.swapDepths(this.queuePlayer);

  // If the new current song is loaded, begin playback. Otherwise, the
  // onEnterFrame() method monitors it until it is loaded, then begins playback.
  if (this.currentPlayer.snd.isLoaded) {
    this.currentPlayer.start();
  } else {
    this.currentPlayer.onEnterFrame = function () {
      if (this.snd.isLoaded) {
        this.start();
        delete this.onEnterFrame;
      }
    }
  }
};
```

```
// Register the class to the corresponding linkage identifier name.
Object.registerClass("JukeboxControllerSymbol", JukeboxController);

#endinitclip
```

The JukeboxController component code is not very difficult once you examine it more closely.

To begin with, it creates two instances of the SoundController component. One controller is visible while the other is hidden. We set the _alpha property to 0 instead of setting the _visible property to false. This hides the second controller but also allows us to fade visually between the two controllers. We create two properties that references the two controller instances, allowing us to switch between them easily.

```
function JukeboxController () {
   this.attachMovie("SoundControllerSymbol", "player2", _root.getNewDepth());
   this.attachMovie("SoundControllerSymbol", "player1", _root.getNewDepth());
   this.player2._alpha = 0;
   this.currentPlayer = this.player1;
   this.queuePlayer = this.player2;
}
```

The *startNext()* method is responsible for switching between the two sound controllers. First, it calls the custom *MovieClip.fade()* method to fade visually between the two controller instances. If we simply set the _visible properties of the two controllers to true and false, there is no need to change the depths. However, because we adjust the _alpha property instead, we must ensure that the controller for the current song has the greater depth using the *swapDeths()* method. If the target sound for the new current player is loaded, we play it immediately. Otherwise, it begins playing as soon as it has loaded. In later sections, you'll see that the code also fades in sounds as they start and fades out sounds as they stop.

```
JukeboxController.prototype.startNext = function () {
   this.currentPlayer.fade(5);
   this.queuePlayer.fade(5, true);
   var tmp = this.currentPlayer;
   this.currentPlayer = this.queuePlayer;
   this.queuePlayer = tmp;
   this.currentPlayer.swapDepths(this.queuePlayer);
   if (this.currentPlayer.snd.isLoaded) {
     this.currentPlayer.start();
   } else {
     this.currentPlayer.onEnterFrame = function () {
       if (this.snd.isLoaded) {
         this.start();
         delete this.onEnterFrame;
       }
     };
   }
};
```

Creating the Main Jukebox Movie

The final step in the jukebox application is to create the main jukebox Flash movie that incorporates all of the other elements. The jukebox movie has the following functionality:

- A text field in which a URL/path to an MP3 file can be typed directly to be added to the playlist
- Buttons that open the local and server MP3 selectors
- A menu in which the playlist is displayed (items can be reordered and deleted)
- A jukebox controller to control the playback of the MP3s

Here are the steps you should complete to create the main jukebox movie:

1. Open *jukebox.fla* if it is not already open.
2. Add the following code to the default layer of the main timeline:

```
// Include Sound.as from Chapter 13 and Forms.as from Chapter 11.
#include "Sound.as"
#include "Forms.as"
// Include DataGlue.as and RecordSet.as,
// which come with the Flash Remoting components.
#include "DataGlue.as"
#include "RecordSet.as"

// The init() function creates a local connection that listens for songs that
// have been added via the local or server MP3 selectors. Additionally, the
// init() function creates a recordset to hold the playlist information.
function init () {
  receiver = new LocalConnection();
  receiver.receivePathInfo = function (path) {
    if (path != "" && path != undefined && path != null) {
      _root.addSongToList(path);
    }
  };
  receiver.connect("pathSendConnection");
  songsList = new RecordSet("url, snd");
}

// The createElements() method creates all the component instances and text
// fields.
function createElements () {
  _root.attachMovie("FListBoxSymbol", "songsListBox", _root.getNewDepth());
  _root.createAutoTextField("newSongURLLabel", _root.getNewDepth(),
                            0, 0, 0, 0, "URL to MP3:");
  _root.createInputTextField("newSongURL", _root.getNewDepth());
  _root.attachMovie("FPushButtonSymbol", "moveUpBtn", _root.getNewDepth());
  _root.attachMovie("FPushButtonSymbol", "moveDownBtn", _root.getNewDepth());
  _root.attachMovie("FPushButtonSymbol", "removeBtn", _root.getNewDepth());
  _root.attachMovie("FPushButtonSymbol", "addSoundBtn", _root.getNewDepth());
  _root.attachMovie("FPushButtonSymbol", "startPlayBtn", _root.getNewDepth());
  _root.attachMovie("FPushButtonSymbol", "getLocalBtn", _root.getNewDepth());
```

```
_root.attachMovie("FPushButtonSymbol", "getServerBtn", _root.getNewDepth());
_root.attachMovie("JukeboxControllerSymbol", "jukeboxCtrl", _root.getNewDepth(
));

    addSoundBtn.setLabel("Add Song");
    moveUpBtn.setLabel("Move Up");
    moveDownBtn.setLabel("Move Down");
    removeBtn.setLabel("Remove Song");
    startPlayBtn.setLabel("Begin Playback");
    getLocalBtn.setLabel("Get Local MP3");
    getServerBtn.setLabel("Get Server MP3");
    addSoundBtn.setClickHandler("addSound");
    startPlayBtn.setClickHandler("startNextSong");
    moveUpBtn.setClickHandler("moveSongUp");
    moveDownBtn.setClickHandler("moveSongDown");
    removeBtn.setClickHandler("removeSong");
    getLocalBtn.setClickHandler("getMP3");
    getServerBtn.setClickHandler("getMP3");
}

// The layoutElements( ) function positions the components and text fields in a
// table.
function layoutElements ( ) {
  tc0 = new TableColumn(5, songsListBox);
  tc1 = new TableColumn(5, startPlayBtn, moveUpBtn, moveDownBtn, removeBtn);
  tc2 = new TableColumn(5, newSongURLLabel, newSongURL, addSoundBtn,
                        getLocalBtn, getServerBtn);
  tc3 = new TableColumn(5, jukeboxCtrl);
  tr0 = new TableRow(5, tc0);
  tr1 = new TableRow(5, tc1, tc2);
  tr2 = new TableRow(5, tc3);
  t = new Table(5, 0, 0, tr0, tr1, tr2);
}

// The formatSongsList( ) function is used by the DataGlue.bindFormatFunction( )
// call in updateListView( ) to format each element in the song list.
function formatSongsList(element) {
  // Get the name of the MP3 from the URL/path. If you split
  // the URL using "/" as the delimiter, the name of the MP3 is
  // the last element of the resulting array.
  var urlAr = element.url.split("/");
  if (urlAr.length == 1) {
    urlAr = element.url.split("\\");
  }
  var name = urlAr[urlAr.length - 1];

  // Create the object to return to bindFormatFunction( ). The data should be the
  // element itself, and the label should be the name of the MP3 file.
  var obj = new Object();
  obj.data = element;
  obj.label = name;

  // If the song is already loaded, display its duration next to the name.
  // Otherwise, display the percentage that has loaded.
  if (element.snd.isLoaded) {
```

```
    obj.label += " (" + SoundController.timeDisplay(element.snd.duration) + ")";
  } else {
    obj.label += " [" + element.snd.percentLoaded + "%]";
  }
  return obj;
}

// The updateListView() function is called continually to update the playlist
// menu to reflect load progress while any songs are loading.
function updateListView () {
  var selected = _root.songsListBox.getSelectedIndex();
  DataGlue.bindFormatFunction(_root.songsListBox, _root.songsList,
                              _root.formatSongsList);
  _root.songsListBox.adjustWidth();
  _root.songsListBox.setSelectedIndex(selected);
}

// The addSongToList() function adds a song to the playlist from a URL.
function addSongToList (url) {

  // Load a sound into a new sound object created using the custom
  // createNewSound() method from Recipe 13.1.
  var mySound = Sound.createNewSound();
  mySound.loadSound(url);

  // Add the song to the songsList recordset.
  songsList.addItem({url: url, snd: mySound});

  // Create an onEnterFrame() method that calls updateListView() continually
  // until the song is loaded.
  mySound.mc.onEnterFrame = function () {
    _root.updateListView();
    if (this.parent.isLoaded) {
      delete this.onEnterFrame;
    }
  };
}

// The startNextSong() function plays the next song in the playlist.
function startNextSong () {

  // The counter variable keeps track of which song is currently being played. If
  // it is undefined or greater than the number of songs, reset it to 0.
  if (counter >= songsListBox.getLength() || counter == undefined) {
    counter = 0;
  }

  // Highlight the current song in the playlist.
  songsListBox.setSelectedIndex(counter);

  // Get the sound object for the current song.
  var snd = songsListBox.getItemAt(counter).data.snd;
```

```
    // Set the sound to fade in for the first five seconds
    // and to fade out for the last five seconds.
    snd.fadeIn(5000);
    snd.fadeOut(5000);

    // When the song fades out, call this function (startNextSong()) again.
    snd.setOnFadeOut("startNextSong");

    // When the song ends (as opposed to when it starts fading out), call
    // stopPlayer() to stop the song.
    snd.setOnStop("stopPlayer");

    // Load the new song into the queue and tell the
    // jukebox controller to play the next song.
    jukeboxCtrl.loadQueue(snd);
    jukeboxCtrl.startNext();
    counter++;
}

// When the end of the song is reached, this function stops the song.
function stopPlayer () {
  _root.jukeboxCtrl.queuePlayer.stop();
}

// The addSound() function is the click handler for the Add Song button; it adds
// a song to the playlist from the URL typed into the text field.
function addSound () {
  var url = newSongURL.text;
  newSongURL.text = "";
  addSongToList(url);
}

// The moveSongUp() function moves a song up in the playlist.
function moveSongUp () {

  // Get the index of the of playlist item the user has selected.
  var selected = songsListBox.getSelectedIndex();

  // Move the song only if it isn't already first in the list.
  if (selected > 0) {

    // Insert the item into the list at one index prior to its current position.
    songsList.addItemAt(selected - 1, songsListBox.getItemAt(selected).data);

    // Remove the item from its original position in the list.
    songsList.removeItemAt(selected + 1);

    // Update the view of the playlist and set the selected index such that the
    // song that was moved is highlighted.
    updateListView();
    songsListBox.setSelectedIndex(selected - 1);
  }
}
```

```
// The moveSongDown( ) function does the opposite of the moveSongUp( ) function.
function moveSongDown ( ) {
  var selected = songsListBox.getSelectedIndex( );
  // Move the song only if it isn't already last in the list.
  if (selected < songsListBox.getLength( ) - 1) {
    songsList.addItemAt(selected + 2, songsListBox.getItemAt(selected).data);
    songsList.removeItemAt(selected);
    updateListView( );
    songsListBox.setSelectedIndex(selected + 1);
  }
}

// The removeSong( ) function removes a song from the list.
function removeSong ( ) {

  // Get the index of the selected song in the playlist.
  var selected = songsListBox.getSelectedIndex( );

  // Make sure a song is selected before trying to remove one.
  if (selected != undefined) {

    // Get the sound associated with the song.
    var snd = songsList.getItemAt(selected).snd;

    // Remove the song from the playlist.
    songsList.removeItemAt(selected);
    updateListView( );

    if (selected < counter) {
      // If the index of the deleted song is less than counter (the index of the
      // song that is currently playing), decrement counter.
      counter--;
    } else if (selected == counter) {
      // If the deleted song was the current song, fade out the song from its
      // current play position.
      snd.fadeOut(5000, snd.position);
    }
  }
}

// The getMP3( ) function is the click handler for the
// getLocalBtn and getServerBtn buttons. It opens the HTML
// pages for the selectors in new browser windows.
function getMP3 (btn) {
  if (btn == getLocalBtn) {
    this.getURL("javascript:void(window.open('localFileForm.html',
               '_blank', 'width=300,height=150'))");
  }
  else if (btn == getServerBtn) {
    this.getURL("javascript:void(window.open('directoryBrowser.html',
               '_blank', 'width=210,height=360'))");
  }
}
```

```
init( );
createElements( );
layoutElements( );
```

3. Save the Flash document and publish the .swf and .html files.

At this point, you have completed the entire jukebox application. You can test it by opening *jukebox.html* in a web browser. If you are using the server MP3 selector, you need to open *jukebox.html* so that it is served by the web server. For example, if you have a web server running on your local machine, you can use *http://localhost:8500/ jukebox.html*.

Most of the code in the main jukebox movie becomes clearer with a little further examination, so let's take a look at some of the code elements in more detail.

The *init()* function creates the local connection object that listens for communications from both MP3 selectors. Both MP3 selectors send messages over the connection named "pathSendConnection" to a *receivePathInfo()* method, and they pass that method the URL/path to the selected MP3. The *receivePathInfo()* method passes the URL/path along to the *addSongToList()* function to add the song to the playlist. The *init()* function also creates a recordset that is used to keep track of the songs in the playlist. A recordset is convenient for populating a list box with complex data, which in this case is a URL/path to the MP3 file as well as a *Sound* object for the song.

```
function init () {
  receiver = new LocalConnection( );
  receiver.receivePathInfo = function (path) {
    if (path != "" && path != undefined && path != null) {
      _root.addSongToList(path);
    }
  };
  receiver.connect("pathSendConnection");

  songsList = new RecordSet("url, snd");
}
```

The *formatSongsList()* function is a formatter function that is used by the *DataGlue.bindFormatFunction()* method in the *updateListView()* function. The playlist displays the name of each song as well as the duration of the song or the percentage that has loaded. These values are obtained from the songsList recordset. Each record has a url column that contains the URL/path to the MP3 file. You can extract the name of the MP3 from this value using the same technique discussed earlier (in the MP3 selector code), in which you split the URL/path into an array using "/" as the delimiter. If the url value is a URL, it should be split using a forward slash (/) as the delimiter. However, if the MP3 has been added to the playlist from the local MP3 selector, the url can potentially use backslashes. In that case, split the value into an array using the backslash (\) as the delimiter. Don't forget to escape the backslash delimiter. Additionally, each item in the playlist list box should contain a data value that includes both the URL/path to the MP3 as well as the *Sound* object into which the song has been (or is being) loaded. You can accomplish this by setting the list box element's data property to the record from the recordset.

```
var urlAr = element.url.split("/");
if (urlAr.length == 1) {
  urlAr = element.url.split("\\");
}
var name = urlAr[urlAr.length - 1];
var obj = new Object( );
obj.data = element;
obj.label = name;
```

If the song has already loaded, you can use the duration property to determine its length in seconds. The *SoundController* class (the class for the SoundController component) includes a static *timeDisplay()* method to format the time in standard minutes and seconds. Otherwise, if the song has not yet loaded, you cannot access the duration, so you should display the percentage that has loaded instead.

```
if (element.snd.isLoaded) {
  obj.label += " (" + SoundController.timeDisplay(element.snd.duration) + ")";
} else {
  obj.label += " [" + element.snd.percentLoaded + "%]";
}
```

The *updateListView()* function is called to update the playlist display, such as when a new song is added or an old one is moved or removed. Also, the display is updated to show a song's load progress. The *updateListView()* function uses the *DataGlue.bindFormatFunction()* method to update the contents of the list box. However, there are a few other things that need to be done for formatting and display to be correct. First of all, because the MP3 names can vary in length, use the *adjustWidth()* method to resize the list box to fit its contents. Also, call *setSelectedIndex()* to reselect the item that was selected before *updateListView()* was invoked.

```
function updateListView ( ) {
  var selected = _root.songsListBox.getSelectedIndex( );
  DataGlue.bindFormatFunction(_root.songsListBox, _root.songsList,
                              _root.formatSongsList);
  _root.songsListBox.adjustWidth( );
  _root.songsListBox.setSelectedIndex(selected);
}
```

The *addSongToList()* method is called when the user clicks the Add Song button or adds a song via the local or server MP3 selector. The function adds the new song to the songsList recordset. The URL value is passed automatically to the *addSongToList()* function, so that part is already known. For the snd column, the function creates a new *Sound* object and loads the song into it. Finally, *addSongToList()* attaches an *onEnterFrame()* method to the mc property of the *Sound* object—the mc property is a reference to the sound-holder movie clip created automatically by *Sound.createNewSound()*. The *onEnterFrame()* method calls the *updateListView()* function continually until the song has completed loading.

```
function addSongToList (url) {
  var mySound = Sound.createNewSound();
  mySound.loadSound(url);
  songsList.addItem({url: url, snd: mySound});
  mySound.mc.onEnterFrame = function () {
    _root.updateListView();
    if (this.parent.isLoaded) {
      delete this.onEnterFrame;
    }
  };
}
```

The *startNextSong()* function is interesting in that it is both the click handler function for the Begin Playback button and the *onFadeOut* callback function for each song. When the function is invoked, it starts the next song in the playlist. The code in this function is central to the core functioning of the jukebox, so let's look at each piece of it. First, it uses the counter variable to keep track of which song is being played. The *startNextSong()* function increments counter each time it completes. Therefore, if counter is greater than the number of songs in the playlist, start back at the beginning of the playlist by setting counter to 0.

```
if (counter >= songsListBox.getLength() || counter == undefined) {
  counter = 0;
}
```

Each time the next song starts, you want to highlight that song in the playlist. You can do this with the *setSelectedIndex()* method:

```
songsListBox.setSelectedIndex(counter);
```

Each item in the playlist list box has data that includes both url and snd properties. The snd property is a *Sound* object into which the song has been loaded, and we can use it to instruct the song to begin playing. To perform a cross-fade between songs, each song should fade in for five seconds at its beginning and fade out for five seconds at its end. The next song should start when the *onFadeOut* event occurs within the current song. This way, the next song begins playing at the point that the previous song begins to fade out.

```
var snd = songsListBox.getItemAt(counter).data.snd;
snd.fadeIn(5000);
snd.fadeOut(5000);
snd.setOnFadeOut("startNextSong");
snd.setOnStop("stopPlayer");
jukeboxCtrl.loadQueue(snd);
jukeboxCtrl.startNext();
counter++;
```

The *moveSongUp()* and *moveSongDown()* functions change the order of the selected song in the playlist. They first insert a copy of the selected item into the playlist at the new position using the *addItemAt()* method, which automatically shifts the subsequent items in the list box. Then, they simply delete the selected song from the original position using the *removeItemAt()* method. Here is the code for *moveSongUp()*; *moveSongDown()* is similar:

```
function moveSongUp ( ) {
  var selected = songsListBox.getSelectedIndex( );
  if (selected > 0) {
    songsList.addItemAt(selected - 1, songsListBox.getItemAt(selected).data);
    songsList.removeItemAt(selected + 1);
    updateListView( );
    songsListBox.setSelectedIndex(selected - 1);
  }
}
```

The *removeSong()* function is the click handler function for the Remove Song button. The function makes sure that a song is selected before trying to remove anything. If the *getSelectedIndex()* method for songsListBox returns undefined, the function doesn't remove anything. If a song is selected, the function does several things. First, it retrieves the *Sound* object associated with the song (because it cannot get the reference after deleting it). It then removes the song from the playlist by deleting it from the recordset and calling *updateListView()* to refresh the playlist's display. If the removed song is currently playing, it fades out the song using *fadeOut()*. Because of the way that you have configured each song in the *startNextSong()* function, when the current song is instructed to fade out, the next song automatically starts.

```
function removeSong ( ) {
  var selected = songsListBox.getSelectedIndex( );
  if (selected != undefined) {
    var snd = songsList.getItemAt(selected).snd;
    songsList.removeItemAt(selected);
    updateListView( );
    if (selected < counter) {
      counter--;
    } else if (selected == counter) {
      snd.fadeOut(5000, snd.position);
    }
  }
}
```

Wrapping It Up

As with any application, there is not one "right" way to plan and develop the jukebox application. However, I hope you have gained some insights and ideas related to good practices working with *Sound* objects, custom components, FLASHVARS, recordsets, local connections, and Flash Remoting.

## CHAPTER 27

A Personalized My Page Application

Personalization is an important part of many web applications, as seen in so-called *My Page* applications, such as those available at My Yahoo!, My Excite, and My MSN. Typical My Page applications offer *modules* that the user can turn on or off and position within the page. A module can be a *.swf* file that gives access to a web service or performs some service function, so we often use the terms "service" or "service module" interchangeably with "module," even if the module is not a formal web service. Examples of modules offered by My Page applications include:

- Scheduler
- Email
- News
- Weather
- Stocks
- Web search
- Shopping

These modules usually can be customized according to the user's preferences. For example, if the user activates a weather module, he is given the option of specifying the city for which to display the weather forecast.

In this chapter, you will create a My Page application in Flash. This application draws on many skills detailed throughout recipes in previous chapters, including:

- Local shared objects
- Loading and processing XML
- Using predefined components
- Creating custom components
- Using the Drawing API's methods
- Loading external SWFs

- Using Flash Remoting to consume web services
- Controlling movie clips with ActionScript

Formulating the Application Overview

Before starting any application, formulate a plan. Clarify the project goals and map out a strategy to meet them. A My Page application requires a framework that allows various modules to be added, as illustrated in Figure 27-1.

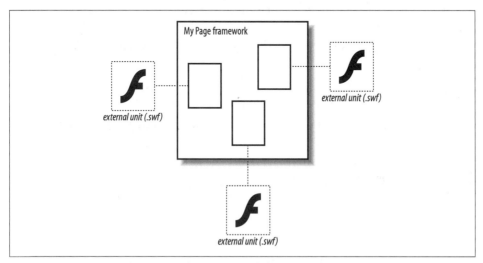

Figure 27-1. A conceptual overview of the My Page framework

The application should have a scalable architecture that allows the developer to offer more modules and allows the user to add more of these modules to his customized page. The My Page framework should not care about the particulars of each module and should treat all modules uniformly.

The sample application code that is provided in this chapter includes the following files:

myPage.fla
   The My Page framework document

notes.fla
   A note module

addressBook.fla
   An address book module

search.fla
   A web search modular service (uses Google's web service)

services.xml

An XML document that tells the framework which modules are available

SupportFunctions.as

An ActionScript file with functions that are shared by multiple movies

The final files can be downloaded from *http://www.person13.com/ascb*.

Creating the Framework

The My Page framework is a single Flash movie, *myPage.fla*, which performs the following tasks:

- Loads available module types from an XML file, which it uses to populate a menu
- Creates a new visual container (a custom component instance) when a user chooses a module and loads the module into it
- Remembers each module's position and state between sessions using a local shared object

Sharing Common Functions

The first step in creating the framework is to create the *SupportFunctions.as* file, which is shared among all the Flash movies, including *myPage.fla*. *SupportFunctions. as* should contain the following code:

```
MovieClip.prototype.getNewDepth = function () {
  // If no currentDepth is defined, initialize it to 1.
  if (this.currentDepth == undefined) {
    this.currentDepth = 1;
  }
  // Return the new depth and increment it by 1 for next time.
  return this.currentDepth++;
};
```

This code adds a *getNewDepth()* method to the *MovieClip* class such that all *MovieClip* objects inherit it. The *getNewDepth()* method generates a unique depth each time it is called. This is important because this chapter creates all application elements at runtime via ActionScript. Each dynamically created element must reside on its own depth to prevent elements from overwriting each other.

Configuring the Available Modules

Later in this chapter we create three modules that are made available to the framework. However, the framework should be able to accommodate other modules as well. We achieve this flexibility using an XML document that contains information about the available modules the framework should load. For now, create *services.xml*

---

as shown in the following example, which lists the three modules that we'll create shortly.

```
<choices>
  <choice title="Address Book" source="addressBook.swf" />
  <choice title="Notes" source="notes.swf" />
  <choice title="Search the Web" source="search.swf" />
</choices>
```

Adding a Component

The next step in the framework development is to create a custom component—the instances of which act as the containers into which each module is loaded. The main module container component actually uses another custom component, so there are two steps in this process. First, you should define the child component, *UnitComponentBar*, which is used as the title bar for the main module container component. Then, you should define *UnitComponent*.

Defining UnitComponentBar

Follow these steps to define *UnitComponentBar*:

1. Within *myPage.fla*, insert a new movie clip library symbol named *UnitComponentBar*.

2. Set the symbol to Export for ActionScript and Export in First Frame using the Linkage option under the Library panel's Options pop-up menu.

3. Give it the linkage identifier *UnitComponentBarSymbol*.

In the following example, you can see the code that you should place on the first frame of the default layer of the *UnitComponentBar* symbol. We'll examine portions in more detail following the code listing.

The *getNewDepth()* method is used within the component class even though you cannot yet see how it has been made available. We will #include it in the framework document later. Because *getNewDepth()* is defined as a method for all *MovieClip* objects, it is accessible from any timeline once it has been loaded in a movie.

```
// #initclip with an option of 0 means that this code loads
// before anything else, which is important, since it must be
// defined before it can be used in UnitComponent.
#initclip 0

// The constructor is called when a new UnitComponentBar instance is created.
function UnitComponentBar () {

  // Create the movie clip into which the bar is drawn.
  this.createEmptyMovieClip("barHolder", this.getNewDepth());
  // Create the title text field.
  this.createAutoTextField("title", this.getNewDepth());
  this.title.selectable = false;
```

```
    // Create a movie clip for the Close button that lets users close the module.
    this.closeSquare = this._parent.createEmptyMovieClip("closer",
                       this._parent.getNewDepth());
}

// UnitComponentBar extends the MovieClip class.
UnitComponentBar.prototype = new MovieClip();

// The draw() method draws the title bar with the given width, height, and fill
// color. It also aligns the title bar to the parent UnitComponent instance
// according to the margin parameter, m, and sets the color of the text.
UnitComponentBar.prototype.draw = function (w, h, m, fillColor, titleColor) {

    // Draw the title bar.
    with (this.barHolder) {
      lineStyle(1, 0, 100);
      beginFill(fillColor, 100);
      drawRectangle(w + m, h, 0, 0, (w + m)/2, h/2);
      endFill();
    }

    // Set the text color
    this.title.textColor = titleColor;

    // Draw the Close button.
    with (this.closeSquare) {
      lineStyle(1, titleColor, 100);
      beginFill(0, 0);
      drawRectangle(10, 10, 0, 0, 5, 5);
      endFill();
      _x = w - m - 5;
      _y = 5;
    }

    // Invoke the close() method to remove the module if the Close button is clicked.
    this.closeSquare.onRelease = this.close;
};

// This function sets the text of the title bar.
UnitComponentBar.prototype.setTitle = function (titleText) {
  this.title.text = titleText;
};

// When a title bar is clicked, make its parent UnitComponent instance draggable.
UnitComponentBar.prototype.onPress = function () {
  this._parent.startDrag();

  // Check for overlapping siblings.
  this._parent.onEnterFrame = this._parent.checkOverlaps;
};

// Stop the dragging when released.
UnitComponentBar.prototype.onRelease = function () {
```

```
  // Stop dragging the item.
  this._parent.stopDrag();

  // Notify all listeners of the unit's new position
  var l = this._parent.listeners;
  for (var i = 0; i < l.length; i++) {
    l[i].onMoved(this._parent);
  }

  // Disable hit testing now that the drag event is over.
  delete this._parent.onEnterFrame;
};

// Close the parent UnitComponent instance.
UnitComponentBar.prototype.close = function () {
  this._parent.onClose();
  this._parent.removeMovieClip();
};

// Register the class.
Object.registerClass("UnitComponentBarSymbol", UnitComponentBar);

#endinitclip
```

This constitutes a rather long listing with some important code that we should look at more closely.

To begin with, it is important that the #initclip directive include the load order parameter. In this case, use the value 0 because the code enclosed between #initclip and #endinitclip should load before any other code in the movie. This is because *UnitComponentBar* instances are created within *UnitComponent* objects (as you will see in the next section), and, therefore, the definition must be loaded first to be accessible.

```
#initclip 0
```

The *UnitComponentBar* constructor creates the close box movie clip with the *createEmptyMovieClip()* method. Notice, however, that the method is invoked from this._parent instead of just this. The reason for this is that the close box instance must be on top of the *UnitComponentBar* instance to function properly. For convenience, a reference to the close box movie clip created in the parent is set to a property named closeSquare:

```
this.closeSquare = this._parent.createEmptyMovieClip("closer",
                     this._parent.getNewDepth());
```

The *onPress()* and *onRelease()* event handler methods are defined for all *UnitCompontBar* instances by defining them on the prototype property of the class. Both of these definitions, as well as the *close()* method, invoke methods defined for the parent *UnitCompont* instance by using this._parent to reference it:

```
UnitComponentBar.prototype.onPress = function () {
  this._parent.startDrag();
```

```
    this._parent.onEnterFrame = this._parent.checkOverlaps;
};

UnitComponentBar.prototype.onRelease = function () {
    this._parent.stopDrag();
    var l = this._parent.listeners;
    for (var i = 0; i < l.length; i++) {
        l[i].onMoved(this._parent);
    }
    this._parent.onEnterFrame = null;
};

UnitComponentBar.prototype.close = function () {
    this._parent.onClose();
    this._parent.removeMovieClip();
};
```

Finally, the class must be registered to be associated automatically with new
instances of the movie clip library symbol in which it is defined. The linkage identifier *UnitComponentBar* is passed as the first parameter, and a reference to the class is
passed as the second parameter to the *Object.registerClass()* method to accomplish
this:

```
Object.registerClass("UnitComponentBarSymbol", UnitComponentBar);
```

Defining UnitComponent

Now that we've defined the *UnitComponentBar*, let's define the *UnitComponent* that
contains it:

 1. Within *myPage.fla*, drag an instance of the ProgressBar component from the Com-
    ponents panel to the Stage in order to add it to the Library. After doing so, you can
    delete the instance from the Stage.
 2. Insert a new movie clip library symbol named *UnitComponent*.
 3. Set the library symbol to Export for ActionScript and Export in First Frame using
    the Linkage option under the Library panel's pop-up Options menu.
 4. Give it the linkage identifier *UnitComponentSymbol*.

Here is the code that goes on the first frame of the default layer of the new symbol.
Look over the code briefly. We'll examine aspects of it in more detail shortly.

```
// Load this code second by using the load order parameter value of 1.
#initclip 1

// The UnitComponentGroup class keeps track of each UnitComponent instance that is
// created within the same timeline.
function UnitComponentGroup () {}

// groupMembers is an associative array that holds references to each sibling
// instance (i.e., other members of the group).
UnitComponentGroup.prototype.groupMembers = new Object();
```

```
// The onNew( ) method is called when a new UnitComponent instance is created.
UnitComponentGroup.prototype.onNew = function (newUnit) {

  // Add the new UnitComponent instance to the groupMembers array.
  this.groupMembers[newUnit._name] = newUnit;
  var sibs;

  // Loop through each sibling (each UnitComponent).
  for (var unit in this.groupMembers) {
    sibs = new Array( );

    // Loop through all the groupMember elements to create an array of siblings (not
    // including itself) for each UnitComponent instance.
    for (var sib in this.groupMembers) {
      if (this.groupMembers[unit] != this.groupMembers[sib]) {
        sibs.push(this.groupMembers[sib]);
      }
    }

    // Call the UnitComponent instance's setSiblings( ) method with a reference to the
    // newly created sibs array.
    this.groupMembers[unit].setSiblings(sibs);
  }
};

// The constructor creates the movie clip and text field objects for a module.
function UnitComponent ( ) {

  // Create the outline box and title bar movie clips.
  this.createEmptyMovieClip("outline", this.getNewDepth( ));
  this.attachMovie("UnitComponentBarSymbol", "bar", this.getNewDepth( ));

  // Add the placeholder for the loaded module.
  this.createEmptyMovieClip("loadPlaceHolder", this.getNewDepth( ));

  // Obtain a unique depth for the new module.
  this.index = this.getDepth( );

  // Create a unit grouping to contain this and any sibling modules (see the
  // discussion following this example).
  if (this._parent.unitGroup == undefined) {
    this._parent.unitGroup = new UnitComponentGroup( );
  }
  this.group = this._parent.unitGroup;
  this.group.onNew(this);
}

// UnitComponent extends the MovieClip class.
UnitComponent.prototype = new MovieClip( );

// Set the default attributes of all units.
UnitComponent.prototype.barColor = 0x000000;
UnitComponent.prototype.titleColor = 0xFFFFFF;
UnitComponent.prototype.listeners = new Array( );
```

```
// Define the following properties and set them to null. They will be assigned a
// value by other methods.
UnitComponent.prototype.index = null;
UnitComponent.prototype.siblings = null;
UnitComponent.prototype.group = null;

// Load an external .swf file into the component.
UnitComponent.prototype.load = function (url) {

  // Load the module into loadPlaceHolder.
  this.loadPlaceHolder.loadMovie(url);

  // Create a text field to label the progress bar.
  this.createAutoTextField("loading", this.getNewDepth());
  this.loading.text = "loading...";

  // Create a progress bar using the ProgressBar component.
  this.attachMovie("FProgressBarSymbol", "progress", this.getNewDepth());
  this.progress._y = this.loading._height + 5;

  // Start an onEnterFrame() loop to update the progress bar.
  this.onEnterFrame = this.onLoading;
};

// The onLoading() method updates the progress while loading and then performs
// actions when the module has loaded.
UnitComponent.prototype.onLoading = function () {

  // Update the loading module's progress bar with the loaded and total bytes.
  var lBytes = this.loadPlaceHolder.getBytesLoaded();
  var tBytes = this.loadPlaceHolder.getBytesTotal();
  this.progress.setProgress(lBytes, tBytes);

  // If the module has loaded completely, then do the following:
  if (this.progress.getPercentComplete() == 100) {

    // Remove the progress bar and its label text field.
    this.progress.removeMovieClip();
    this.loading.removeTextField();

    // Call the drawOutline() and the UnitComponentBar.draw() methods with the
    // loaded module's dimensions. This creates a placeholder rectangle for the newly
    // loaded module.
    var margin = 5;
    var w = this.loadPlaceHolder._width + (margin * 2);
    var h = this.loadPlaceHolder._height + (margin * 2);
    this.drawOutline(w, h, margin);
    this.bar.draw(w, 20, margin, this.barColor, this.titleColor);

    // Create a table to position the title bar and the outline. Use a spacing of -1
    // so that there are no spaces between the two.
    var t = new Table(0, 0, 0, new TableRow(0,
                      new TableColumn(-1, this.bar, this.outline)));
    this.loadPlaceHolder._x = this.outline._x + margin;
    this.loadPlaceHolder._y = this.outline._y + margin;
```

```
    // Stop the onEnterFrame() loop by deleting it.
    delete this.onEnterFrame;
  }
};

// Set the siblings property to an array containing references to all other
// UnitComponent instances.
UnitComponent.prototype.setSiblings = function (s) {
  this.siblings = s;
};

// Draw the outline and background for the component.
UnitComponent.prototype.drawOutline = function (w, h, margin) {
  with (this.outline) {
    lineStyle(1, 0, 100);
    beginFill(0xFFFFFF, 100);
    drawRectangle(w + margin, h + margin, 0, 0, (w + margin)/2, (h + margin)/2);
    endFill();
  }
};

// Set the title of the component, as displayed in the title bar.
UnitComponent.prototype.setTitle = function (title) {
  // Call the UnitComponentBar instance's setTitle() method.
  this.bar.setTitle(title);
};

// Check whether the instance is overlapped by another component instance.
UnitComponent.prototype.checkOverlaps = function () {

  // Loop through all the siblings.
  for (var i = 0; i < this.siblings.length; i++) {

    // If the instance is overlapped by a sibling—hitTest() is true and the sibling's
    // depth is greater than this instance's depth—swap the depths.
    if (this.hitTest(this.siblings[i]) &&
        this.siblings[i].getDepth() > this.getDepth()) {
      this.swapDepths(this.siblings[i]);
    }
  }
};

// Add a listener object (an object with an onMoved() method defined), which is
// called automatically when the component instance is moved (see the onMoved() call
// made from this.bar.onRelease() within drawBar()).
UnitComponent.prototype.addListener = function (listener) {
  this.listeners.push(listener);
};

// Register the class to a symbol linkage name.
Object.registerClass("UnitComponentSymbol", UnitComponent);

#endinitclip
```

Some of the code in preceding example requires illumination. The example code first defines a helper class, *UnitComponentGroup*. The *UnitComponentGroup* class is used to keep track of all the *UnitComponent* instances that are within the same timeline. Each time a new instance is created, it is added to the *UnitComponentGroup* instance. I refer to the *UnitComponent* instances within the same timeline as *siblings*. These siblings are stored within a groupMembers associative array property of the *UnitComponentGroup* object.

```
function UnitComponentGroup () {}
UnitComponentGroup.prototype.groupMembers = new Object( );
```

The *UnitComponentGroup* class defines only one method, *onNew()*, which is invoked whenever a new *UnitComponent* is created. It is passed a reference to the new *UnitComponent*, and it adds that reference to it's groupMembers property. Then, it loops through all the siblings and updates their sibs properties so that each maintains a current list of all its siblings. This array is used by the *UnitComponent* instances whenever they are being dragged by the user to perform hit tests with its siblings (because siblings love to hit one another).

```
UnitComponentGroup.prototype.onNew = function (newUnit) {
  this.groupMembers[newUnit._name] = newUnit;
  var sibs;
  for (var unit in this.groupMembers) {
    sibs = new Array( );
    for (var sib in this.groupMembers) {
      if (this.groupMembers[unit] != this.groupMembers[sib]) {
        sibs.push(this.groupMembers[sib]);
      }
    }
    this.groupMembers[unit].setSiblings(sibs);
  }
};
```

Next, the *UnitComponent* class is defined to extend the *MovieClip* class. This is important since *UnitComponent* instances have a visual representation.

```
UnitComponent.prototype = new MovieClip( );
```

The constructor method for *UnitComponent* instances does a few interesting things. For one thing, it creates an instance of the *UnitComponentBar* component by calling *attachMovie()* with a symbol linkage identifier of "UnitComponentBarSymbol". Because the symbol linkage identifier "UnitComponentBarSymbol" is registered to the *UnitComponentBar* class, the *UnitComponentBar* constructor is called.

```
function UnitComponent () {
  ...
  this.attachMovie("UnitComponentBarSymbol", "bar", this.getNewDepth( ));
  ...
}
```

Also within the constructor, the instance is assigned a *UnitComponentGroup* object. If none exists, one is created on the parent timeline. Then, the group's *onNew()* method is invoked and passed a reference to the new *UnitComponent*.

```
function UnitComponent ( ) {
  ...
  if (this._parent.unitGroup == undefined) {
    this._parent.unitGroup = new UnitComponentGroup( );
  }
  this.group = this._parent.unitGroup;
  this.group.onNew(this);
}
```

The purpose of the *load()* method—repeated in the following excerpt—is straightforward once you take a step back from the minutiae. It loads the external *.swf* module (located at the specified *url*) into the component. It also creates a progress bar and a text label that says "loading…". The trickiest technique is the *onEnterFrame()* event handler used to detect whether the *.swf* file is loaded, which is assigned a reference to the *onLoading()* method. This means that the *onLoading()* method is called continuously as the playhead waits in the frame.

```
UnitComponent.prototype.load = function (url) {
  this.loadPlaceHolder.loadMovie(url);
  this.createTextField("loading", this.getNewDepth(), 0, 0, 0, 0);
  this.loading.text = "loading...";
  this.loading.autoSize = true;
  this.attachMovie("FProgressBarSymbol", "progress", this.getNewDepth( ));
  this.progress._y = this.loading._height + 5;
  this.onEnterFrame = this.onLoading;
};
```

The *onLoading()* method is called repeatedly until the module loads completely. The *onLoading()* method checks the status of the loading module using *getBytesLoaded()* and *getBytesTotal()* and updates the progress bar using *setProgress()*. When the module is loaded, the progress bar and its label are removed, since they are no longer needed. At that time, the *drawOutline()* method and the title bar's *draw()* method are called once to draw the container to the proper dimensions for the loaded module. (Both methods are passed the values of the loaded module's dimensions.) Finally, the *onEnterFrame()* event handler method is deleted since it is no longer needed once the module finishes loading.

```
UnitComponent.prototype.onLoading = function ( ) {
  var lBytes = this.loadPlaceHolder.getBytesLoaded( );
  var tBytes = this.loadPlaceHolder.getBytesTotal( );
  this.progress.setProgress(lBytes, tBytes);
  if (this.progress.getPercentComplete( ) == 100) {
    this.progress.removeMovieClip( );
    this.loading.removeTextField( );
    var margin = 5;
    var w = this.loadPlaceHolder._width + (margin * 2);
    var h = this.loadPlaceHolder._height + (margin * 2);
```

```
        this.drawOutline(w, h, margin);
        this.bar.draw(w, 20, margin, this.barColor, this.titleColor);
        var t = new Table(0, 0, 0, new TableRow(0,
                            new TableColumn(-1, this.bar, this.outline)));
        this.loadPlaceHolder._x = this.outline._x + margin;
        this.loadPlaceHolder._y = this.outline._y + margin;
        delete this.onEnterFrame;
    }
};
```

The *checkOverlaps()* method also benefits from explanation. This method is called
continuously while a user drags the instance. It checks whether the dragged instance
is overlapped by any of its siblings in the siblings array. It uses *hitTest()* to see if the
current and sibling instances overlap in the coordinate space, and it compares the
depths of the current and sibling instances to see if the sibling appears above the current instance. If these two conditions are met, it calls the *swapDepths()* method to
put the current instance above the sibling.

```
UnitComponent.prototype.checkOverlaps = function () {
    for (var i = 0; i < this.siblings.length; i++) {
        if (this.hitTest(this.siblings[i]) &&
            this.siblings[i].getDepth() > this.getDepth()) {
            this.swapDepths(this.siblings[i]);
        }
    }
};
```

Setting Up the Framework Form

Now that the component container has been defined, the only thing left to do for the
framework is add the code for the movie's main routine on the first frame of the
default layer of the main timeline.

Before adding the code to the main timeline, you need to make sure that the Flash
document has all the required component symbols in the library. In addition to the
custom components you created in the previous sections in this chapter, the framework also uses the ComboBox and PushButton components. So the first thing you
should do is add the corresponding component symbols to the document's Library.
You can do this by dragging instances of each of the components on the Stage, and
then deleting those instances. The symbols are retained in the Library.

The following code creates the form that allows the user to add modules to his page,
and it remembers the user's page settings using a local shared object (and loads the
form if it was created previously). This code constitutes the main routine in *mypage.fla*.

```
// Include the necessary libraries.
// Include MovieClip.as from Chapter 7.
#include "MovieClip.as"
//Include Table.as and Forms.as from Chapter 11
#include "Table.as"
#include "Forms.as"
```

```
// Include TextField.as from Chapter 8 and DrawingMethods.as from Chapter 4.
#include "TextField.as"
#include "DrawingMethods.as"

// Create a new local shared object (LSO) if it doesn't yet exist.
// Otherwise, reload the saved page state from the existing shared object.
function initLSO () {
  lso = SharedObject.getLocal("myPage");
  // Create a new local shared object, if necessary.
  if (!lso.data.exists) {
    lso.data.exists = true;
    lso.data.opened = new Object();
  } else {
    // Otherwise, load the saved state from the existing local shared object.
    var o = lso.data.opened;
    var newUnit;
    for (var item in o) {
      newUnit = openUnit(o[item].title, o[item].source, item);
      newUnit._x = o[item].x;
      newUnit._y = o[item].y;
    }
  }
  // The LSO is notified whenever a unit moves, so it can resave the page state.
  lso.onMoved = saveUnitPosition;
}

// Save the current position of a unit to the shared object.
function saveUnitPosition (unit) {
  this.data.opened[unit.index].x = unit._x;
  this.data.opened[unit.index].y = unit._y;
  this.flush();
}

// Read the module information from the XML document into an array
// and pass the array to initForm().
function loadXML () {
  servicesXML = new XML();
  servicesXML.formFunction = initForm;
  servicesXML.ignoreWhite = true;
  servicesXML.load("services.xml");
  servicesXML.root = this;
  // Define an onLoad() handler to parse the data into an array.
  servicesXML.onLoad = function () {
    var services = new Array();
    var items = this.firstChild.childNodes;
    var attribs;
    for (var i = 0; i < items.length; i++) {
      attribs = items[i].attributes;
      services.push({label: attribs["title"], data: attribs["source"]});
    }
    this.root.initForm(services);
  };
}
```

```
// Create a combo box populated with the array of modules passed to the function.
// Include a button to add the currently selected module to the page.
function initForm (services) {
  this.attachMovie("FComboBoxSymbol", "choicesMenu", this.getNewDepth());
  choicesMenu.setDataProvider(services);
  choicesMenu.adjustWidth();
  this.attachMovie("FPushButtonSymbol", "addBtn", this.getNewDepth());
  addBtn.setLabel("add to my page");
  addBtn.setClickHandler("addUnit");
  var t = new Table(10, 10, 10, new TableRow(5, new TableColumn(5, choicesMenu),
                                            new TableColumn(5, addBtn)));
}

// The addUnit() function is the callback function for addBtn.
function addUnit () {
  var si = choicesMenu.getSelectedItem();
  openUnit(si.label, si.data);
}

// Open a module unit based on the title and source parameters passed
// to it. If index is null, the unit is new, so assign a new index.
// Otherwise, restore the index, as loaded from the shared object.
function openUnit (title, source, index) {
  var u = this.attachMovie("UnitComponentSymbol",
                           "unit" + this.getNewDepth(),
                           this.getNewDepth());
  u.setTitle(title);
  u.load(source);
  // Delete the unit if the user clicks the close box.
  u.onClose = function () {
    delete this._parent.lso.data.opened[this.index];
  };
  if (index != null) {
    u.index = index
  } else {
    var openUnit = new Object();
    openUnit.title = title;
    openUnit.source = source;
    lso.data.opened[u.index] = openUnit;
    lso.flush();
  }
  u.addListener(lso);
  return u;
}

// Call initLSO() and loadXML() to start the movie.
initLSO();
loadXML();
```

The main routine of the framework application, as shown in the preceding example, consists of just a few major functions. To better understand some of the inner workings of these functions, let's examine them more closely.

The *initLSO()* function is responsible for opening the local shared object (LSO) and handling any stored data. First of all, it uses the *SharedObject.getLocal()* method to try to locate the shared object named "myPage". If such an object exists, it is opened; otherwise, it is created. If the object did not exist previously, the exists property would not be true. When working with shared objects, you can often benefit from setting such a Boolean property. In this case, the object should be initialized by defining the exists property so that, in future sessions, the framework knows that the object is no longer new.

Additionally, you should define the opened property as a new associative array to store the modules' states. If the object already exists from a previous session, the function uses a *for...in* loop to iterate through the opened associative array and calls *openUnit()* to open any modules that were open in the previous session. Finally, for each module, the *openUnit()* function sets the local shared object as a listener (see next listing). Because the listener objects for *UnitComponent* instances look for an *onMoved()* method for callbacks, you should create a method of this name for the shared object.

```
function initLSO () {
  lso = SharedObject.getLocal("myPage");
  if (!lso.data.exists) {
    lso.data.exists = true;
    lso.data.opened = new Object();
  } else {
    var o = lso.data.opened;
    var newUnit;
    for (var item in o) {
      newUnit = openUnit(o[item].title, o[item].source, item);
      newUnit._x = o[item].x;
      newUnit._y = o[item].y;
    }
  }
  lso.onMoved = saveUnitPosition;
}
```

The *openUnit()* function opens a new module for a given source using the *attachMovie()* method. Notice that the *attachMovie()* method returns a reference to the movie clip it creates. Setting a local variable (u) to this reference is handy because it can save having to type out the full path to the movie clip within the function. Because the name "UnitComponent" is registered to the *UnitComponent* class, the newly created unit is actually a *UnitComponent* instance. Therefore, the methods of the *UnitComponent* class can be invoked from this object.

The *setTitle()* and *load()* methods are called to perform the necessary tasks, and the *onClose()* callback method is defined such that when a unit is closed, the reference to it in the local shared object is removed. The next part of the function checks to see if the function has been passed a value for an index. An index value is passed only when the unit is being reopened from a previous session. ActionScript functions do not validate the number of parameters passed to the function, so if index is not passed to the function, it is simply undefined when used within the function.

```
function openUnit (title, source, index) {
    var u = this.attachMovie("UnitComponentSymbol",
                             "unit" + this.getNewDepth( ),
                             this.getNewDepth( ));
    u.setTitle(title);
    u.load(source);
    u.onClose = function () {
        delete this._parent.lso.data.opened[this.index];
    };
    if (index != undefined) {
        u.index = index
    } else {
        var openUnit = new Object( );
        openUnit.title = title;
        openUnit.source = source;
        lso.data.opened[u.index] = openUnit;
        lso.flush( );
    }
    u.addListener(lso);
    return u;
}
```

The framework also uses the *loadXML()* function to load the values for the available modules. The *loadXML()* function uses an XML object to load the values from *services.xml*. Generally, you should consider loading content into a Flash movie from XML documents or other sources. When you do this, you effectively separate content from functionality to make for cleaner code.

The loaded results are handled within the *onLoad()* method, as defined for this object. The *onLoad()* method loops through each of the modules of the loaded document and creates an array of objects with label and data properties. This array is in the format that can be used to populate a ComboBox component easily. After the array is assembled, the *onLoad()* method invokes the *initForm()* function on the main timeline and passes it the array.

The *initForm()* function call is a little bit tricky because it is invoked from the root property of the *servicesXML* object. The root property is a custom property (see bolded line in the following code) that is defined as a reference to the main timeline. When you set a reference to another object by way of a property, such as root in this example, you can maintain relative relationships. For example, because *initForm()* is called from within the *XML* object's *onLoad()* method, it is impossible to call it without making an absolute reference (*_root.initForm()*) unless a reference property is set, as is done here.

```
function loadXML () {
    servicesXML = new XML( );
    servicesXML.ignoreWhite = true;
    servicesXML.load("services.xml");
```

```
    servicesXML.root = this;
    servicesXML.onLoad = function () {
      var services = new Array();
      var items = this.firstChild.childNodes;
      var attribs;
      for (var i = 0; i < items.length; i++) {
        attribs = items[i].attributes;
        services.push({label: attribs["title"], data: attribs["source"]});
      }
      this.root.initForm(services);
    };
  }
```

Creating Service Modules

The My Page framework does not know or care which modules are being loaded, so you can add any kind of service module you want, using the three sample modules as exemplars. Remember to use relative addresses; avoid absolute references using _root. Because the service module movies are loaded into movie clips, _root refers to the framework's main timeline and not to the main timeline of the service *.swf*.

Making Notes

A common feature of My Page applications is the ability to make notes that are stored between sessions. This feature might be used for making daily goals lists, reminders, directions, or phone numbers. The notes module is instructional in that it uses a local shared object to store information—the user's notes—between sessions.

The notes module uses the ScrollBar component, so add the component symbol to the *notes.fla* document's Library by dragging an instance from the Components panel to the Stage (and then deleting the instance from the Stage).

The following example shows the code for *notes.fla* as it should appear on the first frame of the main timeline:

```
// Include MovieClip.as from Chapter 7 and TextField.as from Chapter 8.
#include "MovieClip.as"
#include "TextField.as"

// Create the form elements used.
function initNotes () {

  // Create the text field used for accepting user input and displaying notes.
  this.createInputTextField("notes", this.getNewDepth(), 0, 0, 100, 200);
  notes.multiline = true;
  notes.wordWrap = true;

  // Create the scrollbar for the notes text field.
  this.attachMovie("FScrollBarSymbol", "sb", this.getNewDepth());
```

```
// Set the notes field width to 200 pixels, counting the scrollbar.
notes._width = 200 - sb._width;

// Tie the scrollbar to the notes field and position it at the field's right.
sb._x = notes._width;
sb.setSize(notes._height);
sb.setScrollTarget(notes);
}

// This function opens the LSO and reads and writes the user's notes.
function initLSO () {

    // Open the local shared object named "notes".
    notesLSO = SharedObject.getLocal("notes");

    // Create a temporary property that references the notes field.
    notesLSO.notesRef = notes;

    // If the shared object has any stored values, display them in the notes field.
    notes.text = notesLSO.data.notes;

    // Set up notesLSO to listen for changes made to the notes field.
    notes.addListener(notesLSO);
    notesLSO.onChanged = function () {
        this.data.notes = this.notesRef.text;
        this.flush();
    };
}

// Call initNotes() and initLSO() to start the movie.
initNotes();
initLSO();
```

The notes module is a relatively short application, and it uses much of the same logic as the framework if you look closely. There are only two functions in the entire application. The first one, *initNotes()*, performs the straightforward task of creating the *TextField* and *ScrollBar* objects that are used to accept user input and display the notes.

The *initLSO()* function is a little more complex, so let's examine it more closely. The function first opens an LSO named "notes", if one exists; otherwise, a new LSO is created. Next, a reference to the notes text field is assigned to a custom property of the shared object named notesRef. This is so that within the *onChanged()* method of the shared object, it can address the notes text field in a relative fashion. The relative addressing is extremely important in the case of a movie such as this one that will be loaded into a movie clip within another movie. Because *SharedObject* and other non-*MovieClip* objects do not have timelines, it is not possible to make relative addresses using _parent, so creating a reference property is a great way to achieve the desired results. The shared object is added as a listener to the notes field, and an *onChanged()*

---

method—which is invoked automatically when the contents of the notes field change—is defined.

Keeping Track of Addresses

Another useful service module is one that keeps track of email addresses and names.

The address book module uses the PushButton and ListBox components. Therefore, you should add the corresponding component symbols to the *addressBook.fla* document's Library by dragging instances from the Components panel to the Stage (and deleting the instances).

The following example shows the code that you should place on the first frame of *addressBook.fla* to implement an address book. This module uses a local shared object to store the addressees' information.

```
// Include MovieClip.as from Chapter 7 and TextField.as from Chapter 8.
#include "MovieClip.as"
#include "TextField.as"
// Include Table.as from Chapter 11
#include "Table.as"

// Set up the address book form, including input fields, buttons, and a list box to
// display the results of a search.
function initForm ( ) {

  // Create the text field for the column headings (name and email address).
  this.createTextField("nameLabel", this.getNewDepth( ), 0, 0, 75, 20);
  nameLabel.text = "Name";

  // Position the email label dynamically to the right of the name label.
  this.createTextField("emailLabel", this.getNewDepth( ), 0, 0, 75, 20);
  emailLabel.text = "Email";

  // Create the text field for the addressee's name and email address.
  this.createInputTextField("name", this.getNewDepth( ), 0, 0, 75, 20);
  this.createInputTextField("email", this.getNewDepth( ), 0, 0, 75, 20);

  // Create an Add button used to add a new addressee to the address book.
  this.attachMovie("FPushButtonSymbol", "addBtn", this.getNewDepth( ));
  addBtn.setLabel("add entry");
  addBtn.setClickHandler("addEntry");

  // Add a search field.
  this.createTextField("searchLabel", this.getNewDepth( ), 0, 0, 75, 20);
  searchLabel.text = "Search";
  this.createInputTextField("search", this.getNewDepth( ), 0, 0, 75, 20);

  // Add a Search button for submitting the entry search.
  this.attachMovie("FPushButtonSymbol", "searchBtn", this.getNewDepth( ));
  searchBtn.setLabel("search for entry");
```

```
// Create the callback for the Search button.
searchBtn.setClickHandler("searchEntries");

// Create the list box that displays search results.
this.attachMovie("FListBoxSymbol", "output", this.getNewDepth());
output.setSize(180, 40);

// Create a button that removes entries from the address book.
this.attachMovie("FPushButtonSymbol", "removeBtn", this.getNewDepth());
removeBtn.setLabel("remove entry");
removeBtn.setClickHandler("removeEntry");

// Use a table to position all the elements.
tr0 = new TableRow(5, new TableColumn(5, nameLabel, name),
                      new TableColumn(5, emailLabel, email));
tr1 = new TableRow(5, new TableColumn(5, addBtn));
tr2 = new TableRow(5, new TableColumn(5, searchLabel, search, searchBtn));
tr3 = new TableRow(5, new TableColumn(5, output, removeBtn));
t = new Table(5, 0, 0, tr0, tr1, tr2, tr3);
}

// Open the shared object and, if it is new, initialize a blank address array.
function openSharedObject () {
  addressLSO = SharedObject.getLocal("addressBook");
  if (addressLSO.data.entries == undefined) {
    addressLSO.data.entries = new Array();
  }
}

// Add an entry to the shared object (called from the Add button).
function addEntry () {
  var entries = addressLSO.data.entries;
  entries.push(name.text + " [" + email.text + "]");
  entries.sort();
  addressLSO.flush();
  name.text = "";
  email.text = "";
}

// Search the entries array for any entries containing the specified substring.
function searchEntries () {
  var entries = addressLSO.data.entries;
  var matches = new Array();
  for (var i = 0; i < entries.length; i++) {
    // Keep a record of all matching entries.
    if (entries[i].indexOf(search.text) != -1)
      matches.push(entries[i]);
  }
  // If there are matches, display them.
  if (matches.length > 0) {
    output.setDataProvider(matches);
  } else {
```

```
      // Otherwise, tell the user that none were found.
      output.removeAll();
      output.addItem("no matches found");
    }
  }

  // Remove the selected entry from the entries array (triggered by the Remove button).
  function removeEntry () {
    var entries = addressLSO.data.entries;
    var val = output.getValue();
    // Remove the item from the ListBox.
    output.removeItemAt(output.getSelectedIndex());
    for (var i = 0; i < entries.length; i++) {
      if (entries[i] == val) {
        // Remove the addressee and update the stored data.
        entries.splice(i, 1);
        addressLSO.flush();
        break;
      }
    }
  }

  // Call initForm() and openSharedObject() to start the movie.
  initForm();
  openSharedObject();
```

The address book module consists of five functions. Two of the functions, *initForm()* and *openSharedObject()*, handle initialization actions for the application. The other three functions are callback functions for the form buttons.

Although *initForm()* is a relatively long function, no single aspect is too complicated. The function is responsible for creating the form using functions such as *createTextField()* and *attachMovie()*; it then sets properties for the created objects.

The *openSharedObject()* function simply opens the shared object and, if it is a new object, initializes the entries array as a new property.

The *addEntry()* function adds a new entry to the array stored in the shared object. It adds the text from the name and email text fields to the array, and then sorts the array alphabetically before saving it using the *flush()* method. For more information, see Recipe 16.4.

You are not strictly required to use the *flush()* method on the LSO to save the data. However, there are several reasons why you should do so here. First of all, as in any situation, there is always the possibility that the data may not save if the user's settings are not correct and you leave it to the automatic save feature. Another reason is that calling *flush()* saves the data immediately; otherwise, the attempt to save data occurs when the movie is closed.

```
  function addEntry () {
    var entries = addressLSO.data.entries;
    entries.push(name.text + " [" + email.text + "]");
```

```
        entries.sort( );
        addressLSO.flush( );
        name.text = "";
        email.text = "";
    }
```

When the user clicks on searchBtn, the *searchEntries()* function is called. This function loops through each of the values stored in the entries array of the shared object. It uses the *indexOf()* method to determine if each entry contains the value entered into the search text field. If so, the entry is added to an array which is then used to populate the output list box. The need to manually implement a search function is typical, and searches are usually accomplished using *indexOf()*. Because *indexOf()* searches strings and not arrays, we search each element of the array separately. Beware, however, that for large text fields, or when searching very large numbers of array elements, *indexOf()* may prove to be slow.

```
    function searchEntries ( ) {
        var entries = addressLSO.data.entries;
        var matches = new Array( );
        for (var i = 0; i < entries.length; i++) {
            if (entries[i].indexOf(search.text) != -1)
                matches.push(entries[i]);
        }
        if (matches.length > 0) {
            output.setDataProvider(matches);
        } else {
            output.removeAll( );
            output.addItem("no matches found");
        }
    }
```

The *removeEntry()* function removes the selected value from the list box and from the shared object. You should remove the entry from both so that not only is the display updated to reflect the deletion but so is the actual data store. The function removes the item from the list box using the *removeItemAt()* method. The function loops through all the entries stored in the shared object until it finds the one that matches the selected entry, and then removes it with the *splice()* function and saves the updated shared object. In this example, a *break* statement is used after a matching entry is found and removed. This is a good practice because it ensures that the program does not needlessly loop through the remaining values. However, if you want the function to remove all entries (even duplicates) that match the value selected, remove the *break* statement.

```
    function removeEntry ( ) {
        var entries = addressLSO.data.entries;
        var val = output.getValue( );
        // Remove the item from the ListBox
        output.removeItemAt(output.getSelectedIndex( ));
        for (var i = 0; i < entries.length; i++) {
            if (entries[i] == val) {
```

```
            // Remove the addressee and update the stored data
            entries.splice(i, 1);
            addressLSO.flush( );
            break;
        }
    }
}
```

Searching the Web Using Google

Another common and useful service is one that enables the user to search the Web from his My Page application. This service module uses Flash Remoting for ColdFusion MX. Alternatively, if you are using Flash Remoting for .NET, you can use the same code and adjust the gateway URL to point to an *.aspx* page. The rest of the code remains the same. No matter which server platform you are using, however, you must obtain a developer's key, which is free, from Google by registering at *http:// www.google.com/apis/*.

Note that the *gateway* URL depends on your Flash Remoting set up, such as ColdFusion, .NET, J2EE, or PHP. (Refer to Chapter 20 for more details on Flash Remoting.) On the other hand, the URL of the Google web service used in the call to *getService()* is always the location of the *.wsdl* file provided by Google (this is the same URL used by everything that calls the Google web service). You, as a Google developer accessing its web service, are identified by the unique Google key—specified in the params object created within *doSearch()*—and not via a unique URL.

The search service requires both the ScrollBar and PushButton components. So the first thing you should do is add the corresponding component symbols to the *search.fla* document's Library by dragging instances from the Components panel to the Stage.

The following example shows the code that you should place on the first frame of the main timeline for *search.fla*:

```
// Include NetServices.as for the Flash Remoting API.
#include "NetServices.as"
// Include MovieClip.as from Chapter 7 and TextField.as from Chapter 8.
#include "MovieClip.as"
#include "TextField.as"
//Include Table.as from Chapter 11.
#include "Table.as"

// The initForm( ) function creates the form elements used by the search service.
function initForm ( ) {

    // Create the input text field that allows the user to enter a search string.
    this.createInputTextField("searchString", this.getNewDepth( ), 0, 0, 150, 20);
    searchString.text = "<type search string here>";
```

```
// When search field gains focus, remove any existing text (such as the initial
// <type search string here> value).
searchString.onSetFocus = function () {
  this.text = "";
};

// Create a Search button to initiate the search.
this.attachMovie("FPushButtonSymbol", "searchBtn", this.getNewDepth());
searchBtn.setLabel("Search");
searchBtn.setClickHandler("doSearch");

// Create a text field to display the search results.
this.createTextField("searchResults", this.getNewDepth(), 0, 0, 300, 100);
searchResults.multiline = true;
searchResults.wordWrap = true;
searchResults.html = true;
searchResults.border = true;

// Add a scrollbar for the search results.
this.attachMovie("FScrollBarSymbol", "sb", this.getNewDepth());
sb.setScrollTarget(searchResults);
sb.setSize(searchResults._height);

// Add a Previous button to get the previous 10 search results.
this.attachMovie("FPushButtonSymbol", "prevBtn", this.getNewDepth());
prevBtn.setLabel("Previous 10");
prevBtn.enabled = false;
prevBtn.setClickHandler("doSearch");

// Add a Next button to get the next 10 search results.
this.attachMovie("FPushButtonSymbol", "nextBtn", this.getNewDepth());
nextBtn.setLabel("Next 10");
nextBtn.enabled = false;
nextBtn.setClickHandler("doSearch");

// Create a table to properly align the searchResults text field
// and the scrollbar to one another.
scrollerTr0 = new TableRow(0, new TableColumn(0, searchResults),
                              new TableColumn(0, sb));
scrollerTable = new Table(5, 0, 0, scrollerTr0);

// Create a table to position the form elements, including the scrollerTable
// subtable.
tr0 = new TableRow(5, new TableColumn(5, searchString),
                new TableColumn(5, searchBtn));
tr1 = new TableRow(5, new TableColumn(5, scrollerTable));
tr2 = new TableRow(5, new TableColumn(5, prevBtn), new TableColumn(5, nextBtn));
t = new Table(5, 0, 0, tr0, tr1, tr2);
}
```

```
// The initNetServices() function initializes the Flash Remoting objects.
function initNetServices () {

  // This uses the default localhost standalone CFMX installation URL. If you use a
  // different one, change this code appropriately. See Chapter 20 for details on how
  // to make a connection and create a service object.
  gwUrl = "http://localhost:8500/flashservices/gateway/";
  NetServices.setDefaultGatewayURL(gwUrl);
  conn = NetServices.createGatewayConnection( );

  // This is the service object for the Google Web service WSDL.
  srv = conn.getService("http://api.google.com/GoogleSearch.wsdl");
}

// Create the response object.
res = new Object( );

// When the result is returned, format the contents and display them in the
// searchResults text field as HTML.
res.onResult = function (result) {
  var r = searchResults;
  r.html = true;
  r.htmlText = "";
  var re = result.resultElements;

  // Loop through the search results and add them as HTML to the searchResults field.
  for (var i = 0; i < re.length; i++) {
    r.htmlText += "<font color=\"#FF\"><a href=\"" + re[i].url +
                  "\">" + re[i].title +
                  "</a></font>" + "<br>";
    r.htmlText += re[i].snippet + "<br>";
    if (re[i].summary != "") {
      r.htmlText += re[i].summary + "<br>";
    }
    r.htmlText += "<br><br>";
  }

  // Reset the vertical and horizontal scroll positions.
  vsb.setScrollPosition(0);
  hsb.setScrollPosition(0);

  // Get the estimated total number of results.
  var count = result.estimatedTotalResultsCount;

  // Enable the Previous 10 results button if we're
  // not already viewing the first page.
  if (result.startIndex > 0) {
    prevBtn.enabled = true;
  } else {
    prevBtn.enabled = false;
  }
```

```
    // If the ending index is less than the estimated total number of results,
    // enable the Next 10 results button, but otherwise disable it
    // so that users cannot try to load results past the last page.
    if (result.endIndex < count) {
      nextBtn.enabled = true;
    } else {
      nextBtn.enabled = false;
    }

    // Set the next and previous starting indexes.
    nextBtn.start = result.endIndex;
    if (result.startIndex - 10 < 0) {
      prevBtn.start = 0;
    } else {
      prevBtn.start = result.startIndex - 11;
    }
};

res.onStatus = function (status) {
  trace(status.description);
};

// Perform the search.
function doSearch (cmpnt) {
  var start = 0;

  // If the calling component is the next or previous button,
  // set the start value appropriately.
  if (cmpnt._name != "searchBtn") {
    start = cmpnt.start;
  }

  // Create the parameter object that the
  // doGoogleSearch( ) web service method expects.
  var params = new Object();
  params.key = "xxxxxxxxxxxxxxxx"; // Your Google registration key goes here.
  params.q = searchString.text;
  params.start = start;
  params.maxResults = 10;
  params.filter = true;
  params.restrict = "";
  params.safeSearch = false;
  params.lr = "";
  params.ie = "";
  params.oe = "";
  srv.doGoogleSearch(res, params);
}

// Call initNetServices( ) and initForm( ) to start the movie.
initNetServices();
initForm();
```

The search service is the longest of the three modules we've implemented, and quite a bit of its code warrants further explanation.

The *initNetServices()* function uses the *NetServices* object's methods in the standard ways. The gateway URL used in the example code points to the Flash Remoting gateway for the localhost, as it would be installed for a standard installation of ColdFusion MX as a standalone server on port 8500. The service object is opened using the URL to the Google web service *.wsdl* file as the service name. This is the standard way in which web services are consumed directly from a Flash movie using Flash Remoting (for ColdFusion MX), as discussed in Recipe 20.24.

```
function initNetServices () {
  gwUrl = "http://localhost:8500/flashservices/gateway/";
  NetServices.setDefaultGatewayURL(gwUrl);
  conn = NetServices.createGatewayConnection( );
  srv = conn.getService("http://api.google.com/GoogleSearch.wsdl");
}
```

Web services can also be consumed directly from Flash movies if you are using Flash Remoting for .NET, in which case only the gateway URL differs. In that case, point the gateway to an *.aspx* page that exists within the root directory of the IIS web application in which Flash Remoting is installed.

Thus, when using ASP.NET, change gwURL, as follows:

```
function initNetServices () {
  gwUrl = "http://yourservername/yourWebApplication/gateway.aspx";
  ...
}
```

To perform a Google search, attach the required search parameters as properties of a generic object and pass the object to the Google web service, as shown in the *doSearch()* method. For example, the q property specifies the search string and the start property specifies the starting record requested from the search.

The response object's *onResult()* method receives the search results returned from the Google web service. The return value is an object containing several properties, including an array containing the matches for the search.

The names and datatypes of the properties of both the submission and return objects are determined by the web service's *.wsdl* file (open the *.wsdl* file in a text editor to explore them further). The return properties that we are most interested in with regards to this example are the following:

estimatedTotalResultsCount
> The total number of results from the search (estimated).

startIndex
> The index of the first returned result relative to the total results (not just the one page of results).

endIndex

    The index of the last returned result relative to the total results.

resultElements

    An array of results. Each element in the array is an object whose properties are:

    url

        The URL to the web page associated with a search result

    title

        The title of the web page

    snippet

        A text snippet from the web page

    summary

        A textual summary of the web page

The *onResult()* method loops through each of the elements in the resultElements array and displays the values in the searchResults text field. The code uses the searchResults field's htmlText property so that HTML tags such as <a href> can be used to create links, and the <font> and <u> HTML tags can be used to create formatting easily. I have chosen to display each search result's title, snippet, and summary. I made this decision in keeping with the conventions for how search results are displayed on the Google web page; however, you are free to experiment with how the results are displayed. In this example, the result's title is made into a hyperlink to the URL associated with the page. This is accomplished using an <a href> HTML tag. Also, because links do not automatically have formatting applied to them in Flash (as they do in most HTML browsers), I have added a <font> tag to color the title blue and a <u> tag to underline the title.

```
res.onResult = function (result) {
  var r = searchResults;
  r.html = true;
  r.htmlText = "";
  var re = result.resultElements;
  for (var i = 0; i < re.length; i++) {
    r.htmlText += "<font color=\"#0000FF\"><u><a href=\"" + re[i].url +
                  "\">" + re[i].title + "</a></u></font><br>";
    r.htmlText += re[i].snippet + "<br>";
    if (re[i].summary != "") {
      r.htmlText += re[i].summary + "<br>";
    }
    r.htmlText += "<br><br>";
  }
  ...
};
```

The *onResult()* method also ensures that the user cannot browse to results that do not exist (prior to the first page or after the last page). The example enables and disables the prevBtn and nextBtn instances, as appropriate, when the user is on the first or last page of results. If the result object's startIndex is not greater than 0, it means that the first page of results is being displayed, so the prevBtn is disabled. Likewise, if the endIndex is not less than the estimatedTotalResultsCount property, the nextBtn is disabled. Additionally, both the nextBtn and prevBtn objects store a value in a custom property named start. I define the start property here so that the program can keep track of the starting index of the next and previous set of search results. Each time a new page of results is returned to the *onResult()* method, the start property for nextBtn and prevBtn is updated to reflect the change. The next page of results always has a starting index that is one more than the endIndex value of the current set. Likewise, the previous page of results will always be the startIndex value of the current page minus 11 (assuming that there are 10 results per page) because Google adds 1 to the start parameter passed as part of the search request. Just in case the indexing is skewed at some point in browsing next and previous pages, you should make sure that the start property for the prevBtn is never less than 0. In the event that it is, simply reset it to 0.

```
var count = result.estimatedTotalResultsCount;
if (result.startIndex > 0) {
  prevBtn.enabled = true;
} else {
  prevBtn.enabled = false;
}
if (result.endIndex < count) {
  nextBtn.enabled = true;
} else {
  nextBtn.enabled = false;
}
nextBtn.start = result.endIndex;
if (result.startIndex - 10 < 0) {
  prevBtn.start = 0;
} else {
  prevBtn.start = result.startIndex - 11;
}
```

Finally, there is the *doSearch()* function, which calls the Google web service. This function, for all its importance, is surprisingly short. The function is set as the callback function for the Search button (searchBtn) instance and also for the Previous and Next buttons (prevBtn and nextBtn). This is because each time the user wants to view another page (next or previous) of search results, the Flash movie needs to call the web service method again. While the actions taken are the same no matter which button invokes the function, the start value sent to the web service differs. If searchBtn invokes the function, the starting index is 0, and the web service returns the first page of results. However, if prevBtn or nextBtn invokes the function, the starting index is passed in as a property of the calling component (cmpnt.start). In this way, the pages of results returned have different starting indexes instead of always beginning with 0.

Other than the *if* statement that handles the starting index, the rest of the function is the same whether initiated by the Search, Previous, or Next button. It creates the params object containing the search parameters and sends it to the web service method. Each of the properties of the params object are required and defined by the *.wsdl* file for the web service. The only property that changes dynamically within this example is the start property. In the example, the maxResults property is set to a fixed value of 10 so that the number of results per page is always 10. The value 10 is the maximum value allowed by Google. However, you could also set the value to any number between 1 and 9. You could also allow the user to select the number of results to return per page. One possible approach to this would be to add a *ComboBox* instance with values from 1 to 10, and to dynamically set the maxResults property according to the selected value.

 You must specify your Google registration key as the params.key property.

The srv object on which the Google service is called is the one returned by the earlier call to *getService()*. The *res* parameter passed to *doGoogleSearch()* is the results text field defined earlier (and used here as the result object).

```
function doSearch (cmpnt) {
  var start = 0;
  if (cmpnt._name != "searchBtn") {
    start = cmpnt.start;
  }
  var params = new Object( );
  params.key = "XXXXXXXXXXXXXXXXX"; // Your Google registration key goes here.
  params.q = searchString.text;
  params.start = start;
  params.maxResults = 10;
  params.filter = true;
  params.restrict = "";
  params.safeSearch = false;
  params.lr = "";
  params.ie = "";
  params.oe = "";
  srv.doGoogleSearch(res, params);
}
```

Putting It All Together

You should make sure that you have exported all the *.swf* files for the service modules and the framework. Place all the *.swf* files and the *services.xml* document in the same folder and run the *myPage.swf* movie. You should be able to open the services, move them around, close them, etc. Between sessions, the framework should remember your user preferences.

Extending the Framework

As it is presented, the framework stores the user's settings in a local shared object on the user's computer. Ideally, however, the application should save the data in a way that the user's preferences can be retrieved from any computer. This can be accomplished in a variety of ways. The data could be stored to a database, a text file, an XML file, or using a FlashCom Server remote shared object. The following example stores the data to an XML document on the server. Without relying on a FlashCom server remote shared object or other proprietary system, the solution uses an ActionScript class, a simple server-side script for file I/O operations, and an XML document. Refer to Chapter 19 for more information on saving and retrieving XML.

Making a Server-Side Shared Object

Without much modification to the framework movie, you can have it use a server-side faux shared object instead of a local shared object (or instead of a true FlashCom server remote shared object). First, let's understand how the process works. Using an ActionScript class, *FauxSharedObject*, you can mimic the operations of a local shared object. You can perform the saving and retrieval operations by serializing and deserializing the data with XML, and then use a server-side script (ColdFusion in this case) to perform the file operations.

Save the *FauxSharedObject* class definition, shown in the following example, in an ActionScript file named *FauxSharedObject.as* and place it in Flash's *Include* directory:

```
// Include NetServices.as for Flash Remoting API.
#include "NetServices.as"

// FSOResponse is a response object used for the Flash Remoting
// service function calls made by FauxSharedObject.
function FSOResponse (parent) {
  this.parent = parent;
}

FSOResponse.prototype.onResult = function (result) {
  if (result != null) {
    this.parent.setData(FauxSharedObject.deserializeObject(result));
    this.parent.onLoadPath[this.parent.onLoadCB]( );
  }
};

// The constructor accepts a filename and a gateway URL
// used by the Flash Remoting connection.
function FauxSharedObject (name, gwURL) {
  this.name = name;
  this.openRes = new FSOResponse(this);
  this.saveRes = new FSOResponse( );
  this.initNetServices(gwURL);
}
```

```
// Define the properties of the class.
FauxSharedObject.prototype.data = new Object();

// Initialize the Flash Remoting connection and service. The service object
// connects to FauxSharedObject.cfc, as shown in "Performing File Operations."
FauxSharedObject.prototype.initNetServices = function (gwURL) {
  NetServices.setDefaultGatewayURL(gwURL);
  var conn = NetServices.createGatewayConnection();
  this.srv = conn.getService("FauxSharedObject");
};

// A static method that serializes an object to XML.
FauxSharedObject.serializeObject = function (obj) {
  var sb = "<obj>";
  if (obj instanceof Array) {
    sb = "<obj type=\"array\">";
  }
  for (var i in obj) {
    sb += "<index name=\"" + i + "\"";
    if (obj[i] instanceof Object) {
      sb += ">";
      sb += FauxSharedObject.serializeObject(obj[i]);
      sb += "</index>";
    } else {
      sb += " val=\"" + obj[i] + "\" />";
    }
  }
  sb += "</obj>";
  return sb;
};

// A static method that deserializes XML to an object.
FauxSharedObject.deserializeObject = function (source) {
  XML.prototype.ignoreWhite = true;
  var sXML = new XML(source);
  var cn = sXML.firstChild.childNodes;
  var items = new Object();
  if (sXML.firstChild.attributes.type == "array") {
    items = new Array();
  }
  var attribs, childCn;
  for (var i = 0; i < cn.length; i++) {
    attribs = cn[i].attributes;
    childCn = cn[i].childNodes;
    if (childCn.length > 0) {
      items[attribs.name] = FauxSharedObject.deserializeObject(childCn[0]);
    } else {
      items[attribs.name] = attribs.val;
    }
    items[attribs.index] = new Object();
    for (var j in attribs) {
      items[attribs.index][j] = attribs[j];
    }
  }
}
```

```
      return items;
};

// Load an object from the server by calling Flash Remoting's open() method.
FauxSharedObject.prototype.load = function () {
  this.srv.open(this.openRes, this.name);
};

// Save the object in serialized form to the server, calling Flash Remoting's
// save() method. Mimics the shared object flush() method.
FauxSharedObject.prototype.flush = function () {
  this.srv.save(this.saveRes, this.name,
                FauxSharedObject.serializeObject(this.data));
};

// Called automatically when the object has loaded from the server
FauxSharedObject.prototype.setData = function (val) {
  this.data = val;
};

// Allow the user to define a callback function for when the object has loaded.
FauxSharedObject.prototype.setLoadHandler = function(functionName, path) {
  if (path == undefined) {
    path = this._parent;
  }
  this.onLoadPath = path;
  this.onLoadCB = functionName;
};
```

Now that you have had an opportunity to look over the code in the preceding example, let's look more closely at the parts that make up the *FauxSharedObject* class and its helper class, *FSOResponse*.

The code first defines the *FSOResponse* class, which is a Flash Remoting response object class used by *FauxSharedObject*. I chose to separate the response object portion into its own class in keeping with object-oriented design. The constructor method takes a reference to the *FauxSharedObject* that instantiates it, and it sets its custom parent property to that reference. This reference is used within the *onResult()* method to invoke the *loadHandler()* method of the parent *FauxSharedObject* when results are returned. The parent property is another example in which using a reference can be useful in establishing relationships between objects. Because *FauxSharedObject* and *FSOResponse* are not *MovieClip* classes, you cannot rely on the _parent property or similar means to relate the objects. A reference such as parent provides this bridge between the objects.

```
function FSOResponse (parent) {
  this.parent = parent;
}

FSOResponse.prototype.onResult = function (result) {
  if (result != null) {
```

```
      this.parent.setData(FauxSharedObject.deserializeObject(result));
      this.parent.loadHandler.call( );
    }
};
```

The constructor method for the *FauxSharedObject* class takes parameters indicating the name of the object that is stored on the server (which is the same as the username in this example) as well as the Flash Remoting gateway URL to use for the Flash Remoting calls.

 The decision to save the file on the server by the username is perfectly valid as long as you can ensure that the username is always unique. In this example application, for the sake of simplicity, there is no user registration that would allow users to create accounts with unique usernames.

The constructor also creates the response objects as *FSOReponse* instances and invokes the *initNetServices()* method to initialize the *NetServices* objects:

```
function FauxSharedObject (name, gwURL) {
  this.name = name;
  this.openRes = new FSOResponse(this);
  this.saveRes = new FSOResponse( );
  this.initNetServices(gwURL);
}
```

The *FauxSharedObject* class defines a data property as an associative array to closely mimic the functionality of local shared objects. Creating a property of the same type, with the same name, and with the same intended functionality as with an LSO, you can ensure that minimum modifications are needed to integrate *FauxSharedObject* instances in place of *SharedObject* instances in existing applications.

```
  FauxSharedObject.prototype.data = new Object( );
```

The *FauxSharedObject* class serializes and deserializes data and sends it between the Flash movie and the server. Serialization converts a reference datatype (an object), which cannot be stored in a file or database on the server, into a format that can be saved. The code uses a custom XML-based structure to perform the serialization. Objects are converted to <obj> elements with nested <index> elements. The <index> elements always have a name attribute, which is the name of the variable/property for the object. If the <index> represents a primitive datatype, it also has a val attribute holding the value of the variable. On the other hand, if the <index> represents an object, it has a nested <obj> element. Here is an example of an object and the corresponding serialized form:

```
  obj = new Object( );
  obj.prop1 = "a value";
  obj.prop2 = "another value";
  obj.prop3 = {a: "eh", b: "bee"};
```

```
/*
<obj>
  <index name="prop1" val="a value" />
  <index name="prop2" val="another value" />
  <index name="prop3">
    <obj>
      <index name="a" value="eh" />
      <index name="b" value="bee" />
    </obj>
  </index>
</obj>
*/
```

To convert objects to their serialized forms, the *FauxSharedObject* class defines a static method, *serializeObject()*. A static method is one that is invoked directly from the class rather than from instances of the class. Because *serializeObject()* and *deserializeObject()* do not need to be used from specific instances of the class, it makes sense to define them as static methods. To define a static method attach it to the *FauxSharedObject* top-level object and not to its prototype.

The *serializeObject()* method accepts an object as a parameter and converts the object properties to <index> elements that are appended to a string. The *serializeObject()* method uses the *instanceof* operator to check whether an object contains a property that is itself an object. If so, that object is passed to *serializeObject()* in a recursive manner (i.e., the function calls itself). Recursion allows a function to handle an arbitrarily nested data structure, such as an object that contains other objects or a directory structure with nested subfolders. See Recipes 7.10 and 19.7 for more examples of recursive functions.

```
FauxSharedObject.serializeObject = function (obj) {
  var sb = "<obj>";
  if (obj instanceof Array) {
    sb = "<obj type=\"array\">";
  }
  for (var i in obj) {
    sb += "<index name=\"" + i + "\"";
    if (obj[i] instanceof Object) {
      sb += ">";
      sb += FauxSharedObject.serializeObject(obj[i]);
      sb += "</index>";
    } else {
      sb += " val=\"" + obj[i] + "\" />";
    }
  }
  sb += "</obj>";
  return sb;
};
```

The counterpart to serialization is deserialization—the conversion of XML data back to the original object. The static *deserializeObject()* method takes an XML string and parses it into an XML object. It then loops through all the child nodes of the root

`<obj>` element and converts them back to properties of an object. If a child node contains nested elements, the node represents an object. As with the *serializeObject()* method, *deserializeObject()* calls itself recursively, passing in the next `<obj>` element, to handle child nodes that contain nested objects.

```
FauxSharedObject.deserializeObject = function (source) {
  XML.prototype.ignoreWhite = true;
  var sXML = new XML(source);
  var cn = sXML.firstChild.childNodes;
  var items = new Object();
  if (sXML.firstChild.attributes.type == "array") {
    items = new Array();
  }
  var attribs, childCn;
  for (var i = 0; i < cn.length; i++) {
    attribs = cn[i].attributes;
    childCn = cn[i].childNodes;
    if (childCn.length > 0) {
      items[attribs.name] = FauxSharedObject.deserializeObject(childCn[0]);
    } else {
      items[attribs.name] = attribs.val;
    }
    items[attribs.index] = new Object();
    for (var j in attribs) {
      items[attribs.index][j] = attribs[j];
    }
  }
  return items;
};
```

The *load()* method calls the Flash Remoting service object's *open()* method to open the shared object data from the server:

```
FauxSharedObject.prototype.load = function () {
  this.srv.open(this.openRes, this.name);
};
```

The *FauxSharedObject.flush()* method mimics a local shared object's *flush()* method by calling the service object's *save()* function to save the data to the server. The *flush()* method, as with the data property, uses the same name and performs the same function as its analog in the *SharedObject* class. This is a good practice when writing custom classes to perform similar tasks as existing classes because it makes the classes largely interchangeable.

```
FauxSharedObject.prototype.flush = function () {
  this.srv.save(this.saveRes, this.name,
          FauxSharedObject.serializeObject(this.data));
};
```

Finally, the *setLoadHandler()* method provides a means for a function to be set as a callback function for when the shared object data is loaded. The *FSOResponse* object's *onResult()* method automatically tries to call this function if it is defined. This is important because, unlike local shared objects, the *FauxSharedObject* is asynchronous. This means that, unlike a local shared object, in which the data is retrieved from the user's computer immediately, the *FauxSharedObject* might take milliseconds or even seconds to retrieve the data from the server. The rest of the ActionScript code continues to execute while the *FauxSharedObject* data is being retrieved, so any functionality that relies on the retrieved data must be handled only after that data has been returned. The *RSOResponse* instance is automatically called (because of Flash Remoting) when a response is returned from the server. By setting a *loadHandler()* method for automatic callback, you can define custom functions for each *FauxSharedObject* instance to know how to handle the particular results returned from the server.

```
FauxSharedObject.prototype.setLoadHandler = function (functionRef) {
    this.loadHandler = functionRef;
};
```

Performing File Operations

Our example My Page application requires that the data sent between the Flash movie and the server be saved to a file on the server side. The following example shows how to save the data using a ColdFusion Component (CFC). You should save the CFC to the server's web root as *FauxSharedObject.cfc*, since this is the service name that Flash looks for. If you are comfortable with another language/platform that works with Flash Remoting (e.g., ASP.NET or J2EE), you can easily adapt this code. See Chapter 20 for examples in various server-side languages.

```
<cfcomponent>
  <cffunction name="save" access="remote">
    <cfargument name="name" type="string" required="true">
    <cfargument name="data" type="string" required="true">
    <cffile action="write"
     file="#GetDirectoryFromPath(GetBaseTemplatePath())##name#.so"
     output="#data#" nameconflict="overwrite">
    <cfreturn #GetDirectoryFromPath(GetBaseTemplatePath())#>
  </cffunction>
  <cffunction name="open" access="remote">
    <cfargument name="name" type="string" required="true">
    <cffile action="read"
     file="#GetDirectoryFromPath(GetBaseTemplatePath())##name#.so"
     variable="data">
    <cfreturn #data#>
  </cffunction>
</cfcomponent>
```

The ColdFusion Component in the preceding example consists of only two functions: *save* and *open*. The <cffunction> and <cfargument> tags define the functions and the parameters they accept. You should recognize these functions from the *FauxSharedObject* ActionScript class, since it makes calls to them by way of Flash Remoting. Each of these two functions performs basic file operations made available by the ColdFusion <cffile> tag. The *save* function writes the data to a file in the same directory with the name specified by the name parameter followed by the *.so* extension. The *open* function does the reverse by reading the contents of the specified file. The `<cfreturn>` tags merely return the results to the calling function.

If you want to adapt this code to another language/platform, refer to the language's file I/O API. You should create a script or program that is accessible to Flash Remoting with the service name "FauxSharedObject." Also, within the script or program should be two methods: one named *save* that saves the specified data to a given filename, and one named *open* that reads the contents of a given file and returns the result.

Modifying the My Page Framework

We're almost done adapting the framework to store the data remotely. One more round of modification is needed to make the framework work with the server-side shared objects. The following example shows the changes to *myPage.fla* in abridged format. Notice that much of the code remains the same as the version from "Setting Up the Framework Form" earlier in the chapter, but some of it is placed into new functions to support the asynchronous callback functionality that is now required.

```
// Include MovieClip.as from Chapter 7 and TextField.as from Chapter 8.
#include "MovieClip.as"
#include "TextField.as"
// Include Table.as and Forms.as from Chapter 11.
#include "Table.as"
#include "Forms.as"
// Include DrawingMethods.as from Chapter 4.
#include "DrawingMethods.as"
// Include the FauxSharedObject class from earlier in this chapter.
#include "FauxSharedObject.as"

// Open the movie with a login form to determine
// for which user to retrieve the settings.
function initLogin ( ) {

    // Create a text field to label the input field.
    this.createAutoTextField("usernameLabel", this.getNewDepth( ));
    usernameLabel.text = "username:";

    // Create the input text field.
    this.createInputTextField("username", this.getNewDepth( ));

    // Create the Login button for logging in.
    this.attachMovie("FPushButtonSymbol", "loginBtn", this.getNewDepth( ));
    loginBtn.setLabel("login");
    loginBtn.setClickHandler("initLSO");

    // Place the form in the center of the movie.
    var x = Stage.width/2 - (usernameLabel._width + username._width)/2;

    loginTr0 = new TableRow(5, new TableColumn(5, usernameLabel),
                       new TableColumn(5, username));
```

```
    loginTr1 = new TableRow(5, new TableColumn(5, loginBtn));
    loginTable = new Table(5, x, Stage.width/2, loginTr0, loginTr1);
}

// Opens the FauxSharedObject determined by the username entered.
function initLSO () {
    // Get username.
    var name = username.text;

    // Remove login form now that it is no longer needed.
    usernameLabel.removeTextField();
    username.removeTextField();
    loginBtn.removeMovieClip();

    // Open the FauxSharedObject.
    gw = "http://localhost:8500/flashservices/gateway/";
    lso = new FauxSharedObject(name, gw);
    lso.setLoadHandler("soCallback", this);
    lso.load();

    // Load the XML for the services menu.
    loadXML();
}

// Some of this function is the same as what used to be in initLSO() but is moved
// here because it has to be opened on callback now that Flash Remoting is used.
function soCallback () {
    trace("called");
    if (lso.data.opened == undefined) {
        lso.data.opened = new Object();
    }
    var o = lso.data.opened;
    var newUnit;
    for (var item in o) {
        newUnit = openUnit(o[item].title, o[item].source, item);
        newUnit._x = o[item].x;
        newUnit._y = o[item].y;
    }
    lso.onMoved = function (unit) {
        this.data.opened[unit.index].x = unit._x;
        this.data.opened[unit.index].y = unit._y;
        this.flush();
    };
}

function loadXML () {
    // Remains the same as original
}

function initForm (services) {
    // Remains the same as original
}
```

```
function addUnit () {
  // Remains the same as original
}

function openUnit (title, source, index) {
  // Remains the same as original
}

// This call to initLogin( ) replaces the calls to
// initLSO( ) and loadXML( ) in original.
initLogin( );
```

The *myPage.fla* code does not change a tremendous amount. The changes, as shown in the preceding example, involve the following:

- A new function, *initLogin()*, creates a login form.
- *initLSO()* is modified to create a *FauxSharedObject*.
- *soCallback()* is a new function that does much of what *initLSO()* did previously, but it is now a separate function that is called automatically when the shared object data is loaded from the server.
- Instead of invoking *initLSO()* and *loadXML()* at the beginning of the movie, *initLogin()* is invoked.

The login form needs to be added so a user can identify himself to the My Page application so that his stored settings are loaded. This example does not provide any password security, but you might want to experiment by adding a password field and integrating the login form with a Flash Remoting back end to perform validation. You may want to refer to Chapter 28 for how such a system can be implemented.

The primary technical modification to *myPage.fla* is that it now uses a *FauxSharedObject*. Because the *FauxSharedObject* class uses Flash Remoting, the operations are asynchronous. This means that it might take a moment for the data from the server to load.

 Due to the asynchronous nature, you must place any operations that depend on the loaded data within a callback function that will be called when the data is loaded, and not before.

These actions are now all placed within *soCallback()*, which is set as the callback function for the *FauxSharedObject* in the *initLSO()* function:

```
function initLSO () {
  ...
  lso.setLoadHandler("soCallback", this);
  ...
}
```

The code within the *soCallback()* function is the same code that was contained within the *initLSO()* function. If you have any questions regarding that functionality, refer to the discussion of *initLSO()* in "Setting Up the Framework Form."

Reexamining the Services

The Google search service does not rely on local shared objects at all and thus will work perfectly regardless of which computer is used to access it. The notes and address book modules, on the other hand, rely on local shared objects for saving their information. Try to adapt each of these services to use either *FauxSharedObject* or your own Flash Remoting code.

Wrapping It Up

This chapter should have given you a solid foundation upon which to build your own My Page application. I hope it has sparked a lot of ideas for your own further development. Experiment to develop this application further. See XMethods (*http://www.xmethods.net*) and SalCentral (*http://www.salcentral.com*) for lots of interesting web services that you may want to incorporate into your application. Perhaps you might want to incorporate stock ticker services, email-sending services, or news services—all of which you can find at XMethods and SalCentral.

CHAPTER 28

A Scheduler Program

In the preceding six chapters, we created a variety of applications that drew on skills learned in recipes from earlier chapters. In this chapter, we develop a scheduler application, which, not surprisingly, relies on the *Date* class covered in Chapter 10 and various techniques you've learned in other chapters. The completed version of the application is available at *http://www.person13.com/ascb*.

Designing the Application Structure

The first thing to do when developing this scheduler program is to determine which pieces should make up the entire application, and how they fit together. We'll design the first version of the application to write data to a local shared object. Later, we'll revise the application so that it can be written to disk and retrieved from any computer. Initially, the entire application can be built using a single Flash document (though later we will add a server-side script as well). This application depends on the Calendar component available as part of the Flash UI Components Set 2. You must drag an instance from the Components panel to the Stage to add it to the Library.

In the course of the chapter, we will create the following custom components:

Time selector component (TimeSelector)
> This component is composed of a menu of 24 button movie clips (TimeSelector-Item components). Each item in the menu represents an hour of the day.

Time selector item component (TimeSelectorItem)
> These components make up the time selector menu. When a user has added schedule information to the hour that corresponds to the time selector item, the item is highlighted.

Schedule component (Schedule)
> The Schedule component is the framework for each of the schedule dates (ScheduleItem components). The Schedule component is analogous to the binder that holds the pages of a day planner.

Schedule item component (ScheduleItem)
> The Schedule component is composed of schedule items. Each schedule item corresponds to a calendar date. A schedule item can have values for the following:

> *Hourly schedule*
>> Contains the user's schedule for each hour of the day

> *Notes*
>> A user's overall notes for the day

> *To do*
>> A user's to-do list for the day

> *Notifiers*
>> An array of events the user has specified he would like to be notified of the day before the event

Notifier displayer component (Notifier)
> This component displays a list of notifications for upcoming scheduled events.

Making the Components

After formulating the general overview of the application's pieces, the next step is to create each of the components. All the components in the subsequent sections should be placed within a single Flash document. To start, create a new Flash document named *scheduler.fla*.

Designing the TimeSelector Component

The TimeSelector component consists of a scroll pane in which 24 TimeSelectorItem instances appear. Additionally, the TimeSelector component should have the following functionality:

- You should be able to make the component selectable or nonselectable. When the user is adding notes or to-do items to a daily schedule, the entire time selector should become nonselectable to signify this.

- You should be able to highlight or remove a highlight from any of the time selector items by index.

- You should be able to set a callback function that is automatically invoked whenever a time selector item is selected.

To create the TimeSelector component, complete the following steps:

1. The TimeSelector component requires you to include the ScrollPane component in your movie. Create a copy of the ScrollPane component in your movie's Library by dragging an instance from the Components panel to the Stage. You can then delete the instance on stage; a copy of the symbol remains in the Library.

2. Create a new movie clip symbol named *TimeSelector*.

3. Open the linkage properties for the symbol.

4. Select the Export for ActionScript and Export in First Frame checkboxes.

5. Give the symbol a linkage identifier of *TimeSelectorSymbol*.

6. Click OK to close the Linkage Properties dialog box.

7. Edit the *TimeSelector* symbol.

8. Add the following code to the first frame of the default layer:

```
#initclip 0

// The constructor creates a scroll pane instance and populates it with 24
// instances of the TimeSelectorItem component.
function TimeSelector( ) {

  // Create the scroll pane instance.
  this.attachMovie("FScrollPaneSymbol", "sp", this.getNewDepth( ));
  this.sp.setSize(150, 380);

  // Create a scroll content movie clip.
  this.createEmptyMovieClip("sc", this.getNewDepth( ));

  // The times property is an array that the component uses to keep track of all
  // the TimeSelectorItem instances.
  this.times = new Array( );
  var time;

  // Perform the same actions 24 times, once for each hour of the day.
  for (var i = 0; i < 24; i++) {

    // Create an instance of the TimeSelectorItem component and set its y
    // coordinate so that it appears directly below the previous
    // TimeSelectorItem.
    time = this.sc.attachMovie("TimeSelectorItemSymbol", "time" + i,
                              this.sp.getNewDepth( ), {_y: i * 20});

    // The TimeSelectorItem.setTime( ) method sets the time displayed by the
    // component based on an integer from 0 (12 A.M.) to 23 (11 P.M.).
    time.setTime(i);

    // The TimeSelectorItem.setOnSelect( ) method sets the callback function that
    // should be invoked when the item is selected by the user.
    time.setOnSelect("onSelectTime", this);
```

```
    // Add the TimeSelectorItem component to the times array.
    this.times.push(time);
  }

  // Set the scroll pane's scroll content.
  this.sp.setScrollContent(this.sc);
}

// TimeSelector extends MovieClip.
TimeSelector.prototype = new MovieClip();

// The setSelectable() method sets whether
// items in the time selector are selectable.
TimeSelector.prototype.setSelectable = function (isSelectable) {

  // If isSelectable is true, enable all TimeSelectorItems and call
  // TimeSelectorItem.grayOut() with a value of false so that the items appear
  // normally. Otherwise, dim and disable the TimeSelectorItems.
  for (var i = 0; i < this.times.length; i++) {
    this.times[i].enabled = isSelectable;
    this.times[i].grayOut(!isSelectable);
  }
};

// The TimeSelector.setHasValue() method calls the
// TimeSelectorItem.setHasValue() method of the item that corresponds to the
// specified index. See TimeSelectorItem.setHasValue() for more information.
TimeSelector.prototype.setHasValue = function (index, hasValue) {
  this.times[index].setHasValue(hasValue);
};

// The onSelectTime() method is the callback function for each of the
// TimeSelectorItem instances (as assigned in the class constructor). The cmpt
// parameter is a reference to the TimeSelectorItem that has been selected.
TimeSelector.prototype.onSelectTime = function (cmpt) {

  // Call TimeSelectorItems.deselect() for every item except the selected one.
  for (var i = 0; i < this.times.length; i++) {
    if (this.times[i] != cmpt) {
      this.times[i].deselect();
    }
  }

  // Invoke the onSelect callback function.
  this.onSelectPath[this.onSelectCB](cmpt);
};

// The setOnSelect() method allows you to define a callback function for the
// TimeSelector component. The functionName parameter is the name of the
// function, and the path parameter is a reference to a timeline in which the
// callback function exists.
TimeSelector.prototype.setOnSelect = function (functionName, path) {
  if (path == undefined) {
    path = this._parent;
  }
```

```
        this.onSelectPath = path;
        this.onSelectCB = functionName;
    };

    Object.registerClass("TimeSelectorSymbol", TimeSelector);

    #endinitclip
```

The TimeSelector component is not very complex. The component loads 24 TimeSelectorItems into a scroll pane and acts as an interface by which some commands can be
sent to the items. The constructor simply creates these instances and places them in a
scroll pane.

```
function TimeSelector( ) {
    this.attachMovie("FScrollPaneSymbol", "sp", this.getNewDepth( ));
    this.sp.setSize(150, 380);
    this.createEmptyMovieClip("sc", this.getNewDepth( ));
    this.times = new Array( );
    var time;
    for (var i = 0; i < 24; i++) {
        time = this.sc.attachMovie("TimeSelectorItemSymbol", "time" + i,
                            this.sp.getNewDepth( ), {_y: i * 20});
        time.setTime(i);
        time.setOnSelect("onSelectTime", this);
        this.times.push(time);
    }
    this.sp.setScrollContent(this.sc);
}
```

The *setSelectable()* method enables or disables all the associated TimeSelectorItems,
graying them out if appropriate. This method is used when the user selects another
entry type (such as notes or the to-do list), and it serves to visually indicate whether
the user is making hourly entries.

```
TimeSelector.prototype.setSelectable = function (isSelectable) {
    for (var i = 0; i < this.times.length; i++) {
        this.times[i].enabled = isSelectable;
        this.times[i].grayOut(!isSelectable);
    }
};
```

When the user selects a TimeSelectorItem, the *TimeSelector.onSelectTime()* method is
invoked automatically (see the constructor in which you set the *onSelect* callback
function for each item). When an item is selected, call the *deselect()* method for all the
other TimeSelectorItems, and call the *onSelect* callback function for the TimeSelector.

```
TimeSelector.prototype.onSelectTime = function (cmpt) {
    for (var i = 0; i < this.times.length; i++) {
        if (this.times[i] != cmpt) {
            this.times[i].deselect( );
        }
    }
    this.onSelectPath[this.onSelectCB](cmpt);
};
```

Designing the TimeSelectorItem Component

The TimeSelectorItem component constitutes the content of the TimeSelector component. Each TimeSelectorItem represents one hour of the day, and it should include the following functionality:

- The component should draw a filled rectangle.
- You should be able to set a time label based on an integer from 0 to 23.
- When the item is selected, the rectangle's outline should be bolded, and when deselected, the outline should not be bolded.
- You should be able to change the rectangle's fill color to highlight the component. (This is used to indicate that an hour has a scheduled event.)
- You should be able to gray out the component to indicate it is disabled.
- You should be able to specify a callback function that is invoked when the item is selected.

To create the TimeSelectorItem component, complete the following steps.

1. Create a new movie clip symbol named *TimeSelectorItem*.
2. Open the linkage properties for the symbol.
3. Select the Export for ActionScript and Export in First Frame checkboxes.
4. Give the symbol a linkage identifier of *TimeSelectorItemSymbol*.
5. Click OK to close the Linkage Properties dialog box.
6. Edit the *TimeSelectorItem* symbol.
7. Add the following code to the first frame of the default layer:

```
#initclip 0

// In the constructor, create the rectangle with a fill and outline and create a
// text field to use as the label.
function TimeSelectorItem( ) {

  // Create a movie clip and two nested movie clips within it, one for the fill
  // and one for the outline.
  this.createEmptyMovieClip("indicator", this.getNewDepth( ));
  this.indicator.createEmptyMovieClip("fill", this.indicator.getNewDepth( ));
  this.indicator.createEmptyMovieClip("outline", this.indicator.getNewDepth( ));

  // Draw the fill as a white rectangle using the drawRectangle( ) method.
  with (this.indicator.fill) {
    lineStyle(0, 0x000000, 0);
    beginFill(0xFFFFFF, 100);
    drawRectangle(150, 20);
    endFill( );
    _x += 75;
    _y += 10;
  }
```

```
    // Call the drawOutline( ) method to draw the outline.
    this.drawOutline( );

    // Create color objects to control the color for both the outline and the fill.
    this.indicator.fill.col = new Color(this.indicator.fill);
    this.indicator.outline.col = new Color(this.indicator.outline);

    // Create a text field in which the time label should appear.
    this.createTextField("time", this.getNewDepth( ), 0, 0, 150, 20);
}

// TimeSelectorItem extends MovieClip.
TimeSelectorItem.prototype = new MovieClip( );

// The drawOutline( ) method draws/redraws the rectangle's outline. If selected
// is true, draw the line with a thickness of 2. Otherwise, use no outline.
TimeSelectorItem.prototype.drawOutline = function (selected) {
  with (this.indicator.outline) {
    clear( );
    if (selected) {
      lineStyle(2, 0x000000, 100);
    } else {
      lineStyle(0, 0x000000, 100);
    }
    drawRectangle(150, 20);
    _x = 75;
    _y = 10;
  }
};

// The static getDisplayTime( ) method takes an integer from 0 to 23 and returns
// a string in the format HH AM/PM (i.e., 12 AM, 3 PM, etc.).
TimeSelectorItem.getDisplayTime = function (timeVal) {
  var time;
  if (timeVal == 0) {
    time = "12 AM";
  } else if (timeVal < 11) {
    time = timeVal + " AM";
  } else if (timeVal == 12) {
    time = "12 PM";
  } else {
    time = (timeVal - 12) + " PM";
  }
  return time;
};

// The setTime( ) method takes an integer from 0 to 23 and it displays the
// corresponding time label in the text field.
TimeSelectorItem.prototype.setTime = function (timeVal) {
  this.timeVal = timeVal;
  this.time.text = TimeSelectorItem.getDisplayTime(timeVal);
};
```

```
// The grayOut( ) method changes the colors of the outline and fill movie clips.
TimeSelectorItem.prototype.grayOut = function (grayOut) {
  if (grayOut) {
    this.indicator.outline.col.setRGB(0xBCBCBC);
    if (this.hasValue) {
      this.indicator.fill.col.setRGB(0xE4E4E4);
    }
  } else {
    this.indicator.outline.col.setRGB(0);
    if (this.hasValue) {
      this.indicator.fill.col.setRGB(0xCCEFFD);
    }
  }
};

// The setHasValue( ) method highlights or removes a highlight from the
// TimeSelectorItem by setting the color of the fill.
TimeSelectorItem.prototype.setHasValue = function (hasValue) {
  if (hasValue) {
    this.indicator.fill.col.setRGB(0xCCEFFD);
    this.hasValue = true;
  } else {
    this.indicator.fill.col.setRGB(0xFFFFFF);
    this.hasValue = false;
  }
};

// When an item is selected, call drawOutline(true) to bold the outline.
TimeSelectorItem.prototype.select = function ( ) {
  this.drawOutline(true);
};

// When an item is deselected, call drawOutline( ) to unbold the outline.
TimeSelectorItem.prototype.deselect = function ( ) {
  this.drawOutline( );
};

// Get the time (an integer from 0 to 23) that
// corresponds to the TimeSelectorItem.
TimeSelectorItem.prototype.getTime = function ( ) {
  return this.timeVal;
};

// When the item is rolled over, set the color of the fill to a light gray.
TimeSelectorItem.prototype.onRollOver = function ( ) {
  this.indicator.fill.col.setRGB(0xDFDFDF);
};

// When the item is rolled out, set the color of the fill to either white (if the
// user has not scheduled anything for the hour) or light blue (if the user has
// scheduled something for the hour).
TimeSelectorItem.prototype.onRollOut = function ( ) {
  if (this.hasValue) {
    this.indicator.fill.col.setRGB(0xCCEFFD)
```

```
    } else {
       this.indicator.fill.col.setRGB(0xFFFFFF);
    }
};

// When the item is clicked on, call the select( ) method and
// the onSelect callback function.
TimeSelectorItem.prototype.onPress = function () {
  this.select();
  this.onSelectPath[this.onSelectCB](this);
};

// Set the onSelect callback function.
TimeSelectorItem.prototype.setOnSelect = function (functionName, path) {
  if (path == undefined) {
    path = this._parent;
  }
  this.onSelectPath = path;
  this.onSelectCB = functionName;
};

Object.registerClass("TimeSelectorItemSymbol", TimeSelectorItem);

#endinitclip
```

Although the *TimeSelectorItem* class has a lot of code, there is nothing within the code that is unusual or complicated. The majority of the code involves either drawing shapes or changing colors.

Designing the Schedule Component

The Schedule component acts as a container for each of the ScheduleItem components. While ScheduleItem components correspond to specific calendar dates, the Schedule component is the framework within which each of these items is stored. The Schedule component should have the following functionality:

- It should allow you to add new schedule items for calendar dates.
- It should keep track of all notifications that a user has set, and it should alert the user at the appropriate interval automatically.
- It should save the data to a local shared object and retrieve that data whenever the application is reopened.

To create the Schedule component, complete the following steps:

1. Create a new movie clip symbol named *Schedule*.
2. Open the linkage properties for the symbol.
3. Select the Export for ActionScript and Export in First Frame checkboxes.
4. Give the symbol a linkage identifier of *ScheduleSymbol*.
5. Click OK to close the Linkage Properties dialog box.

6. Edit the Schedule symbol.

7. Add the following code to the first frame of the default layer:

```
#initclip

function Schedule() {

    // Create associative arrays to keep track of schedule items and notifiers.
    this.items = new Object();
    this.notifiers = new Object();

    // Create a local shared object or open an existing LSO.
    this.so = SharedObject.getLocal("mySchedule");

    // If LSO is not new, populate the schedule
    // application with the retrieved data.
    if (this.so.data.schedules != undefined) {
        for (var i in this.so.data.schedules) {
            var dt = this.so.data.schedules[i].siDate;
            this.addItem(dt);
            this.items[dt].setValues(this.so.data.schedules[i]);
        }
        this.notifiers = this.so.data.notifiers;
    }

    // Run the notifier routine now and call it once per hour.
    this.runNotify();
    this.interval = setInterval(this, "runNotify", 3600000);
}

Schedule.prototype = new MovieClip();

// The save() method is called when the module is closed;
// it writes the schedule data to the local shared object.
Schedule.prototype.save = function () {

    // Create a schedules associative array and fill it
    // with the values from every schedule item.
    this.so.data.schedules = new Object();
    for (var i in this.items) {
        this.so.data.schedules[i] = this.items[i].getValues();
    }

    // Create a notifiers associative array that has the
    // value of the notifiers property of the schedule component.
    this.so.data.notifiers = this.notifiers;

    // Invoke the flush() method to write the data to disk.
    this.so.flush();
};

// The onCloseNotification() method is the callback function
// for when the user closes a notifier window. It removes
// the Notifier component instance from the movie.
Schedule.prototype.onCloseNotification = function (cmpt) {
```

```
      this.noteDisp.removeMovieClip();
};

// Get a schedule item by index (which is a date string).
Schedule.prototype.getItem = function (index) {
  return this.items[index];
};

// Add a new schedule item by index (which is a date string).
Schedule.prototype.addItem = function (index) {
  var uniqueVal = this.getNewDepth();

  // Create a new instance of the ScheduleItem component and assign a reference
  // to the new component to an element of the items associative array.
  this.items[index] = this.attachMovie("ScheduleItemSymbol", "item" + uniqueVal,
                      uniqueVal);
  this.items[index].setDate(index);
};

// The runNotify() method is called at hourly
// intervals to display any new updates.
Schedule.prototype.runNotify = function () {

  // Create a date for tomorrow and get that value as a formatted date string.
  var d = new Date();
  d.setDate(d.getDate() + 1);
  index = d.format("MM-dd-yyyy");

  // Check to see if a notifier exists for that date.
  if (this.notifiers[index] != undefined) {
    var notification = "";

    // Loop through all the elements for that date's notifiers and add them to
    // the notification string.
    for (var i = 0; i < this.notifiers[index].length; i++) {
      if (this.notifiers[index][i]) {
        notification += index + " " +
                        TimeSelectorItem.getDisplayTime(i) + newline +
                        this.items[index].getSchedule(i) + "\n\n";
      }
    }

    // Delete the notifier information so that
    // the user will not be notified again.
    delete this.notifiers[index];

    // Call the displayNotifications() method
    // to display information to the user.
    this.displayNotifications(notification);
  }
};

// Create a new NotifierDisplayer component instance and display the notification
// information to the user.
Schedule.prototype.displayNotifications = function (displayValue) {
```

```
      this.attachMovie("NotifierDisplayerSymbol", "noteDisp", this.getNewDepth());
      this.noteDisp._x = Stage.width/2 - this.noteDisp._width/2;
      this.noteDisp._y = Stage.height/2 - this.noteDisp._height/2;
      this.noteDisp.display(displayValue);
   };

   // The setNotify() method adds a new notifier to the schedule, or, if doNotify
   // is not true, it removes any existing notifiers for the date and time.
   Schedule.prototype.setNotify = function (dt, hour, doNotify) {
      if (doNotify) {
         if (this.notifiers[dt] == undefined) {
            this.notifiers[dt] = new Array();
         }
         this.notifiers[dt][hour] = true;
      } else {
         delete this.notifiers[dt][hour];
      }
   };

   // Call the open() method for a schedule item, which makes it visible, by index.
   Schedule.prototype.openItem = function (index) {
      this.items[index].open();
   };

   // The onClose() method is invoked automatically when a schedule item is closed.
   // This method invokes the schedule's onClose callback function.
   Schedule.prototype.onClose = function () {
      this.onClosePath[this.onCloseCB]();
   };

   // Set the onClose callback function.
   Schedule.prototype.setOnClose = function (functionName, path) {
      if (path == undefined) {
         path = this._parent;
      }
      this.onClosePath = path;
      this.onCloseCB = functionName;
   };

   Object.registerClass("ScheduleSymbol", Schedule);

   #endinitclip
```

Let's examine the Schedule component code more closely to shed light on parts of the code that might be unclear.

When you initialize the Schedule component, it must create properties to keep track of the schedule items and the notifiers. It uses an associative array for each of these properties so that the keys are in the form of formatted date strings (instead of simply integer indexes). Additionally, it creates (or opens) the shared object in which the schedule information is stored. If the shared object already exists, the retrieved data is used to populate the schedule. Finally, it sets up an interval for notifications, which runs once an hour. Although this example auto-saves the data when the user clicks the close box, you could implement a manual save feature using a button instead.

```
function Schedule( ) {
  this.items = new Object( );
  this.notifiers = new Object( );
  this.so = SharedObject.getLocal("mySchedule");
  if (this.so.data.schedules != undefined) {
    for (var i in this.so.data.schedules) {
      var dt = this.so.data.schedules[i].siDate;
      this.addItem(dt);
      this.items[dt].setValues(this.so.data.schedules[i]);
    }
    this.notifiers = this.so.data.notifiers;
  }
  this.runNotify( );
  this.interval = setInterval(this, "runNotify", 3600000);
}
```

The *addItem()* method adds a new schedule item. The index is a formatted date string, and the new schedule item is added to the items associative array using that date string as the key. This makes it easy to retrieve a reference to the schedule item later on.

```
Schedule.prototype.addItem = function (index) {
  var uniqueVal = this.getNewDepth( );
  this.items[index] = this.attachMovie("ScheduleItemSymbol", "item" + uniqueVal,
                     uniqueVal);
  this.items[index].setDate(index);
};
```

The *runNotify()* method is invoked every 60 minutes; it checks for any notifications for the next day. To calculate the date that represents the next day, add one to the current date. From this date, you can create a formatted date string (the format used by the keys of the notifiers associative array) using the *Date.format()* method. Each element of the notifiers associative array is an array of notifications for that day. Therefore, if there is an entry in the notifiers associative array for the next day, loop through all the elements of that array and create a string of those values. Then, run the *displayNotifications()* method to actually open the notifier displayer.

```
Schedule.prototype.runNotify = function ( ) {
  var d = new Date( );
  d.setDate(d.getDate( ) + 1);
  index = d.format("MM-dd-yyyy");
  if (this.notifiers[index] != undefined) {
    var notification = "";
    for (var i = 0; i < this.notifiers[index].length; i++) {
      if (this.notifiers[index][i]) {
        notification += index + " " +
                      TimeSelectorItem.getDisplayTime(i) + newline +
                      this.items[index].getSchedule(i) + "\n\n";
      }
    }
```

```
        delete this.notifiers[index];
        this.displayNotifications(notification);
    }
};
```

Designing the ScheduleItem Component

The ScheduleItem component represents a single calendar date. Each schedule item consists of a time selector, an input text field, and a list box from which the user can select the type of entry he wants to make (hourly schedule, notes, or to-do list). The schedule item should have the following functionality:

- A user should be able to select from different types of schedule entries, and he should be able to make an entry for that type by typing into a text field.
- A user should be able to select from available hours in the time selector and add an entry for that hour. Time selector items corresponding to hours with entries should be colorized to indicate this.
- A user should be able to specify whether the scheduler should notify him of hourly entries on the day before they are scheduled to occur.
- A user should be able to close a schedule item window.

To create the ScheduleItem component, complete the following steps:

1. The ScheduleItem component requires you to include the ScrollBar and Check-Box components in your movie. Create a copy of these components in your movie's Library by dragging an instance of each component from the Components panel onto the Stage and then deleting them. A copy of the symbols remains in the Library.
2. Create a new movie clip symbol named *ScheduleItem*.
3. Open the linkage properties for the symbol.
4. Select the Export for ActionScript and Export in First Frame checkboxes.
5. Give the symbol a linkage identifier of *ScheduleItemSymbol*.
6. Click OK to close the Linkage Properties dialog box.
7. Edit the *ScheduleItem* symbol.
8. Add the following code to the first frame of the default layer:

```
#initclip 2

function ScheduleItem () {

    // Draw the component.
    this.draw();
```

```
// Create arrays to hold information about the hourly schedule entries and any
// entries for which the user has chosen to be notified.
this.hourlySchedule = new Array( );
this.notifiers = new Array( );

// Initialize the component, such that 12 A.M. is the selected hour.
this.selectedHour = 0;

// Initialize the component so that it is not visible.
this._visible = false;
}

// ScheduleItem extends MovieClip.
ScheduleItem.prototype = new MovieClip( );

// Retrieve the schedule item's values.
ScheduleItem.prototype.getValues = function ( ) {
  var valuesObj = new Object( );

  // siDate is the formatted date string that indicates the date to which the
  // schedule item corresponds.
  valuesObj.siDate = this.siDate;

  // These properties are the entries (and notifiers) for the schedule item.
  valuesObj.hourlySchedule = this.hourlySchedule;
  valuesObj.notifiers = this.notifiers;
  valuesObj.toDo = this.toDo;
  valuesObj.notes = this.notes;
  return valuesObj;
};

// The setValues( ) method is used to populate a schedule item when the values
// have been saved to disk and have been retrieved again when the schedule
// application is reopened. The valuesObj is in the same form as the valuesObj
// that getValues( ) returns. Therefore, setValues( ) does essentially the reverse
// of what getValues( ) does.
ScheduleItem.prototype.setValues = function (valuesObj) {
  this.hourlySchedule = valuesObj.hourlySchedule;
  this.notifiers = valuesObj.notifiers;
  this.toDo = valuesObj.toDo;
  this.notes = valuesObj.notes;

  // In addition to setting the properties of the schedule item, call the
  // setHasValue( ) method for the time selector for any times that have entries.
  for (var i = 0; i < this.hourlySchedule.length; i++) {
    if (this.hourlySchedule[i] != undefined) {
      this.times.setHasValue(i, true);
    }
  }
};

// The draw( ) method creates the component on the Stage.
ScheduleItem.prototype.draw = function ( ) {
```

```
// Create a text field for the schedule item title.
this.createTextField("title", this.getNewDepth(), 0, 0, 550, 20);
this.title.selectable = false;
this.title.border = true;
this.title.background = true;
this.title.backgroundColor = 0xDFDFDF;

// Create a TimeSelector instance and set its onSelect callback function.
this.attachMovie("TimeSelectorSymbol", "times", this.getNewDepth());
this.times.setOnSelect("onSelectTime", this);

// Create an input text field so that the user can make entries.
this.createInputTextField("scheduleInfo", this.getNewDepth(), 0, 0, 234, 350);
this.scheduleInfo.multiline = true;

// When the user removes focus from the text field (usually by clicking
// elsewhere in the movie), call the saveInfo() method to save the entry.
this.scheduleInfo.onKillFocus = function () {
  this._parent.saveInfo();
};

// Create a scrollbar for the input text field.
this.attachMovie("FScrollBarSymbol", "sb", this.getNewDepth());
this.sb.setScrollTarget(this.scheduleInfo);
this.sb.setSize(this.scheduleInfo._height);

// Create a movie clip for the notification checkbox.
this.createEmptyMovieClip("notifyBox", this.getNewDepth());

// Draw a filled rectangle as a background.
this.notifyBox.createEmptyMovieClip("background",
                                    this.notifyBox.getNewDepth());
with (this.notifyBox.background) {
  lineStyle(0, 0x000000, 100);
  beginFill(0xFFFFFF, 100);
  drawRectangle(this.scheduleInfo._width + this.sb._width, 30);
  endFill();
  _x = _width / 2;
  _y = _height / 2;
}

// Attach a CheckBox component instance and set the callback function for it.
this.notifyBox.attachMovie("FCheckBoxSymbol", "notifyCheckBox",
                           this.notifyBox.getNewDepth(), {_x: 10, _y: 10});
this.notifyBox.notifyCheckBox.setLabel("notify me");
this.notifyBox.notifyCheckBox.setChangeHandler("notifyChange", this);

// Use a table to position all the elements that you have created thus far.
midTr0 = new TableRow(0, new TableColumn(0, this.scheduleInfo),
                      new TableColumn(0, this.sb));
midTr1 = new TableRow(0, new TableColumn(0, this.notifyBox));
midTable = new Table(0, 0, 0, midTr0, midTr1);
```

```
// Add a list box so the user can select an entry type.
this.attachMovie("FListBoxSymbol", "entryTypeMenu", this.getNewDepth());
this.entryTypeMenu.setSize(150, 380);
this.entryTypeMenu._height = 380;

// Set the values for the list box.
this.entryTypeMenu.setDataProvider(["hourly", "to do list", "notes"]);
this.entryTypeMenu.setChangeHandler("onSelectEntryType", this);
this.entryTypeMenu.setSelectedIndex(0);

// Create a table to position all the elements, including ones from midTable.
tr0 = new TableRow(0, new TableColumn(0, this.title));
tr1 = new TableRow(0,
                new TableColumn(0, this.times),
                new TableColumn(0, midTable),
                new TableColumn(0, this.entryTypeMenu));
t = new Table(0, 0, 0, tr0, tr1);

// Create a button movie clip to let the user close the schedule item window.
this.createEmptyMovieClip("closeBtn", this.getNewDepth());
with (this.closeBtn) {
  lineStyle(0, 0x000000, 100);
  beginFill(0xFFFFFF, 100);
  drawRectangle(10, 10);
  endFill();
  _x = 540;
  _y = 10;
}
this.closeBtn.onRelease = function () {
  this._parent.close();
  // Invoke the save() method of the schedule to
  // save the data when the item window is closed.
  this._parent._parent.save()
};
};

// Return the entry for an hour.
ScheduleItem.prototype.getSchedule = function (hour) {
  return this.hourlySchedule[hour];
};

// The notifyChange() method is the callback function for the notification
// checkbox. This method calls the setNotify() method of the parent schedule and
// adds to the notifiers array property.
ScheduleItem.prototype.notifyChange = function (cmpt) {
  this._parent.setNotify(this.siDate, this.selectedHour, cmpt.getValue());
  this.notifiers[this.selectedHour] = cmpt.getValue();
};

// The onSelectEntryType() method is the callback function that is invoked when
// a user selects an item from the list box.
ScheduleItem.prototype.onSelectEntryType = function (cmpt) {
  var index = cmpt.getSelectedIndex();
  switch (index) {
```

```
    case 0:
      // If the first item (hourly) is selected, make sure the time selector is
      // set to selectable and also enable the checkbox.
      this.times.setSelectable(true);
      this.entryType = "hourly";
      this.selectTime();
      this.notifyBox.notifyCheckBox.setEnabled(true);
      break;
    case 1:
      // If the second item (to-do list) is selected, make sure the time selector
      // is not selectable and disable the checkbox.
      this.times.setSelectable(false);
      this.scheduleInfo.text = "";
      this.entryType = "toDo";
      this.scheduleInfo.text = this.toDo;
      this.notifyBox.notifyCheckBox.setEnabled(false);
      this.notifyBox.notifyCheckBox.setValue(false);
      break;
    case 2:
      // If the third item (notes) is selected, make sure the time selector is
      // not selectable and disable the checkbox.
      this.times.setSelectable(false);
      this.scheduleInfo.text = "";
      this.entryType = "notes";
      this.scheduleInfo.text = this.notes;
      this.notifyBox.notifyCheckBox.setEnabled(false);
      this.notifyBox.notifyCheckBox.setValue(false);
  }
};

// The setDate() method takes a formatted date string as a parameter and sets
// the title text and the siDate property for the schedule item.
ScheduleItem.prototype.setDate = function (val) {
  this.title.text = val;
  var tf = new TextFormat();
  tf.bold = true;
  tf.align = "center";
  tf.size = 15;
  this.title.setTextFormat(tf);
  this.siDate = val;
};

ScheduleItem.prototype.open = function () {
  this._visible = true;
};

ScheduleItem.prototype.close = function () {
  this._visible = false;
  this._parent.onClose();
};

// The saveInfo() method is invoked whenever the text field loses focus.
ScheduleItem.prototype.saveInfo = function () {
```

```
switch (this.entryType) {
  case "hourly":
    // If the user has made an hourly schedule entry, save that entry in the
    // hourlySchedule array and colorize the corresponding time selector item;
    // otherwise, remove any colorization on a time selector item.
    if (this.scheduleInfo.text != "") {
      this.hourlySchedule[this.selectedHour] = this.scheduleInfo.text;
      this.times.setHasValue(this.selectedHour, true);
    } else {
      this.times.setHasValue(this.selectedHour, false);
    }
    break;

  case "toDo":
    // Save the to-do information.
    this.toDo = this.scheduleInfo.text;
    break;

  case "notes":
    // Save the notes information.
    this.notes = this.scheduleInfo.text;
  }
};

// The onSelectTime() method is the callback function
// when a time selector item is chosen.
ScheduleItem.prototype.onSelectTime = function (cmpt) {
  this.selectedHour = cmpt.getTime();
  this.selectTime();
};

// The selectTime() method displays any saved entries for a selected time in the
// input text field. Also, if the user has chosen to be notified for the event,
// the checkbox is checked.
ScheduleItem.prototype.selectTime = function () {
  if (this.hourlySchedule[this.selectedHour] != undefined) {
    this.scheduleInfo.text = this.hourlySchedule[this.selectedHour];
  } else {
    this.scheduleInfo.text = "";
  }
  if (this.notifiers[this.selectedHour] != undefined) {
    this.notifyBox.notifyCheckBox.setValue(this.notifiers[this.selectedHour]);
  } else {
    this.notifyBox.notifyCheckBox.setValue(false);
  }
};

Object.registerClass("ScheduleItemSymbol", ScheduleItem);

#endinitclip
```

Although the ScheduleItem component code is not particularly daunting, it is still worth taking a closer look at some of what is going on here.

The *getValues()* and *setValues()* methods do the reverse of one another. The *getValues()* method is used in conjunction with the Schedule component's *save()* method. It returns an object that contains the user data, which is, in turn, saved to the shared object. Then, when the data is retrieved from the shared object, the same data object is passed back to the *setValues()* method to repopulate the schedule item.

```
ScheduleItem.prototype.getValues = function () {
  var valuesObj = new Object();
  valuesObj.siDate = this.siDate;
  valuesObj.hourlySchedule = this.hourlySchedule;
  valuesObj.notifiers = this.notifiers;
  valuesObj.toDo = this.toDo;
  valuesObj.notes = this.notes;
  return valuesObj;
};

ScheduleItem.prototype.setValues = function (valuesObj) {
  this.hourlySchedule = valuesObj.hourlySchedule;
  this.notifiers = valuesObj.notifiers;
  this.toDo = valuesObj.toDo;
  this.notes = valuesObj.notes;
  for (var i = 0; i < this.hourlySchedule.length; i++) {
    if (this.hourlySchedule[i] != undefined) {
      this.times.setHasValue(i, true);
    }
  }
};
```

The *onSelectEntryType()* method is the change handler function for the entry types list box. Although there are many lines of code in the method, it is really nothing complex. The entire method is a single *switch* statement that sets the time selector's selectable status, the entryType property, and other minor modifications depending on the type of entry the user has selected (hourly, to-do list, or notes):

```
ScheduleItem.prototype.onSelectEntryType = function (cmpt) {
  var index = cmpt.getSelectedIndex();
  switch (index) {
    case 0:
      this.times.setSelectable(true);
      this.entryType = "hourly";
      this.selectTime();
      this.notifyBox.notifyCheckBox.setEnabled(true);
      break;
    case 1:
      this.times.setSelectable(false);
      this.scheduleInfo.text = "";
      this.entryType = "toDo";
      this.scheduleInfo.text = this.toDo;
      this.notifyBox.notifyCheckBox.setEnabled(false);
      this.notifyBox.notifyCheckBox.setValue(false);
      break;
```

```
    case 2:
      this.times.setSelectable(false);
      this.scheduleInfo.text = "";
      this.entryType = "notes";
      this.scheduleInfo.text = this.notes;
      this.notifyBox.notifyCheckBox.setEnabled(false);
      this.notifyBox.notifyCheckBox.setValue(false);
  }
};
```

The *saveInfo()* method is invoked automatically when the user removes the focus from the input text field. This technique ensures that the schedule item's data is updated to reflect the new entry (or entry changes). This method doesn't do anything particularly tricky. It just sets the appropriate schedule item property values depending on the type of entry.

```
ScheduleItem.prototype.saveInfo = function () {
  switch(this.entryType) {
    case "hourly":
      if (this.scheduleInfo.text != "") {
        this.hourlySchedule[this.selectedHour] = this.scheduleInfo.text;
        this.times.setHasValue(this.selectedHour, true);
      } else {
        this.times.setHasValue(this.selectedHour, false);
      }
      break;
    case "toDo":
      this.toDo = this.scheduleInfo.text;
      break;
    case "notes":
      this.notes = this.scheduleInfo.text;
  }
};
```

The *selectTime()* method is invoked whenever a user selects a time selector item. In this method, you should make sure that if the schedule item already has an entry for the selected hour, the text field should be populated with that data. Otherwise, remove any text from the text field. Also, if the user has chosen to be notified for an event stored for that hour, you should mark the checkbox as selected. Otherwise, deselect the checkbox.

```
ScheduleItem.prototype.selectTime = function () {
  if (this.hourlySchedule[this.selectedHour] != undefined) {
    this.scheduleInfo.text = this.hourlySchedule[this.selectedHour];
  } else {
    this.scheduleInfo.text = "";
  }
  if (this.notifiers[this.selectedHour] != undefined) {
    this.notifyBox.notifyCheckBox.setValue(this.notifiers[this.selectedHour]);
  } else {
    this.notifyBox.notifyCheckBox.setValue(false);
  }
};
```

Designing the NotifierDisplayer Component

The NotifierDisplayer component is nothing more than a scrollable text field with a rectangle background and a Close button. This simple component should do the following:

- Draw a rectangle for the background
- Add a text field and a scrollbar that scrolls the text field
- Add a button that enables the user to close the displayer

To create the NotifierDisplayer component, complete the following steps.

1. The NotifierDisplayer component requires you to include the ScrollBar and PushButton components in your movie. You should already have included the ScrollBar component earlier, so you only need to include the PushButton component by dragging an instance from the Components panel to the Stage and then deleting the instance. A copy of the symbol remains in the Library.

2. Create a new movie clip symbol named *NotifierDisplayer*.

3. Open the linkage properties for the symbol.

4. Select the Export for ActionScript and Export in First Frame checkboxes.

5. Give the symbol a linkage identifier of *NotifierDisplayerSymbol*.

6. Click OK to close the Linkage Properties dialog box.

7. Edit the *NotifierDisplayer* symbol.

8. Add the following code to the first frame of the default layer:

```
#initclip 0

function NotifierDisplayer () {

  // Create a movie clip and draw a filled square in it. This serves as the
  // background for the component.
  this.createEmptyMovieClip("background", this.getNewDepth());
  with (this.background) {
    lineStyle(0, 0x000000, 100);
    beginFill(0xFFFFFF, 100);
    drawRectangle(300, 300);
    endFill();
    _x = 150;
    _y = 150;
  }

  // Create a text field in which the notifications can be displayed.
  this.createTextField("notificationText", this.getNewDepth(), 0, 0, 240, 240);
  this.notificationText.border = true;
  this.notificationText.background = true;

  // Create a scrollbar and set its size.
  this.attachMovie("FScrollBarSymbol", "sb", this.getNewDepth());
  this.sb.setSize(this.notificationText._height);
```

```
      // Create a push button that closes the notifier displayer.
      this.attachMovie("FPushButtonSymbol", "closeBtn", this.getNewDepth( ));
      this.closeBtn.setLabel("close");
      this.closeBtn.setClickHandler("onCloseNotification", this._parent);

      // Use a table to position the elements.
      tr0 = new TableRow(0, new TableColumn(0, this.notificationText),
                         new TableColumn(0, this.sb));
      tr1 = new TableRow(0, new TableColumn(0, this.closeBtn));
      t = new Table(5, 30, 30, tr0, tr1);
    }

    // NotifierDisplayer extends MovieClip.
    NotifierDisplayer.prototype = new MovieClip( );

    // The display( ) method sets the notification text.
    NotifierDisplayer.prototype.display = function (value) {
      this.notificationText.text = value;
      this.sb.setScrollTarget(this.notificationText);
    };

    Object.registerClass("NotifierDisplayerSymbol", NotifierDisplayer);

    #endinitclip
```

Putting the Application Together

The final step in creating a working scheduler application is to create the main code routine on the main timeline of the Flash document. Essentially, the main routine is responsible for three things:

- Creating an instance of Macromedia's Calendar component (the FCalendarSymbol must be available in the Library)
- Creating an instance of the Schedule component
- Creating functionality that opens a schedule item that corresponds to a calendar date when the calendar date is double-clicked

All you need to do to complete the scheduler application is add the following code to the first frame of the default layer of the Flash document's main timeline:

```
// Include DrawingMethods.as from Chapter 4.
#include "DrawingMethods.as"
// Include MovieClip.as from Chapter 7 and TextField.as from Chapter 8.
#include "MovieClip.as"
#include "TextField.as"
// Include Date.as from Chapter 10 and Tables.as from Chapter 11.
#include "Date.as"
#include "Table.as"

function init( ) {
```

```
   // Create an instance of the Calendar component.
   _root.attachMovie("FCalendarSymbol", "cal", _root.getNewDepth());
   cal.setChangeHandler("onSelectDate");
   cal.setSize(Stage.width, Stage.height);

   // Create a Schedule component instance.
   _root.attachMovie("ScheduleSymbol", "scheduler", _root.getNewDepth());
   scheduler.setOnClose("onScheduleClose", _root);
}

// The onSelectDate() function is the callback function for the Calendar component.
function onSelectDate(cmpt) {

   // Get the time, in milliseconds, since the movie started playing.
   var currentTime = getTimer();
   var selectedDate = cmpt.getSelectedItem();

   // Select the date that has been clicked in the Calendar component.
   if (selectedDate == undefined || selectedDate == previousDate) {
     cmpt.setChangeHandler(null);
     cmpt.setSelectedItem(previousDate);
     cmpt.setChangeHandler("onSelectDate");
   }

   // If the click is a double-click, open the schedule item that corresponds to the
   // date. If no schedule item for that date has been created, create it first.
   if (currentTime - previousTime < 500) {
     if (scheduler.getItem(previousDate.format("MM-dd-yyyy")) == undefined) {
       scheduler.addItem(previousDate.format("MM-dd-yyyy"));
     }
     scheduler.openItem(previousDate.format("MM-dd-yyyy"));
     cal._alpha = 33;
   }

   // Keep track of the time differences between clicks.
   previousTime = currentTime;

   // Set the previousDate to the date that the user has clicked.
   previousDate = (selectedDate == undefined) ? previousDate : selectedDate;
}

// When the schedule item is closed, reset the calendar's transparency to opaque.
function onScheduleClose() {
   cal._alpha = 100;
}

init();
```

Although the main code routine of the scheduler application is short, it probably requires the most explanation of any of the code in this application thus far. Let's take a look at what this code is doing.

The *init()* and *onScheduleClose()* functions are both straightforward, but the *onSelectDate()* function requires a closer look. The *onSelectDate()* function is the call-back function that is invoked whenever a calendar date is selected. By default, click-ing a date toggles its selection in the Calendar component, but we want a double-click to open the corresponding schedule item. To do this, we need to do several things. First, to determine whether a date has been double-clicked, we need to calculate the time difference between clicks. We start with the current timer value:

```
var currentTime = getTimer();
```

The rest of the code for determining double-clicking comes later in the function, so we'll examine that in a moment.

If the user selects one date and then another, there is no problem. However, if the user clicks a date and then clicks it again, you need to make sure the same date remains selected (instead of toggling to unselected, which is the standard behavior of Macromedia's Calendar component). If a user clicks the same date two or more times in a row, we trick the Calander component by setting the selected calendar item to the previously selected date (which happens to be the same date). The trou-ble with this approach is that it again triggers the calendar's change handler, causing an infinite, recursive loop. To avoid this problem, we temporarily set the calendar's change handler to null just before setting the selected item. Then, immediately fol-lowing that assignment, we reset the change handler.

```
var selectedDate = cmpt.getSelectedItem();
if (selectedDate == undefined || selectedDate == previousDate) {
  cmpt.setChangeHandler(null);
  cmpt.setSelectedItem(previousDate);
  cmpt.setChangeHandler("onSelectDate");
}
```

Returning to detecting double-clicks, you can check for a double-click by comparing the difference between the current timer value and the timer value from when the user last selected a calendar date. If the difference is less than 500 milliseconds (half a second), you should consider it a double-click and open up the schedule item that corresponds to the selected date. If no schedule item for that date has been created, you should create it first.

```
if (currentTime - previousTime < 500) {
  if (scheduler.getItem(previousDate.format("MM-dd-yyyy")) == undefined) {
    scheduler.addItem(previousDate.format("MM-dd-yyyy"));
  }
  scheduler.openItem(previousDate.format("MM-dd-yyyy"));
  cal._alpha = 33;
}
```

Finally, for future calculations, you should store the current timer value as the previ-ous timer value. You should also store the selected date as the previous date for future calculations. The selected date may be undefined because of the built-in toggling functionality of the Calendar component. If this is the case, set the previous date to the value already stored as the previous date:

```
previousTime = currentTime;
previousDate = (selectedDate == undefined) ? previousDate : selectedDate;
```

Making the Scheduler Application Available Online

The scheduler application that you have created thus far retains a user's schedule only when it is run consistently from the same computer. This is because the schedule data is stored in a local shared object. However, with just a few small changes, you can adapt this application so it can be accessed online from any computer. In the next two sections, you can choose from three different alternatives for how to do this.

Using Remote Shared Objects

The easiest way to convert the scheduler application to make it available online is to store the data in a remote shared object instead of a local shared object. However, this option is available only if you have access to a FlashCom server.

To modify the application to use a remote shared object, complete the following steps:

1. Create a new FlashCom application on the server. Name the application *schedulerApp*.

2. Edit the Schedule component code, as shown in the following code block. Most of the code remains the same, so only the code that changes is shown. Modifications are shown in bold.

```
#initclip

function Schedule( ) {
  this.items = new Object( );
  this.notifiers = new Object( );

  // Create a new net connection and connect to the FlashCom application.
  var myConnection = new NetConnection( );
  myConnection.connect("rtmp:/schedulerApp");
  // Create a remote shared object and connect to it. When the shared object date
  // is retrieved, call the setValues( ) method.
  this.so = SharedObject.getRemote("mySchedule", myConnection.uri, true);
  this.so.connect(myConnection);
  this.so.schedule = this;
  this.so.onSync = function( ) {
```

```
      this.schedule.setValues( );
    }
    this.runNotify( );
    this.interval = setInterval(this, "runNotify", 600000);
  }

  Schedule.prototype = new MovieClip( );

  // setValues( ) is called when the remote shared object data is retrieved. The
  // code within the method body is the same code that was previously in the
  // constructor method.
  Schedule.prototype.setValues = function ( ) {
    if (this.so.data.schedules != undefined) {
      for (var i in this.so.data.schedules) {
        var dt = this.so.data.schedules[i].siDate;
        this.addItem(dt);
        this.items[dt].setValues(this.so.data.schedules[i]);
      }
      this.notifiers = this.so.data.notifiers;
    }
  }

  // The remainder of the code does not change.
```

Using Flash Remoting

The second option for saving the scheduler data on a server is to use Flash Remoting. Obviously, this option works only if you have access to a Flash Remoting server. However, you can use this method without Flash Remoting by using the *FauxSharedObject* class from Chapter 27. You need to have the *FauxSharedObject* class ready to include in your Flash document and to also have the ColdFusion Component on the server, as per the instructions from Chapter 27. Once you have that code in place, you can quickly modify your schedule application by changing a small amount of code in the schedule component. The following shows the relevant code with the changes in bold:

```
#initclip
// Include the FauxSharedObject class from Chapter 27.
#include "FauxSharedObject.as"

function Schedule ( ) {
  this.items = new Object( );
  this.notifiers = new Object( );
  // Use a FauxSharedObject in place of the local shared object. Set the load handler
  // to the new setValues( ) method and load the data.
  this.so = new FauxSharedObject("mySchedule",
          "http://localhost:8500/flashservices/gateway");
  this.so.setLoadHandler("setValues", this);
  this.so.load( );
```

```
    this.runNotify( );
    this.interval = setInterval(this, "runNotify", 600000);
    this.saveInterval = setInterval(this, "save", 5000);
}

Schedule.prototype = new MovieClip( );

// The code in setValues( ) was previously included in the constructor.
Schedule.prototype.setValues = function ( ) {
  if (this.so.data.schedules != undefined) {
    for (var i in this.so.data.schedules) {
      var dt = this.so.data.schedules[i].siDate;
      this.addItem(dt);
      this.items[dt].setValues(this.so.data.schedules[i]);
    }
    this.notifiers = this.so.data.notifiers;
  }
}

// The remainder of the code does not change.
```

Using LoadVars and XML

The third way you can modify the scheduler application is to use server-side scripts
that read and write to a file. The ColdFusion versions of these scripts are provided
here in this example, but if you need to use another technology, it is not too difficult. You need two scripts: one to write data and one to read the data. The write
script should take two parameters submitted via HTTP POST: the name of the file to
which to write and the data to be written. Here is the ColdFusion example that you
should name *LoadVarsSharedObjectSave.cfm*:

```
<cffile action="write"
    file="#GetDirectoryFromPath(GetBaseTemplatePath( ))##FORM.name#.so"
    output="#FORM.data#" nameconflict="overwrite">
```

The other script should read the data from the file and return it to Flash. This script
should accept a single parameter submitted via HTTP GET: the name of the file from
which to read. Here is the ColdFusion example. You should name this file *Load-
VarsSharedObjectRead.cfm*.

```
<cfsetting enablecfoutputonly="yes">
<cffile action="read"
    file="#GetDirectoryFromPath(GetBaseTemplatePath( ))##URL.name#.so"
    variable="data">
<cfoutput>#data#</cfoutput>
```

Finally, you should make a few changes to the client-side ActionScript code in the Schedule component. The relevant snippet of code from that component is shown here with changes in bold:

```
#initclip

// The serializeObject() and deserializeObject() functions are the exact same code
// as the serializeObject() and deserializeObject() methods of the FauxSharedObject
// class from Chapter 27. See Chapter 27 for more information on these functions.
_global.serializeObject = function (obj) {
  var sb = "<obj>";
  if (obj instanceof Array) {
    sb = "<obj type=\"array\">";
  }
  for (var i in obj) {
    sb += "<index name=\"" + i + "\"";
    if (obj[i] instanceof Object) {
      sb += ">";
      sb += serializeObject(obj[i]);
      sb += "</index>";
    } else {
      sb += " val=\"" + obj[i] + "\" />";
    }
  }
  sb += "</obj>";
  return sb;
};

_global.deserializeObject = function (source) {
  XML.prototype.ignoreWhite = true;
  var sXML = new XML(source);
  var cn = sXML.firstChild.childNodes;
  var items = new Object();
  if (sXML.firstChild.attributes.type == "array") {
    items = new Array();
  }
  var attribs, childCn;
  for (var i = 0; i < cn.length; i++) {
    attribs = cn[i].attributes;
    childCn = cn[i].childNodes;
    if (childCn.length > 0) {
      items[attribs.name] = deserializeObject(childCn[0]);
    } else {
      items[attribs.name] = attribs.val;
    }
    items[attribs.index] = new Object();
    for (var j in attribs) {
      items[attribs.index][j] = attribs[j];
    }
  }
  return items;
};
```

```
function Schedule () {
  this.items = new Object();
  this.notifiers = new Object();

  // Instead of a shared object, simply create an object with a data property.
  this.so = new Object();
  this.so.data = new Object();

  // Create a flush() method for the object that uses a LoadVars object to send the
  // serialized data to the LoadVarsSharedObjectSave.cfm script.
  this.so.flush = function () {
    serializedStr = serializeObject(this.data);
    var sendLV = new LoadVars();
    sendLV.name = "myScheduleLV";
    sendLV.data = serializedStr;
    sendLV.sendAndLoad("http://localhost:8500/LoadVarsSharedObjectSave.cfm",
                       null, "POST");
  };

  this.so.parent = this;

  // Create a load method for the object that uses an XML object to load the data
  // from the LoadVarsSharedObjectRead.cfm script.
  this.so.load = function () {
    var loadXML = new XML();
    loadXML.ignoreWhite = true;
    loadXML.load(
           "http://localhost:8500/LoadVarsSharedObjectRead.cfm?name=myScheduleLV");
    loadXML.parent = this;

    // When the data loads, deserialize it and then call the setValues() method.
    loadXML.onLoad = function () {
      this.parent.data = deserializeObject(this);
      this.parent.parent.setValues();
    };
  };
  this.so.load();
  this.runNotify();
  this.interval = setInterval(this, "runNotify", 600000);
  this.saveInterval = setInterval(this, "save", 5000);
}

Schedule.prototype = new MovieClip();

// The setValues() method contains code that was previously in the constructor.
Schedule.prototype.setValues = function () {
  if (this.so.data.schedules != undefined) {
    for (var i in this.so.data.schedules) {
      var dt = this.so.data.schedules[i].siDate;
      this.addItem(dt);
```

```
        this.items[dt].setValues(this.so.data.schedules[i]);
    }
    this.notifiers = this.so.data.notifiers;
  }
};

// The remainder of the code stays the same.
```

Wrapping It Up

Well, we've completed our scheduler application and even enhanced it to work online. We've come a long way since the initial recipes of Chapter 1. Even though this book is task-oriented, I hope you've gained the experience, perspective, and knowledge to apply the lessons you've learned to a wide variety of problems, including those not specifically addressed by a pre-built recipe. Good luck with all your future ActionScript programming.

Unicode Escape Sequences for Latin 1 Characters

Table A-1 lists the characters in the Latin 1 character repertoire, with Unicode equivalents in the range of U+0000 to U+00FF (that is, C0 Controls, Basic Latin, C1 Controls, and Latin 1 Supplemental). It is reproduced from Appendix B of *ActionScript for Flash MX: The Definitive Guide* with the gracious permission of the author, Colin Moock.

The table's first column (labeled *Dec*) lists each character's code point in decimal (the standard ASCII or Latin 1 value), the second column provides the Unicode escape sequence for the character, and the third column describes or shows the character itself.

Table A-1. ISO 8859-1 (Latin 1) characters and Unicode mappings

Dec	Unicode	Description	Dec	Unicode	Description
0	\u0000	[null]	15	\u000f	[shift in]
1	\u0001	[start of heading]	16	\u0010	[data link escape]
2	\u0002	[start of text]	17	\u0011	[device control one]
3	\u0003	[end of text]	18	\u0012	[device control two]
4	\u0004	[end of transmission]	19	\u0013	[device control three]
5	\u0005	[enquiry]	20	\u0014	[device control four]
6	\u0006	[acknowledge]	21	\u0015	[negative acknowledge]
7	\u0007	[bell]	22	\u0016	[synchronous idle]
8	\u0008	[backspace]	23	\u0017	[end of transmission block]
9	\u0009	[horizontal tabulation]	24	\u0018	[cancel]
10	\u000a	[line feed]	25	\u0019	[end of medium]
11	\u000b	[vertical tabulation]	26	\u001a	[substitute]
12	\u000c	[form feed]	27	\u001b	[escape]
13	\u000d	[carriage feed]	28	\u001c	[file separator]
14	\u000e	[shift out]	29	\u001d	[group separator]

Table A-1. ISO 8859-1 (Latin 1) characters and Unicode mappings (continued)

Dec	Unicode	Description	Dec	Unicode	Description
30	\u001e	[record separator]	66	\u0042	B
31	\u001f	[unit separator]	67	\u0043	C
32	\u0020	[space]	68	\u0044	D
33	\u0021	!	69	\u0045	E
34	\u0022	" (straight quotes)	70	\u0046	F
35	\u0023	#	71	\u0047	G
36	\u0024	$	72	\u0048	H
37	\u0025	%	73	\u0049	I
38	\u0026	&	74	\u004a	J
39	\u0027	' (straight apostrophe)	75	\u004b	K
40	\u0028	(	76	\u004c	L
41	\u0029	)	77	\u004d	M
42	\u002a	*	78	\u004e	N
43	\u002b	+	79	\u004f	O
44	\u002c	, (comma)	80	\u0050	P
45	\u002d	– (minus)	81	\u0051	Q
46	\u002e	. (period)	82	\u0052	R
47	\u002f	/	83	\u0053	S
48	\u0030	0	84	\u0054	T
49	\u0031	1	85	\u0055	U
50	\u0032	2	86	\u0056	V
51	\u0033	3	87	\u0057	W
52	\u0034	4	88	\u0058	X
53	\u0035	5	89	\u0059	Y
54	\u0036	6	90	\u005a	Z
55	\u0037	7	91	\u005b	[
56	\u0038	8	92	\u005c	\
57	\u0039	9	93	\u005d	]
58	\u003a	:	94	\u005e	^
59	\u003b	;	95	\u005f	_ (underscore)
60	\u003c	<	96	\u0060	` (accent grave)
61	\u003d	=	97	\u0061	a
62	\u003e	>	98	\u0062	b
63	\u003f	?	99	\u0063	c
64	\u0040	@	100	\u0064	d
65	\u0041	A	101	\u0065	e

Dec	Unicode	Description	Dec	Unicode	Description
102	\u0066	f	138	\u008a	control chr
103	\u0067	g	139	\u008b	control chr
104	\u0068	h	140	\u008c	control chr
105	\u0069	i	141	\u008d	control chr
106	\u006a	j	142	\u008e	control chr
107	\u006b	k	143	\u008f	control chr
108	\u006c	l	144	\u0090	control chr
109	\u006d	m	145	\u0091	control chr
110	\u006e	n	146	\u0092	control chr
111	\u006f	o	147	\u0093	control chr
112	\u0070	p	148	\u0094	control chr
113	\u0071	q	149	\u0095	control chr
114	\u0072	r	150	\u0096	control chr
115	\u0073	s	151	\u0097	control chr
116	\u0074	t	152	\u0098	control chr
117	\u0075	u	153	\u0099	control chr
118	\u0076	v	154	\u009a	control chr
119	\u0077	w	155	\u009b	control chr
120	\u0078	x	156	\u009c	control chr
121	\u0079	y	157	\u009d	control chr
122	\u007a	z	158	\u009e	control chr
123	\u007b	{	159	\u009f	control chr
124	\u007c	|	160	\u00a0	[no break space]
125	\u007d	}	161	\u00a1	¡
126	\u007e	~	162	\u00a2	¢
127	\u007f	[delete]	163	\u00a3	£
128	\u0080	control chr	164	\u00a4	¤
129	\u0081	control chr	165	\u00a5	¥
130	\u0082	control chr	166	\u00a6	¦
131	\u0083	control chr	167	\u00a7	§
132	\u0084	control chr	168	\u00a8	¨
133	\u0085	control chr	169	\u00a9	©
134	\u0086	control chr	170	\u00aa	ª
135	\u0087	control chr	171	\u00ab	«
136	\u0088	control chr	172	\u00ac	¬
137	\u0089	control chr	173	\u00ad	-

Dec	Unicode	Description	Dec	Unicode	Description
174	\u00ae	®	210	\u00d2	Ò
175	\u00af	¯	211	\u00d3	Ó
176	\u00b0	°	212	\u00d4	Ô
177	\u00b1	±	213	\u00d5	Õ
178	\u00b2	^{2}	214	\u00d6	Ö
179	\u00b3	^{3}	215	\u00d7	×
180	\u00b4	´	216	\u00d8	Ø
181	\u00b5	µ	217	\u00d9	Ù
182	\u00b6	¶	218	\u00da	Ú
183	\u00b7	·	210	\u00d2	Ò
184	\u00b8	¸	219	\u00db	Û
185	\u00b9	^{1}	220	\u00dc	Ü
186	\u00ba	º	221	\u00dd	Ý
187	\u00bb	»	222	\u00de	Þ
188	\u00bc	¼	223	\u00df	ß
189	\u00bd	½	224	\u00e0	à
190	\u00be	¾	225	\u00e1	á
191	\u00bf	¿	226	\u00e2	â
192	\u00c0	À	227	\u00e3	ã
193	\u00c1	Á	228	\u00e4	ä
194	\u00c2	Â	229	\u00e5	å
195	\u00c3	Ã	230	\u00e6	æ
196	\u00c4	Ä	231	\u00e7	ç
197	\u00c5	Å	232	\u00e8	è
198	\u00c6	Æ	233	\u00e9	é
199	\u00c7	Ç	234	\u00ea	ê
200	\u00c8	È	235	\u00eb	ë
201	\u00c9	É	236	\u00ec	ì
202	\u00ca	Ê	237	\u00ed	í
203	\u00cb	Ë	238	\u00ee	î
204	\u00cc	Ì	239	\u00ef	ï
205	\u00cd	Í	240	\u00f0	ð
206	\u00ce	Î	241	\u00f1	ñ
207	\u00cf	Ï	242	\u00f2	ò
208	\u00d0	Ð	243	\u00f3	ó
209	\u00d1	Ñ	244	\u00f4	ô

Table A-1. ISO 8859-1 (Latin 1) characters and Unicode mappings (continued)

Dec	Unicode	Description	Dec	Unicode	Description
245	\u00f5	õ	250	\u00fa	ú
246	\u00f6	ö	251	\u00fb	û
247	\u00f7	÷	252	\u00fc	ü
248	\u00f8	ø	253	\u00fd	ý
249	\u00f9	ù	254	\u00fe	þ

Index

We'd like to hear your suggestions for improving our indexes. Send email to *index@oreilly.com*.

N

named functions, 369
  calling, 27
  reusable code and, 27
named parameters, passing to CFC
    methods, 583
named result functions, Flash Remoting, 578
names
  dynamic, movie clips, 162
  XML elements, 548
nested nodes, XML, 536
  attributes and, 536
nesting
  for statements, 22
  movie clips
    accessing, 179
    for...in statements, 179
    parents, 161
.NET
  DataTable objects, 603
  Flash Remoting configuration, 571
  web services, consuming using Flash
    Remoting, 601
net streams, 437
  fast-forwarding, 455
  playback control, 454
  rewinding, 455
NetConnection class, 439, 567
  FlashCom, 439
NetConnection object, connect( )
    method, 439
NetServices.createGatewayConnection( )
    method, 569–570
NetStream.play( ) method, 448–450, 451
NetStream.publish( ) method, 453
new operator, class instances, 365
nextFrame( ) method, 165
nextImage( ) method, 716
noBorder mode, scaling, 45
nodeName property (XML), 548
nodes, XML, 536
  nested, 536
  searching for, 561–564
NOT (!) operator, 18
notation
  array, literal notation, 138
  array-access, movie clip dynamic
    names, 162
notes module, My Page application, 779–781
notes.fla file, 763
NotifierDisplayer component, scheduler
    application, 825–826

notifyIncomingCall( ) function, 690
numbers
  angle values, converting units, 121
  bases, 96–97
    converting between, 98–100
  coin flip simulation, 110–112
  dice roll simulation, 113–115
  formatting, 104–106
    currency, 106–108
  playing card simulation, 115–120
  random, generating, 108–110
  rounding, 100–102
  strings, zeros, leading/trailing, 102–103
  unique, generating, 120
Number.toString( ) method, radix
    parameter, 98

O

Object constructor, associative arrays, 156
object literal notation, associative arrays, 156
Object.registerClass( ) method, 586
objects, 6
  arrays of, 149–151
  client-side shared objects, 493
  FlashGateway.Flash, 581
  hash tables, 156
  instances, adding properties, 367–369
  instantiation, Array( ) function, 138
  introduction, 362
  listener events, 380
  listener objects, 380
    text fields, 227
  LoadVars, submitting forms, 318–324
  LocalConnection, 510
  Math object, 96
  methods, 364
    custom, 369–371
  properties, 364
  shared, 492
    client-side, adding data, 494–496
    local, 492
    remote, 492
    server-side, 493
    server-side, My Page
      application, 793–799
  Sound, 396
  TextFormat, 228
  typed
    receiving with ASP.NET, 588
    receiving with ColdFusion, 587
    receiving with Java, 589
    returning from ASP.NET, 593

substrings
    extracting from strings, 252–254
    searches, 247–251
superclasses, 363
    components, Flash Paint, 620–624
    methods, subclass variations, 379–380
SupportFunctions.as file, 764
swapDepths( ) method, 197, 720
SWF files, loading
    external, 466–468
    to movies, 465
    trusting domains, 468
SWF Studio
    projectors, 51
        dimensions, 52
        location on screen, 53
    Standalone Projectors, 51
SWFKit Standalone Projectors, 51
switch keyword, 15
switch statements, 13–18
    body, 15
    case expressions, 15
    case keyword, 15
    default keyword, 15
    text expressions, 15
symmetric encryption
    data transmission security, 334
    keys, 334
system language, checking, 42–43
System object, 37
System.capabilities object, 37
System.capabilities properties
    hasAudio, 48
    hasMP3, 48
    language, 42
    os, 41
    screenResolutionX property, 44
    screenResolutionY property, 44
System.security.allowDomain( )
        method, 469
System.showSettings( ) method, 49

T

tab order, form elements, 338–340
tabIndex properties, form elements, 339
Table class
    creating, 341
    defining, 342
    render( ) method, 348
TableColumn class, defining, 342

TableRow class
    addColumn( ) method, 348
    defining, 342
    render( ) method, 348
tables, form elements, 340–352
tags, XML, 536
targeting movie clips, 57
    dynamic names, 162
    Sound objects, 397
terminating functions, 32
test expressions, for statement, 20
text
    dynamic, displaying at runtime, 216
    Flash Paint, 620
    formatting, 228
    movie clips, 216
    progress bar, hiding, 490–491
    selecting in text fields, 236
    user input fields
        creating, 211–213
        filtering, 214
        passwords, 213
Text button, Flash Paint application
        toolbar, 624
Text component, Flash Paint, 637–641
text expressions, switch statements, 15
text fields
    backgroundColor property, 211
    backgrounds, 211
    borderColor property, 210
    borders, 210
    Button object properties and, 207
    focus, 236
    fonts, 231
        embedded, 232
    formatting text, 228
        portions of field, 230
    forms, auto-complete, 353–357
    HTML text in, 217–219
    HTML text, whitespace, 220
    hyperlinks, 240
    insertion point, setting, 237
    instance names, 208
    maxchars property, 215
    MovieClip object properties and, 207
    password property, 213
    referencing, 208
    restrict property, 214
    rotating text, 234
    runtime creation, 209

unshift( ) method, inserting array
    elements, 138
update expressions
    for statements, 21
updateListView( ) function, 758, 759
updateViewer( ) method, 711
URLs (Uniform Resource Locators)
    CGI scripts and, 525
    forms
        multipage, 330
        submitting, 318–320
    variables, loading from text files, 522
user input fields
    filtering, 214
    maximum length, 215
    passwords, 213
    responding to input, 239
    text formatting, 230
users
    form validation errors, 324–325
    settings, prompting to change, 49

V

validate( ) method
    form input, 321
    multipage forms, 331
validation
    communication receipt, 515–516
    forms errors, 324–325
    forms input, 321
    forms, multipage, 331
values
    arrays, 138
    checkboxes, 314
        forms, 315
    color values, 55
    copying data by, 147
    radio buttons, selected, 312–313
var keyword, 4, 34
variables
    conflicts, 34
    declaring, 4
        var keyword, 34
    definition, 4
    loading
        formatting, 521
        progress checking, 527
        from server-side script, 525
        from text files, 522–524
    naming, date, 276
    scope, 4

sending, server-side script, 528
server-side processing results, 530
version detection, Flash Player, 37–41
video
    FlashCom, 443–445
        adding at runtime, 441–442
    playback, net stream, 454
    publishing to FlashCom server, 451–453
video chat/message center application
    administrator client component, 685–691
    calling client component, 680–684
    overview, 672
    server-side component, 673–679
volume, 397, 413

W

watch( ) method, listener events, 383
WDDX, data transfer and, 566
web cam as source, 443–445
web cam video, displaying in
    FlashCom, 443–445
Web search module, My Page
    application, 785–792
web services
    Flash Remoting, 601
    .wsdl files, 601
whitespace
    HTML text fields, restricting, 220
    strings, 246
        trimming from, 268–270
    XML objects, removing, 552–554
Windows Projectors, dimensions, 53
words
    parsing strings by, 260–263
    reversing strings by, 270
writing XML, 535–537
.wsdl files, web services and, 601
WSDL (Web Services Description
    Language), 601
wsdl.exe, permission to run, 571

X

_x property, forms, 300
XFactorStudio.com, XPath class, 561–564
XML
    advantages, 533
    animation initialization data,
        loading, 667–671
    attributes, 535, 536
        nested nodes and, 536
    data structure, 532

About the Author

Joey Lott is the author of *Complete Flash Remoting MX* as well as the co-author of the *ActionScript Bible*. Joey teaches ActionScript as well as other Internet technologies. He also consults with companies, assisting with the development of their Internet applications.

Colophon

Our look is the result of reader comments, our own experimentation, and feedback from distribution channels. Distinctive covers complement our distinctive approach to technical topics, breathing personality and life into potentially dry subjects.

The animal on the cover of *ActionScript Cookbook* is a crab-eating opossum (*Philander opossum*). It can be found throughout Mexico, Central America, and South America. The length of the animal can vary, though it is usually between 250 and 350 millimeters. Its prehensile tail often grows to about the same length.

P. opossum is an omnivore. It eats insects, lizards, eggs, worms, frogs, small mammals, and birds, along with seeds, bananas, and leaves. It reproduces all year round, though the number of offspring varies. During the dry summer months when food is scarce, the litters can be as low as one or two young, while as many as seven young can be born during the more plentiful rainy season.

Most opossum nests are built in the low branches of trees, though they can also be found on the ground or in burrows. *P. opossum* spends most of its time on the forest floor, where it forages for food, though it will occasionally take to the trees. It was once thought that *P. opossum* was nocturnal, but it has often been observed scampering and foraging during the day. When it senses danger, *P. opossum* will hiss or yelp, and it can be a capable fighter.

Matt Hutchinson was the production editor and copyeditor for the *ActionScript Cookbook*. Reg Aubry, Sarah Sherman, and Claire Cloutier provided quality control. Johnna Dinse wrote the index.

Emma Colby designed the cover of this book, based on a series design by Edie Freedman. The cover image is a 19th-century engraving from Cuvier's *Animals*. Emma Colby produced the cover layout with QuarkXPress 4.1 using Adobe's ITC Garamond font.

David Futato designed the interior layout. This book was converted by Andrew Savikas to FrameMaker 5.5.6 with a format conversion tool created by Erik Ray, Jason McIntosh, Neil Walls, and Mike Sierra that uses Perl and XML technologies. The text font is Linotype Birka; the heading font is Adobe Myriad Condensed; and the code font is LucasFont's TheSans Mono Condensed. The illustrations that appear in the book were produced by Robert Romano and Jessamyn Read using

Macromedia FreeHand 9 and Adobe Photoshop 6. The tip and warning icons were drawn by Christopher Bing. This colophon was written by Matt Hutchinson.